from post-puritan play

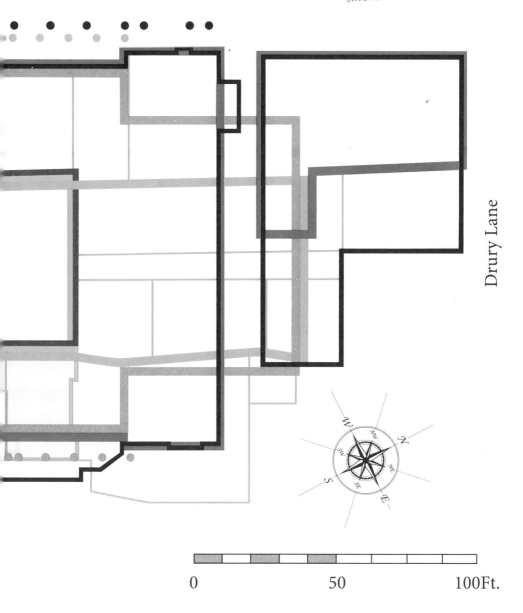

Drury Lane

0   50   100Ft.

The Third Theatre Royal (opened 1794)

The Fourth Theatre Royal (opened 1812)

The Fourth Theatre Royal as it was after the rebuilding of the auditorium in 1921/22

The Other National Theatre

Cover Cast

1 Edmund Kean (1787–1833)
  as Sir Giles Overreach

2 David Garrick (1717–1779)

3 Richard Brinsley Sheridan (1751–1816)

4 Howard Keel (1919–2004)
  as Curly in *Oklahoma!*

5 John Philip Kemble (1757–1823)
  as Hamlet

6 Henry Fielding (1707–1754)

7 Nell Gwynne (1650–1687)

8 Dan Leno (1860–1904)

9 Sarah Siddons (1755–1831)
  as the Muse of Tragedy

10 Grimaldi (1778–1837)

11 John Dryden (1631–1700)

12 Ivor Novello (1893–1951)
  in *Glamorous Night*

13 Colley Cibber (1671–1757)
  as Lord Foppington

14 Mary Martin (1913–1990)
  as Nellie Forbush in *South Pacific*

15 Rex Harrison (1908–1990)
  as Henry Higgins in *My Fair Lady*

16 Julie Andrews (1935–)
  as Eliza Doolittle in *My Fair Lady*

17 Noël Coward (1899–1973)

18 Augustus Harris (1852–1896)

THE OTHER
NATIONAL THEATRE

350 Years of Shows in Drury Lane

Robert Whelan

Published by Jacob Tonson

www.jacobtonson.com

Copyright © Robert Whelan 2013

First published May 2013

Robert Whelan asserts the moral right to be identified as the author of this work

ISBN 978-0-9575980-0-3

Book design and layout by Luke Jefford

Endpapers by Luke Jefford

Cover illustration by Jan Bowman

Printed and bound in Great Britain by Berforts, Stevenage SG1 2BH

For Jim

Drury Lane is to the drama what the Tower of London, Windsor Castle, St James's Palace, Westminster Abbey and St Paul's Cathedral are to the general history of England... It is more than a playhouse, it is a national treasure, and should be loved and revered as such.

W. Macqueen-Pope, *Theatre Royal, Drury Lane*, 1945

Contents

PART FOUR: OUR DRURY LANE

Tables

Illustrations

Colour section *between pages 242 and 243*

Acknowledgements

In his 'Life of Dryden', Dr Johnson wrote that literary history 'is tedious and troublesome; it requires indeed no great force of understanding, but often depends upon enquiries which there is no opportunity of making, or is to be fetched from books and pamphlets not always at hand'. The world has changed a lot since the eighteenth century, and authors can no longer make this excuse for their errors. Libraries, email, the internet and print-on-demand have made those books and pamphlets easier to access, and the enquiries easier to make. Like so many authors before me, I must acknowledge my debt to scholars who have generously shared their expertise and librarians who have shared their books. First and foremost, my thanks go to the Librarian and staff of the London Library, without whom this book could not have been written. The London Library is a wonderful institution which fully deserves the innumerable votes of thanks it receives in lists such as this one. My thanks are also due to the Librarian and staff of the Athenaeum and to Marcus Risdell, the Curator of the Garrick Club.

Everyone who writes on Drury Lane must be aware of the immense debt owed to Dr Francis Sheppard and his team of scholars who produced the Drury Lane/ Covent Garden volume in the Survey of London in 1970. I am grateful to English Heritage, which now manages the series, for their kind permission to reproduce material from this study. Similarly, all theatre historians must acknowledge their indebtedness to the work of the late Richard Leacroft, historian of theatre architecture, whose lifetime of research shone a spotlight into areas that had been dark and confused. His brilliant reconstructions of Drury Lane, from his book *The Development of the English Playhouse* (Eyre Methuen, 1973), are included in Appendix 2 by kind permission of Methuen.

I owe a debt of gratitude to Mark Fox of Really Useful Group Theatres (which includes Drury Lane) who, as a small part of his job, acts as historian and archivist for the RUG theatres. He has helped me with numerous points of the narrative.

Thanks to Luke Jefford for designing and typesetting the book; to Jan Bowman for creating the cavalcade of Drury Lane for the cover; to Gemma Reynolds for taking my picture for the jacket and to Colin Burgoyne for digitally retouching it; to Tanya Lubicz-Nawrocka, Claire Daley, Anna Sonny, Nigel Williams and Catherine Green for help with the text. For any remaining errors, I must accept the responsibility, in the hope that, as they say in the theatre, it doesn't show from the front.

Dates for Shakespeare's plays have been taken from *The Oxford Companion to Shakespeare*, edited by Michael Dobson and Stanley Wells (Oxford University Press, 2001).

Every author who quotes from old books and historic documents has to take a view on stylistic matters such as spelling and punctuation. To modernise completely runs the risk of losing the period flavour; to leave everything as it is in the original runs the risk of making it hard to read. With a few exceptions, I have retained old spellings but modernised punctuation and the use of capital letters.

Finally, I must acknowledge the passion, the dedication, the professionalism and – in some cases – the heroism of the men and women whose belief in theatre in general and this theatre in particular have made the Theatre Royal, Drury Lane, the most important theatre in the world. I have tried to do justice to their stories.

Introduction

The Way to Drury Lane

The Theatre Royal, Drury Lane, has the longest continuous record of performances of any theatre in the world. It opened in May 1663 and has been putting on shows continuously since then, with the exception of the brief periods between the destruction of one building and the opening of the next. No other theatre or company has such a long track record, the nearest competitor being the *Comédie-Française.* However, the *Comédie-Française* opened in 1680 and has moved around Paris, occupying its present site only since 1799. There have been four theatres on the Drury Lane site, each built bigger than the last until the current structure occupies the whole island site bounded by Catherine Street, Tavistock Street, Drury Lane and Vinegar Yard. These four successive structures are shown in Appendix 2, 'The Four Theatres Royal'. There are older theatres in the world, like the theatre at Epidauros, but the theatre at Epidauros isn't doing eight shows a week.

Drury Lane is one of the largest theatres in London, with a capacity of 2,188. Only three houses are larger – the London Palladium, the Royal Opera House and the London Coliseum – and then only by a few seats. However, the Palladium and the Coliseum were both built for variety, not plays. The Royal Opera House, which used to be called the Theatre Royal, Covent Garden, was for 200 years the main rival of Drury Lane and had a long and distinguished theatrical history.

However, it became an opera house in the middle of the nineteenth century, and plays have never been produced in the present building. Drury Lane, on the other hand, can claim to have been a Temple of the Drama (it was often described in those terms) and for hundreds of years it was home to every great actor and every major development in theatre.

Of those three slightly larger theatres, the Coliseum is now the home of English National Opera and is therefore, like the Royal Opera House, in the subsidised sector. Drury Lane, on the other hand, has never received any public subsidy and has to survive on what comes in at the box office.

But why do we call it Drury Lane? There is no obvious reason, because the theatre has never, in any of its various incarnations, had a public entrance on Drury Lane. In fact, until the nineteenth century, the building didn't stretch far enough back from the main entrance to have any frontage on Drury Lane. Drury Lane isn't the only theatre in London to be known by its street name rather than its proper name: the Theatre Royal, Haymarket is known as the Haymarket – but at least it does have its main entrance on the Haymarket, whereas Drury Lane has always been at the backstage end of the theatre. It would have been more logical if the theatre had become known as Catherine Street or Bridges Street (the former name of Catherine Street) which has always been the public entrance.✣ In spite of that, when people say they are going to Drury Lane tonight, we assume they mean they are going to the theatre, which they will enter from Catherine Street, and not to any of the various premises in Drury Lane.

This has been so for a long time. When Samuel Pepys was keeping his diary between 1660 and 1669, he at first referred to the theatre as the Theatre Royal, then as the King's house or the King's playhouse. He never connected it with Drury Lane, and when he went to have a

---

✣ The epilogue to Thomas Southerne's *The Disappointment* (1684) refers to the theatre as being in Bridges Street, and in the following year the epilogue to John Crowne's *Sir Courtly Nice* claims that 'Our Bridges Street is grown a strumpet fair'. The preface to the anonymous *Love the Leveller* in 1704 describes the play as having been 'acted at the Theatre Royal in Bridges Street, Covent Garden' but the connection with Bridges Street didn't last much longer.

look at the site in February 1663, three months before the opening, he described it as being in Covent Garden.♣ However, a playbill advertising 'A new play called Henry II' on 9 November 1692 described the theatre as 'the THEATRE ROYALL in Drury-Lane'[1] and in 1699 James Wright referred to 'the Theatre Royal in Drury Lane' in *Historia Histrionica*. In 1701 George Farquhar complained, in the prologue to his play *Sir Harry Wildair,* that Aristotle's doctrine of the three unities of the drama was being used to stifle modern playwrights. He uses 'Drury Lane', without any mention of a theatre, knowing that his reference will be immediately understood by the audience:

> *Athenian rules must form an English piece,*
> *And Drury Lane comply with ancient Greece.*

In 1702, the anonymous author of *A Comparison Between the Two Stages* refers to the Theatre Royal throughout as 'Drury-lane', sometimes abbreviated to 'D.Lane'. Then, in 1708, John Downes, who had been prompter for the Duke's Men (rivals to Drury Lane) published his theatrical memoirs under the title *Roscius Anglicanus*, in which he refers throughout to 'the Drury-Lane company' and 'the Drury-Lane house'. So, for over three centuries, Drury Lane has meant the Theatre Royal, approached from the other side of the block. It is probably futile to seek the reason now.

The real question is: why was a theatre built there in the first place? To answer that, we have to go a long way back in history, to the struggles between Roundhead and Cavalier that tore the nation apart in civil war.

♣ When Thomas Shadwell's play *The Miser* was published in 1672 it was described as 'the last play acted at the King's Theatre in Covent Garden before the fatal fire'. As late as 1720, when the Lord Chamberlain silenced the theatre, the order was issued to 'the managers of the theatre in Drury Lane, Covent Garden'. Following the opening of the rival company in their new theatre in Bow Street, just around the corner, in 1732, Covent Garden meant – in theatrical terms – that other theatre. It still does, although its correct name now is the Royal Opera House.

A Puritanical view of the stage

The conflict between Charles I, who believed that he had been appointed by God to rule without impediment, and those who felt that parliament had a role to play in government, would plunge the country into civil war in 1642. The parliamentarians, or Roundheads, did not believe that Charles I was God's representative on earth. This was not because they were irreligious: on the contrary, they were so fiercely devout that they prayed and sang psalms before going into battle. (This was one of the things that caused them to be feared throughout Europe.) They were Puritans, or fundamentalist Protestants, seeking the purity and simplicity of the early church. One of their strongest objections to Charles I was a religious one: they felt he was taking the country back to Catholicism with his Catholic Queen, his toleration of Catholic practices and his collection of Catholic art.

They disliked a lot of things about Charles I and his court, one of which was its love of the theatre. They were particularly scandalised by the court masques, which were fabulously extravagant productions for invited aristocratic audiences in which women appeared on the stage – and not only women but the Queen herself and female members of the nobility. One of the first things the Puritans did when they gained power in 1642 was to shut down all theatres and ban the performance of plays 'to appease and avert the wrath of God'.[2] They took particular pleasure in pulling down 'the Queen's dancing barn'[3] – the specially erected structure in the Palace of Whitehall where the masques were performed.

The actors, suddenly thrown out of work, joined the army of Charles I if they were young enough and, according to James Wright's nostalgic account of the good old days in the theatre, *Historia Histrionica* (1699), 'served their old master, though in a different, yet more honourable capacity'. After the execution of Charles I and the triumph of the Roundheads, things looked bleak for the actors, playwrights and everyone else who had been connected with the theatre. They gathered together in a sort of 'scratch' company and tried to keep the flame burning by giving surreptitious performances in private houses of the nobility or – with as little fuss as possible – in the theatres that were still standing. It usually ended in tears, with raids by the army and the destruction of everything the soldiers could lay their hands on.

During this dark age of the theatre, there was one important development. Sir William Davenant, who had established himself as a playwright before the Civil War and who had gone into exile in France with Charles II, was captured by parliamentary forces when he was attempting to sail to America on a mission for Henrietta Maria, the widowed Queen of Charles I. He was imprisoned in the Tower of London as an 'active enemy of the Commonwealth' and faced the death penalty. However, he was released after a few months and decided to have a go at getting theatre going again. He tried to curry favour with the Puritans by publishing a proposal 'For the Advancement of Morality by a New Way of Entertainment of the People', in which he argued for theatrical productions that would teach moral values to the lower classes by means of plays involving scenery and music. This was predictably unsuccessful, as the Puritans took the view that going to the theatre was just about the last thing likely to teach moral values to the lower classes.

Nothing daunted, in May 1656 Davenant put on an 'entertainment' (not a play, of course) in his own house involving some speeches and some music which he described as 'our Elyzian field, the Opera'. This was the first appearance of the word in English. Having received no visit from the soldiers, Davenant took a bolder step and put on *The Siege of Rhodes,* which is generally regarded as the first English opera, also in his own house. Finding himself still a free man, he took the even bolder step of moving the production into the old Cockpit Theatre in Drury Lane, and followed it up with *The Cruelty of the Spaniards in Peru* (which was intended to flatter Oliver Cromwell) and then, in 1659, with an 'entertainment' based on Sir Francis Drake that was clearly, whatever he might call it, a play.

By this time, Oliver Cromwell was dead and his son Richard, who made a brief and unsuccessful attempt to step into his father's shoes, demanded to know by what authority Davenant was putting on public performances at the Cockpit. However, fortunately for Davenant and for all theatre-lovers, time was running out for the Puritans, and the nation soon invited Charles II to return from exile in France and sit on the throne. The republican experiment was over, and with it went the ban on theatre. As Davenant reminded Charles in the prologue to the very first play performed before him at court on 19 November 1660:

> This truth we can to our advantage say,
> They that would have no KING would have no PLAY:
> The Laurel and the Crown together went,
> Had the same foes, and the same banishment.[4]

They would have the same restoration as well.

The return of the King

On 23 May 1660 Charles II set sail from the Hague to Dover to reclaim his throne. Amongst the many passengers on his ship (renamed *The Charles* the day before) was Samuel Pepys, whose famous diary provides us with an invaluable record of day-to-day life in the tumultuous years of the 1660s. As the ship made its way across the channel in fine weather, the King walked up and down on the deck, conversing in a friendly and familiar fashion with many 'persons of honour', including a certain Thomas Killigrew:

> …a merry droll, but a gentleman of great esteem with the King),
> who told us many merry stories: one, how he wrote a letter three
> or four days ago to the Princess Royal, about a Queen Dowager
> of Judaea and Palestine, that was at the Hague incognita, that
> made love to the King, &c., which was Mr. Cary (a courtier's)
> wife that had been a nun, who are all married to Jesus.[5]

It must have been the way he told 'em. However, as Thomas Killigrew is one of the most important people in the history of Drury Lane, we need to know a bit more about him than his complicated jokes.

Killigrew was 48 when *The Charles* set sail. He was a courtier from a family of courtiers: that is to say, he was accustomed to supporting himself by serving the monarch and members of the royal family in various capacities. He had fought on the King's side in the Civil War and went into exile with Charles II. He was appointed by Charles to act as an ambassador, trying to win the support of the Italian states for the royalist cause, and he spent two years in Venice, until the Venetian senate requested his recall. It has often been said that this was because his scandalous behaviour outraged the Venetians, but it is much more likely that they simply didn't want to be seen to be aligning themselves with Charles while Oliver Cromwell was still firmly in control in England. As a republic, the Venetians felt closer to the idea of a commonwealth than a monarchy anyway.

Thomas Killigrew had been theatre-mad from boyhood. There is a story that he used to hang around the Red Bull in Clerkenwell – an inn where plays were performed – trying to get in. When the man responsible for getting local lads to play walk-ons shouted: 'Who will go and be a devil, and he shall see the play for nothing' (presumably in *Dr Faustus* or some similarly supernatural story), young Thomas would rush forward to take up the offer. He began writing plays when he was in his twenties. The first of these were performed in the public theatres, but he continued writing when he was travelling in Europe and during his exile with Charles II, when presumably his plays were intended to be read rather than acted.

Unlike his brothers, Thomas did not receive a university education, or indeed anything much by way of formal education. He was accustomed to living on his wits, and this proved a valuable training for his years in exile. Charles was the Merry Monarch: he valued wit and good company above almost anything else in his companions, and Killigrew got himself into the King's favour by making him laugh.

As a courtier, he never had what would be regarded by most people as a 'proper job'. He was used to being supported by the royal family, either with a regular income for services rendered, or by means of sinecures – jobs in government which carried a salary, but for which the gentlemen holding them were seldom if ever expected to turn up in the office, because the work was done by clerks. Killigrew acquired a reputation for being relentless in asking the King for every sinecure that came up, and because he could keep Charles in a good humour, he often got them. Writing in 1668, Pepys recorded that:

> Tom Killigrew hath a fee out of the Wardrobe for cap and bells, under the title of the King's fool or jester; and may with privilege revile or jeer anybody, the greatest person, without offence, by the privilege of his place.[6]

It would be tempting to dismiss this as a piece of malicious gossip, were it not for the fact that the Lord Chamberlain's records contain a copy of a warrant dated 12 July 1661 'to deliver to Mr. Killegrew thirty yards of velvett, three dozen of fringe, and sixteene yards of Damaske for the year 1661'. The heading of this entry is 'Livery for ye jester'.

A warrant to open a theatre

One of the things that the stage-struck Killigrew asked for from the King, no doubt in the midst of one of their laughing bouts, was permission to run a theatre company. The King said yes, and on 9 July 1660 Killigrew received a royal warrant authorising him to open the King's Company of actors. However, Thomas Killigrew was not the only person to spot a valuable business opportunity here, with the Puritans out of the way. Sir William Davenant also cherished ambitions to be a theatre manager, and what's more, he had a prior claim. In March 1639, before the outbreak of the Civil War, Davenant had obtained a warrant to build and run a theatre on the north side of Fleet Street. He had never carried this out, but his authority to build a playhouse predated Killigrew's.

As a result, a second warrant was issued on 12 August giving both Killigrew and Davenant authority to build theatres, hire actors and charge admission to plays. The King notes, in this warrant, that plays are already being performed in London that contain filth and blasphemy and 'tend to the debauching of the manners of such as are present at them'. Nevertheless, the King notes that there is no need to close down theatres entirely (the Puritan approach), but rather to manage them so well that they 'might serve as moral instructions in human life'. Killigrew and Davenant were ordered to read through all old plays before they were performed and strike out any smut or blasphemy. Furthermore, to prevent the spread of such filthiness, the warrant decreed that there should be no other theatre in London than these two.

Presumably, the idea that Killigrew and Davenant were going to turn the stage into a pulpit to preach higher moral standards was regarded as a huge in-joke, and the way in which theatre developed in subsequent decades must have given many Puritans the opportunity to say 'I told you so'. The two men showed very little inclination to go through plays striking out the dirty bits – quite the reverse, their critics would have said. However, they took the other part of the licence very seriously indeed: they had a monopoly – or rather a duopoly – over theatre in London. Although the two companies they founded were for many years engaged in the most bitter rivalry, this was one thing they always agreed upon: the terms of this warrant issued to both managers would be ruthlessly enforced to stamp out any competition.

This royal warrant was followed up by two patents which confirmed the powers granted in the warrant and added more. Killigrew's patent was issued on 25 April 1662; Davenant's on 15 January 1663. Davenant's company would be under the protection of the Duke of York, Charles II's brother and later James II: it would be known as the Duke's Men, just as Killigrew's company would be the King's Men. The wording of both patents was virtually the same and repeated the claims that the morals of the people were being debauched at unregulated playhouses in London, and that Killigrew and Davenant would have a duopoly over dramatic presentations in London, but the patent added a very significant rider. The powers granted were to the patentees (Killigrew and Davenant), their 'heires and assignes'. In other words, they were granted *in perpetuity*.

The two men could bequeath their patents, with all the privileges these involved, to their successors, or they could assign them – i.e. transfer them to someone else. Whoever was in possession of the patent could put on plays in London. It was not unusual at that time for monarchs to grant their favourites special privileges by way of monopolies, licences and patents, but these arrangements normally lasted for the lifetime of the monarch or the lifetime of the person who benefited. To make a grant perpetual was extremely unusual, as no one could foresee the future. The terms of these patents would have a huge influence over the way theatre developed in England for nearly two centuries.

The patents both contained another clause that had not been included in the warrant of 1660. They permitted women to appear on the stage, thus overturning the pre-Civil War tradition of teenage boys playing female parts. The patents noted that 'some have taken offence' at the acting of women's parts 'by men in the habits of women', and that if women can be allowed to appear, this will benefit the public by giving 'useful and instructive representations of human life'.[7]

Presumably, like the clauses obliging Killigrew and Davenant to go through all plays striking out the dirty bits, this was an in-joke. It is doubtful if anyone thought that bringing women onto the stage would improve the moral tone, especially as no respectable women could work in a theatre;✤ and those who disliked the theatre altogether certainly didn't feel that actresses made things better. The diarist John Evelyn, never keen on theatre, complained of: 'fowle and undecent women now, and never 'til now, permitted to appear and act'.[8] However, as we shall see, by the time the patents were issued permitting women to play female parts, it was a case of opening the stable door long after the horse had bolted.

✤ Thomas Brown, the seventeenth-century writer and wit, wrote that it was 'as hard a matter for a pretty woman to keep herself honest in a theatre, as 'tis for an apothecary to keep his treacle from the flies in hot weather; for every libertine in the audience will be buzzing about her honeypot, and her virtue must defend itself by abundance of fly-traps, or those flesh-loving insects will soon blow upon her honour, and when once she has a maggot in her tail, all the pepper and salt in the kingdom will scarce keep her reputation from stinking.' (*The Works of Mr Thomas Brown,* 1720, ii, 303, quoted in Wilson [1958] 26.)

So where were these playhouses that were apparently debauching the morals of Londoners with their filthy plays, and which the King was so keen to close down? With the loosening of the grip of the Puritans, actors had started to put on plays, even before Charles II landed, at three of the old, pre-Civil War theatres: the Red Bull in Clerkenwell, the Cockpit in Drury Lane and the theatre in Salisbury Court, south of Fleet Street. The Red Bull was an old Elizabethan-style inn theatre, open to the elements and with the audience sitting in galleries surrounding the yard. The Cockpit and the Salisbury Court were known as 'private houses', which is confusing as they weren't private houses at all but theatres open to the paying public. However, they were very small; they were roofed-in, so they acted by artificial light; and they had high prices so the audience would have been upper-class.

There is absolutely no evidence that these companies of actors were debauching the morals of the town by putting on filthy plays. They were performing plays by pre-Civil War authors, mainly Fletcher, Beaumont, Jonson and Shakespeare, and they were no more disorderly than theatres were expected to be at that time. The claim that the duopoly was necessary to protect public morals was simply an excuse to divert attention from the way in which Charles II was using an old trick of monarchs to repay obligations by granting special privileges. Charles was indebted to a lot of people who had supported himself and his father during the bad times, and these debts couldn't always be repaid financially.

Although the patents were a couple of years in the future, the royal warrant gave Killigrew and Davenant enough security to get their operations up and running in the autumn of 1660. They lost no time in letting the actors know that, under the terms they had extracted from the King, actors could work for one or other of their companies or not at all. The ending of Puritanism had not created a free market in theatre.

Killigrew took over the troupe acting at the Red Bull which included experienced actors from before the Civil War period, some of whom had fought bravely for the royalist cause like Michael Mohun and Charles Hart. Davenant took over the troupe acting in the Cockpit in Drury Lane under the direction of John Rhodes, a bookseller. These were younger and less experienced actors, but fortunately for Davenant they included the young Thomas Betterton, an apprentice bookbinder, who would become the greatest star of the Restoration stage.

After a few weeks of performances at the Red Bull, Killigrew moved his company – the King's Men – into an indoor tennis court known as Gibbons's tennis court in Vere Street, Clare Market. There are no images of this building apart from an aerial view in Wenceslaus Hollar's 1658 map of the Covent Garden district, and Vere Street itself has long since vanished, but the stage arrangement was probably no more than a simple platform at the end of an oblong room, creating the basic acting conditions, without scenery, that Shakespeare would have known. However, Davenant had more ambitious ideas which would soon force Thomas Killigrew to up his game.

When the scenery started to move

William Davenant and Thomas Killigrew were both theatre-lovers who had been involved with the professional theatre before the Civil War, so they could both claim to be heirs to the great tradition. However, they came from different social backgrounds, and this would have counted for a lot more at the time than it would today.

Killigrew was a courtier from a family of courtiers. Davenant's background, on the other hand, was not gentry but trade. As a knight, he outranked Killigrew, but he was awarded his knighthood for conspicuous valour at the siege of Gloucester in 1643. Davenant earned his social status; Killigrew inherited his.

Davenant's parents kept a tavern in Oxford where, according to a legend promoted by Davenant himself, Shakespeare used to stay when he was travelling between London and Stratford. Davenant's mother was a handsome woman, and when he was in his cups Davenant liked to hint that his own talent as a writer could have been derived from his mother's attractiveness to the great William Shakespeare. According to the diarist John Aubrey, as a result of this foolish boasting Davenant's mother acquired the reputation of being a very great whore, which probably wasn't what her son intended. It is, in fact, extremely unlikely that Shakespeare was Davenant's father, although he probably was his godfather.

Following the death of Davenant senior, young William travelled to London and went into service. He began writing plays which were performed in the public theatres, as well as plays for the court, and especially for the Queen Henrietta Maria. He entered the Queen's service, and she brought him together with Inigo Jones. Jones was an architect – many would say the greatest English architect – who virtually single-handedly introduced into England the classical style of architecture. Jones had studied the works of the ancient Roman and Italian Renaissance architects and decided to introduce their style into a country where the classical rules were almost unknown. His most famous work, the Banqueting House, Whitehall, is now surrounded by other buildings in a classical style, but it must have really stood out when London was a mass of half-timber, Dutch gables and thatch.

One of the roles of the Banqueting House was to house the extravagant court masques so beloved of the Stuart dynasty. These affairs were sumptuous musical entertainments involving bits of acting, lots of singing and lots of dancing, all conveying some allegorical message – often the divine right of the king to rule without interference from anyone else. Jones was employed to design the sets and costumes for these events and he introduced, for the first time in England, the moveable scenery, painted in perspective, that he had seen on his travels in Italy. Wings and shutters could slide in grooves to change the scene before the eyes of the spectators. It must have seemed like magic, especially as the public theatres of the time used no scenery at all beyond a few hangings and props.

Inigo Jones had originally collaborated with Ben Jonson on these masques, but they fell out over a question of precedence: were the dramatist's words more important than the designer's sets? Jonson felt they were, but the King and Queen were so entranced by Inigo's magical spectacles that Jonson found himself on a losing wicket, and Jones looked for other collaborators. For several of the masques presented at court in the 1630s, the author of the lines was William Davenant.

Davenant wrote the scripts for *The Temple of Love* (1636), *Britannia Triumphans* (1638) and *Salmacida Spolia* (1640), the last, most spectacular and most completely pointless of the Stuart court masques. Both the King and Queen appeared in *Salmacida Spolia*, the King as Philogenes – the 'lover of his people' who is doomed to live in such sad times that his people fail to understand him. Two years later the Civil War broke out and seven years after that the 'lover of his country' was beheaded on a scaffold outside Inigo Jones's Banqueting House.

William Davenant thus had the chance to see at close quarters what could be achieved by moveable scenery painted in perspective. As the son of a tradesman, he would probably have been more closely involved with the production process than a gentleman like Killigrew. He got to see how things worked and, being six years older, he saw more of professional theatre before the Puritans shut it down. Most of Killigrew's plays were written during the period of his European exile with Charles II and so were not performed in London. If they were performed at all, it would have been for a private audience of courtiers – not much more than amateur dramatics.

Davenant, on the other hand, was in London during most of the period of the Commonwealth where, as we have seen, he put on some musical entertainments which he called 'operas' and got away with it on the understanding that these were not plays. However, his opera *The Siege of Rhodes* was described as a 'Representation by the Art of Prospective' (*sic*) and had scenery designed by John Webb, the son-in-law and assistant of Inigo Jones. The designs have survived and show three pairs of wings, painted in perspective, in front of three sets of sliding shutters that would draw apart to reveal the one behind. Davenant's next opera *The Cruelty of the Spaniards in Peru*, presented at the Cockpit Theatre in Drury Lane, was also described as relying on 'the Art of Perspective in Scenes', so there must have been a similar arrangement. His excuse for this one was that it complimented Cromwell's foreign policy (parliament had just declared war on Spain) by representing the Spanish in a bad light.

At the end of 1660, with Killigrew's rival company established in the tennis court on Vere Street, Davenant took his company into the old Salisbury Court Theatre off Fleet Street, but he had already signed a lease for another tennis court – Lisle's court in Lincoln's Inn Fields – in the previous March. It was only a few hundred yards away from Killigrew's tennis court, but it was larger. In fact, it was big enough to install the machinery for moving scenery.

On Friday 28 June 1661, the Duke's Men opened in their new theatre in the converted tennis court. The show was Davenant's own *The Siege of Rhodes* and it had the sort of moving perspective scenery that Davenant had seen in Inigo Jones's court masques and had tried out himself in *The Siege of Rhodes* and *The Cruelty of the Spaniards in Peru*. By now it was more elaborate, as he had the theatre as a permanent base, and there was no need to fear a raid from Cromwell's soldiers to close the show down. It was a huge success and ran uninterrupted (except for Sundays) for twelve days, which was considered a long run. Three days into the run the King attended with the Duke of York. It was the first visit to a public theatre by Charles, and indeed the first ever by a reigning monarch. Davenant followed the *Siege* with his own play *The Wits*, written before the Civil War but 'never acted yet with scenes' as Pepys observed.[9] It was another great success, with the King and the Duke of York turning up again for the first performance. In the following week he presented Thomas Betteron as Hamlet, 'done with scenes' as Pepys once again noted,[10] showing the importance people attached to the new perspective scenery. Davenant had worked for the King's Men – Shakespeare's company – before the Civil War and had seen an actor called Taylor play Hamlet. Taylor was said to have been instructed in the part by Shakespeare✤ and Davenant taught Betterton to play it in the same way. Pepys was blown away by the young actor, only just 26, who had been an apprentice bookbinder the year before. 'Beyond imagination' was his verdict, and it was a general one. It was one of those star-is-born moments.

✤ It is more likely that the actor Joseph Taylor was instructed in the part by Richard Burbage, the original Hamlet, as Shakespeare was dead by the time Taylor joined the King's Men.

The introduction of the new scenery was a development that could have been foreseen. Indeed, the warrant issued to Killigrew and Davenant in August 1660 had specifically stated that they could set prices of admission at a level to reflect 'the great expencese of scenes, musick, and such new decorations as have not been formerly used'.[11] However, Davenant, with more experience of trends in professional theatre, had been more alert to the need than Killigrew, who seemed to have been caught on the hop.

This was having a bad effect on business in Vere Street. During the first full week of performances of *The Siege of Rhodes* at Lincoln's Inn Fields, Pepys went to see the King's Men in Vere Street and had no difficulty in finding a seat. 'Strange to see this house, that used to be so thronged, now empty since the opera begun; and so will continue for a while, I believe.'[12] The fact that the play being performed was *Claricilla*, written by Thomas Killigrew himself, would probably not have made the manager feel any better about it. If Killigrew was going to keep up with the Duke's Men, he needed a bigger theatre where he could have moving scenery. He searched for a site where he could trump Davenant's efforts with a purpose-built theatre designed to accommodate the latest theatrical trends. He found it behind some buildings on Drury Lane.

PART ONE

Killigrew's Drury Lane

1

Curtain Up

Drury Lane is an ancient thoroughfare, described as an 'old way' in 1199, leading out of London to the north-west. In the thirteenth century it was known as Aldewichstrate; in the early sixteenth century it was known as Fortescu Lane after Sir John Fortescu, who leased the Covent Garden estate to the west. Later in the sixteenth century, Sir Thomas Drury built himself a handsome house towards the southern end, and the road has been known by his name ever since.

When Sir Thomas lived there, he had a fine view of open countryside in most directions. London still consisted of two separate cities: the City of London (home to commerce) and the City of Westminster (home to the court and government). They were linked by the Strand, but the authorities were keen to prevent the two cities from becoming joined-up through ribbon development, as it was felt that it might be difficult to maintain order outside the tightly regulated City of London. New building was strictly controlled and strongly discouraged.

However, things were about to change. Drury Lane marked the eastern edge of the Covent Garden estate, belonging to the Abbey, or Convent (Covent), of St Peter, which we know as Westminster Abbey. As its name suggests, it was open land, laid out as orchards, pasture and market gardens. In 1536 Henry VIII acquired most of the land from the Abbey by swopping it for an estate in Berkshire. Four years later, by which time the monasteries had been suppressed and their lands seized, Henry VIII helped himself to the remaining parcel of land to the south-east, roughly where the Strand Palace Hotel now stands, which was known as Friars Pyes. All of this land was given to John Russell, whom Henry had created the first Earl of Bedford, under two grants: one made by Henry in 1541 and the other by his son Edward VI in 1552.

Thus, in the early years of the next century, Francis Russell, the fourth Earl of Bedford, found himself in possession of a very large site, bounded by Drury Lane on the east, the Strand on the south, St Martin's Lane on the west and Longacre on the north. It struck him as being – as we would now say – ripe for development. The obstacle was the official ban on new building in London, which he had to get around by persuading the authorities that some sort of development was going to take place anyway, and it would be best if he had control of a discrete area where he would build high-quality houses for the gentry, using Inigo Jones – the favourite architect of the court – to design them. He paid £2,000 for the licence and was fined another £2,000 for starting work before the licence was issued.

The development of Covent Garden was a huge success, attracting just the sort of upper-class residents the Earl had promised,✢ and he made a great deal of money from it. At the same time, Inigo Jones had also been called in to advise on laying out Lincoln's Inn Fields as a similar development of terraced housing looking onto an open space. The plan was obstructed by the lawyers in Lincoln's Inn for as long as they could and it got off to a patchy start. However, these two developments on either side of Drury Lane sparked off an explosion of house-building that created a new, fashionable residential quarter covering most of the land between Chancery Lane and St Martin's Lane and between the Strand and Holborn. The area benefited from being equidistant from the City and Westminster, but still preserving a quiet

---

✢ Thomas Killigrew lived in the Piazza from 1636-1640.

and respectable air. A number of aristocratic mansions were built along Drury Lane, and Oliver Cromwell lived there for a while during the Commonwealth. The area would soon go into decline, as fashion moved westwards to St James, and the area became known for its taverns and brothels, but when Thomas Killigrew turned up looking for a site it was still a respectable residential area. The presence of the theatre was probably one of the factors that changed that.

The plot which Killigrew found for his theatre was far from ideal. It was a slightly irregular oblong, 112 feet in length and between 58 and 59 feet wide. This would seem to us a very small plot for a theatre, but it wasn't regarded as too small at the time. The real problem was access. It had no street frontage at all, being hemmed in by the backyards of houses fronting onto Drury Lane, Russell Street, Bridges Street (now Catherine Street) and Vinegard Yard. Access was by means of two passageways running in one direction to Bridges Street and in the other to Drury Lane. To make matters worse, although the landlord was William Russell, the fifth Earl of Bedford, he didn't control most of the sites surrounding the plot. These had been sold off by his ancestors between 1635 and 1659 under an arrangement known as 'fee farm', which effectively meant they passed out of the Russell family's control. This would cause problems in later years as the theatre needed to expand.

In the leisure industry, location is vitally important, and it is not a good idea to set up any business venture out of sight of passing trade. Presumably Killigrew felt this was the best he was going to get, given the resources available. There were no large sites left in the immediate area with a street frontage, and he was already on the edge of town. London stopped at the end of Drury Lane, where it met Holborn: after that it was fields.

The Earl of Bedford issued a lease for 'the Rideing Yard' for 41 years from Christmas 1661 at an annual rent of £50. In return, the lessees undertook to spend £1,500 on building a theatre to open by Christmas 1662. These lessees were a group of people known as the building shareholders. The value of the lease had been divided into 36 parts or shares. Each share cost one-thirty-sixth of the capital required and the shareholder in return would receive one-thirty-sixth of the rent that would be paid by the sub-lessees – the actors putting on shows. Killigrew had nine of these original 36 shares, and Sir Robert Howard also had nine. Lacy (an actor) had four while Burt, Cartwright, Clunn, Hart, Mohun, Shatterell and Wintershall (all actors) had two each. The building shareholders then issued a sub-lease to a group of thirteen actors who undertook to pay rent of £3 10s. per acting day.

This created a tripartite structure. Killigrew held a patent which entitled him to build a theatre and put on shows, while the building shareholders erected a building in expectation of receiving rent from the actors performing in it. There was considerable overlap. Killigrew was the patentee and owned a quarter of the shares in the building. Eight of the building shareholders, with a total of 18 (half) of the building shares were actors who were also members of the group of 13 actors contracted to put on the shows.

This complicated system could only get worse as the years went by, because the shares, like all shares, could be traded. As people died or retired, their shares passed to others, sometimes even sub-divided, so that the number of people involved, nominally at least, with running the theatre got larger. Many of these people had no professional experience of the theatre, and some of them never went near it. The shares were regarded as an investment to produce income. Whether the investors ever saw much by way of dividends was another matter, but the structure was guaranteed to make management of the theatre extremely difficult. To make matters worse, Killigrew started to raise money by mortgaging his patent.

However, in 1661 when the lease was signed, these difficulties were in the future. There must have been a sense of excitement about creating the first purpose-built theatre in London since the Puritans had shut them all down in 1642. Not only that, but it would be a theatre like none that had gone before, built to reflect the very different requirements of actors and audiences in post-Restoration London. In a sense, the first Theatre Royal is the direct ancestor of the theatres in London's West End now. A modern theatre-goer who was transported back to Shakespeare's theatre of the early 1600s would find it a very different experience from seeing a show now. If that theatre-goer could sit in the pit at Drury Lane in the late 1600s, it would be different in some ways, but recognisably the same experience.

This makes it all the more frustrating that we have no idea of what that first Theatre Royal looks like. There are no surviving illustrations of it, inside or out, no plans, and we don't know who the architect was. There is a sketch by Sir Christopher Wren for an unknown theatre which some people have thought might be the Theatre Royal, but there is no real evidence to connect it, and it looks more like the sort of theatre that might have been built for court performances. The most likely architect/builder of this first theatre is Richard Ryder, a carpenter who lived in a house on Russell Street backing onto the site of the Riding Yard✢ which he had rented from the Earl of Bedford before it was leased to the theatre shareholders. Ryder was a speculative builder and surveyor to the Earl of Bedford. He was also the King's Master Carpenter and we know that he had worked on some theatrical projects at court.

The little that we know of this theatre, which lasted only nine years, comes from brief descriptions by theatre-goers. Samuel Pepys missed the opening night but was there the next night when he tells us only that the passages into the pit (what we call the stalls) were too narrow; some of the boxes were so far from the stage that they must have difficulty hearing; and some of the musicians were sitting under the stage which muffled the sound.[1] Two weeks later a French visitor described the theatre as the most beautiful he had ever seen, the boxes lined with green baize and trimmed with gold leather bands, and the benches of the pit curved into a semi-circular shape, with each row a little higher than the row in front.[2] A visitor in 1669 describes the auditorium as being circular, which probably means that the front of the stage was concave to reflect the curve of the benches in the pit.[3] We know there was a small dome or cupola on the roof because Pepys reports that, when it rained, the people sitting in the pit got wet.[4]

And that, unfortunately, is pretty much all we have to go on. The architect and theatre historian Richard Leacroft used plans,

---

✢ The similarity between Ryder (sometimes spelt Rider) and Riding Yard is purely co-incidental. The site was called the Riding Yard because it had formerly been a riding school and stables.

illustrations and descriptions to create images of many old theatres and their auditoria, including the three buildings that have stood on this site since the first Theatre Royal burned down, but he attempted only an outside view of this one. As can be seen in Appendix 2, he envisaged it as a two-storey building with windows at first floor level, dormer windows on the sloping roof and a cupola on the crest. We also know that it had a ten-foot yard in front.

Opening Night

The first Theatre Royal, Drury Lane, opened on 7 May 1663 with a performance of *The Humorous Lieutenant* by John Fletcher and Francis Beaumont. It was five months late (according to the agreement with the Earl of Bedford, which stipulated Christmas 1662) and it was way over budget. It had cost £2,500 instead of the budget figure of £1,500.

What would that first performance have been like? For one thing, it would have started very early by our standards of theatre-going, probably at 3:30 p.m. The windows would have allowed the afternoon light into the auditorium to supplement the hundreds of candles in the candelabras and chandeliers. No other form of lighting was available, and there was no way of controlling the level of lighting. It would have been constant throughout the performance, with the auditorium lit to the same level as the stage. Putting the house lights down during the show would not be a possibility for many years.

The seating was divided into three areas: pit, boxes and gallery. The pit was what we would call the stalls, where a seat cost 2*s.* 6*d.* (12.5p) surrounded by a tier of boxes, where a seat cost 4*s.* (20p). Above the boxes were two galleries, costing 1*s.* 6*d.* (7.5p) for the lower gallery, which was probably partly divided into boxes, and 1*s.* (5p) for the upper one which had continuous bench seating for lower-class patrons. The boxes were not quite what we understand by boxes today, as they were not occupied by a group of people who came together. They might seat between ten and twenty people who all bought their seats independently. Unless you were royalty or some other sort of V.I.P., the only way to get a place was physically to occupy it on one of the benches, or send your servant ahead to do it for you. For popular shows, like the first performance of a new play, people would turn up several hours before curtain-up to do this.

The boxes were for the gentry (probably on the first tier) or professional people (on the second tier).✣ The pit was the next best area, favoured by middle-class theatre-goers and single men, especially those who regarded themselves as dramatic critics. The gallery was for working-class patrons.

Physically, the division of patrons by using different prices in different areas of the theatre is still familiar to us. So is the fact that everyone was sitting down in an enclosed structure, sheltered from the weather (apart from the rain coming through the cupola). The indoor environment meant that elaborate scenery could be used, lit by artificial light, so daylight and weather became unimportant. This changed the nature of the theatre 'season': the open air theatres of Shakespeare's day had been restricted to playing during daylight in the warmer months of the year. The season, as it developed after the Restoration, moved from summer to winter: it opened in September/October and finished in May/June when the aristocracy went out of town to their country estates.

These are elements we can still recognise in modern theatres, but the huge difference between us and the first audiences of that seventeenth century theatre would be the way in which the spectators watched, or didn't watch, the play. We now take it for granted that the audience is seated when the play starts; latecomers may have to wait for a break in the programme before being admitted; and everyone sits quietly listening to the actors until the end. Talking is frowned on and likely to be shushed. The ringing of mobile phones is now the greatest challenge to an actor, and has sometimes drawn a rebuke from the stage.

✣ Samuel Pepys sometimes sat in a box if he felt like being extravagant, but he was more likely to be in the pit.

The actors who worked for Killigrew and Davenant had a very different situation to deal with. First of all, audiences did not all arrive and leave together: they came and went as they liked. Plays were written in five acts. Spectators could 'sample' by seeing the first act without paying, then leaving if they didn't like it. Anyone arriving after the third act got in for half price.✢ Members of the audience talked to each other, often calling from one box or bench to another part of the theatre, or simply walking around to talk to their friends. They could sit on the stage and go behind the scenes to watch the actresses getting dressed and undressed. They also didn't hesitate to let the actors know what they thought of the play. Booing and throwing brickbats – especially fruit – were common. The critics of the pit would loudly pronounce their judgement on the play, favourable or unfavourable. Food and drink were consumed during the show. If audiences were unhappy with some aspect of the management's policy, they were quite capable of stopping the show and demanding an account. On many occasions in the history of Drury Lane, and indeed all the early theatres, there were riots when audiences felt they were being ill-treated, particularly in the matter of seat prices.

Every house was potentially a rough house. The noise and lack of respect for the actors and the play would seem intolerable today. However, on the plus side, all classes of society met at the theatre, from the king and the aristocracy in the boxes to the labourers in the gallery. Theatre brought people together then in a way that it doesn't now that it has become largely middle-class. As a result, what happened on the stage was much more important than it is today. So there has been a trade-off. But what exactly was happening on the stage?

✢ This custom seems to have been introduced in the 1670s.

2

Which Show Goes On?

One of the big differences between London theatre now and then was the repertory system. We take it for granted, at least in the commercial theatre,✣ that a play will run at a particular theatre for as long as the public can be persuaded to buy tickets; hopefully for several months if it is to stand any chance of making its money back, and, in the case of big shows, for years. When the play closes, that is usually the end of the production, unless it goes out on tour. It probably won't be seen in London again.

This system would have been impossible in the seventeenth century when the potential theatre-going population was small. London was so much smaller then that you could walk across it in an hour. There were no railways or buses and international tourism was hundreds of years away. Most of the people at Drury Lane on any given night would have been Londoners who had either walked there or come in a coach or sedan chair. It has been estimated that there were probably not more than 30,000 people from whom both theatres could hope to draw their

✣ The repertory system still survives in the subsidised sector. The National Theatre and Royal Shakespeare Company play in rep, as do the Royal Opera House and English National Opera.

audiences[1] and, as Dr Johnson would put it, looking back from the next century, 'the audience, consisting nearly of the same people, could be drawn together only by variety'.[2]

This meant that long runs, as we understand them, were out of the question. There just weren't enough potential punters. Plays were only announced a day or two in advance, because the size of the house would determine whether or not the play was kept on for another night. If the house were thin, another play would be announced for the following night. The plays in the repertoire would go round and round: they were brought back during the season and, if popular enough, in later seasons, for as long as an audience could be found for them. It meant that regular theatre-goers might see the same play several times over the course of a few years, but people thought this no more odd than seeing *Cosi Fan Tutti* or *Swan Lake* several times today, if you like opera or ballet. The repertory system meant that actors had to carry in their heads dozens of parts for each season, as there would be very little time to rehearse before the next play opened. Repertory is expensive in terms of the numbers of stage-hands required to change the sets, although in those days stock sets would have been used for a 'palace', a gentleman's lodgings in St James or the park.

But what were the plays that drew the town when the first theatres opened their doors after the Restoration? Initially, they were old plays, because the theatres had been closed for 18 years and no one had been writing for the stage, with the notable exceptions of William Davenant's 'operas'. The only way to get the theatres open again was to perform the plays by authors who had been popular in the pre-Civil War theatres: Ben Jonson, Shakespeare, James Shirley, Richard Brome and – most notably – John Fletcher (with or without his various collaborators).

The play chosen to open the first Theatre Royal in 1663 was *The Humorous Lieutenant* by John Fletcher and Francis Beaumont. The play and its two authors are now scarcely known except to scholars of the drama, but at the time Fletcher was regarded as the greatest English playwright – way above Shakespeare. Shakespeare was thought to be not correct enough for a more polite age: his plots are all over the place, his stories unfold over years, his characters use vulgar language and clowns keep coming on to make fart jokes, even in the tragedies. Fletcher, on the other hand, was both correct and witty. Ben Jonson was learned and able to write in the classical style, although this could be bit dull, which was why people normally put him just below Fletcher, certainly in terms of box-office appeal. James Shirley had been a prolific author of the period just before the Civil War and had a reputation for churning out solid hits that weren't too demanding.

In 1965, William Van Lennep and a team of scholars based at the University of Southern Illinois began publication of a remarkable series of volumes entitled *The London Stage 1660–1800*. They combed through archives for every playbill, newspaper advertisement, diary entry, letter or printed source that gave details of any performance in any London theatre over that period. Inevitably, the records for the later years are fuller, and those for 1660-1700 are particularly patchy. There were no daily newspapers in those days, so we can't look for advertisements, and most publicity was done by way of playbills that were distributed around London on the day, giving details of that night's performance. Very few of these have survived, so we have to recognise that the plays listed do not represent all plays performed, but only those of which we have some record. Nevertheless, there is no reason to suspect any bias in what has been preserved, so the list does give us a pretty good idea of what was popular with Restoration audiences.

The table on page 30 shows the number of plays by Shakespeare, Fletcher, Ben Jonson and James Shirley performed at the Theatre Royal over the period 1663-1672. Fletcher is the clear winner, with 15 separate plays in four seasons. Shakespeare comes in an embarrassing fourth, with only five separate plays in four seasons, and nothing at all for the first three. One of those five is *Sauny the Scot*, a version of *The Taming of the Shrew* which had been heavily rewritten by John Lacy, the company's most popular comic actor, to provide himself with plenty of low comedy. For many years to come, Shakespeare's plays would be presented almost exclusively in rewritten versions which were felt to be an improvement on the vulgarity and disorderliness of the originals.

Known performances at the first Theatre Royal, 1663 - 1672, Shakespeare and other selected pre-Civil War playwrights.

Theatre Season	Shakespeare (including adaptations)	Fletcher with or without Beaumont and/or Massinger	Jonson	Shirley
1662–63		The Humorous Lieutenant		The Changes or Love in a Maze
1663–64			The Silent Woman The Alchemist	The Court Secret
1664–65			Volpone	
1665–66				The Traitor
PLAGUE AND GREAT FIRE OF LONDON				
1666–67	Sauny the Scot or the Taming of a Shrew, adapted by John Lacy The Merry Wives of Windsor	The Maid's Tragedy The Humorous Lieutenant The Scornful Lady The Chances Rollo, Duke of Normandy The Custom of the Country	The Silent Woman Bartholomew Fair	The Cardinal The Changes or Love in a Maze
1667–68	Sauny the Scot or the Taming of a Shrew, adapted by John Lacy Henry IV Part 1	The Scornful Lady The Storm (The Sea Voyage) Philaster The Wild Goose Chase The Maid's Tragedy Beggar's Bush	Catiline His Conspiracy Bartholomew Fair	Love's Cruelty The Changes or Love in a Maze The Cardinal Hyde Park The Traitor
1668–69	Henry IV Part 1 Othello	Rollo, Duke of Normandy The Faithful Shepherdess The Island Princess The Coxcomb King and No King The Spanish Curate	The Silent Woman Catiline His Conspiracy The Alchemist	
1669–70			Every Man in His Humour	
1670–71				
1671–72	Julius Caesar			
25 January 1672:	**The Theatre Royal is destroyed by fire.**			
TOTALS	5 plays in 4 seasons	15 plays in 4 seasons	6 plays in 6 seasons	6 plays in 5 seasons

30

For the first three years after the Restoration, almost no news plays were presented by either company. The diet for theatre-goers was composed almost exclusively of plays written for their parents and grandparents. The few exceptions were the work of gentlemen amateurs: in 1662 Sir Robert Howard, who owned 25 per cent of the shares in the King's Company, produced *The Committee* and *The Surprisal*; Sir Samuel Tuke wrote *The Adventure of Five Hours*, apparently at the command of Charles II, which was a hit at Lincoln's Inn Fields in early 1663; and Roger Boyle, the Earl of Orrery, tried his hand at writing dramas in rhyming verse, which the King liked so much he promised to put them on at Drury Lane 'as soone as my company have their new stage in order'.[3]

This was all very well, but where were the professionals? Killigrew and Davenant, the two patentees, were the only people left alive and active who had written plays for the London theatres before the Civil War, and although they were happy to revive their old plays, they wrote no new ones. Davenant was a dab hand at translations✢ and adaptations, particularly of Shakespeare, but he didn't trouble the public with any new work of his own. There seems to have been a reluctance about trying to do anything in a literary form that had been officially suppressed for 18 years. All of the arts had suffered under the Puritans, but theatre was the only one to have been actually banned. What would a new play look like? How would it reflect the concerns and anxieties of a generation who had lived through Civil War and Commonwealth; who had seen a king executed and his son restored to the throne; who had seen their country and its institutions torn apart and then reconstituted in the name of religion? This was a very different world to that of the generations for whom Ben Jonson and John Fletcher had been writing.

✢ Davenant's rather strange portmanteau entertainment *The Playhouse to be Let* (1663) contains a translation of Molière's *Sganarelle* which was the first translation of Molière into English. *The Man's the Master* (1668) is a free translation of Scarron's *Le Maitre Valet*.

John Dryden and Dramatic Poesie

John Dryden (1631-1700) was the first professional dramatist of the post-Restoration theatre. He would write plays for over thirty years, becoming the most important formative influence on the drama, not only through his plays but also through his criticism. He has a good claim to being the first literary critic in the English language, and he used his long years of experience in the theatre and his status as the leader of the world of letters (he became poet laureate) to get people to think about what theatre should be doing.

Dryden was born into a family of minor gentry in Northamptonshire, the eldest of fourteen children. There was a strong Puritan tradition in the family, so Dryden's relations were not well disposed towards the court. Dryden had an excellent education at Westminster School followed by Trinity College, Cambridge. He could have become a don, but realised that the academic life was not for him. In the words of one of his contemporaries, he 'went to London in gayer company, & set up for a poet'.[4] As he arrived in 1654, at the height of the Commonwealth, London probably wasn't that gay, and he took a job in Cromwell's civil service. When Charles II was restored to the throne in 1660, Dryden wrote two poems celebrating the event. He had a small income from the family estates, but not enough to live in any degree of comfort, so he needed to think about supporting himself by his pen. He was lodging with Sir Robert Howard, who was theatre-mad,✤ and Dryden's thoughts turned to supporting himself by writing plays. The method of paying playwrights had changed since the pre-war days. Instead of paying a lump sum to the author for the rights to a play, theatre companies had developed a system of allowing the author to receive the third night's takings, after deducting management costs. This might amount to between £100 and £150, less £30 or £35 for the costs, which represented a considerable sum of money in those days.

✤ Howard would become a playwright himself and a major shareholder in the new Drury Lane theatre. His three brothers, Henry, Edward and James, also wrote plays, so it must have run in the family.

Of course, it depended on the play enjoying an uninterrupted run of three nights. If it closed on the first or second night, the author got nothing.

Dryden's first play was called *The Wild Gallant*. It was performed in February 1663, when the King's Company was still appearing at the tennis court in Vere Street, waiting for the new theatre to open. Two weeks later, it was performed at court. Dryden wrote a prologue in which he spoke of the problem for anyone setting up as a playwright in a theatre that was still dominated by plays written in the first part of the century by acknowledged masters like Ben Jonson and John Fletcher. Dryden compared them to the elder brothers who had come into the estate of 'wit' and spent the lot, leaving nothing but scraps for the next generation. He would use the same image two years later in his *Essay of Dramatic Poesie*: 'We acknowledge them [the earlier playwrights] our fathers in wit; but they have ruined their estates themselves before they came into their children's hands.'[5] By 'wit', Dryden meant much more than jokes. Wit in the seventeenth century meant the faculty of understanding the world and sharing that understanding through the skillful use of language.♣ Humour came into it: the ability to make brilliant conversation, whether on the stage or in real life, was highly prized, as it was thought to reflect an intelligent grasp of the world and society. Dryden would later compare those pre-Civil War playwrights to giants who lived before the Great Flood: a race of beings so extraordinary that moderns can only limp along in their shadow.[6]

Dryden had good reason to fear comparison: *The Wild Gallant* was such a mess that Pepys said he couldn't work out which character was meant to be the gallant. The King apparently disliked it. Nothing daunted, Dryden set to work on another play, *The Rival Ladies*, which opened at Drury Lane the following year to greater success. He then began work with Sir Robert Howard on a drama in rhyming couplets called *The Indian Queen*. We do not know how much each contributed

---

♣ Dryden described wit as 'a propriety of thoughts and words' in the preface to *Albion and Albanius* (Dryden, *Of Dramatic Poesy*, ii, 34).

towards the collaboration, nor what Dryden thought of the literary skills of this gentleman amateur, but the blunt fact was that Howard was a major shareholder in Drury Lane and could get anything he wrote staged. Also, Howard's play *The Committee* had been much more successful than Dryden's *Wild Gallant*. A month before the play opened, Dryden became the brother-in-law of his collaborator when he married Lady Elizabeth Howard.

The Indian Queen was a great success when it opened in January 1664, exploiting the capacity of the new theatre for spectacle. It enjoyed a successful run in its first season and was still being performed at Drury Lane thirty years later. Encouraged by this, Dryden went on to write a sequel (alone this time), *The Indian Emperor*, which opened in April 1665. Then the plague broke out and the theatres were closed in June. They would not re-open until November of the following year.

Cut off from his principal source of income, and anxious to escape infection, Dryden spent the period at the home of his father-in-law, the Earl of Berkshire, in Malmesbury. He treated this period of enforced leisure as an opportunity to write free from the disturbances of the theatre, and to sort out his ideas on the role of the theatre. The *Essay of Dramatic Poesie* that he produced is the first extended piece of literary criticism in the English language and contains the first critical analysis of Shakespeare's plays.

The essay takes the form of a dialogue between four characters, all based on real-life originals. Neander (the new man) represented Dryden himself; Crites (the critic) his brother-in-law Sir Robert Howard; Eugenius (the well-born one) Charles Sackville, Lord Buckhurst; and Lisideius (a Latinised anagram of Sir Charles Sedley). They decide to spend a summer's afternoon in a barge on the Thames, discussing various questions that seemed important at the time to people who were trying to re-establish theatre as a significant part of the culture. Crites argues that the dramatists of ancient Greece and Rome were better than the moderns. Eugenius responds that modern plays are much better. Lisideius weighs in with the claim that, amongst the moderns, French plays are better than English plays. This wouldn't have been the case forty years earlier, but the disruption caused by the

Civil War and Commonwealth had destroyed the progress of the arts: 'we have been so long together bad Englishmen that we had not leisure to be good poets'.[7] The French, especially Corneille, write better than English playwrights because they are more 'correct': they observe the three unities of time, place and action.

Neander (Dryden) is having none of that. English plays are livelier and closer to nature than the French ones, which are more like long lectures on religion and politics than plays. Neander gives his view of the early seventeenth century playwrights, comparing Ben Jonson, Beaumont and Fletcher with Shakespeare. Jonson, Fletcher and Beaumont are more witty and correct, but Shakespeare had the greater soul and vaster imagination. To those who argued that the grammar-school boy from Stratford 'wanted learning' compared with university-educated wits, Dryden came up with a reply that has echoed down the centuries: '[Shakespeare] needed not the spectacles of books to read nature; he looked inwards and found her there.'[8]

Having heaped praise on the playwrights of the time of Elizabeth I and James I, with which Lisideius would not have disagreed, Neander/Dryden then moves on to his contemporaries, the men who were writing for the re-opened theatres of the Restoration, and makes the bold claim that: 'We have seen since his Majesty's return many dramatic poems which yield not to those of any foreign nation… our present poets… have far surpassed all the Ancients, and the modern writers of other countries.'[9]

Neander wisely refrains from naming any of these contemporaries who have put the Ancients and the modern French writers to shame, as it would be hard to find any play written between 1660 and 1667 (the date of publication of the *Essay*) that would stand up to much scrutiny. Dryden's own pre-plague efforts were the best of a bad (and very small) bunch. But Dryden seems to have felt that the theatre could become part of a glorious cultural renaissance for England after the horrors of the Civil War and the repression of the Commonwealth; and he was right. The next two decades would see the creation of some of the most brilliant plays in the language, many of which still hold the stage today. A lot of them had their first performances at Drury Lane.

Restoration comedy and heroic tragedy

The question facing would-be playwrights of the 1660s was: what would these glorious cultural artefacts look like? Writing pale imitations of Beaumont and Fletcher wouldn't get them very far, nor would endless translations from the French and Spanish. The age needed its own unique voice, and it would find it in the fields of both comedy and drama.

Theatre in the last part of the seventeenth century became a part of that great project of the age, the scientific revolution that developed the techniques of data collection, analysis and experimentation to find out how the world works. In 1660 the Royal Society was founded, with Charles II as its patron, only months after the Restoration of the monarchy. The fellows of the Royal Society followed the 'empyrical' approach to learning about the world developed earlier in the century by Francis Bacon, the Lord Chancellor. Instead of studying the works of Aristotle and the ancient authorities, the fellows of the Royal Society collected evidence, formulated a hypothesis, performed an experiment and published the results in their journal, *Transactions of the Royal Society*. This would be studied by other scientists who would repeat the experiment. If the results were the same, the hypothesis was taken to be correct. If not, start again.

This seems to us the obvious way to learn about things, but it was revolutionary at the time. The motto of the Royal Society was *Nullius In Verba*, roughly translated as Take No One's Word For It. Many people were shocked that the authority of Aristotle and the learned authors of Greece and Rome was being challenged. 'The fashion of the age is to call everything into question', wrote John Tillotson, the Archbishop of Canterbury.[10] That was true of religion, science and everything else, including the social structures and conventions governing the relationships between men and women.

'We live in an age so sceptical, that… it takes nothing from antiquity on trust,' Dryden wrote, 'And I profess to have no other ambition…

than that poetry may not go backward, when all other arts and sciences are advancing.'[11] Going backward, in terms of poetry (which included plays in Dryden's terminology) meant writing like the authors of the pre-Civil War period. There had to be something fresh. 'Restoration comedy' is a genre that is now instantly recognisable, but perhaps it would be best to start with the age's more curious experiment with heroic drama in rhymed verse.

Charles II had grown up in exile in France as the guest of Louis XIV, so he and his courtiers were very familiar with the conventions of French culture. When the theatres re-opened there was a desire to imitate the French dramas, written in rhyming couplets by playwrights such as Corneille. Charles II specifically asked Roger Boyle, the Earl of Orrery, to try his hand at rhymed couplets in a play, and the Earl obligingly produced *The History of Henry V* (1664), *Mustapha* (1665) and *The Black Prince* (1667). However, the first such play to make it to the stage was the Dryden/Howard collaboration *The Indian Queen* (1664) which Dryden followed up with *The Indian Emperor* (1665).

It is hard to understand the popularity of these heroic dramas, which are sometimes described as heroic tragedies although they weren't always entirely tragic. They were so artificial and stilted, with kings and emperors declaiming about their honour while spotless virgins parade their virtue, it is astonishing that they managed to pack the house with ladies and gentlemen whose honour and virtue were perhaps not beyond question. The characters in these plays behave as no men or women ever behaved, but perhaps that was part of the charm. They were precursors of our comic-strip superheroes, charging around the world fighting battles and wooing fair ladies, rather like Don Quixote, except the audience was meant to take it seriously. It would be hard to perform any of them now.

If these heroic tragedies presented an absurdly idealistic view of human nature, Restoration comedy could be said to go to the other extreme. 'Cynical' is an adjective that often comes up in descriptions of it. The men are out for whatever they can get by way of money and sex; the women speak of their virtue but it is all a pretence. No one is guided by religious or philosophical convictions, which are usually held up to ridicule. But the biggest difference between these comedies and the comedies that were being written before the Civil War is in their treatment of sex. Pre-Civil War plays take adultery very seriously. Any character – particularly any female character – who engages in adultery will be either punished or made to repent of their wicked ways. Restoration comedies treat adultery as a joke and as an almost inevitable consequence of being married: you don't want what you can have, you always want the forbidden fruit.

Restoration comedies are often described as 'bawdy romps', as if they were like Carry On films with more complicated syntax. If that were true, and they were nothing more than smut and cynicism, they would not have lasted on the stage for more than three centuries. At their heart, they embodied an attitude not that far removed from the motto of the Royal Society: *Nullius in Verba*, Take No One's Word For It. The society of the first part of the seventeenth century had been deeply religious: too religious, many people would have said, as the bitter disputes over religious observation and the interpretation of scripture had driven the country into Civil War. But in the area of sexual morality, there was no serious argument. Whatever brand of religion people embraced, Christian moral teaching on sex and marriage was to be upheld.

Post-1660, that had changed. Society became much more secular, and indeed Britain would become notorious as a profoundly secular society compared with other European nations throughout the next century. People weren't prepared to take what St Paul says about sex as gospel. *Nullius in Verba*. How should men and women relate to each other? Should people marry for love, or should financial arrangements predominate? When divorce is impossible, how realistic is it to think that you will remain in love with a spouse for the rest of your life? Is hypocrisy loathsome, or just the necessary glue to hold the social order together? These are all serious questions which still occupy us today in our own highly secular society. The feelings of men and women for each other don't change, but social conventions do. We can change the way in which we think about relationships, and the comic dramatists of the Restoration period certainly got the ball rolling. Plays like *The*

Country Wife, The Man of Mode and *The Way of the World* are much more than 'bawdy romps': they are serious, albeit very funny, attempts to work out how men and women relate to each other under a social order from which the Ten Commandments have been deleted.

Which still begs the question: how could the same audiences have enjoyed *The Indian Queen* and *The Country Wife*? The absurdly idealistic view of human nature expressed in the heroic tragedies and the rather cynical view of the comedies don't seem to belong in the same philosophical universe. There has been some speculation that the tragedies were written for women and the comedies for men, but there is no evidence to support this. In fact, the rakes and libertines who are the heroes of the comedies are in some ways similar to the great warriors of the tragedies: they defy bourgeois morality. As Dr Johnson said of Almanzor, the hero of Dryden's *The Conquest of Granada*: 'He is above all laws; he is exempt from all restraints; he ranges the world at will, and governs wherever he appears.'[12] The heroes of these tragedies are torn between the most extreme demands of love and honour, in situations completely remote from the everyday lives of most of us. The interest, for the original audiences, seems to have lain in seeing how people behave when placed in extreme conditions where bourgeois morality counts for nothing. It's an experiment, not unlike those being conducted by the fellows of the Royal Society.✤ Almanzor goes charging around the world leading armies into battle and claiming:

> *I am as free as nature first made man,*
> *'Ere the base laws of servitude began,*
> *When wilds in woods the noble savage ran.*[13]

This is the first use of the term 'noble savage', and it indicates an interest, still strong today, in how people behave in a state of nature before they have been 'corrupted' by social conventions. In this sense, the heroes of the tragedies are not a million miles away from the fine

---

✤ Dryden was briefly a fellow of the Royal Society, elected to their committee to improve the English language.

In Rep: Plays Performed at Drury Lane During April 1668
These represent known performances, not all performances
Date in brackets is year of first performance

Date of performance, *Play* and playwright

Wednesday 1 April, *The Black Prince* by Lord Orrery (1667)
Tuesday 7 April, *The English Monsieur* by James Howard (1666)
Tuesday 14 April, *Love's Cruelty* by James Shirley (1631)
Wednesday 15 April, *The Maid's Tragedy* by Francis Beaumont and
John Fletcher (1608-11)
Friday 17 April, *The Surprisal* by Sir Robert Howard (1662)
Saturday 18 April, *The Great Favourite or The Duke of Lerma* by Sir
Robert Howard (1668)
Tuesday 21 April, *The Indian Emperor* by John Dryden (1665)
Friday 24 April, *Beggar's Bush* by John Fletcher *et al.* (1622)
Monday 27 April, *The Cardinal* by James Shirley (1641)
Tuesday 28 April, *The Changes or Love in a Maze* by James Shirley (1631)

---

ladies and gentlemen of the comedies, who are trying to find out how they can have a reasonable relationship in a society in which they absolutely must get married, but the omens for success aren't good.

Here come the girls

When Dryden returned to London after the plague, he had more than the *Essay of Dramatic Poesie* in his luggage. He had used his time in the country to write another play: *Secret Love or the Maiden Queen*. This was what was called a tragi-comedy because it had two plots. The serious one concerned a queen who is faced with rebellion. The comical one featured two lively young lovers called Florimel (the Queen's maid of honour) and Celadon (a courtier). In the play's second scene, Florimel meets Celadon whilst she is walking in the park, wearing a mask. It was not unusual then for ladies to wear masks when in public, especially if they were going to places that weren't all that ladylike, such as the theatre. Celadon and Florimel begin to flirt, and Florimel asks Celadon to describe the sort of looks that attract him. 'Oval face, clear skin, hazel eyes, thick brown eye-brows,' he replies, 'a turned-up nose that gives an air to your face... two dimples when you smile.' Celadon threatens to pull the mask from Florimel's face to see how it conforms, at which point she runs off. Had the mask come off, it would have revealed a face exactly matching Celadon's description: it belonged to Nell Gwynne.

Nell Gwynne was one of the first women to take advantage of the new custom of having female parts played by women rather than teenage boys. She was not the first professional actress on the London stage: that accolade belongs to an actress who played Desdemona at a performance of *Othello* given by the King's Company in December 1660 when they were still at the converted tennis court on Vere Street. Unfortunately we don't know the name of this proto-actress, although a prologue to the play drew attention to the novelty and helpfully informed the audience that she was unmarried.[14] Within a matter of weeks, actresses had completely replaced the boys as the public appetite for seeing women on the stage proved irresistible. By the following year, the rolls of both companies show that they had their compliment of actresses.✣ Nell was not amongst them at that stage, and we don't know exactly when she first appeared. There is a frustrating lack of evidence about Nell's early life. We can't be sure where she was born or when, but the most likely date is 1650 and the most likely place an alleyway off Drury Lane. Her mother kept a brothel and Nell was employed as a girl serving drinks to the customers. She probably started working as an orange-seller at the Theatre Royal in 1664. She caught the attention of Charles Hart, the company's handsome leading man, and became

---

✣ The popularity of actresses was such that many plays were written or revived that involved 'breeches' parts, which meant that female characters dressed as men for various plot reasons, thus giving the actresses a chance to show their legs. John Wilson calculated that, of about 375 plays produced in the London theatres between 1660 and 1700, 89 contained breeches parts. Thomas Killigrew even started putting on plays in which all the parts were played by women. We know of all-female productions of his own *The Parson's Wedding*, Dryden's *Secret Love* and Beaumont and Fletcher's *Philaster*. (Wilson [1958] 73 & 82.)

his mistress. He seems to have given her some acting lessons, and within a short time she was playing walk-ons. Her career hadn't progressed much further than that when the plague closed the theatres.

Following the re-opening of the theatres in November 1666, she got bigger parts, and when *Secret Love* opened in February 1667 she was a sensation. Samuel Pepys went to see it on 2 March, on the same night as the King and the Duke of York, and was completely blown away by Nell: 'there is a comical part done by Nell... that I never can hope to see the like done again, by man or woman... so great a performance of a comical part was never, I believe, in the world before as Nell do this.'[15] He went to see the show eight times, in spite of the fact that Pepys was trying to break himself of his theatre-going habit, and the King was so pleased he called it 'his play' and ordered a performance at court.

It is noticeable that Pepys was already calling her 'Nell', as if she needed no other name to be recognised. And she didn't. Almost as soon as she began appearing on the stage she was known as Nell to everyone, in spite of the convention of referring to actresses as 'Mrs' (pronounced Mistress) to make them sound a bit respectable. Nell was the first female star of the British stage, but she went beyond that. The catalogue of an exhibition at the National Portrait Gallery called *The First Actresses* puts Nell forward as the first female 'brand': 'long before "Beyoncé" or "Kylie" there was "Nell"... "Nell" was not respectable but she was folkloric, even mythic... plaques mark her places of residence, and pubs bear her name.'[16] Nell was so famous that, even today, people who have no interest in theatre know the name of Nell Gwynne, who sold oranges at Drury Lane.

What makes this even more remarkable is that her career on the stage lasted for only seven years and none of the plays she appeared in are remembered, except by theatre historians. But then, her success didn't depend entirely on her acting. Nell oozed sex appeal and every man who saw her wanted her. In the summer of 1667 she handed in all her parts at Drury Lane and said she was leaving the stage to become the mistress of Lord Buckhurst (the Eugenius of Dryden's *Essay of Dramatic Poesie*). She went to live with him in Epsom for £100 a year, but it didn't work out and within a month she was picking up her parts again at Drury Lane. She neeedn't have worried: by January 1668 Pepys was reporting that the King was sending for her. She became one of Charles II's mistresses on a much more generous salary: £5,000 a year with a house in Pall Mall and other perks.✣

Nell enjoyed being a royal mistress more than she enjoyed the drudgery of turning up at the theatre every day to rehearse and perform, and left the stage when she was still only 21. In those few years, however, she and Dryden had a few happy collaborations. After *Secret Love*, she appeared in his *An Evening's Love* (1668); *Tyrannic Love* (1669); and finally *The Conquest of Granada* (1670-1671). In fact, she seems to have come out of her second retirement from the stage to do her friend a favour, because in 1669 she had given birth to her first child by Charles II and felt no urge to act again. However, in December 1670 she came out onto the stage of Drury Lane for her final role as Almahide in Dryden's massive, two-part blockbuster of a heroic tragedy, *The Conquest of Granada*. It would mark the start of a brilliant twelve months for both Dryden and Drury Lane.

✣ Nell objected to living in leasehold accommodation and insisted on receiving the freehold of the house. The building on the site remains the only property on the south side of Pall Mall which does not belong to the Crown Estate.

3

The Annus Mirabilis of 1671

When **Dryden was spending** his enforced year of rural retreat in Wiltshire during the plague, he was certainly productive. As well as his *Essay of Dramatic Poesie* and the play *Secret Love,* he wrote a long heroic poem called *Annus Mirabilis*. The Latin title means 'Year of Wonders' and was intended to commemorate the events of the second Anglo-Dutch War. When Dryden had finished the poem, he heard of the Great Fire of London and added verses praising God for saving the City from utter destruction, and prophesying that it would rise in even greater magnificence.

When he got back to London with his three works ready for publication and production, Dryden had a pretty good year of his own in 1667. His new play *Secret Love* was a great hit. His earlier play *The Indian Emperor* was still being performed, and such was his standing that even the rather unsuccessful first play, *The Wild Gallant*, was revived with alterations. Sir William Davenant, proprietor of the rival Duke's company, thought he needed a bit of this sort of success, and tempted Dryden to write for his company. First, in August Dryden produced a farce called *Sir Martin Marall*. He was working in collaboration with William Cavendish, the Duke of Newcastle – another of the theatre-mad aristocrats who played such an important part in Restoration theatre – but it seems that the Duke simply made a literal translation of Molière's play *L'Etourdi* and Dryden did the rest. It was a huge success and remained in the repertoire for years. John Downes the prompter wrote in his theatrical memoirs *Roscius Anglicanus* that this play and *Love in a Tub* 'got the company more money than any preceding comedy'. Three months later, an adaptation of Shakespeare's *The Tempest* appeared, co-written by Dryden and Davenant, which was a travesty of Shakespeare's text but which certainly appealed to the taste of the town. It was such a success that, six years later, the company added some songs and a few more spectacular scenic effects and turned it into an opera. It remained in the repertoire for decades and was the most successful show ever until *The Beggar's Opera* in 1728.

By this time, with five plays by Dryden all playing to good houses in one year and the opposition sniffing around, the company at Drury Lane thought they ought to make sure of their man. He was offered a contract under the terms of which he would become a shareholder in the King's Company, without having to put up any cash, in return for writing three plays a year. This was an ambitious target and Dryden never fulfilled it, but he would remain the house playwright, under exclusive contract, for the next ten years. Around the same time, in April 1668, Sir William Davenant died suddenly and Dryden succeeded him as Poet Laureate. Things were looking good for Dryden and for Drury Lane.

In December 1670 Dryden presented to the astonished audience at Drury Lane his heroic drama to end all heroic dramas: *The Conquest of Granada*. Written in two parts, it is really one play which is so long it takes two sessions to get through it. The plot is immensely complicated and involves the most incredible displays of courage, honour, virtue and chastity. 'Over the top' doesn't begin to describe it. According to the diarist John Evelyn's wife, 'love is made so pure, and valour so nice, that one would imagine it designed for an Utopia rather than our stage',[1] and Dr Johnson pretty much had a handle on it when he attributed to Dryden a determination 'to glut the public with dramatic wonders; to exhibit… a theatrical meteor of incredible love and impossible valour, and to leave no room for a wilder flight to the extravagance of posterity'.[2]

The plot concerns the successful expulsion by the Spanish from Granada of the 'Moors' (Muslim Arabs) in 1492. However, the play is much more about the Moors and their various factions than the Spanish. Almanzor, the Achilles-like hero, is in love with Almahide, who is betrothed to Boabdelin, the King of the Moors. She loves Almanzor but will not betray her vows. Boabdelin knows of Almanzor's love for his fiancée, but cannot do anything about it as he needs Almanzor leading his troops. During the play Almanzor discovers that he is the long-lost son of a Spanish Duke, but he continues to fight for the Moors as he must keep his word.

This was a huge hit. The audiences couldn't get enough of the fantastic twists of the plot, of the spectacular scenery,[3] and of their beloved Nell playing the romantic heroine Almahide. The two parts ran until the end of February 1671 when Nell left the stage for the last time, having done her friend Dryden a huge favour.

Love in a Wood

March saw the première at Drury Lane of William Wycherley's first comedy *Love in a Wood* or *St James's Park*, one of the earliest confident, fully-fledged Restoration comedies. Of the four great masters of the form – Sir George Etherege (1635-1691), William Wycherley (1641-1716), Sir John Vanbrugh (1664-1726) and William Congreve (1670-1729) – Etherege wrote for the Duke's company; Wycherley mainly (three out of four plays) for the King's Company; Congreve and Vanbrugh divided their loyalties. Etherege was first in the field with *Love in a Tub* in 1663 and *She Would if She Could* in 1668, but Wycherley was next. He was 30 when *Love in a Wood* opened, but claimed to have written it when he was 19. This was almost certainly untrue, although he may have worked on it for a few years, but it is in any case an extraordinarily good piece of work for a first play. All the familiar ingredients of Restoration comedy are here: the priapic young blades of St James who pursue as many women as possible; the sensible young women who want their lovers to be faithful; women of the other sort who want sex or money and preferably both together; the miserly puritanical Alderman who inveighs against the wickedness of the age but chases after young flesh; the impoverished and foolish knight who needs to marry a fortune; the fop who also wants to marry a fortune and gets the Alderman's daughter, only to find that she is six months pregnant and the Alderman intends to disinherit her by marrying the daughter of a bawd who has already had £500 off him by threatening to cry rape and begetting a son. All good filthy fun. The extraordinary thing about the plot is the extreme personal freedom that all of the main characters enjoy, which manifests itself in night-time rambles in St James's Park, with the ladies wearing masks. We would call it cruising, but it would be harder today as the Park is fully lit after dark, and we don't expect to see ladies masked any more. The whole point about the set-up is that anonymity dissolves social norms since, in the words of Lady Flippant, 'Joan's as good as my lady in the dark'.[4]

One of the influences on *Love in a Wood* was probably James Shirley's 1632 play *Hyde Park*, in which some of the action takes place in Hyde Park, only recently opened to the public. However, the completely different tone of the two plays shows how radically social attitudes and the theatre had changed since the Civil War. There is nothing in the slightest bit improper about the behaviour of the main characters in *Hyde Park*. The ladies are conventionally virtuous and the scenes in the park take place in daylight. The idea of ladies walking alone in any public place after midnight and looking to pick up men would have seemed too disgusting to put on the stage in the 1630s.

In spite of everything, the two young ladies of the plot agree to marry their lovers in the last scene, hoping for the best in spite of everything. 'If I could be desperate now,' says Lydia to Ranger, 'and give you up my liberty, could you find in your heart to quit all other engagements, and voluntarily turn yourself over to one woman, and she a wife too? Could you away with the insupportable bondage of matrimony?' Ranger replies with a couplet that closes the play:

> *The end of marriage now is liberty,*
> *And two are bound to set each other free.*[5]

In spite of the artificiality of rhymed couplets, it has a modern ring about it.

The performance of the play had an unexpected consequence for Wycherley. As he was riding in Pall Mall in a coach, he passed the coach of the Duchess of Cleveland, Charles II's mistress, travelling in the opposite direction. He was astonished when she leant out of the window and shouted: 'You, Wycherley, you are the son of a whore.' He soon realised that this was meant as a compliment, in reference to a song in *Love in a Wood* that contains the verse:

> *Great wits and great braves*
> *Have always a punk to their mother.*[6]

A punk was a prostitute, so the Duchess was actually telling him he was a great wit. Wycherley immediately ordered his coachman to turn around and overtake the Duchess's coach. After a very elaborate exchange of compliments through coach windows, the Duchess agreed to see the play again that night, when she sat in the King's Box. Wycherley sat in the pit and flirted outrageously with her throughout the show. They became lovers, very much to the advantage of Wycherley's career. It was good from the Duchess's point of view as well because Wycherley was a looker, built and reputedly good in bed – in short, he was like one of the rakes in his own plays. There is something so improbable about the whole incident that it sounds more like something from a play than real life, but that is true of a lot of things that have happened in the Theatre Royal.

Marriage à la Mode

Shortly after the successful opening of *Love in a Wood*, the Duchess of York died and the theatres had to close for six weeks. Dryden used the time to start work on a new comedy which he called *Marriage à la Mode*. According to Dryden's preface to the printed edition, it received some polishing from John Wilmot, the Earl of Rochester, who added sparkle to the courtly conversations whilst they spent time together at Windsor over the summer. We can't be sure of the date of the première, but it was probably in October or November 1671.

Once again, Dryden went for the double-plot structure. The serious plot concerns the usurping King of Scicily and two young people, brought up by a peasant in rural innocence, who are in fact the long-lost son of the deposed King and the long-lost daughter of the usurper. The young man and woman are in love, but as first one and then the other is presented as the long-lost child of the usurper (he doesn't know the sex of the child his long-lost wife gave birth to), the course of their true love doesn't run smooth. When the young woman thinks that she is the usurper's child, she is torn between loyalty to her putative father and love of the young man who is leading a rebellion against him. Typical love-and-honour stuff, then.

The comical plot concerns two couples, one married and one engaged, in which each man and each woman is pursuing the partner of the other. Every attempt they make at coition is frustrated, and in the end they decide they might as well stick with the partners allocated to them. There is virtually no connection between the two plots, and the comical plot would later be separated from the serious one and acted on its own.

The play opens with a witty and elegant lyric which is very anti-marriage:

> *Why should a foolish marriage vow,*
> *Which long ago was made,*
> *Oblige us to each other now,*
> *When passion is decayed?*
> *We loved, and we loved, as long as we could,*
> *'Till our love was loved out in us both;*
> *But our marriage is dead, when the pleasure is fled:*
> *'Twas pleasure first made it an oath.*

This sets the tone of the play, in which the characters in the comical plot ring endless changes on the notion that you are never satisfied with what you can easily have, you'd like a bit of what your friend's got as well. Here is a comparison made by the 'gallant' gentlemen between a husband and a lover:

> RODOPHIL: There's something of antipathy in the word marriage to the nature of love; marriage is the mere ladle of affection, that cools it when 'tis never so fiercely boiling over...
>
> PALAMEDE: O what a difference will she find between a dull resty husband and a quick vigorous lover! He sets out like a carrier's horse, plodding on, because he knows he must, with the bells of matrimony chiming so melancholy about his neck, in pain till he's at his journey's end... I take heat after heat, like a well-breathed courser.[7]

And here they are again on the benefits of an open marriage:

> RODOPHIL: If they would suffer us but now and then to make excursions, the benefit of our variety would be theirs; instead of one continued, lazy, tired love, they would, in their turn, have twenty vigorous, fresh and active lovers.
>
> PALAMEDE: And I would ask any of them, whether a poor narrow brook, half-dry the best part of the year, and running ever one way, be to be compared to a lusty stream, that has ebbs and flows?
>
> RODOPHIL: Ay, or is half so profitable for navigation?[8]

This is witty, in the seventeenth-century meaning of the word: it is funny, it is brilliantly phrased, and it says something about the human condition by drawing an analogy with natural phenomena of just the sort that interested fellows of the Royal Society: tidal rivers, like the Thames, are better for trade.

Some people have taken the anti-marriage sentiments of the play as an indication that Dryden's own marriage was in trouble, and it is true that he took as his mistress at this time an actress in the Drury Lane company called Anne Reeves, who was in the cast of *Marriage à la Mode*. However, this attitude towards marriage was absolutely standard in the comedies of the time. The nature of relationships between men and women was a pre-occupation not just of the theatre but of the wider society. The social and economic order was based on marriage; cohabitation wasn't an option, nor was divorce; and spinsterhood was difficult for women, not least financially. So, for all its imperfections, the married state had to be made to work, just as the two couples in *Marriage à la Mode* decide to make it work by accepting that they are stuck with each other and may as well make the best of it.

Marriage à la Mode was a success and Dryden would later describe himself as having 'swept the stakes' in 1671, but his luck was about to change.

The Rehearsal

While *Marriage à la Mode* was enjoying its first run, another play was in preparation that would make profits for Drury Lane whilst at the same time making fun of Dryden, its in-house dramatist. It was called *The Rehearsal* and it was written by George Villiers, the second Duke of Buckingham. The Duke was another of those theatrical aristocrats who made such an important contribution to late seventeenth-century theatre, like the Earl of Orrery, the Earl of Rochester and the Duke of Newcastle. What was it about theatre in those days that attracted the highest in the land to get their hands dirty in the day-to-day business of running theatres and putting on plays? One nineteenth-century theatre historian speculated that theatre then was rather like the turf in his own day.[9] Just as Victorian gentlemen did not feel it beneath their dignity to concern themselves with the breeding of horses and the management of jockeys, so their forebears thought it no disgrace to write plays and coach actresses. Of all the aristocrats who tried their hand at script-writing, the Duke of Buckingham was the most successful. *The Rehearsal* was a hit and held the stage for over a century, long after the Earl of Orrery's tedious tragedies had been forgotten. Not only was the Duke one of the highest-ranking members of the aristocracy, he was also one of the most powerful members of the government – Buckingham gave the 'B' to Cabal. Under the circumstances, one would have expected a dignified heroic drama, or at least a witty comedy. In fact, *The Rehearsal* is a satirical farce.

The Duke wanted to make fun of certain absurdities in the theatre of his time, and he did so by having a vain and foolish playwright called Bayes take two gentlemen to see a rehearsal of his absurd new tragedy about the two rival kings of Brentford. The two gentlemen play the 'straight' role, asking how the audience can be expected to sit through such wildly improbable and over-written scenes, but Bayes blithely dismisses their quibbles, justifying his play in such a way as to make himself appear a fool and an egotist. Bayes was immediately recognised as Dryden, the in-house dramatist at Drury Lane. First of all, the name of the character referred to Dryden's status as poet laureate – entitled to the wreath of bay or laurel leaves that crowns poetic excellence. Secondly, the play contain parodies of numerous passages in Dryden's plays, including his hits of that year *The Conquest of Granada* and *Marriage à la Mode*. Here is a tender passage about cooing turtle-doves from *The Conquest of Granada*:

> So, two kind turtles, when a storm is nigh,
> Look up; and see it gath'ring in the sky:
> Each calls his mate to shelter in the groves,
> Leaving, in murmurs, their unfinished loves.
> Perch'd on some dropping branch they sit alone,
> And coo, and hearken to each other's moan.

Here is the Duke of Buckingham's take on it:

> So boar and sow, when any storm is nigh,
> Snuff up, and smell it gath'ring in the sky:
> Boar beckons sow to trot in chestnut groves,
> And there consummate their unfininish'd loves.

Pensive in mud they wallow all alone,
And snort, and gruntle to each other's moan.[10]

There was much more like this. *The Rehearsal* opened at Drury Lane
on 7 December 1671, and it is part of theatre-lore that the Duke of
Buckingham tricked Dryden into sitting in his box so that everyone in
the audience could enjoy the discomfort of the poet laureate. The Duke
was also said to have coached Lacy, the comedian who was playing
Bayes, in Dryden's speech and mannerisms, and had him dressed and
made up as his victim.[11] Whether or not Dryden sat in the Duke's box,
it is inconceivable that he didn't know what was coming. Dryden was
a shareholder in the theatre and was actively involved in its
management, as well as being the principal playwright. He would have
been in and out on a daily basis during rehearsals for *Marriage à la
Mode*, which had opened only a few weeks before, and his mistress
Anne Reeves was in the cast of *The Rehearsal*.

So why didn't Dryden use his influence to stop it? Probably because,
as a shareholder, he wanted hit shows, and *The Rehearsal* was certainly
a hit. It outlasted the plays it was making fun of to such an extent that
in 1704 a *Key to the Rehearsal* was published, explaining the parodies.
We know of over 300 performances during the eighteenth century.
Colley Cibber and his son Theophilus Cibber both took the part of
Bayes, while Garrick chose it for his first performance at Drury Lane
in 1742. Then, in 1779, Sheridan gave it a new lease of life when he
rewrote it as *The Critic*. Laurence Olivier scored a great success as
Sheridan's Mr Puff – the descendant of Bayes – as late as 1946.

Dryden made no counter-attack on *The Rehearsal* which, given his
propensity for bitter literary feuds, was surprising. He claimed many
years later that he wasn't particularly bothered by it and didn't take it
personally. However, he did have his own back ten years later when
he portrayed the Duke of Buckingham as Zimri in his poem *Absalom
and Achitophel*:

A man so various that he seemed to be
Not one, but all mankind's epitome;

Stiff in opinions, always in the wrong,
Was everything by starts and nothing long;
But, in the course of one revolving moon
Was chymist, fiddler, statesman and buffoon.[12]

Dryden stopped writing heroic tragedies shortly after *The Rehearsal* and it has often been said that he was embarrassed by the ridicule. It is more likely that he just moved on as a writer. The success of *The Rehearsal* certainly did nothing to drive the plays it targeted from the stage: heroic tragedy remained popular until the end of the century. It was a burlesque – or spoof as we would now say – and burlesque is fundamentally an affectionate form. The *Scream* spoof-horror franchise of films didn't stop people from going to see horror films, and most of the people who go to *Forbidden Broadway* are fans of the musicals that are being mocked: you can laugh at things you like.

The end of the first Theatre Royal

Dryden's poem *Annus Mirabilis* had been written in 1666 to commemorate the extraordinary events of the previous year, and was actually finished when the Great Fire of London broke out. Dryden had to go back into his work to give it another ending. Unfortunately 1671, the *annus mirabilis* of Drury Lane, also led to a conflagration. On 25 January 1672, a fire started under the stairs at the back of the theatre where Orange Moll, who held the concession for selling fruit, kept her stock. It soon consumed the backstage area, including the sets and costumes. A south-westerly wind blew the fire into the houses on Russell Street and Drury Lane where, to prevent the spread of the blaze in a densely built-up area, a number of houses were blown up. A promising young actor called Richard Bell died in one of these explosions. The first Theatre Royal had lasted for less than nine years.

PART TWO

Garrick's Drury Lane

PART TWO

4

A Downward Spiral

The situation facing the King's Company following the fire was extremely serious. Their purpose-built theatre had been destroyed after less than nine years; the entire stock of scenery and costumes had gone; they needed to raise the funds to build a new theatre; and they had somehow to keep working or they would all starve. The one bright spot in all of this was that there was a vacant theatre to let in London. The reason for this (which wasn't quite so good) was that the rival Duke's Company was doing so well.

The Duke's Company had flourished under the capable management of Sir William Davenant, the holder of the other patent. He was a professional man of the theatre (unlike Thomas Killigrew) who also had the good fortune to sign up Thomas Betterton, acknowledged to be the greatest actor of the age. His grasp of the mechanics of stage spectacle had allowed him to steal a march on the opposition with his moveable perspective scenery. Davenant had an instinct for what the public wanted and could spot talent. He had discovered Sir George Etherege, the first of the great writers of Restoration comedy, and his bastardised versions of Shakespeare's *Macbeth* and *The Tempest* (with Dryden) held the stage for decades. Then, in 1668, he suddenly dropped dead. His son, Charles, was only

---

Prologue by John Dryden, spoken by Michael Mohun at the opening of the King's Company at Lincoln's Inn Fields, 26 February 1672

So shipwracked passengers escape to land,
So look they, when on the bare beach they stand,
Dropping and cold, and their first fear scarce o'er,
Expecting famine on a desert shore.
From that hard climate we must wait for bread,
Whence even the natives, forced by hunger, fled.
Our stage does human chance present to view,
But ne'er before was seen so sadly true;
You are changed too, and your pretence to see
Is but a nobler name for charity.
Your own provisions furnish out our feasts,
While you, the founders, make yourselves our guests.
Of all mankind beside Fate had some care,
But for poor wit no portion did prepare;
'Tis left a rent-charge for the brave and fair.
You cherished it, and now its fall you mourn,
Which blind unmannered zealots make their scorn,
Who think that fire a judgement on the stage,
Which spared not temples in its furious rage.
But as our new-built city rises higher,
So from old theatres new may aspire,
Since Fate contrives magnificence by fire.
Our great metropolis does far surpass
Whate'er is now, and equals all that was:
Our wit as far does foreign wit excel,
And, like a king, should in a palace dwell.
But we with golden hopes are vainly fed,
Talk high, and entertain you in a shed:
Your presence here, for which we humbly sue,
Will grace old theatres, and build up new.

---

eleven, so his widow took over the management of the company on Charles's behalf. Realising she needed help, she asked the actors Thomas Betterton and Henry Harris to manage with her. Betterton soon established himself as the dominant partner and became, in effect, the first of a long line of actor-managers who had such an enormous impact on the development of theatre in Britain.

The Duke's Company now began to plan an escape from their converted tennis court in Lincoln's Inn Fields to a new, purpose-built theatre that would allow them to rival the spectacular scenic effects of Drury Lane. The new theatre, possibly designed by Sir Christopher Wren, was built on the riverside at Dorset Garden, a little south of Salisbury Square, off Fleet Street,[1] and opened on 9 November 1671 with Dryden's farce *Sir Martin Marall*. The Dorset Garden Theatre was the last word in luxury, with the very latest stage machinery, and was said to have cost the staggering amount of £9,000. Even without the destruction of the old Drury Lane, it would have constituted a formidable rival.

The Lincoln's Inn Fields theatre had, therefore, been empty for only two months when Drury Lane went up in smoke, so the King's Company was able to move in and put on its first performance in the building a month after the fire. On 26 February 1672 they opened with John Fletcher's play *Wit Without Money* – the choice of play being clearly ironic, as the company was in the most serious financial position. Charles II was in the audience, no doubt to encourage his devastated company, and when the curtain went up, the actors were 'discovered on the stage in melancholick postures' while Michael Mohun spoke Dryden's specially-composed prologue. Dryden thanked his audience for supporting them, which he compared to an act of charity as they were reduced to performing in 'a shed', and with the brilliance that made him the most sought-after author of prologues and epilogues of the time, he compared the destruction of Drury Lane to the destruction of the City of London by the fire of 1666. Just as London had arisen in an even more magnificent guise since the fire, he prophesied, so would another Drury Lane arise from the ashes:

> *So from old theatres new may aspire,*
> *Since Fate contrives magnificence by fire.*

We don't know what that first performance looked like. There is speculation that the Duke's Company may have left behind their old scenery which wouldn't fit into the new theatre, but we don't know. The stage probably looked bare and, at a time when audiences had become used to elaborate sets and costumes, this was going to put the company at a serious disadvantage.

The King's Company would be at Lincoln's Inn Fields for two years, during which their repertoire was not particularly inspiring. Thomas Killigrew, thinking that if the public liked looking at actresses' legs, the more women onstage the better, put on an all-female version of his old play *The Parson's Wedding*. Dryden wrote two new plays: *The*

Assignation, which flopped, and a crude piece of anti-Dutch propaganda called *Amboyna*, which didn't do much better. The Duke's Company, meanwhile, had *The Gentleman Dancing Master* by Wycherley; *Epsom Wells* by Thomas Shadwell; and then really ramped up the competition with *The Empress of Morocco* by Elkanah Settle. This production was designed to make the most of the new machinery at Dorset Garden and had such spectacular sets that, when the play was published, it contained engravings of each scene. This was the first time anything of the sort had been done, and these illustrations provide us with the closest thing we have to an accurate representation of what a Restoration show actually looked like. The King's Company took itself off to Oxford for a summer season, where Dryden wrote an epilogue complaining bitterly, in terms that would become wearily familiar as the centuries rolled by, of the way in which serious plays were being out-competed by spectacle and novelty:

> But when all failed, to strike the stage quite dumb,
> Those wicked engines, called machines, are come.[2]

He meant the machines that were shifting the sets for *The Empress of Morocco*, but 'machines' would become an intrinsic part of the whole debate surrounding what theatre was about for generations to come.

The opening of the second Theatre Royal

Meanwhile, the second Theatre Royal was rising from the ashes. When the first theatre burnt down, the building shareholders lost their entire investment and had to start from scratch, with only 30 years left on the lease (which the Earl of Bedford refused to extend). They appealed to the King for a subsidy, on the grounds that the new theatre would cost 'neere two thousand pounds more than it did when it was first built'. The King promised £2,000 and the Duchess of Cleveland promised £1,500, but there is no record of the payments being made.

However, there was a 'brief' sent out in 1673 to all parish churches in England asking them to take up a collection. Given the hostility that many churchgoers still felt towards the theatre, this seems a strange request, and it raised little money.✦ One way or another, the building shareholders came up with the cash, which was more than their estimate. While the original building had cost £2,500, their budget for the replacement seems to have been around £3,400. In fact, the best evidence we have suggests it cost just under £4,000.

It stood on the same site and had the same footprint, except that the ten-foot yard in front of the main entrance disappeared and the space was incorporated into the building. They also built themselves a new scenic workshop to the south of the main structure, but this was on land that was no longer controlled by the Earl of Bedford, having been let out on 'fee-farm', so the acting shareholders came to an arrangement with another landlord. Each shareholder had to pay £160 towards the cost of the structure, while Dryden (who had one-and-a-quarter shares) paid £200, so it must have been large. It seems that the actors also took leases on some of the smaller properties that lined the passage leading from the back of the building to Drury Lane, and these became incorporated into the structure of the theatre.

Once again, there is a tradition that Christopher Wren designed the theatre. We can't be sure, but this time there is at least some documentary evidence. The collection of Wren's papers at All Souls College, Oxford, contains a sectional drawing of a theatre that is just captioned 'Playhouse', but the dimensions correspond to the known dimensions of the Drury Lane site, and most scholars accept it as a representation of that second Theatre Royal. Now, at last, we can get a fairly accurate idea of what confronted the people who paid to see the play.

The auditorium was, once again, divided into pit, boxes and gallery. The pit benches were curved and set on a stepped, sloping floor, rising up to what was called the amphitheatre. The amphitheatre held the

---

✦ The parishioners of Caversham collected six shillings, Berwick sent two shillings and Symondsbury in Dorset another two shillings. (*The London Stage 1660-1800*, Part I, xli.)

best seats in the house, and was probably divided into boxes, although once again we need to remember that the group of people sitting in a box had not necessarily all arrived together. There were two tiers of boxes flanking the pit, which would have given a restricted view of the stage but which, on the other hand, gave the audience a very good view of whoever was sitting in the boxes. This was a time when people came to the theatre 'to see and to be seen'. Above the amphitheatre were two galleries, with the cheapest seats in the top gallery occupied by working-class patrons. The audience in the middle gallery would have been more middle-class. The best estimate for the capacity of the auditorium is 1,000.

However, no member of the audience would have been far from the actors because they appeared on what was called the proscenium, but which we would call the forestage or thrust-stage, projecting out into the auditorium to the extent that some of the occupants of the boxes were actually beside the actors. What we would call the proscenium was an arch dividing the forestage from what was called the scenic stage, where the wings and shutters slid in and out to change the scene behind the actors. The actors could not appear on this scenic stage because the scenery was painted in perspective, so that actors would have been as tall as the trees and buildings at the back. For really big sets and for the processions that were so popular in shows, the back set of shutters could draw back to reveal a space behind known as the vista stage. As years went by and managements tried to increase the capacity of the house, this forestage would be cut back, eventually disappearing in the nineteenth century, so that actors would appear behind the arch (what we call the proscenium) and within the sets.

The new theatre opened on 26 March 1674 with a performance of John Fletcher's play *Beggar's Bush*. The fact that plays by Fletcher had now been chosen to open both the first and the second theatres on the site, as well as the company's first night at Lincoln's Inn Fields, is a measure of the high esteem in which this now-forgotten playwright was held. John Dryden, the house dramatist, made his usual contribution of a witty prologue and epilogue to make the evening memorable, and he obviously decided that modesty in the face of fierce competition would

Prologue by John Dryden, spoken by Michael Mohun at
the opening of the second Theatre Royal, 26 March 1674

A plain-built house, after so long a stay,
Will send you half unsatisfied away;
When, fallen from your expected pomp, you find
A bare convenience only is designed.
You, who each day can theatres behold,
Like Nero's palace, shining all with gold,
Our mean ungilded stage will scorn, we fear,
And for the homely room disdain the cheer.
Yet now cheap druggets to a mode are grown,
And a plain suit, since we can make but one,
Is better than to be by tarnished gawdry known.
They, who are by your favours wealthy made,
With mighty sums may carry on their trade;
We, broken banquiers, half destroyed by fire,
With our small stock to humble roofs retire;
Pity our loss, while you their pomp admire.
For fame and honour, we no longer strive;
We yield in both, and only beg to live;
Unable to support their vast expense,
Who build and treat with such magnificence,
That, like the ambitious monarchs of the age,
They give the law to our provincial stage.
Great neighbours enviously promote excess,
While they impose their splendour on the less;
But only fools, and they of vast estate,
The extremity of modes will imitate,
The dangling knee-fringe and the bib-cravat.

Yet if some pride with want may be allowed,
We in our plainness may be justly proud;
Our royal master willed it should be so;
Whate'er he's pleased to own can need no show;
That sacred name gives ornament and grace;
And like his stamp, makes basest metals pass.
'Twere folly now a stately pile to raise,
To build a playhouse, while you throw down plays;
Whilst scenes, machines and empty operas reign,
And for the pencil you the pen disdain;
While troops of famished Frenchmen hither drive,
And laugh at those upon whose alms they live:
Old English authors vanish, and give place
To these new conquerors of the Norman race.
More tamely than your fathers you submit;
You're now grown vassals to them in your wit.
Mark, when they play, how our fine fops advance
The mighty merits of these men of France,
Keep time, cry Bon, and humour the cadence.
Well, please yourselves: but sure 'tis understood,
That French machines have ne'er done England good.
I would not prophesy our house's fate;
But while vain shows and scenes you overrate,
'Tis to be feared—
That as a fire the former house o'erthrew
Machines and tempests will destroy the new.

be the best approach. He described the new building as a 'plain-built house' and 'a bare convenience', which it can't have been after spending so much more than the first theatre cost, but it must have seemed plain compared with the luxury of Dorset Garden. However, Dryden excuses the plainness of the theatre by saying that it would be a bad investment to spend money on a good theatre dedicated to drama when the public just want musical spectaculars:

> 'Twere folly now a stately pile to raise,
> To build a playhouse, while you throw down plays;
> Whilst scenes, machines and empty operas reign,
> And for the pencil you the pen disdain.

The reference to the pencil and the pen needs a bit of unpacking now, but would have been immediately understood at the time. Those who believed that the theatre should concentrate on what we call straight plays emphasised the importance of the text – written with a pen. They contrasted this with the delights of spectacular scenery that was drawn with a pencil and then painted with a brush. Dryden ends his brilliant prologue with a warning:

> 'Tis to be feared–
> That as a fire the former house o'erthrew
> Machines and tempests will destroy the new.

Dryden's reference to 'tempests' is double-edged: tempests, like fires, are regarded by insurers as 'acts of God' that no one can foresee, and of course a fire had destroyed the first Theatre Royal. But Dryden is saying that the second theatre could be destroyed, not by an act of God, but by the corrupted taste of the town. In 1667 Dryden had collaborated with Sir William Davenant on an 'adaptation' of Shakespeare's *The Tempest* that had been very successful. In fact, it had been so successful that in 1674, just as the new Theatre Royal was getting ready to open, the management of the Duke's Company called in Thomas Shadwell to revamp the text, mauling what little was left of Shakespeare's original and Dryden's thoughtful alterations, to turn it into an 'opera' – that is to say, a show with lots of songs and spectacular scenic effects. According to John Downes, the prompter of the Duke's Company who wrote his memoirs in 1708, 'not any succeeding opera got more money'.[3] It remained in the repertoire for decades, the seventeenth-century equivalent of *The Phantom of the Opera*. For Dryden, who regarded Drury Lane as the home of the drama, this was a serious threat. What would happen to the tradition of Shakespeare, Ben Jonson and John Fletcher if the public just wanted musical spectaculars? This conception of Drury Lane as a stronghold of the national tradition of drama would be a potent one for centuries to come.

Heading for a merger

It would be good to be able to say that the company swiftly recovered from the devastating effects of the fire and two years spent in a less-than-ideal theatre, but they didn't. In fact, the years that followed were marked by disputes, debts and several closure notices. Dryden had described the company in his prologue as 'broken banquiers [bankers], half destroyed by fire', and certainly the finances never recovered from the effects of the blaze, but the problem was much more deep-seated than that: the King's Company suffered from chronically bad management. A comparison with the rival company makes it clear what went wrong.

Sir William Davenant was a professional man of the theatre whose background had been in trade: his parents were tavern-keepers. He knew what it took to run a business, and when he opened the Duke's Company in the converted tennis court in Lincoln's Inn Fields he moved into a house attached to the building so that he could keep a close eye on it. Four of the actresses lived in his house, not – as people have often assumed – for immoral purposes, but so that he and his wife could look out for their welfare. When he died, his wife, a sensible and capable woman, took over, with the help of Thomas Betterton and Henry Harris. Things were managed in an orderly and efficient way.

In Rep: Plays Performed at Drury Lane During November 1674

These represent known performances, not all performances
Date in brackets is year of first performance

Date of performance, *Play* and playwright

Monday 9 November, *Rollo, Duke of Normandy (The Bloody Brother)*
by John Fletcher *et al.* (1612-1624)
Tuesday 10 November, *The Indian Emperor* by John Dryden (1665)
Thursday 12 November, *The Alchymist* by Ben Jonson (1610)
Monday 16 November, *Aglaura* by John Suckling (1637)
Thursday 19 November, *The Mock Tempest* by Thomas Duffett
(premiere)
Thursday 26 November, *The Changes or Love in a Maze* by James
Shirley (1632)
Monday 30 November, *Bartholomew Fair* by Ben Jonson (1614)

Thomas Killigrew, on the other hand, was a courtier. He had been used to getting money by sponging off the royal family. He knew nothing about running a business and seemed to think that the theatre would run itself while he collected the rent and the dividends. Unfortunately, theatres are very complex organisations: they require the full-time, hands-on attention of a manager or management company to make them work. Drury Lane never had that and it soon started to come apart at the seams. The fire just exacerbated problems that were already there.

By the time the new theatre opened, Killigrew had handed over the management of the company to two of the actors, Michael Mohun and Charles Hart. He had also pawned his interest both in the building shares and the patent to raise cash. This made the legal complexities of the management structure even worse than they had been, as more and more people had a piece of the theatre, and most of them had no relevant experience. Business was terrible, to the extent that, after paying the rent, there was virtually nothing left for the actors. Several of the leading actors threatened to leave, and the theatre did actually close in February 1676. The King expressed his extreme displeasure and ordered the actors to get back to work. The situation was so bad that Killigrew, who was pretty much hated by everyone at this stage, asked his son Charles to sort it out. It was such a thankless task that he promised Charles that he would hand over the patent and all his interest in the theatre to him, if he could do so. Charles did manage to sort it out, mainly by bribing the ringleaders, and the shows continued. Killigrew senior then refused to hand over his interest to his son. The dispute became so bitter that the Lord Chamberlain placed the management of the company in the hands of four of the actors, later reduced to one – Charles Hart – when they couldn't agree. Charles Killigrew went to court to force his father to honour the agreement, at which point the people to whom his father had mortgaged his interest came forward, pointing out that it wasn't his to offer. The court found in favour of Charles Killigrew, who discovered that all the profits from his father's interest were in any case being paid to his creditors. At this point, February 1677, Thomas Killigrew, the creator of the original Theatre Royal, Drury Lane, exits from its stage for the last time. He died six years later.

As the finances of the company lurched from bad to worse, scarcely anyone could get paid. John Dryden was now finding his arrangement as a shareholder in the company was a liability rather than a source of income. When he wrote *All For Love*, his take on Shakespeare's *Antony and Cleopatra*, in 1677, he insisted on returning to his previous arrangement and receiving the third night's profits. (On becoming a shareholder, he had forfeited this right.) In the following year he broke his agreement with the King's Company completely and gave his *Oedipus* to the Duke's Company.

If Dryden couldn't get a living from Drury Lane, how much worse must it have been for the actors? We can get some idea of their situation from the number of times actors in the King's Company were pursued for debt. Members of both companies were sworn in as members of the royal household, under the authority of the Lord Chamberlain. This was necessary to protect them from the vagrancy laws, as actors were still classed as rogues and vagabonds, and could be charged with vagrancy just for putting on a play unless they were protected by a powerful person. Being members of the royal household didn't amount to very much: each actor received an allowance of scarlet cloth to make an outfit with whenever they were required to walk in processions on state occasions. However, there was a valuable fringe benefit: members of the royal household could not be arrested or sued for debt without the permission of the Lord Chamberlain. In the period up to 1682, there were numerous requests to the Lord Chamberlain to waive this privilege, most of them relating to actors in the King's Company.[4] The actors' salaries were weeks or even months in arrears, and on one occasion Thomas Killigrew complained that they had 'violently shared' the contents of a cash box they got their hands on after a particularly good night at the box office. It is almost certain that the play which caused this completely understandable rush for the cash box was one of the greatest in the history of Drury Lane, and indeed in the language: William Wycherley's *The Country Wife*, which opened at Drury Lane in January 1675. This would not be the last time that a masterpiece appeared at Drury Lane in the midst of such chaos that you wonder how they managed to get the curtain up at all. Wycherley followed it, in December 1676, with *The Plain Dealer*, another complex and sophisticated comedy that stands in a different league to the rather simplistic play by Molière (*Le Misanthrope*) that inspired it.

In 1679 things became so bad for the actors that a group of them left and went to Edinburgh. Charles Killigrew, who was having difficulty in getting together enough people to cast any play, wrote to tell them that all the problems had been resolved and that if they came back to London he would reimburse them for their travel. This was a lie and when they came back he refused to reimburse them. The problems seemed to be never-ending.

As if the troubles in Drury Lane weren't bad enough, the whole country was put into an uproar by Titus Oates and his claim of a Popish Plot. Dozens of innocent people were put to death on totally fabricated and preposterous charges of treason. The atmosphere was anything but cheerful, and people stopped going to the theatre. The King's Company went to Oxford to try to make some money, and Dryden wrote a prologue for them which began, with more frankness than tact, by comparing the state of the King's Men with the state of the country as a whole under the Popish Plot:

Discord and plots, which have undone our age,
With the same ruin have o'erwhelmed our stage.[5]

He described the company as a 'broken troop', which was true, but you don't usually announce this sort of thing to the audience.

Back in London, Killigrew tried to keep things going by forming a sort of company within a company, coming to new arrangements with some sharers and excluding others, which was, of course, illegal and resulted in further legal actions. In the spring and summer of 1681, business was so poor that on some nights the takings fell to below £4.[6] As a full house was worth about £150, the actors must have been facing rows of empty benches. On several nights they refused to go on and refunded the money, then they stopped acting altogether for weeks at a time.

By this time there were enough storm clouds gathering to make Drury Lane look like a scene from the operatic version of *The Tempest*. Clearly, this could not go on. The King's Company was exhausted, not least by the simple passage of time which had pushed most of the company's great acting names – Charles Hart, Michael Mohun and others – either towards retirement or the grave. It was inevitable that the company would either have to go under or merge with the Duke's Company. They chose the latter. Charles Killigrew drew up an agreement in May 1682 with representatives of the Duke's Company: Charles Davenant (who had by this stage taken over from his mother), Thomas Betterton and William Smith. Under its terms, the King's Company would be dissolved and Drury Lane handed over to the merged company. Once again, Killigrew was acting *ultra vires*: he was not the sole proprietor of Drury Lane, nor was he even a majority shareholder. Other sharers objected and took legal action. Eventually everyone had to agree to the merger, because the company was going to go bust anyway. By the summer the merger had been effected, and the new company was called the United Company. The King's Company, or His Majesty's Comedians as they were sometimes known, ceased to exist, but Drury Lane stayed open. The new company would operate between Dorset Garden and Drury Lane, but Drury Lane was used far more often and would long outlast its former rival.

5

The United Company

T he merger of the two companies brought to Drury Lane the man who was regarded as the greatest actor of his time, Thomas Betterton. According to Colley Cibber: 'Betterton was an actor, as Shakespeare was an author, both without competitors! Formed for the mutual assistance and illustration of each other's genius!'[1] But while Betterton was certainly famous for his Shakespearean roles, especially Hamlet and Macbeth, he also created the rakes in a series of Restoration comedies: Dorimant in *The Man of Mode*, Valentine in *Love for Love*, and Fainall in *The Way of the World*. He was a thoughtful actor: he took his parts seriously and amassed a considerable library for private study. He married Mary Saunderson, one of the first actresses in the Duke's Company, and they formed the first husband-and-wife team to dominate the London stage. Betterton was sober and prudent: he managed his own finances carefully and became prosperous as an actor, shareholder and eventually manager of the Duke's Company.

When Lady Davenant asked for his help in managing the company after her husband's death, he was co-manager with fellow actor/shareholder Henry Harris. However, while Harris did the PR – he was handsome, debonair and popular at court – Betterton was the more hands-on of the two. Crucially, Betterton took charge of the company's accounts, which were open to scrutiny by fellow-members. No one would have trusted Harris with this job as he was utterly reckless with money. Betterton could be kind and generous with struggling actors and playwrights – he was once described as 'kind Banker Betterton' and managed to keep the highly unstable Thomas Otway solvent for long enough to write a series of successful plays – but he was cautious to the point of being ruthless where his own money was concerned. He came from a humble background, having trained as a bookbinder, but he had reached the top of his profession and intended to live like a gentleman, in so far as an actor could hope for that.

Henry Harris retired in 1678 and his managerial role was taken over by another actor, William Smith. Thus, when the United Company was formed four years later, Betterton and Smith were technically co-managers. In reality, Thomas Betterton was regarded by everyone as being in charge.

He was not, of course, the legal owner of the company, which was still jointly owned by the sons of the original patentees, Charles Killigrew and Charles Davenant. Killigrew didn't want to be involved any further than drawing an income from the theatre and left running it to Davenant. Davenant was happy for Betterton to be, in effect, artistic director.

When the two patents had been granted to William Davenant and Thomas Killigrew, the rights to perform old plays had been divided between them. However, it was a very unfair division, because Killigrew claimed that as his company was the King's Company, he should have the rights to all of the plays performed by the King's Men (Shakespeare's company) at the Globe and the Blackfriars theatres up to the closure of the theatres. Davenant thought this was a bit much, as it would have given Killigrew the rights to plays he (Davenant) had written, as well as leaving Davenant very short of anything to put on. He petitioned the Lord Chamberlain who, in December 1660, allocated to Davenant the rights to his own plays plus nine by Shakespeare and a handful of others.

When the two companies merged in 1682, this division of pre-Civil War plays became irrelevant, and Betterton found himself able to tackle roles that had previously belonged to the rival company. Michael

Mohun and Charles Hart, the leading actors of the King's Company, retired on pensions at the merger, which meant that a lot of parts were suddenly up for grabs. Betterton was able to add Brutus and Othello to his Hamlet, Macbeth and Henry VIII.

With competition eliminated, and only one company operating its repertory between two theatres, which didn't both perform on the same night, the pressure to attract the town with new plays was eased. New plays were a financial risk, and the author had to be given the third night's profits. Old plays were much safer, and if the public could be persuaded to keep coming back to see them again, so much the better. Seeing new actors – not just Betterton but the rest of the former Duke's Company – playing roles that had belonged to others seems to have been novelty enough for a while, and the number of new plays fell sharply compared with the previous decade. As Adam Smith would observe a hundred years later, monopolies seldom benefit the public – or the arts.

However, when Drury Lane re-opened in November 1682, after several months of being dark, it was with a new play: John Dryden's *The Duke of Guise*. It was so controversial that the King had initially banned it because it was thought to contain scandalous reflections on the King's favourite but wayward illegitimate son, the Duke of Monmouth. However, Dryden promised that no such reflection was intended, and it opened for a fairly short run. After that, the repertoire was composed of tried and trusted old favourites, with the actors moving between Drury Lane and Dorset Garden, as required.

After a couple of seasons of this, Betterton was ready for something new, and the impetus for the big new show seems to have come from the King himself. Charles II had grown up in France and always regarded the arts in France as being ahead of their British counterparts, especially opera and ballet. He wanted a big English opera, something that would put him on a par with Louis XIV whose opera company in Paris, run under a monopoly arrangement by Jean-Baptiste Lully, was regarded as the best in the world.

So, after the closure of the 1682/83 season, Betterton and some colleagues set out for Paris on an official visit, arranged by the English ambassador, to persuade Lully to bring his company to London. This proved to be impractical, but Betterton by this time had the bit between his teeth, and signed up a French composer called Louis Grabu to write the music for a big show, for which Dryden would supply the script. It was called *Albion and Albanius* and it would turn out to be a financial disaster on a scale that had never been seen before.

The show was in preparation for a year, during which parts of it were performed for the King in the apartments at Whitehall of the Duchess of Portsmouth, Charles's French mistress. Dryden even went to Windsor to read some bits of it to the royal supporter. Then, just when all the money had been spent and the management was hoping to see a return at the box office, Charles died in February 1685 and the theatres were closed for four months as a mark of respect. By the time they finally re-opened in June, the management was desperate to get some of the money back as quickly as possible, as the show was rumoured to have cost £4,000 at a time when that represented more than the entire production budget for the year. On 3 June 1685, *Albion and Albanius* finally opened at the Dorset Garden Theatre, which was needed to cope with the spectacular scenic effects. It had to do twelve performances to cover its costs, which was a risk as such a run would have been unusual for a new show at the time. On the day of the sixth performance, news arrived in London that the Duke of Monmouth had landed at Lyme Regis and was marching on London with his rebel army. Once again, the theatres closed, and *Albion and Albanius* came to the end of its short run. It was never revived. The loss to the company was colossal and must have infuriated Betterton's fellow shareholders. Charles II had wanted an English opera that would allow him to look Louis XIV in the eye, but whereas Louis XIV made sure that the state picked up the bills for his operas, Betterton's company had to cover its costs from ticket sales.

Albion and Albanius was the first full-length, sung-through English opera to be performed in a London theatre, with recitative and arias, as opposed to a play with musical interludes. The allegory of the plot was, as Dryden admitted, so obvious that it didn't need explaining.

The brothers Albion and Albanius (i.e. Charles and James Stuart) are favoured by Apollo as the wise rulers of their country.

> *All hail, ye royal pair,*
> *The gods' peculiar care!*
> *Fear not the malice of your foes;*
> *Their dark designing,*
> *And combining,*
> *Time and truth shall once expose.*

When Charles II died, all Dryden had to do to make it performable was to arrange for Albion to be taken up into heaven on a cloud at the end, leaving his brother in charge. The show has been described as the last of the Stuart court masques, and it certainly was equally out of touch with reality. The last masque performed for Charles I had been *Salmacida Spolia*, written by William Davenant, which portrayed the King as Philogenes, the wise ruler of his people. Two years after the curtain came down, the Civil War broke out. *Albion and Albanius* was just about as politically astute. The Duke of Monmouth's rebellion, which ended the run, was defeated, but three years later James II would be driven into exile by another invader who landed in the West Country and marched on London with 'For Liberty and the Protestant Religion' on his banners.

An old snarling lawyer takes over

Although *Albion and Albanius* knocked a hole in the company's profits for the year, things soon got back onto an even keel and the United Company was making money again. When James II was driven into exile in 1688 as a result of his attempts to return England to Catholicism, this could have been difficult for Betterton's company as it had been, until the merger in 1682, under the patronage of James as the Duke of York's Company. It also had a history of supporting the claims of the House of Stuart and the Tories against the Whigs, who were now in control. However, Betterton was able to go with the flow and revived Dryden's mildly anti-Catholic play *The Spanish Friar* (written before Dryden became a Catholic) to ingratiate himself with the new régime. The United Company suffered no setbacks in the changed political landscape.

Charles Davenant decided to bail out while the going was good and in August 1687 he sold his shares to his younger brother Alexander. Alexander, in turn, appointed another brother, Thomas, to manage the company. Betterton was given extra shares in lieu of the £100 a year he had received as manager, and he seems to have been quite happy with the arrangement. In reality, he was still in charge, as Thomas Davenant was only 24 and had no experience of theatre management.

However, there was a problem that no one knew about at the time: Alexander did not have the money to buy his brother's shares. He had borrowed most of it from two lawyers, Thomas Skipwith and Christopher Rich. He was never able to pay back the loan, and so assigned the dividends to his creditors, and eventually the shares themselves. Alexander Davenant was a fraudster who created such financial havoc in what had been a well-run and profitable company

---

In Rep: Plays Performed at Drury Lane During January 1687
These represent known performances, not all performances, Date in brackets is year of first performance, Following the merger in 1682, it is not always possible to tell if performances took place at Drury Lane or Dorset Garden.

Date of performance, *Play* and playwright

Monday 3 January, *The Rehearsal* by George Villiers (1671)
Thursday 6 January, *A King and No King* by Francis Beaumont and John Fletcher (1611)
Monday 10 January, *The Spanish Curate* by John Fletcher and Philip Massinger (1622)
Tuesday 11, *Sir Courtly Nice* by John Crowne (1685)
Thursday 20 January, *The Rehearsal* by George Villiers (1671)
Friday 28 January, *The Maid's Tragedy* by Francis Beaumont and John Fletcher (1608-11)

that an audit of the company's books by Sir Robert Legard, Master in Chancery, was ordered. It was published in July 1693, and in October Alexander Davenant fled to the Canary Islands to escape prosecution once his frauds had been discovered. (Selling the same property twice and borrowing against properties he didn't own were favourite tricks.) In December, to the astonishment of the actors, Skipwith and Rich came forward with the document that showed them to be in charge of the company. Skipwith left the management to Rich, who seized the opportunity with relish.

In the course of Drury Lane's history, there have been a number of rather dubious characters, but for sheer nastiness and capacity to inspire feelings of hatred, no one comes close to Christopher Rich. He was described by the anonymous author of *A Comparison Between the Two Stages* (1702) as an 'old, snarling lawyer… a waspish, ignorant, pettifogger in law and poetry; one who understands poetry no more than algebra'[2] and by Colley Cibber, who worked for him for 16 years, as 'as sly a tyrant as ever was head of a theatre'.[3] Whereas Betterton had acquired a reputation for being strict but fair, Rich was as deceitful and unfair as he could get away with being. He cut back on every cost and kept his actors and his creditors waiting for as long as possible before paying them. He could have been the model for Max Bialystock of *The Producers*: he liked flops more than hits, because good returns at the box office made it more difficult to find excuses to get out of paying people.[4] Rich was so underhand and unpleasant, even when it was not in his own interest, that it is difficult not to suspect some sort of personality disorder. His behaviour provoked a walkout by all of his best actors, who set up a rival company, not once but twice. He was silenced on several occasions by the Lord Chamberlain, the last time permanently, and he was eventually evicted from his own theatre. Rich is the only important figure in the history of Drury Lane of whom no likeness is known to exist. He would have been too mean to commission a portrait himself, and the detestation in which he was held by everyone who knew him made sure that no one else did. If the history of Drury Lane were to be turned into a pantomime, Christopher Rich would be King Rat.

The arrival of Rich put Betterton in an impossible position. Betterton was a company man with company values. He respected his fellow performers and his authors, and would help them when in trouble. He had a high conception of the importance of theatre in the culture, and was prepared to take risks to push the art form forward. This was especially noticeable in the field of opera, which was only just being introduced into England at this time. In spite of the financial disaster of *Albion and Albanius*, Betterton continued to explore the form with *The Prophetess*, adapted by himself from a play by John Fletcher and Philip Massinger with music by Henry Purcell, in June 1690. This was followed in the next season by *King Arthur*, with a script by Dryden and music by Purcell; then in May 1692 by *The Fairy Queen*, based on Shakespeare's *A Midsummer Night's Dream* with music by Purcell. These were not what we would understand as opera, with arias and recitative: the actors would leave the stage at the end of their scenes to be replaced by singers, who played no important part in the plot. *Albion and Albanius* had been groundbreaking in that it was sung-through, but that would not become the accepted mode of presenting opera for a few more years. All of these productions were put on at Dorset Garden, which had the necessary stage machinery and, according to surviving accounts, they must have looked wonderful. The finale of *The Fairy Queen* involved a brilliantly-lit Chinese garden with a waterfall and exotic birds circling above the trees. It didn't have much to do with Shakespeare, but it certainly had the wow-factor.

However, even when these big productions didn't actually lose money, like *Albion and Albanius*, they didn't contribute much towards profits, owing to the enormous costs. 'The court and town were wonderfully satisfy'd with it,' said John Downes of *The Fairy Queen*, 'but the expenses in setting it out being so great, the company got very little by it.'[5]

When Christopher Rich took over, he put a stop to any new operas. Betterton belonged to the tradition of developing productions that might appeal more to the 'best judges' – people who were seriously interested in theatre – than the general public. This was anathema to Rich. According to Colley Cibber: 'He look'd into his receipts for the value of a play, and from common fame he judg'd of his actors.'[6] A play that took money was a good play to Rich; actors who pulled the crowds were good actors. He couldn't care less what the 'best judges' thought.

David Roberts, the biographer of Thomas Betterton, puts up the only possible defence of Rich (if this can be called a defence) by presenting him as the first Thatcherite in the arts. He didn't believe in subsidies: shows had to pay their way. He inherited a theatre company that had been run for many years by an actor-manager with a great respect for art, tradition and his fellow professionals. Rich seems to have formed the view that the company was in fact being run for the benefit of the people working for it rather than to produce dividends for shareholders, as a commercial operation should. In what David Roberts describes as 'the conflict of feudalism and capitalism',[7] Rich set about dismantling the 'old Spanish practices' that were rife.

For a start, he began redistributing parts, including Betterton's. In those days actors 'owned' their parts. They could go on playing them for their whole careers, with the easily foreseeable result that the sprightly young lovers in a comedy could be played by an arthritic old gentleman in his sixties and a stout lady in her fifties. Rich complained that Mrs Betterton was receiving 50s. a week even though she was well past her sell-by date and was not appearing 'in any parts to ye satisfaction of ye audience'.[8] When Betterton made his last appearance as Valentine, the romantic lead in Congreve's Love for Love, he was so afflicted by gout that he had to be supported by his two leading ladies standing on either side of him. Although this is an extreme example, it illustrates the problem.

Rich put Betterton and Mrs Barry under pressure to accept reduced terms. If the older actors wanted to go, that didn't bother Rich at all. He regarded them as completely expendable and easily replaceable. He started taking roles away from established actors and giving them to younger members of the company. This might have been better artistically, but that wasn't why he did it. Young actors were cheap because they hadn't had time to settle in and make demands on the management. His main purpose was to maximise profits by cutting costs. That meant paying actors less, and keeping their pay in arrears. He announced penalties for actresses who became pregnant and stopped investing in the company's physical stock of buildings, sets and costumes.

The United Company splits

Thomas Betterton, the greatest actor of his age and now a venerable old man of the theatre approaching 60, was humiliated by all of this. He organised a 'Petition of the Players' on behalf of fourteen other actors and himself to the Lord Chamberlain, complaining that the new style of management overturned 'the whole course and method' of established practice and was 'tending to the ruine and destruction of the company'. Aware of their status as sworn members of the royal household, the actors complained that they were being treated 'not as... the Kings and Queenes servants but... slaves'.[9]

The Lord Chamberlain arranged for a meeting of the two warring factions on 17 December 1694, and a few days in advance he received a long and detailed rebuttal of all the rebels' accusations from Thomas Skipwith, on behalf of the management. It concluded with a request that no one should be allowed to open another theatre in London without their permission. If the tone of this response was arrogant, it was because Skipwith and Rich were both lawyers and they knew they were in the right. The old customs they were disturbing were just that – customs without the force of law. As owners of the company, they could take whatever action was necessary to increase profits. In a modern, capitalist economy, who could argue with that? Finally, there was what the two lawyers regarded as the clincher: in the 1660s Charles II had issued two patents, entitling the holders to the exclusive right to open theatres in London. Upon the merger of the two companies in 1682, both of those patents came together, and they were now both controlled by Rich and Skipwith. If they were worth the parchment they were written on, no other theatre could open in London.

However, they were too confident. The theatre world of the 1690s wasn't Wall Street: it still depended to a great extent on social contacts, aristocratic patronage and influence at court. Skipwith and Rich, representing the new order, failed to take this into account.

The Lord Chamberlain at the time was Charles Sackville, the Earl of Dorset, formerly Lord Buckhurst, who had a lifelong interest in the theatre. He had been the original for Eugenius in Dryden's *Essay of Dramatic Poesy*, published in 1667, and in the same year he had persuaded Nell Gwynne to hand in all her parts at Drury Lane to come and live with him in Epsom. (She was back in a month.) He had ultimately been Betterton's landlord at the Dorset Garden theatre, built in the grounds of his London mansion, Dorset House, on the Strand. He knew and admired Betterton, and he particularly admired Anne Bracegirdle, the beautiful young actress who had been brought up by the Bettertons as virtually their adopted daughter. She was the muse of William Congreve and starred in all his plays. Congreve was madly in love with her, and probably used his influence with the Earl of Dorset, whom he also knew, to plead the case for the breakaway group of actors. So much influence was exercised from various quarters that Betterton, Anne Bracegirdle and the actress Elizabeth Barry were actually granted an audience with William III to plead their case.

As Lord Chamberlain, however, the Earl of Dorset was in a difficult position. There seemed to be little doubt that the two lawyers had the law on their side. He therefore took legal advice, and the advice was that the power of a monarch to grant patents or other permissions to perform plays could in no way impair the right of his successors to do likewise. The Lord Chamberlain therefore issued a licence – not a patent – to allow Betterton and his group of rebel actors to open another theatre.

Rich and Skipwith were stunned. When they realised that their legal rights in their property were going to be overruled, they offered to reach a compromise with the actors, but it was too late. Only a few days after the stormy meeting organised by the Lord Chamberlain between the two factions, Queen Mary died and the theatres closed for three months. This gave Betterton and Co. time to get themselves organised, and in March 1695 they signed a lease on the old Lisle's Tennis Court in Lincoln's Inn Fields. It hadn't been used as a theatre since the King's Company had moved back into the rebuilt Drury Lane in 1674, and it appears to have reverted to its original use as a tennis court. It had to be fitted up from scratch, and of course Betterton and his actors had left all of their costumes and scenery behind at Drury Lane. Various members of the aristocracy got up a subscription to raise funds for the new company, showing how popular Betterton was with the cultured classes and how hated Rich's management had become. But what would be the opening production? They needed something striking and new, and William Congreve came to the rescue.

Congreve was one of the last, and the greatest, of the writers of Restoration comedy. He was born in 1670, so he was 40 years younger than Dryden, the greatest living dramatist and man of letters. Dryden, who felt he was coming towards the end of his career, was looking for a successor, and when he saw the manuscript of Congreve's first play, *The Old Batchelor*, he felt he had found him. He said it was the best first play he had ever seen and it just needed a bit of polishing to give it 'the fashionable cutt of the town'.[10] Congreve took Dryden's criticisms on board, wrote another draft, and the play opened at Drury Lane in March 1693. It had a top-class cast, including Betterton, Anne Bracegirdle, Elizabeth Barry, Elizabeth Bowman and Susanna Mountfort. When the four women appeared together in the last scene, the audience burst into loud applause 'struck with so fine a groupe of beauty'. The play was a huge success, running for fourteen consecutive performances and going through three printed editions in a month. The music was by Purcell.

The following October saw the opening of Congreve's second play, *The Double Dealer*, with much the same cast and music once again by Purcell. It was a success, but not such a huge success as *The Old Batchelor*, which disappointed Congreve. It was written in a very 'correct' style, observing the three unities of time, place and action, and it pleased 'the best judges… who are commonly the fewest'.[11] The fact that *The Double Dealer* appeared at a time when Drury Lane was experiencing the seismic shock of Alexander Davenant fleeing to the

Canary Islands to escape prosecution for fraud, is another extraordinary demonstration of the way in which masterpieces sometimes happened, almost by accident, at the most surprising times.

Congreve was working on his next play, *Love for Love*, when it became obvious that the company was going to split. The play was accepted for production at Drury Lane, but Congreve delayed signing the contract until he could be sure of what was happening. He wanted his play to be performed by the best possible cast, and all of the good actors were leaving with Betterton, including his beloved Anne Bracegirdle. Congreve threw his lot in with the rebels and was made a shareholder in the company in reward, on condition that he would write one play a year for them.

When the theatres were allowed to open again, after the period of mourning for Queen Mary, Christopher Rich was in a hurry to be first in the field before the rebels could get themselves organised. On 1 April he re-opened the theatre with a revival of Mrs Aphra Behn's play *Abdelazar*, with a new score by Purcell. The first performance was well attended, probably out of curiosity to see how the management could put on a play at all when most of their actors, including all of the stars, had decamped. By the second performance, they were playing to a very thin house. Rich followed this up with a revival of Dryden and Howard's *The Indian Queen*, now 30 years old, again with new music by Purcell. This was given at Dorset Garden, as Rich was still operating between the two theatres, to allow for more spectacular scenic effects than Drury Lane could manage.

By the end of the month, the rebels were ready to declare war. They opened on 30 April 1695 with Congreve's *Love For Love* at what was now to be called the New Playhouse[12] in Lincoln's Inn Fields. William III, no great lover of the theatre, was at the first night to show his support for the rebels. It was a great success and had an uninterrupted run of 13 performances. The success was partly due to the play, which is a masterpiece, and to the cast, which was the best that could be seen, but there was also the sympathy factor. 'The town' wanted to show support for Betterton and his comrades in the face of intolerable oppression by the hated Christopher Rich.

Things at Drury Lane were looking bad. With scarcely enough actors to scratch together a cast for any play, the company was reduced to waging a war of attrition against the enemy using tactics that seem to us puerile, but were normal in the London theatre at the time. So, when the rebels announced on a Saturday that Betterton would be playing Hamlet on the following Tuesday, the Drury Lane company said they would do it on Monday. Not wanting to be upstaged, the rebels said they would do it on Monday as well. The Drury Lane actors realised that it would very unwise to go head-to-head with Betterton in his greatest part and so they changed their bills and announced Congreve's *The Old Batchelor* instead – which the rebels had originally announced for Monday. Just to spice it up, George Powell, by now the leading actor of the depleted troupe, announced that he would play the leading part 'in imitation of the original' – that is, he intended to impersonate Betterton throughout. By this stage they had six hours to curtain-up and no one had acted in *The Old Batchelor* before. They sent to a bookseller for copies of the play and set to work for some pretty intensive mugging-up on the lines. At that point, they realised that no one had been appointed to play Alderman Fondlewife, a small but important part that had been created by Thomas Doggett, one of the most popular comic actors of the time. Someone remembered that a stage-struck young man, who had been hanging around Drury Lane for the last few years without being given anything much to do, had once said he would like to have a go at the part. He was sent for and told to be ready within a few hours, no doubt encouraged by Powell's remark to the company: 'If the fool has a mind to blow himself up at once, let us ev'n give him a clear stage for it'.[13]

This was another of those star-is-born moments so beloved of theatrical legend. The young man was Colley Cibber, who would become the most important person in the theatre of his day and one of the most important figures in the history of Drury Lane. He scored a hit as Alderman Fondlewife, taking a leaf out of Powell's book and playing the part in exact imitation of Doggett, who was sitting in the pit, down to the costume and the voice. His first exit was greeted by thunderous applause.

Part of Colley Cibber's importance to us is that he wrote the first theatrical autobiography: *An Apology for the Life of Colley Cibber*. Published in 1740, it gave a view of half-a-century on the London stage during which he had been a key player. Whilst making every allowance for Cibber's bias in favour of himself, he gives us the first complete, first-person narrative of the development of the theatre as it went through important changes. Whilst we sometimes struggle to get a feel for events prior to the 1690s, when Cibber arrives, we feel that there is at least a possibility of getting a real handle on events.

Colley Cibber was the original stage-struck teenager who mortifies his parents by refusing to get a proper job. His father was Caius Gabriel Cibber the sculptor, whose most famous works were the statues of Melancholy and Raving Madness over the entrance to Bedlam. Cibber senior got to meet titled and influential people in the course of his work, and was hoping that the Duke of Devonshire, for whom he was working at Chatsworth, would come up with something for young Colley. Colley, meanwhile, was kicking his heels in London, where he became obsessed with the idea of going on the stage: 'I saw no joy in any other life but that of an actor... preferable to all that camps and courts could offer me!'[14] In 1690, at the age of 19, he joined the United Company at Drury Lane where the custom was to make aspiring actors work for nothing for at least six months. Cibber was not in the least deterred by this: 'Pay was the least of my concern; the joy and privilege of every day seeing plays for nothing, I thought was a sufficient consideration.'[15] The way in which he was eventually taken onto the payroll became a theatrical legend: he had messed up a small part so badly that an irate Thomas Betterton told the stage manager to fine him five shillings. The stage manager pointed out that they weren't paying him anything, to which Betterton replied: 'Put him down for ten shillings and forfeit him five.'[16]

6

Sentimental Comedy and the Last of the Rakes

C ibber is very frank in his *Apology* about his lowly status in the company. When Betterton led his rebel group of actors to Lincoln's Inn Fields in 1695, Cibber wasn't asked to join them as no one had a high opinion of him. He thought that after he had saved the day by playing Alderman Fondlewife at a few hours' notice, he might get offered better parts, but this didn't happen. He eventually decided to write a good part for himself.

Cibber's first play, *Love's Last Shift or the Fool in Fashion*, opened at Drury Lane in January 1696. Cibber had resisted the temptation to give himself the lead, as he knew he was not physically suited to romantic or heroic roles, but took instead the key part of Sir Novelty Fashion, one in a long line of absurd fops who entertained the audiences of Restoration comedies.

Love's Last Shift is such a peculiar play that it has been credited with changing the direction of comedy writing. It is like a typical Restoration comedy in many ways, except that it makes a big thing of championing virtue, particularly in sexual relationships. The heroine, Amanda, has married a faithless rake called Loveless at the age of 16. He ran through her fortune in gambling then deserted her to go to Europe in order to escape his creditors. The action of the play begins ten years later when he arrives back in London, broke. He believes Amanda to be dead and feels quite cheerful about that. However, Amanda is not dead and has been absolutely faithful to her husband, in spite of the way he has behaved towards her. She talks constantly of her virtue: 'All the comfort of my life is, that I can tell my conscience, I have been true to virtue.' Her friend Young Worthy persuades Amanda to try to win her husband back by pretending to be a town flirt attracted to Loveless. Worthy persuades Amanda that, although she is still beautiful, she has changed in ten years and Loveless won't recognise her. She has concerns about whether arousing impure desires (they would be impure for Loveless as he wouldn't know she was his wife) is consistent with her virtue, but is persuaded that, as the aim is to restore marriage, it is acceptable. Loveless is brought into her house by the garden gate. She pretends that he is not the man she sent her servant out to fetch, but after first refusing, she agrees to have sex with him. He is driven mad with desire, on which her observation is: 'Oh, why has hateful vice such power to charm, while poor abandon'd virtue lies neglected?' After a night of passion she reveals herself to be his wife and Loveless is converted to virtue: 'Let me kneel and pay my thanks to her, whose conqu'ring virtue has at last subdued me. Here will I fix, thus prostrate, sigh my shame, and wash my crimes in never-ceasing tears of penitence.'

To say the least, this is psychologically unconvincing, but because the play acquired a reputation for championing virtue and marriage, it gained a high reputation. According to the anonymous author of *A Comparison Between the Two Stages* (1702): 'That play... did wonders... there being few comedies that came up to 't for purity of plot, manners and moral'.[1] However, it is only the ending that is moral. For most of the play, the characters talk and behave like the most abandoned rakes of Restoration comedy, and Cibber acknowledged this in his epilogue, spoken by Cupid:

> *T'embrace a dull chaste wife:*
> *Such out of fashion stuff! But then again,*
> *He's lewd for above four acts, gentlemen!*
> *Four acts for your coarse palates were design'd,*
> *But then the ladies' taste is more refin'd.*

86

In fact, the play is considerably more unpleasant in some respects than even the lewdest works of Wycherly and Etherege, because it involves a sub-plot in which a servant rapes a maid by pulling her into a cellar, which is regarded as a huge joke, and is then bribed by Loveless to marry her for a stipend of £30 a year. What the woman thinks of being forced to marry her rapist is never discussed. The cynical attitude towards marriage is expressed by this servant who says, when he finds he must marry his victim and that Loveless was actually sleeping with his wife unawares: 'Ah! Little did my master and I think last night that we were robbing our own orchards.'

However, it was this Janus-faced aspect of the play that made it a success. People could enjoy the smut and still tell themselves they had seen a virtuous play. Cibber hit exactly the right note to suit the changing taste of the times, because the composition of the audience was changing.

The middle-class audience

The aristocracy played an important part in getting theatre started again post-1660. Aristocrats sponsored companies, became shareholders in theatres, wrote plays and coached actresses. They saw characters like themselves appearing in the leading parts in every play. Their lifestyles were depicted on the stage; their values reflected back at them.

That is not to say that the theatre was their exclusive province. All classes of person could – and did – pay for admission, and sat in their respective parts of the auditorium: upper classes in the pit and boxes, working classes in the gallery. The class that wasn't largely represented was the middle class. When middle-class people did attend the theatre, they weren't particularly welcome. 'Not so well pleased with the company at the [play]house to-day, which was full of citizens,' wrote Pepys in 1662, 'there hardly being a gentleman or woman in the house.'[2] One reason for the small middle-class contingent was the timing of performances. In the 1660s shows started at 3:00 p.m. or 3:30 p.m., which made it difficult for anyone in business to attend. It meant leaving the office or shutting up shop early. Another disincentive to middle-class theatre-goers was the way in which middle-class characters were represented on the very rare occasions when they were seen on the stage. London was really two cities then, the City of London and the City of Westminster. Business was done in the former, and the people who worked in the various trades were referred to disparagingly by authors as 'cits'. When cits appeared as characters in comedies, they were almost invariably depicted as avaricious, puritanical, hypocritical and absurd, with their noses stuck in their account books while the rakes of St James debauched their pretty young wives. This wasn't much of an incentive for middle-class people to go to the theatre.

In the decades following the Restoration, the City of London grew in importance, becoming a word centre for trade and financial services. Banks were developed there, including the Bank of England, and joint-stock companies offered the opportunity to trade on a scale never seen before. The population of the City grew, as did the disposable incomes of the cits. Theatre managers, looking to fill their benches, couldn't ignore them.

Curtain-up became later, moving to 4:00 p.m. by the 1690s and 5:00 p.m. by the end of the century. In the first decade of the next century it settled at 6:00 p.m. More importantly, plays began to reflect middle-class values and concerns. When we talk about Restoration comedy, or the Restoration theatre, we are speaking as if the period from 1660 to 1700 were a homogenous one. In fact, there was a huge cultural shift when, in 1688, the serious-minded Dutch Calvinist William III ascended the throne previously occupied by the Merry Monarch and his Catholic brother. Betterton, sensing the change in the *zeitgeist*, began to put on plays championing middle-class values of decency and morality, such as Shadwell's *Bury Fair* in April 1689, which opposed the simple goodness of country people to the corruption of the town.

Of course, things didn't change completely overnight. They never do in the arts, and the rakes of St James had a few years of life left in them yet. However, it was no longer taken for granted that virtue was a joke and a sham; and this was the atmosphere in which Cibber's first play hit the stage.

A relapse

One member of the audience who sat through *Love's Last Shift* and wasn't convinced by the reclamation of a libertine through the love of a good woman was John Vanbrugh. Vanbrugh – 32 at the time to Cibber's 25 – had no professional experience of the theatre. His career to date had included several years of imprisonment in France, including the Bastille, on a trumped-up charge of spying, followed by a captaincy in the navy. However, Vanbrugh was so disgusted by the hypocrisy of Cibber's ending that he decided to take the unprecedented step of writing a play using the same characters, but showing how they would really behave. He called his play *The Relapse* to emphasise that, in real life, there is no 'happy-ever-after'.

Once again we meet the rake Loveless, now supposedly reformed and faithful to his wife Amanda. As soon as he sets eyes on Berinthia in a box at the theatre, he falls in love with her and seduces her. The two of them decide that the easiest way to cover their affair is to arrange an affair between Amanda and Worthy, who has also been carried over from Cibber's play. Worthy comes very close to seducing Amanda but her virtue prevails. Berinthia reveals to Amanda that Loveless has been unfaithful but Amanda's virtue is not shaken: 'This poor relapse should only move my scorn.' This is left unresolved at the end of the last act.

The play concludes with a masque of Hymen (god of marriage) and Cupid, which contains the chorus:

> *For change, we're for change, whatever it be,*
> *We are neither contented with freedom nor thee.*
> *Constancy's an empty sound.*
> *Heaven and earth and all go round;*
> *All the works of nature move,*

And the joys of life and love
Are in variety.

To this Hymen adds:

I have not pretended, for many years past,
By marrying of people, to make 'em grow chaste.

This takes us back to the rather cynical view of marriage that characterised the earlier Restoration comedies.

The play has a sub-plot that brings in another of the characters from Cibber's play, and the one that had given him his greatest part: Sir Novelty Fashion, now elevated to the peerage as Lord Foppington. Cibber, who knew when he was on to a good thing, went completely over the top with his costumes for the part, wearing a wig that was so enormous it looked like hat and cloak combined. When George Powell, the leading actor of the depleted company, saw Cibber about to make his first entrance in *The Relapse*, he was furious to see how much money had been spent on Cibber's costume and complained to Christopher Rich that he had to play Caesar Borgia in a much cheaper outfit. Cibber's retort (probably not delivered at the time, as he was not yet in charge of the company) was that Mr Powell failed to consider that Lord Foppington always played to full houses, while his Caesar Borgia scarcely paid for the candles in the chandeliers.[3]

Love's Last Shift and *The Relapse* have often been seen as representing a tussle between the cynical, aristocratic scepticism of Restoration comedy and the middle-class values of what would become known as sentimental comedy. Given the general smuttiness and hypocrisy of *Love's Last Shift*, this is stretching the case a bit far, but if we do see them as representatives of different styles, there is no doubt about who won. Vanbrugh was writing at the absolute fag-end of a tradition that was about to expire. *The Relapse* succeeded because it is brilliant: strongly structured, elegantly written and extremely funny. However, the taste for this sort of comedy was declining and would soon disappear. The plays of Wycherley, Congreve, Etherege and

Vanbrugh were too good to vanish completely from the stage, and some of them remained in the repertory throughout the next century, albeit in censored and softened versions, but there would be no more like them after the turn of the century. And Vanbrugh was about to find himself on the receiving end of the most savage and threatening attack made on the theatre since the days of the Commonwealth.

In Rep: Plays Performed at Drury Lane During May 1697
These represent known performances, not all performances
Date in brackets is year of first performance

Date of performance, *Play* and **playwright**

Saturday 8 May, *A Plot and No Plot* by **John Dennis** (first performance)
Monday 24 May, *Aesop* by **John Vanbrugh** (1696)
Tuesday 25 May, *The Tempest* by **William Shakespeare, adapted by Dryden, Davenant and Shadwell** (1674)
Wednesday 26 May, *Don Sebastian* by **John Dryden** (1689)
Thursday 27 May, *The Lancashire Witches* by **Thomas Shadwell** (1681)
Monday 31 May, *The Sham Lawyer* by **James Drake** (first performance)

A short view of the stage

On 21 April 1698, a controversial clergyman called Jeremy Collier published an attack on the theatre called *A Short View of the Immorality and Profaneness of the English Stage*. As critics have been pointing out ever since, it was anything but short, running to 288 pages of highly-wrought abuse of the stage, which Collier saw as a source of moral contagion, poisoning the wider society with blasphemy and obscenity. He objected to the plays of his own time on a number of grounds: they showed vice rewarded and virtue unrewarded; aristocratic characters were shown behaving badly, thus reducing respect for social distinctions; women, who should be modest, were shown as lewd and shameless; marriage was ridiculed while adultery and fornication were presented as acceptable; religion was travestied by showing clergymen as foolish and mercenary; and the name of God was taken in vain by the constant swearing of oaths.

Collier made his point by scanning dozens of plays and plucking out the dirty bits. This selective quotation had the desired effect of making them seem worse than they really were and, as Dr Johnson put it, 'the wise and the pious caught the alarm, and the nation wondered why it had so long suffered irreligion and licentiousness to be openly taught at the publick charge'.[4] Collier had public opinion on his side, which was a novelty for him as he was, and would remain for the rest of his life, an outlaw. He was a non-juring clergyman, that is to say, a member of the Church of England who refused to swear an oath of loyalty to William III, the defender of liberty and the Protestant religion. Like many others, he regarded William III as a usurper and James II, living in exile in France, as the rightful king. He could therefore hold no position in the Church of England and had been thrown into prison twice on suspicion of treason. He then made things far worse by granting absolution on the scaffold at Tyburn to two men who were being executed for plotting to assassinate the King. The men had never repented of their actions, so Collier's absolution was taken to imply that he didn't regard the assassination attempt as sinful. A warrant was issued for his arrest and he went into hiding.

The reception of his *Short View* turned him into a champion of traditional moral values and he was able to appear openly again.✢ He wasn't the first person to object to the theatre of his day,♣ but his powerful and bitter attack acted as a focus for the views of all those, from the King down, who felt that moral standards were declining and something had to be done about it. Although Collier maintained that

---

✢ Colley Cibber claimed that William III was so grateful to Collier for his attack on the stage that he issued a writ of *Nolo prosequi* to allow him to come out of hiding, but there is no evidence for this.

♣ In the previous year, the Lord Chamberlain had issued orders regarding the 'profaneness and immorality of the theatre', which is probably where Collier got his title from.

he didn't want to close the theatres down altogether, plenty of his supporters did.

Collier started off with an uncompromising statement of his position: 'The business of plays is to recommend virtue and discountenance vice.' He poured scorn on John Dryden who had written that: 'delight is the chief, if not the only end of poesie; instruction can be admitted but in the second place, for poesie only instructs as it delights'.[5] Collier was having none of this namby-pamby aestheticism: he regarded the stage as a pulpit from which the audience should be taught how to live. Collier's special targets were John Vanbrugh and William Congreve, then at the height of their success.

The playwrights who felt his lash responded immediately, afraid that, not only were their careers about to be cut short, but they could very well be prosecuted for obscenity and blasphemy. Vanbrugh and Congreve had their replies out within weeks. They adopted the traditional defence of the satirist: they had depicted bad and foolish behaviour in order to make it ridiculous, so that the audience would learn to avoid such failings. 'The stage is a glass for the world to view itself in,' wrote Vanbrugh, 'if it makes their faces too fair, they won't know they are dirty, and consequently neglect to wash 'em… what I have done is in general a discouragement to vice and folly – I am sure I intended it.'[6] Congreve's response was even more feeble.

Collier had the best of the pamphlet war, which went on for the next twenty years, because none of his critics could challenge him on his principal assumption that 'the business of plays is to recommend virtue'. Vanbrugh and Congreve couldn't say that the business of plays is to explore issues that concern the audience and help them to understand themselves and the society they are living in; and that preaching morality is best left to the church. This was partly because the terms for such critical discourse didn't yet exist, and partly because, however sceptical you might be in private, it was absolutely vital to uphold Christianity if you wanted to participate in the public debate about anything. To admit that the stage was not in the business of promoting Christian moral values would have been to invite intervention from the government.

Almost immediately, the prosecutions began. Betterton, Congreve, the dramatist Thomas D'Urfey and others were dragged before the Middlesex Justices in May 1698, charged with 'debauchery and blasphemy' in relation to *Love for Love* and *Don Quixote*. In 1701 members of both theatre companies were up before the King's Bench, charged with 'using indecent expressions in some late plays'. When Vanbrugh's *The Provok'd Wife* was revived, the author and actors were fined £5 each (about £700 in today's values); in 1700 Betterton's company were in trouble for a revival of *Love For Love*, even though it had been staged to raise funds for a Christian charity, and in 1701 and 1702 there were further prosecutions over *Love for Love* and *The Provok'd Wife*. No one went to prison, but it put the frighteners on everyone, and led to an innovation: the playbill for a 1699 revival of Congreve's *The Double Dealer* carried the author's name – 'a new manner of proceeding, at least in England', according to Dryden.[7] It seems doubtful that Congreve was thrilled by the honour: the sole intention was to let the magistrates know who should be prosecuted in the event of a complaint. The playbill carried the ominous words: 'with severall expressions omitted'. The stage was censoring itself. ❖

Perhaps the most surprising thing about the Collier controversy was the level of support Collier received from within the profession and from theatre-lovers. Colley Cibber, who had escaped fairly lightly over *Love's Last Shift*, believed that Collier's 'calling our dramatick writers to this strict account had a very wholesome effect upon those who writ after this time'.[8] In the anonymous dialogue *A Comparison Between the Two Stages* (1702), which carries the authentic note of theatre gossip across the ages, the bitching eases off when the speakers approach the subject of the *Short View*. 'Our audiences are really mended in their taste of plays,' says Sullen, 'it must be confest, that he has done the stage good service in correcting some of their errors.' 'I don't know much in Mr Collyer's book that's to

---

❖ Susanna Centlivre admitted in the preface to her play *The Perjur'd Husband* (1701) that, since Collier's broadside, she had been watching her language to avoid anything suggestive.

be blamed,' replies Critic. 'I'm sure 'twas high time to preach up reformation, when the stage was sunk to such a pitch of infamy.'[9]

March 1700 saw the first performance of William Congreve's masterpiece *The Way of the World*, which he gave to Betterton's company at Lincoln's Inn Fields. The play is not only the greatest of all the Restoration comedies, it is the last. The cool, urbane, rational and sophisticated mood that characterised the *genre* was now out of fashion. People wanted warm-hearted sentimentality, not scepticism about happy-ever-afters. The plot of *The Way of the World* is famously difficult to follow, and the reception wasn't good. It wasn't a disaster, but it wasn't a great hit either. Congreve wrote a tetchy introduction to the printed edition saying that the audience couldn't appreciate subtlety, and he never wrote another play.

The death of Dryden

News of the 'moderate success' of 'Congreve's new play'[10] was brought to John Dryden, who was dying at his house in Gerrard Street, Soho. Dryden had fallen on difficult times. He had converted to Roman Catholicism at the time when James II was trying to return England to the Roman Catholic faith and, when James went into exile, Dryden stuck to his by-now very unpopular religious affiliation. He therefore lost his official positions as Poet Laureate and Historiographer Royal, while his income from the stage was much diminished by the success of other, younger playwrights more attuned to the changing taste of the times. He spent his last years making translations from the classical authors, including his brilliant verse translation of Virgil's *Aeneid* which is still read today, when his plays are unperformed. However, translation was time-consuming work and didn't pay as well as the author's third-night benefit at the theatre, so his last years were beset with money worries. His relations with Drury Lane had experienced their ups and downs since he walked out of his contract with them in 1678, but he was, nevertheless, the Grand Old Man of the theatre, and they decided to do something for him. John Vanbrugh had written an adaptation of John Fletcher's play *The Pilgrim*, and Dryden was asked if he would like to have a benefit performance of it – in other words, the proceeds of the third night after deducting management costs. He said yes, and offered to write a new prologue and epilogue, as well as a short musical piece which he called *A Secular Masque*, looking back over the last century and forward to the coming one.

Dryden had a reputation for being the best writer of prologues and epilogues of his time, but he did himself no credit on this last occasion. The prologue was a crude attack on a literary rival, and in the epilogue he tried to throw the blame for all the faults Jeremy Collier was finding with the stage on the court of Charles II, returning from exile in France and bringing vicious tastes to London:

> *Perhaps the parson stretched a point too far,*
> *When with our theatres he waged a war.*
> *He tells you that this very moral age*
> *Received its first infection from the stage;*
> *But sure, a banished court, with lewdness fraught,*
> *The seeds of open vice returning brought...*
> *The poets, who must live by courts or starve,*
> *Were proud so good a government to serve;*
> *And, mixing with buffoons and pimps profane,*
> *Tainted the stage for some small snip of gain.*

This was really pathetic. It would have been better to go out with a blaze of defiance to censorship than grovelling to Jeremy Collier by blaming everything on the Merry Monarch, who had been in his grave for 15 years. But the *Secular Masque* was much better, and constitutes the dying man's last thoughts on the stage of his time. Chronos, or Old Father Time, lays down the globe and declares himself exhausted by the struggles of the seventeenth century. Momus, the god of mirth, tells him he is taking everything too seriously and should learn to laugh at the world and its follies. The goddess Diana speaks of the elegant courts of James I and Charles I at the beginning of the century; Mars represents the Civil War; Venus speaks of the joys of love that characterised the court of Charles II. The characters all join in a final chorus describing the dying century:

> *All, all of a piece throughout;*
> *Thy chase had a beast in view;*
> *Thy wars brought nothing about;*
> *Thy lovers were all untrue.*
> *'Tis well an old age is out,*
> *And time to begin a new.*

Dryden's old age was indeed out and he didn't live to see his benefit. The show opened on 29 April 1700 and he died in the early hours of 1 May. The proceeds of the benefit went to his son, at his request. But Dryden was right about beginning a new age in the theatre. The comparative failure of Congreve's *The Way of the World* indicated the change in public taste. Audiences wanted something kinder and less abrasive. The serendipity that seems to have guided Drury Lane through the centuries had already produced the man to oblige, in the person of George Farquhar.

Henry Purcell: in-house composer

Another famous figure had departed the stage of life in the last decade of the century. Henry Purcell (1659-1695) is regarded by many people as the greatest English composer. He was born in the year before the restoration of the monarchy to a family already well connected in musical circles. He became a chorister in the Chapel Royal and, when his voice broke, continued to work in the Chapel Royal and Westminster Abbey in various capacities. He was appointed organist in the chapel and 'composer in ordinary' to Charles II, then organist in Westminster Abbey. As a composer, his early work was almost entirely in the form of sacred music for the two churches and odes and other pieces for the court.

When Charles II was succeeded by his brother James in 1685, things changed for Purcell. The new king and queen were both Roman Catholics and thus did not worship in the Chapel Royal, which lost status. There was an even bigger change in 1688 when William of Orange and his wife Mary were crowned in place of James, who had fled to France. William of Orange was a Dutch Calvinist who wanted no trace of Catholic ritual in the Chapel Royal. The violin orchestra in the Chapel Royal was disbanded and services became much simpler.

In need of another outlet for his talents, Purcell looked to the stage. This was not an entirely new departure for him as he had composed music for Nathaniel Lee's play *Theodosius* in 1680, but between 1689 and his death in 1695 most of Purcell's work was for the theatre. The United Company was operating at two theatres, Drury Lane and Dorset Garden, using Dorset Garden for the more elaborate productions and Drury Lane for straight plays. However, even a 'straight' play contained a good deal of music in those days. A full orchestra would play three pieces before the rise of the curtain with further musical interludes between each of the five acts of the play. In addition, songs in plays were extremely popular and audiences demanded more and more. Many of these songs became the hit singles of their time, performed out of context by both amateurs and professionals.

Purcell wrote all or some of the music for 37 of these plays after 1689. Twenty-six of them were performed at Drury Lane, two at Dorset Garden, and nine could have been in either theatre. Some of the plays were revivals and some were new plays. 'Nymphs and shepherds come away' was composed for a revival of Thomas Shadwell's 1675 play *The Libertine*, while the two most important new plays for which Purcell wrote the music were Congreve's *The Old Batchelor* and *The Double Dealer* (both 1693). His incidental music for a revival of Mrs Aphra Behn's play *Abdelazar* in 1695 contained the famous rondeau that became the basis for Benjamin Britten's *Young Person's Guide to the Orchestra*.

In addition, Purcell wrote some of the first English operas. 'Opera' didn't have quite the same meaning in those days as there was no distinction made between plays that had a lot of music (sometimes called semi-operas) and a sung-through piece. The audience would expect more music from what were called 'dramatic operas' than from a 'straight play', but opera was defined as much by its spectacular scenery as by the music. For this reason, Purcell's operas were produced at the Dorset Garden theatre.

The first was *The Prophetess, or the History of Dioclesian*, an old play by John Fletcher which was given a musical make-over with the addition of a dance of the Furies, a dance of butterflies and a chair dance. It opened in June 1690 and was a great success. This was followed in 1691 by *King Arthur*, with a script by Dryden. Dryden was such a great admirer of Purcell, whom he described as 'an *English-man equal with the best abroad*',[11] that he agreed to alter his verses to fit the music. The opera for 1692 was *The Fairy Queen*, an adaptation of Shakespeare's *A Midsummer Night's Dream*, which was so spectacular it failed to make a profit, in spite of good houses.

The expense of *The Fairy Queen* ruled out a new opera for 1693, but in 1695 Purcell was set to work on an operatic revival of Dryden's early success *The Indian Queen*, now more than thirty years old. While this was in preparation, Betterton led his revolt of the actors and the most experienced of them decamped to Lincoln's Inn Fields, leaving behind a company consisting of 'for the most part Learners, Boys and Girls, a very unequal match for them who revolted'.[12] Fortunately, there were some good singers amongst this remnant and Purcell's operatic *Indian Queen* was a success when it opened in April.

In November of the same year Purcell died, at the tragically young age of 36, whilst working on the incidental music for the third part of Thomas D'Urfey's stage version of *Don Quixote*. He was buried in Westminster Abbey to the accompaniment of his own music, composed earlier in the year for the funeral of Queen Mary II. Dryden wrote the funeral ode.

7

A Tumultuous Decade

Dryden was buried on the day after his death in the parish church of St Anne' s, Soho. A group of his admirers decided that this wasn't good enough for a man who had dominated the literary scene for best part of 40 years and so, a few days later, they had him exhumed, embalmed and reburied in considerable state in Westminster Abbey. A young playwright who attended this second funeral was bemused by the pomp and splendour of it. His name was George Farquhar.

Farquhar was born in Kilkenny and came to London in 1698 with his first comedy in his pocket. It was called *Love and a Bottle* and opened at Drury Lane to a successful run in December 1698. In the following year, Farquhar's next play, *The Constant Couple or A Trip to the Jubilee*, opened at Drury Lane in November and scored a major hit. It received 53 performances in its first season, a record not broken until *The Beggar's Opera* in 1728, and introduced the character of Sir Harry Wildair. Robert Wilks, the actor who played Sir Harry, scored such a triumph that he was known by the character's name afterwards, and Farquhar wrote a sequel called *Sir Harry Wildair* that opened in 1701. Farquhar got married in 1703 to a woman he thought rich, only to find that she had deceived him and had no fortune at all. With theatre work not producing enough money, he signed up as a lieutenant with the grenadiers and went recruiting for the army in Shrewsbury. His experiences there gave him the material for his next comedy, *The Recruiting Officer*, which opened at Drury Lane on 8 April 1706 where it provided its author with another triumph. The play would remain one of the most popular in the repertory throughout the eighteenth century and had the honour of being the first play ever performed in Australia (by convicts in 1789). It ran through more than 50 editions during the century.

His next play would be his last and his masterpiece. Farquhar had never enjoyed good health, and by now he was seriously ill. He is thought to have suffered from rheumatic heart disease which can lead to a fatal decline over the course of a few months. The story is that Robert Wilks, realising he hadn't seen Farquhar around the theatre for a while, went to visit him at his lodgings. He discovered that his friend had moved to a garret at the back of a house on St Martin's Lane, where he was very poor and very ill. Wilks left Farquhar some money and suggested he try his hand at another comedy. Over the course of a few weeks, during which he knew that he was dying, Farquhar produced *The Beaux' Stratagem*, one of the sunniest and most good-humoured plays in the language. It opened on 8 March 1707, and two months later Farquhar died at the age of 39.

Because his comedies involve some of the stock characters and situations of Restoration comedies – young men in search of pretty women, trying to marry a fortune, setting up elaborate plots and disguises – Farquhar is sometimes spoken of as the last writer in the Restoration comedy tradition. In fact, there is a huge difference in tone. Farquhar's comedies lack the bite of Wycherly, Vanbrugh and Congreve. He was known as a good-hearted man, utterly devoid of malice, and this comes through in his plays. He liked people too much to satirise them, and he didn't accept the casual attitude towards human frailty, which could amount to cruelty, of his predecessors. In *The Beaux' Stategem*, Aimwell, one of the young heroes, announces his intention to debauch a maid. His companion, Archer, tells him that if Aimwell even attempts such a thing, he (Archer) will wreck the plot they are working on. The debauching of a maidservant would have been a bit of light relief in the 1670s.

Unlike all of Farquhar's other plays, *The Beaux' Stratagem* was not produced at Drury Lane. This was because of an upheaval in the world of London theatre that would set everything at sixes and sevens for several years, and to understand it we have to go back to the exhumation and reburial of John Dryden.

The Kit-Cat Club and the theatre in the Haymarket

The removal of Dryden's remains to Westminster Abbey had not been the result of an act of individual philanthropy: it was a group effort. The transfer of the former Poet Laureate from Soho to Poets' Corner was the work of the Kit-Cat Club, a dining club of which the membership was a mixture of high-powered aristocrats and politicians and the writers who needed their patronage and who would disseminate their ideas. They initially met for regular dinners at a pie shop in Gray's Inn owned by Christopher Catt, whose speciality was a mutton pie – the Kit-Cat.

The Kit-Cat Club was founded, towards the end of the 1690s, by the London bookseller Jacob Tonson who had made his money in a series of successful publishing ventures, including Milton's *Paradise Lost* and Dryden's translation of Virgil. He would later publish the first edited collection of Shakespeare's plays in 1709 and Alexander Pope's translations of Homer. The Kit-Cat Club was, first and foremost, a Whig society: it was dedicated to liberty and the Protestant religion. This was much more than just a form of words. James II was living in exile in France, awaiting his opportunity to lead an invasion backed by Louis XIV's army to regain the throne. He never got another chance after the botched attempt to get into England through the back door of Ireland that led to his defeat at the Battle of the Boyne in 1689. However, his son James Edward Stuart ('The Old Pretender') would invade in 1715 and his grandson Charles Edward Stuart ('The Young Pretender') in 1745. There was a real danger that England's constitutional monarchy might be overthrown and replaced with an absolutist monarchy based on the model of Louis XIV's France.

So how did Jacob Tonson think he was going to avert that by setting up a dining club? There was never any Kit-Cat manifesto, so we have to judge their intentions by their actions. However, the Kit-Cat Club had such a wide-ranging programme, involving political and cultural reform, that Ophelia Field, the historian of the Club, gave her book the sub-title: 'Friends Who Imagined a Nation'. The political agenda is easier to understand than the cultural one. They supported the constitutional monarchy achieved by the Glorious Revolution of 1688; they supported the Act of Union that joined Scotland and England as one country; and they supported the installation of the House of Hanover to replace the Stuarts as the ruling dynasty, following the death of Queen Anne in 1714 without an heir. Horace Walpole said of the Kit-Cats that although they were 'generally mentioned as a set of wits, [they] were in reality the patriots that saved Britain'.[1]

The cultural agenda was all a part of the same project, to create an English identity that would be strong and confident, embracing the best of European culture and anglicising it. Given Tonson's connections, it was inevitable that literature would be a major interest, and the creation of the original *Spectator* and *Tatler* magazines by Kit-Cats Joseph Addison and Richard Steele would do more than anything else to forge an image of the English character: tolerant, rational, wary of extremism and enthusiasm, but passionate about the defence of individual freedom. Addison and Steele were careful not to make their essays seem politically partisan: the most brilliant part of the project lay in the way the Kit-Cats made their ideas seem, not Whig ideas, but just common sense.

After literature, the main thrust of their cultural activities was in developing an appreciation of music that would lead to a more vigorous native tradition. English music was acknowledged to be uninspiring, with the exception of the Purcell brothers, so the Kit-Cats decided to bring Italian opera to London to move things along. That meant they needed an opera house.

John Vanbrugh, no doubt feeling bruised by the Collier controversy and weary of being dragged into court to defend his plays, became increasingly involved with architecture, and is today mainly famous as the architect of Blenheim Palace and Castle Howard. He seems to have originally intended to build the new theatre in the Haymarket as a private venture but, as delays pushed up costs, the Kit-Cats (of which he was a leading member) stepped in to raise a subscription. Ophelia Field compares the subscription got up by the Kit-Cats to fund the opera house with the subscription organised by the Royal Society in the 1670s to build the Royal Observatory in Greenwich.[2] It became a matter of national pride for aristocrats to put their hands in their pockets to create a centre of excellence.

There was, of course, the small matter of getting permission to open. It wasn't possible for just anyone to open a theatre: they needed a patent, or at least a licence. Currently, Christopher Rich held both of the patents issued by Charles II and was using the Davenant patent to run Drury Lane while the Killigrew patent remained dormant. Thomas Betterton and the troupe of rebel actors he had led from Drury Lane were appearing in the old converted tennis court in Lincoln's Inn Fields under a licence procured for them from William III by the Earl of Dorset – a founder member of the Kit-Cats. Betterton was approaching 70 and must have felt he couldn't go on running a theatre company forever, so he agreed to give up his licence in favour of Vanbrugh, who by this time had taken Congreve into partnership. Betterton and his company would close Lincoln's Inn Fields and move to the Haymarket.

In November 1704, Queen Anne was invited to attend a preview performance in the new and very magnificent theatre. She sat under a dome painted with scenes illustrating 'Queen Anne's Patronage of the Arts' (in fact she scarcely patronised the arts at all) and listened to a concert. In the following month she was pleased to issue a licence for the new theatre 'reposing especial trust and confidence in our trusty and well-beloved' servants Vanbrugh and Congreve to reform 'the abuses and immorality of the stage'.[3]

This sounded like a bad joke to the followers of Jeremy Collier, who had singled these men out for special criticism. The Society for the Reformation of Manners published an open letter of protest, addressed to the Archbishop of Canterbury, describing Vanbrugh and Congreve as the two worst people who could have been chosen to run a theatre as they were 'in equal abhorrence of the church and state' and singling out Vanbrugh as 'a man who had debauched the stage beyond the looseness of all former times'.[4]

In Rep: Plays Performed at Drury Lane During w/c 20 November 1704
Date in brackets is year of first performance

Date of performance, *Play* and playwright

Monday 20 November, *Tunbridge Walks* by Thomas Baker (1703)
Tuesday 21 November, *The Rehearsal* by George Villiers, Duke of Buckingham (1671)
Wednesday 22 November, *The Albion Queens or the Death of Mary Queen of Scotland* by John Banks (1704)
Thursday 23 November, *The Committee* by Sir Robert Howard (1662)
Friday 24 November, *The Northern Lass* by Richard Brome (1629)
Saturday 25 November, *King Henry the Fourth with the Humours of Sir John Fasltaffe* by William Shakespeare, adapted by Thomas Betterton (1700)

Nevertheless, the new theatre, which was called the Queen's Theatre, opened on 9 April 1705 with the Italian opera *The Loves of Ergasto*. It was a disaster, messed up by a company of singers hired by Lord Manchester in Venice and described as 'the worst that e're came from thence'.[5] The Queen's immediately ran into financial trouble and by the end of the year Congreve had resigned, saying it had earned him nothing.[6] Vanbrugh started negotiations to merge the company with Christopher Rich's company at Drury Lane.

So, once again, there were two theatres operating in London. Dorset Garden was virtually out of action since Christopher Rich had been kicked out in 1699 for not paying the rent. There were a few occasional performances after that, but the splendid building was demolished in 1709, having lasted less than 40 years. Vanbrugh's approach to Christopher Rich to merge the companies came to nothing, but he appointed as his manager Owen Swiney, an Irishman who had been working as Rich's assistant at Drury Lane for the last three years. Rich was not at all averse to Swiney leaving him to run the Queen's.

He thought that he would be able to control the rival theatre without paying for it by getting his man in there, and was happy for Swiney to take all of his leading actors to the Haymarket, as he intended to concentrate on what Cibber described as 'singing and dancing and any sort of exotick entertainments',[7] for which he didn't need many actors. Rich had enjoyed a great success with Thomas Clayton's opera *Arsinoe*, the first opera written in the Italian style but sung in English, and he saw opera as a moneyspinner for Drury Lane. He still had a few actors, so he could continue to put on plays, but he was just as happy with rope-dancers and acrobats.

The only actor he wouldn't let go was Cibber. This was not because he had a particularly high opinion of Cibber, but simply because Cibber could do useful stock characters like the villain or the old miser. Without Cibber, it would be difficult to do any plays at all. Cibber, realising that his stock had risen, asked for better terms. When Rich refused to be pinned down, he went to the Haymarket and joined Swiney's troupe. Swiney had opened his season in October 1706 and Cibber arrived in November. Under the terms of the agreement with Rich to surrender his best actors to Swiney, the Haymarket company was permitted to perform plays only without any musical entertainments, even music between the acts, but Drury Lane was not limited in its repertoire: it could put on operas or plays with musical interludes.

The Kit-Cats supported their old friend Betterton and the troupe at the Haymarket by organising a subscription season of 'three plays of the best authors', which turned out to be Shakespeare's *Julius Caesar*, *The King and No King* by Beaumont and Fletcher and a composite made from the comic scenes of two plays by Dryden, *Marriage à la Mode* and *The Maiden Queen*.[8] Each subscriber paid three guineas and received three tickets for the first performance of each play. It was the first time that a subscription season had been used for plays and proved a great success when the plays were performed in January and February 1707. The aim was to encourage drama in the face of competition from the Italian opera. The company followed this with the first production of *The Beaux' Stratagem* in March.

The arrival of Colonel Brett

Things were not going quite so well at Drury Lane, where Joseph Addison's attempt to create an English opera with *Rosamund* flopped in March. Addison's remarks on opera in *The Spectator*, never very sympathetic, became more acidic after this. But then something strange happened that changed the set-up at Drury Lane quite significantly.

Rich had now been pursuing his dishonest methods at the Lane for over a decade, keeping the financial affairs in such chaos that no one knew where they were with him. Dividends were never paid, and if investors tried pursuing Rich through the courts, he simply used delaying tactics until his adversaries gave up in exhaustion. Rich's partner, Sir Thomas Skipwith, who was in fact the majority shareholder in the patent, had not received any benefit from it for so long that he considered his share worthless. Whilst staying with his good friend Colonel Henry Brett in Gloucestershire for a few days, Skipwith offered his share of the patent to Brett, observing that, with Brett's political connections, he might actually manage to make something of it. What started as a joke turned into a legal conveyance in October 1707,[9] making Brett a joint-patentee with Christopher Rich.

Brett was not going to be a sleeping partner, as Skipwith had been. He turned up at the theatre and introduced himself to a no doubt astonished Rich as his co-manager, then began actively to involve himself in the affairs of Drury Lane. Brett was, as Skipwith had suspected, a much more capable man than his predecessor, being good-looking, intelligent and very well connected. He could see that the Haymarket was flourishing with all the best actors, so he lobbied the Marquis of Kent, who was Lord Chamberlain, to get them back to Drury Lane. Vanbrugh, who wielded considerable political influence of his own, was equally keen to get opera into the Queen's. On 31 December 1707, the Lord Chamberlain obliged them both by decreeing that the Haymarket must be used exclusively for opera, and the actors must return to Drury Lane, which would have the monopoly on straight plays.

Cibber was delighted to have the whole company together again at Drury Lane, putting on plays and leaving what he considered the fripperies of opera to the other house. Drury Lane was flourishing, as Brett was a good manager and made his company as happy as Rich had contrived to make them discontented. All seemed set for a fair future, except that Rich found himself sidelined. The fact that affairs were prospering was as nothing to him compared with the fact that Brett was now more highly regarded in the theatre than he was. Rich was determined to get rid of Brett, and came up with a cunning strategy: he actually started paying dividends. When the outside investors – who were known as 'adventurers' – found that they were making money from an investment which they had long ago written off as a dead loss, they became very interested in the theatre and started to involve themselves more in its affairs. Rich's intention was to let Brett see that, by the time all the creditors had been paid, there wouldn't be enough left to make it worth Brett's while to stay, but he couldn't have anticipated quite how successful the policy would be. When Sir Thomas Skipwith found that he had given away a valuable property, he served Brett with a subpoena in Chancery claiming that the share of the patent had only been given in trust, and now he wanted it back. This was dishonourable and untrue: there was no mention of a trust in the deed they had both signed, but Brett was too much of a gentleman to want a fight in the courts with an old friend, so he resigned his share. Needless to say, no more dividends were paid after that, so the 'adventurers' melted away and Christopher Rich was left in charge of Drury Lane.

The last straw

Rich was now in the position he wanted: he was in sole charge of the sole theatre in London licensed to present plays. His monopoly allowed him to tyrannise over his actors, since they could not work anywhere else, and he proceeded to do so. Once again, he was cheating and chiselling everyone who worked for him in lots of ways, large and small, but his final and fatal attempt to cheat the actors was to interfere with their benefits.

Actors' benefits had been introduced in the 1680s as a means of rewarding actors who were especially popular with the public and valuable to the company. They worked like author's benefits: the recipient could keep the receipts of the house after paying the management's costs, at this time between £30 and £40 out of possible takings of £100 to £150. Elizabeth Barry had been the first actor to receive a benefit, and no more were awarded until after the division of the companies in 1695, when they started to become common for senior members of the company. In Rich's company, especially, the benefits were vital, because salaries were kept months or even years in arrears, with no realistic prospect of being paid. The proceeds of the benefit could very well exceed everything else the actor earned that year, and they were paid promptly.

Rich cast an envious eye over these benefits which he thought were eating unfairly into his profits, and he announced that in future the management would take a third of the profits, as well as deducting costs. The actors protested, but the arrangements for benefits had never been put in writing. Now, actors were required to sign an agreement to the new terms before a benefit would be granted. If they refused to sign, the offer would be made to a more junior actor in the company.

The actors, as usual, took their complaints to the Lord Chamberlain, who issued an order on 30 April 1709 commanding Rich to deduct no more than the £40 for costs.[10] Rich's protestation that actors had signed up to the new system were dismissed on the grounds that they had been coerced. Rich decided to ignore the Lord Chamberlain, and this was the last straw. The Marquis of Kent was the fourth Lord Chamberlain to have to deal with complaints about Rich, and he decided that enough was enough: he would issue an order of silence to put Rich out of business. However, he didn't do so immediately as negotiations were going on, with his knowledge and permission, to allow the actors from Drury Lane to go back to the Haymarket and work with Owen Swiney again, putting on both plays and operas.✤ When these negotiations were complete, the order of silence was issued on 6 June.

✤ Owen Swiney had by this time taken over the theatre on a lease from John Vanbrugh, who had bailed out after ruinous losses on operas. Under Swiney, the company would settle into a routine of plays four nights a week and Italian opera on the other two nights.

The best part of Colley Cibber's *Apology* is his account of this wonderful moment when Rich found that he had gone too far.[11] Cibber, who was just the sort of person to be up and down the backstairs at Whitehall, happened to be in the Lord Chamberlain's office where he saw the order of silence lying on a table, signed and ready for delivery. He rushed back to the theatre, where a rehearsal was in progress which he should have been attending. When Rich asked him where he had been, he replied: 'Sir, I have now no more business here than you have. In half an hour you will neither have actors to command nor authority to employ them.' Rich was so shocked by the boldness of this strange statement that he could only reply that if Cibber wouldn't work, then he shouldn't be paid. At that moment Sir John Stanley arrived from the Lord Chamberlain's office and Cibber made a great play of formally introducing him to Rich and explaining that he had an important message. As Rich unrolled the order, Cibber turned on his heel and walked out, tossing his head and uttering the terrible words delivered by Henry VIII to Cardinal Wolsey in Shakespeare's play: 'Read o'er that! And now – to breakfast with what appetite you may.'[12] This must be the best exit line ever produced by an actor in real life, and the fact that Cibber was able to dredge it up from a memory stuffed with speeches from dozens of plays at this critical moment gives some idea of why he became the most powerful person in the theatre for the next twenty years.

Cibber took most of the leading actors with him to join Owen Swiney at the Haymarket where he and fellow actors Robert Wilks, Thomas Doggett and Anne Oldfield joined the management. They were all to be 'sharers', until Doggett objected to having a woman involved with management, and proposed that Anne Oldfield should be allowed to fix her own terms instead. She asked for £200 a year and a benefit clear of all charges, which the others were glad to agree to as she was a huge draw, and the first actor to be described as a 'star'.[13]

Under a licence issued by the Lord Chamberlain on 8 July 1709, the actors could put on plays at the Queen's on four nights a week, with the other two nights kept for opera. They spent the summer recess getting ready for an autumn opening, and did as much as they could to improve the theatre's terrible acoustics. Although it had always been intended for both plays and operas, Vanbrugh's magnificent architecture of vast columns topped by a dome caused the loss of so much sound that members of the audience could scarcely hear enough of the dialogue to follow a play. The dome had been blocked off very early on, but there were still problems, so the new team set to work to lower the ceiling and reduce the width of the auditorium. Cibber's intention was to recreate the layout of the original auditorium at Drury Lane before Rich altered it. The thrust stage used to protrude so far into the auditorium that the actors, who did most of their acting at the front of this thrust, were never far from any member of the audience. Rich had spotted the opportunity to get a few more benches into the pit and sliced off four feet from the thrust. He then built 'stage boxes' – that is to say, boxes which were actually at the side of the thrust stage, so that actors had to keep behind these boxes or the people sitting in them would be looking at their backs. This put the actors a good ten feet further back from the audience. However, Cibber's attempt to recreate the earlier layout of Drury Lane at the Haymarket was frustrated by lack of time. They had to be ready for the new season, and they opened on 15 September 1709 with Betterton as Othello.✣

Storming Drury Lane

When Christopher Rich had been served with the writ silencing him, he hadn't been very alarmed. He had been silenced before, but the orders were lifted after a few days or a couple of weeks. As the weeks turned into months, he must have realised that this time he had gone too far, but he wasn't the sort of man to admit defeat. He tried re-opening in September and the audience was actually in the theatre

---

✣ Betterton was 74 by this time. He had retired from management in 1705, but continued to act until the time of his death. His last performance was in *The Maid's Tragedy* by Beaumont and Fletcher on 13 April 1710, when his gout was so bad he had to go onstage in slippers. He died two weeks later.

awaiting a performance of *The Recruiting Officer* when an order arrived forbidding the performance.

On 19 November, while Rich was still occupying Drury Lane, the Lord Chamberlain issued another licence to run a theatre. The new licensee was William Collier, a lawyer and Member of Parliament for Truro. He was also, importantly, a Tory and extremely well connected politically with the current Tory administration. He owned a share of the Drury Lane patent, and like other sharers had received nothing from it for a long time. With the theatre silenced, that income stream was well and truly blocked off. He was told that he would receive his licence on condition that he gave up his share in the patent, which was now worthless anyway. He thus found himself with a licence to run a theatre but no theatre to run, while Rich, who regarded possession as nine points of the law, still occupied Drury Lane with his remaining crew, holding both of the patents issued by Charles II, although he couldn't put on plays. Collier approached the building shareholders who had been receiving no rent since June, as rent was only payable on acting days, and had no difficulty in persuading them to issue him with a new lease, especially as he was promising to pay rent of £4 per acting day rather than the £3 that Rich was supposed to pay them. He then decided to break the impasse by using force.

On 22 November 1709, Collier made a bonfire outside the theatre and gave money to the actors who had remained with Rich to drink the health of the Queen and the Lord Chamberlain. These actors were in a very low condition as they were only paid on acting days, and the theatre had been silenced since June. When Collier showed them a letter from the Lord Chamberlain authorising him to start putting on plays again as of the next day, they joined with Collier in storming the theatre. As a back-up for this task-force of tipsy thesps, Collier had brought along soldiers armed to the teeth with swords and muskets. (Collier later claimed that he hadn't asked them to come and didn't know why they were there, which seems improbable.) They soon broke down the doors and took possession of the theatre, only to find that Rich had been warned of the plan and had stripped it the day before of everything that wasn't screwed to the floor, including the valuable stock of costumes.

Richard Steele wrote a mock-heroic account in *The Tatler*[14] of the storming of Drury Lane, describing how residents of the area were astonished to see a procession from the theatre of Rich's remaining staff wearing all the costumes they could squeeze into: 'doorkeepers came out clad like cardinals, and scene-drawers like heathen gods. Divito himself [Rich] was wrapped up in one of his black clouds, and left to the enemy nothing but an empty stage, full of trap-doors, known only to himself and his adherents.'

Empty stage or not, the show had to go on as there had been no money coming in for months, and they opened the next night with Dryden's *Aurung-Zebe*. The actors wore their own clothes.

This marked the end of Christopher Rich's career at Drury Lane, although not the end of his career in the theatre. He had lost everything because he alienated those he needed to keep on his side by lying, swindling and thoroughly dishonourable conduct. Colley Cibber, who was a shrewd judge of character and who worked for Rich for best part of sixteen years, said that, although people attributed everything Rich did to elaborate plots and cunning, he thought the chaos that characterised Rich's time at Drury Lane simply indicated a man who was out of his depth. 'His parts were too weak for his post... no creature ever seemed more fond of power, that so little knew how to use it.'[15]

8

A Triumvirate (Plus One)

William Collier, who had no experience of theatre at all, decided to appoint a manager to run Drury Lane. This was a wise decision, but he rather surprisingly chose a young man called Aaron Hill who had no more experience of theatre than Collier himself. Aaron Hill was a precocious young man who had left Westminster School at the age of 14 to go on his travels to the Ottoman Empire in Turkey. He stayed with the British ambassador, Lord Paget, in Constantinople, whence he travelled to Greece, the Holy Land and Egypt. Hill then returned to England in the entourage of Lord Paget (who was a distant relative), passing through Bulgaria, Germany, Austria and Holland. He arrived back in London, an amazingly well-travelled 18-year-old, and worked as a private tutor before founding a magazine called *The British Apollo*. In 1709, at the age of 24, he published *A Full and Just Account of the Present State of the Ottoman Empire*, and it was probably on the basis of this that he persuaded Collier to let him manage Drury Lane.

The fact that he was able to get *Aurung-Zebe* on the stage the day after the theatre had been stormed and found to be devoid of any moveable stock shows that Hill must have been a capable organiser. However, he inherited a tricky situation. Under Christopher Rich, the actors had been left pretty much to manage themselves, and seven of them were described as 'managers'. Hill found himself being second-guessed by these other 'managers', and he responded to a dispute over casting by telling them they were dismissed from any involvement in the management of the company. They all went on strike. Hill then rather unwisely went away for a few days on personal business, leaving his 20-year-old brother in charge. He was soon summoned back to the theatre by a letter telling him that there was a full-scale revolt in progress. After a very bitter interview with the ringleaders, Hill was tipped off that they intended to storm the building on 2 June. He ordered the doorkeepers to keep the doors shut, but the actors got in through a side-entrance and broke open the main door from within. A crowd of actors and their supporters surged into the theatre, and the audience arriving for that night's performance of *The Fair Quaker of Deal* found themselves witnessing a full-scale battle with real swords drawn. Hill was then locked out of his own theatre and the show went ahead. Before he was ejected, he saw Christopher Rich being hailed by the actors in the corridor and suspected, no doubt correctly, that Rich was behind the whole thing. After this outrageous behaviour, the Lord Chamberlain ordered that the actors responsible should be sacked or suspended, and Drury Lane closed for the rest of the season.

Things were not much better over at the Haymarket. Running an opera company and an acting company together was difficult and unprofitable, especially for the actors who had only four nights a week instead of the normal six. There was so much uncertainty about the way forward for the London theatres that the new season didn't open as normal in September, and only limped into action in November. Business was not good and Swiney was reduced to hiring a Dutch contortionist to appear between the acts of the plays, and then to exhibiting 'the Four Indian Kings' who had recently arrived in London. Cibber and his fellow actor-managers must have been infuriated by this betrayal of their 'legitimate' ideals and they were arguing with Swiney before the end of the season.

It was obvious that actors and singers didn't get on together, so the idea of awarding each theatre a monopoly of one type of entertainment made sense. Drury Lane was better suited to plays and the Haymarket to operas, so it was all-change again for the 1710/11 season, with the Lord Chamberlain giving Swiney, Cibber, Wilks and Doggett the monopoly on plays at Drury Lane, while Collier got the monopoly on opera at the Haymarket. Collier, no doubt frustrated by the collapse of Aaron Hill's attempts at management and the early closure of Drury Lane in June, thought he might like to try his hand at opera, and he had enough political clout to make sure it wasn't a fair swop. The management at Drury Lane had to pay £200 a year to the Haymarket for the privilege of their monopoly of drama and – much worse – were forbidden from acting on Wednesdays in competition with the opera in the Haymarket.✣ This meant that their possible takings were reduced from six nights a week to five nights, and so most of the actors, who were only paid on acting days, were a day short on their money every week. Cibber describes this arrangement as 'making the day-labouring actors the principal subscribers' to the opera.[1] It was certainly a very early example of government subsidy (given that it was imposed by political lobbying) and evidence that opera would always struggle to survive on box-office takings.

The licence from the Lord Chamberlain to Swiney, Cibber, Wilks and Doggett was issued on 6 November 1710, and on 20 November, without any fanfare, the new team opened at Drury Lane with Wilks starring in *The Unhappy Favourite, or the Earl of Essex* by John Banks. The new management at the Haymarket opened two nights later with the opera *Hydaspes* by Mancini and Pepusche. Once again, Collier had entrusted the management to Aaron Hill, still only 25, in spite of the fiasco at Drury Lane earlier in the year. However, this was not a salaried position: it seems that Hill paid Collier a flat fee of £600 a year to manage the theatre, meaning that everything was being done at his own risk. (Hill had just married the daughter of a wealthy tradesman who came with a dowry of £800, which paid for this venture.) The risk element was considerable because operas were much more expensive to stage than plays, partly owing to the staggeringly high fees paid to

---

✣ Although the houses acted against each other on Saturdays.

the Italian stars, and yet the audience for opera was so limited that it could only be performed twice a week: Wednesdays and Saturdays. For the first few months Hill seems to have just about broken even, but then in February 1711 he put on the very first opera written by Handel for the London stage: *Rinaldo*. Hill co-wrote the libretto (he seems to have written it in English from which it was translated into Italian) and spent a lot of money on the most spectacular scenic effects available. It was a great success with audiences, who loved being able to see a new opera by the most famous new name in opera in Europe, with the composer himself in the pit playing the harpsichord. However, on 3 March Collier resorted to violent methods once again to take back control of his theatre, expelling Hill and his staff, probably because the show was losing too much money. Audiences had been between 180 and 260 people a night, which wasn't enough to cover costs.[2] Hill found himself liable for the debts contracted, although the money paid in advance by aristocratic subscribers was still being held by Collier. Collier was ordered to give it up, but neglected to do so, probably because he was finding the debts unpayable. He was losing as much money as Hill and, incredibly, he began to think, once again, of a switch.

Realising that opera on its own would never be a money-maker, Collier set his sights on Drury Lane again. Being, as Cibber memorably put it, 'a true liquorish courtier',[3] he managed to get his friends in high places to agree to yet another swap of the two theatres. And so, on 17 April 1712, two new licences were issued: one to Owen Swiney to run the opera at the Haymarket, and one to Cibber, Wilks, Doggett and – this time – Collier, to put on plays at Drury Lane. The prohibition against Drury Lane acting on Wednesdays was dropped, but the management of Drury Lane was obliged to pay Swiney £100 a year 'towards defraying the expences of the opera' and not to put on the first night of a new play or an actor's benefit when it clashed with the opera.[4]

Given the well-known financial problems at the opera, why did Swiney agree to it? It seems he had no choice. He had fallen out with Cibber, Wilks and Doggett, who discovered that they no longer needed him and managed effectively to exclude him from the management, paying him a stipend of £600 a year to stay away.[5] Furthermore, Sir John Vanbrugh, who was still the landlord of the Haymarket and was himself well-connected politically,✤ told Swiney that, if he didn't accept the Haymarket position, he would find himself with no position in either theatre. When Swiney got to the Haymarket he found the finances to be as bad as everyone had been saying they were. In January 1713 he fled to Europe, together with the previous night's takings from Handel's *Teseo*, and was declared bankrupt. Thus, at the end of this three-year game of musical chairs with the London theatres, Swiney found himself without a seat when the music stopped – ironically, at the opera. He must have felt cheated, but there was a happy ending: he established himself in Venice as an agent for the Italian opera in London, and for English collectors seeking Italian paintings. He was largely responsible, in this latter role, for the popularity of Canaletto in England.

The triumvirate

William Collier must have realised by now that theatre management wasn't his forte, and he wanted to have nothing more to do with Drury Lane on a day-to-day basis. He had used political influence to get a licence to put on shows, to get control of Drury Lane, to swap it for the Haymarket and to swap again for Drury Lane. So far, he had seen little by way of profits, which was his only reason for getting involved in the first place, as he appears to have had no interest in theatre. Now he wanted the money but not the hassle.

He told Cibber, Wilks and Doggett that he regarded his position at Drury Lane as a sinecure. They were to pay him £700 a year for the privilege of running his theatre, and he wouldn't trouble them with

---

✤ John Vanbrugh had been the first person to be knighted by George I when he stepped off the boat from Hanover.

any interference. The three actor-managers, who would soon become known as the triumvirate, were not happy about working to support a drone, but they knew they had no choice, owing to Collier's political influence. If they didn't agree, he could easily get rid of them. They offered him an equal share in the proceeds, but having seen the state of the box office for the last three years Collier said no, he wanted the flat fee of £700. The triumvirate had no option but to agree to his terms, but it was a source of satisfaction to Cibber that, by refusing the equal share, Collier did himself a disservice, because Drury Lane was about to enter into a long period of stability, success and profitability – the first in its so-far troubled history. Cibber claimed that there was no year in which the triumvirate paid themselves less than £1,000 each (the equivalent of over £100,000 now).

Cibber attributed the success of the triumvirate to the fact that they were all professional theatre people, unlike the 'former managers, who were only idle gentlemen'.[6] They had their differences, and in fact Cibber describes their respective temperaments as so 'vexatiously opposite' they were like 'fire, air and water',[7] but they knew that, whatever their personal feelings, the show had to go on. They knew that actors were reasonably easy to manage if they were fairly treated and paid on time; that suppliers had to be paid; and that the shows they put on had to get bums on seats without upsetting anyone in authority. In his *Apology* Cibber paints himself as the peacemaker between the other two, using tact and diplomacy to smooth feathers ruffled by displays of temperament, and this is probably not far from the truth. Cibber was prepared to swallow any sense of resentment at the behaviour of the other two because 'the sweet morsel of a thousand pounds a year was not be met with at every table',[8] and he used the same reasoning to placate Wilks and Doggett when they were on their high horses. The fact that the arrangement with Doggett broke down in the year after they took over Drury Lane he attributes to the fact that as Doggett 'had more money than I, he had not occasion for so much philosophy'.[9] As usual with theatrical upheavals in those days, the breakdown was the result of political interference.

Cato and liberty

One of the things that makes theatre so interesting is its unpredictability. Like horse-racing, it can throw up the most surprising winners. Seasoned theatregoers are amazed to find Greek tragedy or German romantic dramas cleaning up on Shaftesbury Avenue, while shows with all the ingredients of a sure-fire hit close at the end of the week.

The year 1713 threw up just such a surprise hit in Joseph Addison's *Cato*. It is an account of the last hours of a virtuous Roman senator who refuses to accept the crushing by Julius Caesar of the ancient Roman republic, and who commits suicide rather than witness the destruction of his country's liberties. This sounds like pretty heavy stuff, and Addison's ponderous, solemn and preachy tone made it worse than it need have been. Addison was far from being a man of the theatre, although he recognised the importance of theatre in the culture. Together with Richard Steele, he had founded *The Spectator* and *The Tatler* to raise the tone of cultural life by bringing 'philosophy out of closets and libraries... to dwell... at tea-tables and coffee-houses'.[10] Both publications had carried numerous articles on the importance of theatre, praising good plays and actors and urging 'the town' to support the best in drama. However, there is a big difference between being a theorist of the drama and putting on a hit show, and Addison had been humiliated in 1707 when his attempt to establish an English style of opera with *Rosamund* flopped at Drury Lane. He was essentially an academic, who preferred the cloisters of his beloved Oxford to the rough-and-tumble of a raucous auditorium.

Addison had written most of *Cato* by 1703, a full ten years before its production, when he read the first four acts to Richard Steele and Colley Cibber. Both men urged him to let it be produced, but Addison took the view that it was better for reading in the study than acting on the stage. (He was right about that.) However, by 1712 things were looking decidedly bad for the Whigs, and Addison, who was a staunch Whig and member of the Kit-Cat Club, was urged to allow the play to be put on to help the cause. Queen Anne, a Tory herself, always favoured Tory ministers, but she was coming to the end of her life. She had no children, so the succession was a big issue. James Edward

Stuart, 'The Pretender', was just across the water, waiting for the chance to return and reclaim the throne his father, James II, had vacated. The Tories were negotiating with him to bring this about, their only condition being that he had to renounce his Roman Catholicism. The Whigs, on the other hand, had reached an agreement to pass the throne to the Elector of Hanover which would preserve Protestantism as the national religion and, it was felt, the liberty of the British people.

The Kit-Cats thought that *Cato* was just what was needed to remind everyone of the importance of liberty, which for them meant keeping the Pretender, with his Roman Catholicism and his family tradition of the Divine Right of Kings, in France where he belonged. However Addison, who was rather a timid person, was understandably nervous about being too political. It was not at all uncommon for critics of the government to find themselves being prosecuted for criminal libel, or even sent to the Tower of London on a charge of treason, as Sir Robert Walpole had been. Addison therefore went to see Lord Bolingbroke, the Tory Secretary of State, to ask him what he thought about the play. Bolingbroke spotted an opportunity for a PR coup: if the Whigs were intending to cheer Cato as the representative of British liberty, the Tories would cheer even louder.

The first night of *Cato*, therefore, turned into a cross-party event. Drury Lane was packed, with the Tories occupying the pit underneath Lord Bolingbroke's box while the Whigs clustered under the Kit-Cats' boxes on the other side of the auditorium. Addison was so nervous that he had arranged for a table spread with Burgundy and champagne to be set up in his box, to fortify himself against possible booing. He needn't have worried. The audience went wild, cheering even during the prologue that had been written by the Tory Alexander Pope. The play was full of lines like:

> *A day, an hour of virtuous liberty*
> *Is worth a whole eternity in bondage* [11]

which set off wave after wave of cheers, with Tories trying to drown out the Whigs and vice-versa. At the end of the show, Lord Bolingbroke summoned Barton Booth, who was playing Cato, to his box, where he presented him with a purse containing 50 guineas 'for his honest opposition to a perpetual dictator, and his dying so bravely in the cause of liberty'.[12] For the Whigs, the 'perpetual dictator' they feared was the Pretender; for the Tories, it was the Duke of Marlborough, now living in exile, as he was felt to harbour unconstitutional ambitions for permanent command of the armed forces. No matter, the show was a hit. It had twenty consecutive performances, apart from two Monday nights when the theatre had already been booked for an actor's benefit and a performance of *Richard III* 'at the desire of several ladies of quality'.✢

Barton Booth had not been the most obvious casting for Cato, as he was not a favourite with the triumvirate. When Colley Cibber had led the walkout of actors from Drury Lane to the Haymarket in 1709, Booth was one of the few actors who stayed behind with Christopher Rich, so he played no part in the sequence of events that led to the actor-managers gaining control of the theatre. He certainly wasn't Cibber's first choice for the part: when Cibber had first heard Addison reading *Cato* in 1703, he had envisioned Betterton in the lead, but Betterton had died in 1710. Booth did, however, have one very important thing going for him: he was a Tory, and could expect favourable treatment under a Tory ministry.

Doggett, who was a virulent Whig, was furious when he heard about Lord Bolingbroke's purse of 50 guineas, not because he begrudged Booth the money, but because he didn't want the Tories claiming Cato as one of their own. Doggett told Wilks and Cibber that they should make Booth a present of another 50 guineas from the management as a token of their appreciation. Wilks was enthusiastic, but Cibber said that they should wait and see what happened before throwing away 50 guineas, as Booth might be expecting a good deal more as a reward for *Cato*: he might be looking for a share in the management. Wilks wasn't

---

✢ The unusually long first run posed problems for Mrs Oldfield, playing Cato's virginal daughter, whose pregnancy was so far advanced that a midwife was kept in the wings for the last performances.

worried and Doggett assured Cibber that no one could take their property away from them, so the gift was made.

Cibber's assessment of the situation proved to be the right one. Booth applied to Bolingbroke, and on 11 November 1713 a new licence to run the theatre was issued to Collier, Cibber, Wilks, Doggett *and* Booth. Since Collier was still insisting on his flat fee of £700 per year, this meant that remaining profits now had to be divided four ways instead of three. Wilks and Cibber realised that they could do nothing against such powerful political forces, but Doggett was adamant: he wouldn't give up his property and he wouldn't negotiate. He walked out of the theatre and refused to act or to be involved in the management any more. Booth agreed to pay £600 for the share he was being given in the business, and this £600 would be paid to the others out of his share of the annual profits. According to Cibber, it was repaid within a year.

Doggett, however, was still demanding his share of the profits, even though he was playing no part in the theatre's affairs. The new triumvirate offered him a half-share as a sincecure, but he refused: he wanted his share and the whole share. Cibber managed to tie the matter up in the courts for two years until eventually Doggett was given £600 plus back-interest for his share. This was much less than the half-share would have been worth to him, without all the litigation.

The new triumvirate of Cibber, Wilks and Booth would run Drury Lane for nearly twenty years, but the fourth name on the licence would soon change, again for political reasons. In August 1714 Queen Anne died and in the next month George, Elector of Hanover, landed at Greenwich. On 20 October he was crowned George I. He distrusted the Tories, whom he suspected of plotting to bring back the Stuart dynasty, and when he announced his first ministry, it was 100 per cent Whig. At the general election in the following spring, the Whigs won a large majority. The Tories would be out of office for a long time.

This meant changes at Drury Lane, because the licence under which Collier and the triumvirate operated the theatre was held 'at pleasure', i.e. at the pleasure of the monarch who issued it and expiring with that monarch. A new licence was needed, and the triumvirate knew they would be in a weak position if they were applying in partnership with a Tory MP. Collier was unceremoniously dumped, and they asked Richard Steele if he would like the job.

Richard Steele and the reform of the stage

Steele was, in many ways, the perfect choice. Politically, he was as sound as a bell. Not only was he a Whig, he had been such a bitter opponent of the claims of the Jacobite Pretender, and such a staunch defender of the claims of the House of Hanover to the British throne, that he had actually been expelled from the Tory-dominated House of Commons on a charge of seditious libel. Who could have a better claim to the new king's gratitude? Furthermore, he was a Kit-Cat, and Kit-Cats were everywhere in the new administration, showered with honours.✢ It was unlikely that Steele would be refused any position he asked for.

Equally important was the fact that Steele would not be a carpet-bagging opportunist like Collier: he was passionate about the theatre and was both a successful playwright and an effective advocate. His three comedies *The Funeral* (1701), *The Lying Lover* (1703) and *The Tender Husband* (1705) had all been hits at Drury Lane, while in *The Tatler* and *The Spectator*, which he produced with Joseph Addison, the state of the theatre had been one of the regular topics for discussion. Both men felt that theatre was important.♣ They would promote plays and actors who seemed to them to be aiming high in cultural terms, and these articles would immediately be followed by full houses for the shows concerned.

But there was even more to it than that. The controversy stirred up by Jeremy Collier in 1698 about the profaneness and immorality of the stage had not gone away. There was a widespread concern amongst

---

✢ 'Only four of thirty-nine Kit-Cat members did not hold some government or Court office immediately following George's accession.' (Field, 307)

♣ 'There is no human invention so aptly calculated for the forming a free-born people as that of a theatre.' *The Tatler* No 167, 2-4 May 1710.

the cultural classes that the corruption of the stage was a serious issue and should be addressed. The question was, who would have the time, the talent and the energy to do it? In this respect, Steele was the perfect choice. He was a devout Christian who believed that the business of the stage was to instruct audiences in the moral virtues. He was by far the most influential of all those who sided with Collier, and had written a bitter attack in *The Spectator* on the character of the 'fine gentleman' in Restoration comedies. He took as his text *The Man of Mode* by Sir George Etherege and its hero Dorimant:

> I will take for granted, that a fine gentleman should be honest in his actions, and refined in his language. Instead of this, our hero in this piece is a direct knave in his designs, and a clown in his language... This whole celebrated piece is a perfect contradiction to good manners, good sense, and common honesty; and... there is nothing in it but what is built upon the ruin of virtue and innocence...[13]

This passage is so close to the denunciation of the fine gentleman of Restoration comedy by Jeremy Collier that Steele must have had Collier's book open in front of him when he wrote it, but there is a difference. Collier chose to attack Valentine, the hero of Congreve's *Love for Love* (1695), a purely fictional character, whereas Steele took Dorimant, who had been recognised, as soon as the play appeared in 1676, as a portrait of John Wilmot, second Earl of Rochester. The Earl made every effort to live up to his sulphurous reputation as the most debauched libertine at the court of Charles II✠ and, four years after the first performance of *The Man of Mode*, he died of syphilis after a spectacular deathbed conversion in which he repented of his wickedness. Steele firmly believed that the whoring, drinking, gambling and dishonesty of the characters held up for admiration in

---

✠ In his 1676 poem 'To the Postboy', Rochester reports an imaginary conversation between himself and a postboy that begins: 'Son of a whore, God damn you! Can you tell/A peerless peer the readiest way to Hell?' It ends with the postboy's reply: 'The readiest way, my Lord's, by Rochester.'

Restoration comedies would bring people to a bad end, and that it was the business of the stage to warn them against it.

Steele was due a reward for his services to the House of Hanover, and several of his admirers felt that Drury Lane was just the place for him. Steele soon received a message from the King saying that he was being lobbied to give Drury Lane to Steele, and asking if Steele really wanted this himself, or if it was just his friends' idea. Steele replied that he did want it, and the licence was issued on 18 October 1714. The triumvirate, feeling that they were on a roll with Steele, asked him to move things up a notch and ask for a patent, which would put their operation on a much more secure footing than a licence, that could be revoked at any time. The patent came through on 19 January 1715. Shortly afterwards, Steele was knighted.

The patent was not perpetual but limited to Steele's life plus three years. Steele claimed that he had asked for this because of the difficulties that had arisen with the two perpetual patents issued by Charles II as they passed through different hands. Both of these patents were now held by Christopher Rich, who couldn't use them since he has been silenced, but the issuing of a third patent to Steele, in spite of the assurances of the first two that no one but the holders of them would be allowed to run a theatre in London, raised tricky legal issues. Some years later, when Steele was locked in a bitter dispute with the Lord Chamberlain's office, the Lord Chamberlain took legal advice on Steele's patent and was told not to raise it, as it was of very questionable legal authority. Nevertheless, things were looking good for the triumvirate plus one at the dawn of the new Georgian age.

Steele was appointed 'governor' of Drury Lane and retained the title until his death. It had never been used before, and suggested that its holder was in some way superior to a mere 'manager'. The wording of patent was explicit and highly significant. Its preamble complained that:

> …instead of exhibiting such representations of human life as may
> tend to the encouragement and honour of religion and virtue…

> the English stage… hath given great and insufferable scandal to religion and good manners… by indecent and immodest expressions, by profane allusions to Holy Scripture, by abusive and scurrilous representations of the clergy, and by the success and applause bestowed on libertine characters…

This could have been straight out of Collier and the fact that it was included in a patent for Drury Lane shows how far the ideas of a rebellious clergyman, who was at one time facing prosecution for treason, had permeated mainstream thinking. Steele had been appointed as governor, the patent stated, because of 'his publick services to religion and virtue' as well as 'his steady adherence to the true interest of his country', and 'we do hereby command and enjoyn that no new play, or any old or revived play, be acted… containing any passages or expressions offensive to piety and good manners, until the same be corrected and purged by the said governor…' Furthermore, Steele was instructed to ensure that nothing critical or defamatory of 'the Christian religion in general or the Church of England' be performed, nor anything that might undermine government policy.[14]

Of course, language like this had been used before and no one had taken it very seriously. There had never been any real expectation that Thomas Killigrew, William Davenant, John Vanbrugh or William Congreve were going to purge plays of 'passages offensive to piety', but this time it was different. Steele took the job seriously, and informed the readers of his periodical *Town Talk* that he intended to run Drury Lane along the lines laid down by the patent:

> If everything that be represented is not virtuous, at least let it be innocent. This will bring a new audience to the house; and it is in the hope of entertaining those who at present are terrified at the theatre, that the sharers may hope for their success hereafter.[15]

Throwing over your existing audience for a different sort of audience you hope to attract is a perilous business, as Steele soon discovered.

He persuaded Addison to let him stage a comedy Addison had written several years before called *The Drummer*, which was an attempt to meet Collier's demands by writing something both funny and virtuous. Addison had reservations about it, and with good reason. *The Drummer*, which opened in March 1716, stood four-square behind the institution of marriage, complaining that for too long 'the poor wedded pair' had been the butt of every playwright looking for a cheap laugh. Unfortunately it was deathly dull and only just made the third night – the author's benefit – before it disappeared. Addison never acknowledged it and it was not included in the complete edition of his works that was published after his death. Meanwhile, an unwelcome development in London theatre had made the task of putting on morally uplifting plays at Drury Lane more difficult.

In Rep: Plays Performed at Drury Lane During w/c 17 October 1715
Date in brackets is year of first performance

Date of performance, *Play* and playwright

Monday 17 October, *The Busy-Body* by Susanna Centlivre (1709)
Tuesday 18 October, *Jane Shore* by Nicholas Rowe (1714) followed by *The What D'Ye Call It* by John Gay (1715)
Wednesday 19 October, *Sir Courtly Nice* by John Crowne (1685)
Thursday 20 October, *The Constant Couple* by George Farquhar (1699)
Friday 21 October, *Cato* by Joseph Addison (1713)
Saturday 22 October, *The Careless Husband* by Colley Cibber (1704)

9

A Christian Hero
at Drury Lane

W hen **Christopher Rich** was kicked out of Drury Lane, everyone assumed that would be the end of his troublesome career in the London theatre. Rich, however, was a man who seemed to be constitutionally incapable of even contemplating defeat, so when he realised that his time at Drury Lane was at an end, he turned his attention to the theatre that was now standing empty in Lincoln's Inn Fields.

From as far back as 1708, when things were getting rocky, Rich had been paying rent on the Lincoln's Inn Fields building, which had been unused since Betterton took his company to the Haymarket in 1705. With Drury Lane now occupied by his enemies, Rich began what was virtually a reconstruction of the old tennis court to turn it into a serious rival to his former theatre. There was one huge problem: although he held both patents issued by Charles II, he had been silenced, so even if he had a theatre, he couldn't put on plays. However, with a new monarch on the throne and a new Lord Chamberlain in office, he thought he would try again, and he got one of his well-connected investors in the Lincoln's Inn Fields project to speak to the King. George I probably knew little and cared less about Rich's management of Drury Lane, and simply said that, when he used to visit London as a young man, there were two theatres, and he didn't see why there shouldn't be two theatres again. (The King's Theatre in the Haymarket was now an opera house.) The order of silence was lifted, and Rich spent the autumn of 1714 getting ready for a re-opening. However, he didn't live to see it. Christopher Rich died on 7 November, leaving the majority interest in the new venture to his son John, who opened the new theatre on 14 December 1714 with a performance of *The Recruiting Officer*.

John Rich had no formal education, and was said to be illiterate. This must have been an exaggeration, but he may have been dyslexic. He stumbled over words and claimed not to be able to remember people's names. (He always called Garrick 'Griskin'.) He came to theatre management blissfully unburdened by any high-falutin' ideas about the role of theatre in the culture: as far as he was concerned, it was just about getting bums on seats, and he soon found a brilliant way to do that. After a few attempts at acting, he discovered his true vocation as a dancer. He began to appear as Harlequin, which he made into a non-speaking part so that he wouldn't have to remember lines, and was known professionally as Lun.

Rich played a key role in the development of pantomime, which emerged at this time and became a vital part of theatre culture, to the despair of those who wanted theatre to be an intelligent and verbal experience. It had all started so innocently – over at Drury Lane.

The Loves of Mars and Venus

John Weaver (1673-1760) was a dancer, choreographer and theorist of dance who has been described by one dance historian as 'the major figure in British dance before the present [twentieth] century'.[1] He studied the history of dance, which he wanted to promote as an art form in its own right, 'worthy the regard and consideration... of the learned world',[2] rather than just a bit of light relief between the acts of a play. He was particularly interested in the *pantomimi*, the dancers of the ancient Greek and Roman theatre who could tell a story without the need of words, and in March 1717 he put on at Drury Lane *The Loves of Mars and Venus*, which was described on the playbill as 'a new dramatick entertainment of dancing after the manner of the antient pantomimes'.[3] This was the first time that a show had been described as a pantomime – Greek for 'all in mime' – and the name stuck. *The Loves of Mars and Venus* was not a full evening's entertainment but an afterpiece, meaning a short entertainment which would follow the five-act play that was the main business of the evening. Afterpieces had become popular by the early years of the eighteenth century, and made for a very long evening in the theatre of four hours or more, although not everyone would stay for the complete bill of fare. Pantomimes would remain as afterpieces for many years.

Weaver followed this in April with *The Shipwreck, or Perseus and Andromeda*, which he described as 'a new dramatick entertainment of dancing in grotesque characters'.[4] The 'grotesque characters' were Harlequin and his companions from the harlequinade, who impersonated the characters of the myth: Harlequin was Perseus and Colombine was Andromeda, the princess he rescues from a sea-monster. Weaver described his grotesques as 'a faint imitation of the Roman pantomimes'. This was the moment that pantomime assumed the form it would hold for the next century: a serious story, often from classical mythology, would be mixed up with a ludicrous story using the characters of the harlequinade. Sometimes the plots would run in parallel, alternating serious scenes and comic scenes, sometimes the characters would appear together, and sometimes the serious characters would be transformed into the characters of the Harequinade. Pantomime came to mean a mixture of certain elements: a story from mythology, legend, fairy tale or nursery rhyme; a harlequinade; singing, dancing, mime; special effects (especially transformations) and spectacular scenery. None of these elements were new. Singing and dancing had been an important component of theatrical performances since the Restoration; spectacular scenery and transformation scenes likewise. These had been brought together in opera, but since the vogue for Italian opera had begun, opera appealed only to élite audiences who could understand Italian (or pretend to). The singing in pantomimes was in English, which made them more accessible. Masques involving classical gods and heroes had cropped up from time to time in the theatres. Harlequinades were also very familiar on the London stage, and John Rich had already made a name for himself as Harlequin. Seeing the popularity of the new form, Rich put on an afterpiece at Lincoln's Inn Fields in November 1717 called *Mars and Venus or The Mousetrap* which was a spoof of Weaver's show at Drury Lane, with Harlequin and Scaramouche invading the serious part of the plot. He followed it up in January 1718 with *Amadis or the Loves of Harlequin and Columbine* which was a spoof of Handel's opera *Amadis*, but this time with the serious and comic characters kept separate.

The speed with which the public took to pantomimes surprised everyone. Within a very short time, they were the most popular shows on the stage. Even though they were still only afterpieces, their attractions often outweighed the mainpieces they were supposedly supporting.✣ The competition between the two theatres was so intense they would go head-to-head with pantomime versions of the same stories: after Perseus and Andromeda there were rival productions of Orpheus and Eurydice and the Rape of Proserpina. But nothing compared with the square-off that took place in 1723 when Dr Faustus was selling his soul to the devil at both Drury Lane and Lincoln's Inn Fields.

There was a feeling amongst the theatre-going public that Lincoln's Inn Fields had the advantage in pantomime, largely because of John Rich's brilliant performances as Harlequin. He could transform himself into a dog, fall to pieces on the gallows and put himself back together again, and one of his most famous routines involved his birth from an egg. So, in November 1723 the triumvirate at Drury Lane tried to gain the initiative by pulling out all the stops for *Harlequin Doctor Faustus*, a pantomime version of the legend of the man who sells his soul in exchange for infernal powers while he lives. The nub of the

---

✣ The expense of the spectacular scenery caused prices to be raised for plays that would be followed by a pantomime afterpiece, to the fury of theatre-lovers who complained that they were being made to pay for nonsense they didn't want to see. As a concession, the managements agreed to refund the difference to anyone who left before the start of the overture to the pantomime.

show was taken up with the tricks that Faustus (played by Harlequin) performs courtesy of these powers: he cuts off his own leg and replaces it, then makes asses' ears appear on Scaramouche, Pierrot and Punch. At the end he is dragged off to hell while the gods of Mount Olympus perform a ballet to celebrate his death.

This time, the verdict of the town was that Drury Lane had scored a triumph over Lincoln's Inn Fields in the pantomime department – until John Rich put on *The Necromancer, or Harlequin Doctor Faustus* a month later. It was bigger and better in every way and ended up with Faustus being taken to hell by a huge dragon. *The Necromancer* became one of the greatest hits of the eighteenth century, notching up over 300 performances between 1723 and the retirement of John Rich from the stage in 1753.

Colley Cibber, meanwhile, was watching all of this with a sense of mounting horror, and must have felt at times as if he had made his own pact with the devil. Cibber was a man who regarded a good play, well acted, as one of the highest accomplishments of art, and the most rational and rewarding shared experience a community can engage in. He didn't have much time for opera, which he regarded as an 'entertainment so entirely sensual, it had no possibility of getting the better of our reasons',[5] but he really loathed 'the decorated nonsense and absurdities of pantomimical trumpery' which he regarded as 'so much rank theatrical popery'.[6] What made it worse, as he had to admit, was that Drury Lane had started the trend with its production of *The Loves of Mars and Venus*, which had seemed inoffensive enough at the time, although the managers didn't spend much on it as they doubted its box-office appeal. 'From this original hint then… sprung forth that succession of monstrous medlies that have so long infested the stage.' Writing his *Apology* in 1740, more than 20 years after the monstrous birth, Cibber could only wish that the authorities would intervene to put down 'these poetical drams, these gin-shops of the stage, that intoxicate its auditors, and dishonour their understanding, with a levity for which I want a name.'[7]

Cibber was far from being alone in his strong reaction to the dominance of the stage by pantomime. Many cultural gatekeepers saw it as a serious threat, ✤ including Alexander Pope. In *The Dunciad*, Pope's mock-heroic poem of 1728 on the decadence of the culture, the Doctor Faustus pantomimes of 1723 are seen as a defining event, while for Dr Johnson, looking back from 1747, rational entertainment on the stage had died when 'great *Faustus* lay the ghost of wit'.

The silencing of Drury Lane

In spite of his personal aversion to pantomimes, Cibber had to keep putting them on in order to keep Drury Lane open. As he frequently reminds the readers of his *Apology*, theatre managers must respond to public taste, whatever their own feelings: 'If they [the multitude] will have a maypole, why, the players must give them a maypole.'[8] So what had happened to Sir Richard Steele's earnest intentions to reform the stage and make it a place of moral and rational entertainment?

It had got off to a good start. Steele and his three actor-managers got on well because they were all serious about theatre. Steele wasn't going to be a renter, like his predecessors, only interested in extracting money from Drury Lane: he intended to be involved in the management. He clearly wouldn't be involved with the day-to-day business of running the theatre: as a member of parliament and a busy professional author he had too many other irons in the fire. However, he was involved with selecting plays and hiring performers, and he used his social and political contacts to advance Drury Lane's interests. He respected the professionalism of the triumvirate, and they respected the fact that he gave them political influence that they would not otherwise have enjoyed.[9] Steele even used his experience of periodical

---

✤ Theatre-lover Gabriel Rennel published a bitter attack on the Drury Lane management for going head-to-head with Lincoln's Inn Fields in the pantomime department: 'For by introducing new and ridiculous inventions into the playhouse, and by prostituting the use and dignity of the stage, they have brought their theatre into contempt.' *Tragicomical Reflections... occasioned by the present state of the two rival theatres in Drury-Lane and Lincolns-Inn-Fields*, London, 1723, quoted in Loftis, 226.

publishing gained through *The Spectator* and *The Tatler* to launch a new publication – *Town Talk* – which ran theatrical stories and puffs for forthcoming productions at Drury Lane. He also used *Town Talk* to publish in full the text of his patent, charging him with cleaning up the stage, and promising to purify Drury Lane.[10] This was unfortunate, because he couldn't deliver on the promise, and he had no shortage of enemies waiting to point this out.

The repertoire at Drury Lane remained much the same under Steele. It was still putting on the same mixture of pre-Civil War plays by Shakespeare, Fletcher and others; Restoration comedies by Congreve, Vanbrugh and Etherege; and more recent plays by Farquhar, Addison and Rowe. Although the odd smutty line or scene may have been deleted, Steele's enemies attacked him for putting on the very plays he had criticised for their immorality in *The Tatler* and *The Spectator* such as Wycherley's *The Country Wife* and Etherege's *The Man of Mode*. Nor did he stick to what he called 'rational entertainments' – i.e. straight plays rather than musical pieces, farces and variety acts. On the contrary, we know that he was actively involved in hiring a successful Harlequin in Paris to bring to Drury Lane. Steele's defence was that he could not have anticipated the re-opening of Lincoln's Inn Fields under John Rich. Rich felt himself under no obligation to 'improve' the stage and drew the public with all sorts of 'irrational' entertainments, so if Drury Lane wanted to stay in business, it had to compete. Steele's sense of helplessness can be gauged from a couple of lines that he wrote on the back of a Drury Lane playbill found lying on a table in Button's coffee-house:

> *Weaver, corrupter of this present age,*
> *Who first taught silent sins upon the stage.*[11]

John Weaver, the dancing master at Drury Lane, was actually on Steele's payroll, but Steele felt impotent in the face of the taste of the town. He promised the stage reformers that, as soon as he had dealt with the threat to Drury Lane from Lincoln's Inn Fields, he would get on with purifying the stage.[12] That didn't happen.

To make matters worse, Steele was a hopeless man of business and completely incompetent when it came to handling money. He was always in debt, no matter how much he was earning, and always in need of ready cash. Like other patent-holders before him, he sought to raise funds by mortgaging his patent. This would have been questionable even if it had been done in a regular way, given his brief from the King for moral reform, but Steele fell into the hands of con-men who tied him up in such a mesh of mortgages and remortgages that it is almost impossible now to understand it. Steele very nearly lost his patent to them altogether, which would have left a gang of crooks involved in the management of the theatre of which he had been appointed governor. His fellow sharers in the patent – the triumvirate – watched in horror as Steele put their enterprise at risk, and it is significant that from the time that these financial shenanigans started, Steele's involvement with the running of Drury Lane seems to have diminished.

Worse was to come, in the form of a show-down with the Lord Chamberlain over the powers conferred by a royal patent to run a theatre. In the years before the Civil War, legal control of all theatres was vested in the office of the Lord Chamberlain, who delegated most of the day-to-day management to his subordinate, the Master of the Revels. In 1660, with Killigrew and Davenant negotiating with Charles II to obtain powers under a patent to open theatres and maintain a monopoly, Sir Henry Herbert, the Master of the Revels, became seriously concerned about the undermining of his authority and, more specifically, the income to his office, that a patent would confer. He expected £2 to license a new play and £1 for an old one, but under the terms of the warrant issued to William Davenant and Thomas Killigrew in August 1600, they were required to 'peruse all plays... and to expunge all profaneness and scurrility'.[13] So why would they also pay fees to the Master of the Revels? From the time of his appointment in 1660, soon after the restoration of the monarchy, Herbert began a flurry of legal actions against Killigrew, Davenant and various actors to protect the rights of his office. In June 1662 Killigrew reached an agreement with Herbert to pay the fees demanded, although it may not have gone on for very long.✤ The Lord Chamberlain or the Master of the Revels would sometimes intervene directly and decisively in the affairs of the theatre either to ban plays or force cuts on political grounds, but the legal authority of the Lord Chamberlain's office over a patent was a moot point. At least it was, until Colley Cibber decided to force the matter.

Soon after the granting of the patent to Richard Steele, Cibber received one of the customary demands from the Master of the Revels for a fee of £2 to license a new play. Cibber decided to knock this one on the head once and for all and went to see the Master of Revels, who at this time was Charles Killigrew, son of Thomas and still part-owner of the Drury Lane patent. Cibber said that he and his fellow-managers would be happy to pay the fees demanded, if Killigrew could produce any legal authority for them. If he could not, and if the supposed authority of the Lord Chamberlain and his officers over patent theatres were no more than an ancient custom, Cibber felt that he could not oblige the Master of the Revels to the extent of meeting financial demands for which there was no statutory basis. In spite of being pressed several times on the question, Killigrew was unable to give any legal basis for his claim to authority and Cibber thought he had won the day.[14] However, civil servants don't like to be defeated, and the permanent officials of government departments have long collective memories. The retaliation took a few years to come, but when it did it was serious.

On 13 April 1717, Thomas Pelham-Holles, the Duke of Newcastle was appointed Lord Chamberlain, in charge of the royal household and its dependencies – including Drury Lane, as he was determined to show. Newcastle's appointment should have been good news for Steele: they had been on friendly terms for years as they were both members of the Kit-Cat Club, and Newcastle had actually provided Steele with his parliamentary seat in Boroughbridge in Yorkshire, one of more than a dozen constituencies that were within his gift. Newcastle was

---

✤ The timing is curious because, just before this agreement, Killigrew had received his patent that contained a clause not in the original warrant, stating that he was authorised to enjoy his rights: 'peaceably and quietly without the impeachment or impediment of any person or persons whatsoever'. It could easily have been assumed that the Master of the Revels was one of these 'persons'.

fabulously wealthy and a man of the greatest political and social standing. He was only 23 when he became Lord Chamberlain, which meant that Steele, at 45, was old enough to be his father. They had been used to meeting on conditions of intimacy at the Kit-Cat Club, but Newcastle was fiercely ambitious – he would later become prime minister twice – and was determined to stamp his authority on the office. Friendship wasn't going to get in the way of that.

Newcastle almost immediately summoned Steele and his three actor-managers to his office and told them he wanted them to surrender their patent and accept a new licence. This was an offer that the patentees would have been very foolish to accept, as a licence gave them much less protection than a patent, so they said no. Nothing happened immediately, but Newcastle was taking advice as to the best way to deal with these rebellious people at Drury Lane who challenged the authority of his office. There had been several skirmishes since Cibber's interview with the Master of the Revels, all of them fairly minor, but adding to the feeling within the Lord Chamberlain's office that something was going to have to be done.

In October 1719 it all blew up over what must have seemed at the time a very minor issue. Newcastle instructed the actor-managers that he wished the Irish actor Tom Erlington to be given the part of Torrismond in a revival of Dryden's play *The Spanish Friar*. Cibber replied that this was impossible as the part belonged to one of the managers. When he was urged to respect the authority of the Lord Chamblerain, Cibber replied, with a laugh, that 'they were a sort of separate ministry'[15] at Drury Lane, with the implication that they were beyond the control of politicians. This may have seemed like a piece of witty repartee at the time, but the Duke of Newcastle was not the sort of man to tolerate the open defiance by an actor of a department of state of which he stood at the head. On 19 December, Newcastle wrote to Steele, Barton Booth and Robert Wilks telling them that Cibber was banned from acting or participating in any way in the management of Drury Lane. Steele replied protesting that this action was an invasion of his property rights, and would cause hardship as Cibber was a popular actor. He received a reply from Henry Pelham, Newcastle's brother and his secretary, telling him that he must not attempt any further communication with His Grace.

Things then got even more serious. Newcastle had been taking legal advice as to the best way of dealing with Drury Lane, and he had been advised to leave the patent well alone. The status of the patent issued by George I to Steele was dubious, as it clearly violated the terms of the two patents granted by Charles II to Killigrew and Davenant, giving the holders exclusive rights to run theatres in London. Both of these patents were at the time held by John Rich at Lincoln's Inn Fields. However, if it were held to be valid, it might very well confer the powers that the patentees were claiming. It was much safer to go after the licence on the basis that, even with a patent, no one could run a theatre without a licence.

Newcastle summoned Barton Booth, one of the two remaining actor-managers, and told him that he intended to silence Drury Lane with a sign manual. This was about as serious as things could get, because a sign manual was a direct royal command that could not be challenged in the courts. Arguments about the powers conferred by the patent would become irrelevant. Steele, as a parliamentarian, realised the significance of this and responded in the only way now left to him: he started another periodical called *The Theatre* which ran from January to April 1720, putting his own side of the dispute. To admirers of the urbane, balanced and conversational tone that Steele had pioneered in *The Tatler* and *The Spectator*, the self-pitying, self-justifying tone of *The Theatre* comes as a disappointment, but it is understandable. Steele was feeling himself overwhelmed by forces he could no longer influence.

On Saturday 23 January 1720, George I issued a warrant revoking the licence granted to Steele, Cibber, Wilks and Booth in 1714. That night an order was read out from the stage at Drury Lane banning all performances until further notice. Two reasons were given for the order: the defiance of the authority of the office of the Lord Chamberlain and the frequent raising of prices by the managers.✤ It seems strange to us now that a politician should be in any way involved in fixing the prices

---

✤ In the days before inflation, theatre prices were regarded as being fixed at the same level they had been at when the theatres re-opened in 1660. The management at Drury Lane – like the rival management at Lincoln's Inn Fields – would occasionally announce higher prices for a new play, for example, or an expensive pantomime. These raised prices were bitterly resented.

of seats in a theatre, but it shows the extent to which the theatre was regarded as coming under the direct control of the government.

On 27 January a new licence was issued, signed both by the King and the Duke of Newcastle, addressed to Cibber, Wilks and Booth. Steele was to be excluded from the management of Drury Lane. This new licence had the effect of lifting the order of silence imposed on Cibber. Steele was understandably furious and wrote to the actor-managers forbidding them to recommence performances. They decided to ignore him and were summoned to the Lord Chamberlain's office to swear an oath of obedience to the Lord Chamberlain and his subordinates. 'The Lord Chamberlain's authority over the playhouse is restor'd, and the patent ends in a joke' was Sir John Vanbrugh's assessment of the situation.[16]

The Lord Chamberlain lost no time in asserting his authority. On 2 February he ordered the managers to permit no actors' benefit performances earlier in the season than those for Mrs Oldfield and Mrs Porter (earlier benefits brought higher returns) and told them they must not raise prices for any performance without clearing it with him first. He told them to put on a tragedy by John Hughes called *The Siege of Damascus*, which appeared on 17 February, and to follow it with a 'pastoral tragedy' by John Gay called *Dione*.[17] The latter was, in fact, never acted, probably because it is so bad that even the Duke of Newcastle couldn't force audiences to sit through it, but the triumvirate were now left in no doubt as to who was in charge.

Meanwhile Steele was left with no involvement with Drury Lane, no share of its profits and no means of redress. It says a great deal for his fighting spirit that he continued to be active in political life and fiercely to oppose his own Whig party in government over an issue that he regarded as a point of conscience: the South Sea Scheme. The directors of the South Sea Company were offering to take over the substantial government debt that had been accrued under Queen Anne over years of warfare with Louis XIV. They promised to turn this into a huge profit for their shareholders by means that would take too long to go into here. (If this sounds improbably optimistic, it is perhaps worth observing that it was no more fantastic than some of the 'financial products' that brought the entire banking system to the verge of collapse in 2008.) Steele smelt a rat and used several issues of his periodical *The Theatre* to oppose the Bill. In April 1720 the South Sea Bill was passed and Steele ceased to publish *The Theatre*. Steele's strongest ally in opposing the South Sea Bill had been Robert Walpole, a fellow member of the Kit-Cat Club. This would turn out to be fortuitous for him in respect of Drury Lane.

The South Sea Bubble set off a frenzy of stock-jobbing as share prices rose and rose until, in 1721, the bubble burst and thousands of people, including many of the richest and most powerful men in the land, faced catastrophic losses. Public fury demanded, and got, heads on the block. Ministers resigned, and Robert Walpole, as the highest-profile opponent of the South Sea Bill, was made First Lord of the Treasury and Chancellor of the Exchequer. From this point on, Robert Walpole is regarded as our first Prime Minister (although no such job description existed at the time) because he acquired such complete control over parliament that he could get any bill passed. Within a month, he had ordered that his friend and ally Sir Richard Steele must be re-instated as the governor of Drury Lane. On 2 May 1721 the Duke of Newcastle instructed Cibber, Booth and Wilks that Sir Richard Steele was indeed re-instated and that all profits that would have been due to him, had he not been barred, must be paid in full. Newcastle probably cared very little one way or the other about this, as the principle for which he had fought – that Drury Lane was to be subject to the authority of the Lord Chamberlain – had been won.

The Conscious Lovers

Steele was deeply relieved to be governor of Drury Lane once again, as he desperately needed the money that his share in the patent gave him. However, his involvement with the management of the theatre ceased. He stopped going in and played no further active part in the enterprise. The triumvirate resented the fact that he wanted to take his share of the profits without doing any work, so they started making a charge of £5 a day for their own time which was deducted from the takings before calculating profits. Steele went to court to challenge this, but the ruling went against him.✤

Ironically, it was during this period when his relations with the triumvirate were at a low point, and he was no longer involved with running Drury Lane, that Steele made his most important contribution to the project that had been occupying him for over twenty years: the reform of the stage. For years, Steele and others had been complaining that the stage was corrupting society by presenting dissolute characters as smart, witty and successful. The patent issued to Steele by George I in 1714 had specifically mentioned this problem of 'applause bestowed on libertine characters', while clergymen and sacred scripture were ridiculed and the Lord's name profaned. Steele had often called for a new type of hero – a Christian hero who would behave virtuously and inspire his audiences to do likewise. But who was going to write a play with such a hero? Nobody was rushing forward to take up the challenge, especially after the failure of Addison's pro-marriage play *The Drummer* in 1716, with the result that Drury Lane under Steele's governorship continued to put on the bad, bawdy old Restoration comedies.

With his health failing, his political influence waning and his debts growing, Steele made a last effort to pull together ideas he had been turning over in his mind for over a decade and he wrote *The Conscious Lovers*, which opened at Drury Lane in November 1722. The play came as anything but a surprise to the town, as Steele had been plugging it relentlessly for years. He seems to have devised the outline of it by 1710,[18] and by 1714 Swift was satirising the plot in a poetical squib.[19] Just before the play opened, John Dennis, who loathed the whole Drury Lane management, wrote sarcastically that Steele had read the play to everyone he could get to sit still for long enough between Wales

---

✤ Cibber gives a detailed account of this legal action without mentioning anything about the silencing of Drury Lane, the expulsion of Steele or his re-admittance to the management. This is an extraordinary gap in a narrative that claims to be frank and transparent. Cibber probably felt that it would be impossible to give an account of the events without showing himself in a bad light: Steele had stood by him when he was attacked, but Cibber didn't back Steele at the critical moment.

and Edinburgh.[20] So it was no secret that Steele had written a play with the express intention of showing that 'to be charming and agreeable shall appear the natural consequence of being virtuous'.[21] The question was, would it work on the stage?

Steele's original title for the play had been *The Fine Gentleman*, because he wanted to create a hero who would be as attractive as the fine gentlemen of Restoration comedies, but who acted in strict compliance with Christian teaching. This paragon is called Bevil Junior, and he is in love with Indiana, an orphan without means. Young Bevil pays for her support, but in spite of the fact that he loves her, he never tells her as it would be ungentlemanly to take advantage, and absolutely no impropriety has taken place. Sir John Bevil wants his son to marry Lucinda, daughter of a wealthy City merchant called Mr Sealand, and Bevil won't go against his father's wishes as it would be undutiful. Lucinda is in love with Bevil's friend Myrtle and Myrtle with her. Mr Sealand knows that Young Bevil is paying for the support of a woman and determines to find out what is going on. He visits Indiana and speaks to her as if she were a kept woman; she haughtily rebuffs him and he realises she is a lady; her bracelet falls off and he discovers that Indiana is his long-lost daughter by his first wife. Indiana can therefore marry Young Bevil with the blessing of both parents as she now stands to inherit a fortune and Sealand agrees to give Lucinda to Myrtle.

Whilst there is no doubting Steele's serious moral purpose in trying to make virtue appealing, it is unfortunate that he created in Bevil Junior the most sanctimonious, prissy milksop ever to tread the boards of Drury Lane. 'I'll take this opportunity to visit her,' he says of his beloved Indiana, 'for though the religious vow I have made to my father restrains me from ever marrying without his approbation, yet that confines me not from seeing a virtuous woman that is the pure delight of my eyes and the guiltless joy of my heart.'[22] After an evening of this, the audience must have been pining for Horner, Dorimant and the rakehells of Restoration comedy. None of the characters are convincing as they are all brought on the stage to lecture us on virtue rather than behave in any remotely convincing way. In the last scene Myrtle says to Bevil Junior: 'I rejoice in the pre-eminence of your virtue',[23] which isn't the way in which young men normally speak to their best friends, and Steele uses an interview between Indiana and Bevil Junior to let us know that, not only is she beautiful and virtuous, but she prefers Shakespeare to opera.[24] This is just the sort of thing to inflame a young man's passions. Steele contrives a particularly unconvincing scene to give us his opinion on the evils of duelling, and it seems he regarded this as one of the chief beauties of the play.

The Conscious Lovers is now unactable and almost unreadable, but in 1722 it hit the spot. The managers gave it a lavish production, all three appearing in it themselves,✤ and it made more money that any play ever put on at Drury Lane. It had an uninterrupted first run of eighteen performances, which was unheard of. The success of the play was partly the result of relentless plugging by Steele over more than a decade which raised expectation to fever pitch by the time it finally opened. Here, at last, was to be the answer to objections that had been raised to the stage for years, that it encouraged vice by rewarding immoral characters at the end of the play. Steele's play was described as the first 'exemplary comedy', which is to say, the characters are being held up as examples of good behaviour. In fact, it wasn't the first but it was certainly the most influential, and its success was another nail in the coffin of the more robust comedies of the previous generation. John Dennis, now known to us chiefly as the butt of Alexander Pope's diatribes, was one of the few critics to protest against the trend. His pamphlet, *A Defence of Sir Fopling Flutter*,[25] which defended the muscular satire of Ben Jonson, Wycherley, Congreve and Vanbrugh, was almost a lone voice. The Restoration comedies didn't disappear from the stage altogether, but they were performed less frequently, and in increasingly bowdlerised versions. *The Conscious Lovers* set a new benchmark for comedies that were respectable and to which a man

---

✤ The plot of *The Conscious Lovers* had been taken from the *Andria (The Girl From Andros)* of the Roman dramatist Terence. By a strange co-incidence, Bevil Junior was played by Barton Booth, who had played Pamphilus – the equivalent character in the *Andria* – in a Latin production at Westminster School in 1695. Booth ran away from school three years later, at the age of 17, to join a troupe of strolling players in Dublin.

could take his wife without fear of offence. It would remain popular for the rest of the century.

One reason for the triumph of the new form was the increasing presence of middle-class theatregoers in the audience. The character of Mr Sealand makes a significant defence of middle-class values:

> Give me leave to say that we merchants are a species of gentry that have grown into the world this last century, and are as honourable, and almost as useful, as you landed folks, that have always thought yourselves so much above us; for your trading, forsooth, is extended no farther than a load of hay or a fat ox. You are pleasant people, indeed, because you are generally bred up to be lazy; therefore, I warrant you, industry is dishonourable.[26]

It was no longer going to be possible for playwrights to hold up the 'cits' to ridicule: they represented too large a proportion of the potential audience. The aristocratic contempt in which working for a living was held by the heroes of Restoration comedies wouldn't be acceptable any more.♣ Mr Sealand was far from being Steele's first attempt to promote middle-class values in polite society. In *The Spectator*, which he had created with Addison, the character of the merchant Sir Andrew Freeport had represented the advantages of hard work and fiscal prudence coupled with generosity of spirit. The aims of *The Spectator* had been just as didactic as *The Conscious Lovers*: 'to enliven morality

---

♣ On 4 July 1724 the *Universal Journal* published a letter complaining about the stereotyping of merchants in plays: 'In the City may be found a very great number of learned, polite and honest generous men.' A sign of the increasing dominance of middle-class and mercantile values in the theatre can be seen in the success of George Lillo's 'bourgeois' tragedy *The London Merchant* (also known as *George Barnwell*), about an apprentice who becomes involved with a prostitute, steals from his master, commits murder and is hanged. It was customary to take apprentices in London to see a play annually on apprentice day, and since about 1675 the play chosen had always been Edward Ravenscroft's *The London Cuckolds*, in which the wives of three city merchants cuckold their husbands with their apprentices. This was felt to be sending out the wrong message, and soon after the first performance of *The London Merchant* at Drury Lane in 1731, it was staged for this annual apprentice show until 1819. The moral tone was certainly higher, but perhaps not quite so much fun for the apprentices.

with wit, and to temper wit with morality, till I have recovered [my readers] out of that desperate state of vice and folly, into which the age is fallen'.[27] While *The Conscious Lovers* now seems absurd, the *Spectator* essays are still regarded as being amongst the finest in the language. For some reason, the stage doesn't make a good pulpit.✤

Steele received an enormous amount of money from *The Conscious Lovers* since, in addition to the share of the profits that he already received as a manager, the triumvirate allowed him the proceeds of his benefit nights – the third, the sixth and the ninth nights. He dedicated the published version to George I and received a reward of £500. Nevertheless, it represented the end of his association with Drury Lane. His plans to follow it with other plays came to nothing, and in 1724 he left London to live in Wales, where he died in 1729. His share in the theatre went to his daughters, as the patent had been drawn up to run for Steele's life plus three years, but the triumvirate knew that the clock was ticking. If they wanted to stay in business, they needed to get another patent by 1732.

The end of the old order

Fortunately for the triumvirate, Colley Cibber had increased his already considerable stock of political leverage when, in 1730, he had been created Poet Laureate, an official, salaried, government position. Although we know nothing of the negotiations that lay behind it, a new patent was issued to Booth, Wilks and Cibber, to become effective for 21 years from 1 September 1732 – the day on which the Steele patent expired. The wording of the patent was almost the same as before, and it was assignable – that is to say, it could be traded. Booth, who hadn't acted since ill health forced his retirement in 1728, was the first to take advantage of this.

✤ Hazlitt called Steele's plays 'homilies in dialogue, in which a number of pretty ladies and gentlemen discuss… fashionable topics… with a sickly sensibility'. Quoted in Fitzgerald, p.413.

> **In Rep: Plays Performed at Drury Lane During w/c 4 January 1725**
> Date in brackets is year of first performance
>
> Date of performance, *Play* and playwright
>
> Monday 4 January, *The Plain Dealer* by William Wycherley (1676)
> Tuesday 5 January, *King Lear* by William Shakespeare (1605)
> Wednesday 6 January, *The Tempest* by William Shakespeare (1611)
> Thursday 7 January, *The Careless Husband* by Colley Cibber (1704)
> Friday 8 January, *Rule and Wife and Have a Wife* by Francis
> Beaumont and John Fletcher (1624) followed by *Harlequin Doctor
> Faustus* (1723)
> Saturday 9 January, *Vertue Betray'd* by John Banks (1682)

Before the patent had even come into effect, in July 1732 he sold half of his one-third share for £2,500 to a gentleman called John Highmore who fancied himself as an amateur actor. He also appointed Highmore to manage the half-share which he retained. Then, in September, Robert Wilks died and his widow assigned the management of her share to John Ellys, a portrait painter. Cibber began to have doubts about whether he wanted to continue in partnership with two people, neither of whom had any experience of professional theatre, so he rented his own share to his son Theophilus for the 1732-33 season and put himself on a generous salary. Then in March 1733, before the season was over, Cibber sold his one-third share in the patent to Highmore for £3,000 guineas, giving Highmore 50 per cent of the patent and the management of the remaining half of the Booth share. Highmore was now in charge.

Theophilus Cibber was furious that his father had sold his share without even telling him or offering him the chance to acquire it, but then the relationship between the Cibbers, father and son, had always been terrible. Theophilus proposed to Highmore that he should be in charge of the company on Highmore's account, but Highmore refused and told Theophilus to leave at the end of the season. Theophilus Cibber was a diffiicult man who managed to upset almost everyone, and it seems he had already irritated Highmore sufficiently. He then drew up a plan of attack.

It seems that the actors at Drury Lane didn't much like the new management of the company by amateurs, and they were particularly upset that Highmore was negotiating with John Rich at Covent Garden to re-establish a cartel: neither theatre would employ actors from the other theatre, thus putting the managements into a very strong bargaining position with the actors, who would not be able to defect to the rival house. Theophilus persuaded the actors to rebel against the management in order to get better terms. His battle plan was simple but deadly: he knew that the new patentees did not have a formal lease on the building, so he negotiated with the building shareholders for a new lease to himself and the rebel actors. This would have left Highmore with a patent but no theatre in which to put on plays. Highmore found out about it and at midnight on Saturday 26 May 1733 he sent in the heavies to eject the rebel actors and barricade the theatre against them. The actors brought an action against the patentees for ejecting them from their own building but the case took months to reach the courts. Meanwhile, both sides kept up a barrage of pamphlets attacking each other and staking their claims to legality. In one of these documents, *A Letter from Theophilus Cibber, Comedian, to John Highmore Esq*, Cibber complained of the unfitness of Highmore and Ellys to run a theatre; brought up the cartel issue; then offered the patentees £1,200 a year if they would let the actors back into Drury Lane to run it for them. This offer was turned down.

On 24 September, Drury Lane re-opened with a scratch company drawn from the rag-tag-and-bobtail of the profession, semi-professionals and people who normally performed in fairground booths. The rebel actors, comprising almost every star name of the day, opened at the Little Theatre in the Haymarket two days later. This relatively tiny house, next to the site of the present Theatre Royal Haymarket, had been built by a carpenter called John Potter in 1720 and let to a visiting company of French actors sponsored by the Duke of Montagu. The theatre had no licence to operate so it was, strictly speaking, illegal, but the Duke's patronage seems to have been enough to get them through the first season. After that, it had been used for occasional performances by foreign companies, amateurs or scratch companies put together to do a few shows. As long as they didn't do anything controversial, the authorities were prepared to turn a blind eye.

The position of the rebels at the Little Theatre was precarious and could only be temporary, as the house was too small to cover their running expenses, but the situation of the patentees at Drury Lane was worse. Only a handful of the original company had stayed with them, so there were problems with getting a cast together for any play. Standards were low and audiences were thin. Highmore was facing heavy losses. With things looking bleak all round, Barton Booth's widow decided to get rid of her remaining half of Booth's original one-third share, which she sold for £1,350.[28] The buyer was Henry Giffard, the manager of yet another 'illegal' theatre that had opened in a converted workshop in Goodman's Fields, Whitechapel. Giffard was operating precariously, always at risk of being shut down by the authorities, and seems to have wanted to go legitimate.

Highmore, increasingly desperate, tried to get the rebel actors arrested under the Vagrancy Act as 'rogues and vagabonds'. The case failed, but only on a technicality.✣ On 12 November 1733 the action for possession of Drury Lane by the rebel actors was heard in King's Bench and was granted. The judge took the view that they held a valid lease on Drury Lane and were entitled to occupy it: the fact that they didn't have a patent or licence to perform was irrelevant to the consideration of the lease. With the rebels set to return from the Haymarket to Drury Lane, this was the end of the road for Highmore, who bailed out. He sold his 50% share of the patent to Charles Fleetwood for £2,250 – less than half of what he paid for it. Fleetwood also bought the one-third share originally allocated to Robert Wilks from his widow for £1,500, which meant that he owned the whole patent apart from the one-sixth share which Giffard had bought from Mrs Booth.[29] He immediately entered into negotiations with the rebels, and on 8 March 1734 they moved back to Drury Lane on vastly improved terms, with Theophilus Cibber as deputy manager. Fleetwood took on their lease.

✣ The brief for the patentees spoke of 'rogues *or* vagabonds', but the lawyers representing the rebels objected that the wording of the act was 'rogues *and* vagabonds'.

10

The Great Playwright
We Never Had

One person who suffered as a result of the upheavals at Drury Lane was a man who, under different circumstances, might have become one of our greatest playwrights: Henry Fielding. Fielding is known as the Father of the English Novel. *Joseph Andrews* (1742) is often cited as the first work of fiction which is recognisably what we expect a novel to be, and *Tom Jones* (1748) is undoubtedly one of the greatest novels in the language. However, Fielding didn't set out to write prose fiction, he wanted to be a playwright. At the astonishingly early age of 20, his first play was accepted for performance at Drury Lane. It was called *Love in Several Masques* and it opened on 16 February 1728 – not great timing as it was in competition with the first run of *The Beggar's Opera* at Lincoln's Inn Fields. The play lasted only four nights, possibly because the town was flocking to the other theatre, but also because it wasn't a very good play. A traditional five-act comedy of romantic intrigue, it was unoriginal and not all that competent.

It seems likely that Fielding's cousin, the bluestocking Lady Mary Wortley Montague, may have used her influence to get his comedy accepted at Drury Lane. However, having obliged Lady Mary once, the triumvirs weren't inclined to cover the costs of young Fielding's learning curve, and turned down the next play he offered them. Rather offended, he gave *The Temple Beau* to the 'illegal' theatre in Goodman's Fields, Whitechapel, where it had a modest success. It was another traditional five-act comedy which showed no great originality. He took his next play, *The Author's Farce*, to the other theatre operating without any licence, the Little Theatre in the Haymarket, and this is where things start to get interesting.

The Author's Farce

For *The Author's Farce*, instead of writing in traditional forms, Fielding tried his hand at a ballad-opera that satirised all of the popular entertainments of the day. The hero of his play is an impoverished playwright who puts on a puppet show called 'The Pleasures of the Town' in which the Queen of Nonsense presides over a court of easily recognisable characters, including Sir Farcical Comick (Colley Cibber), Monsieur Pantomime (John Rich) and Signor Opera (Senesino, the famous castrato singer). The Goddess of Nonsense has fallen in love with Signor Opera, preferring him over all the other idiotic pleasures of the town, and intends to marry him. The constable arrives to arrest the master of the puppet show for libelling the diversions of 'people of quality'. It was absurd and funny and completely original, with lots of musical numbers thrown in to lighten the satire. Fielding was making a serious point about the decline in cultural standards but in a good-humoured way. *The Author's Farce* opened on 30 April 1730 and was a success, with 41 performances in its first season: Fielding had found his voice on the stage.

A few weeks after *The Author's Farce* had opened, Fielding added a new afterpiece: *Tom Thumb, A Tragedy*. This was not a tragedy at all but a very funny burlesque of heroic tragedy which exploits the diminutive stature of its hero for all sorts of bathetic effects. Tom escapes an attempted poisoning (a monkey is poisoned by mistake) only to be swallowed by 'a cow of larger than usual size'. Every absurd situation is expressed in high-flown verse that recalls the heroic tragedies of the previous century, some of which were still being performed. In spite of the efforts of some modern critics to read political satire into it, *Tom Thumb* was harmless fun.

Fielding's next play for the Little Theatre was a five-act comedy called *Rape Upon Rape*, which is much more traditional in its structure but in which the authentic Fielding tone can be heard, especially in the characters of the corrupt Justice Squeezum and his terrifying wife Mrs Squeezum, who blackmails him by threatening to expose his rackets. Although Fielding has a reputation for bawdiness, he was a man of serious moral purpose. He would later become a magistrate and establish the Bow Street Runners, London's first modern police force. He was a devout Christian and a firm believer in marriage and fidelity. Sometimes this made him a bit preachy, but *Rape Upon Rape* is a funny treatment of serious themes, and it represents the only play of Fielding's that might be known to modern theatregoers as it formed the basis of Lionel Bart's musical *Lock Up Your Daughters* which opened the Mermaid Theatre in 1959.

Fielding was back at the Little Theatre in the Haymarket in 1731, by which time the theatre's unofficial status was encouraging people to get, as Ben Elton would say, a little bit political. Fielding's next ballad-opera, *The Welsh Opera*, was ostensibly about a ridiculous Welsh family consisting of Squire Ap-Shrinken, his domineering wife Madam Ap-Shrinken, his useless son Master Owen and the butler Robin, who has been stealing his master's silver. Everyone in the audience knew that these characters represented George II, Queen Caroline, the Prince of Wales and Sir Robert Walpole. This was very daring, as any representation of the royal family on the stage was completely forbidden. However, it was all good knockabout fun. The much more serious challenge to Walpole's authority came from another play in the Little Theatre repertoire, not written by Fielding: *The Fall of Mortimer*.

This play, which was anonymous, belonged to a tradition known as 'majesty misled'. To depict a foolish or corrupt king, even from the past, was extremely risky. It was therefore common to show how the king had been misled by wicked ministers who were responsible for the monarch's loss of the love of the people. The Mortimer of the title was Roger Mortimer, Earl of March, who became the lover of Edward II's Queen and arranged the deposition and murder of the King. Mortimer became the effective ruler England, as Edward III was only 14 when he succeeded to the throne. At the age of 17, Edward got his act together and had Mortimer executed on a charge of usurping the prerogatives of the crown. Once again, everyone in the audience knew that Mortimer was Walpole.

Walpole took this very seriously, and on 21 July 1731 the High Constable was sent to the theatre to arrest the actors on a charge of sedition, which was no laughing matter. They scarpered when they heard who was coming to the show. The theatre tried to re-open a few weeks later, but once again the constables were sent round, this time to arrest the actors on the charge of being rogues and vagabonds. Once again, they ran away and warrants were issued for the arrest of anyone who had appeared in *The Fall of Mortimer*. The Little Theatre in the Haymarket was eventually allowed to get back in business on condition that there were to be no more controversial shows like *The Fall of Mortimer*.

Fielding at Drury Lane

Then things took a turn for the better for Fielding: he was invited back to Drury Lane. It may seem strange that Colley Cibber and Robert Wilks✣ should have been prepared to forgive and forget the pasting Fielding had given them in *The Author's Farce* only two years before, but you have to be pretty hard-nosed to survive in show-business. A 'star', in whatever role, can get bums on seats, and Fielding was the star playwright of his time, at the age of only 24. Drury Lane needed hits, and if Fielding could provide them, what was a little personal abuse?

✣ Wilks had been depicted in *The Author's Farce* as Sparkish, a foolish character who repeats everything the Cibber character says. Barton Booth, the third member of the triumvirate, had retired on health grounds in 1728, so he escaped the satire.

Things got off to a good start with *The Lottery*, another ballad opera, in January 1732. Fielding followed this with *The Modern Husband*, a successful comedy with serious and indeed quite dark elements, in February. June saw a double bill: *The Old Debauchees* and *The Covent Garden Tragedy*. They flopped so badly that *The Covent Garden Tragedy* was withdrawn after its first performance, allegedly because the audience would not tolerate a play set in a brothel.❖ Fielding made good three weeks later with *The Mock Doctor*, a brilliant adaptation of Molière's *Le Médecin Malgré Lui*.

By the autumn of that year things were changing at Drury Lane as the rock-solid management of the triumvirate began to disintegrate, and Fielding must have wondered how this would affect him, with amateurs replacing the professionals. Nevertheless, he was still in fine form for the 1732/33 season, producing in February 1733 *The Miser*, a version of Molière's *L'Avare* that is so good it could be argued that it improves on its French original. It was a huge success and became Fielding's most successful mainpiece, remaining in the repertoire for the rest of the eighteenth century. In April, Fielding's farce *Deborah* flopped, but *The Miser* was still packing them in when Drury Lane was closed by the actor rebellion in May.

When Theophilus Cibber led the rebel actors out of Drury Lane, Fielding had to decide whose side he would take in the dispute, and he threw his lot in with the Drury Lane management. We can only speculate on his motives, but one reason may have been that the only leading actor to remain at Drury Lane was Kitty Raftor, later Kitty Clive, who seems to have become something of a muse for Fielding. She was a brilliant light comedienne and he wanted to go on writing for her. His next play for her, *The Intriguing Chambermaid*, was a farcical afterpiece that appeared in January 1734. The problem was the play it came after.

❖ *The Grub Street Journal* (15 June 1732) suggested that, instead of performing the play again, the 'young managers' of Drury Lane should just take their audience to one of the brothels for which Drury Lane was famous and let them have a look at the whores and their customers. 'There would be no difference in the entertainment.' (Milhous & Hume [1991] 784-85)

Fielding had decided to revive his hit of four years earlier, *The Author's Farce,* with additions to bring it up to date. Robert Wilks had died, so his character of Sparkish was replaced by Marplay Junior, a theatre manager clearly based on Theophilus Cibber, who runs the theatre by using the cheap tricks pioneered by his father Marplay Senior (Colley Cibber). Fielding added a very funny new scene in which Marplay Senior passes on the tricks of the trade to his son – how to suppress rival authors, how to force rubbish on the public – and tries to steel his rather pathetic son against hissing. 'Idle young actors are fond of applause,' he tells his stupid offspring, 'but, take my word for it, a clap is a mighty silly, empty thing and does no more good than a hiss; and therefore if any man loves hissing he may have his three shillings worth at me, whenever he pleases.' Colley Cibber was famous for his brass neck – 'Corinthian brass' as he describes it to Marplay Junior, telling him that this inheritance will be of more use to him than gold: 'Gold thou might'st have spent, but this is a lasting estate, which will stick by thee all thy life.'

When Fielding wrote these scenes he presumably thought that the rebel actors would lose their action against the Drury Lane management. By the time they were performed, the case had been won and it was obvious that the rebels, led by Marplay Junior, would soon be making a triumphant return to the Lane. Fielding had shot himself in the foot.

In the space of two years, Fielding had supplied eight new plays of various kinds for Drury Lane. This was a great achievement, especially when we remember that Dryden, under contract as the house playwright, had never been able to provide the three plays a year stipulated. Admittedly, Dryden's were all five-act plays, whereas many of Fielding's plays were short afterpieces, but the sheer fizz of Fielding's brilliant efforts is still impressive, especially given the daring originality of some of them. What would become of him now? Unlike Dryden, he had no contract with Drury Lane, and he seems to have developed an antipathy towards Theophilus Cibber (as had almost everyone who ever met him) who was going to be, in effect, artistic director.

When the rebels returned to Drury Lane, Fielding wasn't exactly banned, but it would be a year before another new piece by him was put on there. On 6 January 1735, Fielding's ballad opera farce *An Old*

Man Taught Wisdom, once again starring Kitty Clive, appeared as the afterpiece to a performance of *Venice Preserv'd*. It was a smash hit and, under its alternative title of *The Virgin Unmask'd*, it would become Fielding's most performed play to the end of the century. Fielding probably regarded it as no more than a bit of hack-work, but he was more serious about his next play, *The Universal Gallant*, that opened at Drury Lane in February. It was a five-act comedy in which Fielding attempted serious social satire, and it flopped, closing on the third night. Fielding was devastated. He was a would-be social reformer who wanted to use his art to improve people's lives, just like his friend Hogarth whose engravings he would praise in his novels. Unfortunately, the harder he tried, the more he lost the audience.

In Rep: Plays Performed at Drury Lane During w/c 3 November 1735
Date in brackets is year of first performance

Date of performance, *Play* and playwright

Monday 3 November, *The Double Gallant* by Colley Cibber (1707) followed by *Harlequin Restor'd* (unknown author, 1732)
Tuesday 4 November, *Tamerlane* by Nicholas Rowe (1701) followed by *Columbine Courtezan* by John Lampe (1734)
Wednesday 5 November, *Tamerlane* by Nicholas Rowe (1701) followed by *Columbine Courtezan* by John Lampe (1734)
Thursday 6 November, *The Rover* by Aphra Behn (1677) followed by *The Devil to Pay* by Charles Coffey (1731)
Friday 7 November, *Oroonoko* by Thomas Southerne (1695) followed by *Harlequin Restor'd* (unknown author, 1732)
Saturday 8 November, *The Double Dealer* by William Congreve (1693) followed by *Harlequin Restor'd* (unknown author, 1732)

The Great Mogul of the Haymarket

Perhaps because of the frustrations he had encountered in working with the gentleman amateur Charles Fleetwood and his obnoxious manager Theophilus Cibber, Fielding decided that the time had come to set up as an impresario. Describing himself in press advertisements as 'The Great Mogul', he signed an agreement to rent the Little Theatre in the Haymarket and hired his own troupe of actors to put on his new play *Pasquin*, which opened on 5 March 1736. For *Pasquin* Fielding went back to the play-within-a-play format of *The Author's Farce*, but with two playwrights this time: Trapwit is rehearsing his comedy about a corrupt country election and Fustian is rehearsing his tragedy on 'The Life and Death of Common Sense'.

The theme of the comedy is bribery and corruption: the election is being fought between Lord Place and Colonel Promise for the court party (the Whigs) and Sir Henry Fox-Chace and Squire Tankard for the country party (the Tories). All candidates rely on bribing voters, Lord Place by promising places at court (i.e. government sinecures) and Sir Henry by promising to make large purchases from the tradesmen who make up the tiny electoral roll in this rotten borough. At one point Trapwit has his actors line up across the stage so that the candidates can go down the line bribing away 'to right and left'. 'Is there nothing but bribery in this play of yours, Mr Trapwit?' asks Fustian. 'Sir, this play is an exact representation of nature', replies Trapwit.[1] This is followed by Fustian's play 'The Life and Death of Common Sense' which attacks the cultural decline manifested by the now familiar targets of opera and pantomime.

Pasquin was a huge success, achieving 60 performances in its first season – only two short of the record set by *The Beggar's Opera*.✣ Fielding made so much money that he began to think in terms of building himself a new theatre, or at least pulling down the Little Theatre in the Haymarket and rebuilding it on a grander scale. Whilst he was working on these plans and preparing for his second season as a manager at the Little Theatre, Fielding wrote what would be his last new piece for Drury Lane.♣

✣ *Pasquin's* uninterrupted first run was 39 performances – longer than that of *The Beggar's Opera*.

♣ Two earlier plays would appear years later, after Fielding had ceased to write for the stage and, in one case, long after Fielding's death. Garrick put on *The Wedding Day*, written in 1729, in 1743. *The Good Natur'd Man*, written in 1735, would be presented at Drury Lane in 1778.

Eurydice, or the Devil Henpeck'd was a farcical ballad opera which travestied the Orpheus and Eurydice myth to suggest that hell is much like life in fashionable London. Eurydice is unwilling to be taken back to earth by Orpheus because she is having so much fun in Hades with Pluto. It was performed on 19 February 1737 as an afterpiece to Addison's *Cato*, but the evening turned out to be memorable for all the wrong reasons.

Back in the 1690s, Christopher Rich had decided to boost business at Drury Lane by giving the servants of his rich patrons in the boxes a free seat in the second gallery. His thinking was that, if the servants enjoyed a show, they might persuade their masters to come later. This turned out to be a really bad idea because, although a certain level of boisterousness was expected amongst audiences in those days, the footmen in the gallery took pride in their ability to disrupt and even halt performances by their barracking. Eventually, other theatre patrons began to object to this, as it was felt that the lowest social class in the audience was being allowed to dictate what could and couldn't be acted. On the night of Saturday 19 February 1737, the patrons of the pit and boxes decided that enough was enough when some of the footmen who were holding places for their employers in the boxes began shouting insults at patrons in the pit. The footmen were ejected and told they would not be admitted to the footmen's gallery that night. They tried to break in between the acts and several arrests were made.[2] In the uproar, poor *Eurydice* was well and truly damned. There was no attempt to give it another performance, although it had nothing to do with the riot. It was an unfortunate note on which to sever the connection between Fielding and Drury Lane.

A month later, Fielding opened the season at the Little Theatre in the Haymarket with a play, anonymous and now lost, called *A Rehearsal of Kings*. It only lasted for three performances, after which there was one performance of *Pasquin* then, on 21 March a revival of George Lillo's play *Fatal Curiosity*. There was nothing very controversial about Lillo's play, but the new afterpiece that Fielding wrote to follow it would become famous as the play that led to the censorship of the stage: *The Historical Register for the Year 1736*.

The title refers to the publication *The Historical Register* that had appeared annually since 1716, giving details of public affairs that were usually extracted from newspapers and journals. Sometimes these extracts were linked with new copy, but often the different bits of information followed each other inconsequentially. This gave Fielding his format, which is so loose it is more like a satirical review than a play. The centrepiece of the play is a surreal auction of lots such as 'a most curious remnant of political honesty'(£5); 'a most delicate piece of patriotism' (no bids); 'three grains of modesty' (no bids – it is out of fashion with the ladies); and 'a very neat clear conscience' (no bids). But when 'a very considerable quantity of interest at court' comes up, the bidding reaches a thousand pounds in seconds. Other targets include the (mis)management of Drury Lane by Charles Fleetwood, 'Apollo's bastard son', who is so incompetent he has to depend on the advice of his prompter, and Theophilus Cibber, 'who fancies himself of great consequence and is of none'. What really caused the trouble, however, was the satire on Sir Robert Walpole's government contained in the political scenes, in which the politicians show themselves to be mainly interested in raising taxes ('Hang foreign affairs, let us apply ourselves to money') and bribing opponents into silence. (Walpole's most famous saying was that 'every man has his price'.)

This put *The Historical Register* in a different category of risk to *Pasquin*. *Pasquin* did not, to put it mildly, present an elevated view of the political process. ('How can a man vote against his conscience who has no conscience at all?… I think it is quite out of character for the mayor to be once sober during the whole election' and so on.[3]) However, it was at least even-handed in its satire against both Whigs and Tories. *The Historical Register* was Walpole-specific and drew furious comment from the government press. 'There are things which… ought to be sacred, such as government and religion,' thundered the *Daily Gazetteer*, a pro-government paper, accusing the play of abusing 'liberty of the subject' to such an extent that it 'might make a RESTRAINT necessary'.[4] The restraint wasn't long in coming.

Robert Walpole had already made one attempt to impose stage censorship. In 1735 Sir John Barnard had introduced a bill to restrict the number of playhouses to those holding royal patents or licences –

Drury Lane, Covent Garden and the King's Opera House in the Haymarket – and close down the 'illegals' like Goodman's Fields and the Little Theatre in the Haymarket. The bill had widespread support and would have passed, had Walpole not tried to tack on another clause at a late stage giving the Lord Chamberlain powers of stage censorship. This was unacceptable to the sponsors of the bill, who withdrew it.

Two years later, with the *Historical Register* packing 'em in, Walpole decided to try again. His supporters introduced a bill on 20 May 1737 with the same purpose as Barnard's earlier bill – to close the illegal playhouses by reforming the law on rogues and vagabonds. Just as before, Walpole then added an extra clause giving the Lord Chamberlain powers of censorship. To get it accepted this time, he produced in the House of Commons the script of a play called *The Golden Rump* which he claimed was about to be produced. The passages he read aloud were so stuffed with obscenity and treason that the honourable members had no scruples about increasing the powers of the Lord Chamberlain and the government over the theatre.[5] Of course, there had been no such play as *The Golden Rump* until Walpole commissioned it for this express purpose.[6]

Even at this stage, it seems Fielding had no idea of what was about to hit him. On 12 May, *The Historical Register* was published with a 'Dedication to the Public', in which Fielding announced his scheme to rebuild and enlarge the Little Theatre in the Haymarket. He promised that: 'If nature hath given me any talents at ridiculing vice and imposture, I shall not be indolent, nor afraid of exerting them while the liberty of the press and stage subsists.'[7] On 25 May he announced two new plays: *Polly in India* and *The King and Titi*. The effrontery of this was astonishing. *Polly in India* was clearly *Polly*, the sequel to *The Beggar's Opera*, that had been banned before it ever got to the stage, although it had been published.[8] We don't know much about *The King and Titi* although it seems likely that it was another satire on the bad relationship between George II and the Prince of Wales. The Licensing Act wouldn't become law until the end of June,[9] and Walpole decided not to wait. Somehow contact was established with John Potter, the landlord of the Little Theatre in the Haymarket, who was becoming concerned about the activities of his controversial tenant. Walpole promised to reward him if he closed the theatre down. Potter sent in workmen who dismantled the stage and filled the building with lumber to make it unusable. The performance of *The Historical Register* on 23 May proved to be the very last that Fielding's little company would give.

A broken wit

Henry Fielding's career as a playwright was now at an end. Deprived of his main source of income, he turned to other styles of writing, notably journalism and then novels. Because his novels are so good, it has become conventional to regard the plays as a sort of mechanical apprentice work which led him to something better. However, in his study of Fielding's involvement with the stage, Robert Hume has challenged that view. Because none of the plays is good enough to merit a revival, it is easy to ignore the brilliant flashes that occur throughout several of them. Fielding started off trying to write traditional five-act comedies of manners and it took him a while to discover that this genius lay in burlesque and satire.✤ Hume argues that we should not be so complacent about the fact that Fielding was forced to abandon the stage, because we don't know what he would have gone on to write. He used to say of himself that 'he left off writing for the stage when he ought to have begun',[10] meaning presumably that he felt he was just hitting his stride. Fielding regarded himself as the English Aristophanes, and the comparison was not absurd. He had the intelligence, the perverse sense of humour and the strong moral compass that make for great satire. George Bernard Shaw regarded him as the 'greatest practising dramatist' in England, bar Shakespeare, between the middle ages and the nineteenth century.[11]

✤ His friend William Hogarth travelled the same road. Hogarth wanted to be a history painter (the noblest category of art) but excelled in his satirical 'modern moral subjects' like *Marriage à la Mode* and *The Rake's Progress*.

His brilliant short plays brought a new audience into the theatre and challenged the risk-averse policies of the patent theatres with regard to new writing. Hume has demonstrated that, when Fielding first set up as a playwright, the repertoire of both patent houses was stuck in the past, with endless revivals of plays from the previous century. New plays were so rare that it had become impossible for any writer to earn a living from the theatre. Competition from the 'illegal' theatres, and especially from the plays of Fielding, forced the patentees to up their game. More new and recently written plays were mounted, and in 1732 Fielding was taken on by Drury Lane specifically to provide them with new material. The Licensing Act crushed competition, giving Drury Lane and Covent Garden an iron-clad monopoly over plays in London, with predictably stultifying effect. It has become a truism to say that the eighteenth century was an age of great acting and mediocre playwriting. The Licensing Act was at least partly to blame.

Goodbye to Colley Cibber

Colley Cibber was delighted by Fielding's downfall, which is understandable given the amount of satirical abuse he had come in for (although there was plenty more of that to come in Fielding's journalism and novels). However, the events at the Little Haymarket had only confirmed Cibber in his strongly held view that competition was bad because it would drive down standards to the lowest level. He accuses Fielding (whom he refuses to name except as 'a broken wit') of raking the channel for the 'trash and filth of buffoonery and licentiousness' that would 'knock all distinctions of mankind on the head: religion, laws, government, priests, judges and ministers, were all laid flat at the feet of this Herculean satirist'.[12] This sort of thing would have genuinely alarmed the conformist Cibber, and he conveys his relief at the outcome with a brilliant image drawn from those scraps of a classical education he had managed to pick up along the way: 'like another Erostratus [Fielding] set fire to his stage, by writing up an act of parliament to demolish it.'[13]

Cibber was in a bit of a bind in supporting censorship because, as a staunch Whig, he had always championed liberty, which included a free press. He was reduced to using a casuistical argument, taken from Jeremy Collier of all people, that the stage stands in greater need of regulation than the press, because the image of a man exhibited on the stage will fix itself more strongly in the spectator's mind than something that has simply been printed: 'He that is made a fool in a play, is often made one for his life. 'Tis true, he passes for such only among the prejudic'd and unthinking, but these are no inconsiderable division of mankind.'[14] After being pilloried as Sir Farcical Comick, Marplay Senior and Ground-Ivy✤ (because he was a creep), Cibber knew whereof he spoke.

With the passing of the Licensing Act and the defeat of the independent theatres, Colley Cibber exits from our story. He had disposed of his share in Drury Lane in 1733, and although he came out of retirement in 1745 to appear in his own adaptation of Shakespeare's *King John*, which he had turned into anti-Catholic propaganda as a response to Bonnie Prince Charlie's invasion, his involvement with theatre management was over. He was a rich man and a prominent member of society. He remained Poet Laureate until his death in 1757. His *Apology for the Life of Colley Cibber*, published in 1740, was a great success, going through four editions in his lifetime, and has been frequently reprinted. It has been described as 'smug, self-regarding and cocksure',[15] but Cibber's real passion for theatre shines through it all. He really loved the theatre and had the highest opinion of its importance in the culture of a civilised society. He was a good businessman, and realised that to stay in business the theatre had to give the public what they wanted. This might include opera, pantomime and other things he disliked, but through it all his commitment to 'a good play, well acted' as 'the most valuable entertainment of the stage'[16] never wavered. He tells a story about the time when Christopher Rich hired some rope dancers to appear at

---

✤ Cibber appears as Ground-Ivy in *The Historical Register,* insisting that no play is any good until he has altered it, especially Shakespeare's. 'Shakespeare was a pretty fellow, and said some things which only want a little of my licking to do well enough.'

Drury Lane in the intervals between the acts of a play in which Cibber was playing a leading part. Cibber regarded this as a step too far and went into the auditorium before curtain-up to tell the audience that he 'declined acting upon any stage that was brought to so low a disgrace'.[17] This was accepted by the audience, and the actors admired him for standing up to Rich, who backed down over the rope dancers.

It is Cibber's misfortune that he got on the wrong side of the greatest writers of the age, notably Pope, Swift and Fielding, and that in so far as he is remembered at all, it is courtesy of their satirical attacks. Pope made Cibber the chief dunce in the 1743 version of his mock epic poem *The Dunciad*, and Henry Fielding developed something of an obsession with Cibber whom he never tired of ridiculing. This was partly political: Pope and Swift were Tories while Cibber was a Whig who made Drury Lane a Whig house for as long as he was in charge. This didn't mean that Drury Lane put on Whig propaganda, but that it could be relied on not to stage anything to undermine the fundamental Whig principles of liberty and the Protestant religion by, for example, staging plays about the sufferings of overthrown kings that might cause audiences to think about James II and his descendants, languishing in exile in France.✤ There was also professional jealousy: when Cibber was made Poet Laureate in 1730, Pope, who was undoubtedly the greatest living poet, felt the job should have been his. This was also to do with politics: a Whig government wanted a Whig laureate and put political dependability above poetic genius. In his *Apology*, Cibber expresses amazement at the venomous attacks on himself, asking what he has done beyond writing a few not-very-good poems, but there was a bit more to the Pope/Cibber feud that wasn't quite so high-flown in its motives as a concern for the purity of poetry.

✤ Strangely, Cibber himself had fallen foul of the authorities on this point with his adaptation of Shakespeare's *Richard III*. On its first appearance in 1699, the Master of the Revels had struck out the whole of the first act in which Cibber filled out the back-story by incorporating material from Shakespeare's other history plays. Cibber was accused of causing people to reflect on the situation of James II in France by depicting the distress of the deposed Henry VI. Cibber objected that the Master of the Revels was really straining for this historical parallel, but nevertheless for several years the whole act had to be omitted. (Cibber, 152.)

In 1717 Drury Lane had staged a farce called *Three Hours After Marriage*, written as a joint effort by Pope, John Gay and John Arbuthnot. It appears that, half-way through the first performance, Cibber realised that the character he was playing was a satire on himself. Unhappy about being made fun of in his own theatre, Cibber retaliated a month later by reviving the Duke of Buckingham's ever-popular *The Rehearsal* with a new scene ridiculing *Three Hours After Marriage*. Pope stormed backstage after a performance and told Cibber he deserved a good thrashing. As he was dwarfish and hunch-backed, Pope couldn't deliver this himself, but the next night John Gay came round and really set about Cibber.

Ten years later, Gay turned up at Drury Lane with the manuscript of *The Beggar's Opera*. It was unlike anything ever seen before, being what was described as a 'ballad opera', that is, a play with musical numbers of which the tunes were taken from folk songs, but the lyrics were new. The characters were whores and criminals who compared their behaviour favourably at every turn with that of their betters. Cibber turned it down, probably because it looked too weird and also because it looked like a satire on Sir Robert Walpole's government. Gay took it to John Rich at Lincoln's Inn Fields who said yes and staged it in January 1728. It proved to be the most successful show ever, with an uninterrupted first run of 32 performances and 62 performances in the first season. It became a staple of the repertoire and *The Beggar's Opera* remains one of the very few eighteenth-century plays still to hold the stage.

The Beggar's Opera was said to have made Gay rich and Rich gay. It also made Rich rich. He used the money to build himself a beautiful new theatre in Covent Garden, only a few paces from Drury Lane, which is now, after two rebuilds, the Royal Opera House. It opened on 7 December 1732 with *The Way of the World*. In his *Apology*, Cibber says nothing about his decision to turn down *The Beggar's Opera*, which is understandable. Not only was it one of the worst management decisions in show business history – on a par with the record company executive who turned down the Beatles – but it had long-term consequences for Drury Lane, whose main rival was now established just round the corner in Covent Garden. As the eighteenth century progressed, fashionable London moved westwards with the creation of Mayfair and other aristocratic estates, so a theatre in Covent Garden would stand a much better chance of success than one in Lincoln's Inn Fields, which ceased to be a fashionable residential area. The rivalry between the two companies, which had always been intense, would now be ratcheted up. This was an indirect result of Cibber's refusal of *The Beggar's Opera*, but we can hardly blame him for it. However ridiculous his enemies made him out to be, Colley Cibber was a great man of the theatre and one of the most important people in the history of Drury Lane. One thing is certain: whatever else you might say about him, Cibber wasn't a dunce.

11

The Coming of Garrick

By the time the Licensing Act provided the two patent theatres with protection against competition, Drury Lane needed all the help it could get. Charles Fleetwood had proved to be as hopeless as other gentleman-managers who saw the theatre purely as a source of profit. He was a gambler who had run through a very substantial estate and acquired the Drury Lane patent with the last remnant of what had been a considerable fortune. He is sometimes compared with his successor at the Lane, Thomas Brinsley Sheridan, who also used the takings from Drury Lane to fund his lifestyle. Another characteristic they shared was the ability to turn on a devastating charm and win over everyone they had borrowed from and everyone they owed money to.

When the rebel actors returned to Drury Lane in March 1734, Fleetwood wisely decided that, with no professional theatre experience himself, he should put the running of the theatre into the hands of people who knew more about the business than he did. He therefore chose two members of the acting company, Theophilus Cibber and Charles Macklin, to be joint managers. This was always going to be an explosive pairing. Theophilus Cibber was brash and difficult to deal with. He was known as Pistol after the braggart character in Shakespeare's *Henry IV*

Part 2 which he played so well. In *The Historical Register*, Fielding has the bastard son of Apollo (Fleetwood) ask who is going to play the king in a forthcoming production, to which his prompter answers: 'Pistol, sir, he loves to act it behind the scenes.'[1] But Charles Macklin was no pushover either. He was one of the actors who had joined the company in 1733 when John Highmore was desperate to get absolutely anyone who could remember a few lines, after the walk-out by all of his star performers led by Cibber. Being a lot better than some of his fellows, he stepped straight into leading roles that ordinarily he would have waited years for. Following Fleetwood's purchase of the patent and the return of the rebels to Drury Lane in March 1734, Macklin spent the next few months appearing at other theatres but then, in September, he was signed up as a member of the Drury Lane regulars.

Almost immediately, Macklin's fiery temper got him into trouble. On 10 May 1735 he got into an argument with another actor in the Green Room about the wearing of a wig, thrust his walking stick towards his antagonist and pierced his eye. The stick lodged in the brain and the actor died. Macklin was charged with murder and conducted his own defence at the Old Bailey. He was able to get witnesses to acknowledge that it had been an accident and was convicted of manslaughter, for which he was 'to be branded on the hand and discharged'.[2]

Theophilus Cibber had to leave Drury Lane in 1739, having annoyed everyone, especially Fleetwood, so much that no one wanted to work with him. Fleetwood had also lost interest by this time, having acquired a passion for refereeing boxing matches at Tottenham Court, so he left his treasurer in charge of the finances and Macklin in charge of the plays. Macklin made good use of his opportunity and decided to put on *The Merchant of Venice* with himself as Shylock.

The Jew that Shakespeare drew

The Merchant of Venice had not been performed from the time of the Restoration until 1701, when George Granville adapted it as *The*

Jew of Venice, a more 'proper' version from which most of the humour, like the two Gobbos, had been excised. The character of Shylock was simplified to remove any ambiguity that might trouble the audience: he was a wicked old man at whose downfall we can all rejoice. 'Today we punish a stock-jobbing Jew', announces the ghost of Shakespeare in the prologue. It was put on at Lincoln's Inn Fields with Thomas Doggett playing Shylock for laughs in a red beard and a style that was closer to the Pantaloon of harlequinade than Shakespeare's original. Following Doggett's departure from the stage, the part was given to the low comedian of the company, receiving its last performance in 1729. It was never performed at Drury Lane.

Macklin realised that he had the opportunity to do something fresh and he took it. He read *The History of the Jews* by Josephus and studied the behaviour of Jews in the coffee-houses around the Exchange. He restored much of Shakespeare's text, and henceforth the play would be known by its original title. Macklin's début in the role, on 14 December 1741, was a sensation and elicited the famous epigram from Pope: 'This is the Jew/ that Shakespeare drew.' His Shylock wasn't funny but nor was he noble: he was absolutely terrifying. It is said that, when Robert Walpole was having difficulty in getting a bill through the House of Commons, George II advised him to threaten them with the Irishman playing Shylock at Drury Lane. Macklin experienced not just a personal triumph, but a triumph for his view that it was time for a more realistic style of acting to replace the declamatory style left over from the days of Betterton. Unfortunately for him, he wasn't the only person with this idea.

A gentleman who never appeared on any stage

The theatre in Goodman's Fields, Whitechapel, which should have been closed down by the 1737 Licensing Act, was in fact still operating. Henry Giffard was using the transparent ploy of advertising a concert (which was legal) in the interval of which a play would be performed 'free'. For the time being, the authorities were letting him get away with it. He wasn't a great rival to the patent houses as they were in the West End and he was east of the City. His audience was mainly drawn from the population of the Square Mile, which was still large, rather than the fashionable districts further west. However, in October 1741 he put on an attraction that had Fleet Street and Ludgate Hill jammed with the coaches of the gentry. A performance of *Richard III* was announced for 19 October 1741 with the part of the King played by 'a GENTLEMAN (*who never appear'd on any stage*)'. This wasn't strictly true. The gentleman was David Garrick and he had played a season in Ipswich during the summer, but this was certainly his first professional appearance in London. The house wasn't full for that first appearance, but word went around like wildfire that there was a new acting sensation in Goodman's Fields, and the fashionable world flocked to see him. One night Garrick heard that Alexander Pope was out front, which gave him palpitations, but he needn't have worried. Pope's verdict was that: 'I am afraid the young man will be spoiled, for he will have no competitor.'[3]

Garrick did a run of seven performances as Richard, then appeared in a variety of other plays for the rest of the season: comedies, tragedies and farces from *King Lear* to *The Rehearsal*. He was initially billed as 'the gentleman who performed King Richard', although everyone knew his name by now. The reason for this was the disapproval of the stage felt by his respectable Huguenot family, and their strongly expressed view that he had disgraced them. He was upset and tried to placate them: 'I hope when you shall find that I may have ye genius of an actor without ye vices, you will think less severe of me',[4] he wrote to his brother Peter. But he wasn't going to back down. At the age of 24, he was the most celebrated actor in London, credited with introducing a new and more naturalistic acting style that caused people to see plays in a new light. He had also proved a successful playwright with his afterpiece *Lethe* and his farce *The Lying Valet*. For a young man who had only recently arrived in London from Lichfield to set up as a rather unsuccessful wine merchant in Durham Yard, the prospects were dazzling.

Garrick comes to Drury Lane

The managers of both patent houses were after Garrick, but he chose to go to Drury Lane where the by-now desperate Fleetwood made him the sort of unprecedented offer he couldn't refuse: 500 guineas (£525) for a season and a clear benefit – i.e. a benefit performance from which the management would deduct no charges. Garrick gave his last performance at Goodman's Fields on 24 May and two days later opened at Drury Lane as Bayes in *The Rehearsal*. Two days after that he performed *King Lear*, then the next night he closed the Drury Lane season with *Richard III*. This time it was a royal command performance and his name was very definitely on the bills. As Garrick's biographer Ian McIntyre says, Drury Lane is only a few miles west of Goodman's Fields, but the unsuccessful wine merchant from Lichfield had come a long way in seven months.[5] It was the eighteenth-century equivalent of going from a room over a pub to the National Theatre.

The 1742-43 season was Garrick's first full season at Drury Lane and it only added to his bag of triumphs. After appearing in some of his already familiar roles, including Richard III, he gave the public his first Hamlet and appeared as Abel Drugger in Ben Jonson's *The Alchymist*, which would remain one of his most popular parts throughout his career. However, the company was in a bad way under Fleetwood's incompetent management: actors went unpaid for months and there were visits from the bailiffs on more than one occasion. By the close of the season, Garrick's salary was over £600 in arrears and other actors, on much lower salaries, were suffering real hardship. Under Garrick's direction, twenty of them agreed to give Fleetwood a list of demands, threatening to leave unless they were met. Charles Macklin took the wise precaution of getting them all to sign an agreement that they would stand or fall together: no one was to make individual terms with Fleetwood.

The ultimatum, presented early in September, was dismissed by Fleetwood out of hand. He still had enough actors left to put on shows, so he told the twenty they could go. The question was, where to? They applied to the Lord Chamberlain for a special licence to put on plays at the opera house in the Haymarket, but this was refused in October, so they had nowhere to act and no money coming in. Having failed to get the licence, most of the actors took the view that the agreement between them was over, and all they could do was make terms with Fleetwood to go back to Drury Lane. Fleetwood was keen to get Garrick and offered him a salary increase – thought to be somewhere between £600 and £700 a year. Others were offered three-quarters or less of what they had been earning. Macklin he refused to have back on any terms after what he regarded as an act of gross betrayal: he had stood by Macklin when he was accused of murder, allowed him to come back the theatre when he was convicted of manslaughter, and to top it all they had been gambling buddies at White's. As far as Fleetwood was concerned, Macklin would never act at Drury Lane again.

Macklin reminded Garrick of their agreement: one for all etc. Garrick, like the other actors, wasn't prepared to see his career collapse, especially as Theophilus Cibber was now back at Drury Lane taking back his old parts. On the other hand, he felt a sense of obligation to Macklin. Macklin, as the older and more experienced actor, had always been helpful to Garrick, and for a while Garrick and his partner, the actress Peg Woffington, had lived at Macklin's house in Bow Street, Covent Garden. Garrick did everything he could to mediate. He offered money to Fleetwood; he offered to act as guarantor of Macklin's good behaviour; he tried to get work for Macklin and his wife at Covent Garden, or in Dublin. All in vain: Fleetwood wouldn't have Macklin at Drury Lane and Macklin refused to work anywhere else. He remained unemployed while the other actors went back to Drury Lane, and a bitter pamphlet war broke out. When Garrick made his return to Drury Lane on 6 December, playing Bayes in *The Rehearsal*, a group of Macklin's supporters disrupted the performance. For his next appearance, Garrick brought in a bunch of prizefighters who beat up Macklin's men and drove them out of the pit. Things settled down, but Garrick hadn't come out of it well, although, under the circumstances, it is difficult to see what else he could have done.

Exit Fleeetwood, enter Lacy

There would be more rough stuff in the pit in the following year, but this time it was nothing to do with Garrick. In spite of his victory over the rebel actors, Fleetwood was in a perilous condition. In an attempt to stave off bankruptcy (resulting from his habit of gambling with the takings) he mortgaged his patent for £3,000 to Sir John de Lorme and secured a further £7,000 loan from an upholsterer called Mure who thought that he was clearing the mortgage and the theatre's debts and acquiring the patent. This didn't solve the problem, so Fleetwood resorted to the dangerous expedient of 'advanced prices', which had been a bugbear with the theatregoing public for years and had already provoked riots. When Drury Lane had been silenced by the Lord Chamberlain in 1720, the frequent raising of prices by the management had been given as one of the two reasons. When a new licence was issued to re-start performances, one of the conditions had been that the management must never raise prices without clearing it with the Lord Chamberlain's office. This put managers in a difficult position when the public demand for spectacle and more items on the bill was raising the costs of production.

People expected prices to stay where they were set in 1660: 4s for a seat in a box; 2s 6d in the pit; 1s 6d first gallery; 1s second gallery. There was a grudging acceptance that the first performances of a new production, or a revival of an old production with new sets and costumes, might occasion a rise in seat prices to cover the capital costs: 5s; 3s; 2s 6d; 2s. Prices were expected to fall to the usual levels pretty quickly. The advent of pantomimes posed new problems for the management, because the large numbers of dancers and the elaborate machinery required for the transformations and special effects meant that the running costs were much higher, even after capital costs had been cleared. On nights when a pantomime afterpiece was played, therefore, it could be argued that advanced prices were justified.[6]

This didn't go down well with the public, and on Saturday 17 November 1744 a riot broke out during a performance of *The Conscious Lovers*, with benches being ripped up and light fittings thrown onto the stage. The rioters demanded to see the manager but Fleetwood replied rather grandly that he was not an actor and was not obliged to appear on the stage. This was a mistake, as people expected theatre managers to be subservient to their public, and Horace Walpole stood up in his box to call Fleetwood 'an impudent rascal'. Fleetwood agreed to meet a delegation in his office, where he agreed a compromise: anyone not wanting to pay the advanced prices could have the difference refunded if they left before the start of the afterpiece. This should have satisfied the malcontents but it didn't. On the Monday night there was a worse disturbance, and Fleetwood seems to have decided that it was time to bail out. A few weeks later he sold the patent to two bankers called Norton Green and James Amber. The price was £3,200 plus an annuity to Fleetwood of £600 during the life of the patent.[7] They also had to square Mure, as he realised when the sale of the patent was announced that he had been defrauded. Green and Amber were bankers with no experience of theatre, so they approached James Lacy, John Rich's assistant manager at Covent Garden, and asked him to run the theatre for them in return for a share in their partnership. He could repay the value of his one-third share out of profits from the theatre, and would then become co-owner. Lacy was a failed actor who had proved himself to be a successful entrepreneur by creating the Ranelagh pleasure gardens to rival those at Vauxhall. He had sold the lease of the gardens in 1742 for £4,000.

Fleetwood went to France to escape his creditors, just pausing long enough to persuade his good friend the poet Paul Whitehead to guarantee a bill for £3,000. Whitehead spent the next few years in debtors' prison as a result.

The relationship between Lacy and Garrick got off to a difficult start, with Lacy refusing to admit responsibility for £250 of back-pay that had been owed to Garrick by Fleetwood. There was also a dispute over the frequency of Garrick's appearances. Lacy wanted his biggest star onstage as often as possible, but Garrick protested that he couldn't act every night. Nevertheless, the rest of the season went well for Garrick. He played Sir John Brute in Vanbrugh's *The Provok'd Wife*, which became one of his most popular roles, and he persuaded Lacy to let him revive

Shakespeare's *King John* in competition with Colley Cibber's 'improved' version, *Papal Tyranny in the Reign of King John*, at Covent Garden. Garrick used Shakespeare's text (or most of it) and played the King; Cibber played Cardinal Pandulph in his adapted version. The reason for this sudden interest in what has never been one of Shakespeare's most popular plays was the upsurge of patriotism in anticipation of that year's invasion from France by Charles Edward Stuart – 'Bonnie Prince Charlie'. The Roman Catholicism and tendency towards absolutism of the Stuarts were regarded as the antithesis of the political settlement achieved by the Glorious Revolution of 1688, and the theatres lost no time in putting on anything with an anti-Catholic bias to let people know what was in store for them if Charles Edward Stuart were successful.

In Rep: Plays Performed at Drury Lane During w/c 11 November 1745
Date in brackets is year of first performance

Date of performance, *Play* and playwright

Monday 11 November, *Lady Jane Gray* by Nicholas Rowe (1715)
Tuesday 12 November, *Lady Jane Gray* by Nicholas Rowe (1715) followed by *The Old Debauchees* by Henry Fielding (1732)
Wednesday 13 November, *The Nonjuror* by Colley Cibber (1717) followed by *The Old Debauchees* by Henry Fielding (1732)
Thursday 14 November, *The Relapse* by John Vanbrugh (1696) followed by *The Old Debauchees* by Henry Fielding (1732)
Friday 15 November, *The Relapse* by John Vanbrugh (1696) followed by *The Old Debauchees* by Henry Fielding (1732)
Saturday 16 November, *The Beaux' Stratagem* by George Farquhar (1707) followed by *The Old Debauchees* by Henry Fielding (1732)

God Save The King

King John **gave Garrick his first opportunity** to act opposite Susannah Cibber, who would become his leading lady for many years. She was the wife of Theophilus Cibber, whose brutal treatment of her eventually led to a separation, and the sister of Thomas Arne, the in-house composer for Drury Lane. In 1740 Arne had composed the music for a masque about Alfred the Great that was performed for the Prince of Wales at Cliveden. 'Rule Britannia' formed part of the score. In March 1745, as part of the patriotic response to Bonnie Prince Charlie, *Alfred* was performed as an oratorio at Drury Lane, thus marking the first public performance of the song that has become a sort of alternative national anthem. Later in the same year, Arne came up with the actual national anthem for Drury Lane.

In September, with Bonnie Prince Charlie marching south from Scotland, John Lacy decided to form the actors at Drury Lane into a volunteer force 'in defence of His Majesty's person and government' as the *Daily Advertiser* put it on 28 September 1745. The same edition of the paper also reported that, on the previous Saturday, the audience at Drury Lane had been 'agreeably surprised by the gentlemen belonging to that house performing the anthem "God Save Our Noble King". The universal applause it met with being encored with repeated Huzzas sufficiently denoted in how just an abhorrence they hold the arbitrary schemes of our invidious enemies and detest the despotic attempts of papal power.' Apparently Lacy had told Arne that a patriotic song was needed p.d.q., and Arne put together a tune and some lyrics, both of which had been circulating in different forms for some time, to create what is now the national anthem in its current form. It came at just the right time. At 4:00 a.m. on that Saturday morning the rebels had defeated the King's forces at the Battle of Prestonpans and were marching on London. 'God Save Our Noble King' was such a hit that the Covent Garden management also began to add it to performances, using a different arrangement by Arne's pupil Charles Burney, and it started a tradition that lasted until the 1960s of playing the national anthem at theatrical performances.

Back to the Lane

By this stage, Garrick wasn't at Drury Lane. He had declined to sign a contract with Lacy for the 1745-46 season, as he was still angry about the refusal to cough up the £250 of back-pay. There was a possibility that he might sign with Covent Garden, but to keep his options open for a bit he went to Dublin to perform for Thomas Sheridan (Richard Brinsley Sheridan's father) with whom he shared the management of the Smock Alley Theatre. He had a successful season there, but while he was away there was a crisis in the finances of Drury Lane. The bankers Amber and Green went bust✣ in a run on banks precipitated by the Jacobite rebellion, and Lacy himself very nearly went under. Garrick was receiving a stream of letters from Susannah Cibber begging him to come back to London, where she was convinced the two of them could put together a bid to get hold of the Drury Lane patent for themselves. Garrick wasn't sure about this, and he was particularly unsure about entering into any business arrangement with Susannah Cibber as her appalling husband would try to interfere. He returned to London in May and gave a few performances for John Rich at Covent Garden during the last weeks of the season. He then signed for the 1746-47 season at Covent Garden.

The Covent Garden company for this season was a strong one, comprising both Garrick and James Quinn, the arch-representative of the old declamatory style of acting which Garrick was replacing. 'If this young man is right,' Quinn was widely quoted as having said when Garrick burst upon the town, 'then we have all been wrong.' The public looked forward to sparks flying, but in fact the two men got on well and established a good working relationship. The management pitted them against each other as Falstaff (Quinn) and Hotspur (Garrick) in *Henry IV Part 1*, and Garrick seems to have come off worse. He dropped Hotspur after a few performances and didn't go back to the part. The company also included the brilliant Susannah Cibber and Hannah Pritchard, the great tragedienne of the day. Horace Walpole called it 'the best company that perhaps ever were together'.[8] Garrick also produced his farce *Miss In Her Teens* for the Covent Garden season. It was enormously popular and would remain one of his most performed plays for the rest of the century.

✣ In his 1971 history of Drury Lane, Brian Dobbs describes the financial uncertainty of the time as 'a red light for Green and Amber' (101). Norton Amber became the pit-doorkeeper in the theatre he had co-owned (McIntyre, 198).

Around the corner at Drury Lane, Lacy was contemplating the future of the theatre. The 21-year patent granted to the triumvirate in 1732 had only six years to run, and renewal had to be thought about sooner rather than later. Lacy knew that, in spite of his differences with Garrick, the two of them together stood the best chance of getting another patent. Garrick was not only universally acknowledged to be the greatest actor of his generation, but he also had experience of management from his time in Dublin with Sheridan. Throughout the spring of 1747, negotiations were carried on to establish an agreement for a joint bid. Lacy would undertake to obtain a new patent and Garrick would pay him £12,000 for a half-share. They would be jointly liable for debts accrued – a mortgage, back-pay to actors, a lump sum to Fleetwood to buy out his annuity – up to the value of £12,000. Above that level, Lacy would be liable. They would both draw an annual salary of £500, and Garrick would receive a further 500 guineas for his acting, plus a benefit free of charges.

Lacy and Garrick signed their agreement on 9 April, and on 4 June 1747 a new patent was granted to Lacy and Garrick to run for 21 years from the expiry of the existing patent in September 1753. Lacy and Garrick mortgaged both patents to a city merchant called James Clutterbuck for £12,000 which they used to clear all outstanding debts and charges against the theatre. They would open their first season together on a sound financial basis and with good prospects for artistic success. The golden age of Drury Lane was about to dawn.

12

The Fourth Estate

The opening night of the Garrick/Lacy regime took place on Tuesday 15 September 1747. Garrick chose not to act himself, and the play was *The Merchant of Venice* with Charles Macklin as Shylock. One of the first things Lacy had done, when he took over the management of Drury Lane from Green and Amber in 1744, had been to re-hire Macklin, who would both act and write for Drury Lane, on and off, for the remainder of his long life. In spite of this, Macklin's breach with Garrick was never healed.

The first night under new management is remembered less for the play than for the prologue, spoken by Garrick and written by his old friend Samuel Johnson, who had come down to London from Lichfield with him in 1737. Johnson had failed in his attempt to run a school near Lichfield, in which Garrick was one of only three pupils, so they both decided to try their luck in the capital. While Garrick had risen to fame, Johnson was still working as a literary drudge. He was compiling his great *Dictionary of the English Language* which would establish him as the leading man of letters on its publication in 1755, but in 1747 he wasn't famous. The Drury Lane prologue gave him an unexpected taste of success.

Prologues and epilogues were popular elements of a visit to the theatre from the 1660s to the early part of the nineteenth century,

Prologue by Samuel Johnson for the opening of Drury Lane under the
management of David Garrick and James Lacy on Tuesday 15 September 1747

When learning's triumph o'er her
barb'rous foes
First rear'd the stage, immortal
SHAKESPEARE rose;
Each change of many-colour'd life he drew,
Exhausted worlds, and then imagin'd new:
Existence saw him spurn her bounded reign,
And panting time toil'd after him in vain:
His pow'rful strokes presiding truth
impress'd,
And unresisted passion storm'd the breast.
Then JONSON came, instructed from
the school,
To please in method, and invent by rule;
His studious patience, and laborious art,
By regular approach essay'd the heart;
Cold approbation gave the ling'ring bays,
For those who durst not censure, scarce
could praise.
A mortal born he met the general doom,
But left, like Egypt's Kings, a lasting tomb.
The wits of Charles found easier ways
to fame,
nor wish'd for JONSON'S art, or
SHAKESPEARE'S flame,
Themselves they studied, as they felt,
they writ,
Intrigue was plot, obscenity was wit.
Vice always found a sympathetick friend;
They pleas'd their age, and did not aim
to mend.
Yet bards like these aspir'd to lasting praise,
And proudly hop'd to pimp in future days.
Their cause was gen'ral, their supports
were strong,
Their slaves were willing, and their
reign was long;
Till shame regain'd the post that
sense betray'd,
And virtue call'd oblivion to her aid.
Then crush'd by rules, and weaken'd
as refin'd,
For years the pow'r of tragedy declin'd;

From bard, to bard, the frigid caution crept,
Till declamation roar'd, while passion slept.
Yet still did virtue deign the stage to tread,
Philosophy remain'd, though nature fled.
But forc'd at length her ancient reign to quit,
She saw great Faustus lay the ghost of wit:
Exulting folly hail'd the joyful day,
And pantomime, and song, confirm'd
her sway.
But who the coming changes can presage,
And mark the future periods of the stage?
Perhaps if skill could distant times explore,
New Benns, new Durfeys, yet remain
in store.
Perhaps, where Lear has rav'd, and
Hamlet died,
On flying cars new sorcerers may ride.
Perhaps, for who can guess th' effects
of chance?
Here Hunt may box, or Mahomet
may dance.
Hard is his lot, that here by fortune plac'd,
Must watch the wild vicissitudes of taste;
With ev'ry meteor of caprice must play,
And chase the new-blown bubbles of
the day.
Ah! let not censure term our fate our choice,
The stage but echoes back the publick voice.
The drama's laws the drama's patrons give,
For we that live to please, must please
to live.
Then prompt no more the follies you decry,
As tyrants doom their tools of guilt to die;
'Tis yours this night to bid the
reign commence
Of rescu'd nature, and reviving sense;
To chase the charms of sound, the pomp
of show,
For useful mirth, and salutary woe;
Bid scenic virtue form the rising age,
And truth diffuse her radiance from
the stage.

and many of the leading authors of the day tried their hand at this demanding form. The obvious aim was to recommend the show to the audience and to disarm criticism, but they had also assumed, from the very start, a critical role. Prologues and epilogues were often used to rebuke the audience for their vanity, poor behaviour and lack of taste. The boorish gallery who disrupted what they couldn't understand; the captious critics of the pit who damned a play in advance; the fops and flirts of the boxes who came not so much to see as to be seen: all felt the lash of the prologue and epilogue writer's satire. It might seem a strange way to get the audience on your side, but it was expected, in the same way that auditors of a sermon expect to be reminded of their sins. Dryden had been regarded as the greatest writer of prologues and epilogues, and his imitators knew that the knack of writing a successful one was to season the criticism with wit. Johnson's prologue, reprinted here, is the greatest example of the form ever written and was recognised as such immediately. It was called for again and again throughout the season, and has given us the couplet that sums up the dilemma of the manager of a commercial theatre: 'The drama's laws the drama's patrons give,/ For we that live to please, must please to live.' No one had a firmer grasp of that reality than David Garrick, and it was one of the factors that made Drury Lane, under his management, the most famous theatre in Europe.

For most of his time at Drury Lane, however, Garrick was not acting alone. His partnership with John Lacy lasted until Lacy's death in 1774, in spite of a good deal of inevitable friction. Because Garrick was the public face of the partnership, as star actor as well as manager, Lacy tends to get forgotten, or just remembered as the annoying money-man. This is unfair because, without Lacy, Garrick would not have had the chance to manage Drury Lane at all. Lacy was the established manager, already in control of Drury Lane after the bankruptcy of his backers Green and Amber, and it was he who decided to ask Garrick to join him, in spite of the considerable ill-will that had already built up between them over Lacy's refusal to meet Garrick's back-pay demands. There is a danger of thinking of Garrick as the 'artistic' one and Lacy as the financial controller, but in reality they were both men of the theatre and they were both businessmen, serious about making money from Drury Lane. Lacy wasn't telling Garrick to forget his airy-fairy ideas about Shakespeare, he just wanted them to pay – and so did Garrick. Playing to empty benches held no appeal to the man who was known as Roscius, after the greatest actor of the ancient world.

Both men realised that there would be disagreements, and they were sensible enough to agree from the very start about how to handle them. Neither would go public with a pamphlet war or letters to the papers. Intermediaries would be called in if the two men could not resolve things themselves and, in the event of a complete breakdown which necessitated the dissolving of the partnership, they agreed the terms in advance to avoid lawsuits. Garrick complained constantly and bitterly about Lacy to his friends, and no doubt Lacy had plenty to say about Garrick that hasn't come down to us, but there was only one occasion when things got so bad that Garrick seriously considered splitting up, and that was avoided by the skill of the intermediaries who found that Lacy was genuinely upset at such a prospect and prepared to build bridges again.

When Lacy and Garrick took over, they owned their own patent which would kick in as soon as the old patent issued to Colley Cibber and his fellow managers expired in 1753. Admittedly, they had mortgaged the patent to raise the funds to clear all outstanding claims against the theatre, but that mortgage would soon be repaid, and the patent would never, under their management, be split up and sold in shares to outsiders who would then be able to interfere with the affairs of the theatre.

The lease under which they held the theatre was still the strange, cobbled-together effort of 1733 when Theophilus Cibber and his rebels had persuaded the building shareholders to issue a sub-lease to them instead of John Highmore, who was actually supposed to be in charge at the time. This sub-lease was due to expire in 1748, and after that the ground lease issued by the third Duke of Bedford to the building shareholders had only another five-and-a-half years to run. To gain the stability required for major investment, Garrick and Lacy needed a new lease from the fourth Duke to replace the sub-lease from the building shareholders, and as it was his family's practice to issue a lease

Samuel Johnson at Drury Lane

Two years into his management, Garrick was able to repay the favour of Johnson's prologue by staging his tragedy *Irene*.[1] It opened on 6 February 1749 and Garrick really did his friend proud, appearing in the top-notch cast himself. Unfortunately Johnson was the last person who should have set up shop as a playwright as he completely lacked what Oscar Wilde called the touch of vulgarity that makes the whole world kin. *Irene* is so turgid that no one would read it now for pleasure. Garrick struggled to keep it going for nine nights, so that Johnson would get his author's benefit for the third, sixth and ninth nights. It was normal to put on a new play without an afterpiece, but by the sixth night it looked as if it might not make the ninth. Garrick added three copper-bottomed hit afterpieces for the next performances: Edward Ravenscroft's farce *The Anatomist*, Garrick's own *The Lying Valet* and Fielding's *The Virgin Unmask'd*. The combined takings for the three benefit nights came to £384, from which Garrick deducted £189 as house charges, so Johnson ended up with £195, plus the £100 he received for publication rights.

Johnson had been made welcome in the Green Room during rehearsals and developed a habit of dropping in to enjoy some theatrical gossip. Eventually he had to bring these backstage visits to a close for moral reasons: 'I'll come no more behind your scenes, David,' he is supposed to have said, 'for the silk stockings and white bosoms of your actresses excite my amorous propensities.' That, at least, is the official version. Boswell's notes reveal that Johnson actually said 'for the white bubbies and silk stockings of your actresses excite my genitals.'

to the tenant in occupation, this was soon agreed. On 24 August 1748, at the end of the new management's first season, the Duke issued a ground lease to Garrick and Lacy which would begin when the existing lease expired and would end in 1774.

This represented the end of the tripartite structure of ownership that had bedevilled the theatre for nearly 90 years, with a patent owned by shareholders; a building owned by a different set of shareholders; and an acting company paying a nightly rental for the use of the building. Garrick and Lacy would be in control in a way in which no former managers had been, and the stability this provided would not only benefit Drury Lane, but would be instrumental in raising the whole status of theatre in society.

In Rep: Plays Performed at Drury Lane During w/c 19 April 1756
Date in brackets is year of first performance

Date of performance, *Play* and playwright

Monday 19 April, *The Fair Quaker of Deal* by Charles Shadwell (1710) followed by *The Genii* by Henry Woodward (1752)
Tuesday 20 April, *Hamlet* by William Shakespeare (1600) followed by The Devil to Pay by Charles Coffey (1731)
Wednesday 21 April, *The Alchymist* by Ben Jonson (1610) followed by *The Anatomist* by Edward Ravenscroft (1696)
Thursday 22 April, *The Earl of Essex* by Henry Jones (1753) followed by *Lethe* by David Garrick (1740)
Friday 23 April, *The Beaux' Stratagem* by George Farquhar (1707) followed by *The Intriguing Chambermaid* by Henry Fielding (1734)
Saturday 24 April, T*he Drummer* by Joseph Addison (1716) followed by *The Maiden Whim* by John Hill (first performance)

Increasing the size of the house

The new lease which the Duke of Bedford granted was particularly interesting because it didn't just cover the footprint of the main theatre building. The Duke was promising the reversion of the leases on some of the properties backing onto the theatre and fronting onto the surrounding streets. The reason was that the auditorium had to be expanded, and expansion was particularly difficult on this site.

Garrick and Lacy took the view that they needed more customers to make Drury Lane profitable, as their capacity was about 30 per cent below that of their rival, Covent Garden. This brings us to the vexed question of what the capacity of the theatre actually was. We are used to knowing exactly how many seats there are in a theatre, because there is a seating plan which, in most cases, can be seen online, and you can count them. This was not the case in the eighteenth century, because most of the patrons were not in seats but on benches. This meant that the idea of a 'full house' was a flexible one. If people were standing at the door with money in their hands, the temptation for the management was to keep cramming an extra person onto the end of the bench until it became physically impossible to get another body in. Managers didn't talk of their capacity in terms of number of people, they spoke of the gross takings. Thus, a £40 house would be a thin house that didn't cover costs; a £200 house was a great success. Increases in the size of the audience would be described as 'adding £30 to the house'.

Nevertheless, there are a number of performances for which we have records of the takings, and in some of these the takings are broken down by the three divisions of the house – pit, boxes and galleries. As we know the price of admission to each part of the house, it is possible to work out how many people were present on a given night. If we make the calculation for a show which was known to be popular – for example the first night of a new play or the benefit performance of a popular actor – we can get an idea of how many people the house held when it was 'full'.

With all due allowance for the considerable amount of guesswork involved in these figures, it seems that when Garrick and Lacy took over, the capacity of Drury Lane was about 1,000 people, compared with 1,335 at Covent Garden. The two men got the builders in immediately and, by the time their first season opened in September 1747, they had added another 270 people to the capacity.[2] We don't know how they got these extra people in because the process of acquiring the surrounding properties had not begun, and the verbal and visual descriptions of the auditorium throughout the period are extremely limited. However, this was the start of a process which would go on throughout the next thirty years. As the years went by, leases fell in and Garrick and Lacy were able to incorporate more and more of the buildings that surrounded the theatre. Since the Duke of Bedford did not own all of these buildings, as his ancestors had sold some of them under a fee-farm arrangement in the 1630s, the managers had to carry out their own negotiations with the individual leaseholders.

In 1762 Garrick and Lacy decided to have a major push to increase the capacity of the house, partly because they wanted to end the practice of members of the audience sitting on the stage. Although it seems strange us, it was not at all uncommon for people of quality to demand to be seated actually on the stage so that actors had to push past them to get on and off. This was particularly true of benefit nights for popular actors, when a whole bank of seats would be erected beside and behind the actors, leaving a tiny amount of floorspace in the middle where the actors were supposed to do their acting.✦ This custom was so likely to lead to disorder that it had frequently been banned by proclamations of the Lord Chamberlain. The fact that these proclamations were made over and over again shows that they were not being heeded.

Garrick and Lacy decided to grasp the nettle and deal with this once and for all, but they knew that they would face opposition from their own actors if the value of the house was reduced for a benefit performance. The only way round that was to increase the capacity so much that, even with no one sitting on the stage, the actors would still be quids in.

The building work of 1762 achieved this. The capacity of the house was very nearly doubled to 2,362, putting it way ahead of Covent

---

✦ An account of Mrs Oldfield's benefit had appeared in the *Universal Spectator* (8 March 1729) describing 'the house so excessive full, stage and all, that the actors had scarce room to perform' (Milhous & Hume [1991] ii, 739).

Garden.[3] Once again, we have no detailed record of where these extra people were sitting, but the endpapers to this volume show how it was done. The plots shaded in pale green represent the leases that Garrick and Lacy had acquired from the fourth Duke of Bedford, plus those they had negotiated themselves, between 1747 and 1776 when Garrick sold his share following Lacy's death. The enormous increase in space which this allowed the managers is obvious, and although not all of the space had been added by 1762, most of it had. This made it possible to start moving ancillary functions outside the footprint of the principal plot: box office, staircases, foyers, offices, storage and even rooms for the organ and the fire engine. As the plot became larger, the back wall of the theatre started moving east. The dark green line represents the main building in 1776, by which time the back wall had moved 100 feet to the east of Christopher Wren's original.

Garrick's repertoire

The 29 years of Garrick's management represent the most intensely studied period in the history of Drury Lane, owing to his unique status. Not only was Garrick universally acknowledged to be the greatest actor of his age, he was a supremely successful theatre manager. Together with Lacy, he made Drury Lane into the most important theatre in Europe, and one of his first biographers, Arthur Murphy, memorably summed up the tremendous cultural status of Garrick's Drury Lane: 'The theatre engrossed the minds of men to such a degree that there existed in England a *fourth estate*, King, Lords, Commons and Drury Lane playhouse.'[4]

Garrick embarked on his management with the words of Johnson's prologue ringing in his ears: 'We who live to please, must please to live.' In truth, he didn't need to be reminded of that. The reason for his phenomenal success was the way in which Garrick combined great acting ability with a shrewd head for business. He was a highly intelligent man with a love of literature in general and drama in particular. He saw himself, with justification, as something of a scholar and antiquary. But he knew that, in the theatre, the bottom line is getting bums on seats. No one would have agreed more wholeheartedly with the observation of Aaron Hill, who had briefly struggled with Drury Lane before him, that 'he could not think it was the business of the directors to be wise to empty boxes'.[5] So how to fill those boxes, without emptying the pit and galleries?

Garrick's repertoire has been comprehensively analysed, down to the number of shows and the number of performances of each show,[6] so we have a pretty good idea of what his public liked. Garrick put on a grand total of 377 productions, including afterpieces, and we can rank them in order of popularity. The table on pages 194-195 shows the top 50.

There are some noticeable changes from the previous century. Leaving Shakespeare to one side, the Elizabethan and Jacobean dramatists, who had been the stalwarts of the repertoire at the end of the seventeenth century, were losing ground. Two of Ben Jonson's plays – *Every Man in His Humour* and *The Alchymist* – were still crowd-pleasers, in the case of the latter because the character of Abel Drugger had been one of Garrick's earliest and greatest successes. However John Fletcher's plays, which had swept all before them when the theatres re-opened in the 1660s, were now rarities, with only *Rule a Wife and Have a Wife* and *The Chances* (adapted by the Duke of Buckingham) appearing in the top 100 (at 71 and 100 out of 377 respectively). One play of Massinger's appeared at 223 (*A New Way to Pay Old Debts*) but it had only lasted for four performances, while Brome and Shirley had disappeared from the repertoire. These theatrical patriarchs, described by Dryden as 'our fathers in wit',[7] seemed just too far away by the middle of the eighteenth century.

The more relevant inheritance came from the writers of the Restoration, those controversial figures who had been lambasted by Jeremy Collier for corrupting the morals of the nation. The charges of obscenity and blasphemy had stuck, so their plays had to be handled gingerly, with lots of cuts. Nevertheless, as Steele had discovered long before Garrick's arrival, they were brilliant plays and you couldn't ignore them, however much some people might want to turn the stage into a pulpit. A play either works on the stage or it doesn't, and that consideration will generally trump any amount of moralising. Of course, the tragedies of the Restoration period were unobjectionable, and it is surprising to see how popular they remained – surprising because they are so formal and wooden as to be unperformable now. All of Congreve's five plays were still in the repertoire, but the most popular (33 in the ranking) was his one tragedy, *The Mourning Bride*. Otway's tragedies *The Orphan* and *Venice Preserv'd* come in at 38 and 47. Even Nathaniel Lee's dreadful old fustian could still pack 'em in from time to time: *The Rival Queens* was revived for 10 seasons and comes in at 102 on the full list.

The Restoration comedies were more problematic because of their reputation for filth. Congreve had given up writing plays after the lukewarm reception for *The Way of the World* in 1700, but it was recognised as a masterpiece during his lifetime and still comes in at 59 under Garrick. *Love For Love* was also in the top 100 (at 79). Etherege's *The Man of Mode or Sir Fopling Flutter*, with its dangerously seductive anti-hero Dorimant, got a few performances, but it was regarded as strong meat by Garrick's time. The most interesting example of a Restoration comedy being given a respectable eighteenth-century afterlife was Wycherley's *The Country Wife*, the funniest and the filthiest of them all. It appears to have been given three performances in its original version and a few more after being rewritten as a two-act farce. Garrick decided to take it in hand and re-wrote it in 1766 as *The Country Girl*, taking out the dirty bits, which is to say most of it. Garrick's version was so different that it can scarcely be called an adaptation at all. One critic accused him of changing 'a whore of Wycherley's lewd pen' into 'a flabby Magdalen'[8] – i.e. a reformed prostitute. But Garrick knew that it was this or nothing for his audience, and *The Country Girl* was a success, coming in at 107.

By far the most successful of the Restoration comedies, coming in at 25, was *The Provok'd Wife* by Sir John Vanbrugh. It had first appeared in 1697 with Betterton as Sir John Brute, the boorish, bullying husband of the title character. It was an immediate success,

and contained a scene in which Sir John disguises himself as a
clergyman to escape the pursuit of the night watch, then makes a
drunken scene with the constable, swearing, fighting and calling for
a whore, to the great scandal of the cloth. Unsurprisingly, Jeremy
Collier made a special attack on the play in his *Short View* and
Betterton, Anne Bracegirdle and Vanbrugh were fined £5 'for using
indecent expressions' in it.✢ As public toleration of indecency
decreased, the play dropped out of the repertoire until 1726, when it
was revived as a command performance, according to Colley Cibber.[9]
The scene with Sir John Brute as a clergyman was just too risky, so
Vanbrugh was prevailed upon to rewrite it with Brute dressing up as
his wife. This is the version that Garrick took on (and it is the version
still performed, as it is actually much funnier). He cleaned up the
script a bit, removing sexual references and jokes about religion, and
first appeared in the character in November 1747, only a few weeks
after the start of his management. Garrick's Sir John Brute was a huge
success and he would play the part more often than any other in his
career with the exception of Benedick in *Much Ado about Nothing*
and Ranger in *The Suspicious Husband*.

By Garrick's time, the plays by authors of the Restoration period
had something like classic status, and people were prepared to make
some allowances for the coarseness of a less polite age. This latitude
would not have been afforded to the authors of new plays, who were
expected to take account of the refined sensibilities of the ladies in the
audience. The result, predictably, was a lot of very dull plays. 'The
refiners of the purity of the stage,' wrote Horace Walpole to a friend,

---

✢ On 18 February 1699 the Lord Chamberlain warned Betterton and the actors at
  Lincoln's Inn Fields about 'severall new plays... containing expressions contrary to
  religion and good manners'; on 14 October 1699 'the grand jury presented [against]
  The Provok'd Wife, a play, as obscene'; on 20 November 1701 there was a King's
  Bench indictment against Betterton, Bracegirdle, Vanbrugh and others 'for using
  indecent expressions in some late plays, particularly *The Provok'd Wife*'; on 16
  February 1702 they were tried before Lord Chief Justice Holt on the basis of
  testimonies from informers in the audience. They pleaded innocent but the plays
  were introduced as evidence and 'the judge declared to the jury the ill consequence
  of such profane wicked speeches' and they were all fined £5 and ordered 'not to
  commit the like again'. (Milhous and Hume [1991] i, 335, 339, 354, 355-56, 357.)

'are most woefully inspid.'[10] Comedy was worse affected than tragedy, with the development of what had been called sentimental or exemplary comedy from the beginning of the century. Sentimental comedy involved polite ladies and gentlemen who often suffered misfortune, but were able to support their spirits with noble sentiments concerning the wisdom of providence, the consolation of a clear conscience and the cast-iron confidence that comes from doing your duty. Although they ended happily, sentimental comedies often contained scenes of pathos and suffering, and were described as *comédies larmoyantes*, or tearful comedies. In many cases, they were so profoundly unfunny that the term 'laughing comedy' was coined to describe plays of the old school, that actually gave you a laugh rather than a catechism.

Garrick's preference was for what he called 'the high-seasoned comedies' over 'the pap and loplolly of our present writers'.[11] 'The *comédie larmoyante* is getting too much ground upon us,' he wrote to an author, 'and if those who can write the better species of comic drama don't make a stand... the stage in a few years will be (as Hamlet says) like Niobe, all tears.'[12] However, in this as in other areas of the repertoire, he had to yield to public taste. Garrick was a successful playwright himself, and always encouraged new writing for Drury Lane, but there was a limit to how far he could go. Most of the new plays he staged would be regarded as insufferably dull or trite nowadays, and the only one which still gets revived from time to time is the comedy he wrote with George Colman in 1766, *The Clandestine Marriage*. This makes it all the more strange that he missed the opportunity to stage the comedy that was conceived as a standard-bearer for laughing comedy and became such a great success that it remains a firm favourite in the repertoire today: Oliver Goldsmith's *She Stoops To Conquer*.

Goldsmith's masterpiece of brilliant, good-natured and really funny comedy opened at Covent Garden on 15 March 1773. Why Garrick let it go to the rival house is something of a mystery, as he and Goldsmith knew each extremely well. They had been meeting for years as members of the Literary Club set up by Dr Johnson and Sir Joshua Reynolds, although the relationship between them may have been a bit edgy.✤ However, Garrick had turned down Goldsmith's earlier play, *The Good-Natur'd Man*, six years earlier and that had been put on at Covent Garden.

Everyone, including Goldsmith, expected *She Stoops to Conquer* to flop. George Colman, who had worked with Garrick for many years at Drury Lane, had now taken over at Covent Garden. He sat on the script for so long that Goldsmith took it back and asked Garrick to do it. Samuel Johnson told Goldsmith that he mustn't break an agreement and that he must return the play to Covent Garden where eventually, according to Johnson, Colman was 'prevailed upon by... a kind of force to bring it on'.[13] The leading actors refused to appear in it and Goldsmith's friends urged him to hold it back until the next season. Goldsmith refused, which was just as well as he died the following year. To soften the audience up for a play which – amazingly, it seems to us – was regarded as coarse, Goldsmith published an essay in the *Westminster Magazine* two months before the first night, defending laughing comedy against sentimental comedy and warning that, as a result of 'our being too fastidious... humour at present seems to be departing from the stage'.[14] Goldsmith's friends from the Literary Club turned out in force for the first night, with Garrick providing a prologue attacking sentimental comedy and Johnson sitting in the front of a box, daring the audience not to laugh. It was a huge success and the *London Magazine* announced that the fightback against 'that monster called sentimental comedy' had begun.[15]

✤ One night when Goldsmith couldn't attend a meeting of the Literary Club, the other members amused themselves by composing mock epitaphs on him. Garrick's was the best and was repeated all over town: 'Here lies Nolly Goldsmith, for shortness call'd Noll,/ Who wrote like an angel, but talked like poor Poll.' Goldsmith was well known for making a fool of himself in conversation, but he didn't appreciate having attention drawn to this. He responded with a mock epitaph on Garrick that contained the lines: 'On the stage he was natural, simple, affecting,/'Twas only that when he was off he was acting.'

Comedy, tragedy – and Harlequin

Watching the crowds gathering at the rival house, Garrick must have wished he had taken a chance on his old friend, but in truth the choice of different types of comedy was a minor issue when it came to filling the house at Drury Lane. For lovers of the drama, the question was not sentimental comedy *v.* laughing comedy or Jacobean plays *v.* Restoration plays, but whether straight plays could survive at all in the face of competition from pantomime. For the opening of his very last season at Drury Lane in 1775, Garrick wrote a 'musical prelude' called *The Theatrical Candidates* which summed up, in a light-hearted but truthful way, the reality of managing a theatre. Melpomene, the Muse of Tragedy, and Thalia, the Muse of Comedy, are arguing about who should rule the stage. Each states her case and slanders the other, then they ask the audience to choose between them. Suddenly Harlequin bounds onto the stage, representing pantomime and demanding his share of the glory:

> *Should Harlequin be banished hence,*
> *Quit the place to wit and sense,*
> *What would be the consequence?*
> *Empty houses,*
> *You and spouses,*
> *And your pretty children dear,*
> *Ne'er would come,*
> *Leave your home,*
> *Unless I came after.*

At this point Mercury appears with the judgment of Apollo. Thalia and Melpomene must both respect each other as they play different roles, but they must also share the stage with Harlequin. This little piece of classical allegory came straight from Garrick's heart. He disliked pantomime just as much as Colley Cobber, but like Cibber he also realised that there is no fighting public taste if you want to survive in show business.♣

♣ In 1724 Cibber, Wilks and Booth had written to Richard Steele asking him to agree to sell the patent, as Drury Lane could no longer compete against the pantomimes at Lincoln's Inn Fields and 'nonsense of different kinds' at the other theatres. A year later, Cibber was boasting in the epilogue to his *Caesar in Egypt* that Drury Lane was now competing on the same ground: 'And tho' w'are but beginners there, we'll drudge,/And entertain as low as crowds can judge.' (Loftis, 227-78.)

GARRICK'S TOP 50: MOST POPULAR SHOWS IN THE

Ranking	Production	Author
1	Queen Mab	Henry Woodward
2	The Genii	Henry Woodward
3	Harlequin's Invasion	David Garrick
4	Fortunatus	Henry Woodward
5	The Anatomist	Edward Ravenscroft
6	Lethe	David Garrick
7	The Jubilee	David Garrick
8	The Devil to Pay	Charles Coffey
9	Romeo and Juliet	William Shakespeare
10	The Padlock	Isaac Bickerstaffe
11	High Life Below Stairs	James Townley
12	The Chaplet	Moses Mendez
13	The Suspicious Husband	Benjamin Hoadly
14	Miss In Her Teens	David Garrick
15	The Beggar's Opera	John Gay
16	Hamlet	William Shakespeare
17	The Elopement	Unknown
18	The Lying Valet	David Garrick
19	Much Ado About Nothing	William Shakespeare
20	The Witches	James Love
21	The Beaux' Stratagem	George Farquhar
22	Richard III	William Shakespeare
23	Cymbeline	William Shakespeare
24	The Conscious Lovers	Richard Steele
25	The Provok'd Wife	John Vanbrugh
26	Harlequin Ranger	Henry Woodward
27	The Intriguing Chambermaid	Henry Fielding
28	The Clandestine Marriage	David Garrick & George Colman
29	Polly Honeycombe	George Colman
30	King Lear	William Shakespeare
31	The Provok'd Husband	John Vanbrugh & Colley Cibber
32	Every Man in His Humour	Ben Jonson
33	The Mourning Bride	William Congreve
34	The Tempest	William Shakespeare
35	The Wonder	Susanna Centlivre
36	The Deuce in in Him	George Colman
37	Macbeth	William Shakespeare
38	The Orphan	Thomas Otway
39	The Jealous Wife	George Colman
40	The Fair Penitent	Nicholas Rowe
41	The Alchymist	Ben Jonson
42	Duke and no Duke	Nahum Tate
43	The Englishman in Paris	Samuel Foote
44	Jane Shore	Nicholas Rowe
45	The Way to Keep Him	Arthur Murphy
46	A Peep Behind the Curtain	David Garrick
47	Venice Preserv'd	Thomas Otway
48	Zara	Aaron Hill
49	Cymon	David Garrick
50	The West Indian	Richard Cumberland

Source: *Drury Lane Calendar 1747-1776,* MacMillan, 1938; *The Theatrical Public in the Time of Garrick,* Pedicord, 1954; plus author's calculations

DRURY LANE REPERTOIRE 1747-1776

Type	# Performances	1st Perf.	Panto	Shakespeare	% of Total
Pantomime	259	1750	259		
Pantomime	207	1752	207		
Pantomime	171	1759	171		
Pantomime	158	1753	158		
Farce	157	1697			
Farce	154	1740			
Entertainment	153	1769			
Ballad opera	143	1731			
Tragedy	142	1595		142	
Comic opera	142	1768			
Farce	140	1759			
Masque	129	1749			
Comedy	126	1747			
Farce	125	1747			
Ballad opera	119	1728			
Tragedy	116	1600		116	
Pantomime	110	1767	110		
Comedy	106	1741			
Comedy	105	1598-99		105	
Pantomime	103	1762	103		
Comedy	100	1707			
History/ tragedy	100	1592-3		100	
Tragedy	98	1610		98	
Comedy	96	1722			
Comedy	95	1697			
Pantomime	94	1751	94		
Farce	92	1734			
Comedy	87	1766			
Farce	86	1760			
Tragedy	83	1605-6		83	
Comedy	82	1728			
Comedy	82	1598			
Tragedy	79	1697			
Comedy	79	1610-11		79	
Comedy	78	1714			
Farce	78	1763			
Tragedy	77	1606		77	
Tragedy	77	1680			
Comedy	75	1761			
Tragedy	74	1703			
Comedy	74	1610			
Farce	72	1684			
Comedy	72	1753			
Tragedy	65	1714			
Comedy	65	1760			
Burletta	65	1767			
Tragedy	64	1682			
Tragedy	64	1735			
Dramatic Opera	64	1767			
Comedy	63	1771			
Total Shakespeare				800	15%
Total Pantomime			1102		21%
Grand Total	5245				

Somehow pantomime, tragedy and comedy had to be made to live together, if the legitimate drama was to survive at all. It was Garrick who associated pantomime with the Christmas period and introduced the custom, followed well into the twentieth century, of opening new pantomimes on Boxing Day.

The table on pages 194-195 shows just how important pantomime had become to Drury Lane. Out of the 377 productions of all sorts that Garrick staged during his 29-year management, the four top attractions, by a long way, were pantomimes. If we just consider the 50 most popular productions, representing a total of 5,245 performances, pantomimes represent 21 per cent of those. Without Harlequin to 'come after', there was a real chance that Thalia and Melpomene would have found themselves out on the street begging for bread.

But that is not to say that the case was entirely lost for good straight plays. After the four pantomimes, numbers five and six in our chart were farces, and numbers seven and eight an extravaganza and a ballad opera. These were all afterpieces. Our first mainpiece, coming in at number nine, was *Romeo and Juliet*, more popular than Congreve, Vanbrugh, Steele and Farquhar. Whatever else was going on, Shakespeare was doing pretty well at Drury Lane. There was a reason for that.

The god of our idolatry

In the last half of the seventeenth century, Shakespeare had not achieved iconic status. He was the author of some old-fashioned plays that were not particularly highly esteemed, compared with those of his contemporaries Ben Jonson and John Fletcher. By the beginning of the eighteenth century this had begun to change and Shakespeare was being afforded a very high cultural status – in fact, he was beginning to represent the very idea of high culture as opposed to popular trash. In December 1700, the epilogue to Nicholas Rowe's play *The Ambitious Stepmother* complained about public taste:

Show but a mimic ape or French buffoon,
You to the other house in shoals are gone...
Must Shakespeare, Fletcher and laborious Ben
Be left for Scaramouch and Harlequin?

Although pantomime would not emerge until 1717, harlequinades were already familiar and the plays of Shakespeare, John Fletcher and the pedantic Ben Jonson were seen to be under threat from them. A few years later, Rowe was chosen by the publisher Jacob Tonson to produce the very first edited collection of Shakespeare's plays. Tonson had made his fortune by spotting candidates for canonical status – he had done it with Milton's *Paradise Lost* – and Shakespeare was now important enough to have his text sorted out and cleansed of errors. Shakespeare's classic status rapidly took hold, with the feeling that his plays were important enough to be protected from market forces: they *ought* to be staged and people *ought* to go to see them, even if they weren't as much fun as a harlequinade. In 1707, when the Kit-Cat Club got up their subscription to support 'three plays of the best authors', one of them was *Julius Caesar*. Then, in 1736, there was an unusual development that we still don't completely understand.

A literary pressure group called Shakespeare's Ladies was formed, with the aim of getting the London theatres to put on more performances of Shakespeare's plays. The Ladies were very successful: the theatre seasons of 1736/37 and 1737/38 were so dominated by Shakespeare that theatregoers must have wondered what was going on: not only did managements trot out the old war-horses like *Richard III* and *Hamlet*, but they put on plays hadn't been seen for decades and in some cases scarcely since Shakespeare's time: *Richard II* ('Not acted these forty years'); *Henry V* ('Not acted these forty years'); *Henry VI Part 1* ('Not acted these fifty years'); and *Much Ado About Nothing* ('Never acted there before'). In the 1735/36 season, the plays of Shakespeare had constituted 14 per cent of all performances given in London theatres; in the following season this figure was 17 per cent and in the next one 22 per cent.[16] The Ladies were praised in the newspapers and in prologues and epilogues for persuading 'the Town' to 'neglect and despise Harlequin and his harlot Columbine for Shakespeare and his lawful spouse Common Sense'.[17] They were credited with awakening the 'manly genius of Eliza's days', in contrast to the effeminacy of Italian opera.[18]

But how did they do it? How did they get John Rich, despised by all right-thinking people for debasing the stage with pantomimes,[19] to put on four Shakespeare plays at Covent Garden in five months that had rarely been seen in the eighteenth century? Did the Ladies offer managers some sort of subsidy or subscription, whereby ticket sales would be guaranteed up to a certain level? We don't know, nor do we know who Shakespeare's Ladies were: not a single name has surfaced in the records. However, they left a physical memorial of their veneration for the Bard which would have a long-lasting influence. On 28 April 1738, Drury Lane put on a performance of *Julius Caesar* 'towards raising a fund for erecting a monument to the memory of Shakespeare'. Nearly £200 was raised for a monument that was unveiled in Westminster Abbey on 29 January 1741. Designed by William Kent, it contained a statue of Shakespeare by the Flemish sculptor Peter Scheemakers, showing him in the now familiar pose of leaning on a plinth and pointing to a scroll containing lines from *The Tempest*. Shakespeare was now well and truly part of the establishment, his image surrounded by those of kings, queens and heroes in the national Valhalla.

David Garrick had a genuine love of Shakespeare and a sense of national pride in the greatness of the plays. He also had a strong desire to link himself with Shakespeare in the public mind, and to make Drury Lane a temple to his god:

> *Sacred to Shakespeare was this spot design'd,*
> *To pierce the heart and humanize the mind.*[20]

As the table opposite shows, he achieved a considerable measure of success. He burst upon the public as Richard III and soon added more of the great Shakespearean roles to his repertoire, like Hamlet, Macbeth and Romeo. However, he didn't just stick with the established

Shakespeare's Plays by Number of Performances under Garrick's Management

Title of Play	Total # of Performances	Performances with Garrick Acting	Place in Ranking*
Romeo and Juliet	142	64	9
Hamlet	116	56	16
Much Ado About Nothing	105	104	19
Richard III	100	35	22
Cymbeline	98	16	23
King Lear	83	56	30
The Tempest	79	0	34
Macbeth	77	21	37
As You Like It	59	0	54
Henry VIII	54	0	61
Othello	52	7	65
The Merchant of Venice	52	0	66
Catharine and Petruchio (The Taming of The Shrew)	48	0	75
Twelfth Night	47	0	77
The Winter's Tale	25	23	121
Measure For Measure	22	0	134
Henry IV Part 2	21	15	139
King John	20	8	145
Merry Wives of Windsor	17	0	158
Henry IV Part 1	12	0	188
Timon of Athens	11	0	206
All's Well that Ends Well	9	0	221
Coriolanus	9	0	225
Antony and Cleopatra	6	6	256
Two Gentlemen of Verona	6	0	261
Henry V	5	0	267
A Midsummer Night's Dream	1	0	357

* Ranking in the 377 productions presented by Garrick between 1747 and 1776

Source: *Drury Lane Calendar 1747-1776*, MacMillan, 1938; *The Theatrical Public in the Time of Garrick*, Pedicord, 1954; plus author's calculations

favourites: he put on the first production of *Antony and Cleopatra* since Shakespeare's day and made Benedick in *Much Ado About Nothing*, which had scarcely been performed in the eighteenth century, into his most popular Shakespearean role. The texts in use at the time were not pure Shakespeare: they had been 'improved' by various hands since the Restoration in order to make Shakespeare acceptable to a more polite age. Garrick took over these 'improved' versions – he performed King Lear in Nahum Tate's version with the happy ending – but he also did a lot of work on the texts to put back more of Shakespeare's lines. Garrick was able to work with the greatest Shakespearean scholars of the day, not only his old friend Samuel Johnson but also William Warburton and Edward Capell, who would both bring out important editions of Shakespeare's plays. Garrick restored hundreds of lines and whole scenes that had been cut for years: his Shakespeare wasn't undiluted Shakespeare, but it was certainly a purer mixture than anything seen since the reopening of the theatres in 1660.

Garrick is often credited with the creation of Bardolatry:[21] the idea that Shakespeare wasn't just another playwright, he was the greatest writer in the history of literature and the greatest Englishman who ever lived, a man whose pre-eminence on the stage was a symbol of Britain's superiority over other nations. Garrick certainly had a better claim to being the first priest of this cult than anyone else, as he actually built a temple to Shakespeare in the garden of his riverside villa at Twickenham in 1755.✢ Designed by Garrick's friend Robert Adam, the temple contained a statue of Shakespeare that Garrick commissioned from the French sculptor Louis Francois Roubiliac. This work, which now stands in the entrance to the British Library, is a masterpiece of a completely different order to the rather pedestrian figure in Westminster Abbey. It shows Shakespeare leaning on his writing desk,

---

✢ The actor and satirist Samuel Foote wrote that 'Mr Garrick... has... dedicated a temple to a certain divinity... before whose shrine frequent libations are made, and on whose altar the fat of venison, a viand grateful to the deity, is often seen to smoak' (McIntyre, 99). There was a legend that Shakespeare had to flee Stratford after being caught poaching deer in Charlecote Park.

> **In Rep: Plays Performed at Drury Lane During w/c 18 November 1765**
> Date in brackets is year of first performance
>
> Date of performance, *Play* and playwright
>
> Monday 18 November, *The London Merchant* by George Lillo (1731) followed by *Harlequin's Invasion* by David Garrick (1759)
> Tuesday 19 November, *The School for Lovers* by William Whitehead (1761) followed by *Harlequin's Invasion* by David Garrick (1759)
> Wednesday 20 November, *Cymbeline* by William Shakespeare (1610) followed by *Daphne and Amintor* by Isaac Bickerstaffe (1765)
> Thursday 21 November, *Tancred and Sigismunda* by James Thomson (1745) followed by *Harlequin's Invasion* by David Garrick (1759)
> Friday 22 November, *Much Ado About Nothing* by William Shakespeare (1598) followed by *The Devil to Pay* by Charles Coffey (1731)
> Saturday 23 November, *King Lear* by William Shakespeare (1605) followed by *Harlequin's Invasion* by David Garrick (1759)

a quill pen in his right hand and his chin thoughtfully resting on his left hand. Garrick is said to have been the model, which may account for the paunch bursting through the buttons of Shakespeare's waistcoat.

Towards the end of the next decade, an opportunity presented itself to Garrick to identify himself even more clearly with his idol. The corporation of Stratford-upon-Avon had decided to rebuild their town hall, and they had the bright idea of getting a contribution towards it from Garrick. A councillor called Francis Wheler, who was Steward of the Stratford Court of Records, wrote to Garrick asking if the town might be permitted to honour him for his work in raising the reputation of Stratford's most famous son by including in this new town hall either a statue or a portrait of Shakespeare, together with another of Garrick, 'that the memory of both may be perpetuated together in that place which gave him birth'.[22] Garrick was supposed to pay for these. As a sweetener, they offered to make him a Freeman of the borough.

Garrick was delighted, and could see immediately the value of linking his name with Shakespeare's in a more lasting way than his acting ever could. He agreed to the request and spoke to Gainsborough about a painting of Shakespeare. Garrick changed his mind when Gainsborough made what he considered disrespectful remarks about the Bard, and he gave the commission to a lesser artist called Benjamin Wilson. However he had also decided to present the borough with a statue of Shakespeare to fill an empty niche on the front of the new town hall. He didn't intend to part with his beautiful statue by Roubiliac, nor did he want to commission a copy as the original had cost him £315, but he found a cheaper solution. A man called John Cheere was running a successful workshop at Hyde Park Corner churning out lead copies of famous statues to be used as garden ornaments. Garrick commissioned a lead statue of Shakespeare, based on the Scheemakers figure in Westminster Abbey. By this stage Garrick, who was careful with money, thought that he had spent enough, and suggested to the town council that they should bear the cost of the portrait of himself to hang beside the one of Shakespeare. The councillors agreed and found themselves committed to paying 60 guineas – £63 – to Thomas Gainsborough, the leading portrait painter of the day (who had been forgiven for his earlier saucy remarks).❖

The scroll awarding Garrick the freedom of the borough was to be presented to him in a wooden box carved from mulberry wood. This wood had supposedly come from the mulberry tree in the garden of Shakespeare's last house in Stratford, New Place, that had been cut down in an act of cultural vandalism by the owner of the house in 1756. The logs were purchased by a local entrepreneur who produced so many mulberry wood souvenirs that nothing less than a forest of mulberries would have sufficed. Nevertheless, Garrick was delighted with the tribute, and received the box, and the scroll, from a deputation of members of the Corporation who travelled to London and met him at his house in Southampton Street on 8 May 1769. The next day, the *St James's Chronicle* carried an account of the presentation, together with the announcement that, to celebrate the creation of Stratford's first Freeman, a jubilee would be held in Stratford the following

---

❖ The lead statue still graces the front of the Town Hall in Stratford, but Gainsborough's portrait, which Mrs Garrick pronounced the best likeness of her husband ever painted, was destroyed in a fire in 1946.

September. Garrick would be the steward of the jubilee, 'in honour and to the memory of Shakespeare', and the new town hall would be dedicated to Shakespeare's memory.[23]

This was a bold step. Stratford was a long way from London and travelling there was difficult. It was not a tourist centre: scarcely anyone, beyond a handful of scholars and antiquaries, had thought it worthwhile to visit the birthplace of Shakespeare, so there were few places to stay. Furthermore, Garrick had left himself only four months to organise the Jubilee. Nevertheless, he was at the height of his powers and popularity, and was convinced he could bring it off.

In June he went to Stratford to meet with the councillors and to discuss arrangements. His head was already full of possible events, but the pressing question was, who was going to pay for it? Garrick proposed that costs should be shared between the Corporation and himself, and that any profits would be split between them. The Corporation refused. Plan B then came into place, which was for Garrick to form an *ad hoc* committee of funders, including William Hunt, the Town Clerk, and John Payton, the proprietor of the White Hart, Stratford's only hotel, and a few other enthusiastic supporters. In the end, Garrick bore almost all the costs himself.

In the first week of September, Garrick set out for Stratford, followed by the entire company, orchestra and chorus of Drury Lane. The Jubilee was to run from Wednesday 6 September to Friday 8 September, and the first day went quite well, with an oratorio in the church followed by a dinner and ball in the Rotunda, a large temporary structure erected on what are now the Bancroft Gardens in front of the theatre. The main events were to take place on the Thursday: a pageant of actors dressed as Shakespeare's characters would parade through the town to the Rotunda, where Garrick would deliver an Ode to Shakespeare. In the course of the Ode, Garrick would crown the statue of Shakespeare he was donating to the town with a wreath of laurel, then the statue would be taken through the streets and lifted into its niche on the front of the new Town Hall.

Unfortunately, on the Thursday it poured with rain from before dawn, and the pageant had to be cancelled after James Lacy warned

Garrick that, if it went ahead, he would have to be prepared for £5,000 of damage to the Drury Lane costumes. Garrick had to go into the Ode 'cold', in front of a rather wet and disgruntled audience in the Rotunda. He had written it himself and Thomas Arne had composed the music. For the first time, passages of spoken poetry were interwoven with orchestral and choral music, involving over a hundred musicians and singers. It was a complete triumph, and even the sternest critics of the Jubilee admitted that the Ode represented one of the high points in Garrick's career. The poetry wasn't up to much, and the chauvinistic references to Shakespeare as a demi-god and national hero now seem faintly ridiculous:

> To what blest genius of the isle
> Shall gratitude her tribute pay?...
> 'Tis he! 'Tis he!
> The god of our idolatry!

Nevertheless, Garrick was a master showman, and he held the audience spellbound. When he spoke of 'the silver Avon' and the white swans on its bosom, he had the stagehands throw open the enormous doors at the back of the Rotunda to reveal the actual Avon flowing past. A wonderful *coup de theatre*, but worryingly the Avon was beginning to burst its banks and no swans were to be seen on its now all-too-ample bosom, as they had made themselves scarce in the downpour.

Dinner was to be followed by a magnificent firework display but it turned out to be (literally) a damp squib. Then, at 11 p.m., the masked ball began. By this time, the water was lapping around the edge of the Rotunda, and the guests arrived with mud splattered all over their white silk stockings. Nevertheless, it was all quite jolly until, just after dawn, it was announced that everyone must leave immediately as there was a danger of the Rotunda being washed away in a flood. There was nothing for it but to wade through the water, several feet deep in places, back to dry land, although some of the more gallant gentlemen gave the ladies piggy-backs. Most of the next day's events were cancelled and everyone hurried back to London.

Garrick had lost a lot of money on the Jubilee – something in the region of £2,000 – and it could not be said to have been either a great popular or critical success. The Ode had been a triumph, but the cancelled pageant, soggy fireworks and waterlogged masquerade coloured everyone's view. Those who had mocked the idea of a Jubilee throughout the summer had a field day, but Garrick set about salvaging what he could. On 30 September he gave a performance of the Ode on the stage of Drury Lane, this time with his Roubiliac statue of Shakespeare brought from Twickenham to stand in for the lead figure that now graced the Town Hall in Stratford. It was very well received, and he repeated it several times during the season. But the real payback came on 14 October when the performance of *The School for Rakes* was followed by an afterpiece called *The Jubilee* 'in which will be introduced the pageant as it was intended for Stratford-upon-Avon'.

The Jubilee opened with a scene of comical rustics speculating about the 'Jubillo' and all the fuss it was causing in their little town, threatening to bring Popery and ravishings galore. This was followed by a realistic depiction of the courtyard of the White Hart Inn, with waiters rushing hither and thither attending to the demands of the guests, who all rushed off at the end of the scene to see the pageant. Here was the pageant as it should have been, with the weather firmly under control this time. Every single member of the company had been roped in, supported by 115 extras, the entire wardrobe and scenic resources of the theatre to create a spectacle such as had never been seen before. Groups of characters from 19 of Shakespeare's plays appeared, dancing and miming key scenes: the casket scene from the *Merchant of Venice*; Fluellen making Pistol eat the leek; Beatrice and Benedick teasing each other. Several of the sequences involved spectacular effects: a storm-tossed ship in *The Tempest*; Cleopatra on her barge; Oberon and Titania in a carriage drawn by fairies and butterflies; Falstaff and the Merry Wives of Windsor on horseback. Processions had been popular in theatres since the Restoration, but nothing like this had ever been seen before. It was described by William Hopkins, the prompter, as 'the most superb that ever was exhibited or

I believe ever will. There was never an entertainment produc'd that gave so much pleasure to all degrees, boxes, pit and gallery.'[24]

The Jubilee enjoyed a spectacular and unprecedented success. It was given for 28 nights consecutively and 71 times that season. It remained in the repertoire for years and made so much money that it has been estimated that Garrick recouped his losses on the real Jubilee four times over.[25] It was a triumph for Garrick and his campaign to establish Shakespeare as a writer and national hero of unique stature. The final scene showed Venus, the Muses and the Graces dancing before a magnificent transparency representing Shakespeare being crowned by Tragedy and Comedy, surrounded by his characters. Shakespeare would never again be judged as just another playwright. He had ascended to Mount Parnassus.

The irony was that Garrick had celebrated the genius of Shakespeare as the greatest writer of all time by using techniques of music, spectacle and dancing developed for pantomime. In fact, there were strong echoes in The Jubilee of a pantomime Garrick had written in 1759 called Harlequin's Invasion, in which the powers of pantomime invade the realm of King Shakespeare. They are repulsed, and a final spectacular tableau reveals a huge silk-screen transparency representing a statue of Shakespeare. Harlequin's Invasion was a great success, the third most popular production of Garrick's management, but like The Jubilee (which was the seventh), it allowed the audience to feel good about Shakespeare as a national hero without the effort of sitting through one of his plays. Whatever Garrick's private opinion of pantomime, he wasn't going to deprive the audience of their favourite form of entertainment that paid the bills and made him a rich man. It is greatly to his credit that he was able to perform the balancing act that so many other managers of Drury Lane found difficult, of putting on popular spectaculars and performances of Shakespeare that had people fighting to get in. If pantomimes represented 21 per cent of performances of the top 50 shows under his management, Shakespeare accounted for 15 per cent – no mean achievement given the commercial environment in which Garrick was operating. He would be buried at the foot of Shakespeare's statue in Westminster Abbey with verses on his tombstone that conclude:

Shakespeare and Garrick like twin stars shall shine,
And earth irradiate with a beam divine.

Garrick's name would be forever linked to the god of his idolatry.
He deserved it.

Mezzotint of Gainborough's portrait of David Garrick,
painted to hang in the Town Hall at Stratford-upon-Avon.

13

The Last Years of Garrick's Drury Lane

In January 1774, James Lacy, Garrick's partner of 27 years, died. Under the terms of their agreement, Garrick had first refusal of Lacy's share in Drury Lane, but he did not exercise it, so it went to Lacy's 25-year-old son Willoughby. Garrick had already decided to dispose of his own share in the theatre and retire, so, at the end of the 1774/75 theatre season, he called in the builders for the last time. Over the years he and Lacy had made constant alterations to the structure of the building to increase the capacity of the house from about 1,000 to an estimated 2,362. The building was now a hundred years old and it was time to spruce the old place up and put it into a glittering new garb to get the best price.

Garrick called in his friend Robert Adam to do the job. Adam had designed Garrick's temple to Shakespeare at Twickenham and Garrick had helped Adam out by taking one of the first houses in his bold, speculative development The Adelphi in 1772. Adam's brief was not to increase capacity again: it appears that the house was already quite big enough, if not a little too big, for the level of demand, and it may be that Adam's alterations actually reduced this a bit. Unfortunately it is very difficult to establish exactly what Adam did as no accounts have survived and, although we have engravings of the auditorium after the changes, there are none from before.

The most noticeable and famous of the alterations was the addition
of a handsome new frontage on Bridges Street, giving the theatre its first
architectural presence on what had always been, and still is, the main
entrance. However, this was only a facade: the arches in the classical

Robert Adam's new street frontage for the Theatre Royal
on Bridges Street, 1775.

temple-front simply gave on to the long passages that led to the auditorium, still in the middle of the site. The auditorium was redecorated with the usual elegant Adam motifs and a brilliant arrangement of coloured foil and glass set into the pilasters to give the space more glitter and light, but it is difficult to know what alterations Adam made to the seating. It seems that new side-boxes were created in what had been the slips of the gallery, and the ceiling was raised by twelve feet, which improved the acoustics, but there would not have been time for any major structural alterations. The previous season had closed on 27 May and the new season opened on 23 September, giving Adam just four months. The new dress for the Old Lady of Drury Lane was much admired, and the first night audience burst into applause before the show had even started. Garrick could now begin negotiating the sale.

He had promised first refusal to George Colman, his former collaborator on *The Clandestine Marriage* and now manager of Covent Garden, but Colman was only interested in acquiring 100 per cent and Willoughby Lacy now had his father's half-share. So Garrick sold his half of Drury Lane, for £35,000, to a group of three people: Dr James Ford, Physician Extraordinary to the Queen; Thomas Linley, musician and composer; and Thomas Linley's son-in-law, Richard Brinsley Sheridan. The three partners divided Garrick's £35,000 share between them in £5,000 units: Ford took three, Linley and Sheridan two each. Ford was a wealthy man and seems to have had no difficulty finding the money; Linley was able to mortgage property in Bath; but Sheridan had no ready funds. Garrick must have wondered where his £10,000 was coming from as Sheridan had borrowed £200 from him only a few weeks before. In fact, the only way Sheridan could get the money together was to raise several mortgages against the theatre itself. From the very start, his management of Drury Lane was founded on what his biographer Walter Sichel called 'the quicksands of loans and mortgages'.[1]

The contract was signed on 18 January 1776 and word spread quickly that this was to be the Garrick's last season. He gave farewell performance of his great parts – Benedick, Lear and Richard III – and showed that he had lost none of his power: Joshua Reynolds said it took him three days to get over the emotional trauma of seeing one of the final performances of Lear. Garrick gave what was supposed to be his final performance of Richard III on 3 June, then received a royal command for another, to take place two days later. 'It will absolutely kill me,' Garrick wrote to friend,[2] as he found the part exhausting. The house was so packed, it was found that they had admitted more people than there were places and the disturbance caused the actors to leave the stage while it was sorted out. According to the Drury Lane prompter, 'the King sent two messages to Mr G. to desire that he would not let this noise disconcert him and his Majesty would take care that all should be quiet before the play began'.[3] And then, on 10 June, came the farewell performance. Garrick decided not to go out with a Shakespearean role: he chose a comedy by Susanna Centlivre called *The Wonder* and donated the profits from the evening to the Theatrical Fund charity.✢ He had composed a special prologue to bid farewell, but at the end of the play he came forward to address the audience in plain speech, to avoid 'the jingle of rhyme and the language of fiction'.[4] He thanked the public for kindness and favours shown over many years in that actual building, and, placing his hand on his heart, he promised to be forever grateful for their support. For once, the old expression that 'there wasn't a dry eye in the house' was literally true. The play was meant to be followed by a ballad opera, but the audience didn't want it and the cast were in no state to perform.

At last, the sun had set on the golden age of Drury Lane. Garrick's stature in theatre history is unique, and deservedly so. He had many qualities that contributed to his success. The most obvious one was that he was a truly great actor. Had he never gone into management, he would still have been famous. His success as a manager was due to his strong instinct for what the public wanted, coupled with a sincere desire to raise the level of public taste, especially for Shakespeare. His management had seen many physical changes at Drury Lane, much to the improvement of

---

✢ It was said that Garrick realised that the evening would be an emotional one, and didn't want to cope with the trauma of bidding farewell to his public after a gruelling part like Richard III – the most obvious candidate for a farewell role.

the house. The auditorium had been expanded and all ancillary services improved, on a very difficult site. The theatre had been given an imposing frontage onto Bridges Street. He had cleared spectators from the stage for good. He pioneered advances in lighting by introducing footlights that could sink into a trough and battens of lights set in the wings that could be rotated. It became possible, for the first time, to raise or lower the level of light during a performance and to get rid of the enormous chandeliers that used to hang over the stage. He brought to Drury Lane the brilliant set designer Philippe de Loutherbourg, who tried to co-ordinate all aspects of the look of a show – lighting, scenery, machinery and costumes. This had never been done before. De Loutherbourg achieved extraordinarily beautiful effects and came to be regarded as the most important designer for the stage since Inigo Jones.

Equally important as all of these things, though, was Garrick's absolute decency and integrity. Drury Lane had seen its fair share of swindlers and rogues, and would see many more, but Garrick was completely honest in all of his dealings. Contracts were honoured and actors, staff and suppliers paid on time. The theatre had enjoyed a period of unprecedented prosperity, delighting audiences and making big profits. Garrick's private life was above reproach. He had married for love, at the age of 32, a beautiful young Austrian dancer who performed under the name of Violette. He would not allow her to appear in public after that as it was not considered respectable for a married woman to show her legs on the stage, and he wanted a conventional home life. Neither of them was ever touched by the slightest suggestion of scandal, which was remarkable in view of the fact that most actresses of that time would have regarded it as almost part of the job to exchange sexual favours with the management in return for parts and status in the company.✤ Dr Johnson's tribute

---

✤ Dora Jordan was effectively raped by Richard Daly, the manager of the Smock Alley Theatre in Dublin, when she made her début there at the age of 20. Daly had a reputation for sexually harassing all of his actresses, and Mrs Jordan's first biographer, her friend James Boaden, explained that: 'the resistance of the fair to a *manager* may be somewhat modified by the danger of offending one, who has the power to appoint them to parts, either striking or otherwise' (Tomalin, 22).

to Garrick, that he had 'advanced the dignity of his profession',[5] was true. Actors didn't all become respectable overnight, but they were no longer rogues and vagabonds either. Garrick had made acting, in Burke's words, 'a liberal art'.[6] Writing up the farewell performance in his notebook, the Drury Lane prompter was moved to quote from Hamlet: 'I can only say, "I shall not look upon his like again".'[7]

Another triumvirate

Once again, Drury Lane was under the control of a triumvirate, but this time its members were not equally matched. James Ford was a fashionable gynaecologist who appears to have taken very little active part in running the theatre, which he regarded mainly as an investment. Thomas Linley was a popular musician and the head of a large and talented musical family, but his status was entirely overshadowed by that of his son-in-law, Richard Brinsley Sheridan.

Sheridan's life was so extraordinary that it seems more like something from the Penny Plain, Tuppence Coloured melodramas of Regency toy theatres than real life. The term we would now use for most of it is 'way over the top'. There could scarcely have been a greater contrast between his style of management and Garrick's.

He was born in Dublin in 1751, the second surviving son of Thomas Sheridan, the most famous actor-manager in the country. Sheridan senior came from a family of run-down gentry with a small estate in Cavan. He had been educated at Westminster and Trinity College, Dublin, then at the age of 23 he burst upon an astonished public at the Smock Alley Theatre as Richard III. He had been inspired to act by seeing Garrick at the same theatre in the previous year, and in 1745 Thomas Sheridan took over the management of the theatre, working in partnership with Garrick for a season while Garrick was weighing up the options open to him in London. Garrick was 28 at the time and Sheridan was only 25, but he made a great success of Smock Alley until it was destroyed by a rioting audience in 1754. Sheridan was ruined and came to London, but returned to Dublin two years later to take up the management of the now restored theatre again. This time it was competition that did for him: the actor Spranger Barry set up a rival theatre in Crow Street and took most of his best actors. Sheridan rented out his estate, put the furniture up for auction and went to London again, probably to escape his creditors. Initially Richard stayed behind in Ireland with his sister, but they both joined their parents at their house in Henrietta Street, Covent Garden, when Richard was eight. He never went back to Ireland.

Thomas Sheridan now set himself up as a teacher of oratory and elocution and an educational reformer. The house in Henrietta Street became the haunt of well-known figures from the world of letters, including Dr Johnson, who liked Mrs Sheridan rather more than her husband. Richard was sent to Harrow while his parents, still being pursued by creditors, went to live in France, where his mother died. Richard left Harrow at 17, presumably because there was no more money for fees, and went to live with his father in Frith Street, Soho. Two years later, Thomas Sheridan moved his family to Bath, the most fashionable watering-hole for the gentry in England by that time, where he first tried to start a school, then devised what were called Attic Entertainments, mixing poetry and music.

As a centre for entertainment and the arts, Bath was second only to London. Actors, writers, painters, singers, musicians and architects flocked to the place where large numbers of the idle rich were looking for ways to amuse themselves. When the Sheridans arrived, Thomas Linley's family of brilliant musical siblings, described by Burney as a 'nest of nightingales', was already well-established, and the most celebrated of them all was Elizabeth, a sixteen-year-old beauty. She appeared with Thomas Sheridan in his Attic Entertainments, and soon the young Linleys and the young Sheridans were firm friends. Elizabeth's amazing good looks and stunning soprano voice made her a celebrity. She was painted four times by Gainsborough and was able to command large fees for her appearances. A girl like that was clearly not going to be short of admirers, especially in Bath, which was something of a marriage mart, and both Richard Sheridan and his elder brother Charles were love-struck. Charles decided to put the infatuation out of his head, as he had no intention of marrying into showbusiness, but Richard's attachment was more serious. Thomas Linley had other ideas for his valuable daughter, however, and arranged a marriage with a wealthy man in his fifties, Walter Long. Elizabeth objected and Long behaved like a gentleman: he agreed to be the party responsible for breaking off the engagement and settled £3,000 a year on Elizabeth in compensation. She was then pursued – or stalked, in modern parlance – by a very much less desirable character, a debauched old roué who styled himself, without entitlement, Captain Mathews. Elizabeth seems to have been brought to the verge of a nervous breakdown by Mathews's persistent attentions and contemplated suicide. News of her state of mind came to Sheridan's sisters, who spoke to their brother about a plot to save the young lady. She wished to live in a convent in France until she came of age, and would use part of the money settled on her by Long to compensate her father for his loss of her earnings. Sheridan immediately fell in with this romantic plot and sent a sedan chair to collect her from the Linleys' house in the Royal Crescent and take her to a waiting coach on the London Road. The two of them set out for London, with a maid acting as chaperone, and then across the channel to Dunkirk. Sheridan, who had behaved completely honourably and took care never to allow Elizabeth to be compromised, now told her of his love, which she had not suspected up until that time. Elizabeth was won and they were married in a Catholic church outside Calais. At that point Thomas Linley arrived, pointed out that the marriage was invalid as they were both underage and Protestants, and got them to agree to return to Bath so that Elizabeth could fulfil her commitments.

Once back in Bath, the young couple were forbidden to see each other as both fathers objected strongly to the idea of a union. Thomas Sheridan wanted his son to marry above himself socially, not into the theatre, and Thomas Linley had no intention of allowing his precious daughter to marry a young man with no money and no prospects. Richard and Elizabeth kept in contact through secret letters and meetings, using fictional names, but then Richard discovered that Mathews had inserted a paragraph in the *Bath Chronicle* in his absence calling him a liar and a scoundrel. He challenged Mathews to a duel, which he won, and forced his opponent to make a further announcement in the *Bath Chronicle* retracting his allegations and begging forgiveness. Mathews went back to Wales where he found himself the object of public detestation, so he challenged Richard again. This time he very nearly killed his rival and fled the scene. Sheridan survived and became a romantic hero in Bath, but the lovers were still kept apart and Sheridan was sent by his father to study law in London. Elizabeth bombarded him with love letters but he had made a solemn promise to his father not to be in touch with her and he seems to have kept it, even when she was appearing at Drury Lane in the Lenten oratorios. Eventually she wrote to him to break it off and demanded the return of her letters. Two months later they were married.

Sheridan forbade his wife from ever singing in public again, although it meant turning down engagements that would have brought them thousands of pounds within the first year of their marriage. He was the husband of a very famous wife, but he was determined to make his own way in the world. Success through the law seemed a very slow process, so he gave up his legal studies and decided to set up as a writer. Thomas Harris, the manager of Covent Garden, had become a frequent visitor to the Sheridans' London home, trying to persuade Elizabeth to sing for him. In the course of a conversation, he suggested to Sheridan that he might like to try his hand at writing a play. The play, which opened at Covent Garden on 19 January 1775, was *The Rivals*.

The first night was not a huge success. The play was felt to be too long, the actors seemed under-rehearsed and the character of Sir Lucius O'Trigger was taken as an insult to the Irish. Sheridan withdrew it and spent the next ten days doing a complete rewrite. Its second performance was a great success and made Sheridan the talk of the town. The story of a beautiful young woman in Bath, pursued by rich old men but in love with a handsome young one who wants to elope and who fights a duel for her, reminded everyone of the Sheridans' own romantic story. The play established itself as a popular favourite and has always remained so.

Ten months later, Sheridan followed it with a three-act comic opera called *The Duenna*. He wrote the libretto and got his father-in-law to set the songs, without telling him what the plot was about. This was perhaps because the story of a beautiful young singer who runs away to a convent to escape her parents' attempts to marry her off to a rich old man would have been a bit close to home. Linley was busy in Bath while the show was in rehearsal and couldn't write all of the music, some of which was composed by his more talented son, Thomas junior. Not all of the tunes were original, many being based on Italian operas and Scottish ballads. The show was an even bigger hit than *The Rivals*, with 75 performances in its first season – more than *The Beggar's Opera*.

The Duenna is seldom performed now, although *The Rivals* has never lost its appeal. The fact that Sheridan, coming out of nowhere as it were, had produced these huge hits by the time he was 24 was an indication of his precocious brilliance, and this was the young man who, a few months later, would take over Drury Lane. It looked as if he would have no trouble writing plays to fill the benches, although as Garrick would have been well aware, there is more to running a theatre than that.

In Rep: Plays Performed at Drury Lane During w/c 11 November 1776
Date in brackets is year of first performance

Date of performance, *Play* and playwright

Monday 11 November, *The Maid of the Oaks* by John Burgoyne (1774) followed by *Bon Ton* by David Garrick (1774)
Tuesday 12 November, *Cymbeline* by William Shakespeare (1610) followed by *A Christmas Tale* by David Garrick (1773)
Wednesday 13 November, *The Maid of the Oaks* by John Burgoyne (1774) followed by *The Waterman* by Charles Dibdin (1775)
Thursday 14 November, *The Clandestine Marriage* by David Garrick and George Colman Sr (1766) followed by *A Christmas Tale* by David Garrick (1773)
Friday 15 November, *The Hypocrite* altered from Colley Cibber's *The Nonjuror* by Isaac Bickerstaffe (1768) followed by *Bon Ton* by David Garrick (1774)
Saturday 16 November, *The Roman Father* by William Whitehead (1750) followed by *A Christmas Tale* by David Garrick (1773)

The new régime

The first season under new management at Drury Lane opened on 21 September 1776 with a very full programme. First, there was a specially written 'prelude' called, appropriately, *New Brooms*; this was followed by *Twelfth Night*, then Garrick's popular afterpiece *Miss In Her Teens*. Garrick himself had generously written a prologue to the season to get his successors off to a good start.

In spite of the title of the prelude, there was nothing of the new broom about this first season. It was business as usual, with the repertoire that had worked so well for Garrick. Shakespeare was well represented, with 44 performances of ten plays; the Restoration authors were still strong, both in comedy and tragedy, with popular plays by Congreve, Otway and Lee; Steele's *The Conscious Lovers* and Garrick's *Clandestine Marriage* were trusty old war-horses. The tradition of performing Nicholas Rowe's *Tamerlane* on either 4 November (William III's birthday) or 5 November (the anniversary of his landing at Torbay) was maintained in support of liberty and the Protestant religion;✣ and *George Barnwell* was still giving its uplifting moralising message to the London apprentices.

There was a change in the public taste, however, and Sheridan was quick to detect it. He loved the Restoration authors, and according to his friend and later musical director Michael Kelly, his favourite poet was Dryden: he could quote reams when he was in his cups.[8] Unfortunately the times were becoming more proper, and according to the playwright Frederick Reynolds, who worked with Sheridan and published his memoirs in 1826: 'the dramatists of former periods have been denounced as the cause of corrupting the morals of unsophisticated persons of both sexes; and whilst poor Congreve, Vanbrugh and Wycherley are said to be suffering in purgatory, Killigrew, Davenant, and other Charles the Second wits, are supposed to be enduring more decided punishment.'[9]

✣ The tradition ended at Drury Lane in 1780, but continued for a few more years at Covent Garden. In Rowe's version of the story, Tamerlane was supposed to represent William III and the tyrant Bajazet Louis XIV.

Tut, tut. We tend to associate prudery with the Victorians and view their Regency forbears as being altogether more laid-back, but at the time people saw themselves as far more refined than their ancestors of a hundred years before. The plays which had set pit, boxes and gallery in a roar at the end of seventeenth century were simply too indecent for the end of the eighteenth. Trying to keep at least some of them in the repertoire, Sheridan revised two of Congreve's plays – *The Old Batchelor*, which hadn't been acted at Drury Lane for 18 years, and *Love For Love* (not acted for five years). He hoped that by taking out the smut and the *double-entrendres* he could keep them going for a bit longer, but he wasn't happy about doing it. 'His plays,' Sheridan told Michael Kelly, 'are, I own, somewhat licentious, but it is barbarous to mangle them; they are like horses, when you deprive them of their vice, they lose their vigour.'[10] That didn't stop him from gelding Vanbrugh's stallion *The Relapse* with a pretty thorough re-write. Sheridan's shortened version, called *A Trip to Scarborough*, took the edge off Vanbrugh's satire with sentiment and moralising. Nevertheless, when it opened on 24 February 1777 it was a success, and stayed in the repertoire for many years.

This modest success was nothing compared with the surprise Sheridan had for his audience in May, when the opening night of his comedy *The School for Scandal* entered theatrical legend. This time, there were no teething troubles, as with *The Rivals*: it seemed to its first-night audience to be absolutely perfect. Its success would be immediate and overwhelming. *The School for Scandal* became the most valuable theatrical property of its day and Sheridan would never allow it to be published during his lifetime, as he wanted to keep it exclusive to Drury Lane. It took £15,000 in its first two seasons and was performed more often than any other play in London until the end of the century. Its first night gave rise to one of the great Drury Lane stories. Frederick Reynolds, then a twelve-year-old schoolboy, was making his way back to Westminster School after visiting a friend in Lincoln's Inn Fields. He was walking past the theatre at nine o'clock when he heard such a roar that he imagined the building was collapsing and fled for his life.[11] The next day he discovered that what he had heard was the reaction of the audience to the falling of the screen in the fourth act, which reveals Lady Teazle to her astounded husband in the rooms of a single man.

In his second season, Sheridan consolidated his control of Drury Lane by increasing his share of the business. Linley, Ford and Sheridan had only acquired Garrick's half-share of Drury Lane: the other half belonged to Willoughby Lacy, the son of Garrick's partner James Lacy. Willoughby Lacy had mortgaged his share to Garrick and was having difficulty in keeping up the payments, so in 1776, just as the triumvirate were taking over, he sold his share to two men called Abraham Langford and Edward Thompson. As soon as the triumvirs heard about it, they claimed that the original agreement between Garrick and James Lacy was still in force, and that Willoughby should have offered them first refusal. Willoughby backed down, but two years later he sold his share to Sheridan for £31,500, plus two annuities of £500 for life to Mrs Lacy and Abraham Langford, to whom Lacy owed a great deal of money. This made Sheridan the majority shareholder, owning nine-fourteenths of the theatre, but raising the money put him in an even more complicated financial position, loaded with

The screen scene from *The School for Scandal* (1777).

mortgages, loans and guarantees. The theatre had just enjoyed a spectacularly successful season, and there was every reason to think that, if Sheridan kept churning out hit plays, the money would come in to service all of these debts. Unfortunately Sheridan was already losing interest in the theatre, and would shortly give up writing plays.

It is one of the great paradoxes of Sheridan that he placed a low value on, and even partly despised, the sphere in which he seemed destined to shine. He used to say that he had never sat through any play from beginning to end except his own, and that may have been true. He didn't particularly enjoy the company of actors and was so awkward when he visited the Green Room that the actors asked him to stay away, as he put a blight on the conversation. In 1775, during Garrick's last season at Drury Lane, he discovered that one of his wife's sisters had been invited to join the company, and wrote to his father-in-law advising against it in the strongest terms. He described the theatre as 'the greatest nursery of vice and misery on the face of the earth' and actresses as 'corrupted by the operation of their trade... everything around them is unchaste – their studies are lessons of vice and passion'.[12] This is the sort of language we would expect from Puritans who closed theatres down, not from the man who was about to take over the management of the Theatre Royal.

Sheridan did not want to be regarded as a man of the theatre. He wanted to be a wit, a member of high society and a gentleman. He was becoming seriously interested in politics, and regarded the House of Commons as a more important platform than the stage of Drury Lane. He was happy to use his proprietorship of Drury Lane as a springboard for these things, but he didn't intend to allow the theatre to engross his time. He needed someone to manage its day-to-day affairs, and in 1780 he appointed his father Thomas. His relationship with his father as manager would be fractious and unsatisfactory, just like his relationships with all of his subsequent managers, because he wasn't prepared to put in the hours and he didn't put the theatre first in his list of priorities. Theatres don't run themselves: they are complex and demanding organisations that require the complete attention of whoever is in charge, and it was for this reason that the affairs of Drury Lane got into a mess almost immediately. The contrast between Sheridan and Garrick, who had lived and breathed the theatre for his whole working life, was quickly commented on. Kitty Clive, one of Garrick's leading ladies, wrote to her old boss: 'Everyone is raving against Mr Sheridan, there never was in nature such a contrast as Garrick and Sheridan.'[13] The contrast would soon become even more poignant following the final exit from the world's stage of the man they called Roscius.

In the autumn of 1778, Drury Lane staged an afterpiece called *The Camp*. Although anonymous, it was probably the work of Sheridan and General Burgoyne, and concerned a threatened invasion by France. It was remarkable for very little apart from the beautiful set representing the camp of the regiment stationed at Coxheath in Kent that had been designed by de Loutherberg. Garrick, who was always willing to help out his successor, attended rehearsals to see the set. The theatre was bitterly cold and he caught a chill that turned into something more serious. He died on 20 January 1779. That night's performance of *Henry IV Part 1* was cancelled as a mark of respect: it was the first time Drury Lane had been dark to honour the death of a commoner since Dryden's death in 1700. Sheridan arranged the funeral, which was as magnificent as any of the pageants that drew the crowds to Drury Lane. The undertaker would later be declared bankrupt as the bill was never paid.

In October of 1779, Sheridan produced another hit. His afterpiece *The Critic* was loosely based on *The Rehearsal*, the Duke of Buckingham's satire on heroic tragedy that had opened at Drury Lane 108 years before. It uses the play-within-a-play format to poke fun as some of the stage conventions of the day, and for that reason it hasn't worn well. We are too far away from the sort of nonsense that is ridiculed in Mr Puff's tragedy *The Spanish Armada* for the jokes to hit home, but Sheridan told Michael Kelly that he valued the first act of *The Critic* above anything else he had written.[14] Not that writing anything came easily to Sheridan: his prevarication in delivering a final script would become legendary. Two days before the first performance, the last scene had still not been written. The actors were becoming nervous, so Thomas King, who was playing Mr Puff, was given the task of getting the last pages out of the author. Thomas Linley, who was by this time fairly familiar with the weaknesses of his son-in-law, devised a plot. An evening rehearsal was called, during which King whispered to Sheridan that he had something particular to tell him. Sheridan stepped into the Green Room, which was furnished with a writing table, paper and ink, a blazing fire and a supply of port and anchovy sandwiches. King immediately stepped out and locked the door. Linley and Dr Ford then told their fellow-sharer that he wasn't going to be let out until he had finished the play. Sheridan enjoyed the joke and did it.[15]

The first night was a huge success, with Charles James Fox and the Duchess of Devonshire applauding from Mrs Sheridan's box. Sheridan had come up with another money-spinner. At the age of 28 he had produced a series of hugely successful pieces, all considered remarkable in their different types: *The Rivals* and *The School for Scandal* (comedy); *The Duenna* (opera); and *The Critic* (satirical farce). No young playwright had ever burst upon the stage with such a string of brilliant hits. Had Sheridan continued to write for the stage, there is no telling what he might have produced. His genius was such, it is not an exaggeration to say that he might have changed the course of English drama, which went through a long period of stagnation in the nineteenth century. He understood that the hard-bitten, cynical tone of Restoration comedies was no longer acceptable, but he could produce witty plays that still make serious points and work brilliantly on the stage. Furthermore, as the playwright Frederick Reynolds pointed out, he did it without recourse to *double-entrendres* (the 'staple commodity' of Congreve and Vanbrugh) and what were known as 'trap-claps': lines about Jolly Jack Tar, England's wooden walls, an Englishman's home is his castle, the liberty of the true-born Englishman, etc., that could be relied upon for an easy round of applause.[16] Unfortunately, at this point Sheridan stopped writing plays. With the single exception of *Pizarro*, an uncharacteristic piece of fustian melodrama in 1799, he gave up as a dramatist. He now wanted to cut a figure on a more important stage: the House of Commons.

In September 1880 Sheridan was elected MP for Stafford, a constituency he would represent for the next 26 years. He had been offered the candidacy as a result of intervention by his friend the Duchess of Devonshire, as the Spenser family had an interest in it. Many years later, when he was asked what had been the happiest moment of his life, Sheridan said it had been after dinner on the day of his election 'when he stole away by himself to speculate upon those prospects of distinguishing himself which had been opened to him'.[17] These prospects of distinguishing himself would draw Sheridan further and further away from giving the affairs of Drury Lane the attention they needed.

It is not a co-incidence that the really serious problems at Drury Lane began with Sheridan's entry into the House of Commons. He wanted to be a statesman, shaping the destiny of the nation, not a playwright or manager moving actors around on the stage. Being master of Drury Lane gave him a certain kudos, but also, more dangerously, it gave him a source of funds to pay for his political career and the extravagant lifestyle which he saw as a necessary adjunct to it. Sheridan began to regard the treasury of Drury Lane as his piggy-bank. He would scoop up the night's takings and use them to pay for other things, with the predictable result that his actors, staff and suppliers often found themselves unpaid.

He still had the problem of finding someone to handle the day-to-day affairs of the theatre for him. The arrangement with his father had come to an end, with considerable bitterness, in the summer of 1780. Thomas Sheridan should have been an ideal deputy. He was passionate about theatre, he had a successful career as an actor/manager behind him, and should have been the ideal person to ensure Drury Lane's prosperity on his son's behalf. Unfortunately, relations had always been strained between father and son, and an attempt to establish him as his son's deputy in 1776 had collapsed because they could not agree terms. The issues were supposedly resolved in 1778, but Sheridan had made it an absolute condition that his father must not act. He was having enough trouble establishing himself as a gentleman in high society without his father exhibiting himself on the stage at Drury Lane to be hissed and booed. Sheridan *père* was furious and regarded this as a plot to undermine him. His already short temper was frayed even further and he became known in the company as Old Surly Boots. Sheridan found himself in the awkward position of dealing with complaints from actors about his own father's behaviour, so they had to part company.

Somehow Sheridan managed to run Drury Lane without a deputy for the next two years, but in the spring of 1782 he was appointed Under-Secretary of State for the Northern Office, and it became pressing to hand over the affairs of Drury Lane to someone else. He chose Thomas King, who had been a leading actor under Garrick and had been the original Sir Peter Teazle in *The School for Scandal*. King was a kind man who was highly respected in the company, but he found the strains of management too great and resigned at the end of the 1782/83 season, leaving Drury Lane altogether to tour the provinces for a year. However, his brief stint as manager had seen a development that would have an enormous impact of the fortunes of Drury Lane: the arrival of Sarah Siddons.

Sibling stars: Siddons and Kemble

This was not, in fact, the début of Mrs Siddons at Drury Lane. She had been invited to join the company in 1775 for Garrick's last season, but she formed the view that Garrick had only engaged her to annoy his three leading ladies, who were giving him a good deal of grief at the time. Aged 21, Sarah Siddons was extremely beautiful and Garrick made a great show of favouring her in front of the other actresses, with the predictable result that they hated her. She appeared as Portia and as Lady Anne to Garrick's Richard III in his final performances, but she didn't make a great impact. Garrick had told her that he would make sure that the incoming management would keep her on, but they didn't. Feeling betrayed, she left London to work in Bristol and Bath.

She established such a reputation for herself at the Theatre Royal in Bath – the most important theatre in the country after Covent Garden and Drury Lane – that people were making the journey to the West Country specially to see her. When she was asked to return to Drury Lane, she hesitated, as she claimed that the previous bad experience had almost destroyed her. However, she eventually agreed terms and opened on 10 October 1782 as the eponymous heroine of *Isabella*, a lurid melodrama adapted by Garrick from Thomas Southerne's tragedy *The Fatal Marriage*. Her reception was rapturous. There was continual clapping throughout the fourth and fifth acts, with a minute of applause following the death scene. Her second 'début' was regarded as the most important since Garrick's and she immediately established herself as the star of the company. She acted 80 times in seven different parts in her first season, with takings that were double what they were on nights when she didn't appear. She excelled in tragedy and was painted by Sir Joshua Reynolds as Melpomene, the Muse of Tragedy. Her Lady Macbeth was regarded as the greatest ever interpretation of the part, and her performances regularly reduced members of the audience to weeping and hysterics.[18] When George III and Queen Charlotte came to see her, the King wept and the Queen had to turn her back to the stage protesting that it was 'indeed too disagreeable'.[19] Siddons carried the manner of the tragedy queen into private life and was reserved and intimidating offstage as well as on. When Sheridan was asked if he had ever made love to her, he replied: 'To that magnificent and appalling creature! I should as soon have thought of making love to the Archbishop of Canterbury!'[20]

Sarah Siddons was a member of a large acting family and, a year after her own sensational triumph at Drury Lane, her brother turned up to carry on the family tradition. In September 1783, John Philip Kemble (Siddons was the name of Sarah's husband, also an actor in her father's company) strode out onto the stage of Drury Lane in black velvet as Hamlet. He was tall and handsome, with a dignified manner that was considered by some people as a bit stiff. His delivery was stately, and it was joked that any night on which he was playing the lead would have a late final curtain. Although he didn't have quite the same impact as his sister, Kemble's London début was well received. He didn't immediately become the star of the company, because the leading actors who were there when he arrived couldn't be deprived of their established parts, but he did well in appearances with his sister in various solemn and tragic roles. They played husband and wife in *The Gamester* and Constance and King John in Shakespeare's play. Kemble's love of Shakespeare was equal to Garrick's and he took care to cultivate the reputation of a scholar, with a large library. The brother and sister would be received into society in a way that was quite new for actors. Garrick had been entertained in the best houses, but he was always ready to oblige his hosts with little performances and mimickry. There was no question of that with Siddons and Kemble: they never let the grand manner slip. They would dominate the profession for more than 30 years. Kemble was also destined to become the most famous in the line of unhappy individuals who managed Drury Lane for Sheridan.

In 1785 the actor Thomas King returned to London from his successful tour of the provinces and was persuaded by Sheridan to take over the management again. We don't know why King accepted after his previous bad experience, but probably Sheridan promised him that things would be different this time. They weren't, and three years later King made a very public resignation from the thankless position with a letter to the newspapers explaining his dilemma:

> Should anyone… ask me: 'What was my post at Drury Lane? and if I was not manager, who was?' I should be forced to answer… to the first, *I don't know* – and to the last, I can't tell. I can only once more positively assert, that I was *not manager*, for I had not the power… to approve or reject any new dramatic work; the liberty of engaging, encouraging or discharging any one performer – nor sufficient authority to command the cleaning of a coat, or adding, by way of decoration, a yard of copper lace; both of which, it must be allowed, were often much wanted.[21]

The obvious choice for a replacement was Kemble, by this stage 31 years old, and he took over within a few weeks of King's resignation. He was in a position to demand better terms than King and was manager in almost all respects, although his title was deputy manager as Sheridan still had to be called the manager. Kemble made sure that he really was in charge and used his authority to increase the number of Shakespearean productions, preparing the texts and directing the cast himself. His greatest part was Coriolanus, in which he was painted by Sir Thomas Lawrence, but he had no objections to playing smaller parts

---

In Rep: Plays Performed at Drury Lane During w/c 8 May 1786
Date in brackets is year of first performance

Date of performance, *Play* and playwright

Monday 8 May, *A Trip to Scarborough* adapted by Richard Brinsley Sheridan from *The Relapse* by John Vanbrugh (1777) followed by T*he Humourist* by James Cobb (1785)
Tuesday 9 May, *Twelfth Night* by William Shakespeare (1602) followed by *The Sons of Anacreon* by Anon (1785) followed by *Bon Ton* by David Garrick (1774)
Wednesday 10 May, *The Clandestine Marriage* by David Garrick and George Colman Sr (1766) followed by T*he Virgin Unmask'd* by Henry Fielding (1735)
Thursday 11 May, **Isabella** adapted by *David Garrick* from Thomas Southerne (1750) followed by *Who's The Dupe?* by Hannah Cowley (1779)
Friday 12 May, *The Heiress* by John Burgoyne (1786) followed by *The Romp* by T.A. Lloyd (1771)
Saturday 13 May, *The Merchant of Venice* by William Shakespeare (1596-97) followed by *Daphne and Amintor* by Isaac Bickerstaffe (1765)

---

if other actors already had the leading roles by right, and he would even appear in the pantomimes. He was completely devoted to the theatre, self-disciplined and expecting others to be similarly committed. He acquired a reputation for being strict and sometimes stubborn, but no one could doubt his passion for his art. However, one part of the manager's role that Sheridan had insisted on retaining was the right to read the scripts of all new plays submitted to Drury Lane. Taken up with politics and other things, Sheridan never got around to reading them, and they formed a mournful pile in his library. As a result, Drury Lane acquired a bad reputation with playwrights, who regarded it as a black hole into which plays would disappear and never be seen again.

The quality of the music at Drury Lane reached new heights at this time with the arrival of the Irish tenor Michael Kelly and the siblings Nancy and Stephen Storace. As teenagers, they had all three performed in Italy, where they first met in Leghorn. They then went to Vienna where in 1786 Nancy, still only 21, created the role of Susanna in Mozart's *The Marriage of Figaro* and Kelly sang the parts of Don Basilio and Don Curzio. In the following year they all travelled to London where Nancy Storace was engaged as *prima donna* at the King's opera house in the Haymarket and Kelly was hired to sing at Drury Lane. He would perform there for the next 20 years, becoming the first stage tenor not to sing his high notes in *falsetto*.

In 1789 the King's Theatre burnt down and Nancy moved to Drury Lane, where the three friends were able to work together until Stephen's death seven years later. They were effective in promoting each other's careers, with Nancy inserting arias by Stephen into any opera she appeared in and Stephen composing operas to showcase the talents of his sister and Kelly. His first work for Drury Lane was an afterpiece, *The Doctor and the Apothecary*, followed in November 1789 by a mainpiece, a three-act comic opera called *The Haunted Tower*. The show was a huge success, with 50 performances in its first season, and established Stephen Storace as the leading composer of English opera.

The auditorium of the second Theatre Royal shortly before
it was pulled down

He effectively took over from an ageing Thomas Linley as musical director of Drury Lane, although Linley held onto the title of 'composer to the theatre' until his death, so Stephen was never on the payroll. Nevertheless, he was in charge of music at Drury Lane where his sister was *prima donna* (she styled herself Signora Storace) and Kelly was the leading tenor. They brought the richness and sophistication of the Italian and Viennese operatic traditions to London and, for a few years, the music at Drury Lane could rival that of any theatre in Europe.

With Thomas Linley handing over many of his responsibilities to Stephen Storace, Sheridan was left in almost complete control. In 1788 Sheridan had paid Richard Ford £18,000 for his share in the business which, after some movement of shares between the three men, left Sheridan with 75 per cent of Drury Lane and Linley, now increasingly unwell and unable to participate to any great degree, with 25 per cent. How he managed to raise this enormous sum, when he owed money all around, was a mystery to everyone, including his wife. Then, in 1791, Sheridan decided to pull the building down.

PART THREE

Sheridan's Drury Lane

14

Old Madam Drury's Successor

On 4 June 1791, the curtain fell for the last time in the theatre that had seen the first performances of masterpieces by Wycherley, Vanbrugh and Farquhar; the acting of Cibber, Macklin and Garrick; the pantomimes of Weaver; and the scenery of de Loutherberg. The play for the night was *The Country Girl*, Garrick's adaptation of Wycherley's *The Country Wife*, followed by *No Song, No Supper*, a comic opera by the brilliant young Stephen Storace, the theatre's recently appointed director of music, that had premièred the year before.

At the end of the performance, the actor John Palmer stepped forward to make an announcement: 'Ladies and gentlemen, on the part of the proprietors, manager, and performers, I have to express their gratitude for the unprecedented support with which you have favoured them, during the past season; when next we have the honour to appear before you on this spot, we trust it will be in a theatre better calculated for your accommodation, more deserving royal countenance, and the patronage of this great metropolis.'[1]

On the following Monday, the *Universal Magazine* gave a humorous account of the last rites:

> Died, on Saturday night, of a gradual decay, in the hundred and seventeenth year of her age, old Madam Drury, who lived in six reigns, and saw many generations pass in review before her. She remembered Betterton in age, lived in intimacy with Wilks, Booth and Cibber, and knew old Macklin when he was a stripling; her hospitality exceeded that of the old English character, even in its earlier days of festivity, having almost throughout the whole of her life entertained from one to two thousand persons of both sexes six nights out of seven in the week.[2]

But why did Sheridan decide to pull his theatre down, when it was making money? One explanation, that a survey had revealed the old building to be structurally unsound, appears to be unsupported by evidence. It was really to do with money. Sheridan regarded Drury Lane as a cash-cow to fund his political career; he wanted to make as much money out of it as possible; and he wanted to do it without much competition.

By the end of the eighteenth century, London was the biggest city on earth and the centre of a vast trading network and empire. In spite of the growth of its population, it still had only two theatres permitted to put on plays, because of the restrictive nature of the patents granted by Charles II in the 1660s. Increasingly, people were complaining about the unreasonableness of this situation. The demand for entertainment was growing, and on nights when popular attractions were presented, both Drury Lane and Covent Garden were dangerously crowded, with fights to get in and fights to get a seat. Many people saw the answer as a third theatre, and indeed Sheridan and Thomas Harris, the proprietor of Covent Garden, had for several years planned to build one at Hyde Park Corner. In the event, they both settled for enlarging their existing buildings to ward off the threat of a competitor.

Garrick had enlarged Drury Lane by acquiring the leases on properties backing onto the theatre and then incorporating them. Sheridan aimed for something far more ambitious: a completely new and enlarged structure that would have frontages onto the surrounding streets – something it had never had so far. Such a plan required one lease for the whole site as no one would put up money for a building that stood on plots belonging to different freeholders, on which the leases would fall in at different times. The problem was that the theatre's landlord, Francis Russell, the fifth Duke of Bedford, did not control most of the sites immediately surrounding the theatre as they had been sold off in fee-farm by his ancestors in the 1630s. Sheridan persuaded the Duke to buy back these plots and to issue a new lease to the theatre for the whole site. The Duke undertook to do this, as it would increase the value of his Covent Garden estate to have one magnificent structure in place of a series of buildings, some of which were looking rather ramshackle by this time. Sheridan appointed as his architect Henry Holland, one of the leading architects of the day and the surveyor of the Duke of Bedford's estate.

Holland's vision was certainly grand enough. He envisaged a magnificent theatre building, with colonnaded entrances on both long fronts, which would be encased at both ends by ranges of coffee-houses, taverns, shops and houses. The whole development, in his elegant classical style, would form one of the most striking architectural improvements in the metropolis and give not only the theatre but the whole area a definite stylistic boost. The alleyway running along the south side of the theatre, by that stage known as Little Bridges Street and Marquis Court, would be replaced by a new road called Woburn Street, so that the new development would form its own block, bounded by Drury Lane on the east, Russell Street on the north, Bridges Street on the west and Woburn Street on the south.

Sheridan, who wasn't short of vision himself, set about raising the funds. He sold 300 shares at £500 each to raise £150,000, which would pay for the new structure and clear the various loans and mortgages which were held against the existing building. Sheridan had no difficulty in finding takers for his shares: some people bought several, such was the confidence in the success of this ambitious venture.

The move to the Haymarket

Meanwhile, the Drury Lane company had to have somewhere to perform while the building work was going on, and here Sheridan was able to profit from the tangled and unsatisfactory nature of affairs over in the Haymarket, at the King's Theatre. The King's was London's third patent theatre, and had been presenting opera throughout the eighteenth century under a series of 21-year royal patents. In 1789 it burnt to the ground, apparently as a result of arson by a disgruntled employee. Its manager, William Taylor, set about rebuilding it, but he neglected to make sure that he would have permission to put on performances when it was finished. Robert O'Reilly, the proprietor of the Pantheon in Oxford Street, spotted an opportunity to supply London's frustrated opera-lovers and applied to the Lord Chamberlain for a patent. The Lord Chamberlain took the view that the patent for the King's had gone up in flames with the building, and that therefore others could apply for the exclusive right to present opera in London. The patent was granted to O'Reilly in June 1790, which was a disaster from Taylor's point of view as his magnificent new building on the Haymarket, designed by Michael Novosielski to be the largest theatre in Europe apart from La Scala, was already half-built.

The Pantheon, designed by James Wyatt in 1772, was based on the Pantheon in Rome and was widely regarded as the most beautiful building in London. It had been used for concerts, exhibitions and masquerades, but Wyatt managed to fit it up with a stage and auditorium, and it began to present operas in February 1791. Meanwhile, the best thing that William Taylor could get from the Lord Chamberlain for the King's was a licence to present concerts and ballet, but not opera.

Concerts and ballet were clearly not going to bring in the sort of audiences Taylor needed to keep his gigantic new theatre solvent, so it was a piece of good luck for him that Sheridan was looking for a temporary home for the Drury Lane company at exactly this time. The troupe moved in over the summer and opened the new theatre season at the Haymarket on 22 September with a short musical interlude called *Poor Old Drury!* by James Cobb with music by Stephen Storace, followed by their earlier successful collaboration *The Haunted Tower*.

In December, the demolition men began to knock poor old Drury down. Sheridan was keen to get the work done as quickly as possible so that he could start earning money from his new theatre and stop paying rent on the King's, but a serious problem emerged which brought work to a halt. It was linked to the tangled history of those two old patents that Charles II had granted to Thomas Killigrew and William Davenant which conveyed to whoever owned them the exclusive right to present plays in London.

The patent solution

Killigrew had used his patent to found the King's Company in Drury Lane, while Davenant took his to Lincoln's Inn Fields for the Duke of York's Company. In 1682 the two companies merged to form the United Company, based at Drury Lane and (by that time) Dorset Garden. Although they were using two theatres, only one patent was required as the same company was performing in both, and as the Duke's had been the dominant party in the merger, it was Davenant's patent that was used. The Killigrew patent became dormant. In 1709, when Christopher Rich was silenced, he was still in possession of both of these patents. He left Drury Lane when it became clear he would not get permission to re-open and he rebuilt the old theatre in Lincoln's Inn Fields. For the rest of the century, Drury Lane would operate under a succession of 21-year patents, which gave less security than a perpetual patent. Rich obtained permission to use one of his patents to open the rebuilt theatre in Lincoln's Inn fields in 1715, although he died before the event. His son John Rich inherited these two patents and continued to use the Davenant patent, which was also used when the company moved to Covent Garden in 1732.

When Sheridan was planning his new and improved Drury Lane, therefore, his rival Thomas Harris at Covent Garden was still in possession of these two patents, with the Killigrew patent dormant. Sheridan's investors realised that there was a serious risk here. Anyone who obtained that patent – which was a tradeable asset – could open another theatre in London, which would constitute increased competition for the two established theatres. The investors refused to let Sheridan see the colour of their money until he had obtained this patent for Drury Lane.

Sheridan entered into negotiation with Harris and a price of £15,000 was agreed. Then it turned out that Harris didn't own the whole of the patent. A man called White owned the reversionary freehold of 14/60, and he had not been consulted about the sale. Eventually it was agreed that Sheridan would give Harris £11,667 for the 46/60 of the patent that he controlled, with £5,000 to White for his 14/60. Unfortunately the deal with White fell through, but Sheridan felt safe enough to proceed with the majority share of the Killigrew patent as it would enable him to block any attempt to use it to build another theatre. This was a good outcome, as work on the theatre, which had ground to halt, was able to get going again, but the money for the patent would have to be found out of the £150,000 that had been promised for the new building plus the clearance of all charges against the old one, so the budget was stretched even before the first brick was laid.

That was not the end of Sheridan's work with patents, however. The situation at the King's, an opera house prohibited from performing opera, was clearly unsatisfactory, and it became more so when the Pantheon burned to the ground in January 1792. Not only was the building in ruins, but the fortunes of it proprietor, Mr O'Reilly, had also combusted. He had racked up debts of £30,000 and fled to Europe to escape his creditors. A committee was put together to sort out the situation and Sheridan, as a prominent Whig MP, a theatre proprietor currently in occupation of the King's and, importantly, a friend of the Prince of Wales, was asked to be a member of the committee. In August 1792 the General Opera Trust Deed was signed by the Prince of Wales, the Duke of Bedford and the Marquess of Salisbury, who was Lord Chamberlain. It awarded to the King's Theatre the exclusive right to perform Italian opera (i.e. sung-through opera rather than semi-opera or what we would regard as musicals) but in exchange William

Taylor had to undertake to pay off the £30,000 of debt run up by O'Reilly at the Pantheon.

In September 1792, the corner stone for the new Drury Lane was laid, and Sheridan, with his new theatre rising before his eyes at last, decided to make as much money as possible while he was waiting for it to be finished. As he was currently in occupation of the King's, he took it upon himself to get the opera going again, and he formed another company under the direction of Michael Kelly and Stephen Storace. Because the audience for opera was so small, it was only performed twice a week, so Sheridan had the idea of putting on operas at the King's on Tuesdays and Saturdays, when the acting company would move across the road to perform in the Little Theatre in the Haymarket. The Little Theatre, standing next to the site of the present Theatre Royal, Haymarket, had a licence to perform in the summer months only when the patent houses were closed. However, Sheridan could use his own patent to cover performances of the acting company there on Tuesdays and Saturdays, as the King's now operated under its own patent for Italian opera.

This is the sort of visionary, lateral thinking that would only occur to someone who didn't actually have to do the work. The logistical complexities of shifting sets and costumes across the road on Tuesdays and Saturdays, then bringing them back on Wednesdays and Mondays, must have turned the air blue in the Haymarket, especially as the Drury Lane scenery was too small for the enormous stage at the King's and too large for the tiny stage at the Little Theatre. The first opera to be presented at the King's under this arrangement was *Il Barbiere di Siviglia* on 26 January 1793, while the actors were across the road giving Nicholas Rowe's *Jane Shore*. The arrangement went on until the end of June when the opera season came to an end.

Opening night in the new theatre

As the beginning of the 1793/94 season approached, it was clear that the new Drury Lane would be ready at some time during the season, so Sheridan decided not to open the season again at the King's. The actors were told that their services weren't required for a few months, so they either went off on tours of the provinces or else they signed up to appear at the Little Theatre in the Haymarket. George Colman the younger, proprietor of the Little Theatre, had agreed to pay Sheridan £15 a night for the privilege of using his patent, while Sheridan didn't require it, to put on shows during the main theatre season. He used it for 50 nights, so the bill came to £750 before the new Drury Lane was ready to open its doors.

The new Theatre Royal was roofed in on 30 October 1793, an event Sheridan celebrated by throwing a party at the Shakespeare Tavern. He was keen to get the building open as soon as possible, even if not everything was ready, and the public were admitted for the first time on 12 March. This fell during Lent, which was not the best time to open a theatre as there were restrictions on performances. Plays were not permitted on Wednesdays or Fridays in Lent, and theatres were closed altogether on Ash Wednesday and during Holy Week. A tradition had grown up of presenting oratorios, usually on sacred themes, on Wednesdays and Fridays in Lent, and these oratorio seasons had become both popular and profitable. Sheridan therefore decided to give his new building what would nowadays be called a soft opening: oratorios on Wednesdays, Fridays and some other nights during Lent prior to a fully-fledged gala opening after Easter.

The performance on 12 March was 'A Grand Selection of Sacred Music from the Works of Handel' and it was performed in a new set representing the interior of a Gothic cathedral.[3] The singers in the chorus were dressed 'with that attention to their attire that rendered the stage respectable'[4] – i.e. no cleavage.

The theatre that greeted the first members of the public to get inside it was certainly impressive. It was a splendid piece of architecture, and certainly the most magnificent building to stand on the site in the history of Drury Lane. Instead of approaching the auditorium through long, narrow passages from Bridges Street or through the various converted houses attached to it on Russell Street and Little Bridges Street, Holland had designed two magnificent colonnaded entrances on the north and south frontages leading to a magnificent set of reception rooms. He had created a sense of occasion with his architecture, allowing the gentry to arrive in their coaches and set down in style. Unfortunately, not everything had gone according to plan. The parliamentary bill to permit the creation of Woburn Street to the south had failed, so that side of the theatre was still bounded by a narrow passageway.✥ It was not possible to get coaches down it, so the whole of the southern approach was for those arriving by foot or sedan chair only.

The much more serious departure from the original plan was the failure to build the rest of the block which was to encase the theatre. The western front of the theatre was still not on Bridges Street, but set back, just as it had been in the previous two structures. It was to be approached down a passageway leading between the elegant buildings that were to complete the block. These were not built when the theatre opened, and never were built, so the western end of the site, on the corner of Russell Street and Bridges Street, was waste land. Nor was the plan completed at the Drury Lane end of the site, which still retained its old buildings. The Duke of Bedford was so annoyed by the failure to carry the plan through that he refused to issue the extended lease he had promised. Holland was mortified that his grand metropolitan improvement scheme was left unfinished and ragged at both ends. Sheridan, in his turn, blamed Holland for going way over budget.

But what had the budget been? The amount raised to create this magnificent structure had been £150,000, to include demolition of the old building and the redemption of all loans and mortgages attached to it. It also had to cover the unanticipated expenditure to acquire the Killigrew patent. Finding out how much was budgeted for the new building is difficult, because nobody, probably not even Sheridan, knew the full extent of the theatre's indebtedness. It seems to have been left very late in the day to get to grips with costs, and in November 1791, when work was just about to start, Holland submitted a budget

---

✥ It still is. It has reverted to the old name of Vinegar Yard and provides the emergency exits from the stalls. Apart from that, there is now no public access on this side of the building.

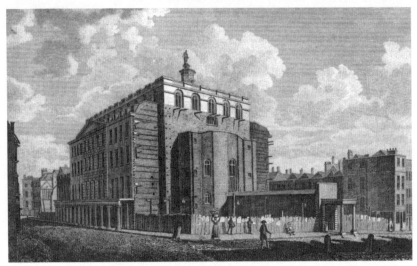

Henry Holland's Theatre Royal development as it was
supposed to look… and as it was left.

of £80,000 for the new theatre. This was £11,000 higher than the budget
he had submitted only a few weeks before, suggesting that costs were
not completely understood, and it was more than double the figure

'The Apotheosis of David Garrick' by George Carter. Actors costumed as Shakespeare's characters look on as Shakespeare descends the slopes of Mount Parnassus to welcome his worshipper.

'The Manager and His Dog – or a New Way to Keep One's Head Above Water' by James Sayers. Frederick Reynolds's play *The Caravan* featured Carlo the dog saving a drowning child. Here the dog is saving Sheridan. Thalia, the Muse of Comedy, covers her eyes in horror.

'Drury Lane Theatre 1795' by Edward Dayes. This is the only image of Henry Holland's auditorium before it was altered.

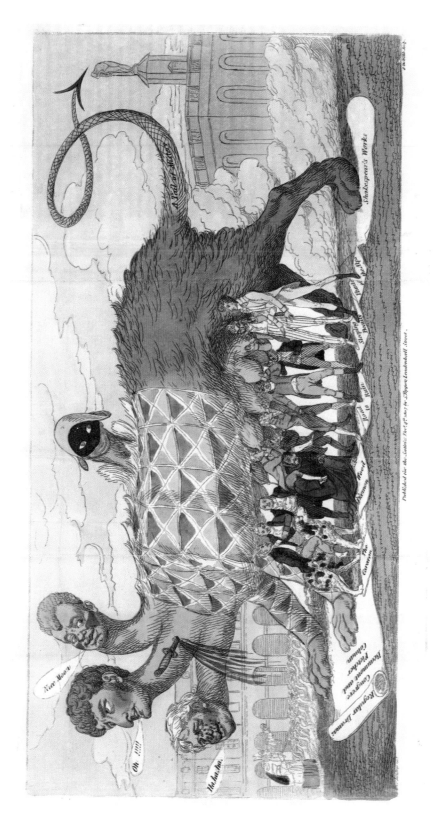

The Monster Melodrama (1807) is half-Harlequin, half-lion, with the heads of Sheridan, John Philip Kemble, Grimaldi and Harlequin. The monster tramples on the works of Congreve and Shakespeare but suckles the authors of worthless melodramas. Frederick Reynolds, author of *The Caravan*, is riding on the back of Carlo the dog.

'Richard III attacks the Poet Bunn'. This is the only known illustration
of the famous assault on Alfred Bunn by William Charles Macready,
incensed by having *Richard III* cut to three acts in order to make time for
two musical extravaganzas. Macready is still in his Richard III costume.

'Isaac Van Amburgh and his animals' by Sir Edwin Landseer.
Landseer carried out his commission from Queen Victoria backstage at Drury Lane.

that Sheridan originally had in his head for the scheme.[5] In 1797, three years after its opening, the trustees for the theatre published their accounts in *The Morning Herald* stating that the theatre had cost £71,419 6*s*. 8*d*.[6] Holland's own accounts, drawn up a few months before, put the cost slightly higher at £78,730 10*s*. 6*d*.,[7] but that included his own fee. Either way, it was within the budget figure, but Sheridan complained that what Holland had undertaken to 'finish for £80,000 will not be finished for £160,000'[8] and would later claim that additional work that had to be carried out after the opening had consumed more than the whole net profits of the theatre.[9] Holland countered that Sheridan was charging to the building fund things like furnishings that had not been included in the estimates. Whatever the truth of matter, there wasn't enough money left to complete the scheme as it had been agreed with the Duke of Bedford, and the theatre stood throughout the short period of its existence looking like a mouth with several front teeth missing.

Monday 21 April 1794 was the night for the grand gala opening of the third Theatre Royal. The play chosen for the occasion was *Macbeth*, with Sarah Siddons frightening the life out of everyone as Lady Macbeth, John Philip Kemble as her terrible husband and their younger brother Charles Kemble making his Drury Lane début as Malcolm. The first and second theatres on the site had opened with plays by John Fletcher, regarded at the end of the seventeenth century as one of the greatest English dramatists. A hundred years later, Fletcher had almost vanished from the repertoire and it would have been unthinkable to open Drury Lane with anyone other than the Swan of Avon. The afterpiece was Fielding's *The Virgin Unmask'd*, still popular after 60 years, which, together with prologue and epilogue, made it a long night. The evening started at 6:15 p.m. and ended at 11:20 p.m., which we would consider quite a marathon, but which seemed normal to the eighteenth-century theatregoer.

The prologue, specially composed by Major General Richard Fitzpatrick, dedicated the house to the immortal memory of Shakespeare, but it is the epilogue that has lingered in theatre lore as a sort of terrible harbinger of disaster – not inappropriate to a theatre that chose the Scottish play to open with. The destruction by fire of both the King's in 1789 and the Pantheon in 1792 had made people more than usually aware of fire hazards in a theatre, so Henry Holland

---

Prologue written by Major General Richard Fitzpatrick
and spoken by John Philip Kemble on the opening of the
Theatre Royal, Drury Lane on Monday 21 April 1794

As tender plants, which dread the boist'rous gale,

Bloom in the shelter of a tranquil vale,

Beneath fair freedom's all protecting wing

The liberal arts, secure from danger, spring;

Through ravag'd Europe now while discord reigns,

And war's dire conflicts desolate her plains,

O, lest they perish in this boasted age,

Once more the victims of barbarian rage,

Her shield to guard them let Britannia rear,

And fix, in safety, their asylum here!

Here, where mild reason holds her temperate sway,

Where willing subjects equal laws obey,

Firm to that well pois'd system, which unites

With order's blessings freedom's sacred rights.

'Midst wrecks of empires, England, be it thine,

A bright example to the world to shine,

Where law, on liberty's just basis rear'd,

Of all the safeguard, is by all rever'd,

And stems alike, when clouds of discord low'r,

The storms of faction, and the strides of pow'r.

Hence have the Muses on the lists of fame,

With pride, recorded many a British name;

And on their votaries, in this lov'd abode,

Bright wreaths of never fading bays bestow'd;

True to the cause of ev'ry English bard,

'Tis yours the just inheritance to guard.

What, though his vaunting Pegasus disdain

The servile check of too severe a rein,

Like untaught coursers of the Arab race,

He moves with freedom, energy, and grace;

With caution, then, the generous ardour tame,

Lest, while you chasten, you repress the flame;

Some licence temper'd judgement will permit

To Congreve's, Wycherly's, or Vanbrugh's wit;

Nor, for an ill-timed ribald jest, refuse

A tear to Otway's, or to Southern's, Muse;

But chief, with reverence watch his hallow'd bays,

To whom this night a monument we raise;

Beyond what sculptur'd marble can bestow—

The silent tribute of surviving woe—

Beyond the pow'rs of undecaying brass,

Or the proud pyramid's unmeaning mass;

A shrine more worthy of his fame we give,

Where, unimpaired, his genius still may live;

Where, though his fire the critic's rule transgress,

The glowing bosom shall his cause confess;

Where Britain's sons, through each succeeding age,

Shall hail the founder of our English stage,

And from the cavils of pendantick spleen

Defend the glories of their Shakspeare's scene.

had installed the latest fire-retardant technology in Drury Lane. Tanks of water in the roof were able to drench every part of the house and the theatre had the very first safety curtain to prevent the spread of fire from backstage into the auditorium.

The epilogue was spoken by the popular actress Elizabeth Farren in the character of a housekeeper, showing off her master's premises to visitors and boasting of the fire precautions:

> The very ravages of fire we scout,
> For we have wherewithal to put it out.
> In ample reservoirs our firm reliance,
> Whose streams set conflagration at defiance.
> Panic alone avoid, let none begin it–
> Should the flame spread, sit still, there's nothing in it;
> We'll undertake to drown you all in half a minute.

As she spoke, the curtain behind her rose to show a man rowing a boat in a large tank fed by a waterfall. The housekeeper went on to promise 'Assurance double sure… your safety yet is certain/ Presto! For proof let down the *Iron Curtain*.' At this point an iron curtain descended and was struck with a hammer to set everyone's mind at rest. It then rose again to reveal a statue of Shakespeare underneath a mulberry tree, with a choir singing 'Behold this fair goblet' from Garrick's afterpiece *The Jubilee*. At least, that was the plan. In what could have been seen as a bad omen, the iron curtain was 'alluded to', in the words of the *Times* reporter,[10] but it wasn't ready until the following week, when they did the whole routine again.

The architecture of the new theatre, in Holland's elegant neo-classical style, was greatly admired, and the auditorium looked especially beautiful in a colour scheme of light blue, white, beige and silver with thirty-five panels on the fronts of the tiers decorated with scenes from classical mythology. With its huge chandeliers and its looking-glass panels set into the fronts of the supporting columns, it must have looked enchanting to that first-night audience. It must also have looked huge. The auditorium of Garrick's Drury Lane had accommodated something in the region of 2,300 people. Holland's magnificent structure, with its pit surrounded by two tiers of boxes, surmounted by a gallery and upper gallery, both of which had further boxes in their slips, sat 3,600. The capacity of the house was increased by over 50 per cent, and this would inevitably affect the sort of shows that could be put on there. For the actors, it was daunting. 'You are come to a wilderness of a place,' wrote Sarah Siddons to an actor joining the company, 'and God knows, if I had not made my reputation in a small theatre I should never have made it.'[11] The auditorium of Covent Garden had been rebuilt the year before, also by Henry Holland and also on a gigantic scale. These auditoria were referred to by Richard Peake, the Drury Lane treasurer, as 'those covered Salisbury Plains'[12] and the popular playwright Richard Cumberland later described the effect of these changes in his memoirs. Henceforth, he wrote, there would be 'theatres for spectators rather than playhouses for hearers... The splendour of the scenes and the ingenuity of the machinist and the rich display of dresses aided by the captivating clamours of music now in a great degree superseded the labours of the poet.'[13] Words became less important in a theatre in which those at the back, or up in the gods, could not easily hear, or even see, the actors. Gestures had to be larger; make-up had to be thicker. 'The nice discrimination of the actor's face and of the actor's feeling are all now lost in the vast void of the new theatre of Drury Lane,' wrote John Byng,[14] a keen theatregoer. In spite of the fine words about Shakespeare that John Philip Kemble delivered in the prologue to the first performance, Drury Lane's status as a temple of the drama was now less important than its capacity to host crowds and spectacle. It would be Sheridan's most important legacy to the Theatre Royal.

15

Spectacle and Melodrama

The shows in the new Drury Lane certainly looked great, whatever drawbacks the vast auditorium held for actors. Managements had always liked to boast of 'new scenes' for their productions, but all of the scenery had to be new after 1794 because the stage was so much bigger than the previous one that the stock of old scenery would no longer fit. Furthermore, Henry Holland had given the theatre a wonderful new device for changing the sets. His Drury Lane was the first with a fly-tower, allowing the scenery to be raised and lowered, rather than sliding in and out. Coupled with the very latest stage machinery, so complicated that the man who was paid to build it had to be employed to run it for the first two years, the scope for spectacle was now immense.

Three months after the opening of the new building, John Philip Kemble decided to mount a lavish production called *Lodoiska*. This dramatic story of a beautiful princess imprisoned in a castle by a wicked baron and rescued from the burning building by a band of Tartars offered obvious scope for the new stage. There had already been two rival operatic versions of the story presented in Paris, so Kemble wrote an English version of the text and gave it to Stephen Storace to arrange the music. Storace put together a composite score, using arias from both Parisian productions by Cherubini and Kreutzer, plus new material of his own. Although *Lodoiska* was an afterpiece, it was an unusually long one at three acts, and an unusually serious one. Afterpieces were normally humorous and light-hearted: *Lodoiska* was fully-fledged operatic melodrama.

The first night certainly went with a bang. At the climax of the show the Princess Lodoiska, played by Anna Maria Crouch, was trapped in a burning tower from which she was to be rescued by the Tartars, led by Michael Kelly. Flames were set up to burn behind the tower, but it seems that a draught backstage caused the flames to blow too close to the scenery. Kelly, seeing Mrs Crouch in real danger, ran across the bridge to the castle to save her, but at that moment a carpenter knocked out one of the supports and the bridge collapsed, throwing him down onto the stage floor. At that moment the tower, by now alight, collapsed, with the screaming Mrs Crouch inside it. Kelly managed to pick himself up and catch her, after which he was so stunned that he staggered towards the footlights holding her up in triumph. The audience loved it and they had to repeat the routine at subsequent performances. It was made all the more exciting by the widely-shared knowledge that Anna Maria Crouch was the love of Michael Kelly's life, which was slightly awkward as 'Mrs' was not a courtesy title in her case. There was a Mr Crouch somewhere, although he had tired of living in a *ménage à trois* and left, 'never appreciating the gem which he possessed' according to Kelly's not entirely accurate account of his departure.[1]

The next year saw an even bigger show: *Alexander the Great* was a dance spectacular 'calculated to show the extent and powers of the new stage'[2] and including a stunning representation of Alexander's triumphal entry into Babylon. The procession involved 200 extras, Darius in a car drawn by three white horses and Alexander in a car drawn by two elephants.✣

✣ These were the first elephants to appear at Drury Lane but they would not be the last. The present theatre has a high access point to the stage platform which is known as the elephant arch.

The Baddeley Cake

January 1796 saw the start of a Drury Lane tradition that continues today: the cutting of the Baddeley Cake on Twelfth Night. Robert Baddeley had been an actor in the Drury Lane company since 1762, playing secondary roles in comedies, especially funny foreigners and Jewish characters. His was the original Moses, the Jewish moneylender, in *The School for Scandal*, and he continued to play the character until, on 19 November 1794, he was taken ill as he was dressing for the part and died the next morning. He had become deeply attached to Drury Lane and made a generous bequest in his will. He left the bulk of his estate, including houses in London and West Molesey, to his partner for her lifetime, to revert on her death to the Drury Lane Theatrical Fund. This fund, the oldest theatre charity in the world, had been established by Garrick for the relief of indigent actors who had delivered lines on the stage of Drury Lane. Baddeley had been one of the original directors of the fund and his estranged wife, Sophia Baddeley, whose successful stage career had been wrecked by a combination of too many men and too much laudanum, had been one of its beneficiaries. He also bequeathed £100 in three per cent consolidated bank annuities to produce the sum of three pounds annually 'to purchase a cake, with wine and punch, of which his Majesty's Company of Comedians appearing at Drury Lane are requested to partake every Twelfth Night in the Great Green Room, so that I might be remembered by them'.[3] Baddeley had been a cook before he became an actor, which no doubt accounts for the saccharine commemoration, but his iced confections have provided him with a monument more lasting than bronze: the Baddeley Cake has been cut and his memory toasted by the cast of the current Drury Lane show on every Twelfth Night since 1796, with the exception of thirteen years when there was no show or when wartime restrictions meant that sugar was rationed.

Raiding the kitty

In March 1796, Stephen Storace died at the age of only 33. He insisted on attending rehearsals for a play by George Colman called *The Iron Chest* for which he had composed the music, in spite of the fact that he was running a fever. He was carried to the theatre in a sedan chair, wrapped up in blankets, but the draughts of the enormous Drury Lane stage made his condition worse. 'He went home to his bed, whence he never rose again,' in the words of Michael Kelly.[4]

Storace was deeply mourned, and the profession turned out in force for a performance to benefit his widow on 25 May 1796. The mainpiece was *Mahmoud*, an opera on which Storace had been working at the time of his death, together with a selection of arias from his other operas and the finale of *The Iron Chest*. The ballet company from the King's Theatre also appeared. The house was full and the takings came to £657 12s. 0d., which would no doubt have been very welcome to Mrs Storace. Unfortunately for her, Sheridan went to the treasury and removed all the night's takings for his own use. He promised to pay the money back in stages, but he already owed Storace hundreds of pounds in unpaid moneys from benefit nights. Money came to Mrs Storace in small amounts over the next few years, but like all of Sheridan's creditors she had to pursue her claim vigorously to get anything.

Defrauding widows and orphans has been regarded as one of the worst things a man can do since biblical times,✥ but the finances of Drury Lane, which had been shaky since the start of Sheridan's proprietorship, were by now truly dreadful. The overspend on the building of the new theatre, coupled with much higher running costs and interest payments on a web of loans and mortgages, meant that there was never enough in the kitty when pay-day came around. The popular performer Fanny Kemble,

---

✥ The theatre historian John Genest relates a similar story about a benefit performance held the following month for the widow and three orphan children of Robert Benson, a member of the Drury Lane company who had committed suicide. 'The house was a very good one, [Mrs Benson stood to gain £465 15s. 6d.] but it has been said that Sheridan went to the treasury and carried off the money, so that Benson's widow and children never got a sixpence.' (Genest, vii, 245.)

whose mother Maria de Camp had married Charles Kemble, left a harrowing account of the way in which Sheridan would fob off his actors and staff, week after week. Every Saturday they would wait for Sheridan in the passages approaching the treasury. When he arrived they would cry out: 'For God's sake, Mr Sheridan, pay us our salaries!' 'Certainly, certainly, my good people, you shall be attended to directly,' he would reply, as he went to the treasury, scooped up the week's takings, and exited by another route.[5] Sheridan's financial problems explain a small but significant change to the layout of the backstage offices in the new theatre: the treasurer's office was moved to the ground floor with a window opening onto the street, allowing easy escape.[6]

Things became so bad that tradesmen were unwilling to supply the theatre and began demanding personal guarantees from John Philip Kemble, who was known to be an honourable man, before they would deliver. Kemble, whose passion for the theatre outran his prudence, would sign these guarantees in order to keep the show on the road. Inevitably, he was arrested for debt when the treasury had failed to honour one. He was furious at being so humiliated and in April 1796 he resigned as manager, although he agreed to stay on in the company as an actor. Just before abandoning his managerial role, however, he had presided over one of the great fiascos in the history of Drury Lane.

Vortigern and Rowena

Thanks in part to the efforts of John Philip Kemble and his sister, Shakespeare had achieved a very high level of popularity at Drury Lane by the end of the eighteenth century. Considering that no subsidies were available, and that every show was expected to make a profit, it is remarkable how many performances of Shakespeare's plays there were. Bardolatry had taken hold, and people were interested in anything that had the name of Shakespeare attached to it.

Samuel Ireland was an engraver who made a living by producing lavishly illustrated travel books. He was also a fanatical admirer of

Shakespeare who made the beauties of the Bard the standard topic of after-dinner conversation in his household. He had a son called William, of whom he had a much lower opinion, regarding him as a lazy good-for-nothing. William found a way to get his father's attention and approval by tapping into the Bardolatry: he claimed to have met a gentleman who had a trunk full of old documents, some of which had Shakespeare's name on them. William was supposedly entitled to remove any of these he wanted, as long as he left a copy. And so it was that William presented his father with, first of all, a legal document signed by Shakespeare, then a letter to Anne Hathaway (or 'Anna Hatherwaye'), letters between Shakespeare and Elizabeth I, and even a letter from Shakespeare to his dear friend 'Master William Henrye Irelande' (a distant ancestor, of course) bequeathing him his manuscripts as a reward for saving the poet from drowning.

These forgeries caused a sensation. Samuel Ireland exhibited them in his house and published them in a deluxe edition called *Miscellaneous Papers and Legal Instruments under the Hand and Seal of William Shakespeare*. William Ireland must have realised he was playing a dangerous game when his forgeries were exposed to the critical examination of the leading Shakespeare scholars of his age, but for the first time in his life he was experiencing approval from his father. He then took things up a notch by declaring that he had found the manuscript of an unknown play by Shakespeare called *Vortigern and Rowena*. Samuel offered it to the two playhouses and Sheridan outbid the opposition. He had not read the play at the time, and wasn't all that worried about its authenticity, but the level of interest in these amazing Shakespeare papers promised a profitable run.

Not everyone was convinced. Sarah Siddons was supposed to be playing the leading lady, but developed a convenient illness. Her brother could not escape it, as both leading actor and manager of the company, but he decided to open the play on 1 April – April Fools' Day. Sheridan saw that one coming and made the first night 2 April 1796. Two days before this, Edmund Malone, the greatest Shakespeare scholar of his generation, published a 400-page hatchet-job on the whole set of Shakespeare papers entitled: *An Inquiry into the*

*Authenticity of Certain Miscellaneous Papers and Legal Instruments…
Attributed to Shakespeare*. This just stoked up public interest even
higher, and the house was absolutely packed for the first performance
of a play about a fifth-century British warlord who gets a mention in
Geoffrey of Monmouth's *History of the Kings of Britain*.

The first three acts went reasonably well, with the audience at least
inclined to give it a fair hearing, but they got restless after that as
absurdity was piled on bathos. There was so much laughter and
groaning that Kemble came down to the front and asked them to give
it a chance, but then he delivered the *coup de grace* himself. In a speech
about death, Kemble had the line: 'And when thy solemn mockery is
over…' Kemble was known for his pauses, but he left a particularly
long one after that line, during which people started to laugh. The
laugher turned to jeering and, after that, nothing could be heard of the
actors until the end of the play. When it was given out for the following
Monday (2 April was a Saturday) the audience booed until *The School
for Scandal* was announced instead. *Vortigern and Rowena* was never
performed again and Sheridan was furious with Kemble for
deliberately wrecking what could have been a nice little earner for at
least a few more nights. Perhaps the saddest part of the story is that,
even after William put his hands up to the forgery, his father refused
to believe him. He simply couldn't accept that his son was intelligent
enough to deceive a Shakespearean scholar like himself. He went to
his grave four years later, convinced that *Vortigern and Rowena* was
the work of his idol. William, meanwhile, found that there was a
market for his forgeries and, having sold them to collectors, developed
a post-modern sideline in selling forgeries of his own forgeries.[7]

Horrors, melodrama and German romanticism

The financial problems of Drury Lane were not the result of poor
houses. On the contrary, the theatre in these years witnessed hit after
hit. The 1797/98 season saw three really big successes: *The Stranger*, a

translation of a play of 'German sentiment' by Kotzebue; *The Castle-Spectre* by Matthew Lewis; and *Bluebeard*, with a script by George Colman and music by Michael Kelly, who had taken over the position of musical director at Drury Lane. They received 26, 47 and 64 performances respectively during the season and remained popular for years, but by the end of the season the theatre had sustained a deficit of £1,000. This was because the running costs of these big shows were so high, especially for *Bluebeard* which brought back the elephants, that they made it almost impossible to turn a profit even on good houses. Sheridan and Kemble would not be the last members of the profession to learn the hard way the difference between gross and net.✤

The success of these three shows tells us a lot about where public taste was going and why serious plays would be less frequently acted at Drury Lane. The works of the German dramatist Kotzebue were immensely popular in London at the end of the eighteenth century, although they are now only interesting as harbingers of the great cultural shift from classicism towards romanticism. Kotzebue will be forever remembered as the author of the highly improper play *Lovers' Vows* that attracts the disapproval of Sir Thomas Bertram in Jane Austen's *Mansfield Park*, and *The Stranger* was also condemned in some quarters for immorality, as it was said to condone adultery. The central character, Mrs Haller, leaves her husband and children for another man, but is eventually re-united with them in a tearful finale. Mrs Siddons made it one of her most popular roles.

The Castle-Spectre was a tale of the supernatural by Matthew Lewis, known as 'Monk' Lewis because he had written the gothic horror story of that name. According to one critic, *The Castle-Spectre* had enough ghosts, hobgoblins and other creatures of the night appearing through trapdoors to be regarded as a 'speaking pantomime'.[8] *Bluebeard* was

---

✤ The playwright Frederick Reynolds wrote in his memoirs (1826) of the difference in profitability between 'what is technically termed a "blue coat and white waistcoat play", and… a "spangled and processional play"'. He contrasted a popular light comedy called *John Bull* with Sheridan's *Pizarro*: '*Pizarro*… brought more money into the theatre; but at the same time, it should be remembered that it also took more money out of it.' (Reynolds, ii, 341-42.)

an early stage treatment of the tale of the much-married serial killer with ghastly scenes of corpses, ghosts and skeletons. Audiences who thrilled to this sort of thing were less likely to want to see serious plays – comedies or tragedies – that explored the human condition without recourse to elephants or horrors from beyond the grave.

In Rep: Plays Performed at Drury Lane During w/c 5 November 1798
Date in brackets is year of first performance

Date of performance, *Play* and playwright

Monday 5 November, *A Bold Stroke for a Wife* by Susanna Centlivre (1718) followed by *Blue-Beard* by George Colman Jr (1798)
Tuesday 6 November, *The Gamester* by Edward Moore (1753) followed by *The Prize* by Prince Hoare (1793)
Wednesday 7 November, *The Castle-Spectre* by Matthew Lewis (1798) followed by *The Shipwreck* by Samuel Arnold (1796)
Thursday 8 November, *The Stranger* by Benjamin Thompson adapted from Kotzebue (1798) followed by *The Liar* by Samuel Foote (1762)
Friday 9 November, *The Jew* by Richard Cumberland (1794) followed by *Blue-Beard* by George Colman Jr (1798)
Saturday 10 November, *The Rivals* by Richard Brinsley Sheridan (1775) followed by *No Song, No Supper* by Prince Hoare (1790)

In 1799 Sheridan took up his pen to write his first full-length play since *The School for Scandal* and the last thing he would ever write for the stage. It was called *Pizarro* and it became the biggest block-buster ever seen. It was based on another of Kotzebue's German dramas called *Die Spanier in Peru (The Spaniards in Peru)*, although Sheridan always insisted that his play was so significantly altered from the German text that it should be seen as an original work. Under normal circumstances, no one would have been very interested in a story about the relationship between Spain and its conquered Peruvian subjects in the sixteenth century, but in 1799 Britain was at war with revolutionary France under the leadership of Napoleon. It was easy to see the freedom-loving Peruvians as the British, leading the coalition against French tyranny. The heroic Rolla, commander of the Peruvian army, puts heart into his soldiers on the eve of battle by comparing the motives of both sides: 'They... fight for power, for plunder and extended rule – we for our country, our altars and our homes. They follow an adventurer whom they fear and obey a power which they hate. We serve a monarch whom we love – a God whom we adore.' Sheridan, who had been praised by Frederick Reynolds for avoiding trap-claps in *The School for Scandal,* was up to his neck in them now. He even inserted into the characters' mouths extracts from his own speeches in the House of Commons.

Pizarro opened on 24 May 1799 with the strongest cast Drury Lane could muster, led by Kemble, Sarah Siddons and Dorothy Jordan, in a magnificent production with new sets and costumes and music by Michael Kelly. Sheridan took his tendency to procrastinate right to the wire this time:[9] when the first performance started, he hadn't written the last scenes of the play. He sat in the prompter's room scribbling at speed and handing the sheets to copyists, who would give the actors their last pages of the script to get by heart during the play. The first performance was a bit ragged and finished five minutes before midnight,[10] but *Pizarro* was an astounding success. It ran for 31 consecutive performances apart from one night when another play had been arranged as a benefit for the theatre's housekeeper. This was unheard of for a tragedy. It took £13,624 9*s.* 6*d.* in its first season – despite opening towards the end of the season – and £16,422 4*s.* 0*d.* in the next season. Such sums had never been known in the theatre before. Once again, Sheridan had displayed his uncanny knack for pulling a rabbit out of a hat at the critical moment.

God Save the King

George III was not often seen at Drury Lane while Sheridan was in charge as he strongly disapproved of Sheridan's politics. Sheridan was not just a Whig but a staunch supporter of Charles James Fox on what we might call the hard left of the party. He had made himself unpopular with the King and many others by his enthusiastic support for the French Revolution in its early days and his strong opposition to war with France. He had made himself doubly unpopular with George III by his friendship with the Prince of Wales and his support for the creation of the Prince as Regent during the King's first onset of porphyria, which was taken to be madness. Following his recovery, the King pointedly made his first public appearance at Covent Garden and rarely visited the rival house.✤ However, *Pizarro* made Sheridan look far more patriotic, and the King decided to visit the Theatre Royal again.

On 15 May 1800, he commanded a performance of Colley Cibber's play *She Would and She Would Not*. As he came into the royal box, a madman in the pit stood up and fired a pistol at him, narrowly missing his head. The King took a step back then, with great courage, advanced to the front of the box, put his opera glass in his eye and looked around the house, to show that he was safe. Sheridan managed to stop the Queen and the princesses from entering the box by telling them that someone was letting off firecrackers, and the Marquis of Salisbury, then the Lord Chamberlain, asked the King to go back into the royal retiring room. 'Sir, you discompose me as well as yourself,' was the reply, 'I shall not stir one step.' The Queen wanted to leave, but the King insisted on staying for the whole performance. After the shock, no one was in the mood for a comedy, and the Queen and princesses were bathed in tears throughout the performance. 'God Save the King' was called for four times, and during the last rendition Michael Kelly, who was leading the singing, was handed a new verse written by Sheridan during the show. He sang:

> From every latent foe,
> From the assassin's blow
> God save the King.
> O'er him thine arm extend,
> For Britain's sake defend
> Our father, prince and friend,
> God save the King.

✤ Between 1785 and 1800 the King and Queen commanded 32 performances at Drury Lane but 119 – nearly four times as many – at Covent Garden. (*The London Stage*, Part 5, i, l.)

Kelly was made to repeat it three times, with the audience joining in, and it became part of the lyrics of the National Anthem. George III was more inclined to patronise Drury Lane after that.

The return of Kemble as manager

At this time, John Philip Kemble was at the height of his powers and reputation as an actor. His resignation as manager four years earlier had freed him to concentrate on his roles and *The Stranger* and *Pizarro* had both given him meaty parts. His standing as leading Shakespearean actor and respected Shakespearean scholar was beyond question. He was also well off financially. In spite of the irregularity of pay-day at Sheridan's Drury Lane ('Tomorrow was always his favourite pay-day' was Michael Kelly's verdict on his boss[11]), Kemble was well-off and in a position to invest in the management of a theatre. He believed that, properly managed, Drury Lane could be as culturally significant as it had been under Garrick and still turn a profit. Sheridan, who had no interest in Drury Lane as a temple of the drama, wanted Kemble's investment and wrote him a flattering letter suggesting that together they could prevent Drury Lane from falling into 'vulgar or illiberal hands'.[12] He invited Kemble to take up the position of manager again and to buy a share in the theatre.

Kemble was seduced by the prospect and agreed. He opened the 1800/1801 season with his own Hamlet, only to find that nothing had changed and that, in spite of money pouring into the treasury from *Pizarro*, there still wasn't enough to pay salaries. This was largely owing to the fact that Sheridan was using the takings from *Pizarro* to pay his other debts. Kemble was reduced to writing a stream of letters to Richard Peake, Drury Lane's treasurer, threatening to withdraw his services and those of his sister unless their back-wages were paid:

> Let me remind you that you are to send the fifty pounds for Mrs
> Siddons today, or we shall have no *King John* on Saturday... They

are standing still in Greenwood's Room for want of a little canvas – Unless you can help us there, we can have no *Cymbeline*, nor no pantomime this Christmas… We are all at a stand for want of colours [paint] – If you help us you shall have *Cymbeline* and full houses – otherwise, we must go on with *The West Indian*… unless you send me a hundred pounds before Thursday, I will not act on Thursday – and if you make me come a-begging again, it will be for two hundred pounds before I set my foot in the theatre.[13]

Poor Richard Peake was in an unenviable position, but so was Kemble. As an actor, it was embarrassing and unpleasant for him to have to keep making threats just to get paid; as a manager, it must have driven him to distraction to see the workshops standing idle for want of paint and canvas with the profitable pantomime season looming.

In the following year the inevitable crunch came. The bankers Messrs Hammersley foreclosed and applied to the Lord Chancellor for first call on all of the theatre's income to clear its debts. This was the sort of crisis that brought out the best in Sheridan and he gave a brilliant account of himself in court, deploying the eloquence that had caused his speeches in the House of Commons to be regarded as some of the best ever delivered there. Sheridan admitted his own failings in the most candid and disingenuous way, but then went on to say that if the bank had first call on the takings, the actors would go unpaid. In such a case, they would withdraw their services and there would be no money to pay anyone. The court found in favour of Sheridan, although a committee was appointed to represent the interests of the creditors. This was a serious blow for Sheridan, as it would prevent him from using the theatre as his piggy-bank in future: takings would actually be used to pay off the debts of the theatre, not his own. Furthermore, the Lord Chancellor took the opportunity to quote the famous conclusion to Dr Johnson's *Life of Richard Savage*: 'Negligence and irregularity, long continued, make knowledge useless, wit ridiculous, and genius contemptible.' So Sheridan didn't completely get away with his attempt to portray himself as a naïve artistic type, unable to get his head around the accounts.

For Kemble, this was the last straw. He realised that a share in Drury Lane would be a share in debt and mismanagement for as long as Sheridan was around, so he announced his departure. He gave a farewell dinner for his friends and colleagues at which Sheridan arrived, uninvited. He took Kemble into another room, and shortly afterwards they emerged in the best of spirits, announcing that Kemble was to remain as manager after all.

What made Kemble change his mind, after all of his bad experiences with Sheridan? Did he really think things would change? The answer lies in the way in which Sheridan could deploy his astonishing personal charm on people who were threatening to derail his plans. Sheridan's charm – 'there has been nothing like it since the days of Orpheus' according to Byron[14] – was a potent weapon, particularly when deployed against angry creditors. There are numerous stories about the way in which Sheridan could charm those who were demanding immediate repayment to the point of getting them to lend him more money before departing. One must suffice, from Michael Kelly's *Reminiscences*.

During the building of the new theatre, when the Drury Lane company was occupying the King's Theatre in the Haymarket, Sheridan was able to use his influence to get a new licence authorising the King's to put on Italian opera. He then set up his own opera company which he placed under the management of Michael Kelly. After several weeks of non-payment, the singers delivered a written demand to Kelly on a Saturday morning, promising not to go on that night unless they received £3,000 in back-pay. Kelly went to the theatre's bank to see the manager, who told him in no uncertain terms that the bank would not advance another shilling either to Mr Sheridan or Drury Lane as they were already too far in arrears themselves. Kelly then went round to see Sheridan at his house in Mayfair to alert him to the crisis. Sheridan kept Kelly waiting for two hours while he got dressed, then, when the situation was explained to him, said nonchalantly: 'Three thousand pounds, Kelly! There is no such sum in nature.' 'Then, Sir,' said Kelly, 'there is no alternative but closing the Opera House.' Sheridan didn't agree and told Kelly to get a hackney coach to take them to the bank. He left Kelly waiting in the coach and, after 15 minutes, emerged with the £3,000 in cash. Handing it to Kelly, he told him to deposit the money with the treasurer, but to keep back enough to buy a barrel of oysters which they would enjoy together that night. 'By what hocus-pocus he got it, I never knew... but certes he brought it to me out of the very house where, an hour or two before, the firm had sworn that they would not advance him another sixpence.'[15]

The departure of Kemble and Siddons

The truce between Kemble and Sheridan didn't last for long. Early in 1802 Kemble was advised by his lawyer, who had been investigating the possibility of Kemble buying a share in Drury Lane, that he could not proceed. Sheridan had enmeshed the theatre in such a tangle of legal and financial obligations that it was by no means clear that he was, in fact, the owner of the business, with the right to sell shares in it. Kemble realised that there was no point in trying to work with Sheridan any longer. At the close of the 1801/02 season he resigned as both manager and actor and departed for Covent Garden, in which he had bought a one-sixth share. He took Mrs Siddons with him.

The loss of these two great actors was a severe blow to Sheridan, but he had no alternative other than to carry on as best he could since the income from Drury Lane was vital to fund his political career. The following year saw another of those amazing stokes of luck that bailed him out, just when things seemed hopeless. It came in the form of a short melodramatic afterpiece called *The Caravan or the Driver and His Dog*, written by Frederick Reynolds. Reynolds had been the 12-year-old Westminster schoolboy who fled at the roar of the audience on the first night of *The School for Scandal* when the screen fell down. He had grown up to be a successful playwright, although his association had been mainly with Covent Garden. However, the plot of *The Caravan* revolved around a dog that would dive into a lake to save a drowning child. The stage of Covent Garden at the time was not up to providing this special effect, but it proved an easy matter to accommodate a lake on the vast and well-equipped stage at Drury Lane. The main issue was casting the part of the dog, which was given to Carlo, a magnificent Newfoundland belonging to a local butcher. Carlo proved a bit difficult at rehearsals as he didn't want to hurl himself down the steep drop from the piece of scenery representing the edge of a cliff into the tank. Eventually, with the aid of some screens to focus his vision and quite probably the toe of someone's boot in his rear end, Carlo got the hang of it and had done the jump a dozen times by the time the show opened. He was a sensation on the first night, receiving such rapturous applause that Sheridan realised he had a much-needed hit on his hands. He rushed into the Green Room ten minutes after the fall of the curtain crying: 'Where is he? Where is my guardian angel?' The prompter told him that the author had left the building a few minutes ago. 'Pooh,' replied Sheridan, 'I mean the dog; actor, author and preserver of Drury Lane Theatre.'✤

The Young Roscius

A year later, another extraordinary piece of luck would give the fortunes of Drury Lane a boost. Towards the end of 1804, London witnessed the arrival of young Master William Betty, a child star whose extraordinary career makes those of all subsequent juvenile prodigies look tame in comparison. Betty, who was 13 when he pitched up in the capital, had begun his acting career the year before in Ireland, where he had grown up. After a four-night stint in Belfast playing in popular

---

✤ Reynolds tells the story of Carlo in his autobiography, i, 349-52. However, there is a very similar story about the dog in Michael Kelly's *Reminiscences* that makes exactly the same point. According to Kelly, Sheridan went into the Green Room just before a performance of *The Caravan* to be told by Charles Dignum, who was appearing in the piece, that it was a terrible thing to allow illness to halt the performance of such a successful play. Sheridan became alarmed and asked him what he meant. 'I am so unwell,' replied Dignum, 'that I cannot go on longer than tonight.' 'You!' exclaimed Sheridan, 'My good fellow, you terrified me; I thought you were going to say that the dog was taken ill!' (Michael Kelly, 177-78)

stock plays of the time – *Zara, Douglas, Pizarro* – he had gone on to Dublin, Cork, Glasgow, Edinburgh and Birmingham. It was while the boy was breaking box-office records in Birmingham that the managers of Drury Lane and Covent Garden became seriously interested and sent their respective agents to secure his services. Mr Macready, manager of the Birmingham theatre and father of William Charles Macready, who later became the leading tragedian of his generation, reported that Betty had played to full houses for fourteen performances, when Mrs Siddons had never got beyond six. Sheridan's agent offered half the takings of a benefit performance in exchange for twelve shows at Drury Lane. Betty senior took a dim view of this and entered into negotiations with Covent Garden, receiving an offer of twelve performances at fifty guineas a performance plus a clear benefit – i.e. the entire takings of the house for the benefit performance with no management charges deducted. These were truly staggering terms: no actor on the London stage had ever come anywhere near them. John Philip Kemble, the acknowledged leader of the acting profession, was receiving £37 16s. a week at Covent Garden.[16]

Sheridan was furious when he found he had lost out to his rivals and foresaw the ruin of his season. He sent his agent chasing after the Betty entourage, which was by this time in Liverpool, to see if the contract with Covent Garden had included a non-compete clause. Amazingly, the Covent Garden management had overlooked that, so Sheridan was able to sign up Master Betty to appear on the same terms at Drury Lane between his Covent Garden appearances. At this stage, neither Sheridan nor Harris, his opposite number at Covent Garden, had seen the boy act.

William Betty's first appearance at Covent Garden was on Saturday 1 December 1804. The atmosphere of anticipation in London had by this time passed from hysterical adulation to potentially riotous. By early afternoon a crowd of people stretched all around the Piazza and police were called to prevent a storming of the theatre. When the doors were finally opened, the theatre filled up in minutes with a seething mass of people, as men climbed over the fronts of boxes to seize places in the pit that was already full. Master Betty's performance in the now forgotten tragedy of *Barbarossa* received such blanket coverage that the Napoleonic wars were driven from the people's minds. *The Times* gave it a quarter of the space available for news in the paper, claiming that: 'the first appearance of Master Betty in London may be considered as a remarkable epoch in the history of the stage.'[17] The Countess of Bessborough wrote to a friend that: 'You would not suspect that... Europe was in a state of warfare and bondage; it seems as if the whole people of England had but one interest, one occupation – to decide on the merits of Master Betty.' Napoleon crowned himself emperor in Paris on the day the reviews appeared, but this was of comparatively little interest. 'The war and Buonaparte were for a time unheeded and forgotten,' said the *Morning Post*.[18]

Betty was due to act at Covent Garden every night for the next week, with his first Drury Lane appearance scheduled for the following Monday. By this time the pressure was beginning to tell and he developed a fever which affected his voice – unsurprisingly, as he needed to project his teenage voice to the back of the gallery, unaided by amplification, in theatres that seated thousands. The Prince of Wales, no less, intervened and told the management not to work the boy so hard. They gave him one night off in the week, and Sheridan announced that he would not be required to appear for more than three nights at Drury Lane the following week.

Drury Lane was no less packed than Covent Garden, although Betty was clearly ill and collapsed the following week, when all performances had to be cancelled. Southampton Row, where the family was staying, was jammed with carriages as persons of quality sought assurances as to the boy's health. Medical bulletins were posted daily on the door of the house – an expedient only used by royalty and the upper echelons of the aristocracy up to then – but he eventually recovered and went to recuperate at Bushey House, where the Duke of Clarence – the future William IV – lived with Mrs Jordan.

On 13 February, Betty was back onstage at Drury Lane and continued to perform there until the end of April. The astonishing financial success of this run – with a gross return from twenty-five performances amounting to more than £15,000 – put Sheridan in the unusual position of operating at a profit. He was able to pay the Duke of Bedford arrears of rent going back several years and to offer six months in advance, which must have come as something of a shock to His Grace.[19]

On 4 March Betty gave his first performance as Romeo at Drury Lane, followed on 14 March by his first-ever Hamlet in London. Betty was promoted as the Young Roscius, which was a bold claim as Garrick had been referred to as Roscius, the most famous actor of ancient Rome. To draw a comparison between a thirteen-year-old and the greatest actor in the history of the English stage was a risky strategy, but it paid off. For a while, he was seriously spoken of as an actor of unparalleled genius and Charles James Fox pronounced Master Betty's Hamlet 'finer than Garrick's'.[20]

In his 1967 book *The Prodigy*, Giles Playfair compared Bettymania with Beatlemania as the only outbreak of mass hysteria over a showbusiness phenomenon that came close. However, Beatlemania affected almost exclusively teenage girls. Bettymania afflicted the whole of society from the royal family down, and it attracted far more men than women. The fans of the Beatles were dismissed by cultural commentators as impressionable girls, but it was the guardians of the culture themselves who were praising Master Betty not only above Kemble and other actors of his time, but even above the great Garrick.

Of course, it ended as quickly as it had begun. William Betty was engaged for another season, still moving between Drury Lane and Covent Garden, but the first flush of hysteria was over, and there was no talk of a third London season. He toured for a few years in the provinces, playing to smaller and smaller houses, until in 1808, at the age of 17, he was admitted to Christ's College, Cambridge. He left two years later without a degree and tried to restart his career as an adult actor. This was a forlorn venture, not helped by the fact that he had now put on a lot of weight, and Betty became so depressed that he twice attempted suicide. (The second attempt failed grotesquely when he tried to throw himself through a window but became stuck in the frame.) He finally admitted defeat in 1824, resigned to being a has-been at 33. He lived out the rest of his long life as a stout, genial and prosperous gentleman of whom his neighbours would have found it incredible that the painter James Northcote had once said of him that 'he and Buonaparte now divide the world'.[21]

16

The Ravages of Fire

Sheridan's first wife, the beautiful and brilliant Elizabeth Linley, had borne him a son before her early death from tuberculosis at the age of 38. Thomas, always known as Tom, was adored by his father and certainly took after him in some respects. He inherited the charm and the wit, but not the driving ambition and certainly not the genius. He drifted through life, getting into scrapes and running up debts, always sure that his father would bail him out. He looked to his father to find him a position, and there was certainly no lack of commitment on his father's part there. He persuaded his friend the Prince of Wales to finance Tom's three attempts – all unsuccessful – to get into parliament, then got Tom into the army for a brief and undistinguished military career. In 1806, Sheridan decided to bring his son into the family business. He gave Tom a 25 per cent share in Drury Lane and appointed him manager. Tom, by this time 31, had no professional experience of the theatre, so it wasn't very likely that he would make a success of a job that had defeated all previous incumbents including John Philip Kemble. As if managing Drury Lane weren't enough of a challenge, he also became joint proprietor and sole manager of the Lyceum Theatre, a few yards down the road on the corner with the Strand. Tom once excused his lack of ambition and his dependence on his father by saying that, ever since he had been a boy, Drury Lane had been set before him as his future inheritance, and this had discouraged him from making efforts in any other area. Unfortunately he would live to see this inheritance go up in smoke – literally.

On the evening of 24 February 1809, Sheridan senior was in the House of Commons where a debate was taking place on the war with Spain. Light from a great blaze was coming through the windows of the chamber and, when news arrived that Drury Lane was on fire, it was proposed that the sitting should be adjourned to allow Sheridan to attend to his interests. Always one for the grand gesture, Sheridan replied that he would not allow his private affairs to interfere with the conduct of the business of the nation. He left to visit the scene with some fellow MPs and found the situation to be hopeless. The fire had broken out in a coffee-house in Bridges Street and spread to the theatre. There had been no performance that night as it was a Friday in Lent, so by the time the blaze was noticed, at 11 p.m., it had taken hold, and within half an hour the roof had fallen in. The treasurers, Mr Peake and Mr Dunne, at great personal risk, managed to bring out an iron chest which contained the theatre's most important documents, including the patent, but nothing else could be saved.

> *The very ravages of fire we scout,*
> *For we have wherewithal to put it out.*

This had been the proud boast of the epilogue delivered at the opening of the theatre, fifteen years earlier. It sounded in retrospect like a horrible example of what happens when you tempt providence. The architect's fire precautions proved to be useless: the iron curtain had rusted into place and been dismantled, while the water tanks in the roof were said to be half empty.[1] Holland's auditorium, although making extensive use of cast iron supports, was encased in a wooden framework that went up like tinder.

As Sheridan sat drinking a glass of wine outside the Piazza coffee-house, one of his companions asked him how he could be so calm as he watched the source of his income going up in flames. 'A man may surely be allowed to take a glass of wine by his own fireside' was his laconic reply.✤

Most people would have been crushed by a disaster of this magnitude, but Sheridan was always at his best in a crisis. The day after the fire, he met with his principal actors, the stage manager and Michael Kelly (who had by this time retired from Drury Lane) to work out a strategy. Sheridan fully intended to rebuild Drury Lane, but meanwhile the most urgent thing was to find somewhere for the company to perform under his patent, 'for though the theatre was destroyed, the patent was not'. The only condition he made, 'which was with him a *sine qua non*', was that the whole company should stick together. He explained that the principal actors would easily get work in other theatres, but what would then happen to other members of the company, both acting and non-acting? 'Elect yourselves into a committee, but keep in your remembrance even the poor sweepers of the stage who, with their children, must starve if not protected by your fostering care.'[2] It was a noble sentiment, but Sheridan would soon discover that the future of Drury Lane was now out of his control and he would no longer be a part of it.

Sheridan's management of Drury Lane has attracted much less attention than that of Garrick. This is partly because his new theatre lasted for only 15 years, but he had been manager for 18 years before that building opened. With 33 years in total, he was manager for longer than Garrick's 29 years and, in terms of the changes that came over Drury Lane, his management was far more significant than Garrick's. The enormous increase in the size of the stage and auditorium made Drury Lane problematic for serious plays, but ideal for spectacle. We can see the change in the repertoire if we compare the productions

---

✤ Like other famous one-liners (e.g. 'Let them eat cake') this one has had its authenticity called into question. It is recorded by Thomas Moore, Sheridan's first biographer, in somewhat cautious terms: 'Without vouching for the authenticity or novelty of this anecdote, (which may have been, for aught I know, like the wandering Jew, a regular attendant upon all fires since the time of Hierocles) I give it as I heard it.' (Thomas Moore, *Memoirs of the Life of the Right Honourable Richard Brinsley Sheridan*, London, 1825, 526.) At this distance, we can only feel that, if Sheridan didn't say it, he should have said it.

Sheridan's Repertoire: Shakespeare and Selected Dramatists

Number of performances in brackets

	1776/1777 (First Season)	Total Performances	1799/1800	Total Performances	1807/08 (Last Full Season)	Total Performances
Shakespeare	As You Like It (2); Cymbeline (2); Hamlet (6); Macbeth (4); Measure for Measure (1); Othello (1); Richard III (2); Romeo and Juliet (4); The Tempest (18); Twelfth Night (4)	44	As You Like It (5); Measure for Measure (1); The Merchant of Venice (3); Much Ado About Nothing (2); Othello (1); Richard III (2); Hamlet (6); The Tempest (2)	22	As You Like It (1); Much Ado About Nothing (3); Romeo and Juliet (3);	7
William Congreve	Love for Love (9); The Old Batchelor (8); The Way of the World (6)	23	Love for Love (4)	4	Love For Love (4)	4
Thomas Otway	Venice Preserv'd (1)	1		0		0
John Vanbrugh/ Richard Brinsley Sheridan	A Trip to Scarborough (10)	10	A Trip to Scarborough (4)	4	A Trip to Scarborough (3)	3
George Farquhar		0		0	The Beaux' Stratagem (1)	1
Nicholas Rowe	The Fair Penitent (1); Jane Shore (2); Tamerlane (2)	5	Jane Shore (2);	2		0
Richard Steele	The Conscious Lovers (2); The Funeral (2)	4		0		0
Joseph Addison	The Drummer (1)	1		0		0
Oliver Goldsmith		0	She Stoops to Conquer (1)	1	She Stoops to Conquer (1)	0
Richard Brinsley Sheridan	The Rivals (10); The School for Scandal (20);	30	Pizarro (36); The Rivals (5); The School for Scandal (4);	45	The Duenna (3); Pizarro (7); The Rivals (1); The School for Scandal (3)	14

that Sheridan put on in his first year as manager (1776/77) with those of his last full season (1807/08).

Shakespeare was less popular and his contemporaries had almost vanished from the stage. Congreve was the last of the great Restoration playwrights to cling on. Vanbrugh was represented only by *The Trip to Scarborough*, Sheridan's version of *The Relapse*. Otway, long regarded as almost equal to Shakespeare, had disappeared, as had Rowe, Steele and Addison. *She Stoops to Conquer* merited only a single performance. Even Sheridan's own showing in the repertoire was heavily dependent on *Pizarro*. The Lane would become known for spectacle and melodrama, not for serious plays, and the saddest thing is that Sheridan himself gave up writing plays so early. We don't know what he would have produced had he continued, but he might have set the English drama on a better course for the new century, which proved to be a barren one for most of its duration. *The School for Scandal* (1777) would turn out to be the last undeniably great play to receive its first performance at Drury Lane. In *English Bards and Scotch Reviewers* (1809), Byron implored Sheridan to try again:

> *Oh Sheridan! if aught can move thy pen,*
> *Let Comedy assume her throne again;*
> *Abjure the mummery of German schools;*
> *Leave new Pizarros to translating fools;*
> *Give, as thy last memorial to the age,*
> *One classic drama, and reform the stage.*

It was not to be. One night, when Queen Charlotte was leaving Drury Lane, she asked Sheridan: 'When shall we have another play from your masterly pen?' Sheridan told her that he was writing a comedy which he expected to finish shortly. Michael Kelly heard about this and later challenged Sheridan, with the frankness of an old drinking partner: 'You will never write again; you are afraid to write.' 'Of whom am I afraid?' asked Sheridan. 'You are afraid,' said Kelly, 'of the author of *The School for Scandal*.'[3]

The bed royal

Ever since women had been appearing on the stage, the theatre had been a happy hunting ground for rich men looking for glamorous mistresses. John Downes, the author of *Roscius Anglicanus* (1708), remembered Mary Davis, who attracted the attention of Charles II by singing a song in a 1664 play that began: 'My lodging is on the cold ground': 'She performed that so charmingly that, not long after, it raised her from her bed on the cold ground to a bed royal.'[4] She was the first of a long line, but Sheridan's period at Drury Lane saw, in close succession, three of the most famous couplings of actresses with aristocrats, including two future kings. This was not, it must be said, owing to any particular moral laxity introduced into the management of the theatre's affairs by Sheridan. For all his failings as a theatre manager, he never exercised his *droit de seigneur* over the actresses: his snobbery and consciousness of his own somewhat fragile social position ensured that he conducted his extra-marital affairs with the wives of gentlemen. Nevertheless, before we leave the Sheridan era behind, we should pay tribute to these sirens of the stage.

Mary Robinson was the first and had the shortest career of the three. She was the daughter of a merchant who had fallen on hard times, but she had been well educated and was extremely beautiful. She joined the Drury Lane company in Sheridan's first season, at the age of 20, making her début as Juliet. She followed this with other Shakespearean heroines including Ophelia, Cordelia and Lady Anne (in *Richard III*). Then, in November 1779, she appeared as Perdita in *The Winter's Tale*. This was the part that changed her life, and she would always be known as Perdita Robinson afterwards. On 3 December there was a royal command performance which was attended by the Prince of Wales, then 17, who fell madly in love with her. He bombarded her with letters, signed Florizel, to which Perdita wrote encouraging replies. They became lovers and he persuaded her to retire from the stage, offering her a bond for £20,000, payable when he should be of age. Unfortunately the Prince, who was somewhat fickle in his amours, almost immediately lost interest and moved on to another mistress. Mrs Robinson, furious that she had given up her career for nothing, threatened to publish his love letters. A deal was reached whereby she handed them back in exchange for £5,000 and an annuity of £500. Perdita was a fashion icon and lived a life of fabulous extravagance. She was befriended by the Duchess of Devonshire, sought out by Marie Antoinette and bedded by Charles James Fox, Colonel Banastre Tarleton *et al.* She was a prolific and successful author, an early feminist and one of the most notorious figures in London. She died at the age of 42 in 1800.

Elizabeth Farren had a very different career. Her parents ran a touring theatre company, so it was inevitable that she would go on the stage. Her father died when she was a child, but her mother ensured that she had a good education and was taught impeccable manners. She made her London début at the Little Theatre in the Haymarket in 1777 and made such a name for herself that the managements of Drury Lane and Covent Garden were soon competing for her services. Drury Lane won, and she remained there for the rest of her career, apart from doing occasional summer seasons at the Haymarket.

Elizabeth Farren was very beautiful and very lady-like. She was a notable Beatrice in *Much Ado About Nothing* and Hermoine in *The Winter's Tale*, but she specialised in 'fine lady' parts, especially Lady Teazle in *The School for Scandal*. She became the object of the affections of the Earl of Derby, who was already married, but it was a marriage of form only. The Countess had left him for the Earl of Dorset, to whom she had borne a daughter. When the relationship broke down, the Earl of Derby allowed his wife to return, and he looked after the child as his own, but he regarded the marriage as effectively over. However, divorce was out of the question and there was no possibility of Elizabeth Farren agreeing to become his mistress. She was deeply respectable and never went anywhere, nor received anyone, without her mother acting as chaperone. The Earl accepted that it was marriage or nothing, and that theirs would be a relationship of passionate celibacy until the Countess should die. The nature of the relationship was so well understood that he had no problem in taking Elizabeth into high society, and was able to arrange for her to manage the amateur theatricals at Richmond House in 1787 and 1788 at which the parts were played by aristocrats and the audience contained the King and Queen.

On 14 March 1797, the Countess of Derby died. On 8 April, Elizabeth Farren made her farewell appearance at Drury Lane as Lady Teazle to a house that contained 3,656 people and was worth £728 14s. 6d. – the most money taken at Drury Lane in the eighteenth century for any show apart from benefit performances (when patrons made donations on top of the ticket price).✤ On 1 May, by this time in her late thirties, she married the Earl and became the new Countess of Derby. Elizabeth had been playing fine ladies for so long that she had no difficulty in keeping up the role in real life. She presided over Knowsley House, near Liverpool, as a brilliant hostess and well-loved figure in the county until her death in 1829.

Dorothy Jordan, or Dora as she preferred to be known, was the most extraordinary of the three actress-mistresses, and indeed her story, so beautifully told by Claire Tomalin in *Mrs Jordan's Profession*, is one of the most moving in the history of Drury Lane. Dora Jordan was the illegitimate daughter of an actress who was abandoned by her lover when Dora was 13. Dora followed her mother onto the stage, appearing first at the Crow Street Theatre in Dublin, then moving to the rival Smock Alley Theatre, run by Richard Daly. Daly had a reputation for sleeping with all of his actresses, and when he couldn't woo them, he was not averse to raping them. We don't know exactly what went on between Daly and Dora but, within a few months of joining the company, she was carrying his child. She was 20, with poor prospects at Smock Alley once Mrs Daly, who was also pregnant, found out what had been going on, so she travelled to England and became a member of Tait Wilkinson's touring company in Yorkshire. Dora was a brilliant performer with a gift for comedy and her reputation soon attracted the attention of London managers. She was engaged to join the Drury Lane company and opened there on 18 October 1785 in *The Country Girl*, Garrick's milk-and-water adaptation of Wycherley's *The Country Wife*. It was her first performance of the part and it was perfect for her, especially as it allowed her to appear dressed as a man in Act Three, showing off her beautiful legs. She was an

---

✤ The largest sum taken on a non-benefit night in the old auditorium had been £377 7s. 6d. on 21 March 1791 when Mrs Siddons was appearing in *Jane Shore*. The difference between these two sums shows why Sheridan wanted a bigger theatre. (*The London Stage*, Part 5, i, clxxxiv.)

immediate favourite, following up with Viola in *Twelfth Night* and Miss Hoyden in Sheridan's *A Trip to Scarborough*. Tomboyish roles were her strong point, including Priscilla Tomboy in *The Romp*, but she could do romantic as well; Rosalind in *As You Like It* would become another triumph for her, allowing her to convey all of the joyous passion of Shakespeare's heroine, whilst also showing her legs as 'Ganymede'. She had a beautiful voice both for speaking and singing and an infectious good nature that carried over the footlights.

Dora joined the company just a few months after Sarah Siddons had made her triumphant appearance as Isabella, but the two women were not in competition for the same parts. Mrs Siddons was painted as the Muse of Tragedy and Mrs Jordan as the Muse of Comedy. They rarely appeared together so they were joint stars rather than rival stars of Drury Lane. Mrs Jordan lasted longer at the Lane than Mrs Siddons, and for more than 20 years she would be a star of Drury Lane, popular both with the general public and with the 'best judges' such as Joshua Reynolds, Leigh Hunt, Lord Byron and William Hazlitt. She was not short of admirers, but she accepted the proposals of Richard Ford, a handsome and sensitive young man of 27 whose father just happened to be the Dr Ford who shared ownership of Drury Lane with Thomas Linley and Sheridan. No doubt that is how they met, but, although both father and son were theatre-lovers, Dr Ford had no intention of allowing his son to marry an actress. Dora agreed to live with Richard on the understanding that they would be married as soon as Richard could overcome his father's prejudices. Dora bore him two children, but no proposal of marriage was forthcoming, although they passed themselves off as husband and wife.

In 1791 Dora received a proposal of quite a different nature. Prince William, Duke of Clarence and third son of George III, had seen Dora on the stage and fallen in love with her. He made his intentions clear over a period of several months, during which it seems Dora used the situation to try to force Richard's hand. When he still declined to propose, she seems to have taken the view that, if she was going to be someone's mistress, it might as well be a royal duke. Ford was sent packing and Dora was offered a settlement of £840 a year by the Duke (out of his total income of £12,000 a year).

There was, inevitably, a public display of outrage by the newspapers and satire by caricaturists, and Dora was accused of being a gold-digger, ditching one keeper (the father of two of her children) for a richer one. However, it was not quite as simple as that, because although the Duke enjoyed a royal lifestyle, he had also run up royal debts, like his brothers. Dora, on the other hand, was earning a great deal of money which she had saved and invested. When the Duke began turning up at the stage door to collect Dora's pay at the end of the week, some satirists got the feel of things:

> As Jordan's high and mighty squire
> Her playhouse profits deigns to skim,
> Some folks audaciously inquire
> If he *keeps* her *or* she *keeps* him.[5]

There was no question at that time of Dora retiring from the stage, as Perdita Robinson had done and Elizabeth Farren would do; the Duke was too keen to exploit her earning capacity to make such a stipulation. Over the course of their relationship, Dora paid some very substantial debts of her 'keeper': in May 1803 she had to give him £455 to clear an outstanding bill with his upholsterer when his bank had stopped payment, and in 1797 she lent him £2,400.[6] When we consider that, in today's money, this would be worth well over a quarter of a million pounds, it gives some idea of Dora's star-power.

But to reduce the relationship to the cash nexus is really to miss the point. Dora and the Duke lived together for 20 years, during which she bore him ten children. They were in love with each other and devoted to their children. Their home life was conventional, with a chaplain to take morning prayers and church on Sundays. Apart from the fact that she was living with a man without benefit of matrimony, Dora's life was respectable and untouched by scandal. To describe her as the Duke's mistress seems out of place; today she would be called his partner.

The King and Queen disapproved strongly of their son's lifestyle, but on the other hand, his life with Dora was quiet and settled – how unlike the home-life of the Prince of Wales, the Queen might have thought. In 1797 George III presented his co-habiting son with the estate of Bushy in Surrey, only two hours by coach from the centre of London which would make it easy for the Duke to get to St James and easy for Dora to get to Drury Lane (although the King probably didn't have Dora's needs in mind). Bushy House was large and pleasant, surrounded by parkland. It would provide an idyllic home for the couple and their growing brood of children, a haven of peace away from the bustle of Drury Lane – but not too far away.

The atmosphere in the theatre must have been slightly odd, with Dora being dropped at the stage door by a coach with the royal coat of arms painted on the door, but she could always put her fellow actors at their ease by telling stories against herself. One concerned her Irish cook, whom she had to sack for insolence, but who threatened to see her at Drury Lane that night: 'Arrah, now, honey… won't I sit in the gallery, and won't your royal grace give me a courtesy, and won't I give your Royal Highness a howl, and a hiss into the bargain!'[7]

In 1809, Drury Lane burnt down, and things started to go wrong for Dora. The Duke decided that he didn't want his partner appearing on the stage, in London at least, so she did not move to the Lyceum with the rest of the company. Instead, she had to go on a series of gruelling provincial tours at a time of life (she was in her late forties) when she would probably have preferred to take things a bit easier. Then, in October 1811, the Duke summoned her to a meeting in Maidenhead at which he told her that he wished to separate from her. We can only guess at his motives, but his brother the Prince of Wales, now Regent, no doubt encouraged him to make a suitable marriage before it was too late, which would result in an increased allowance from parliament (very helpful for clearing debts) plus the possibility of more heirs to the throne. The Prince of Wales had only one legitimate offspring, Princess Charlotte, who would pre-decease her father; his brothers and sisters had none. The Duke of Clarence would eventually marry Princess Adelaide of Saxe-Meiningen, who was only slightly older than some of his daughters. She would bear him two daughters, both of whom died.

Dora was given a settlement of £4,400 per annum, but it depended on her never appearing on the stage again. If she broke this condition, it would go down to £2,100. This clause was probably the work of the Duke's advisers, as he didn't enforce it, and Dora was soon acting again. When the new Drury Lane opened in 1812, she hoped to take up her career again there, but the terms she was offered were so poor she hit the road once more.

Dora knew that she couldn't go on acting forever: she was getting older and her once beautiful figure had turned plump and flabby, making her breeches parts less delightful for the audience. The settlement from the Duke had made her independently wealthy and she was still earning good money, but she felt she could never have enough for her many dependents. She provided for her relations and her numerous children, bailing them out of scrapes and providing substantial dowries to enable her daughters to make respectable marriages. One of these marriages would prove her undoing.

In 1809, her daughter Dorothea (Dodee) had married Frederick March, the illegitimate son of Lord Henry Fitzgerald and the grandson of the Duke of Leinster. In spite of his grand lineage, March was working as a clerk in the ordnance office and he saw in this marriage to the illegitimate daughter of a royal duke and a leading actress the chance to enjoy an altogether more glamorous lifestyle. He regarded his mother-in-law as a source of funds and she went along with it. At some time in 1815, he mentioned to Dora that he was in some slight financial difficulties, and she issued notes to Coutts, allowing him to draw on her account. In September, she found that he had ruined her. Not only had he emptied her account, he had run up enormous and unpayable debts in her name. Dora was confused and badly advised: she thought she was going to be arrested for debt and, reasoning that she wouldn't be able to do much in prison, she decided to flee to France for what she thought would be a short period. She was encouraged by her son-in-law, who was in no danger himself and just wanted to get her out of the way, and by John Barton, an adviser to the Duke (whom she was now not allowed to contact directly). Barton no doubt regarded Mrs Jordan and her tribe of troublesome children as a source of endless potential embarrassment to the royal family and just wanted to put some distance between them. Dora thought Barton would arrange affairs for her, but he did nothing and didn't even tell the Duke what was happening. She took a cottage outside Boulogne where she lived with only Miss Sketchley, the former governess to her children, for company. Her health declined and she died on 5 July 1816, probably of heart disease. Her last months were spent in poverty and she was buried in Saint-Cloud. The funeral expenses were never paid, although, three years later, an English couple, who scarcely knew Dora but admired her, had a headstone erected with an inscription written by John Genest, the theatre historian. It ends: *Mementote lugete*: Remember her and weep.

The conclusion to the story is almost unbearably poignant. In 1830, the Duke of Clarence succeeded his brother and ascended the throne as William IV. One of the first things he did was to commission Francis Chantrey, the leading sculptor of the age, to create a statue of Dora with two of her children. The King intended to place it in Westminster Abbey but the Dean refused to have it, on moral grounds. So did the Dean of St Paul's. It was still in Chantrey's studio at the time of his death, when it was acquired by the Rev. Lord Augustus Fitzclarence – one of Dora's sons – and installed in his church at Mapledurham. It later passed to the fourth Earl of Munster – Dora's great-grandson – and, in 1980, moved from the Munster collection into the Royal Collection. It can now be seen in Buckingham Palace, where William IV was born and where Dora could never be received.

Grim-All-Day

There is one last person we must remember before passing from Sheridan's Drury Lane, as he played no part in the new theatre, but his name is one of the most famous in the history of pantomime: the great clown Joseph Grimaldi.

Grimaldi came from a long line of acrobats, dancers and pantomimists. His grandfather, John Baptist Grimaldi, known as Iron Legs, had been a famous performer in Paris until he did something to upset the authorities and was thrown into the Bastille. On his release, he came to London and joined John Rich's company at Covent Garden as Pantaloon in the harlequinades, but he had to make a quick escape from the country when he swindled Rich out of a lot of money. His son Giuseppe, known as the Signor, followed in the family tradition and joined Garrick's company at Drury Lane, also playing Pantaloon and taking the position of *maître de ballet*. Even in the world of the theatre, the Signor was an extraordinarily larger-than-life character, blustering, unpleasant and a violent bully. He fell out with everyone in the company including Garrick and was called Old Grim or Grim-All-Day. A long-running dispute with Garrick over money concluded when the Signor forced his way into Garrick's office and lowered his trousers, revealing a painted face on his posterior.

The Signor had women and children dotted around London, but when one of these women bore him a son, he was delighted. He showed his approval by moving in with that household, which meant that his partner, the son, christened Joseph, and another son called John, were subject to his sadistic abuse until his death ten years later. He decided to pass on his skills to Joseph, who made his first appearance on the stage at Sadler's Wells at the age of two-and-a-half, dancing with one of his half-sisters. This was not a walk-on but a fully choreographed routine which they performed perfectly, knowing that any mistakes would result in a severe beating. At the age of four, Joe opened on Boxing Day 1782 in the Drury Lane pantomime *The Triumph of Mirth, or Harlequin's Wedding* in which he played Little Clown to his father's Clown. He then joined Sadler's Wells for the summer season, playing various little creatures and fairies. The Sadler's Wells season ran from Easter Monday to late summer, during most of which patent theatres were closed, so they were allowed to operate undisturbed. Nevertheless, Sadler's Wells could not present plays, as the spoken word was still confined to Drury Lane, Covent Garden and the Little Theatre in the Haymarket during the summer. It presented a mixture of pantomimes, dancing, variety acts and what were called burlettas: three-act entertainments consisting of musical numbers interspersed with some speeches in rhyming couplets, but no dialogue. Sadler's Wells was some way out of London, in what was then rural Islington, and catered for a much rougher audience than the patent theatres.

Although still a child, Joe was working full-time, going between Drury Lane and Sadler's Wells, and soon learned the risks of his profession. At Sadler's Wells he played a monkey which was led on a chain by the Signor. The Signor would swing him around faster and faster on his chain, which inevitably broke one night and sent Joe into the back of the pit. At Drury Lane he sustained a more serious injury in the 1785 pantomime *Hurly Burly* in which he played a cat. Unfortunately, no one had thought to cut eyes in the cat costume, so he ran onto the stage and fell through a trapdoor that had been accidentally left open, hitting the floor thirty feet below. He broke his collarbone and was off work until the next season opened at Sadler's Wells at Easter.

In 1788 the Signor died, probably to everyone's relief, but continued to terrify his family even after death. He had entertained a morbid fear of being buried alive, and left instructions that his corpse should be burned with candles, pricked with pins and then decapitated to prevent this horrible occurrence. His oldest daughter Mary had to perform the grisly task, according to the terms of her father's will, although a local butcher was brought in to force the blade of the knife, on which she merely rested her hand while she looked away.

At the age of nine, Joe became the breadwinner for the family. Sheridan, who was always generous to struggling fellow professionals, raised his salary at Drury Lane to 25 shillings a week (£1.25), but it was a different story at Sadler's Wells where it was cut from 15 shillings a week (75p) to three (15p), on the basis that he didn't have his father to teach him pantomime tricks anymore.

Joe continued to work for both Sadler's Wells and Drury Lane, sometimes appearing at both on the same night when the Sadler's Wells summer season overlapped by a few weeks with the main theatre season. This was possible because the evening's entertainment was divided into mainpiece and afterpiece, with pantomimes always being afterpieces. Joe claimed that he learnt to run from one to the other in eight minutes, which indicates considerable agility. He appeared in mainpieces at Drury Lane, such as Sheridan's *A Trip to Scarborough* and *Hamlet*, in which he played one of the gravediggers, but his career really took off at Sadler's Wells where, in 1800, he appeared for the first time as Clown in a pantomime in his own right (i.e. not as an understudy or stand-in). The pantomime was called *Peter Wilkins* and involved two of everything – two Harlequins, two Columbines and two Clowns. Joe was Guzzle the Drinking Clown opposite John Baptist Dubois, London's leading clown, as Gobble the Eating Clown. He was a great success, and went on to play Clown in Drury Lane's next pantomime *Harlequin Amulet*, opening on 22 December 1800. It did so well that it was revived for Christmas 1801, closing in March 1802. Joe then went off to Kent to do some performances for a Mrs Baker who ran theatres in Maidstone and Canterbury and paid well. Unfortunately he found that John Philip Kemble had announced him to appear in the mainpiece at Drury Lane on Easter Monday, which was contrary to the terms of his contract which stated that he could only do afterpieces at Drury Lane once the Sadler's Wells summer season had begun. In fact, he was not claiming the right to appear at Sadler's Wells but in Kent, so he went to see Kemble to explain that he wouldn't be available on the date. Kemble refused to listen and simply insisted he must appear. When he didn't, he received a note telling him that his services would no longer be required at Drury Lane. Fortunately for Joe, this was in June, and Kemble resigned as manager in July, leaving Drury Lane for good. Sheridan soon re-appointed Joe.

It was at this time that Joe came up with his distinctive make-up and costume which changed the look of clowning. Clowns had traditionally worn tatty servants' costumes, with perhaps a red wig and red cheeks. Joe devised the complete mask of white with vivid crescent-shaped cheeks and a huge mouth in red, topped by a highly-coloured Mohican wig. His costume was a brilliant patchwork of squares and triangles of multi-coloured fabrics, covered with spangles and topped with a ruff. He called the look 'Joey', and clowns are known as Joeys to this day.

In November 1803, Joe was involved in a real-life Drury Lane mystery. During a performance of Susanna Centlivre's play *A Bold Stroke for a Wife*, Joe was told that two gentlemen were waiting to see him at the stage door. They were both well dressed and one spoke to

Joe in such familiar language that Joe thought he was being made fun of. He turned to go, but the man opened his shirt and pointed to a scar on his chest, saying: 'Joe, don't you know me now?' Joe realised that this was his brother John who had gone to sea sixteen years before and had been presumed dead, in the absence of any communications. John looked tanned and prosperous, beautifully dressed and carrying a gold-topped cane. Joe told him that he couldn't leave the theatre until the play was over and asked him to come to the Green Room. John's companion left at this point, saying that they would meet at ten the following morning. Joe took John to the Green Room and introduced him to other actors, with whom he chatted until the end of the play. Joe then went to his dressing room to get changed and said he would meet John in a few minutes. When he returned, John was nowhere to be found. Joe was told that he had left minutes before, so he went to various places, including his own house, where John might have gone. Several people had seen him but no one knew where he was. For several days Joe searched the Covent Garden area but could discover nothing. The police conducted a search and the Admiralty became involved, but nothing was ever heard of John again. He had told Joe that he carried £600 in his pocket, and Joe had warned him that it was dangerous to have so much cash on him. John had replied that sailors cared nothing for danger, and he had plenty more anyway. He was probably murdered for this cash, and suspicion naturally fell on the other man, who was unknown and whose features Joe couldn't remember.

In 1805 Joe walked out of Drury Lane and joined the opposition at Covent Garden over a petty dispute that could easily have been avoided. The *maître de ballet* was an important person at Drury Lane as he was responsible for the considerable amount of dance in every evening's programme, and especially the pantomimes. When James Byrne, who had been doing the job for several years, left in the summer of 1805, Joe was asked to take over until a replacement was found. He agreed on condition that his salary would go up from £4 a week to £6 a week, not just until the new person was found but until the end of the season. Byrne had been on £10 a week. This was agreed, and when Joe collected his raised salary for the first time, Peake, the treasurer, showed him a letter from Aaron Graham, the chairman of the board, giving the instruction that the rise should apply until the end of the season. However, on 26 October, after a new *maître de ballet* had been appointed, Joe went to the treasury to find that his salary had gone back down to £4 on the chairman's instructions. Joe was so angry that, a few days later, he went to see Thomas Harris at Covent Garden, who was only too happy to hire him. When Joe went into the Green Room that night, waiting to go on as Pan in a dance extravaganza called *Terpsichore's Return*, he found Graham himself there, and received a dressing down in front of the rest of the cast for disloyalty. Joe gave as good as he got and told the chairman he had seen his letter ordering the reduction in salary, in spite of their agreement. This infuriated Graham even more, and when other company members began to join in, according to Grimaldi's *Memoirs*, 'a rather stormy scene followed'.[8] The next day Joe told Graham that he would be leaving at the end of the following week, at which point Graham threatened to sue him for breach of contract. He went anyway.

Drury Lane thus lost the services of Grimaldi at the point at which he reached the peak of his powers. His engagement with Covent Garden began in the autumn of 1806, and the first pantomime in which he appeared there was *Harlequin and Mother Goose, or the Golden Egg.* It opened on 29 December 1806 and became the most successful pantomime of all time, largely because of Grimaldi. He went from being one amongst a number of London clowns to the greatest clown of them all – a title he still retains. The effect was to change the balance of the pantomime, in which Harlequin had formerly been the most important character. Now it would be Clown. Grimaldi's Clown was a character in a way that other clowns had not been. He was sensual and anarchic, acting on his base instincts and always getting away with it, rather like Mr Punch. He attacked the night-watch, tripped up old ladies and stole sausages. Lord Eldon, who had never seen a pantomime before, came to see *Mother Goose* eleven times in its first season, saying: 'Never, never did I see a leg of mutton stolen with such superhumanly sublime impudence as by that man.'[9] This was high praise from a man who was Lord Chancellor for over 20 years, but part of Grimaldi's fame depended on the way in which he could appeal to the gallery and the boxes. Byron was a fan; and one of his routines, which involved using a basket of Covent Garden vegetables to build a creature who came to life and chased him off the stage, was thought to have influenced Mary Shelley's *Frankenstein*. His memoirs were edited by Charles Dickens and illustrated by Cruikshank.

In his biography of Grimaldi, Andrew McConnell Stott presents him as the archetype of that familiar figure, the clown who is crying beneath his greasepaint. Grimaldi suffered from depression and used to quip of himself: 'I make you laugh at night but am Grim-All-Day'. One of the most famous stories about him concerns his visit to a doctor, seeking some cure for the melancholia that afflicted him. After listening to his symptoms, the doctor advised 'relaxation and amusement… perhaps sometimes at the theatre. Go and see Grimaldi.' 'Alas,' was the reply, 'that is of no avail to me; I am Grimaldi.'[10]

However, depression was not the only thing that made him Grim-All-Day. By the age of 40, his body was showing serious signs of wear-and-tear. The life of a pantomimist was dangerous and unrelenting. Jumping through hoops, taking falls, dropping through traps and screwing the body up into contorted shapes resulted in regular injuries which, even if not fatal or life-threatening, had a cumulative effect. Sprains and fractures were not allowed to heal properly, as a missed performance meant no pay, until deformity and chronic rheumatoid arthritis set in.

When Grimaldi had to cancel shows in Dublin because his body refused to carry on, a local doctor diagnosed 'premature old age'.[11] He was 42. A year-and-a-half later, he was repeatedly collapsing between his scenes at Covent Garden until, on 3 May 1823, he was unable to go on. Charles Kemble, younger brother of John Philip and Mrs Siddons and by this time manager of Covent Garden, kept him on half-salary to the end of the 1823/24 season, after which Grimaldi had no income. Well-wishers organised a benefit for him at Sadler's Wells on 17 March 1828 which went well, after which he applied to Kemble for another one at Covent Garden. In spite of the thousands of pounds he had earned for the theatre over the years, Kemble refused.

Grimaldi then received a generous offer from Stephen Price, the proprietor of Drury Lane, of the use of his theatre free of any charges for a benefit, fixed for 27 June 1828.

It was an emotional occasion, especially as Grimaldi was unable to stand. The only pantomime routine he could perform was one that allowed him to sit in a barber's chair and be shaved. He then changed into evening dress and returned to the chair to read a speech written for him by Thomas Hood:

> Eight-and-forty years have not yet passed over my head, and I am sinking fast. I now stand worse on my legs than I did on my head. But I suppose I am paying the penalty of the cause I have pursued all my life: my desire and anxiety to merit your favour has excited me to more exertion than my constitution would bear.[12]

Grimaldi would live for another nine years, supported by the takings at his benefits and a pension of £100 a year from the Drury Lane Theatrical Fund.

In Rep: Plays Performed at Drury Lane During w/c 16 November 1807
Date in brackets is year of first performance

Date of performance, *Play* and playwright

Monday 16 November, *The Jealous Wife* by George Colman Sr (1761) followed by *The Wood-Daemon* by Matthew Lewis (1807)
Tuesday 17 November, *The Cabinet* by Thomas Dibdin (1802) followed by *Three Weeks After Marriage* by Arthur Murphy (1764)
Wednesday 18 November, *Time's a Tell-Tale* by Henry Siddons (1807) followed by *The Wood-Daemon* by Matthew Lewis (1807)
Thursday 19 November, *All in the Wrong* by Arthur Murphy (1761) followed by *Ella Rosenberg* by James Kenney (1807)
Friday 20 November, *Love in a Village* by Isaac Bickerstaffe (1762) followed by *Ella Rosenberg* by James Kenney (1807)
Saturday 21 November, *A Trip to Scarborough* by Richard Brinsley Sheridan (1777) followed by *Ella Rosenberg* by James Kenney (1807)

PART FOUR

Our Drury Lane

17

From the Ashes

The destruction by fire of Sheridan's Drury Lane was a shocking event, not least because Covent Garden had burnt to the ground the year before. Theatres were beginning to seem very unsafe places, particularly to those who could remember the conflagrations that had destroyed the King's in 1789 and the Pantheon in 1792. Thirty-seven people had died in the Covent Garden fire, but mercifully there were no fatalities at Drury Lane as the fire had broken out on a Friday in Lent, when there was no performance.

The immediate concern was to keep the show on the road, as without performances there would be no money to rebuild the theatre. William Taylor, the proprietor of the King's, gave the company the free use of his opera house for three nights, after which they moved into the Lyceum. It was an obvious choice as it stood only yards from Drury Lane and was managed by Tom Sheridan. Covent Garden was rebuilt in a year, but the Drury Lane company would remain in temporary accommodation for the next three years, as the rebuilding proved to be a long drawn-out business, just like before. In 1791 Sheridan senior had found that he couldn't start work on a new theatre until the question of the dormant patent had been dealt with: this time it was the tangle of debts he had run up.

The indebtedness of Drury Lane, after 33 years of Sheridan's chronic financial mismanagement, was something that Sheridan couldn't even have put a figure on, although it was later calculated to amount to nearly half-a-million pounds. In order to raise funds to rebuild, it was necessary to deal with these creditors, especially those who had put up the £150,000 for the previous building, and who had seen very little by way of returns on their investment. They could, if not agreeable, have claimed the insurance money, although as the theatre had been seriously under-insured (for £35,000), that wouldn't have got them very far.

A committee of gentlemen

Sheridan came up with the idea of a committee of noblemen and gentlemen who would undertake the fundraising for this noble cause. This was mentioned in the course of a conversation with Samuel Whitbread MP, who said that he would not object to becoming a member of such a committee. Sheridan followed up this meeting with a flattering letter stating that: 'you are the man living, in my estimation, the most disposed and the most competent to bestow successfully a portion of your time and ability… Little more is necessary than resolution on my part and for a short time the superintending advice of a mind like yours.'[1] The events that followed would see Sheridan exiled from the theatre he had regarded as his kingdom and Whitbread propelled towards mental breakdown and suicide.

Sheridan no doubt thought that he would be able to manage Whitbread. They knew each other professionally, as Whitbread was a fellow Whig MP, and personally, as Whitbread was one of the trustees of Sheridan's wife's estate. (The second Mrs Sheridan was the daughter of the Dean of Winchester who, knowing all about her future husband's habits, had insisted on a dowry to be tied up in a trust which, theoretically, Sheridan would to be able to get at.) Whitbread was independently wealthy, as heir to the brewery fortune, and extremely well connected. His family and friends begged him not to get involved with Sheridan's smoking heap of debt, but he took it on because, according to his son-in-law: 'He considered the rebuilding of Drury Lane Theatre as a vast, national object... he considered it as a point of duty to attempt the undertaking, thinking that he could be enabled to give the various proprietors and creditors of the old theatre some value for their share of debts which at that moment were worth nothing.'[2]

Whitbread certainly put together a splendid committee consisting of 86 aristocrats, representatives of the royal family, MPs, aldermen and bankers. Many of the members were creditors of the former theatre. They decided to finance the rebuilding of the theatre by forming a joint-stock company, which required an act of parliament. This was passed in June 1810, by which stage Whitbread had discovered a serious problem with regard to fundraising for Drury Lane. The first question anyone asked was: 'Has Mr Sheridan anything to do with it?' Unless he could give them a definite 'No', there would be no money forthcoming.[3] With great reluctance, Sheridan agreed to stand down and sell his interest in the business to the new company.

The preservation of a patent monopoly

In 1810 and 1811 Sheridan performed his last service for Drury Lane by fighting off the proposal to build a third London theatre, which would have threatened the attempt to rebuild Drury Lane. The need for more theatres to serve a growing population was again being raised, this time by a group of people backed by the Lord Mayor and other City interests as well as five MPs. They petitioned the King for a charter to build a theatre in East London which would be able to put on plays during the winter season, just like Covent Garden and Drury Lane. The King referred the matter to the Attorney General and Solicitor General, who found against the petition. The petitioners then sought a hearing before the Privy Council which was granted in March 1810, and which turned into a full-scale examination of the rights and wrongs of monopolies in general and theatrical monopolies in particular.

The counsel for the petitioners argued that Covent Garden and Drury Lane had become so enormous that they weren't even fit for their original purpose of putting on plays, so they had no right to prevent other theatres from being built. The counsel for Drury Lane accused the petitioners of opportunism, raising the matter when Drury Lane was in ashes in such a way as to wreck the chances of those who were trying to raise funds to rebuild it. Sheridan then spoke to argue for the maintenance of the terms of the two original patents issued by Charles II. He claimed that, if these terms were not respected, those who had invested on the strength of them had to be compensated; and that, if a third theatre were deemed desirable, he should be given the first option to build it, using the 'dormant' patent, i.e. the original Killigrew patent. Sheridan had bought this in order to facilitate the building of the 1794 theatre, but it wasn't being used as Drury Lane was still operating under the latest in a series of 21-year patents.

The Privy Council found against the petitioners for a third theatre, but that wasn't the end of it. A year later, in March 1811, a bill called the London Theatre Bill was introduced into the House of Commons to permit the building of a third theatre. Its sponsor spoke scathingly of Sheridan's assurances that Drury Lane was going to be rebuilt: two years after the blaze not a stone had been laid. The fundraising for the new Drury Lane was described as 'a wholesale swindling operation'[4] as it would never happen. Sheridan did his best to excuse the delay, but his credibility was not high, and the situation was only saved when Samuel Whitbread rose to speak as the new champion of Drury Lane. He assured members that rebuilding would soon start, and asked for a six-week postponement of consideration of the London Theatre Bill, after which time he would be in a better position to explain things. This was granted, but at the end of six weeks he could still give no assurances, and asked for the bill to be postponed until the next session of parliament. The sponsors of the bill objected, but Whitbread's reputation for integrity was so great that the House supported the postponement of the bill, which effectively killed it. From here on, the rebuilding of Drury Lane would be Whitbread's project and Sheridan would play no important part. However, although the monopoly of the patent houses had been preserved once more, the hearings before the Privy Council, the debates in the House of Commons and the coverage in the press had given the pent-up resentment against the arrangement its fullest airing. The abolition of patent privileges had been postponed, but not for long.

Rebuilding begins

Following the passage in June 1810 of the act of parliament to establish the joint-stock theatre company, known as the Theatre Royal Drury Lane Company of Proprietors, the members had appointed ten of their number to a managing committee, under the chairmanship of Whitbread, to be responsible for raising £300,000 by selling 3,000 shares at £100 each. Each shareholder would receive a proportion of the profits, and anyone with five shares or more received free admission to all shows during his or her lifetime. The capital would be used to settle all debts and claims on the old building; purchase the shares in the business belonging to Sheridan (50%), his son Tom (25%) and the widow of his old friend Joseph Richardson (25%); acquire the remaining 14/60 share of the Killigrew patent; and build a new theatre. The estimate for the new building was £150,000.

In May 1811, with the threat of a third London theatre averted and with Whitbread's reputation now on the line, the committee finally got busy. A competition was announced to find an architect, and in October 1811 the committee announced that the winner was Benjamin Dean Wyatt, the eldest son of James Wyatt who had enjoyed a brilliantly successful career as one of the country's leading architects since designing the Pantheon in Oxford Street forty years before. His son Benjamin was, however, a strange choice. Originally intended for the law, Benjamin had worked for the East India Company and then became private secretary to Sir Arthur Wellesley, the future Duke of Wellington. When Wellesley was appointed to command the British army in the Peninsula, Wyatt decided to join the family business and went to work in his father's office. This was in the year that Drury Lane burnt down, so the big prize that every architect in London wanted was the design of the new theatre. Winning the commission was an amazing achievement for a 37-year-old with absolutely no track record.

At its first general assembly of the company in October 1811, the committee reported assets of £56,700 (including a £35,000 insurance claim) against debts of £435,000 plus unpaid rent to the Duke of Bedford and an annual rent of £7,500 still payable to the subscribers of the 1794 building. Clearly, there was going to have to be a lot of compromising and goodwill. The Duke of Bedford wrote off the back-rent and almost all of the 1794 subscribers agreed to forego their arrears in return for a nightly rent on the new building and free admission. Creditors agreed to accept part-payment, and that had to extend to Sheridan and his two partners in the business. Sheridan was offered £24,000, Tom £12,000 and Mrs Richardson only £6,000, as her husband had never paid in full for his share. This total of £42,000 represented a fraction of what Sheridan had laid out to acquire control since 1776, and in a typically quixotic gesture he said that he didn't expect to be paid until the theatre had been rebuilt. This would cause problems for him in the future.

The foundation stone was laid on 29 October 1811, 20 months after the fire. The long delay had been caused by the need to establish the joint-stock company, fight off the bid for a third theatre, raise funds and negotiate with creditors. These matters were far from resolved when the new theatre started to rise, and would not be resolved until several years after it had opened. The purchase of the remaining share of the Killigrew patent, which cost £9,562, did not take place until 1813, so in the meantime the company had to obtain another 21-year patent to run from the expiry of Sheridan's patent in 1816. Ominously, the £300,000 of working capital had not been raised: only £120,000 had come in when building started, and although more would follow, the target was never reached. The Duke of Bedford issued a new ground lease to the company to expire at Christmas 1894 at an annual rent of £1,703 15s. 6d.

In spite of the delays, the work, once started, proceeded with astonishing speed and the theatre was ready to open to the public a year later, on 10 October 1812.

Prologue by Lord Byron. Spoken at the opening of the Theatre Royal,

IN one dread night our city saw,
and sighed,
Bowed to the dust, the Drama's tower
of pride;
In one short hour beheld the blazing fane,
Apollo sink, and Shakespeare cease
to reign.
Ye who beheld, (oh! sight admired and
mourned,
Whose radiance mocked the ruin
it adorned!)
Through clouds of fire the massy
fragments riven,
Like Israel's pillar, chase the night from
heaven;
Saw the long column of revolving flames
Shake its red shadow o'er the startled
Thames,
While thousands, thronged around the
burning dome,
Shrank back appalled, and trembled for
their home,
As glared the volumed blaze, and
ghastly shone
The skies, with lightnings awful as
their own,
Till blackening ashes and the lonely wall
Usurped the Muse's realm, and marked
her fall;

Say – shall this new, nor less aspiring pile,
Reared where once rose the mightiest in
our isle,
Know the same favour which the
former knew,
A shrine for Shakespeare – worthy him
and you?
Yes – it shall be – the magic of that name
Defies the scythe of time, the torch of flame;
On the same spot still consecrates the scene,
And bids the Drama be where she
hath been:
This fabric's birth attests the potent spell –
Indulge our honest pride, and say, How well!
As soars this fane to emulate the last,
Oh! might we draw our omens from
the past,
Some hour propitious to our prayers
may boast
Names such as hallow still the dome
we lost.
On Drury first your Siddons' thrilling art
O'erwhelmed the gentlest, stormed the
sternest heart.
On Drury, Garrick's latest laurels grew;
Here your last tears retiring Roscius drew,
Sighed his last thanks, and wept his
last adieu:

Prolegomena

The programme for the opening night of the fourth Theatre Royal consisted of *Hamlet* followed by a musical farce called *The Devil to Pay*. By this stage it would have been unthinkable to open the theatre with anything other than a work by the immortal Shakespeare, especially after the 1794 prologue to open Sheridan's Drury Lane had dedicated the place to him. Oddly enough, however, the most talked-

Drury Lane on 10 October 1812 by Robert Elliston.

But still for living wit the wreaths may bloom,
That only waste their odours o'er the tomb.
Such Drury claimed and claims – nor you refuse
One tribute to revive his slumbering muse;
With garlands deck your own Menander's head,
Nor hoard your honours idly for the dead!
Dear are the days which made our annals bright,
'Ere Garrick fled, or Brinsley ceased to write.
Heirs to their labours, like all high-born heirs,
Vain of our ancestry as they of theirs;
While thus Remembrance borrows Banquo's glass
To claim the sceptred shadows as they pass,
And we the mirror hold, where imaged shine
Immortal names, emblazoned on our line,
Pause – ere their feebler offspring you condemn,
Reflect how hard the task to rival them!
Friends of the stage! to whom both players and plays
Must sue alike for pardon or for praise,

Whose judging voice and eye alone direct
The boundless power to cherish or reject;
If e'er Frivolity has led to fame,
And made us blush that you forbore to blame –
If e'er the sinking stage could condescend
To soothe the sickly taste it dare not mend –
All past reproach may present scenes refute,
And censure, wisely loud, be justly mute!
Oh! since your fiat stamps the Drama's laws,
Forbear to mock us with misplaced applause;
So Pride shall doubly nerve the actor's powers,
And Reason's voice be echoed back by ours!
This greeting o'er – the ancient rule obeyed,
The Drama's homage by her herald paid
Receive our welcome too – whose every tone
Springs from our hearts, and fain would win your own.
The curtain rises – may our stage unfold
Scenes not unworthy Drury's days of old!
Britons our judges, Nature for our guide,
Still may we please – long, long may you preside.

about part of the evening's entertainment was the prologue, spoken by Robert Elliston who was playing Hamlet.

The committee had announced a competition for a prologue to open the new theatre for which the prize would be £100 plus the honour hearing it delivered. The judges were to be Lord Holland, Whitbread himself and Harvey Christian Combe, MP for the City of London. This challenge was enough to set the tribe of poetasters off in search of glory, and almost a hundred entries were received. Unfortunately they were so bad that it was decided to ditch the lot and

Lord Holland asked Byron to write one instead. This was a generous request, considering that Byron had ridiculed him and his wife in *English Bards and Scotch Reviewers* three years before, but Byron was pleased to be asked and produced a prologue. There was a vigorous correspondence back and forth between the two peers that lasted for a month, during which Byron proved to be surprisingly open to suggestions and changes imposed by Holland and his fellow judges. They took the view that insulting the audience was not the best way to get them onside, and removed some lines upbraiding the public for their appalling taste in wanting to see live animals on the stage:

> *Nay, lower still, the Drama yet deplores*
> *That late she deigned to crawl upon all-fours.*
> *When Richard roars in Bosworth for a horse,*
> *If you command, the steed must come in course.*
> *If you decree, the Stage must condescend*
> *To soothe the sickly taste we dare not mend...*

Byron accepted the cut but asked: 'Is Whitbread determined to castrate all my *cavalry* lines?'[5]

As soon as it was announced that Byron's prologue would be spoken, there were howls of protest from the competitors, claiming that the whole thing was a stitch-up and there had never been any intention of using one of their entries. One disappointed prologue-writer, Dr Thomas Busby, organist and composer, was so annoyed that he made a dramatic protest. He went to Drury Lane a few nights after the opening and sat in a stage box with his son, who astonished the audience by climbing over the front of the box onto the stage and starting to deliver his father's lines. He got to the end of the first couplet before the stage manager and a constable dragged him into the wings.

At this point two brothers, James and Horace Smith, decided to have some fun by publishing a collection called *Rejected Addresses*, in which they tried to imagine how the leading poets of the day like Wordsworth, Coleridge and Southey *would* have written a prologue for Drury Lane, if only they had been asked. *Rejected Addresses* is one of the most brilliant literary parodies in the language. It went through 17 editions by 1819 and Sir Walter Scott said that 'his' prologue was so good that he assumed he must have written it and forgotten about it. The pastiche of Byron's *Childe Harold's Pilgrimage* as 'Cui Bono? By Lord B.' is one of the best bits.

In order to defend themselves from criticism, the committee then published *The Genuine Rejected Addresses, presented to the Committee of Management for Drury Lane Theatre: preceded by that written by Lord Byron and adopted by the Committee*. It certainly vindicated their decision not to use any of the submissions, and although not quite as funny as the Smith brothers' collection, it did include the actual prologue submitted by the irascible Dr Busby which was so bad that Byron wrote his own parody of it. Busby's prologue begins:

> *When energising objects men pursue,*
> *What are the prodigies they cannot do?*
> *A magic edifice you here survey,*
> *Shot from the ruins of the other day!*
> *As Harlequin had smote the slumberous heap,*
> *And bade the rubbish to a fabric leap.*

Byron's take on this was called 'Parenthetical Address by Dr Plagiary' and begins:

> *When energising objects men pursue,*
> *Then Lord knows what is writ by Lord knows who.*
> *A modest monologue you here survey,*
> *Hissed from the theatre the other day;*
> *As if Sir Fretful*✤ *wrote the slumberous verse,*
> *And gave his son the rubbish to rehearse.*[6]

This was all good fun, but by this stage the reading public must have been wondering whether these prologues, real and imaginary, were ever going to end.

✤ Sir Fretful Plagiary is a ludicrous author in Sheridan's farce *The Critic*.

Longitudinal section of Benjamin Dean Wyatt's Theatre Royal, taken from *Observations on the Design for the Theatre Royal, Drury Lane*, London, 1813.

What did it look like?

We know almost nothing about the appearance of the first Theatre Royal, and not much more about the second, apart from the illustrations of Robert Adam's alterations in 1775. We have more details about Henry Holland's theatre, but we know pretty much everything about the appearance of Benjamin Dean Wyatt's theatre when it opened in 1812. This is because detailed plans survive and the tyro architect published *Observations on the Design for the Theatre Royal, Drury Lane* to give the public a full account of his achievement. Also, of course, the building is still there.

The major difference between Wyatt's Drury Lane and all its predecessors is that, at last, the front of the building was actually on Bridges Street. The plots of land that had been intended, if Henry Holland's plan had been completed, to accommodate coffee-houses, taverns and shops, were now incorporated into the theatre. This allowed Wyatt to create a magnificent suite of reception rooms: the lobby, rotunda, two double-flight staircases and the Grand Saloon. Members of the audience arriving at Drury Lane today can still enjoy these superb spaces which are unlike anything else in London theatres, and which occupy space that would be almost big enough to accommodate another theatre.

The building didn't extend quite as far back on the site as Holland's theatre, which revealed a curious anomaly: part of the back-end of the previous building had been built on land that didn't belong to the Duke of Bedford, even though it had been included in the lease. The ownership of this nest of plots was so complicated that even the lawyers had been confused by it. When the theatre burnt down, the freeholder of this plot found himself with the smoking remains of the carpenters' shop on his land and no further use for it. He sued the Duke of Bedford, to whose ancestors it had been leased in 1776, for contravention of the terms of the lease and was awarded £1,100. In 1814, two years after the opening, a scenic workshop was built on the corner of the site bounded by Russell Street and Drury Lane, thus taking the theatre, for the first time, from one end of the island site to the other.

The surviving drawings for the building, which show the plans at various stages of their development, demonstrate how ruthless Whitbread was when it came to keeping within budget. There was to be a large Ionic portico built out over the pavement on Bridges Street, and further columns in the middle of the Russell Street frontage. These were scrapped and the building was given a simple but elegant Greek revival style with a minimum of decoration. The Bridges Street front was faced with Roman cement and grooved to look like stone, but the rest of the exterior was left in brick with minimal stone dressings. It all came in for £151,672, only slightly above the budget figure of £150,000.

The most important part of the building, from the point of view of its commercial success, would be the auditorium. Although theatres had grown in size, the basic layout of pit, boxes and gallery had not changed since the 1660s. Wyatt's Drury Lane had a sloping pit of which the rake meant that some boxes could be inserted towards the front of the pit at the sides. Above the pit were three tiers of boxes, the best, called the dress boxes, being on the first tier. The fifth level comprised the first or lower gallery with boxes at the sides, or slips as they were called. The sixth level comprised the second or upper gallery, which was so high and so far from the stage that it rose up above the ceiling of the auditorium. Looking at the cross-section on page 298, the striking thing is how shallow each of the tiers of boxes was – only four rows deep. We are used to seeing the first-floor level of an auditorium, which we now call the dress circle, extending over the ground level, which we now call the stalls, to give a depth of anything up to 20 or 25 rows, but at the time the technology didn't exist to support the weight of so many bodies over a void.

Most people in the theatre were sitting on benches, apart from a small number of individual chairs in boxes. This makes it difficult to give an exact capacity, since on a popular night more people would simply be squashed onto the benches. However, according to Wyatt's own calculations,[7] the pit sat 920, the boxes 1,286, the first (two-shilling) gallery 550, and the second (one-shilling) gallery 350. That gave a capacity of 3,106, but excluded the 14 private boxes beside the pit and the four boxes built into the proscenium. The average capacity of the boxes in the theatre was 15 people, but most of these boxes were not for the use of discrete groups of spectators who came together, but for anyone who was prepared to pay the highest admission price. The private boxes set in the proscenium and lining the pit were, as the name would suggest, for smaller, related groups of spectators, and were let on an annual fee. If we allow an average of six people for each of these smaller boxes, it gives us a capacity of 3,214, approximately 400 below the capacity of Holland's theatre.

It would be nice to think that managements were having a rethink about whether bigger is better for the drama, but the explanation is much more prosaic. Holland's auditorium had rarely been full. True, it relieved the dangerous crush on 'Siddons nights', but one of the lessons you learn in showbusiness is that a house that is packed to the rafters will give you a much better atmosphere than the same number of people spread around double the number of seats. Nothing stimulates the desire to see a show like the thought that you might not be able to get in. Having said all of which, Drury Lane was still a very big theatre and Wyatt estimated that a full house would be worth 'not less than £600, exclusive of the private boxes'. He claims to have been 'aware of the existence of a very popular notion that our theatres ought to be very small', but he decided to ignore this notion as it would not allow the investors to see a return on their money. Nevertheless, he boasts that the distance from the front of the stage to the back of the boxes in his theatre was 53 feet 9 inches, whereas in Holland's theatre it had been 74 feet.[8] On the other hand, Wyatt's auditorium was one tier higher than Hollands – six levels to five.

In his account of the theatre, Wyatt mentions one cost-cutting measure that proved to be a false economy: the proscenium, and consequently the stage, were quite small in relation to the size of the auditorium. Wyatt explains that this was to reduce the size of the scenery, and thus save money on paint, canvas and the manpower required to change sets. There would also be a saving on the number of extras required for 'processions, scenic groupings etc'.[9] However, the smallness of the proscenium was immediately commented on, being compared by playwright Frederick Reynolds to 'a small fire-place in a large drawing-room'.[10] It would later have to be enlarged, at considerable expense.

Wyatt introduced into his design a consideration that would become increasingly important as the nineteenth century progressed: the separation of different classes in the auditorium. The audience of his day was still composed of all classes of society, from the dukes in their boxes to their servants in the one-shilling gallery, but the dukes didn't want to find themselves being jostled by their servants on the way to their boxes. Wyatt's layout was designed to protect 'the more rational and respectable class of spectators from those nuisances to which they have long been exposed, by being obliged to pass through lobbies, rooms, and avenues crowded with the most disreputable members of the community, and subject to scenes of the most disgusting indecency'.[11] He was referring specifically to prostitution, which was accepted as a legitimate activity in a theatre, but there was more to it than that. Moving forward, theatres would increasingly be designed so that each class of patron had their separate entrances, lobbies and refreshment areas. Not everyone was happy with this, and private boxes were particularly controversial. There had been some private boxes in Holland's Drury Lane, but until the end of the eighteenth century, it was first-come, first served for everyone bar the royal family and visiting VIPs. Rich people could buy a ticket for a box in advance, but the ticket didn't guarantee any specific place. You just took whatever was available when you arrived, or else you sent your servant ahead to get in when the doors opened and save a place at the front. When the new Covent Garden theatre had opened in 1809, there had been riots, known as the Old Price or OP riots, that lasted for 67 nights protesting against the raising of seat prices. However, the rioters also objected to the fact that the entire third tier of boxes had been turned into private boxes, which was felt to be unfair. They demanded that the number of private boxes be reduced to three on each side, and the Covent Garden management had to cave in. Drury Lane escaped the riots, but there was a definite unease about the idea that some members of the audience were being treated differently to others. In a way that is hard for us to appreciate now, the two patent theatres were regarded as having a role to play in the constitution of a free people: this was the justification for the protection from competition that the patents afforded them. It was felt that everyone should be able to get in on equal terms to express their view as to what was being presented, whether Shakespeare or pantomime.

Drawn & Etched by F.W.L. Stockdale.

The fourth and current Theatre Royal, Drury Lane,
as it looked when it opened in 1812.

18

A Theatre Run by a Committee

The decision to form a committee of noblemen and gentlemen to rebuild Drury Lane had been a good one. The 86 impressive names had inspired the confidence that people needed to invest in Drury Lane after the chaos of the Sheridan years. By 1812, the theatre had been built; it had come in within budget; a new lease had been obtained from the Duke of Bedford; and substantial progress had been made towards reaching agreements with creditors and securing a new patent. Samuel Whitbread could feel proud of his achievement. He had staked his reputation as an honourable man in public life on the rebuilding of Drury Lane because he considered it 'a vast, national object'[1] and a great service to London, to dramatic authors and to members of the acting profession. The question in 1812 was: who was going to run it?

Whitbread had been approached in March 1812 by a man who offered to lease the theatre from the proprietors, but he opposed the idea, believing that the committee who had saved the theatre should run it. He may have been motivated by the desire to maintain artistic standards, he may have found it an interesting challenge, and there may have been an element of vanity in his decision, but he carried the proprietors with him and they appointed a management committee of five, including Whitbread, to run the theatre. None of them had any relevant professional experience.

The prologue for the opening had been delivered – very badly apparently – by Robert Elliston, who also played Hamlet that evening. Elliston had been playing leading roles at Drury Lane since 1804 and was especially admired for his comic characters, but he came nowhere near the stellar status of John Philip Kemble and Sarah Siddons, who had defected to Covent Garden in 1802, or of Dora Jordan, who had been so disgusted by the terms offered to her by the Drury Lane committee in 1812 that she preferred to go out on tour. The star-power of Drury Lane had been diminished.

When Drury Lane burnt down in 1809, the company moved into the Lyceum for the remainder of the season, which closed in June. When the new season opened there in the autumn, Elliston was no longer a member of the Drury Lane company, having decided to go into management. He took on the lease of the rather seedy Royal Circus in Blackfriars Road, which he renamed the Surrey Theatre, then, a few years later, he bought the Olympic Pavilion, on the other side of Drury Lane from the Theatre Royal. He cheekily renamed it Little Drury Lane for a while, but when the proprietors of the real Drury Lane objected it became the Olympic Theatre. At various times he would run theatres in Croydon, Birmingham, Worcester, Shrewsbury, Leicester, Northampton, Coventry and Leamington Spa, as a result of which he became known as the Great Lessee. In 1819 he would take over Drury Lane.

Edmund Kean saves the day

Following the re-opening in 1812, Drury Lane was a dull place. There was little to draw the public, and it acquired a reputation for lacklustre productions, done on the cheap. Then, at the end of 1813, the committee found what they were looking for: a really big star who would draw the theatre-going public back to Drury Lane and make the whole enterprise profitable. The star was Edmund Kean and, rather like Sheridan, his extraordinary life-story reads more like romantic fiction than real life. He would acquire a reputation, which survived well into the twentieth century, for being the greatest actor ever to appear on the British stage, and he was certainly one of the most spectacularly troubled.

Kean's mother described herself as an actress but was really a prostitute, and his father committed suicide when he was six. He was brought up by a bit-part Drury Lane actress called Charlotte Tidswell – Aunt Tid – who lived with his father's brother, a ventriloquist called Moses. Kean grew up around Drury Lane and did the odd bit of acting as a child. At the performance of *Macbeth* that opened Sheridan's new theatre in 1794, the seven-year-old Edmund was one of a troupe of small boys playing sprites in the scenes with the witches, but he made so much noise backstage that Kemble dismissed the whole lot of them.[2] He was promoted as an infant prodigy and was billed in 1801 as 'The celebrated theatrical child Edmund Carey, not eleven years old' – when he was actually 14. He performed in fairground booths with strolling players as a tumbler, then went between various provincial companies. He was a successful Harlequin as well as playing 'straight' roles. There is no doubt that he experienced poverty, but so did all of his fellow performers at that level of the profession. He certainly made his situation worse than it need have been by his aggressive behaviour and a touchiness that arose from an almost paranoid obsession that his genius was being stifled by malignant people. Whenever it looked as if he might be settling down and progressing with his career, he would upset the boss or someone in authority and get fired or walk out. He had a chip on his shoulder big enough to play Richard III, which would become one of his great roles. Whilst appearing in Cheltenham, he married an Irish actress called Mary Chambers, eight years older than himself. The marriage was a disaster for both of them and was probably the initial cause of his alcoholic binges which would make everything in his life more difficult.

Like many provincial actors, Kean had his sights set on the London theatres, but he was careful about how he made his London début as an adult actor. He didn't want to accept a job playing bit-parts as he knew how easy it was for an actor to get stuck at that level and never move up. Ideally, he wanted an offer from one of the patent houses, because, once an actor had been identified with one of the other theatres (known as 'minors'), Covent Garden and Drury Lane would be wary of taking that person on. In 1813 he was seen in Teignmouth by Dr Joseph Drury, a former headmaster of Harrow, who was struck by his ability and recommended Kean to some of his acquaintances who were members of the Drury Lane committee. As a result, Samuel Arnold, the manager of Drury Lane, was despatched to see Kean, by now in Dorchester, and report back. Arnold saw Kean in a play called *The Mountaineers* by Richard Cumberland on 15 November 1813. He was sufficiently impressed to offer Kean the opportunity to join the Drury Lane company and to open playing any part of his choice. Kean was, of course, delighted. This was his dream come true: he could play one of the great tragic parts for a London audience on the stage of Drury Lane. He accepted gratefully, but neglected to tell Arnold of an important fact. He had just accepted an offer to appear at the Olympic for Robert Elliston as principal actor and stage manager. As a 'minor' theatre, the Olympic could not stage straight plays, so Kean would be appearing in pantomimes and musical entertainments known as burlettas, dancing, tumbling and superintending 'the business of the stage', all for four guineas a week. Kean attached little weight to this earlier agreement and wrote to Elliston on 19 November explaining that he had received a better offer from Drury Lane and that he was sure Elliston would take 'a high and liberal view of the question'.[3] Elliston didn't reply to the letter, but he wasn't inclined to take a very liberal view of breach of contract.

When Kean arrived in London with his wife and child, he presented himself at Drury Lane where he was welcomed by Arnold and paid his first week's salary of £8. By the time he turned up to collect the second week's salary, Arnold had placed a puff in the newspapers for the 'phenomenon... discovered in a provincial theatre... never seen anything comparable to him... since the days of Garrick'[4] and so on. At this point Elliston told Arnold that he had a binding contract with Kean and intended to enforce it. Arnold was furious, as he had put his own reputation on the line with the management committee by persuading them to hire a man none of them had ever seen, so he told Kean that he had been removed from the payroll and that it was up to him to sort things out with Elliston.

For the next few weeks, Kean was running between Arnold and Elliston, neither of whom was eager to receive him, but at last, on Christmas Eve, he obtained the letter he needed from Elliston releasing him from his contract. As part of the deal, the £8 a week he had been promised at Drury Lane was reduced to £6, with the balance going to compensate Elliston. A further condition was that Kean would appear in Elliston's Birmingham theatre when the London season was over. Kean hurried back to Drury Lane with the document, but Arnold told him that it was too late to get him back on the payroll before Christmas, so he spent Christmas Day with no money or food, in a rented room with his wife and sole surviving son, whose elder brother had died the month before with no medical attention. The weather was so cold that the Thames had frozen over, so there can't have been much Yuletide cheer. Even though the circumstances were entirely his own fault, the experience would have soured a sweeter nature than Kean's.

Kean's Drury Lane début was fixed for 26 January 1814 and the choice of play was left to him. He appeared as Shylock, which was the perfect part for a man who felt himself to be an outcast persecuted by lesser men. Kean was unknown in London and the weather was bad, so his first night was far from a full house – probably not more than one-third. Fortunately for him, one of the people sitting in the sparse audience was William Hazlitt, reviewing the performance for *The Morning Chronicle*. Extended reviews of plays in newspapers were a comparatively new phenomenon, and Hazlitt was not only one of the first but one of the greatest critics. He had a passion for Shakespeare in performance and was the perfect person to report on Kean's début. 'For voice, eye, action and expression, no actor has come out for many years at all equal to him. The applause, from the first scene to the last, was general, loud and uninterrupted.'[5] The reaction of the small audience had, indeed, been wildly enthusiastic, as if they realised they were in at the birth of a new acting phenomenon. Word of mouth spread rapidly and the houses got bigger and bigger. On 12 February, Kean appeared as Richard III, another perfect part for a man who felt persecuted by the world and was determined to have his revenge. It was another sensation: the second performance took £600, which represented the capacity of the house as planned by the architect. On 26 February, Samuel Arnold was able to report to the management committee that 'Mr Kean had performed the characters of Shylock and Richard III and had succeeded beyond the capacity of any actor within his recollection'. The committee agreed to raise his salary to £16 a week, with a gift of one hundred guineas to show their appreciation. On 12 March, after Kean's triumph as Hamlet, they raised it again to £20 a week.[6] Money was pouring into the treasury and the theatre's free list was suspended. As Kean liked to remind the committee in later years, when his behaviour became problematic, he had saved Drury Lane from collapse, and not only financially. Hazlitt, Leigh Hunt and other critics acknowledged him as a great interpreter of Shakespeare. Drury Lane was at the top of the critical tree, the place, once more, where you went to worship at Shakespeare's shrine. By the end of the first season Kean had added Othello and Iago to his repertoire. By the end of his second season, he had been provided with a wonderful and literal example of poetic justice for the treatment he had received at the hands of Robert Elliston. As well as running both the Surrey and Olympic theatres, Elliston was still a leading actor in the Drury Lane company to which he had returned in 1812 for the opening of the new building. When he played Othello to Kean's Iago, that didn't cause any problems, but when he was cast as Macduff to Kean's Macbeth, he refused the part and was fined £75. In March 1815, Elliston was given Bolingbroke opposite Kean's Richard II and decided that enough was enough. He resigned at the end of the season.

One reason for Kean's triumph was that he came to symbolise things that were valued by the burgeoning Romantic movement: passion, spontaneity, recklessness. His style of acting was famously compared by Coleridge to reading Shakespeare by flashes of lightning. It was certainly uneven: he could mumble through slow bits, gabble lines and he had a harsh voice. He was the polar opposite of John Philip Kemble, with his stately delivery, weighing every word and timing every pause, and that was the point. Kemble was Classicism and Kean was Romanticism. He represented on the stage what Wordsworth, Keats and Byron stood for in poetry.

George Cruikshank's print *The Theatrical Atlas* (1814) shows Edmund
Kean as Richard III supporting the full weight of Drury Lane.

Kean came from nowhere to become the biggest star in London, although, like other 'overnight' successes, he would have been bitterly aware of the long years of poverty, learning his trade in the provinces. Now he was rich. On top of his Drury Lane salary, he was showered with gifts: a hundred guineas from the Prince Regent, a hundred pounds from Lord Jersey, a gold watch from Mr Coutts the banker. He was able to live in style, taking a house in Mayfair and sending his son to Eton. Had he been a sensible man, a prudent manager like Garrick, he could have settled down to a long, prosperous and illustrious career. But of course, the whole point about Kean was that he wasn't like Garrick. His behaviour to his public and to his management was disgraceful and outrageous. He was passionate, wild and manic, and all of these tendencies would be increased by the copious amounts of alcohol he consumed. His career would lurch from one disaster to another, without ever completely losing his following of faithful admirers. His life was such a grand romantic drama in itself that, three years after his death, Alexandre Dumas père turned it into a play, *Kean, ou désordre et génie* (*Kean, or disorder and genius*), in which he became the living embodiment of the spirit of romanticism.✤

The death of Samuel Whitbread

Samuel Whitbread was under no illusions about Kean's importance to Drury Lane. On 2 September 1814, he told the annual shareholders meeting that: 'It is to [Mr Kean] that, after 135 nights of continued loss and disappointment, the subscribers are indebted for the success of the season'. A dividend of five per cent was declared.[7]

In the first eight months of the year, Kean had earned £4,000, and he was now feeling in a position to throw his weight about. He began performing at other theatres during the main theatre season, which was

---

✤ The play is better known today in Jean-Paul Sartre's 1953 existential reworking of it as *Kean*.

against the terms of his contract, and he demanded to know why he was receiving £20 a week when Robert Elliston was on £30. (The committee put it up to £25 and gave him a gift of £500.) He wanted to choose his roles and direct the productions. This was a response to his failure as Romeo, a part forced on him by the management for which he was unsuitable, being, at the age of 27, clearly too old and bitter to play the naïve young lover. On 4 May 1815, Whitbread was again praising Kean to the shareholders, but his discovery had been the one thing that the committee of amateurs could claim credit for in an otherwise undistinguished régime. One shareholder suggested that Drury Lane should be let to a professional manager, but Douglas Kinnaird, another member of the management committee, objected to allowing Drury Lane to 'fall into the grasp of pecuniary speculators… The present plan is material to the upholding of the real drama – to the interest of the profession which has been so materially served by the rebuilding since it has brought forward the splendid talents of Mr Kean.'[8]

Whitbread was, by this stage, in very poor health, and resigned from the management committee. He had put on an enormous amount of weight and was subject to terrible headaches. His behaviour in the House of Commons had become eccentric; he had developed a persecution complex; and he was worried about money, although he was an extremely wealthy man.

On 2 July, Whitbread made what would turn out to be his last speech in the House of Commons; on 3 July he spent the evening at Drury Lane, discussing the finances, and as he walked home along Piccadilly he said to a friend: 'The world will point and scoff at me. The populace will pull down my house.' The next morning his butler found him on the floor of his dressing-room, his throat cut with a razor. The coroner's inquest returned a verdict of 'died by his own hand – but in a deranged state of mind'. Black-edged bills were posted outside Drury Lane announcing the death: 'There will be no performance this evening.'[9]

Some of those who knew Whitbread well had no doubt about what had caused this 'deranged state of mind'. 'It was the damned theatre', was the verdict of one of his closest friends and political allies.[10] There is no doubt that the strain of sorting out the financial mess in which

Sheridan left Drury Lane would have been enough to distress anyone, especially as no one knew exactly, or even approximately, what the level of indebtedness was. This had led to a falling out with Sheridan that must have been distressing for Whitbread. Sheridan had offered to forego payment for his share of the business until the new theatre should be built, and Whitbread had accepted the offer. It appears that Sheridan thought that he would be able to borrow against the anticipated payment but then found that he could not do so, as no one trusted him with money by this stage. As a result, Sheridan got into serious problems and, when he lost his seat in parliament at the general election in 1812, he blamed Whitbread for keeping him short of the funds he needed for his election campaign. Sheridan's share had been valued at £24,000 and, by this stage, Whitbread had authorised the payment of £12,000. The remainder was held back because Whitbread had been advised by lawyers that, if money were paid out to Sheridan, and creditors later appeared with demands that could not be met, the proprietors could be held liable for those claims.

Losing his seat in parliament had one immediate and very pertinent disadvantage for Sheridan: he could no longer invoke parliamentary privilege to escape being arrested for debt. The Prince Regent, realising the danger, offered Sheridan an apartment in St James's Palace where he could have claimed immunity, but Sheridan refused. As a result, he soon found himself in one of the debtors' prisons known as sponging houses, from which he wrote the most bitter letter to Whitbread: 'Whitbread, putting all false professions of friendship and feeling out of the question, you have no right to keep me here. For it is in truth *your* act. If you had not forcibly withheld from me £12,000... I should at least have been out of the reach of *this* state of insult.'[11] Whitbread immediately went to arrange for Sheridan's release, only to find that he had been bailed by the Prince Regent. In the few remaining years of his life, Sheridan would never escape the bailiffs, and would see the inside of more than one sponging house.

Whitbread had undoubtedly taken on far more than he realised when he accepted Sheridan's invitation to be on the committee to save Drury Lane, and he was particularly concerned that he had persuaded friends to buy shares in the venture from which they were unlikely ever to see a return. However, Whitbread was no stranger to stress, having led an eventful life in politics, and it has been suggested that his disturbed behaviour at the end of his life may have had a physical cause such as Cushing's syndrome.[12] He was much mourned as a decent and honourable man – just the sort of man Drury Lane needed at that moment in its history. When we think of the people who have turned around the fortunes of the theatre over the long course of its history, it is inevitably the triumphs of performers and playwrights that come to mind. Whitbread wasn't like these glamorous figures, but his careful, methodical and unremitting approach to keeping the books straight saved Drury Lane when it could very easily have disappeared forever. He deserved the bust by Nollekens which the committee commissioned, and which still stands in the rotunda.

Byron joins the committee

Following Whitbread's resignation, a new committee of management had been formed with Douglas Kinnaird as its leading light. Kinnaird persuaded his friend Lord Byron to join them and Byron was delighted to accept. He had always been fascinated by the theatre and he enjoyed the backstage politics and drama. The committee seems to have been a rather disorganised affair, meeting on most afternoons and having a quorum of three (out of five), but Byron took it upon himself to be the inspector of plays. He found a stack of about 500 unread plays that had been submitted for consideration and he undertook to clear the backlog, either reading them himself or getting them read. He soon came to the conclusion that they were all rubbish, so he set about encouraging his literary friends to write for the theatre. He persuaded Charles Robert Maturin to write *Bertram*, which was produced successfully in May 1816 with Kean in the title role.

Byron and Kinnaird joined the extras for the 1815 Drury Lane pantomime in which they played guests at a masquerade to honour the

Duke of Wellington. The weird thing was that they had both been at the actual masquerade the year before, so it was a case of art imitating life. Byron found the view of the auditorium from the stage 'very grand'.[13] Lady Byron was less than thrilled by her husband's new-found involvement with Drury Lane as she felt that it was taking up too much of his time on altogether unworthy tasks – superintending candlesnuffers, as she put it.[14] She no doubt liked it even less when Byron took a minor Drury Lane actress, Susan Boyce, as his mistress.

Kinnaird, as part of his plan for 'the upholding of the real drama', wanted to bring forward neglected masterpieces on the stage of Drury Lane, an urge that almost always leads to financial disaster in the theatre. However, by a fluke, he struck gold with this policy when he came up with the idea of reviving Philip Massinger's 1633 comedy/ melodrama *A New Way to Pay Old Debts*. The play had made occasional appearances in the repertoire until the 1780s,[15] after which it dropped out, so most members of the audience would have been unfamiliar with it. Edmund Kean played Sir Giles Overreach, one of the greatest blustering villains ever created for the stage, who ruthlessly tramples on everyone who stands in the way of his own advancement. Kean's performance, in January 1816, gave him one of his greatest stage triumphs. In his death scene, defying all the devils in hell, he terrified the other actors onstage with him, who thought he had actually gone mad this time, and reduced men and women in the audience to hysterics. Even Byron was shaken. The most famous image of Kean is a sketch of him in this scene by George Clint which catches the manic intensity that drove audiences wild with terrified delight. When Kean bought himself an estate on the Isle of Bute, he set the busts of four people he admired on the gateposts. One, inevitably, was of himself; one of Garrick; one of Shakespeare; and one of Massinger. Kean must have realised that, while there would be many Hamlets and many Shylocks, he had made Sir Giles Overreach his own forever.

All this was too much of a challenge for John Philip Kemble, still the star and manager of Covent Garden and still, in his own eyes at least, the leader of the profession. Kemble decided that it was time to go head to head with Kean, and, having played Sir Giles Overreach at Drury Lane in the 1780s, decided to dust down his performance and go for a straight comparison. It was a serious mistake and it backfired. Hazlitt had given Kean an unqualified rave review in the part: 'He is a truly great actor. This is one of his very best parts. He has not a single fault.'[16] His review of Kemble's performance in May was very different: 'We never saw signs of greater poverty, greater imbecility, and decrepitude in Mr Kemble, or in any other actor: it was Sir Giles in his dotage.'[17] Just to push the message home, Hazlitt began his review of Kemble's King John in December with the crushing words: 'We wish we had never seen Mr Kean. He has destroyed the Kemble religion and it is the religion in which we were brought up.'[18] Taking the hint, Kemble retired from the stage a few months later. Sarah Siddons had retired five years before and Dora Jordan was dead, so that school of acting had closed down.

Exit Sheridan

The phenomenal success of Kean as Sir Giles Overreach lured Sheridan into the new theatre for the first time. His anger at his treatment by Whitbread and the committee was so great that he had declined the offer of a free box and steered well clear of Drury Lane since its re-opening. Now, however, with Whitbread in his grave, Sheridan allowed his friend Lord Essex, a member of the committee of management, to persuade him to see the actor all London was talking about. What he thought of the performance we don't know, because during the show Lord Essex noticed that Sheridan was missing from his box and found him in the Green Room, surrounded by actors welcoming him back and wishing that he would 'often, very often, reappear among them'.[19] That was not to be, as Sheridan was about to make his own last exit.

Shortly after that convivial trip to Drury Lane, Sheridan took to his bed in the grip of his last illness. His situation was pitiable: bailiffs were in possession of the house, everything that could be moved had been seized, his wife was dying in one room while he was dying in another; they lacked food and the whole place stank. In a touch of *Grand-Guignol*, the doctor had to stop a bailiff from turfing Sheridan out of his bed by telling him that the shock would certainly kill the patient. A newspaper report was published carrying details of his awful situation and old friends rallied round at the last. He died on 7 July 1816. In a last twist of the narrative, after which irony must pant in vain, Sheridan's remains were carried to their last resting place in Westminster Abbey six days later by a duke, three earls, a peer and the Bishop of London. The funeral cortège was so long that when the head of it reached the Abbey, the tail hadn't left the house in George Street from which he was buried.

They laid Sheridan to rest in Poets' Corner, to which he would certainly have objected. He had wanted to be remembered as a statesman, not as a man of the theatre, but the world has felt otherwise. His political career was unsuccessful, for all sorts of reasons, some to do with his personal failings and some to do with his beliefs. He was anti-slavery, in favour of Catholic emancipation and fair treatment of the Irish, and in favour of reforming rotten boroughs. He took the side of the individual against the state, opposing the suspension of Habeas Corpus in the panic caused by the French Revolution and supporting many other causes that would now be popular, but which were ahead of their time. He upset too many people, from the King down, to play a major role in affairs of state. His plays, on the other hand, have been making audiences laugh for more than two centuries and show no sign of losing their appeal.

There was a feeling that a great man had departed and that, in the words of one of his parliamentary colleagues, 'there is no one to take the chair he leaves'.[20] The regard in which he was held by those who knew and worked with him, even those who knew all about his failings, is remarkable. Peake, the long-suffering treasurer of Drury Lane who had seen Sheridan pocket the takings night after night, named his son Richard Brinsley Peake. Michael Kelly, from whom Sheridan had 'borrowed' thousands of pounds, described him as 'one of the most extraordinary men of the age in which he lived'.[21]

Byron had always idolised Sheridan, and once said of him that: 'Whatever Sheridan has done... has been... always the *best* of its kind. He has written the *best* comedy, the *best* drama... the *best* farce... the *best* address... and, to crown all, delivered the very *best* oration ever conceived or heard in this country.'✤ When this remark was repeated to Sheridan by a mutual friend, the ruined man burst into tears.[22] So, when Byron was asked to write a monody on Sheridan's death to be read from the stage of Drury Lane, he was happy to oblige. He produced a moving tribute in verse to his hero that was delivered several times to applause, but Byron wasn't there to hear it. He had been obliged to flee abroad after his wife had obtained a separation from him and his reputation had been blasted by rumours of incest and sodomy – a capital offence at the time. He had been warned not to go either to Drury Lane or the House of Lords, as his appearance would have provoked a riot. On 25 April 1816, Byron left England, never to return. He would die in Greece eight years later at the age of 36.

If this felt like the end of an era, it really was, at least for Drury Lane. The theatre was about to enter a sixty-year period of almost unrelieved decline that would see it threatened with the prospect of demolition.

In Rep: Plays Performed at Drury Lane During w/c 19 February 1816
Date in brackets is year of first performance

Date of performance, *Play* and playwright

Monday 19 February, *A New Way to Pay Old Debts* by Philip Massinger (1626) followed by *The Poor Soldier* by John O'Keeffe (1783)
Tuesday 20 February, *The Busy-Body* by Susanna Centlivre (1709) followed by *The Poor Soldier* by John O'Keeffe (1783)
Wednesday 21 February, *Richard III* by William Shakespeare (1591/92) followed by *The Poor Soldier* by John O'Keeffe (1783)
Thursday 22 February, *The Will* by Frederick Reynolds (1797) followed by *The Poor Soldier* by John O'Keeffe (1783)
Friday 23 February, *A New Way to Pay Old Debts* by Philip Massinger (1626) followed by *The Poor Soldier* by John O'Keeffe (1783)
Saturday 24 February, *The Haunted Tower* by James Cobb and Stephen Storace (1789) followed by *The Irishman in London* by William Macready (1799)

✤ Respectively: *The School for Scandal*; *The Duenna*; *The Critic*; the monody on Garrick's death; and the speech in the House of Commons calling for the impeachment of Warren Hastings.

19

The Great Lessee

For all of their undoubted enthusiasm for the theatre, the committee of gentlemen amateurs running Drury Lane failed to compensate for their lack of professional experience by any more strokes of inspiration after putting Edmund Kean into *A New Way to Pay Old Debts*. The theatre staggered from one uninspired new play or revival to another, and even Kean, whose novelty had now worn off, could not guarantee full houses. The house was seldom more than half-full for Kean, and less than that when he didn't appear. The only real advance during these years was the introduction of gas lighting to the stage at the beginning of the 1817/18 season, which made it easier to vary the level of light in different scenes.

By that time, receipts for the season were half what they had been for the opening season in 1812/13, and the theatre had racked up debts of £84,800. On 5 June 1819, the theatre closed without warning, announcing debts of £90,922.[1] The sub-committee resigned *en masse* and a select committee was set up to raise £25,000 to clear the most pressing debts. An advertisement appeared asking for bids to lease the theatre, bringing the joint-stock principle of management to a close.

There were four main contenders: Samuel Beasley, a former manager; Edmund Kean; Thomas Dibdin, writer and composer of pantomimes; and Robert Elliston, who by this stage had returned to the acting company, although he was still managing the Olympic. The committee didn't want Kean, whose behaviour was difficult enough as an actor without putting him in charge of the whole operation, and Arnold didn't look like a serious contender, so it came down to Elliston and Dibdin. Elliston initially offered a rent of £8,500 per annum, which he later raised to £10,200 per annum, beating Dibdin's offer by £100. He was able to produce securities for £25,000 and undertook to spend £7,000 on renovating the theatre. On this basis, he was offered a lease for 14 years. The select committee was dissolved and a new sub-committee of the proprietors was formed, but from now on the lessee would be in charge.

Kean, upset at not being chosen as lessee, immediately announced that he would not act under Elliston and that he was going to America to discover new worlds to conquer. Elliston reminded him that his contract with Drury Lane still had one year to run and that he intended to enforce it. Kean's offer to buy it out for £1,000 was refused, and Kean was warned that he could be facing damages of up to £10,000 for breach of contract, so with a bad grace he agreed to carry on for another year.

If it falls now...

Elliston decided that he didn't have time to embark on major structural changes for the coming season, but he had the auditorium completely redecorated and relit, installing three enormous gas chandeliers. He cleared out some dead wood from the company and brought in new talent from the Olympic and from the Theatre Royal in Birmingham that he had also managed. Drury Lane was packed for the opening night of the new management on 4 October 1819 and on this occasion the prologue was written by the indefatigable Dr Busby, who had been so disappointed to have his offering rejected in 1812 that he had pushed his son onto the stage to give an unauthorised reading. Busby made some grand claims for Elliston's approach to management, comparing him to Atlas bearing up his 'mimic world', and promising high standards:

> *The plain, broad road of candour is his course,*
> *The drama's honour his compelling force...*
> *A lib'ral system your support ensures,*
> *Merit he hails! And merit's cause is yours.*[2]

The *Times* critic gave a good review to the opening production, O'Keefe's sentimental comedy *Wild Oats* in which Elliston starred, but left readers in no doubt as to the gravity of the situation: 'Mr Elliston is now fairly embarked in his undertaking, and our best wishes accompany him; a great establishment is committed to his superintendence; he has to raise it from a state of comparative degradation, and to support it when raised. If it falls now, it falls, probably, never to rise again.'[3]

Carrying the weight of this mimic world on his shoulders, Elliston proceeded with a repertoire of old favourites, leading up to an elaborate restaging of Kean's *Richard III* with historically accurate costumes. He followed this with Kean as Coriolanus, not only in accurate costumes but using Shakespeare's unadulterated text for the first time at Drury Lane rather than the standard mixture of Shakespeare's play with another one by James Thompson. In spite of Elliston's efforts, Kean flopped badly as Coriolanus and it ran for only four performances.

On 30 January 1820, George III died, making it possible, for the first time in years, to perform *King Lear*, which had been suppressed during the period of the King's supposed insanity. Elliston decided to set it in the early Saxon period, with a storm scene that was so realistic it made it almost impossible to hear the lines. Elliston decided not to risk unadulterated Shakespeare this time and stuck with the happy ending grafted on by Nahum Tate, on the grounds that 'the public taste long ago decided against the sublime, but terrible, catastrophe of the original'.[4] Kean was a great success in the part, which became one of his most popular.

The most popular show of the season, however, was not authentically costumed Shakespeare, but a saucy afterpiece called *Giovanni in London*. This was a burlesque of Mozart's opera in which the wicked seducer's behaviour is too much for the Devil, who expels Don Giovanni from Hell and sends him to London where he wreaks havoc with various matrimonial arrangements. The part of Don Giovanni was played by a woman as a breeches part and Elliston, who had scored a great success with the show two years earlier at the Olympic, thought he would give it another outing. This time he cast Elizabeth Vestris – always known as Madame Vestris – as the Don. Born into an artistic family in Soho, she had trained as a singer and dancer, appearing in London, Paris and Naples. She was 22 when Elliston engaged her for the Drury Lane company, and her appeal lay not so much in her voice as in her great beauty and perfect legs. The public loved to see her dressed as a man and the show became the most popular afterpiece of Elliston's time at Drury Lane. In Pierce Egan's humorous account of two young men-about-town, *Life in London or, the Day and Night Scenes of Jerry Hawthorn, Esq., and his elegant friend, Corinthian Tom*, his heroes (the original Tom and Jerry) visit the Drury Lane Green Room to meet the cast.✤

By the end of his first season, Elliston had taken £44,000 – £10,000 more than the dismal receipts of the previous season. He then decided to stay open over the summer months, presenting Edmund Kean in a round of all his popular roles prior to his departure for America. The last of these performances took place on 16 September, by which time it was very nearly time to open for the next season. Elliston decided, however, that he needed to smarten up the undistinguished main entrance to the theatre with a portico. As the portico would project over the pavement, permission had to be given by the vestry of St Paul's, Covent Garden, and this was granted on 1 September 1820. Sir John Soane had recently been appointed as supervisory architect to the

---

✤ The adventures of Tom and Jerry appeared in a monthly journal called *Life in London* from 1821-28. William Moncrieff, the author of *Giovanni in London*, would put Egan's characters on the stage in *Tom and Jerry*, a sort of Regency *Beggar's Opera* that enjoyed a great success at the Adelphi in 1821.

theatre, and so should have been in charge of the job, but Elliston managed to upset him at some stage, probably by insulting Soane whilst drunk. When James Winston, Elliston's manager, went to see Soane on 28 September, all Soane wanted to talk about was Elliston's bad behaviour. He absolutely refused to look at the drawings or instruct the builder. Under the terms of the lease, Elliston could not have anything done to the building without the involvement of the architect or a professional person recommended by him, and eventually Soane was prevailed upon to give the name of a man called Spiller. For a long time, Spiller was credited with designing the portico, but in his account of his expenditure on the theatre, Elliston wrote that the work had been 'completed under the sole direction and design of Sir John Soane'.[5] The portico, which cost £1,050 and is still there, was originally crowned by a lead statue of Shakespeare, now in the foyer. It was compared at the time to a cowshed and has never been greatly admired.

Elliston's second season suffered, as far as the straight plays were concerned, by the absence of Kean. However, the sight of Madame Vestris showing her legs cheered everyone up, so Elliston brought back *Giovanni in London* and put on *The Beggar's Opera* with Vestris as Macheath. It was a great success and was followed by other musicals/operas starring Madame Vestris in breeches parts. Elliston's attempt to find a new serious play was less successful. He wanted to stage Byron's Venetian tragedy *Marino Faliero* but Byron refused to allow it on the grounds that it was written to be read, not acted. He described it as 'mental theatre' – no love interest, no cliff-hangers, no 'outrageous ranting villains'.[6] Nothing daunted, Elliston got hold of advance sheets from the printer and put together an acting version which he managed to get licensed by the Lord Chamberlain in time for a first performance on 25 April. Byron, still living in exile, got his publisher John Murray to take out an injunction. The injunction failed, but it was unnecessary. Byron's prediction about the play's appeal to contemporary theatregoers was right: it closed after seven performances.

Financially, it was another good season, grossing £42,000 and enabling the Drury Lane proprietors to announce that their debts of £92,000 had been reduced to £39,800. This was at the expense of straight plays, which were outnumbered by operas and melodramas by two-to-one.[7]

No sooner had the theatre closed for the summer recess than it re-opened with an Elliston special. George IV was crowned on 19 July 1821, and it was traditional for both patent houses to celebrate such events with a production that allowed for a big coronation procession, usually Shakespeare's *Henry VIII* or *Henry IV Part 2*. Elliston decided to go one better and announced that he was going to replicate the actual coronation on the stage of Drury Lane, using sketches of the robes worn and following newspaper accounts of the events. Elliston himself took the part of the King and received a standing ovation on his entry, partly because he bore a physical resemblance to George IV and partly because he could put on a convincing regal manner. It was said that he got carried away and came down to the footlights, extending his arms over the pit and saying 'Bless you, my people', for which he was ridiculed.[8] The show lasted for an hour-and-a-half and was a big hit, clocking up 100 performances by the following January.

Rebuilding the National Theatre

For the opening of the 1822 season, Elliston decided that he needed a big new attraction, and that it would be the theatre itself. He had promised the proprietors when he took out the lease that he would renovate the building, so he instructed the architect Samuel Beazley to come up with a completely new design for the stage and auditorium. The builder, Henry Peto, started work in August and completely ripped out the auditorium, back to the outer walls abutting the surrounding passages. The forestage was reduced, given more space to the pit, and the whole shape of the auditorium was changed from the form of a part-circle to a horseshoe. This gave better sightlines and allowed for additional rows of private boxes, seating six people, to be constructed behind the public boxes, which sat nine. Many of these boxes were furnished with chairs rather than benches, in an attempt to lure the gentry back into theatregoing, on which they were no longer so keen. An elegant decorative scheme included panels representing scenes from Shakespeare's plays on the front of the dress circle (a term that had only recently come into use) and a completely new lighting scheme, including an enormous lotus-shaped gas chandelier hanging from the ceiling. Although there were more boxes, they sat fewer people, and the depth of the auditorium, from the front of the stage to the fronts of the tiers, was reduced. As a result, the capacity of the house went down to 3,060 – a loss of about 150 seats. The ceiling was lowered by 14 feet.

The more important changes were in the stage area. The size of the proscenium arch was increased and a lot of structural work was done backstage to open up more space in the wings. This meant that large sets could slide on and off, increasing the capacity for spectacle.

On 12 October the theatre was re-opened by the Duke of York and four days later the first performance on the new stage was *The School for Scandal*, with Elliston as Charles Surface. He received a rapturous reception from the audience, and he deserved it. To be able to tear apart a vast stage with a 3,000-seat auditorium and rebuild them in two months was an astonishing achievement, and Elliston was justified in installing a brass plaque in the pit engraved with the words:

GEORGE IV KING

THEATRE ROYAL, DRURY LANE

The interior of this National Theatre was entirely pulled down

and rebuilt in the space of fifty-eight days, and re-opened

on the 12th of October, 1822

BY

ROBERT WILLIAM ELLISTON, ESQ.

The work had cost him £22,000[9] – more than three times the amount he had undertaken to spend when he signed the lease, and that was not including the cost of the redecoration in 1819 and the new portico in 1820. Elliston considered it all money well spent. 'You shall have a good company, if you astonish the town with the theatre,' was one of his maxims.[10]

Elliston lost no time in exploiting the potential of his magnificent new stage and auditorium. He began running a multi-star policy, attracting the leading actors from Covent Garden by doubling or trebling their salaries, and then pitting them against the established Drury Lane stars. The public really enjoyed these face-offs, such as Kean playing Othello to the Iago of Charles Mayne Young from Covent Garden. He hired a brilliant young scene designer called Clarkson Stanfield, who produced some beautiful sets for the pantomime *Harlequin and the Golden Axe*,✢ but then really came into his own with *The Cataract of the Ganges*. This was a melodramatic afterpiece written by William Moncrieff, author of *Giovanni in London*, which featured a wedding in a Hindu temple with dozens of dancing girls, two military bands and a gorgeous bridal car pulled by six horses. This was nothing compared with the finale, which involved a full-scale battle from which the hero escaped on horseback, carrying the heroine and galloping up the eponymous cataract amidst blazing fires. The public loved it and the show was a great success, but some people were wondering what had happened to 'the drama's honour', which Elliston had promised to defend in the prologue to his management. The *Morning Chronicle* for 28 October 1823 warned that, if *The Cataract of the Ganges* succeeded, it would be farewell to Shakespeare 'and welcome noise, and nonsense, and all the tinsel and trumpery… to gratify the grown children of the metropolis'.[11] The box office told its own story: receipts for the 1823/24 season stood at a healthy £61,115.

After that, it was more of the same. *Faustus*, which was very loosely based on Goethe's play, opened on 16 May 1825 with a prologue in which the author promised the audience much more than a 'regular play' could offer:

✢ For the following year's pantomime, *Harlequin and the Flying Chest*, Stanfield painted the first diorama to be seen on the British stage. An enormous piece of canvas, 272 feet long, was unrolled across the stage to reveal scenes off Plymouth Breakwater, including a storm at sea and a vessel in distress. It was so popular that it was still being shown after the pantomime had finished. Stanfield followed it with an even bigger one – 482 feet long – for *Zoroaster*, featuring the wonders of Egypt and the East.

Machinery, scenery, music and song,
And all that to Melodrame Muses belong,
He culls to contribute their dazzling aid
And by charming your senses, your judgements evade.[12]

Once again, the public flocked in. Receipts for the 1824/25 season were the highest yet, at £67,000, but the expenses were also at record levels of £56,000. It was the old story of the difference between gross and net. The biggest shows didn't necessarily make the biggest profits for the management. Nevertheless, it is surprising that within months of the close of a record-breaking season, Elliston had been forced into bankruptcy by the Drury Lane committee and ejected from the theatre. We can put together a reasonably full picture of what lay behind this turn of events, because Elliston's manager, James Winston, kept a diary that covered the whole period of Elliston's management, and it has survived.

Elliston 'wide'

James Winston is an important figure in theatre in the first part of the nineteenth century, not least because he became the first secretary of the Garrick Club, but the details of his life are sketchy. He seems to have been the illegitimate son of a nobleman and he inherited substantial property from his grandfather, who brought him up. He was obsessed by theatre from an early age and set up as an actor before going into management. When Elliston took over the lease of Drury Lane, he needed a manager, owing to the fact that he had other irons in the fire. He had given up his lease on the Theatre Royal, Birmingham, and he disposed of the Olympic (which he owned outright) on a ten-year lease when he took on Drury Lane, but he was running what can only be described as a leisure centre, including a theatre, lending library, assembly rooms and lodging houses, in Leamington Spa. This meant that he was moving between London and Warwickshire throughout the year, so he needed someone to handle the day-to-day running of Drury Lane. James Winston was the obvious choice as he had been making a good job of managing the Olympic on Elliston's behalf since 1815.

This would have been a difficult arrangement under any circumstances, but Elliston made things worse by his heavy drinking and womanising. This was an age when men were expected to drink deep, and drunkenness was not necessarily frowned upon or unexpected, but Elliston took it very far indeed. He was warned about his reputation for 'intemperance' by one of his best friends as early as 1811,[13] but the drinking got worse as the years went by. Winston kept his diary partly in a cipher, and was given to using 'wide' as a euphemism for 'drunk' in the parts not written in cipher. The number of days on which Elliston turned up at Drury Lane 'wide' is remarkable. He was 'wide' for days at a time, and often went on stage in that condition, while the running of the theatre was left to his subordinates. His frequent absences from the theatre caused inevitable problems, which Winston records. On 13 March 1824, he reports that Elliston had not been at the theatre since the previous Wednesday: 'Learned this evening he had been all the time at a whore's lodging in Church Street, Soho.'[14] Four months later, Elliston cut it so fine getting back from Leamington Spa that the performance in which he was meant to be acting had already started when he reached Drury Lane at quarter to eight, and Winston had sent on a singer to hold the curtain. 'So much for the proprietor of Drury Lane, considering that theatre of less consequence that acting at Leamington on Monday and running a very great risk of not only disappointing a London audience but of doing great injury to his prospects.'[15] Like Sheridan, Elliston had developed a habit of helping himself from the Drury Lane treasury to pay bills associated with his other ventures, which meant that when pay-day came around there was not always enough in the kitty. 'In consequence of taking Wednesday receipts for private accounts, there was only the receipts of last night to pay the company... I lent £200 that the company might be paid.'[16] Fortunately, Winston was a wealthy man and able to bail his employer out on several occasions, but he strongly disapproved of Elliston's attitude, and he wasn't the only one.

The Drury Lane sub-committee, and especially its chairman John Calcraft, took the view that Drury Lane would be a lot more profitable if it were being managed by someone who could stay sober, at least during working hours. On 10 May 1824, Calcraft gave Elliston a dressing down in front of his staff, telling him that 'he was a disgrace to the theatre, always drunk, had reduced the theatre to as bad a state as it ever was, etc.'[17] This was pretty rich, given the mess that the committee had made of things when they were running Drury Lane themselves, but Calcraft wanted Elliston out and began to look for ways of evicting him. The most obvious excuse would be non-payment of rent leading to a declaration of bankruptcy, in which case the lease was automatically terminated, but as long as Elliston kept up the payments, there was little Calcraft could do.

Winston, who was a shrewd man of the theatre, formed an interesting view of the record-breaking 1824/25 season, which came to an abrupt close when Elliston couldn't raise the money to pay salaries at the normal time of noon on a Saturday in July. He managed to

---

In Rep: Plays Performed at Drury Lane During w/c 25 April 1825
Date in brackets is year of first performance

Date of performance, *Play* and playwright

Monday 25 April, *Virginius* by James Knowles (1820) followed by *Harlequin and the Talking Bird* by Charles Dibdin (1824)
Tuesday 26 April, *The Fall of Algiers* by John Howard Payne and Henry Bishop (1825) followed by *Abon Hassan* by Carl von Weber (1811)
Wednesday 27 April, *Der Freischütz* by Carl von Weber, adapted by George Soane (1821/24) followed by *Harlequin and the Talking Bird* by Charles Dibdin (1824)
Thursday 28 April, *The Winter's Tale* by William Shakespeare (1609/10) followed by *Abon Hassan* by Carl von Weber (1811)
Friday 29 April, *The Fatal Dowry* by Philip Massinger and Nathan Field (1619) followed by *The Rossignol* (unknown author, 1825) followed by *My Uncle Gabriel* by John Parry (1824)
Saturday 30 April, *Der Freischütz* by Carl von Weber, adapted by George Soane (1821/1824) followed by *Abon Hassan* by Carl von Weber (1811)

---

borrow enough from his bank to pay them in the evening, but rumours were already circulating that Drury Lane had stopped payments. 'Thus ended a successful but unprofitable season – the successful pieces so huddled upon one another on some instances as to ruin both, others brought out without any chance of success, bad and expensive engagements.'[18] Then, in August, Elliston had a stroke. He appointed his son, William, to act as his deputy and retired to Ramsgate to recuperate. The sub-committee had no option but to accept this arrangement, but waited for the next instalment of rent to fall due.

The Great Lessee bankrupt

The new season opened at Drury Lane on 18 September 1825 with the inexperienced William Elliston in charge, and predictably things went badly. In November, Calcraft called a meeting of the Drury Lane sub-committee to discuss Elliston's affairs, and he was able to report that the lessee had been forced to move out of his grand house in Stratford Place, north of Oxford Street, and into an area of South London known as 'living within the Rules', where creditors could not be arrested for debt. At this point Calcraft took ultimate control of the theatre away from Elliston, who struggled on for a few more months. He appeared in May 1826 for the first time as Falstaff, but it was not a success, and during one performance he collapsed and had to be carried off. At this point the committee announced that his lease had been cancelled for non-payment of the rent. Their behaviour was ungenerous, as Elliston had by this time spent between £30,000 and £40,000 on improvements to the theatre, when his lease had only obliged him to spend £7,000, and now he had nothing to show for it. He was declared bankrupt on 10 December 1826, with assets of £15,000 and liabilities of £40,000, on the basis of the debt to the proprietors of Drury Lane of £5,670 16s. 8d.[19] Even Winston, whose diary adopts a strongly judgmental tone against Elliston, thought that this was a poor return for his services to Drury Lane: 'This much for gratitude.'[20]

Unlike other Drury Lane bankrupts, Elliston had a happy end to his story. Ruined and in poor health, he managed to scrape together enough money to take on once again the running of the Surrey Theatre in Blackfriars Road. He opened there on 4 June 1827, acting in one of his old favourites, the comedy *Three and a Deuce*. The Surrey patrons were glad to see the return of their old manager, who had made the theatre such a success before, and Elliston entertained them with a mixture of pantomimes, melodramas and Shakespeare. He tried again with Falstaff, and this time he was acclaimed as one of the great exponents of the character. He had the good luck to find another child prodigy – Master Burke, a nine-year-old phenomenon from Galway, who delighted the Surrey audience for several years. But Elliston's greatest discovery, at the very end of his career, was Douglas Jerrold's nautical melodrama *Black-Eyed Susan*. Jerrold was 26, and had written only a few pieces for Sadler's Wells and the Coburg, when Elliston put on three plays by him in 1828. *Black-Eyed Susan* was the third and it swept all before it, running for hundreds of performances. It presented sailors as heroic characters and role models for the working-class audience at the Surrey and set a trend for nautical dramas that continued for decades. Elliston would remain the successful proprietor of the Surrey for another three years, putting on a variety of shows including an updated version of Garrick's *The Jubilee*, the first play about Thomas à Becket and the only play by Sir Walter Scott ever to be staged. Not all of these shows were hits, but Elliston was cushioned against losses by the ongoing success of *Black-Eyed Susan*. He died in June 1831, probably of a cerebral haemorrhage. He had been popular in his community, living in a large house opposite the theatre, and he used to say that he would not leave the Surrey 'to be the king of the first playhouse in London'.[21] For all his failings, personal and professional, Elliston had been a great man of the theatre, and Charles Lamb provided the perfect epitaph for the Great Lessee: 'Wherever Elliston walked, sat or stood still, there was the theatre.'[22]

20

The Monopoly Under Attack

O ne person who was probably glad to hear of Elliston's bankruptcy was Edmund Kean. He had been unsuccessful in his bid for the lease of Drury Lane in 1819, but now he had a second chance.

As the events of 1826 unfolded, Kean was touring North America in an attempt to make some money and shore up his reputation, whilst anxiously trying to get news from London about the situation at Drury Lane. This was actually Kean's second American tour: the first one, from 1820 to 1821, had been going well until he refused to go on for a thin house in Boston and almost provoked a riot. His behaviour was construed as a national insult and he had to leave the country in a hurry. When he got back to London, Elliston gave him unprecedented star treatment, with a triumphal procession to the theatre involving a coach drawn by four grey horses and numerous outriders in the costumes of all nations. Kean's London fans were glad to see him back, and he was playing to reasonable houses when his career was very nearly wrecked by a sex scandal.

Kean had the sexual appetite of a satyr and his womanising was regarded as part of the dangerous, living-on-the-edge defiance of convention of the romantic hero. He needed to have three women in his dressing room just to get through a performance ('two waited while the other was served'[1]) and when he delayed the curtain of a performance of *Venice Preserv'd*, his explanation was: 'I always take a shag before the play begins'.[2] He demanded two private boxes for some performances, 'one for his wife and one for his whore'[3] and once shared with James Winston his philosophy of life: 'Ah, give me bread and cheese and a couple of whores.'[4]

However, it was not his relationships with women of this class that got him into trouble. For several years he had been conducting an affair with Charlotte Cox, wife of a City Alderman who also happened to be one of the shareholders in Drury Lane. Alderman Cox did nothing to stand in their way: on the contrary he seemed to take every opportunity to push them together. He was declared bankrupt while the affair was in full swing, and he was no doubt very happy to be treated everywhere by the most successful actor of the day. At best he was a complaisant cuckold and at worst he was prostituting his wife.

Things came to a head when his wife, who didn't confine her extra-marital attentions to Kean, walked out on the Alderman to live with his clerk. She left behind her all the letters Kean had written to her, conveniently tied up in ribbon. The Alderman brought an action against Kean for criminal conversation with his wife, demanding damages of £2,000. He was actually awarded £800. The trial, on 17 January 1825, was a sensation, as the letters were read out in court and Kean's reputation was destroyed. The criticism he came in for from the press, led by *The Times*, reached an even greater pitch of hysterical self-righteousness when Kean announced that he would be appearing at Drury Lane as Richard III seven days later. 'It is of little consequence,' thundered the voice of the nation, 'whether the character of Richard III or Othello be well or ill acted; but it is of importance that public feeling be not shocked, and public decency be not outraged.'[5] Feeling was running so high that, a few days before the performance, Sir Richard Birnie, the Bow Street magistrate, called on Elliston to ask him to cancel the appearance as it might provoke a riot. Elliston stood by Kean's decision and the performance went ahead, although it was completely drowned out by abuse from the rise of the curtain to its fall. Othello suffered the same fate four days later, but when Sir Giles Overreach got the same treatment, Kean made a speech in which he gave as much of an apology as he was willing to make, claiming that 'I stand before you as the representative of Shakespeare's heroes' and that, if the public wished him to retire from the stage, he would. After this he was allowed to continue, although the protests followed him on his summer tour of the provinces.

Kean decided to escape all this by having another crack at America, which he regarded as his El Dorado, where he had been able to earn a thousand pounds a month. He hoped that the Americans would have forgotten the matter of the no-show in Boston, but he was wrong. News of his immoral behaviour had arrived in American before him and his appearances provoked the same reaction as in London, culminating in a very serious riot in Boston.

Learning of Elliston's troubles, Kean decided that it was time to return to London, and when he sailed on 6 December 1826 it appears that he believed the Drury Lane committee wanted him as the next lessee and all he had to do was show up to assume the mantle. He was bitterly disappointed to find out, when he arrived, that the lease had already been awarded to Stephen Price, an American whom Kean knew well as Price had been the manager of the New York Theatre where Kean had often appeared.

Price had agreed to pay £10,600 per annum to the proprietors, and was no doubt delighted to see Kean back in London as he was still the biggest star of the day. Kean appeared as Shylock at Drury Lane on 8 January and, once again, was welcomed back by his London audience in all his old parts. He wanted to do something new, however, and agreed to star in a play called *Ben Nazir*, written by his old friend Colley Grattan. Kean attended the first two rehearsals then announced that the other actors disturbed his concentration and that he would rehearse the part alone at home. He didn't appear in the theatre again until the first night, when it became obvious to everyone backstage that he had no idea of his lines. The stage manager begged him to postpone but he refused, and the performance turned into a fiasco. He knew so little of his part that the plot became unintelligible, and the audience, at first silent, began to boo. The withdrawal of the play was announced at the end of the evening. Oddly enough, the audience and the newspapers blamed the author for giving Kean such rubbish to learn.

Kean tried to persuade Stephen Price to give him a share in the management of Drury Lane, but Price said no, probably because he was having enough trouble without going into partnership with a man who, at the age of 39, was a physical wreck with a terrible reputation. Kean therefore took himself off to Covent Garden for the next season, and Price responded with a particularly nasty trick. Kean and his wife had both intended that their only surviving son, Charles, would be brought up as a gentleman, and for that reason had sent him to Eton. Mary Kean had demanded and obtained a legal separation from her husband after the Cox scandal, and the ensuing wreck of the family finances meant that Charles had to leave Eton in 1827 at the age of 16. Kean wanted his son to become a cadet in the East India Company but Charles refused. He had sided with his mother since the Cox affair, feeling that she had been badly treated by his drunken, lecherous father. He was determined to do nothing that his father had planned for him, which made him very susceptible to the offer from Stephen Price to go on the stage at Drury Lane, where he would act in competition with his famous father.

Charles Kean made his first appearance on any stage as Young Norval in *Douglas* on 1 October 1827. It was a cruel stunt, as he was a teenager with absolutely no professional experience. He was ridiculed by the critics and appeared only seven times during the season. Nevertheless, he had been bitten by the bug. Sensibly deciding that it might be a good idea to gain some experience in a less exposed situation than the stage of the most famous theatre in the country, Charles Kean took himself off to the provinces to learn his craft.

Edmund Kean was back at Drury Lane for the 1829/30 season, and once again seems to have felt that he needed to add a new role to his very limited repertoire, which the theatregoing public had been seeing over and over again for fifteen years. This time it was Shakespeare, so no one would be able to blame the author if it went wrong, and on 8 March 1830 Kean appeared for the first time as Henry V. Once again, it was a total disaster, with Kean needing a prompt for every line. The audience booed until he came down to the footlights to plead for understanding. 'Time and other circumstances must plead my apology.'[6] He was a pathetic figure, blaming the passage of the years when he was only 42. His memory loss was probably the result of mercury poisoning, mercury being the standard treatment for syphilis at the time. Shortly afterwards, Edmund Kean announced a series of farewell performances that would mark his retirement from the stage in the summer.

In the same month as the doomed *Henry V*, Stephen Price surrendered the lease of Drury Lane. He had failed to solve the financial problems that had beset Drury Lane under Elliston and would continue to do so for another fifty years. He had tried cutting ticket prices, cutting wages and holding down overheads until he acquired the nickname of 'Half-price'. He was, of course, detested by everyone in the company, and one actor called Reading was arrested after calling him 'a Yankee, a thick-headed American, and nothing but his [Reading's] family prevented him from giving him two black eyes. Price came to England,' Reading added, ' to starve the Londoners.'[7]

James Winston, who strongly resented the treatment given to Elliston, had taken a dim view of his successor from the start: 'from the moment he interfered the receipts have been much worse. He is not, in my opinion, properly qualified for a London establishment... Price comes but seldom to the theatre, but when he does 'tis always to find fault and assert things that are not true.'[8] By the end of Price's first season, Winston had had enough. On 30 June 1827 he wrote: 'This night, or rather Sunday morning, it being seven minutes to one when the curtain fell, terminated the first season of the American manager, Price, whose ignorance of theatrical knowledge... has sown the seed of future destruction to the theatre. The season has been carried on with a parsimony unknown in a London theatre.' Two days later the entry reads: 'Attended Drury Lane Theatre and left there at two o'clock, not intending to return.'[9] Thus ends the most gossipy, intimate chronicle we have of the backstage life and dramas of Drury Lane in its whole history.

By Price's fourth season, the Drury Lane committee wanted him out, but he was a lawyer and insisted that, if the terms of his lease were not to be honoured, he must be compensated. He left in March 1830, owing £2,000 in rent, and before the end of the year he had been declared bankrupt.✢

All Change at the Grand Junction

The new lessee of Drury Lane was Alexander Lee, unflatteringly described as a 'broken-down singer at the Haymarket and the keeper of a music-shop in the Quadrant'[10] (in Regent Street). Lee was a singer, conductor and composer of music for plays and operas with a limited track-record of management. He had become a partner in the management of the Tottenham Street Theatre in 1829 but left after a year when the theatre was subject to heavy fines for performing operas without a licence. It was a big leap from Tottenham Street to Drury Lane, and it was said that Lee was driven by his obsession for the popular ballad singer Harriet Waylett, whom he wished to showcase at the Lane. Lee lacked the resources to take on the lease so he started asking everyone he knew for assistance. He got a positive response from Francis Polehill, a captain in the King's Dragoon Guards and later MP for Bedford, who had employed him as a singing teacher for a lady of his acquaintance, and they took a joint three-year lease at £9,000 per annum. This was a drop on the rent paid by Elliston and Price.

Lee adapted Auber's opera *Fra Diavolo* for Drury Lane, but he was out of his depth and, within less than a year, handed over the whole enterprise to Polehill. It was said that his position became intolerable as a result of furious squabbles between Mrs Waylett and Captain

---

✤ In his memoirs, published in 1882, J.R. Planché blamed the greed of the proprietors, in setting an unrealistic rent, for the collapse of Price's management as well as those that followed: 'the infatuated proprietors continued cutting up the goose that laid them golden eggs till they could find no goose green enough to submit to the operation'. (Planché, i, 157.)

Polehill's protégée whom Lee had been hired to coach. This may be just theatrical gossip but, when Mr Waylett died in 1840, Lee married the widow and became her devoted slave.

Drury Lane now presented an unappealing prospect, still pathetically dependent on the increasingly frail Edmund Kean who, after several 'retirements' from the stage, kept returning to earn a bit of cash by trotting out his old parts. Kean tried to borrow £500 from Polehill and took offence when he was refused. He crossed the road to Covent Garden, and Polehill took counsel's opinion on taking out an injunction, but it proved to be unnecessary. Kean's first appearance at the rival house was on 25 March 1833 as Othello, opposite his son's Iago. In the third act, Kean collapsed into Charles's arms saying: 'O God, I am dying, speak to them for me.' He was carried from the stage and died two months later. At the end of the season, Charles returned to the provinces, swearing that he would never appear in London again until he could command £50 a night – a sum only ever paid to his illustrious father.

In July, Polehill negotiated another lease, for six years with a break-clause at three, at the reduced rent of £8,000 per annum, but in December 1834 he threw in the towel. Polehill, described by J.R. Planché as 'a gentleman possessing more money than brains', claimed to have lost £50,000[11] and assigned his lease to Alfred Bunn. The only thing for which Polehill's brief stint as manager of Drury Lane is remembered is the construction of the colonnade of cast-iron columns along the Russell Street frontage in 1831.❖ There have been no significant changes to the exterior of the building since then.

Alfred Bunn was not a newcomer to Drury Lane. In the 1823/24 season he had been Elliston's stage manager, but it ended badly. The account that we have from Winston is biased, because Winston resented having another man brought in as manager when the hierarchy between them was not clearly defined, but nevertheless it appears that Bunn was very lax in the performance of his duties.

❖ It is sometimes said that the columns in this colonnade came from the Quadrant in Regent Street, where the buildings on both sides were originally adorned with colonnades as the street turns through 90 degrees. However, the Quadrant colonnades were not demolished until 1848.

He would arrive late, leave early and, when he was in the theatre, spend most of his time sleeping on the sofa in Elliston's room.[12] Elliston eventually tumbled to this and, during a drunken dinner with his stage manager at the Piazza coffee-house, Elliston stood up on the table and shouted at him: 'You are a great rascal. Out of my company of 150, you can't find three but say you are a shit wig' (sic).[13] Bunn was 'let go' but he returned in September 1831 as manager for Polehill, when Lee departed, so he was around when Polehill wanted to bail out.

When Bunn took over the lease of Drury Lane from Captain Polehill, he was already the lessee of Covent Garden, having taken that over in 1833. However, Bunn had slightly anticipated events[14] by issuing an Address to the public on 27 May 1833 announcing himself as lessee of both Drury Lane and Covent Garden[15] for the purpose of restoring 'the prosperity of that long neglected but rational source of amusement – THE NATIONAL DRAMA'.[16] He called it the Grand Junction.

Bunn's approach to the problems of both patent houses was a daring and innovative one. Both theatres were experiencing severe financial problems, Covent Garden to an even greater extent than Drury Lane. In 1829 the magistrates had put a tax collector in possession of Covent Garden and the furniture and moveables were advertised for sale, so great were the arrears of rates and taxes. Bunn reasoned that it was no longer possible for both establishments to compete in the old way, maintaining four separate companies for tragedy, comedy, opera and ballet at each house. Bunn wanted to combine the resources of both theatres, using Covent Garden for opera and ballet and Drury Lane for straight plays.[17] Rival pantomimes could be avoided by using Covent Garden for pantomime and Drury Lane for equestrian dramas and other suitable Christmas shows.[18] He thought that, as the theatres were only a few yards apart, he could employ one-and-a-half companies between the two theatres, making performers appear in either theatre as required. This occasionally entailed running from one to the other in costume and make-up between the mainpiece and the afterpiece:

> Broad Court and Martlett Buildings from about half-past nine at
> night to a quarter to ten exhibited a most extraordinary scene.

> Actors half-attired, with enamelled faces and loaded with the paraphernalia of their art, were passing and repassing... double-basses, trombones, long drums, books and wearing apparel carried on the heads of figure dancers...[19]

During the Christmas season, when both theatres needed large numbers of dancing girls, local people were treated to the spectacle of troupes of gauzy fairies flitting through the streets six times a night.[20] It didn't all go perfectly to plan: according to J.R. Planché, there would be delays of a quarter of an hour or more as the audience at one theatre waited for a performer to finish at the other, or, even worse, performers would leave without finishing their parts, 'leaving speeches that were indispensable to be spoken by another person'.[21]

The performers probably disliked it, but there was little they could do: with Bunn controlling both patent houses, the bargaining position of actors, musicians and playwrights was weakened. This was, in fact, a key plank of Bunn's policy. He argued that actors' salaries had increased to the point at which they were no longer justifiable. At the beginning of the nineteenth century, £20 a week had been a good salary for an actor, with £30 a week reserved for the stars. For many years there had been an informal understanding between Covent Garden and Drury Lane not to go above this level, and as these were the only two theatres in London permitted to put on plays, they were able to operate a cartel. However, two things happened to change the rules of the game.

The first was the extraordinary success of Edmund Kean, which made the fortunes of Drury Lane dependent on him from the time of his first appearance. His initial three-year agreement for £8 a week in the first year, £9 in the second and £10 in the third year, was almost immediately upped to £20 by a grateful management, but he still complained that he wasn't the highest-paid actor in the company. After the expiry of his three-year contract, he demanded £50 a night.

The second factor precipitating change was Robert Elliston's policy of running multi-star casts at Drury Lane, for which he persuaded the leading members of the Covent Garden company to desert to his banner by offering them two or three times their salary. Thus, Charles Young, who had been on £20 a week at Covent Garden, got that much per night when he moved to Drury Lane.[22] This set off spiralling inflation in actors' pay that Alfred Bunn was determined to crack down on. As the proprietor of both patent houses, he was in a strong position to do so.

The challenge to patent privileges

However, Bunn could scarcely have chosen a worse time for this experiment to reduce competition. The longstanding resentment against the monopoly privileges of the patent houses had reached a tipping point and a bill had been introduced into parliament to abolish them. The patents had, by this time, become completely indefensible. The original justification for them had been the need to maintain standards by limiting competition. It had been felt in the 1660s that, with only two theatres putting on plays in London, those theatres would be able to put on good plays by the best authors if they were protected from a free market in which the winners would be those who catered to the lowest level of public taste. Colley Cibber had felt that even two theatres in London was one too many, as pantomimes at the other house forced Drury Lane to put on pantomimes to stay in business.[23]

By the beginning of the nineteenth century, it was impossible to make this argument. The enormous increase in the size of the auditoria at both Drury Lane and Covent Garden at the end of the previous century had made them unsuitable for serious plays. With many in the audience straining to see or hear the actors, straight plays had to give way to pantomimes, melodrama and sensation dramas, with cataracts, burning castles and cavalry. At the same time, more theatres were being built. The small group of theatres that had existed in the early to middle part of the eighteenth century presented Drury Lane with very limited competition, with only the Little Theatre in the Haymarket allowed to put on plays, and then only in the summer. That had now all changed. Other theatres, called minor theatres, had been licensed, either by the Lord Chamberlain or by local magistrates, to put on musical entertainments. They couldn't perform 'the drama', but they could present pantomimes, singing, dancing, acrobats, animal acts and melodramas, providing nothing was said and everything was conveyed by gesture or by holding up placards to tell the audience what was happening. They could also perform a special form of entertainment which was called a burletta, understood to be a performance of no more than three acts involving songs, dancing and just a few lines spoken in rhyming couplets that had to be accompanied by music.

The demand for entertainment in London was now so great that increasing numbers of these minor theatres were opened: the Royal Circus, later the Surrey Theatre, in Blackfriars Road (1782); Astley's Amphitheatre in Westminster Bridge Road (1794); the Olympic Theatre in Wych Street, now the site of Bush House (1806); and the Sans Pareil, later the Adelphi, in the Strand (1806) among others. The patent houses tried to protect themselves from competition by planting spies in the audiences of these theatres, ready to lay an 'information' before a magistrate if any words were spoken, and in 1789 the actor John Palmer (the original Joseph Surface in *The School for Scandal*) was imprisoned as a vagrant for speaking in a piece called *The Fall of the Bastille* at the Royal Circus. The most famous, because the most absurd, example was the imprisonment of the pantomime clown Carlo Delpini for uttering the words 'roast beef' on the stage of a minor theatre.[24]

The Privy Council hearings in 1810 in the case of the application for a third theatre in London had brought to the surface a lot of simmering resentment against the patent houses, and although Sheridan carried the day on that occasion, times were changing. Successive Lord Chamberlains became less ready to intervene in disputes on the side of the patentees, and magistrates became less willing to convict when charges were brought against minors. The Trojan horse which would eventually bring the patent privileges tumbling down was that harmless-sounding little entertainment the burletta, and the wily Odysseus of this story is none other than the Great Lessee himself, Robert Elliston.

Pushing the boundaries

When Elliston had taken over the management of the Royal Circus in 1809, it was not a very attractive venue. It was in a rough part of South London where taste for theatre was limited, and featured performing animals, acrobats, pantomimes and what were known as 'ballets of actions', involving mime and dance but no dialogue. Elliston was determined to take it upmarket and to change the repertoire, in spite of the restrictions imposed upon him by the licence. His first appearance at the Circus was in a surprising piece for a minor theatre: John Gay's *The Beggar's Opera*, with Elliston as Macheath. *The Beggar's Opera* was a ballad opera, so the plot already depended heavily on the songs, but Elliston had the prose dialogue rewritten in rhyming verse with a musical accompaniment. It was well received, and there was no attempt to intervene by the authorities, so Elliston then took a very bold step indeed: he put on Shakespeare's *Macbeth* as a burletta. The text was cut to three acts, with only 326 lines in rhymed recitative amidst the songs, mime and musical interludes. Banners had to be held up on the stage to tell the audience what was happening: 'THE QUEEN IS DEAD', 'THE WOOD OF BIRNAM MOVES TOWARDS DUNSINANE' and so on. Great attention had been paid to the scenery and machinery, especially in the scenes with the witches. The show was well received and well reviewed, at a time when it was rare for anything at a minor theatre to be reviewed at all. *The Morning Chronicle* for 31 August 1809 reported that: 'with the exception of the dialogue, the performance was almost exactly the play of Shakespeare'. Whilst that is rather a large exception to make, the important thing was that Elliston got away with it again. It raised the question: if the definition of a burletta could be stretched to accommodate *Macbeth*, did it mean anything at all?

Elliston renamed the theatre the Surrey and rebuilt the interior, replacing the circus ring with a pit and the stables with refreshment rooms. He began to attract a more fashionable crowd from outside the immediate area and made the Surrey one of the best-known theatres in London. He continued to defy expectations of what a minor theatre should be presenting, with versions of *The Beaux' Stratagem* and even Walter Scott's poem *The Lady of the Lake* – all pretty smart stuff. He kept the theatre open throughout the winter season, offering a direct challenge to the patent houses. Then he decided to take the battle closer to the enemy camp: in 1813 he bought the Olympic Pavilion, on the other side of Drury Lane from the back end of the Theatre Royal, for £2,800 and cheekily called it Little Drury Lane.❖

Elliston initially intended to run the Surrey and the Olympic together, swapping productions and personnel, but after a year he let the Surrey go to concentrate on turning the Olympic Theatre (as it was now called) into a real rival to the patent houses. (It was at this point that he engaged Edmund Kean to act for him, only to find that Drury Lane had gazumped him.) Elliston ran a winter season to put himself into direct competition with the patents, and he rebuilt the interior of the theatre to make it more elegant. The exterior, auditorium and front of house areas were lit by gas, for the first time in a theatre. Once again, he pushed to boundaries of what a minor theatre could stage, and this time there was a reaction.

On 29 November 1817, Elliston staged a three-act tragedy called *The Italian Wife*. It had been adapted from a five-act original by Henry Hart Milman called *Fazio*, but apart from the cuts, no changes had been made. It was written in blank verse, not rhyme, and it had no musical numbers. If this was a burletta, then clearly the term had ceased to have any meaning at all. The following February, Covent Garden put on the full five-act version, no doubt encouraged by the success of the truncated version at the Olympic, and decided to take action against Elliston. On 14 March 1818, the managements of Covent Garden and Drury Lane submitted a joint memorial to the Marquis of Hertford, then Lord Chamberlain, asking

---

❖ This piece of effrontery was too much for the proprietors of both Drury Lane and Covent Garden, who petitioned the Lord Chamberlain to complain that Elliston was violating the terms of the licence he had taken over from Astley. The Lord Chamberlain agreed and closed down Little Drury Lane. When it re-opened a few months later, the provocative name had been dropped and it was known as the Olympic Theatre. (Nicholson, 292-93.)

him to shut down the Olympic and the Sans Pareil in the Strand on the grounds that they had violated the terms of their licences. The real target was Elliston and his interpretation of burletta. The Lord Chamberlain sent the memorial to Elliston, asking if he would like to reply, which the Great Lessee did, at very great length. He subsequently published the memorial and his refutation of it as a substantial book.

Elliston dealt with all of the issues raised by the patentees point by point, but his most effective thrust went to the very heart of the justification for having a patent monopoly at all. Drury Lane and Covent Garden were meant to be dedicated to the national drama, but they were almost entirely given over to spectacle, melodrama, musicals and performing animals – which were meant to be the stock-in-trade of the minors. The patentees complained of unfair competition, but if anyone was guilty of this, it was the proprietors of Covent Garden and Drury Lane who wanted to engross 'the whole store of stage exhibition, from the deep pathos of tragedy to the highest flights of tightrope dancing – from the amblings of the poet to the amblings of the riding-horse – from the splendid illusions of the scene-painter to the sloppings of the stage with real water – from the Attic playfulness of Congreve to the more congenial playfulness of *Puss in Boots*'. If the minors wanted to compete with the patent houses, they would need to find 'dogs... who should bark more eloquently than the *Dog of Montarges* was engaged to do on the stage of the Theatre Royal, Covent Garden; children must be found to support the dignity of the minor stage as effectively as the dignity of... Drury Lane was supported lately by the little girl who personated Richard III; horses must be found to prance... more classically than those that sustained the "regular" and "national drama" of *Timour the Tartar*.'[25] Elliston rounded off his diatribe by quoting the protest of Philip Astley, famous for his equestrian spectacles at Astley's Amphitheatre, when Covent Garden brought a troupe of horses onto the stage for *Blue-Beard*: 'Why do they take my horses? I never tried to engage Mrs Siddons.'[26]

The Lord Chamberlain found in Elliston's favour. There is a certain irony in the fact that, when Elliston became the lessee of Drury Lane the following year, he provided the classic example of poacher-turned-gamekeeper and became as eager to suppress competition from the minors as he had been fierce in his championing of their freedoms. When he left Drury Lane and took over the Surrey Theatre again, it was the old story: the plays of Shakespeare (*Henry IV Part 1; Hamlet, Othello, Romeo and Juliet*) described as 'burlettas'; then, in 1829, a five-act tragedy in prose about Thomas à Becket, with no songs, by Douglas Jerrold. This had no claim to being a burletta at all and was the first serious, full-length play to be presented at a minor theatre. It represented Jerrold's attempt to cultivate a 'national drama' in opposition to the influence of French melodrama. Of course, this is exactly what the patent houses were supposed to be doing.

A bill in parliament

There was a widespread feeling that patent rights had become, legally, a dead letter, and that something should be done to tidy up the situation and to relieve the managers of other theatres from the constant fear of informers and malicious prosecutions. On 22 May 1832 Edward Bulwer, MP for St Ives, petitioned the House of Commons for a select committee to examine the question of patent rights. Bulwer, who would later change his name to Bulwer Lytton, was already a successful novelist and would soon become a successful dramatist. In his speech to the House of Commons, he focused on the failure of the patent houses to do anything to promote the national drama in exchange for their monopolistic privileges:

> Where are the immortal tragedies, where are the chaste and brilliant comedies? You were to preserve the dignity of the drama from being corrupted by mountebank actors and absurd performances; you have, therefore, we trust, driven jugglers and harlequins from the national stage; you have admitted no wild beasts; you have introduced no fire-eaters and sword-swallowers; you have preserved the dignity of the national drama inviolate;

you have left it such as it was when you took it from the hands of
Ben Jonson or Shakespeare; for if you have not done this, then
you have not fulfilled that object for which we took from your
brethren those privileges we have entrusted to you.[27]

Bulwer asked why, in the growing metropolis, people should be expected
to travel from distant suburbs to Drury Lane or Covent Garden for a
night at the theatre, when all they would find when they got there would
be 'a very bad melodrama – or perhaps, if they were in eminent luck, a
couple of lions and a diorama by way of keeping up the national drama'.

The sarcasm was heavy-handed but it was deserved. The patentees
didn't even bother to defend themselves on this front. All they could
do was keep repeating the mantra of sacred property rights: investors
had ventured hundreds of thousands of pounds on Covent Garden and
Drury Lane in the expectation of monopoly rights. To remove these
rights was an attack on private property. By this stage, however, a lot
of people felt frustrated by the way in which these property rights were
getting in the way of the rights of Londoners to enjoy a good play in
congenial surroundings.

Bulwer got his Select Committee, followed by a bill introduced into
the House of Commons by himself on 12 March 1833 to allow all
theatres to stage 'the regular drama'. The bill passed its third reading
in the House of Commons by 38 to 7, and was then introduced into
the Lords where it was defeated. Apparently there was concern about
the implications of using an act of parliament to abolish patents issued
under the royal prerogative. For the second time, the opportunity
for a sensible and long-overdue reform was missed, but from now on,
as everyone knew, it was just a matter of time.

Bunn, Bulwer and Macready

As the lessee of both Covent Garden and Drury Lane, Alfred Bunn
could scarcely have avoided playing a major part in the debate

surrounding Bulwer's bill, even if he had been of a more shy and retiring disposition than was the case. Bunn persuaded the Duke of Gloucester to present his petition against the bill to the House of Lords, where it was defeated. When this was followed by another attempt to get permission to open a third theatre, he petitioned the King and was again successful. He was the fiercest defender of property rights, arguing that, in the previous year, parliament had voted £20 million to compensate slave-owners, when they abolished slavery, whereas there was to be no compensation for those who had invested in Covent Garden and Drury Lane in expectation of monopoly privileges. Why, he asked, 'if twenty millions were voted by the British Senate to please a given quantity of saints, one million might not have been given to indemnify a quantity of sinners'.[28] This no doubt seemed like a smart remark at the time, but Bunn wasn't helping his cause by comparing Covent Garden and Drury Lane to slave plantations.

Bunn had several meetings with Bulwer, suggesting amendments to his bill that would make it less damaging to the patent houses, but Bulwer was having none of it. He sent Bunn away with a flea in his ear, 'as if the genius and power of King, Lords and Commons lay in one learned and despotic pericranium'.[29] The animosity between the two men which began at this time would have serious consequences, owing to Bulwer's support for the man who would turn into Alfred Bunn's nemesis: William Charles Macready.

21

Bunn Fight

On 25 May 1833 the remains of the great and greatly troubled Edmund Kean were laid to rest beneath the pavement of the parish church in Richmond, Surrey. One of his pall-bearers was William Charles Macready, destined to succeed him as leader of the acting profession, although the two men could scarcely have been more different. Nothing could have been further from Kean's wild, debauched lifestyle than Macready's stiff respectability. The passing of the mantle from Kean to Macready prefigured, in a small way, the transition from the colourful naughtiness of the Regency to the decorum of the Victorian era.

Macready recognised Kean's acting ability but regarded 'his disgusting and reckless dissoluteness' with horror.[1] He had originally planned to excuse himself from attending the funeral, but appears to have changed his mind when he realised that the event would feature virtually every leading figure of the stage. To present himself as Kean's heir, he had to be there, even though he loathed the very profession of which he stood at the head.

Macready had never wanted to go on the stage. One of the stock situations that we come across time and time again in biographies of actors is the rebellion against the wishes of parents who want their child to get a proper job. With William Charles Macready, it was the opposite case. He was born into a theatrical family in which both parents were actors and his father went into management, running theatres in Birmingham, Sheffield and Manchester. The young Macready was sent to Rugby to prepare him for a career at the bar or in the church, but when he was 15 the money ran out and he had to leave. He had told his headmaster that he was determined not to follow in his father's footsteps as he disliked the theatre, but with bankruptcy looming, he had no alternative but to help his father to sort out the family finances. Macready senior had always maintained that the theatre was a profession, and that actors were as entitled to be regarded as professional people as doctors and lawyers. William seems to have gone along with that, although many years later he would confess that he had been mistaken at this critical point in his life. Whereas the church and law automatically confer the status of gentleman on their practitioners, an actor who wants to be regarded as a gentleman has an uphill struggle to endure, working against his calling rather than with it. When he was in his forties and fifties, Macready became a copious diarist, and although the originals were burnt by his grandson, enough of the entries survive to convey the rather shocking way in which Macready despised the theatre and virtually everybody who worked in it. 'What a calling is this!' he confided to his diary, 'How deeply I feel the degradation of belonging to it... I wish I were anything rather than an actor.'[2]

Although he had only been at Rugby for five years, he was always able to hold his own in the company of gentlemen and scholars, but his sense of social inferiority kept gnawing at him, making him ask himself if 'I might have been far happier had my education been level with my situation'. He had planned to go from Rugby to Oxford, and when he was in his twenties and it was still not too late, an old schoolfriend offered to lend him the money to get the degree that would set him on the road to professional status. At the same time, his brother Edward needed money to purchase a commission in the army, so William took his friend's loan, gave the money to his brother, and resigned himself to being an actor. It wasn't a promising start.

Macready cut his teeth on juvenile roles in his father's company for several years before making his London début at Covent Garden on 16 September 1816, at the age of 23, as Orestes in *The Distressed Mother,* an adaptation of Racine's *Andromache* by Ambrose Phillips. He stayed at Covent Garden for seven years, establishing himself as a leading tragedian with his Hamlet, Macbeth and Richard III, then in 1823 he crossed over to Drury Lane in response to the huge salaries Robert Elliston was offering to create his all-star company. He would remain at Drury Lane, on and off, for the next thirteen years, acting under Elliston, Stephen Price, Captain Polehill and then Alfred Bunn.

When Macready heard that Bunn had become the lessee of Drury Lane 'under Polehill's security', he immediately feared the worst: 'a more dishonest choice could not have been made... I know him to be destitute of honesty and honour'.[3] Like Macready, Bunn had been around the Lane for a while, first as Elliston's stage manager, then as manager under Polehill. Macready began his diary in earnest in 1833, just as Bunn was announcing his Grand Junction of Drury Lane and Covent Garden, and the language the tragedian uses of his manager is quite shocking: 'Mr Bunn is destitute alike of honour and common honesty... Mr Bunn is such a blackguard, and so out of the pale of respectability, that I have resolved to have no more dealings with him... one passes by him and his actions, as we would the most offensive nuisance which the negligence of the police has overlooked... this fellow Bunn was, is, and will be a beast until the last days of his disgusting existence.'[4]

What could have occasioned this venomous abuse? Macready and Bunn had been rubbing up against each other at Drury Lane before the Grand Junction, but as far as we know there had been no significant incidents between them. Bunn had done nothing to injure Macready; he was not a crook, nor was he leading a flagrantly immoral life like Edmund Kean. We know that one of the main aims behind Bunn's Grand Junction was to force down actors' pay, and this would certainly have annoyed Macready, whose only motive in acting was to make enough money to retire and live as a gentleman of leisure. However, the real animus for Macready's hatred of Bunn would seem to have been that Bunn was a man of the theatre through and through, while

Macready was not. Bunn was certainly Macready's polar opposite, so much the self-made man that we know nothing at all about his birth, parentage, education or upbringing. He bursts upon the public fully-formed as a theatre manager, taking over the Theatre Royal, Birmingham from Elliston in 1819 and running it until 1824, doubling as Elliston's stage manager at the Lane during the last year. He wasn't a gentleman, in Macready's estimation at least, and this would lead to the most famous bout of fisticuffs in Drury Lane's history.

Being extra legitimate

Bunn's Grand Junction got off to a good start when he opened Drury Lane for the season on 5 October 1833 with *The Tempest* followed by Milton's *Comus* – 'by way of being extra legitimate'.[5] He had promised to do his bit for 'the national drama', and now he was as good as his word. The prologue made this clear:

> Yes – Shakespeare's Tempest, *joined with Milton's masque:*
> *What more can the dramatic critic ask?*
> *And thus you'll find, through all his bold career,*
> *England's best poets represented here.*[6]

To demonstrate what could be achieved by combining the resources of both houses, he then put on a magnificent production of Auber's opera *Gustavus The Third* at Covent Garden that ran for 100 performances during the season. For the Christmas period, Bunn didn't want two pantomimes going head-to-head, so he put on a grand pageant and equestrian spectacle of *St George and the Dragon* at Drury Lane with *Old Mother Hubbard and Her Dog* at Covent Garden. It was a sensible policy and was obviously paying dividends.

Still keen to show himself to be 'extra legitimate', Bunn then decided to stage one of Byron's plays at Drury Lane, in spite of Byron's insistence that his plays were intended to be read not acted. Bunn hit on *Sardanapalus*, the story of an outrageously luxurious and effeminate Assyrian ruler who rouses himself from his bed of lust to defend his country and dies a brave death as Nineveh falls to the enemy. One bonus of the story was that it reminded people of its author, who had died for the cause of freedom in Greece ten years before. Bunn decided that the script needed a makeover so he gave it to the playwright Frederick Reynolds, who was still hanging around Drury Lane thirty years after the triumph of Carlo the Newfoundland dog in *The Caravan*. The play was announced, with Macready in the lead, although he was just about the last person to be convincing as a decadent oriental.

With the play cast and the first night announced, Reynolds came to Bunn with a strange letter he had just received from Paris. It was signed by Charlotte Mardyn, who had been a young and beautiful actress in the Drury Lane company in 1815 when Byron was a member of the theatre's committee. It had been rumoured that she was Byron's lover and that this had led to the breakdown of his marriage, but this was untrue. Byron did have a mistress in the Drury Lane company but it wasn't Charlotte Mardyn, and that wasn't the cause of his separation from Lady Byron. However, Miss Mardyn was now claiming that Byron had told her that the part of Myrrha in *Sardanapalus*, the despot's favourite slave girl, should be played by her if the play were ever staged. She claimed to be perfect in the part, having been coached in every line by Byron himself, and was ready to come to London to act it at Drury Lane.

This was too good an opportunity for Bunn to miss, so he told Ellen Tree, who was rehearsing the part, that her services were no longer required, negotiated terms with Charlotte Mardyn, and announced that the opening night was being delayed to allow for this extraordinary reappearance of a figure from the theatre's past. Macready was disgusted by the early manifestation of celebrity culture at Drury Lane and took the view that, as Charlotte had not been a success when she had youth and beauty on her side, it wasn't very likely that she would make a convincing Myrrha when she was in her mid-forties. He asked Bunn what he would do if she turned out to be terrible in the part. 'Kick her arse and send her back again!' was Bunn's reply, which of course infuriated Macready.

However, as the day of La Mardyn's arrival in London approached, letters arrived pleading ill health and asking for delays, then saying she wouldn't be able to make it at all. Bunn told Ellen Tree she was back in the part, to which she replied that, having been fired once, she didn't want it. Bunn sent her a message telling her she had no option, adding the consoling rider that 'Punch has no feelings'.

The play was a surprising success, largely owing to the spectacular conflagration of the tyrant, his mistress and slaves on a funeral pyre at the end, but Bunn couldn't let the Charlotte Mardyn episode alone. He had enquiries made in Paris and established that no such person was known at the address from which the letters had been sent. It seems to have been a practical joke perpetrated on Bunn by an English playwright called William Dimond who was living in Paris at the time.

The search for subsidy and the end of the Grand Junction

At the end of 1834, when Bunn had just started the second season of the Grand Junction, Captain Polehill withdrew completely from Drury Lane, leaving Bunn in absolute charge but with no backer. 'I had to fight my way single-handed,' he said, 'and such as it was, "alone I did it".'[7] Bunn saw more clearly than anyone else at the time that Covent Garden and Drury Lane had become economically unviable in their existing form, so he came up with the radical idea of asking for a government subsidy. On 17 March 1835, he wrote to the Prime Minister, Sir Robert Peel, drawing attention to the fact that successive managements of both Covent Garden and Drury Lane had struggled with insuperable financial problems, and that 'the leading theatres of France, Italy and Germany receive permanent support from their respective governments'. He had a reply by return of post stating that: 'Sir Robert Peel is wholly unable to hold out to Mr Bunn any prospect of pecuniary aid for the support of theatres from the public funds.' Bunn claimed that he never thought he would get a positive response, but he had to try anyway.[8]

With no backer to inject capital and no possibility of a government grant, Bunn realised that he had to cut his liabilities. He asked the proprietors of both Covent Garden and Drury Lane to reduce the rent by £1,500 a year. The answer was yes from Drury Lane but no from Covent Garden, so Bunn announced that the Grand Junction would reach the end of the line with the end of the 1834/35 season.

As the united company was dissolved, performers could apply to stay with Bunn at Drury Lane or at Covent Garden with the new management there. Almost all wanted to stay with Bunn, including Macready, in spite of the horrible opinions about his manager that he had been confiding to his diary. Macready demanded generous terms, however, including a salary of £30 a week whether he was acting or not, half a benefit night's takings clear of all costs, his benefit to be the first in the season, the right to refuse all parts which he considered to be 'of a melodramatic character', plus he must never be asked to play Sir Giles Overreach in *A New Way to Pay Old Debts*, Joseph Surface in *The School for Scandal* or Rob Roy. There was also an agreement for Bunn to put on a play called *The Bridal*, adapted by Macready from Beaumont and Fletcher's *The Maid's Tragedy*, 'immediately after Christmas', for which Macready would receive the author's royalties.

The contract was heavily weighted in Macready's favour, but Bunn claimed later that he had no choice as he had to have Macready in his company. Macready was widely acknowledged to be the great Shakespearean actor of the day, and if Bunn had not been able to retain him 'there would be an out-cry on the town'.[9]

Covent Garden opened for the 1835/36 season under a new manager called Osbaldiston, who began his reign with the dramatic gesture of slashing prices. Box tickets that had cost 7s. came down to 4s., with corresponding reductions in the rest of the house. This was an act of desperation, as it was going to be difficult to make a profit at the new prices, even with good houses. However, the publicity generated had its effect and business fell off at Drury Lane. In the first two weeks of the season, Bunn lost £1,548 and was facing ruin. He asked the actors if they would agree to accept a one-third reduction in their salaries to tide the theatre over a bad patch, and they all agreed with the exception of Macready and another actor called William Farren.

However, by one of those unforeseen pieces of good luck that make theatre so interesting, Bunn had to reduce the salaries for only one week, because he found himself with not one but two smash hits opening within weeks of each other. The first was Michael Balfe's opera *The Siege of Rochelle*, which opened on 29 October 1835 and ran for 73 performances during the season. Balfe had been a fiddler in the Drury Lane orchestra when Bunn was first engaged as stage manager for Elliston in 1823, but in 1835 he returned trailing clouds of European glory. He had established a brilliant reputation for himself as a singer and composer, with successful ballets and operas performed in France and Italy. *The Siege of Rochelle* was his first work for the London stage, and it would establish a relationship with Bunn that would be profitable to both men.

Three weeks later, Bunn had an even greater sensation with *The Jewess*, adapted by J.R. Planché from Scribe's *La Juive*.✥ It was described as a 'grand operatic drama', but it wasn't really an opera as none of the principal characters sing and the music is confined to choruses that accompany the spectacular set-pieces of the action. However, the drama is certainly grand enough, telling the story of a wealthy Jew and his daughter who are persecuted for their faith in fifteenth-century Constance. The girl falls in love with a married Christian prince who has disguised himself as a Jew to win her. When this is discovered, both father and daughter are sentenced to be burnt for heresy. The father reveals with his dying breath that the girl is not his daughter at all, but the long-lost daughter of the bishop who is presiding over the execution, and who believed his wife and daughter to have perished before he entered the priesthood. The heroine is snatched from the furnace in the nick of time.

✥ Planché was anxious that *The Jewess* should be regarded as an original work rather than a translation 'for the protection of the property that others, as well as myself, retain in the acting... of this drama'. He certainly made a very significant change in the dénouement. In the French play, the heroine is hurled into the furnace just *before* her identity is revealed to her father the bishop. It was felt that London audiences would not put up with this.

This ripe old hokum was a huge success, running for 65 uninterrupted nights, often as an afterpiece to *The Siege of Rochelle*. The two shows were taking so much money♣ that Bunn didn't want to take them off, even as the pantomime season approached. Thus, on 26 December, the evening's entertainment began with the forty-ninth performance of *The Siege of Rochelle*, followed by the thirty-fourth performance of *The Jewess*, followed by the first performance of that year's pantomime, *Dick Whittington*. The evening began at 6:30 p.m. and ended at one o'clock the next morning, which was not ideal for children who only wanted to see the pantomime.

Macready had been offered the part of the Jewish merchant but had declined it, citing the clause in his contract that allowed him to refuse parts 'of a melodramatic character'. However, even he couldn't help but be impressed by the production, which he described as 'the most gorgeous pageant I have ever seen on an English stage – beyond all reach of comparison'.[10] This meant that, for a period of thirteen weeks, he wasn't acting at all, although he was receiving his full salary. Getting bored, he went to play some parts in Bristol for a few days in January without obtaining permission, and when he got back he found a note announcing the first performance of *The Bridal*, his adaptation of *The Maid's Tragedy*, and pointing out that he had missed the read-through when the play had been cast. Macready complained that he had the right to be consulted over casting and he particularly objected to the actress cast in the lead. By this stage, he was refusing to deal with Bunn and insisted on going through John Cooper, the stage manager, who went to see him to explain that the actors thought the play shocking, that Ellen Tree, whom he had wanted for the lead, would have refused the part, and that Bunn would offer him £33 6s. 8d. to withdraw the play. Macready indignantly refused, at which point Cooper asked him on whose authority he had gone to Bristol. Macready roared: 'On my own!' and the interview ended acrimoniously. That was the end of *The Bridal* at Drury Lane.

♣ Planché claimed that, between the opening of *The Jewess* on 16 November and Christmas, receipts averaged over £2,000 per week (Planché, i, 241.)

The next day, Macready complained that his salary had not been paid, and Cooper replied that it had been docked for his unauthorised trip to Bristol, but that Mr Bunn would be prepared to remit it 'if you are disposed to render your best assistance to the management in a more harmonious manner'.[11]

With relations between manager and star going rapidly downhill, Bunn decided to let Macready appear in another new play that he was keen to add to his repertoire, *The Provost of Bruges* by George Lovell. The play did so badly that Bunn threatened to withdraw it if the author didn't agree to a cut in his royalties. Lovell suggested £10 a night rather than £20 a night (the figure negotiated by Macready) and Bunn agreed, but then closed the play after its eighth performance, even though the author was willing to waive his royalties altogether. Bunn said he was losing too much money, but Macready said it was because he wanted the costumes for his new spectacular show by J.R. Planché, *Chevy Chase*, described as a 'grand chivalric romance'.✤

Bunn certainly didn't want to keep putting on plays that were losing money when he had hit shows that the public wanted to see and that were paying everyone's wages. On the other hand, he didn't want to pay Macready for doing absolutely nothing, so he came up with what he regarded as a reasonable compromise. Thus it was that, on 27 April 1836, as Macready was walking to Drury Lane, he was appalled to see a bill announcing the programme for two days ahead: the first three acts of *Richard III*, followed by the first act of *Chevy Chase*, followed by *The Jewess*.

✤ Planché had signed an exclusive contract with Bunn for the 1835/36 season and had written *Chevy Chase* as the Easter piece. However, Bunn sent him to Paris to negotiate with Meyerbeer for a London production of *Les Huguenots* and, although Meyerbeer agreed, Planché told Bunn that to represent the St Bartholomew's Day Massacre on the stage at a time of religious controversy was too dangerous. Bunn saw his point and rushed *Chevy Chase* into production, to the annoyance of Planché who wasn't there to oversee rehearsals. (Planché, i, 250.)

The Bard avenged

There was a sense of shock amongst the cultured classes. It was absolutely normal to follow a Shakespeare play with a musical afterpiece, but no one had ever cut Shakespeare in half to put on *not one but two* extravaganzas. It was as if a line had been crossed, and 'the national drama', in the person of William Shakespeare, was being dishonoured on the boards of Drury Lane. Bunn would later say, in his defence, that actors often played one or two acts of a play in their benefit performances, which was true, but benefits were rather like charity galas today: they didn't represent a normal night in the theatre.

Macready, ready to take offence at any time, really had something for his resentment to work on now. 'What can recompense me for being subject to the spite of such a reptile as Bunn?'[12] He took the slashing of *Richard III* as a grotesque insult to himself and to the memory of Shakespeare, whom he idolised. He thought of walking out, but he would have been subject to a large fine for breach of contract, so he decided to go through with it. It was made particularly galling by the fact that Macready's Richard was said to be not so good in the early part of the play, but tremendous in the last act – which the public wouldn't get to see.

Coming offstage after this truncated Richard, Macready was walking to his dressing room, seething with fury, when he passed the door of Bunn's office. He pushed it open and, unluckily, Bunn was sitting at his desk paying bills. Shouting 'You damned scoundrel! How dare you use me in this manner?', Macready rushed at Bunn and hit him. Bunn, who was working by a desk lamp, with the rest of the room in darkness, literally didn't see it coming. He was accustomed to working with his leg wrapped around the leg of his chair, so he sprained his ankle as he fell to the floor, covered in blood, ink and lamp-oil, with Richard III on top of him, hunchback and all. He asked if Macready intended to murder him and, receiving a reply in the affirmative, he screamed 'Murder!', got hold of Macready by the collar and dragged him to the sofa, biting his finger in the process. At this point the prompter and others came in to separate them. Macready was hurried out of the theatre and back to his lodgings, while Bunn called the police.

Macready suffered agonies of conscience because he had betrayed the ideal of gentlemanly behaviour that meant so much to him. He had lowered himself to the level of the 'reptile' Bunn by engaging in fisticuffs with him and it had been a cowardly attack on a man in a dark room with no warning. This did not stop him from writing to demand his salary. The reply, from Bunn, informed him that his contract was terminated and that he was never to darken the doors of Drury Lane again.

Macready was so ashamed of himself that he began travelling around in a hackney coach to avoid meeting people, and when he saw the newspaper placards announcing 'Great Fight – B-nn and M---y' he felt physically sick. Nevertheless, he was the hero of the hour, regarded as the champion of Shakespeare and the national drama. When he crossed the road to Covent Garden and appeared as Macbeth on 11 May, he received a standing ovation on his entrance. At the end of the play, the audience called for him to appear and he made a speech, declining to go into the details of the unfortunate events that had led to his appearance before them, but mentioning that these events were the result of 'a series of studied and annoying and mortifying provocations, personal and professional'.[13]

When Bunn heard of this remark, he was furious. As far as he was concerned, he was the one who had been subjected to mortifying provocations. Macready had always been a difficult man to deal with: supercilious, proud, humourless, demanding and quick to take offence. Bunn saw himself as the victim, having to humour Macready in order to keep the big star name on board. He genuinely had no idea of the hatred, amounting to mania, that Macready had conceived for him, partly because for some time Macready had insisted on dealing with Cooper, his stage manager, rather than Bunn.✣ On the other hand, it is hard to take at face value Bunn's claim that: 'in making this selection, I had no more idea of wounding Mr Macready's feelings than if he had not been in the theatre. I never once thought whether it would please

---

✣ When Macready received the letter from Bunn telling him that he was fired, he admitted that he didn't recognise the handwriting on the envelope because it was so long since he had been in direct contact with his manager. (*Journal*, 3 May 1836, 65.)

or displease him, my object being solely to make out as effective a bill as I could.'[14] After all the years he had been working in the theatre, Bunn must have understood more of symbolism than that.

On 26 June, Bunn's action for assault against Macready was heard at the Sheriff's Court in Red Lion Square. Macready declined to appear but was represented by his friend Thomas Talfourd, Sergeant-at-Law and later MP for Reading. Talfourd was also a playwright and the author of *Ion*, which Macready had wanted to perform at Drury Lane and which he actually performed at Covent Garden in the fag-end of that season. Macready had instructed Talfourd to offer no defence of his actions, as he regarded them as indefensible, and Bunn was awarded damages of £150.

At the time of the assault, Bunn had been working with Michael Balfe on his next opera, *The Maid of Artois*, for which Bunn had written the libretto. It opened on 27 May 1836, starring the great mezzo-soprano Maria Malibran, and established Balfe as the leading composer of opera in English. Although Thomas Talfourd had been instructed by Macready to offer no defence in court, he had made some suggestions that 'Shakespeare and Shakespeare's representative' had been neglected by Bunn so that 'the songs of *The Maid of Artois* should be given to the public'.[15] The sneer was too much for Bunn, who, in his memoirs, compared the takings of *The Maid of Artois* with those for Macready in Shakespeare.

In the course of the 1835/36 season, Macready had given 24 Shakespearean performances before he was fired, grossing £4,542 – an average of £189 per performance. There were 16 performances of *The Maid of Artois* between its opening in May and the end of the season, grossing £5,690 – an average of £355. As the daily costs of running Drury Lane were in the region of £220, the conclusion was obvious: Shakespeare consistently lost money while a successful opera made money. It is hard to disagree with Bunn's view that Shakespeare's representative protested too much.

The Lord Chamberlain *v.* the patents

When the 1737 Licensing Act was being debated, the only significant opposition to it came from Lord Chesterfield, who made a splendid defence of freedom of speech in the House of Lords. Chesterfield pointed out that the Act conferred enormous discretionary powers on the Lord Chamberlain, making him the effective monarch of the stage. The proprietors of Drury Lane and Covent Garden were very happy with this situation for as long as the Lord Chamberlain acted in their interests, which he did for the most part throughout the eighteenth century. However, by the beginning of the nineteenth century the climate of opinion was moving against patent rights, and this was reflected in the increasing willingness of holders of the office to favour the requests from the minor theatres. The minors could get away with more and more, effectively putting on plays in all but name, while the seasons of the 'summer' theatres like the Little Theatre in the Haymarket were extended to the point at which they were open almost throughout the year.

Then, in May 1835, Francis Conyngham, the second Marquess Conyngham, was appointed Lord Chamberlain. He adopted a policy of making the patents not only worthless to their holders but actually burdensome, so that further parliamentary attempts to repeal them would not be opposed. For some reason, he appears to have entertained a particular dislike of Alfred Bunn and he persecuted him on two fronts. The first was the question of performances in languages other than English; the second was the tradition of closing the theatres on Wednesdays and Fridays during Lent.

Towards the end of the 1834/35 season, when Bunn was still managing both patent houses, he had engaged Maria Malibran to appear at Covent Garden in *La Sonnambula, The Marriage of Figaro* and other operas at the unprecedented sum of £125 per night. The performances were so successful that Bunn extended the engagement by another seven nights, which took place at Drury Lane in July in order to give the box-holders there a chance to see the most popular mezzo-soprano of the time. In August, Bunn received an enquiry from the Lord Chamberlain's office asking under what authority he had been presenting Italian operas at Drury Lane. Bunn replied that the patent issued to Killigrew by Charles II had authorised him to present 'tragedies, comedies, plays, operas, music, scenes and all other entertainment of the stage whatsoever'. This wording had been repeated in all subsequent patents. The reply from the Lord Chamberlain's office stated categorically that: 'His Lordship denies that the power of Killigrew's patent can be extended to any other than English entertainments of the stage' and warned that Bunn's interpretation of the wording of the patent would not be accepted.[16]

As the Malibran performances were now over, it was an academic point, but more trouble was in store. Two years later, Bunn announced that he would be presenting Madame Pasta as Romeo in Zingarelli's opera *Romeo e Giulietta*, and once again this was prohibited. This time, the reason given was that, under the General Opera Trust Deed of 1792, negotiated by Sheridan and signed by the Prince of Wales, a licence for Italian opera was granted to the King's Theatre in the Haymarket with the understanding that Drury Lane and Covent Garden would not perform it. Bunn replied that in 1792 the King's Theatre had been performing opera on only two nights a week, giving only sixty performances in a season. By 1837 they were performing six nights a week as well as doing morning concerts, so the situation was completely different. This cut no ice with the Lord Chamberlain, so Bunn decided to take it right to the top. A 'noble lord', who was no doubt a shareholder in Drury Lane, undertook to take Bunn to Windsor Castle to lobby the King, using his acquaintance with Sir Herbert Taylor, William IV's private secretary, to get them in. Unfortunately, as they were walking across the quadrangle of Windsor Castle, Sir Herbert Taylor was standing by a window talking to the King. Guessing what they wanted to talk to him about, he sent down a note excusing himself on the grounds that he was busy all day, and adding that: 'if it is about the theatre, your lordship must go to the Lord Chamberlain.'[17] A few days later, Bunn was sent for by Lord Foley, the commander of the Honourable Corps of Gentlemen at Arms, of which Bunn was a member. He told Bunn that His Majesty had informed him that 'if Mr Bunn attempted to interfere with His Majesty's prerogative in regard to the patent theatres, he should be under the necessity of requiring him to leave the Corps of Gentlemen at Arms'.[18]

The next year, it all blew up again. In August of 1838, Bunn was approached by the Chevalier Spontini with a proposal for a season of German opera at Drury Lane from April to July in the following year. German opera was becoming very popular and Spontini claimed to have been assured by Lord Conyngham that there would be no problem over a licence. He was about to leave London and wanted to finalise the deal with Bunn, involving an advance of £1,000. Bunn decided to check up on this arrangement with Lord Conyngham, and heard a few days later that no such promise had been made. The correspondence went back and forth between Drury Lane, the Lord Chamberlain's office and Conyngham himself, who was in Paris, until on 10 September Bunn received a definite refusal for German opera at Drury Lane. By this stage Bunn had been obliged to pay Spontini his £1,000 advance to keep negotiations open. Bunn replied by asking if the Lord Chamberlain seriously intended to call into question the legal status of the Drury Lane patent. There was no answer to this, apart from a restatement of Conyngham's ruling that 'only English entertainments were sanctioned at the Theatres Royal, Drury Lane and Covent Garden'.[19] There was no legal basis for this: the language of performance had never been mentioned in the original patents nor in any subsequent document arising out of them, with the sole exception of the General Opera Trust Deed of 1792 which limited Italian opera to the King's Theatre, and which, as Bunn argued, had been superseded by events. But then the Lord Chamberlain didn't need to provide a legal basis for his rulings: under the powers vested in him by the 1737 Licensing Act, they were not open to challenge.

The second issue on which Lord Conyngham went to war with Bunn was the tradition of closing theatres on Wednesdays and Fridays in Lent, which went back to the 1660s. This closure meant a serious loss of revenue to the managements of Drury Lane and Covent Garden, but it did not apply to the minor theatres. They could open and put on any shows they liked, without respecting the liturgical season. In

1837, Bunn decided to sort out this anomaly. He had a successful opera at Drury Lane called *Fair Rosamund* by John Barnett, which opened on Tuesday 28 February and was announced for the following Thursday and Friday – the Friday falling in Lent. On the Thursday evening the prohibition of this performance arrived from the Lord Chamberlain's office, addressed not to Bunn but to the secretary of the Drury Lane committee of proprietors – presumably to indicate the seriousness of the issue. Bunn decided to present a petition to the House of Commons, through the good offices of Thomas Duncombe, the MP for Finsbury, pointing out the absurdity of the situation. While Drury Lane and Covent Garden were forced to observe Lent with fasting and abstinence, the Adelphi, the Strand and the St James, only a few hundred yards away and all under the jurisdiction of the Lord Chamberlain, were presenting comic songs, pantomimes and 'gymnastic exercises by an Indian juggler' on these solemn nights.[20] Duncombe took up the matter with the Chancellor of the Exchequer and was told that he had been advised that if Drury Lane were to open on Wednesdays or Fridays in Lent, the proprietors would expose themselves to prosecution for 'playing without a licence'.[21]

By the following Lent there was another great attraction at Drury Lane: the American lion-tamer Isaac Van Amburgh and his menagerie of wild animals. The great success of this act was bringing much-needed revenue into the treasury of Drury Lane, and Bunn requested special permission from Lord Conyngham to keep the show on during the Wednesdays and Fridays of Lent. 'Those who know Lord Conyngham's manner, and have watched the progress of his lordship's persecution of this theatre, will not be surprised to learn that he refused my petition.'[22] Once again, Bunn petitioned the House of Commons and, once again, Thomas Duncombe took up the matter, proposing a motion to address the Queen. This was felt to be a bit strong, but another motion introduced ten days later was milder: 'That it is the opinion of this House that during Lent no greater restrictions should be passed upon theatrical entertainments within the City of Westminster than are placed upon the like amusements at the same period in every other part of the metropolis.'[23] Opposition to the motion was led by Lord John Russell, Home Secretary and younger son of the sixth Duke of Bedford, landlord of both Drury Lane and Covent Garden, but it was passed by 92 to 72.

Duncombe advised Bunn that he could proceed with shows on Wednesdays and Fridays in Lent on the strength of this, so Bunn announced the opera *Farinelli* for 8 March. Sure enough, like the catastrophe in the old comedy, on 6 March the letter arrived from the Lord Chamberlain's office forbidding the show and claiming to be 'by direction of Her Majesty's ministers', a phrase never used before. Duncombe then tabled a motion on 11 March noting 'with regret and surprise' that Her Majesty's ministers had shown contempt for the will of parliament 'by directing an officer... so as to defeat the manifest object of a resolution of this Commons House of Parliament'. This was getting serious, as the Queen could have been drawn into the argument once a member of her household had been accused of contempt for the House of Commons. Lord John Russell✤ tried to defuse the situation by promising a review of the law to tidy things up. On this basis, Duncombe withdrew his motion.[24]

In the midst of these absurd and vexing disputes, Bunn had one tiny consolation. As the opening of 1837/38 season approached, he received a letter from the Lord Chamberlain's office asking by what authority he was announcing performances. The 21-year patent that had been obtained by Samuel Whitbread during the rebuilding of the theatre, dated to run from 1816, was about to expire, and the officers anticipated another fat fee for negotiating its replacement. They had forgotten that, after obtaining the 21-year patent, Whitbread had raised the money to

---

✤ During the debate, Lord John Russell accused Alfred Bunn of setting 'at nought the prerogative of the crown' by challenging the Lord Chamberlain's authority. This annoyed Bunn, who wrote to *The Times* (13 March 1839) insisting that he had complied with the ban imposed on him, and furthermore that 'her Majesty has not a more loyal or devoted subject in all her dominions than... A.Bunn, Lessee, Theatre Royal, Drury Lane'. Macready wrote in his diary of this letter from 'the contemptible wretch, Mr Bunn,' that 'his anger and indiscretion look as if he were near the end. God grant it!' (Macready, *Journal*, 134.) It is not clear if Macready meant the end of Bunn's management or the end of his life. Either would have pleased the eminent tragedian.

buy the remaining share of Killigrew's perpetual patent, which made the other unnecessary. The Killigrew patent had achieved legendary status by this stage: it had been dormant since 1682♣ and was widely believed to have perished in the fire of 1809. As a result, when Bunn replied that he intended to operate under the authority conferred by the Killigrew patent, he was challenged to produce it. He could have refused, as he took the view that it was the business of the Lord Chamberlain's staff to know where it was, but he allowed himself the pleasure of inviting a functionary to come to his office, where he 'displayed, before the wondering eyes of the disappointed official the document itself, bearing the signature of "Howard" with the appendage of his lordship's ponderous seal of power'.[25]

'The Patents!' Bunn exclaimed later. 'They are literally worthless to their possessors, and harmless to those they are supposed to injure.'[26] He was right, and within a few years they would be done away with altogether. It was Bunn's misfortune to be in the hot seat when the Lord Chamberlain decided to help the process along by making life difficult at Drury Lane. The farcical proceedings relating to Lenten performances and foreign-language productions had cost Bunn a great deal of money when his management was already in financial trouble. Just in the course of the 1838/39 season, which would end in his bankruptcy, he had lost the £1,000 downpayment to Spontini for German operas plus the revenue he would have received from presenting Van Amburgh and his lions continuously throughout Lent. He had been told by Sir Robert Peel that the government would not consider a subsidy for the theatre, but his management was being endangered by an unelected officer of the Queen's household. He deserved his little moment of triumph, producing the dusty old Killigrew patent from a tin box in his office, but for all the good it did him, it might just as well have gone up in smoke in 1809.

♣ With the possible exception of the brief period when John Rich was running the old theatre in Lincoln's Inn Fields after opening Covent Garden. Had he been challenged on his authority for running two theatres, he could have claimed that he owned both the Killigrew and the Davenant patents. In fact, the question didn't arise.

22

The First Theatre
of the Empire

Wourdilliam Charles Macready was much more than a successful actor: to many people, he was the torch-bearer for high culture in the theatre. His attack on Bunn had just confirmed his status as the man of culture who struck a blow (literally) for the Bard. There was a widespread view that the drama was in decline and that, if anyone could restore standards, it would be Macready. As a result, a coterie of writers, artists and intellectuals gathered around the eminent tragedian to support not just his career, but the cause of the drama on the London stage. This little group included Charles Dickens, Edward Bulwer, Robert Browning, Daniel Maclise and John Forster, literary passe-partout of mid-nineteenth century London and the first biographer of Dickens.✥ They were described as the cabinet or, less flatteringly by Alfred Bunn, as 'the sycophants who buzz about Mr Macready' or 'Mr Macready and his toadies'.[1]

The cabinet believed that Macready, as not only the leader of the acting profession but a man of great culture, should take over the management

---

✥ When Dickens and Forster called on Macready to offer him a stage version of *Oliver Twist*, Macready 'told them of the utter impracticality of *Oliver Twist* for any dramatic purpose'. (10 November 1838, Macready, *Journal*, 126.) Dickens would dedicate *Nicholas Nickleby* (1839) to Macready.

of one of the two patent houses to show just what could be done. Macready had been thinking about going into management himself, and in 1837 he signed a very unusual agreement with the proprietors of Covent Garden. Instead of paying the usual rent of £8,800 per annum, he would go into a profit-sharing arrangement. He agreed to pay £40 a night for 180 nights to the proprietors; he paid himself £30 a week; while the remainder of the takings would be split 60/40 between the proprietors and himself until the full sum of £8,800 should be reached.[2] Out of his 40 per cent, Macready had to pay for running the company, and anything left over would be his profit. He was to have complete artistic control, with no interference whatsoever from the proprietors.

It was still a big risk and Macready had misgivings about it, but he seems to have taken the view that it was now or never for the patent houses. They had fallen so low, with whole hordes of bankrupts in their wake, that almost no one wanted to take them on. Macready believed that it was still possible to manage them profitably, or at least not at a loss, while putting on good plays, old and new. Now he was going to find out if he was right.

He put together the strongest company he could muster, persuading everyone to take less than their usual salary for the sake of the venture, and issued a manifesto declaring that 'the decline of the drama, as a branch of English literature, is a matter of public notoriety' and that his aim was 'to advance the drama as a branch of national literature and art'. This provoked Alfred Bunn to announce the new season at Drury Lane with his own manifesto, blaming the decline of the drama on 'the exorbitant demands made by certain professors'. Bunn defended his policy of using crowd-pleasers like *The Jewess* and *The Siege of Rochelle* to subsidise loss-makers like Shakespeare and Ben Jonson on the grounds that 'public pleasure and private enterprise have been equally consulted', and he promised 'to sustain the character Drury Lane has long enjoyed of being THE FIRST THEATRE OF THE EMPIRE.'[3]

Macready opened with *The Winter's Tale* and ran a programme of his already established successes: *Venice Preserv'd, The Stranger* and Byron's *Werner* – one of Macready's most popular roles – but also plays by living authors like Sheridan Knowles's *Virginius* and a new play that

---

In Rep: Plays Performed at Drury Lane During w/c 16 October 1837
Date in brackets is year of first performance

Date of performance, *Play* and playwright

Monday 16 October, *Pizarro* by Richard Brinsley Sheridan (1799)
followed by *The Child of the Wreck* by J.R. Planché (1837) followed
by *Black-Eyed Susan* by Douglas Jerrold (1829)
Tuesday 17 October, *She Stoops to Conquer* by Oliver Goldsmith
(1773) followed by *The Child of the Wreck* by J.R. Planché (1837)
followed by *The Maid of Cashmere* by Edward Fitzball (1833)
Wednesday 18 October, *As You Like It* by William Shakespeare
(1599) followed by *The Child of the Wreck* by J.R. Planché (1837)
followed by *Cinderella*
Thursday 19 October, *The Belle's Stratagem* by Hannah Cowley
(1780) followed by *The Child of the Wreck* by J.R. Planché (1837)
followed by *The Devil on Two Sticks* by Charles Coffey (1728)
Friday 20 October, *The Merry Wives of Windsor* by William
Shakespeare (1597) followed by *The Child of the Wreck* by J.R.
Planché (1837) followed by *The Brigand* by J.R. Planché (1829)
Saturday 21 October, *Gustavus III* by Daniel Auber/J.R. Planché
(1833) followed by *The Child of the Wreck* by J.R. Planché (1837)
followed by *Masaniello* by James Kenney (1829)

Edward Bulwer had written for him, *The Lady of Lyons*. For all his loathing of pantomime, it was absolutely necessary for the finances to have a successful one, and *Harlequin and Peeping Tom of Coventry* went off well, with a moving diorama painted by Clarkson Stanfield showing the scenery of a journey from northern Italy to the English Channel. Macready followed this with an extremely important Shakespearean production: the first *King Lear* since the seventeenth century to get rid of Nahum Tate's happy ending and restore the character of the Fool. The production looked magnificent and was a great success. John Forster wrote a review of it, entitled 'The Restoration of Shakespeare's "Lear" to the Stage', describing it as 'The only perfect picture that we have had of Lear since the age of Betterton'.[4]

Macready's success, which drew the young Queen Victoria several times to Covent Garden, created a challenge to Drury Lane that Alfred

Bunn met in characteristically showmanlike fashion: he offered Charles Kean the £50 a night he had been holding out for to act his father's old parts at Drury Lane. Kean junior had been enjoying great success in the provinces, but this was his first appearance in London since the 1833 season in which his father had dramatically collapsed into his arms. Kean's Hamlet in January 1838 was a triumph, quickly followed by Richard III, Shylock and Sir Giles Overreach in *A New Way to Pay Old Debts*. The audiences loved him, probably more for the sake of his dead father's memory than for his performances.

Macready was not a generous actor: he made sure the spotlight stayed on him, he resented other actors' successes and gloated over their failures. Nevertheless, the members of his Covent Garden company realised that he was trying to do something special and called him into the Green Room one night to present him with a salver engraved with their names. The actor, George Bartley, congratulated him on giving them a season 'equal in its effects to the best days of the drama within the memory of the oldest actor'.[5] Macready replied, assuring them that his intention had been to 'elevate my art, and to establish an asylum for it, and for my brothers and sisters who profess it'.[6] He could certainly look back with pride on his first Covent Garden season, with 55 nights of Shakespeare and more performances of straight plays than opera and pantomime. A few weeks later, he agreed to a request from the Covent Garden proprietors to continue the arrangement for another year, in spite of the fact the he estimated himself to be £2,500 worse off, compared with what he could have earned as a touring star performer.[7]

The Lion King at Drury Lane

Bunn was having a harder time at Drury Lane. The season had lost money, as had every season since he took on the management, and he wanted to bail out. The proprietors advertised, but were unable to find anyone else to take on the lease. They told Bunn that, if he continued the management, they wouldn't press him for the rent, which had been reduced to £6,000 per annum since the start of the 1836/37 season, and he agreed. It would prove to be a fatal mistake for him, but he went into it with his eyes open. He wrote in his diary: 'As they cannot convert any other reasonable being into a jackass, they are willing to continue to make one of me... But what fearful odds one has to fight against! Macready re-opens Covent Garden and his followers have clubbed together a large sum of money, to prevent... his becoming a loser by his speculation.'[8] Bunn, on the other hand, had been operating without a backer since the departure of Captain Polehill in December 1834.

As was often the way with Bunn, an unexpected success came along to lighten his load and put a cheerful aspect on things. In October he opened a spectacular production of *Charlemagne* which featured the American animal tamer Isaac Van Amburgh with his lions and tigers. Macready recorded in his diary 'the failure of the "horse and beast" piece at Drury Lane... I do feel thankful for the defeat of this bad man's attempt to debase still lower the arts',[9] but he spoke too soon. *Charlemagne* was a huge success, almost entirely due to Van Amburgh. In fact, the lions and tigers were still performing after *Charlemagne* had closed, either in other shows or on their own. Queen Victoria came to see them six times in six weeks, on one occasion making it a command performance. The Queen expressed the wish to see the animals after one of the performances, so it was arranged that she should witness them being fed. To make sure the beasts put on a good show, they were starved for 36 hours beforehand, which nearly led to a mishap on the night. One of the highlights of the show involved putting a lamb into the cage to fulfil the prophecy of Isaiah that the lion shall lie down with the lamb.[10] As soon as the starving lion saw the lamb, it pounced, and only a liberal application of Mr Van Amburgh's whip prevented a scene that would have distressed the Queen and disproved the prophecy. The Queen commissioned Landseer to paint the handsome young American and his animals, and Bunn had to arrange for 'this gigantic genius, this prince of painters'[11] to execute his commission backstage at Drury Lane. Bunn applied to the Lord Chamberlain for permission to run Van Amburgh's show throughout Lent but, as we have seen, this was refused. The 'Lion King' (as he was known) therefore took advantage of one of the 'dark' nights to give a magnificent dinner in the Grand Saloon of the theatre to thank the Drury Lane company for his success.

This was Bunn's last piece of luck, and it came too late to save him. The heavy losses of the season, aggravated by the Lord Chamberlain's vindictiveness, were pushing him towards bankruptcy. On 7 March, Bunn was to have his benefit performance at Drury Lane and the cast offered to perform for nothing as a sign of their esteem for him. He thanked them and said he would use their contribution to purchase a memento engraved with their names – no doubt remembering the salver the Covent Garden company had given to Macready. In the event, the finances were so bad he had to put all the money taken that night into the treasury just to stay afloat.

In April, the Drury Lane proprietors asked Bunn to surrender his lease and said that they wished to advertise for a new lessee immediately. Bunn was pinning all his hopes on a production of Auber's opera *The Fairy Lake*, for which he had translated the libretto, and he asked that the lease should not be advertised before he had got the show onto the stage as it would prejudice his chances. The proprietors agreed but, just before the first night, the principal performer, Madame Albertazzi, said that she was going to return to Paris a few days after the opening as she was pregnant. Bunn abandoned the production, at a considerable loss, and shortly afterwards Drury Lane closed before the end of the season.

On 24 July there was a meeting of the proprietors of Drury Lane at which the secretary reported that Bunn had agreed, at very short notice, to take on the lease for the 1838/39 season to avoid the necessity of closing the theatre. However, the theatre had closed early in the season with £12,000 owing in rent, as Bunn had paid only £6,000 in the previous three seasons. One of the proprietors, Mr George Robins, took a far less charitable view of Bunn's exertions as lessee, observing that: 'The boards upon which the plays of the immortal bard had been represented... had been disgraced by an exhibition worthy only of Bartholomew Fair – wild beasts, monkeys, and horses, and asses, have polluted the fair fame of that once classic temple'.[12] This was, of course, a reference to Van Amburgh and his lions, but Mr Robins was only repeating what a lot of people had been saying about Bunn: that he had degraded the temple of the national drama. As a result, Bunn set himself to work on a memoir which he hoped would clear his name with posterity. He called it *The Stage, Both Before and Behind the Curtain*, and it was published in 1840, by which time he had been declared bankrupt.

Bunn fights back

'The gravest charge… that has been preferred against me,' Bunn told his readers, 'consists of my having neglected the legitimate drama, and infected its dominions with gewgaw and pageantry, wherein SENSE had been compelled to give way to SHOW.'[13] This is one of the earliest uses of the term 'legitimate' to describe what we would call straight plays as opposed to musicals, variety and other entertainments. It had first been used in an 'extravaganza' called *The Drama's Levée* written by J.R. Planché for the Olympic Theatre in April 1838. The central character in Planché's plot had been The Drama ('in a critical state of health') and her two sons The Legitimate Drama and The Illegitimate Drama, described as being 'on the worst possible terms with each other'. The Legitimate Drama, representing comedy and tragedy and dressed in a Roman toga, complains that his illegitimate brother has impoverished him. The Illegitimate Drama, representing pantomime and sensation dramas, dressed 'half-harlequin and half melodramatic', replies that his legitimate brother has been stealing his toys ever since they were children:

> *Stole from the nursery of my best hopes,*
> *My rocking horses and my skipping ropes,*
> *And took my harlequins from loss to save you,*
> *And now you blame the punches that I gave you.*[14]

Bunn was the first author of a serious book on the theatre to take over the terminology, and he defines the legitimate drama by drawing the old distinction between what comes in through the ear to the brain and what comes in through the eye to the senses:

> ...under the head of LEGITIMATE DRAMA may be classed all the works of Shakespeare, Ben Jonson, Massinger, Beaumont and Fletcher, Rowe, Otway, Lee, Southern, Addison, Garrick, Cibber, Goldsmith, Vanbrugh, Steele, Colman the younger, Sheridan, Cumberland, Murphy, Young, Centlivre, Cowley, Lord Byron, Joanna Baillie, Knowles, &c. &c. most of whose writings are of a high mental order, and most of them appealing rather to the ear than to the eye.[15]

He then gives a breakdown of the repertoire for those seasons during which he was responsible for programming at Drury Lane (and Covent Garden for two years) to show that he maintained a respectable balance between legitimate and illegitimate entertainments:

The Legitimate Drama at Drury Lane and Covent Garden Under Alfred Bunn		
THEATRE SEASON	PERFORMANCES OF PLAYS BY SHAKESPEARE	PERFORMANCES OF OTHER LEGITIMATE DRAMAS
1832-33	33	49
1833-34	56	113
1834-35	39	64
1835-36	29	20
1836-37	42	28
1837-38	63	32
TOTAL (568)	262	306

Source: *The Stage, Both Before and Behind the Curtain* by Alfred Bunn, 1840, ii, 225-8.

NOTE: Bunn dates his responsibility for the repertoire to 1832, when he was managing Drury Lane for Captain Polehill. For the two seasons 1833/34 and 1834/35, Bunn was managing both Drury Lane and Covent Garden.

Admittedly, Bunn had expanded his definition of legitimate drama somewhat to include other authors than those just mentioned (including himself), but he boasts that these 568 night on which he was presenting the legitimate drama represented very nearly half of all the nights on which he was responsible for one or both theatres. It was all to no avail. He complained that those who alleged, contrary to the evidence, that 'Mr Bunn never played the legitimate drama... could have no other object than to degrade me in public opinion and to do me essential injury',[16] but the charge stuck. Almost every reference to Bunn, from those by his contemporaries through the long line of Macready's biographers to historians of Drury Lane, have made him out to be the arch-philistine, pandering to the lowest possible public taste and desecrating the hallowed boards of Old Drury with the pad of leonine paws. In vain did Bunn protest that quadrupeds had been prowling the boards in the golden age of Sheridan and Mrs Siddons (and long before that, he might have added); the fact that he had presented the first British performance of Rossini's *William Tell*, the first English-language production of Mozart's *The Magic Flute* and the last performances of Ben Jonson's *Every Man in His Humour*✤ to be seen at Drury Lane would count for nothing when weighed in the scales against lions and tigers. He would always be the vulgar populist in the Drury Lane story, a sort of grotesque Dickensian caricature.♣ By the time Bunn wrote his memoir, his hatred of Macready was almost as pathological as Macready's for him, and there is an element of paranoia about the whole thing. However, as the old saying goes, just because you're paranoid doesn't mean they're not out to get you. Bunn was correct in his view of Macready's cabinet, that a well connected clique of writers and intellectuals can influence the public perception of a person, almost regardless of the facts.

✤ It lasted for two nights.

♣ Although he never appeared in a novel by Dickens, Bunn was the original for Mr Dolphin, the theatre manager in Thackeray's *Pendennis* (1848-50): 'a portly gentleman with a hooked nose and a profusion of curling brown hair and whiskers; his coat was covered with richest frogs, braiding and velvet'.

The feeling that the drama was in a bad way was general amongst cultured people of the time, and there were many reasons for that. Unfortunately for Bunn, he became a sort of lightning rod for these concerns, as if he were responsible for the problem, when in fact he understood the situation more clearly than most. Having been manager of both theatres, he knew that Covent Garden and Drury Lane could not survive in the forms they presented in the mid-nineteenth century: 'The position of these two theatres will be defined sooner than is expected by the rude hand of necessity… the ploughshare passing over the ruins of both, his grace the Duke of Bedford will turn one into a brewery, and extend Covent Garden market into the body of the other.'[17]

The prophecy of prop-swords into ploughshares would very nearly come true in both cases.

23

The End of the Monopoly

When Alfred Bunn was drawing up his list of productions
that came under the heading of the 'legitimate drama',
he warned his readers that: 'One legitimate drama was
played nearly as often as all the rest put together, and that was THE
ROAD TO RUIN.'[1]

Bunn was on this road himself, and on 17 December 1839 he
presented himself before the commissioners for bankruptcy. On his
way to the court, he happened to meet his successor as lessee of Drury
Lane, William Hammond, who had signed a three-year lease at £5,000
a year. The fact that the rent was now less than half of what the
proprietors had been able to get from Elliston in 1819 is sufficient
indication of the dire state of the patent houses by this stage.
Hammond was an actor-manager who had been running the Strand
Theatre since 1836, where he had appeared very successfully as Sam
Weller in two stage versions of *The Pickwick Papers*. Bunn, however,
took the view that he was not up to the task ('His place is in a *sloop*,
not on the quarter-deck of a seventy four') and greeted him with the
cheery remark: 'If you don't look much sharper after matters than you
do, you'll go where I am going.' 'Where may that be?' asked
Hammond. 'To the Court of Bankruptcy,' replied Bunn.[2]

Although Bunn felt the humiliation keenly, the commissioners gave him a gentle ride. He was complimented on keeping accurate and clear accounts, and on living a frugal lifestyle. His debts were almost all to do with the theatre, but they were substantial, amounting to £23,052 11s. 5d. His responsibility for the finances of Drury Lane began in December 1834, when he formally took over the lease from Captain Polehill, and he had lost money in every season since then. The losses had been manageable for most of those years, at between £1,600 and £3,000 per annum, but the 1838/39 season had been a complete disaster, with losses of £15,264. Mr Commissioner Merivale observed that the income fluctuated greatly, from £57,000 in 1835/36 down to £29,000 in 1838/39, and he asked if that was because ticket prices had been reduced. The answer was that it was partly due to reduced prices and partly to 'the loss of public inclination for the last two seasons'. Even in that most successful season of 1835/36, expenses had outstripped income by £2,000 owing to the enormous costs involved in staging the operas and *The Jewess*.[3]

Bunn's gloomy prophecy about Hammond turned out to be correct. Hammond, who was known as an actor of low comedy parts, yearned to go upmarket, so he hired Macready as his principal actor and undertook to present a new tragedy by James Haynes called *Mary Stuart*. Macready was glad to be back at the Lane, where he was welcomed as a returning hero, but was dismayed by Hammond's inability to control the company. *Mary Stuart* opened on 22 January 1840 to reasonable reviews and a good reception. It ran for twenty nights, interrupted by some performances of *Macbeth*, but then on 28 February it was discovered that Hammond had decamped with the takings. He was arrested and declared bankrupt for £8,000. Unlike Bunn, he spent over a year in prison.

Facing closure, the actors approached Macready and asked him, if they would guarantee his salary, to act for one week while they tried to sort something out. Macready said he would act for them free of charge as long as they paid James Haynes his royalties for *Mary Stuart*.

Drury Lane lurched along under a series of short-term arrangements for the next year until the proprietors were able to find another lessee. He was none other than William Charles Macready.

The Macready manner

Macready had not much enjoyed his experience of managing Covent Garden from 1837 to 1839, because the duties of management distracted him from his own performances. Time and again he records that his performance had been less than brilliant because he had not had time to prepare for it properly. To make matters worse, he became involved in a bitter dispute with the Covent Garden proprietors over what he regarded as duplicity over the terms of their agreement, claiming that, rather than being lessee, he found himself in the position of 'salaried foreman'.[4] On 30 June 1839, when the experiment was coming to an end, he wrote in his diary: 'Came to the conclusion that if it were ever proposed to me to undertake the management of a theatre again, I should give no answer *until I had read carefully over the diaries of the two years now past*.'[5]

In spite of this, less than two years later he agreed to take on Drury Lane. He once again allowed himself to be persuaded that he alone could save the legitimate drama and restore the artistic integrity of the patent houses, which were commonly referred to by this time as 'the national theatres'. His management of Covent Garden had been regarded as a triumph, and if it didn't make him a lot of money, it didn't lose money either. Now it was time for the other one.

We know very little about the terms of his agreement with the proprietors, beyond an entry in his diary for 23 March 1841 stating his conditions for taking it on: 'liberty to close at a day's notice; no compulsion to pay any rent; no rent to be paid before Christmas; my salary to be included amongst the working expenses of the theatre; the theatre not to be opened before Christmas; to be mine in virtue of a clear lesseeship'.[6] Macready had been on what was basically a profit-sharing arrangement at Covent Garden: if the money didn't come in, then the proprietors didn't get their rent. This must have been what led to his fury at being treated as a 'salaried foreman'. This time he was definitely going to be the lessee, but the reference to 'no compulsion to pay rent' is puzzling, as is the insistence on the right to close at a day's notice. They probably meant no more than that, if he closed before the end of the agreed period, he wouldn't have to pay rent after vacating the premises.

Lord Glengall, the chairman of the Drury Lane proprietors, was eager to get Macready to take over the running of the theatre and agreed to his terms. Although we don't know the details of these terms, it seems that Macready signed up to more risk than he envisaged. He later claimed that the theatre was in a poor state when he moved in, with the women's wardrobe not worth £40, not a scene fit to be put on the stage and not a single rope working to shift the scenery. He agreed a reduction of the rent in lieu of the money he was going to have to spend, but it wasn't enough to compensate him, 'and thus the burden of restoring the various departments of this large establishment from decay and ruin to their present state has really fallen upon myself'.[7] Before the start of his second Drury Lane season (1842/43), he wrote in his diary that his losses were in the region of £8,000 and had cost him his life's savings.[8] It is hard to know if this figure represented an actual loss, or was in part the result of his calculations of what he could have earned as a star player working for other managements. A loss of £8,000 would have been a shattering blow to a man who worried constantly about his finances, and whose main aim in life was to accumulate sufficient funds to retire and live as a gentleman. But this is jumping ahead.

On 4 October 1841, Macready wrote in his diary: 'On this day I enter upon the lease and management of Drury Lane theatre. I humbly implore the blessing of Almighty God upon my efforts.'[9] The extent to which members of his company shared his vision is shown by the fact that the leading actors agreed to a reduction of a third of their normal salary, on the understanding that the deficiency would be made good if finances allowed it. (They were eventually paid in full.) The season opened on 27 December with *The Merchant of Venice*, followed by a new pantomime *Harlequin and Duke Humphrey's Dinner, or Jack Cade, Lord of the London Stone*. Macready followed this up with *The Two Gentlemen of Verona*, in which he played Valentine. Still committed to new writing, he mounted a handsome production of a tragedy set in the ancient world called *Gisippus* by Gerald Griffin. This was not a great success but it was followed by another new play, *Plighted Troth: A Dramatic Tale* by C.F. Darley, which lasted for only one performance. The turgid nature of the writing was mainly to blame, although it didn't help that an actor trod on Macready's hand when he was lying on the floor, supposedly dead. Macready sat up shouting 'Beast of Hell!', then had to die all over again, to the joy of the audience.

The big hit of the season was, surprisingly, an opera. Macready shared the literary intellectuals' view of opera as a nonsensical farrago of sights and sounds, but decided to try to do something to make it more rational. He chose Handel's *Acis and Galatea*, with its libretto by John Gay, as just the sort of quintessentially English show to suit a national theatre. The sets and costumes were stunning, the chorus of shepherds and shepherdesses danced and sang to perfection, and it enjoyed a huge success. It could easily have run for the rest of the season, but Macready believed that the repertory system, with its frequent changes of programme, was an essential element of 'national theatres', so he only

---

In Rep: Plays Performed at Drury Lane During w/c 10 October 1842
Date in brackets is year of first performance

Date of performance, *Play* and playwright

Monday 10 October, *Hamlet* by William Shakespeare (1600) followed by *The Follies of a Night* by J.R. Planché (1842)
Tuesday 11 October, *The Stranger* by Benjamin Thompson adapted from Kotzebue (1798) followed by *The Follies of a Night* by J.R. Planché (1842)
Wednesday 12 October, *As You Like It* by William Shakespeare (1599) followed by *The Follies of a Night* by J.R. Planché (1842)
Thursday 13 October, *Marino Faliero* by Lord Byron (1821) followed by *The Follies of a Night* by J.R. Planché (1842)
Friday 14 October, *As You Like It* by William Shakespeare (1599) followed by *The Follies of a Night* by J.R. Planché (1842)
Saturday 15 October, *The Rivals* by Richard Brinsley Sheridan (1777) followed by *The Follies of a Night* by J.R. Planché (1842)

---

allowed it 43 performances. It still brought in so much money that it compensated for the failure of the two new plays.

The season came to an early close on 23 May with Macready playing Iago, 'very poorly... I have had too much upon my head'. He had just heard that a summons had been issued against him for non-payment of the rates – 'the first I had heard of it'.[10]

His second Drury Lane season opened on 1 October 1842 with *As You Like It*, in which Macready played Jacques – an unusually small part for him. It was followed by *King John*, then a revival of the Dryden/Purcell opera *King Arthur* which was meant to repeat the success of *Acis and Galatea*. It was certainly spectacular, with a cast including 79 members of the regular company, a chorus of 100 and 116 extras. It was well received but didn't do as well as its predecessor, running for 31 performances.

A new play called *The Patrician's Daughter*, which was a modern tragedy based on class distinctions written in blank verse, enjoyed only a very modest success and the next new play – Robert Browning's *A Blot in the 'Scutcheon* – was a resounding flop, closing after three nights. Macready blamed its failure on the fact that he had not appeared in it: it was becoming so difficult to find an audience for a serious new play that star-power offered the only chance of success. The depression he felt about the state of the drama increased when both of his next new plays, *The Secretary* by Sheridan Knowles and *Athelwold* by William Smith, flopped badly. A new production of *Much Ado About Nothing* was a moderate success, with Macready as Benedick – an unusual part for the eminent tragedian, who was described by one of his fellow actors as being as cheerful in the part as a hearse in a snowstorm.[11]

The season was due to close on 12 June with a performance of *Macbeth*, Macready's favourite and greatest role, but Queen Victoria commanded *As You Like It* on that night instead. Macready had no choice but to play it, but then made the actual closing night two days later.

Always inclined to look on the gloomy side, Macready regarded his Drury Lane experiment as a failure that just confirmed his view that the drama had gone to the dogs. This view was not shared by others, and certainly not by his cabinet, who thought he had achieved something brave and noble. In the last season of 183 nights, he had put on 96 performances of Shakespeare and 177 of other plays, as opposed to 148 performances of pantomimes and operas. Artistically, the standards were so high that it became customary to speak of 'the Macready manner' as an approach to putting on a play in such a way as to do everything possible to bring out the full meaning of the author's words. This was Macready's real legacy to the theatre, from which we are still benefiting.

Up until his time, rehearsals had been a perfunctory affair, normally taken by the stage manager. The main aim was to get everyone on and off the stage without falling over the furniture. Leading actors like Garrick and John Philip Kemble might direct rehearsals of a new production, but mainly with the aim of making sure that no one stole their limelight. Macready, on the other hand, insisted on many long days of rehearsal for a new production in which he would ensure that all of the actors understood his vision of the play and gave their best possible interpretation of whatever part they were playing. He was very much the star, but that didn't mean he wanted everyone else to be rubbish to set him off. He was what we would now call the director of the play, although the term wasn't used then. He persuaded his actors to give their best, even when they were in parts they regarded as too small for their status, and to set an example he took Friar Lawrence in *Romeo and Juliet* and Jacques in *As You Like It*. When he reflected on the difference between his productions and other people's, he decided that it lay in this: 'I thought for and acted to myself every character and supernumerary figure, and taught them to act as I would have done had I been cast in their places.'[12]

Macready's other innovation was in the field of design. Although managements had been boasting on their playbills for hundreds of years of 'entirely new scenes and dresses' for a new production, it was almost unheard of for a new show to be designed completely from scratch. The theatre held a stock of wings and backdrops from which any scene could be cobbled together, no matter if the backdrop of Julius Caesar's forum had the wings of Shakespeare's London. Costumes were a matter of personal choice for the actors: they could get a dress out of the wardrobe or provide their own. Whether it matched anything else in the show was irrelevant. Macready was the first person to insist on a design concept: he made sure that *Romeo and Juliet* showed Verona in 1200 and *The Two Gentleman of Verona* in 1500. *The Merchant of Venice* was the result of a great deal of research into how Venice looked in 1300, and how its Senate worked. For his Drury Lane season, Macready made small playbills available in the auditorium giving the details of each scene, who had painted it and what research had been done into it. If we could see these productions now, they would probably seem over-elaborate to us, and Macready himself acknowledged that his successors allowed the designs to dominate the play, whereas his intention had always been to bring out the poetry. Nevertheless, the Macready manner was a vast improvement on what had gone before. It was also a heavy drain on Macready's resources, because, as lessee, he had to pay for the productions, but the sets and costumes were handed over to the proprietors when the lease came to an end.

We have to make some allowances for Macready's gloomy view of everything, but nevertheless he was determined to make his second season his last. When the Drury Lane proprietors asked him if he would like to renew for 1843/44, he submitted a list of demands that he knew they would not agree to. Macready's first biographer, the critic William Archer, astutely observed that Macready went into management with a negative mindset, almost willing it to fail and make a martyr of him. 'This was not the temper to set about the reform of the drama.'[13] Macready could have made more money if he had followed what was increasingly becoming the trend in theatre of long, continuous runs for his successful productions like *Acis and Galatea* but he insisted on sticking to the promises he had made to the public. 'He had promised variety, and he would be conscientious.'[14] As Archer pointed out, Macready was trying to run theatres as they had been run in the days of Davenant, when there were only two theatres in London catering for the taste of a smaller but more homogenous playgoing public. All of that had now changed, and 'he was trying to continue the system of monopoly management under the conditions of free-trade'.[15]

He would never manage a theatre again, but would instead concentrate on building up his assets until he could bid farewell to the stage forever, which he did on the boards of Drury Lane eight years later.

Establishing a free market in plays

Macready was a radical in his politics but deeply conservative in everything else. He had tried to make the patent theatres work as they were intended: using their special status, guaranteed by monopoly powers, to put on high quality plays, especially those of Shakespeare. He had tried his hand at both theatres and the experiment had failed, not artistically but financially. It simply wouldn't work without a subsidy, and there was no chance of any government subsidy of the theatre in the first half of the nineteenth century. The old system had come to the end of the road.

In his farewell speech on the last night of his Drury Lane management, Macready revealed that, several years before, he had applied to the Lord Chamberlain for a licence to run his own theatre company, but that this had been refused. As a result, if he were to mount a play by Shakespeare in a theatre licensed for the appearance of 'brutes and brute-tamers', he would risk prosecution. 'May I not ask for what public benefit such a law is framed, or for what one good purpose it is persisted in?'[16] This rhetorical question was about to be answered, and the restrictive law abolished.

In the following month, on 26 July 1843, the Theatre Regulation Bill was introduced into parliament, abolishing the patent privileges. There was no opposition to the central idea that the patents were outdated and actually damaging to the health of the drama, and the bill went rapidly through both houses of parliament, receiving royal assent on 22 August. As *The Times* would say, a few years later: 'In the drama, as in all things else, the world has arrived a period when the order of the day is Free Trade.'[17]

Before the bill reached the statue book, *The Spectator* had already pronounced the eulogy over the coffin of the old system:

> The 'Patent' monopoly has finished its work. The 'legitimate drama', for the support of which the two great theatres were endowed with exclusive privileges, has ceased to exist – at least in so far as they are concerned... the 'legitimate drama' has fallen a victim to protection. Mr Macready, its fast and best friend, tried every effort to revive it; but in vain.[18]

A few months after the passage of the Theatre Regulation Act 1843, the originator of the term 'legitimate theatre', J.R. Planché, wrote yet another of his extravaganzas to explain the new situation to the theatregoing public. Entitled *The Drama at Home*, it opened at the Haymarket on 8 April 1844. It is set in 'the ruins of the ancient temple of the drama', where the character of The Drama reviews the goings-on at Drury Lane and Covent Garden and decides that she is not welcome at either. Mr Puff the Critic advises her to emigrate, but then Portia appears with news of the change in the law, which means that The Drama can appear wherever she likes:

> *Sheridan now at Islington may shine;*
> *Marylebone echo 'Marlowe's mighty line';*
> *Otway may raise the waters Lambeth yields,*
> *And Farquhar sparkle in St George's Fields;*
> *Wycherley fluster a Whitechapel pit,*
> *And Congreve wake all 'Middlesex to wit'.*[19]

Puff tells The Drama that she has always had a home at the Haymarket, but she replies that it is only open for the half the year. (The Haymarket had a licence to present plays, but only in the summer when the patent houses were closed.) Portia announces that the change in the law means that the Haymarket can now stay open throughout the year, and Ariel sings that: 'the drama feels at home/'neath this cosy little dome.'

By the time the Theatre Regulation Act 1843 was passed, Covent Garden had virtually ceased to function as a theatre and was being used for public meetings and promenade concerts. In 1847 it would become the Royal Italian Opera and has remained an opera house ever since, although it also staged pantomimes until 1882. That left Drury Lane as the only large theatre in the central London area still presenting plays. But what sort of plays would attract support in the new competitive environment, in which smaller theatres could offer a more sympathetic setting for 'the legitimate drama'? That was a puzzle that would see several more lessees making their way down the road to ruin.

24

More Lessees

There are numerous deeply unflattering references to Alfred Bunn in Macready's diary during the period of his Drury Lane management. This may have been partly because being back at the Lane brought back memories of the punch-up, but it was mainly because Macready's hatred of Bunn had reached the level of an obsessive mania. When the management of Madame Vestris and her husband Charles Matthews collapsed at Covent Garden, they were replaced by Bunn. Macready believed that he had been appointed by the Covent Garden proprietors as 'the person most inimical to me'.[1] Two months later, he heard that the actors at Covent Garden had accepted Bunn's request to work for half-salary: 'The wretches! They deserve the fate they have mainly contributed to bring on themselves.'[2] Two months after that, the Bunn management at Covent Garden collapsed and Macready told his diary that, although he didn't want to be vindictive, 'I cannot but regard with satisfaction the termination of this wretched attempt to degrade our miserable art still further... by the obtrusion of such... a villain as Bunn.'[3]

It must, therefore, have been mortifying for Macready in the highest degree when he found that Bunn was to succeed him as lessee of Drury Lane. 'This is, on the part of the committee, shameful – to the art, actors, and the public.'⁴ The committee probably didn't regard it as shameful at all. If the high-minded Macready wanted to throw in the towel, someone had to keep the doors open, and Bunn had a lot to recommend him by way of managerial experience.

Alfred Bunn didn't trouble himself too much with the legitimate drama this time. His passion had always been mainly for opera and ballet, so he effectively turned Drury Lane into an opera house. He would present 11 new operas over the next four years, including several by Michael Balfe, with whom Bunn liked to work as librettist. Things got off to a very good start when, on 27 November 1843, *The Bohemian Girl* opened at Drury Lane with music by Balfe and a libretto by Bunn. It ran for more than a hundred nights and was the only English opera to achieve international fame, with versions in Italian, French and German. It contained the song 'I dreamt I dwelt in marble halls' which became a standard in the repertoire of concert singers, and *The Bohemian Girl* itself was still being performed in the 1930s. Other Balfe operas for Bunn's second spell as manager of Drury Lane included *The Bondman* (1846) and *The Maid of Honour* (1847). The enormous sums that Balfe's operas brought into the Drury Lane treasury were recognised in the colossal statue of him, by Louis Auguste Malempré, that was erected in the rotunda of the theatre after his death, and which puzzles many theatregoers today who have absolutely no idea of who he was.

Bunn had a less happy experience with soprano Jenny Lind, the 'Swedish Nightingale', whom he engaged to appear at Drury Lane in 1845. She reneged on the agreement and he sued for breach of contract, claiming to have lost £10,000. He was eventually awarded £2,500 in damages.

Bunn carried on until March 1848 when he gave up for the second time, as he was losing too much money. He had been sub-letting the theatre to a flamboyant French musical impresario called Louis Jullien, famous for his 'monster concerts' involving hundreds of singers and musicians, with some dramatic special effects. His flashy dress sense, coupled with a nose for publicity, made him a celebrity, and many regarded him as a charlatan, although it would be fairer to describe him as a populariser. He specialised in promenade concerts, which originally meant a concert during which you could walk around.

However, his were so popular that movement was impossible. He made good music available to a wide public at low prices, and was successful for many years.

When Jullien took over the Drury Lane lease from Bunn, one of his first acts was to present the Théâtre Historique from Paris. Founded by Alexandre Dumas in the 1840s, the company had decided to visit London in order to escape riot-torn Paris, but they walked straight into a demonstration of nationalistic feeling that made them wonder why they had bothered. They were to present a ten-act version of their founder's novel *The Count of Monte Cristo* over two nights, but their arrival sparked off a controversy about the extent to which French influences were dominating the British stage. One pamphleteer attacked British playwrights 'who suck forth Frenchmen's brains through a quill and void the diluted matter forth as specimens of British society and manners'.[5] Having a company of French actors appear at the national theatre was a step too far, and as soon as the curtain went up on the first part of the play, a chorus of boos and catcalls began which drowned out the actors. Louis Jullien tried to calm the audience, but he was warned that the protest would be continued if he tried to present another performance. The protesters were as good as their word and, after a second night of this, the French actors decided that, if they were going to have to put up with riots, they might as well go back to Paris. They did two final performances at the St James Theatre, where there were no demonstrations. 'Taking-the-bread-out-of-the-mouths-of-British-actors' had only been an issue at Drury Lane. Undaunted in his Frenchness, M. Jullien then presented a Gallic circus, the Cirque National de Paris, followed by a season of German opera. Both passed off without incident.

Farewell to Macready and the threat of demolition

In December 1849 the lease of Drury Lane was taken over by James Anderson, a Scottish actor who had made his London début with Macready's company at Covent Garden in 1837. Anderson, who had been a good-looking young man, played Florizel in Macready's production of *The Winter's Tale* and got such a good reaction from the audience that Macready, always nervous of the success of other members of his company, rushed to the prompter's box to ask what the noise was all about.[6] He remained with Macready for the seasons at Covent Garden and Drury Lane, so he was well acquainted with Macready's difficult and demanding nature. Macready had by this time accumulated enough money to achieve his highest goal as an actor: to leave the stage forever and live the life of a gentleman. He chose Drury Lane for his farewell to the public on 26 February 1851, appearing as Macbeth. Cantankerous to the last, he objected when Anderson inserted his own name and those of some leading members of the Drury Lane Company into the bills amongst the singing witches. This was meant as a friendly gesture but Macready described it as 'a piece of vulgar insolence without parallel' and insisted on their removal.[7] Things got worse when Macready found that Anderson had told members of the Drury Lane company that they could watch the performance from backstage. The eminent tragedian said that if Anderson insisted on this, he would find another theatre for his farewell. Anderson was mortified by Macready's behaviour, which he regarded as proud and dictatorial.[8] In spite of all this, the event was a great success, with a packed theatre and hundreds turned away. A crowd of three thousand was outside the theatre at six-thirty to see the audience arriving. The performance had been sold out for days, and the reaction to Macready, when he appeared and when he made his farewell speech, was overwhelming. The tragedian and his audience were in tears as he told them he wanted to retire while his powers were still intact, rather than decline before their eyes. He was proud of restoring Shakespeare's texts, but he regretted that his 'ambition to establish a theatre, in regard of decorum and taste, worthy of our country, and to have in it the plays of our divine Shakespeare fitly illustrated, was frustrated by those whose duty it was... to have undertaken the task.'[9] When Macready walked off the stage, it was for the last time. He resisted all requests for comeback appearances, and dedicated himself to living the life of a gentleman and doing good works in his local community of Sherborne. He did agree to give public readings of *Macbeth* to raise funds for the purchase of Shakespeare's Birthplace for the nation.

Macready's obstreperousness was not the only obstacle James Anderson faced. He had been hoping to profit from the crowds arriving in London for the Great Exhibition of 1851 but his losses were becoming unsustainable. He had reduced prices to: stalls 5s., boxes 4s., pit 2s., first gallery 1s., second gallery 6d., but to no avail.[10] He had to withdraw in June 1851, by which time he had lost £9,161 in only two seasons. For the rest of the year Drury Lane was occupied by a very popular American equestrian troupe called McCullock's, followed by promenade concerts organised by Louis Jullien. Then, in December 1851, Alfred Bunn was back. He redecorated the theatre in Louis XVI style and put on a season of operas, including Michael Balfe's *The Sicilian Bride* in March 1852. In June, Bunn left Drury Lane for good, the only person to have held the lease more than once. His managerial style was described by J.R. Planché as 'sheer gambling of the most reckless description',[11] but, with the wrecks of so many managements piling up, only a gambler with a strong stomach for risk would have taken on Drury Lane at all.✤

In July, Bunn was succeeded by an American called Sheridan Smith who took the lease 'for a brief period', but it turned out to be briefer than he thought because he decamped at the end of the first week, unable to pay the wages. The proprietors managed to let the theatre until December to Louis Jullien and Frederick Gye, who was also running Covent Garden, for a series of winter concerts. A more permanent arrangement was struck with Edward Smith to take over the lease in December at the astonishingly low rental of £3,500 per annum.

A rent that was less than one-third of what had been demanded in 1826 shows the desperate state of Drury Lane. During the summer, Christopher Haedy, the Duke of Bedford's London agent, had written

---

✤ Planché wasn't entirely hostile: 'To do him justice, Bunn had all the courage as well as the recklessness of the inveterate gamester, and bore his misfortunes with more equanimity, indeed, than he did his successes.' (Planché, i, 274.)

to the Drury Lane treasurer warning that the ground rent to the Duke was now so far in arrears that Drury Lane might have to be demolished to make way for buildings on which the rent might actually be paid. A few weeks later, Haedy wrote to Francis Russell, the seventh Duke of Bedford, advising him not to take possession of Drury Lane just yet as he had been promised that the rent paid by Gye and Jullien would be used to reduce the arrears of ground rent. This seems not to have happened and, in February 1853, Haedy recommended the Duke to vacate the lease and demolish the theatre. He said that Drury Lane had survived longer as a theatre than Covent Garden, which was now an opera house, but that:

> …there is now strong reason to fear that its days, as a theatre, are numbered, every attempt to let it as a theatre ending in failure. The rent payable to your Grace for it is getting into arrear and it appears to be far from improbable that either the lease of it will be surrendered to your Grace, or that you will have to resort to legal proceedings for vacating it. This has so long appeared to be probable as to have made it necessary to consider what would be the best use it could be put to in the event of the surrender and avoidance of the lease. The result of much consideration is that it is incapable of being applied as a building to any profitable purpose, and that the best thing to do with it will be to take it down, sell the materials, and let the site of it as building ground.[12]

This was no doubt sensible advice, but, for whatever reason, the seventh Duke neglected to act on it. A year later Haedy was singing a different tune, telling the Duke that 'contrary to what was expected', the arrears of rent had been diminished and 'for the present at least the necessity for taking steps to vacate the lease has ceased'.[13]

This skin-of-the-teeth escape from demolition was due, in some part, to the success of the new lessee, Edward Smith.

Everything by turns

Edward Smith was the sort of man who, at one stage, would have stood no chance of acquiring the lease of Drury Lane. He had been a Bow Street Runner, a restaurateur and landlord of the Coal Hole in the Strand. When Mrs Amelia Bloomer launched her eponymous items of underwear, Smith made his barmaids wear them. In 1850 he had taken the lease of the Marylebone Theatre in Edgware Road. He was well down-market of Drury Lane, but the theatre was in a desperate condition which was reflected in the rent.

Smith got off to a good start, opening his first season on 27 December 1852 with a stage version of Harriet Beecher Stowe's recently published novel *Uncle Tom's Cabin* followed by the pantomime *Harlequin Hudibras*. Uncle Tom lasted for two weeks but the pantomime ran continuously until 12 February, as the afterpiece to a number of different mainpieces.

The first season was financially successful, and Smith negotiated a seven-year lease with the proprietors at the higher rate of £4,000 a year. Like other Drury Lane managers, he had to present a variety of attractions to keep the theatre full, alternating straight plays with Chinese conjurors and the final performances of the great tragedienne Madame Rachel in Racine and Molière with a man who could walk on the ceiling like a fly. He tried a season of Italian opera at popular prices: stalls 4s.; dress circle 2s. 6d.; second circle and pit 1s.; the two galleries 6d.[14] The experiment was a failure, but it is interesting to see the old division of the auditorium into pit, boxes and gallery making way for the classifications we use today. Managements had realised that the seats in the front of the pit were actually amongst the best in the house, so there was no need to let them go for the second price. A barrier was introduced to divide the front rows from the rest of the pit, and this new area was called orchestra stalls, as they were sitting next to the orchestra. Patrons of the orchestra stalls sat on chairs, not benches and, as the nineteenth century progressed, the barrier would move further and further back until the pit disappeared altogether, although it would last longer at Drury Lane than at most other London theatres.

The 'dress circle' was in the tier that had been called dress boxes, and the term 'boxes' for which the charge was one guinea (£1.05) represented a private area where a small group of people who had arrived together would sit, rather than a seat in a large enclosure of twenty or so people. Patrons sitting in the dress circle and orchestra stalls would have been expected to wear evening dress.

Smith introduced what he called morning performances to Drury Lane. These actually took place in the afternoon, and were not unknown at the time for charity galas, children's entertainments like puppet shows and the occasional royal command performance for visiting dignitaries. However, Smith was the first theatre manager to see that the large number of children in the audience for a pantomime would be much happier (or at least their parents would) if they could be home by bedtime rather than staying up until midnight. Pantomimes were still afterpieces at this time, so a child who was only interested in the antics of Clown and Pantaloon would first have to sit through the mainpiece, which might be unsuitable for children. For example, the 1854 Boxing Day première of *Jack and Gill, or Harlequin King Mustard and the Four-and-Twenty Blackbirds Baked in a Pie* followed *George Barnwell*, a tale of lust, murder and execution that had been used to put the fear of God into London apprentices for many years.[15] 'Morning performances', which actually started at 2.00 p.m., gave children the opportunity to see the pantomime on its own and be home in time for tea. The original misnomer is responsible for the fact that we still use the term 'matinée' to describe a performance that takes place in the afternoon.

Smith's entrepreneurial drive was by no means satisfied just by being the lessee of Drury Lane. He became the proprietor of a circus and of the Royal Panopticon in Leicester Square which he renamed the Alhambra. He took over Her Majesty's Theatre in the Haymarket and put on the first pantomime ever seen there, then leased Cremorne Gardens in Chelsea. The reader will probably be anticipating the word 'bankrupt' fairly soon in this narrative, but oddly enough Edward Smith was one of the few nineteenth-century lessees of Drury Lane not to end up in the bankruptcy courts. At the end of his seven-year lease he negotiated another one, but by the end of his tenth year, he was

---

In Rep: Plays Performed at Drury Lane During w/c 20 March 1854
Date in brackets is year of first performance

Date of performance, *Play* and playwright

Monday 20 March, *The Corsican Brothers* adapted by Dion Boucicault from Alexandre Dumas (1852) followed by *Grand Ballet Divertissment*
Tuesday 21 March, *A New Way to Pay Old Debts* by Philip Massinger (1626) followed by *Léonie* by Joseph Duggan (1854) followed by *Grand Ballet Divertissment*
Wednesday 22 March, *Léonie* by Joseph Duggan (1854) followed by *My Cook and My Housekeeper* (unknown author, 1854)
Thursday 23 March, *Virginius* by James Knowles (1820) followed by *My Cook and My Housekeeper* (unknown author, 1854)
Friday 24 March, *Léonie* by Joseph Duggan (1854) followed by *My Cook and My Housekeeper* (unknown author, 1854)
Saturday 25 March, *Hamlet* by William Shakespeare (1600) followed by *Grand Ballet Divertissement*

---

beginning to feel it was time to move on, especially as the theatre was due for repairs. He asked Dion Boucicault, the most successful dramatist of the day, if he would like to acquire his lease. 'Only six thousand pounds, my boy. You walk in, I walk out.' 'Very good, Smith,' replied Boucicault, 'I should want you to give me six thousand, and then I should not walk in but keep out.'[16] However, Boucicault did take a short sub-lease towards the end of 1862.

He was having an unprecedented success with his play *The Colleen Bawm* at the Adelphi, where it became the longest-running play ever seen in London: it opened on 10 September 1860 and ran for ten months, with only a short Easter break. This was unheard of. The advent of the long run would soon drive the repertory system off the London stage and transform the way in which actors were hired, replacing engagements for a theatrical season with a run-of-the-play contract. Boucicault developed a system of sending out his own touring companies to perform the play in the provinces, instead of licensing other theatre managements to produce it, which made him even richer.

Queen Victoria came to see the play three times at the Adelphi, and the third visit was the last she ever made to a public place of entertainment, as Prince Albert died shortly afterwards.

Boucicault was able to insist on a partnership arrangement with Benjamin Webster, the lessee of the Adelphi, which was so much in his favour that he was virtually running the theatre.✣ In spite of this, he was dissatisfied, unable to tolerate the idea that Webster was somehow making money out of him. Boucicault's difficult and grasping nature made it impossible for him to sustain a long-term working relationship with anyone and he began looking for ways to break his agreement with Webster. Webster eventually solved the problem for him by locking him out of the Adelphi as a response to his outrageous behaviour.

Boucicault then took a short-term lease on Drury Lane and moved *The Colleen Bawm* in there, although the show had to be rebuilt as Webster refused to hand over the sets and costumes. It opened at Drury Lane on 23 June 1862 and had a successful run until Boucicault replaced it with *The Relief of Lucknow* on 15 September. This had to close on 8 November, because Smith had finally managed to dispose of his lease. During its run, Boucicault wrote to *The Times* complaining about the antiquated condition of the Theatres Royal. He alleged that they were overcrowded, insanitary, inefficient and lacked leg-room: 'a spectator is a human being, not a sardine'. Boucicault was trying to raise funds to build a theatre of his own, but in the course of his letter he revealed that he was paying rent 'at the rate of £7,800 a year for Drury Lane'.[17] We don't know what rent Smith was paying the proprietors of Drury Lane for his lease to replace the seven-year lease at £4,000 per annum, but it sounds as if he was making a reasonable profit from Boucicault for this short season.

✣ He was able to negotiate a percentage payment for himself as author for every performance of one of his plays. This was the first time that an author had broken free from the flat-fee arrangement that had persisted from Elizabethan times, and theatre managers were horrified when it became known what Webster had agreed to. Difficult and demanding as he was, Boucicault made it possible for successful playwrights to become rich, instead of seeing others reap the fruits of their labours.

To be able to run one play continuously for three months, followed by another play for two months, was something new at Drury Lane. The 1850s marked a watershed in theatrical practice in London, as the growing population, increasing affluence and expansion of the railways made a long, continuous run of the same play possible. Charles Kean's production of *The Winter's Tale* had run for 102 nights at the Princess's Theatre in 1856, and thirteen productions would have runs exceeding 100 nights during the decade.[18] For Drury Lane, with its 3,000 seats to sell, a run of this length was hard to achieve, but we can see Smith working towards it during his management. He was able to hold productions for longer, perhaps a week or two weeks, and rotate a smaller number of mainpieces and afterpieces throughout the season. On 1 March 1858 he introduced a new ballad opera called *William and Susan* and was able to run it continuously until 21 March; the 1860 pantomime *Peter Wilkins or Harlequin and the Flying Women of the Loadstone Mountain* followed a play called *The Billet-Doux* starring Charles Matthews which ran continuously, with the pantomime, from 27 December 1860 to 26 January 1861. There ensued a month of Shakespearean performances by Charles Kean (still followed by the panto), then Charles Matthews returned in a melodrama called *The Savannah* which ran continuously from 7 March until 21 March 1861. Whilst we would not regard two or three weeks as a long run, it was very different from the nightly change of programme that would have seemed normal to Garrick and Sheridan.

Smith, who has been described as 'a most wonderful and indefatigable impresario, a kind of English Barnum',[19] was by no means out of ideas by the time he left Drury Lane. He took on the Surrey Theatre, the Alexandra Theatre and the Regent Music Hall; he opened several restaurants and owned *The Sunday Times* for a while. He was well liked and trusted, a generous supporter of charities and an all-round good egg. His ten-year stint at Drury Lane was far from being a brilliant period in the theatre's history, but it wasn't a disaster either. Compared with some of his predecessors and successors, he got off lightly.

25

Poets and Profits

In December 1862, Edward Smith managed to transfer the lease of Drury Lane to Edmund Falconer. Falconer was an Irish actor and playwright who had made a success of managing the Lyceum for several years, where his play *Peep O' Day* opened in November 1861 and enjoyed an uninterrupted run of thirteen months. The £13,000 he had earned from this and other successful comedies enabled Falconer to take on Drury Lane, where he thought his plays would earn him even more money. He wrote *Bonnie Dundee* to open his management and followed it with other self-penned efforts including *Nature's Above Art, Love's Ordeal* and two Irish plays, *The O'Flahertys* and *Galway-go-bragh*. Unfortunately, according to one contemporary theatre historian, he was misled by 'a partiality for his own writings that the public did not reciprocate',[1] and he lost a lot of money. His management wasn't entirely an exercise in vanity playwriting, however: he put on a series of high-quality Shakespeare productions including *Macbeth, Cymbeline, As You Like It* and *Henry IV Part 1*, as well as Byron's *Manfred* and Milton's *Comus*. He employed leading actors and some of these productions had beautiful scenery designed by William Beverley, but nothing succeeded.

In 1863, he took his acting manager Frederick Chatterton into partnership, and by 1866 he had spent all of his capital and had to withdraw. According to Chatterton, the partnership was terminated 'through differences of opinion on the mode of conducting the business of the house',[2] so there may have been artistic disagreements as well. The proprietors issued a new lease to Chatterton on condition that he had to clear all of Falconer's debts. The rent was £6,000 per annum, with £10 per night for every night over 200 in the year.✛ This additional charge reflected a change in London theatregoing: the old idea of a theatre season that lasted from September to June was dying out. The huge and ever-changing population of London created a demand for entertainment all the year round, so that closing theatres in the summer months while the aristocracy went to their country estates had become an anachronism.

Frederick Chatterton had entered into the management of Drury Lane with the highest goals. He wanted 'to restore Old Drury to its position as the home of the poetic drama'[3] and he issued a manifesto stating that he had resolved 'to place his reliance on a series of Shakespearean performances of the drama'. Within a few years, he had been accused of betraying this pledge and 'desecrating the National Theatre',[4] a charge that stung him eventually to commission from a playwright and critic called Charles Kenney in 1875 an examination of the repertoire and balance sheet of Drury Lane over the first ten seasons of his management. The resulting pamphlet, published under the title *Poets and Profits at Drury Lane Theatre,* gives one of the sharpest accounts we have of the way in which successive managers of Drury Lane had struggled on the horns of a dilemma, trying to run 'a national institution' and 'the leading theatre of the kingdom'[5] without a subsidy and without going bust. Kenney breaks his account down by seasons, as follows:

FIRST SEASON, 1866/67: Chatterton started as he would have liked to go on, with productions of *Macbeth, King John* and *The Comedy of*

✛ According to the contemporary theatre historian Dr John Doran, Falconer had been paying £4,500 a year with £5 for every night over 200, so the rent was on an upward trajectory again. (Macqueen-Pope [1955] 186.)

Errors, followed by *The Beggar's Opera* and a lavish musical version of
Goethe's *Faust*. Helen Faucit played a short engagement in *As You Like
It* and *The Lady of Lyons*, followed by a revival of *The Hunchback* and
a performance of *Hamlet*. This got Chatterton to the all-important
pantomime season, and Kenney gives a good account of what this had
come to mean to managers:

> The pantomime safely reached, the Manager of Drury Lane
> Theatre leaves for a time all his troubles and anxieties behind
> him… the annual rising of the Nile fructifying the Egyptian valley
> and covering the arid soil with golden harvests is not looked
> forward to with more eager anticipation… than is the advent of
> the Christmas holiday season by the lessee of this Temple of the
> Drama, especially if he has been sacrificing too freely to its all
> devouring idols, Shakespeare and Legitimacy. In fact, but for the
> golden tide which now flows into the exchequer to fill up ugly
> deficits, and make all smooth and pleasant again, it would be
> impossible to pay the least regard to the exacting requirements
> of those local deities.[6]

The pantomime that year was *Number Nip*, written by Edward Leman
(E.L.) Blanchard and designed by William Beverley. Chatterton was
fortunate to have inherited this brilliant pantomime team from his
predecessors. Blanchard, who wrote the Drury Lane pantomimes for
nearly forty years, was the literary genius of pantomime: he could weave
together fairy tales, nursery rhymes and legends to make clever and
funny plots, involving lots of elegant rhyming verse, songs, ballets and
a moral. The moral was important to Blanchard, but it wasn't laboured.
Harlequin Hudibras (1852/53) brought together Antiquity and the
Spirit of Improvement to preserve the best of the old whilst embracing
progress; *Little Jack Horner* (1857/58) pitted Intelligence, supported by
Imagination, Discovery and Invention, against Prejudice and
Superstition.[7] The scenery for Blanchard's pantomimes was designed
by William Beverley, who was regarded as having inherited the mantle
of Clarkson Stanfield as the greatest scene-painter of the age. Not only

did he have great artistic skills, he also understood the way in which technology was increasing the possibilities of the stage machinery. The transformation scene had always been an important part of pantomimes, but under Beverley it achieved new wonders, as tons of scenery seemed to dissolve before the eyes of the spectators. Like Blanchard, Beverley had joined the Drury Lane team under Smith's management: he arrived at the Lane in 1854 and remained until the end of Chatterton's management in 1879. From 1868 to 1879 Beverley was working exclusively for Drury Lane, designing most of the productions.

The success of the pantomime made up for the losses of the season to date, but it was followed by a revival of *Faust*, a musical version of *Rob Roy* and some 'old comedies' like *John Bull* and *The Man of the World*. None of these made money and the first season came to an end.

Chatterton didn't want to leave the theatre dark over the summer, so he commissioned Andrew Halliday to write a melodrama that would utilise the resources of the vast Drury Lane stage. Halliday came up with *The Great City*, a drama of high and low life which became famous for bringing a real horse and cab onto the stage, together with thieves' dens and burglars on the rooftops of London making their escape by telegraph wires. It ran for 100 performances. However, 'though *The Great City* brought a welcome flow of gold into the treasury, it was only looked upon for the present as a summer frolic – a midsummer night's dream – and to be followed by an awakening to the stern reality of the classic muse'.[8]

SECOND SEASON, 1867/68: The second season started off with more performances of *Faust*, followed by a revival of the old melodrama *The Miller and His Men*. Both flopped. After some more performances of *King John* and *Macbeth*, Chatterton put on a lavish adaptation of Byron's *Marino Faliero* called *The Doge of Venice*, with sets by William Beverley in the style of Canaletto. It closed after a short run with a loss of £5,000. The pantomime, *Jack the Giant Killer*, was followed by *Richard III*, *Othello*, *The Merchant of Venice* and old comedies like *The School for Scandal*. The season ended with a substantial loss 'as a memento of the reward to be expected in the disinterested pursuit of classical literature'.[9]

'Young Supernumeraries at Drury Lane', *The Illustrated London News*, 7 December 1867.

THIRD SEASON, 1868/69: Chatterton needed to find a way of drawing the public in sufficient numbers to pay his bills and satisfying those who saw Drury Lane as a temple of the drama. He hit on the happy idea of dramatising the Waverley novels of Sir Walter Scott, which seemed to tick all the boxes. Sir Walter was an eminent figure in the literary pantheon: his novels had exciting (dare one say melodramatic) plots; and they offered scope for scenes of action well suited to the resources of the vast Drury Lane stage. Chatterton set his in-house dramatist Andrew Halliday to work on *The Fortunes of Nigel*, which emerged as a play called *The King of Scots*, with the focus now on James I. It worked well, with beautiful scenes of old London by William Beverley, and made a profit. The pantomime was *Puss in Boots*, but the 'partial return to the old legitimate repertoire'[10] in the spring wiped out most of the profits.

FOURTH SEASON, 1869/70: Chatterton's next season gave him what he desperately needed: a stonking great hit in the form of Dion Boucicault's *Formosa or the Railroad to Ruin*. This was a melodrama that built up to the rowing of the Oxford v. Cambridge Boat Race onstage, which would have been sensational enough, but what really stimulated public interest was the fact that several scenes of the play took place in the home of Formosa, a woman who lived by her feminine charms. Formosa was supposedly based on Mabel Gray, a well known high-class prostitute, and there was outrage that this sort of immoral behaviour was being presented on the stage of the national theatre. One angry correspondent to *The Times* complained that: 'Not only is the harlot the heroine of the piece, but her harlotry is made one of its most prominent features. To assist the effect, there were three or four subordinate harlots.' Boucicault, who had absorbed from Phineas T. Barnum the philosophy that all publicity is good publicity, knew that such controversies were always good for business. He began writing pseudonymous letters to the papers attacking his own play so that he or Chatterton could respond. The objections to the play fell under two headings: first, it glorified immoral behaviour by presenting a prostitute as a main character; secondly, Drury Lane should not be staging sensational melodramas. It was agreed that Boucicault would answer the first point and Chatterton the second.

It was in one of these responses that Chatterton used the phrase that would stick to him forever. He said that those who believed Drury Lane should only present the higher drama needed to recognise that, in the experience of people who had run the theatre, 'Shakespeare spelt ruin and Byron bankruptcy'.[11] Boucicault's biographer Richard Fawkes believes the letter to have been written by Boucicault and only signed by Chatterton, to maintain the division of responsibilities. If so, Chatterton must have bitterly regretted his part in the deceit, because the epigram entered the public discourse in a way that he came to feel was extremely damaging to himself. Whilst no one could deny the truth of what he had said, there were many who professed themselves appalled that such a vulgarian had been put in charge of the National Theatre. Boucicault was right about the publicity, however. *Formosa* enjoyed a run of 117 nights and made more than £10,000 for the two men.

It was followed by *Beauty and the Beast*, which was the first pantomime to bring the Vokes family to Drury Lane. Frederick (Fred), Jessie, Victoria and Rosina Vokes were the children of Frederick Vokes, a theatrical costumier. They all appeared on the stage as child actors, but when Fred developed a strange style of acrobatic dancing, they combined to appear in pantomimes together as the Vokes family. They were popular and swelled the size of their 'family' by bringing in Fred's wife, Bella, then a man called Walter Fawdon, who wasn't related at all and had to appear as Fawdon Vokes. They would appear in every pantomime to the end of Chatterton's management in 1879 except for one, taking most of the leading roles in a way that would ultimately have disastrous effects for him. The pantomime was followed by a revival of *Peep O' Day* by former lessee Edmund Falconer, which cleared a profit of £2,000.

FIFTH SEASON, 1870/71: Chatterton splashed out some of his profits on painting the auditorium white and gold, then mounted another staged version of a Sir Walter Scott novel. This time it was *Kenilworth*, under the title of *Amy Robsart*, with a magnificent depiction of the revels staged at Kenilworth Castle by the Earl of Dudley for the Virgin Queen. It made a profit of nearly £10,000 before it had to make way for the pantomime, which was *The Dragon of Wantley*. When the panto closed, *Amy Robsart* was brought back for the rest of the season, making even more money for the treasury.

SIXTH SEASON, 1871/72: On the principle that, when you have a winning horse, you might as well ride it into the ground, Chatterton next set Andrew Halliday to work on *Ivanhoe*, which emerged in dramatic form as *Rebecca*. With its huge cast, knights in armour, jousting with real horses and Robin Hood and his Merrie Men, it was another huge hit and made a profit of £8,000 – 'more than Sir Walter received for the original romance',[12] according to Edward Stirling, whose was responsible for the staging. Even the pantomime took up the Merrie England theme, being *Tom Thumb, or Harlequin King Arthur and the Knights of the Round Table*. This was followed by another revival of *Amy Robsart*, which was still making money.

SEVENTH SEASON, 1872/73: When Chatterton put on a version of Sir Walter Scott's poem *The Lady of the Lake*, he found he had gone to the well too often. It flopped badly. The manager couldn't wait to get the pantomime on. As Kenney rather colourfully expresses it: 'the arrival of Clown, Harlequin and Pantaloon was hailed as a detachment of surgeons would be on the field of battle after a severe engagement'.[13] *The Children in the Wood* was another triumph for E.L. Blanchard and William Beverley and made up for the losses incurred by *The Lady of the Lake*. When it closed, it was replaced by yet another revival of *Amy Robsart*.

EIGHTH SEASON, 1873/74: Chatterton decided to give Scott a rest and to placate 'the spirit of Shakespeare',[14] who had been neglected in the midst of so many Highland romances, with a huge production of the sort that only Drury Lane could do. He chose *Antony and Cleopatra*, which was still one of the most rarely performed Shakespeare plays, and pulled out all the stops. James Anderson, another former lessee, was brought back to play the hero and William Beverley was given a huge budget to recreate the glory of the ancient empires. Cleopatra's barge sailed across the stage; the battle of Actium was fought by triremes on the stage; and the Temple of Isis, where Cleopatra committed suicide, was stunning to behold. Unfortunately, the production fell between two stools. Shakespeare-lovers were outraged that the text had been cut from 34 scenes to 12 to make way for the spectacle, while people who enjoyed spectacle didn't want to see *Antony and Cleopatra*. It lost between £4,000 and £5,000. Chatterton followed it with a revival of William Moncrieff's old war-horse *The Cataract of the Ganges* which had made so much money for Elliston, but Kenney describes it as not so much a revival as a disinterment,[15] since the old nag was as dead as doorknockers.

The 1873/74 pantomime, *Jack in the Box*, was without the Vokes family, as they were touring the USA. This was unfortunate from the point of view of their posthumous reputations as *Jack in the Box* was analysed by the greatest of all Victorian cultural commentators, John Ruskin. Ruskin's standing as a cultural and social critic is hard to appreciate today as his work went out of fashion after his death in 1900, and there is no one alive today who enjoys the same stature. He moved from writing about art to writing about the kind of society that produces great art. He was the champion of the Pre-Raphaelites, the pioneer of the Gothic Revival and the fiercest critic of the industrial capitalist system that had made the British economy the largest in the world, at the expense, he argued, of the quality of life of those who produced the wealth. His most famous aphorism was: 'There is no wealth but life.' Ruskin was a man of towering intellect and passionately held moral convictions, so it is perhaps surprising to find that he was so fond of pantomimes that he would visit his favourites over and over again.

In 1871, Ruskin had begun publishing a series of letters addressed 'to the workmen and labourers of Great Britain' called *Fors Clavigera*, in which he shared his views on life, art and everything else. The March 1874 letter described how he had spent most of his leisure-time during three weeks in the New Year going between performances of *Jack in the Box* at Drury Lane and *Cinderella* at Hengler's Circus (now the site of the London Palladium). As he walked through the streets of Soho, he was struck by the contrast between the children in the pantomimes – beautifully dressed, well-behaved, a delight to look at – and the children

Jack in the Box from The Illustrated London News, 10 January 1874.

in the street – 'ill-dressed and ill-taught, and ill-behaved, and nobody cares to look at them'.✣ If only life could be more like a pantomime:

> At Drury Lane there's just everything I want people to have always, got for them for a little while… Mushroom Common, with its lovely mushrooms, white and grey,♣ so finely set off by the incognita fairy's scarlet cloak; the golden land of plenty with furrow and sheath… they can't have enough, any more than I can, of the loving duet between Tommy Tucker and Little Bo Peep… and yet contentedly return to what they call the necessary state of things outside, where their corn is reaped by machinery, and the only duets are between steam whistles… they return to their underground railroad, and say, 'This, behold – this is the right way to move and live in the real world.' [16]

E.L. Blanchard would probably have been amazed had he known his work would provoke such profound reflections by one of the greatest thinkers of the age, but he took care to embed a moral in all of his pantomimes, and the moral message of *Jack in the Box* was that girls should learn the wifely virtues of patience, economy, industriousness and humility.[17] This is a message that would have resonated strongly with Ruskin, whose own marriage had been annulled in humiliating circumstances.

Chatterton was so relieved to have survived to the end of the pantomime season that he decided not to take any more risks that year and shut the theatre early.

✣ Ruskin was not the first to make this comparison. Dr John Doran had written an account of his visit to the last rehearsal of the 1865 pantomime which made the same point: 'Outside were blasphemy and drunkenness. Inside, boundless activity, order, hard work and cheerful hearts.' Doran gave some interesting statistics: there were over 200 children in the cast who got a shilling per night and 'about five dozen' ladies of the ballet. The show had to take £160 per performance just to cover its running costs. (Macqueen-Pope [1955] 185-86.)

♣ 'In this pantomime occurred the wondrous stage effect, which none who witnessed can forget, in the Mushroom Valley, where the fungi were seen to develop, according to their wont, with a rapidity of vegetation that has made them proverbial, and where others became transformed into hundreds of little children, their button tops forming the head gear of the army of little people.' (Kenney, 46.)

NINTH SEASON, 1874/75: Chatterton was in the habit of sub-letting Drury Lane to Colonel Mapleson during the summer for a season of Italian opera, and during the summer of 1874 Mapleson put on the posthumous première of Michael Balfe's operatic version of Sir Walter Scott's novel *Talisman*. Still unwilling to believe that the public might have had enough of Scott, Chatterton decided to put on *Talisman* as a play, under the title of *Richard Coeur de Lion*. It opened on 26 September 1874, which Kenney describes as well-timed since the statue of Balfe, who had died in 1870, had been unveiled the day before in the rotunda of Drury Lane. Whether this really was good timing is open to question, as it reminded people that they were being given the second version in one year of one of Scott's weakest novels. It flopped with losses in the same region as *Antony and Cleopatra*. This year it was the turn of *Aladdin* to repair the damage to the treasury.

TENTH SEASON, 1875/76: Chatterton really needed a hit now, so he was glad to receive Dion Boucicault's proposal to give the first London production of his new play *The Shaughraun* at Drury Lane. *The Shaughraun* had opened in New York in the previous year to record-breaking business, making more than half a million dollars for Boucicault, who was also starring in the play as Conn, the shaughraun or vagabond. He was fifty-five but played a young man so convincingly that no one commented on the incongruity. *The Shaughraun* is a brilliant play and one of the very few Victorian melodramas that can still be performed successfully; it would deservedly become Boucicault's greatest success. However, there was one drawback for Chatterton. He hadn't forgotten the abuse he had received over *Formosa*, and the terrible slip he had been betrayed into with that never-to-be-forgotten epigram about Shakespeare and Byron. The awful memory of this is what prompted him to commission Charles Kenney to write *Poets and Profits*: he was desperate to convince the public that he wasn't a philistine, and that he really wanted to do the legitimate drama. Only the tyranny of the box office was holding him back. In his foreword, Chatterton complains that he was accused of 'desecrating the National Theatre' when he put on *Formosa*, and now that he is about to present 'another drama by the same author which in the strict sense is not termed legitimate',[18] he wants to lay his case before the public. In spite of the pretext that *Poets and Profits* would be a work of independent research, it soon becomes clear to the reader that Kenney was no more than the lessee's mouthpiece. The pamphlet was published just before *The Shaughraun* opened and its last eight pages (out of 58) are nothing but an extended puff for the forthcoming production.

Fortunately for Chatterton, *The Shaughraun* was a huge success. It opened at Drury Lane on 4 September and ran to packed houses until 18 December, when it had to be taken off to make way for the pantomime. It made £14,000 for Chatterton and Boucicault, and moved to the Adelphi (which Chatterton was also managing) for another month.

No one could have taken a more down-to-earth view of the public taste than Boucicault. He believed that, when the public wanted art, another Shakespeare or another Garrick would appear.[19] Meanwhile, the old hokum he could churn out would do. 'I can spin out these rough-and-tumble dramas as a hen lays eggs,' he wrote to Edward Stirling. 'It's a degrading occupation, but more money has been made out of guano than poetry.'[20]

This was not Chatterton's view. He wanted to do poetry, not guano, and his little commissioned pamphlet contains the pithiest summing up of the unenviable position of the theatre manager who is torn between the box office and the demands of 'the higher drama':

> To keep up the glorious traditions of its past history, to pay a due tribute of reverence to its high intellectual and artistic associations, constitutes, let it be freely admitted, a primary responsibility assumed by anyone who takes the reins of a theatre which, like Drury Lane, is at the same time a sort of national monument. But since, unlike similar establishments in other countries, Drury Lane has no State allowance awarded to it... to enable it to keep up its dignity without regard to those strictly commercial principles which exact a balance of profit at the end of the year, there is no other way out of the dilemma than to let this quasi-national theatre occasionally derogate from its high

position, and stoop to follow the evanescent fashions of the day, balancing legitimacy and high art that will not pay with the sensational drama and realism that will... To put the matter figuratively, if Apollo's lute is to be heard at Drury Lane, Pan with his less elegant but more popular instrument must be allowed his turn, or there will be no one to 'pay the piper'.[21]

Chatterton's policy was that of so many managers of Drury Lane before him: to use pantomime, melodrama and spectacle to cross-subsidise Shakespeare and the legitimate drama. In the absence of subsidy, it was the only way to make Drury Lane work as the National Theatre. He had made a pretty good job of it in his first ten years but, in spite of the success of *The Shaughraun*, it was all about to unravel.

The 1878/79 season was Chatterton's thirteenth, so he had lasted longer than any other lessee so far. He signed a new lease for five years at the same rate of £6,000 per annum with £10 a night for every night over 200 in the season. He opened with a big production of *The Winter's Tale* that failed badly. He followed it with *Othello* and *Macbeth*, which also failed, so he was more than usually dependent on that year's pantomime, Blanchard's *Cinderella*. For once, the Fairy Godmother's wand didn't work. In February, Chatterton found himself unable to pay the weekly wage bill and had to ask the performers to wait. The Vokeses withdrew their labour, which meant the pantomime had to close since they were playing most of the leading parts. On 4 February 1879, Chatterton posted a notice on the doors announcing: 'Owing to a combination of unforeseen circumstances, this theatre is unavoidably closed for the present. F.B. Chatterton, Sole Lessee and Manager.'

Chatterton privately blamed the Vokeses. He told the actor-manager John Coleman, who published *Players and Playwrights I Have Known* in 1888, that he had paid them more money every season as they increasingly dominated the pantomime, but by 1879 'their attraction was over'.[22] William Beverley wrote a letter to *The Daily News* implicitly blaming the Vokeses (without naming them) for putting the whole company out on the street, as the other members would have been willing to give Chatterton some time to recover.[23] Whilst the Vokeses can certainly be criticised for cutting Chatterton no slack at all, after making a great deal of money at Drury Lane over the previous decade, they weren't the cause of the problem. Chatterton admitted that he had lost £7,000 on the season by the time the pantomime opened, but that wasn't the full extent of his financial problems. He petitioned for bankruptcy with assets of £1,500 and liabilities of £38,690,[24] and a large part of his indebtedness was owing to the fact that he had gone into partnership with Benjamin Webster to run the Adelphi and the Princess's theatres. He described this decision as 'suicidal', as the losses on those theatres had absorbed whatever profits he could make at Drury Lane, forcing him to borrow money at what he called 'usurious interest'.[25]

There are several points in the Drury Lane story where the words 'end of an era' come to mind, and this is one of them. The collapse of Chatterton's management was the end of an era in two ways. First, Chatterton was the last in the long line of Drury Lane bankrupts: no subsequent proprietor or lessee would go through that humiliation. Second (closely related to the first) is that Chatterton was the last person in charge of Drury Lane to feel torn between the two goals of running at a profit and maintaining the status of Drury Lane as 'a sort of national monument' with 'high intellectual and artistic associations'. From now on, Drury Lane was in business to make money. The shade of the immortal Shakespeare could look for sacrificial offerings elsewhere.

26

Druriolanus

Drury Lane presented a distinctly unappealing prospect in 1879. Ever since the committee of proprietors had started issuing leases in 1819, most of the lessees had been bankrupted by it. Chatterton's fate was particularly horrible: to go bust in the middle of *Cinderella* has a sort of iconic awfulness about it, as *Cinderella* is the most popular pantomime, and pantomimes had traditionally kept the doors of Drury Lane open. As the playwright George Sims put it: 'Shakespeare had spelt ruin, Byron bankruptcy, and pantomime had put up the shutters.'[1] There seemed no reason to doubt that the line of Drury Lane bankrupts would stretch, like Banquo's posterity, to the crack of doom.

The committee interviewed a few applicants for the lease, none of whom was appealing. One of them was Chatterton, now discharged from his bankruptcy thanks to the reasonableness of his creditors, and eager to get back in the saddle. As soon as he had petitioned for bankruptcy, his lease had fallen in and the committee had confiscated the £1,500 deposit he had paid as guarantee for the rent. As he didn't actually owe any rent at the time, the trustee of his bankruptcy took the view that this £1,500 should be returned and began legal proceedings to that effect. When Chatterton applied for a new lease, he was told that the committee could not commence dealings with him unless he persuaded his trustee to withdraw this action. He did so, and then found they had awarded the lease to someone else: Augustus Harris.

Harris was an actor and stage manager, whose father had been stage manager at Covent Garden. He was only twenty-seven and had no experience of theatre management but he was forceful and convincing, and the committee told him that he could have the lease if he produced a down-payment of £1,000 on the rent. He said that was no problem and the deal was agreed at a rent of £6,000 per annum.

In fact, as Harris never tired of telling people later, his total capital at the time was £3 15s., so he had to raise not only the £1,000, but enough to put on his first show, for which he estimated he needed another £2,000. He managed to borrow £2,000 from William Rendle, one of his rivals for the lease, whom he met at the Aquarium Restaurant in Westminster, £250 from a refreshment contractor, £250 from a relative and £250 from a friend.✤ He thought this was good enough, and went ahead slightly short of his £3,000 total.

With nothing ready, he sub-let the theatre to the actor George Rignold just to get the place open again. Rignold wanted to appear as Henry V, and his production, with lots of horses and banners, was well received. 'The entire production augured well for Mr Harris's enterprise and seemed to be the dawn of a new day in the history of Drury Lane,' according to *The Era*.[2] In fact, it had nothing to do with Mr Harris's enterprise. He didn't mind bringing in the occasional visiting company to do Shakespeare, particularly if someone else was taking the risk, but he had no intention of committing financial suicide by dedicating his Drury Lane to the Swan of Avon. There would be no in-house production of a Shakespeare play at Drury Lane for more than forty years.

Henry V did what he was supposed to do: he got Harris to the pantomime season and his first in-house production. It was *Bluebeard*, with a script by E.L. Blanchard and yet another outing for the Vokes family, who played most of the leading roles. Harris produced it

---

✤ His friend George Sims warned him of the risk: 'Look at the managers the Lane has ruined. It may ruin you.' 'It can't,' replied Harris, 'I've got nothing to lose.' (Sims, 75.)

himself, as he would do every pantomime under his management, and, without being anything particularly out of the ordinary, it was well done. On the first night, Harris appeared before the curtain at the end, in evening dress and Inverness cloak, and asked the audience: 'Well, are you satisfied?' They shouted 'Yes!' This would become an invariable tradition of Harris's management, and as the years went by, the roars of assent from the audience just got louder and louder.

Bluebeard ran for 81 performances and provided Harris with the working capital he needed for his next venture, which would define his management. Meanwhile, he put on a production of a comic opera called *La Fille de Madame Angot*, paid for by a man who presumably had a friend in it whom he wanted to support. The opera wasn't new and this wasn't a particularly good production of it. When he was later criticised for putting on such a weak production so early in his management, Harris's response was: 'If you had to pay a thousand pounds for rent, and hadn't got it, and if a friend turned up and offered to find the shekels if you'd produce *Madame Angot* – what would you do?'[3]

To buy more time, Harris followed *Madame Angot* by bringing in Marie Litton's company. Marie Litton was an actor-manager who had run the Court Theatre (now the Royal Court) in Sloane Square, then the Imperial Theatre in Westminster (where Methodist Central Hall now stands). She excelled in comedy roles such as Lady Teazle in *The School for Scandal* and Kate Hardcastle in *She Stoops to Conquer*, but her biggest success was as Rosalind in *As You Like It*. This production ran for 100 nights at the Imperial before transferring to Drury Lane, where it ran from May to July. Once again, Harris was happy to have Shakespeare at the Lane as long as he wasn't producing it. Throughout June, Marie Litton added what were described as 'Saturday morning performances' (although they started at 2.30 p.m.) of the classic comedies *She Stoops to Conquer*, *The Rivals* and *The Beaux' Stratagem*. In his book *Old Drury Lane*, published in the following year, Edward Stirling claimed that this indicated 'a revival of the taste for the higher class of drama'.[4] In fact, it indicated the reverse. Sheridan, Farquhar and Goldsmith, who had been mainstays of the Drury Lane repertoire for generations, were now too risky for evening performances.

Marie Litton's run at Drury Lane ended on 10 July 1880, making the 1879/80 season 'the longest season on record', according to Stirling. When Augustus Harris opened his next offering on 31 July 1880, Stirling pronounced this 'the earliest date on record for the opening of a winter season'.[5] What this actually meant was that the theatre 'season' had ceased to have any meaning. Harris knew that London was always full of people looking for entertainment, which he intended to give them, and this was the production that was going to show what he could offer.

To describe *The World*, co-written by Harris and Paul Merritt, as a melodrama doesn't really do it justice. Melodramas were nothing new at Drury Lane: they had been around for the best part of a century. What was new was the professionalism and the scale of it. Harris understood that if you do something well enough, even people who would normally be sniffy about that sort of thing will come to see it. His melodramas were unlike any previous melodramas at Drury Lane. They had strong scripts which focused on modern situations and amazing spectacle. The extremely complicated plot of *The World* involved an explosion on a ship at sea, a scene in which the survivors cling to a raft on the billows of the ocean, and – another nascent Harris tradition – a scene in a well known London location, in this case the aquarium at Westminster. As if writing and producing weren't enough, Harris appeared as one of the villains (there were seven of them) who met a satisfying end by plunging down a lift-shaft. When he asked: 'Are you satisfied?', the response was thunderous.

The World took Harris as far as the next pantomime, which was really the first one he could completely control. He rid himself of what he described as the 'tyranny'[6] of the Vokes family and hired a less demanding cast for *Mother Goose and the Enchanted Beauty*, with a script by E.L. Blanchard. The Sleeping Beauty story was decorated with a ballet of dolls and white rabbits, and another of Dresden china figurines in the style of Watteau. The transformation scene, the Fountain of Love, was so effective that Harris and his scene painter Henry Emden were called onto the stage for a round of applause. A short harlequinade was followed by the Reflected Statue Ballet, in which a huge plate-glass mirror at the back of the stage reflected groups of dancers posed as statues and the audience watching them.

Pantomime as a national institution

Harris would turn the Drury Lane pantomime into a national institution, rather like the Last Night of the Proms today: even people who didn't go to them understood their cultural importance. They got bigger and bigger, involving casts of up to 500, thousands of costumes and tons of scenery. They lasted for between four and five hours. Audiences would emerge shell-shocked by the scope and the spectacle, conscious that they had seen something the like of which had never been seen before. They usually cost between eight and ten thousand pounds, although *The Forty Thieves* in 1886 cost £65,000 – well over three million pounds in today's values.[7] *Robinson Crusoe* in 1881 introduced a procession of the trades through the City of London. These processions would become a feature of Harris's pantomimes, getting longer and more elaborate: 'A Dream of Fair Women' in *Aladdin* (1885); 'Shakespeare's Heroines' in *Jack and the Beanstalk* (1889); 'Nursery Rhymes' in *Little Bo Peep* (1892). In 1882 *Sinbad the Sailor* included a procession of kings and queens of England from William the Conqueror onwards, featuring Shakespeare presenting his plays to Elizabeth I, Guy Fawkes riding on a barrel of gunpowder and Napoleon surrendering his sword to the Duke of Wellington. In 1894 Harris returned to the theme in *Robinson Crusoe* with an even bigger montage of monarchs: William the Conqueror was seen to stumble as he disembarked on English soil and to grab two handfuls of sand; King John was forced to sign Magna Carta; Sir Walter Raleigh laid down his cloak for the Virgin Queen; and Charles II appeared with Nell Gwynne and other ladies of easy virtue. The *Times* critic thought that 'pantomime… would have been well-advised to omit the preliminaries to the execution of Charles I', although he didn't object to 'the two pretty little Princes in the Tower'.[8]

The biggest procession of them all, however, occurred in *The Forty Thieves* (1886). Harris had been reluctant to stage this particular tale from the Arabian Nights because forty was too small a number to fill the Drury Lane stage. He wanted to increase the number of thieves but was told that children would object, as the size of the cohort was legendary. He therefore decreed that every thief must have a retinue of

The caption to this 1879 cartoon in *Entracte* read:
'Master Gussy Harris – What will he do with it?'

servants. In the cave scene, in which Ali Baba's brother Cassim forgets the password 'Open Sesame' and is trapped in the cave until the forty thieves get back, the arrival of the thieves and their retinues took forty minutes and filled the stage with 500 people in gorgeous oriental costumes. Now that any cast of over 30 is considered large, it is difficult for us to appreciate the impact of spectacle on this scale. As if this were not enough, there was another procession in the pantomime representing the territories of the British Empire. No wonder the first performance started at 7:30 p.m. and came down at 1.00 a.m.

It was recognised that the Drury Lane pantomime was in a category of its own. 'The traditions of Boxing Day at the "National Theatre" are upheld', said the *Times* critic in his review of *Whittington and His Cat* in 1884, noting that there was no other pantomime in London that Christmas.[9] Covent Garden gave up on pantomime after 1882 as competition with Harris seemed futile.

The Drury Lane pantomime changed a great deal under Harris, and in the opinion of many cultural commentators it was a change for the worse. The harlequinade had been the mainspring of pantomime since its emergence in the eighteenth century, but it diminished in importance in the nineteenth century. Harris cut it back to a very brief interlude and sometimes omitted it altogether. He said that the emergence of Clown was a sign for a lot of people to head for the exits.[10] Harris continued to use E.L. Blanchard as his script-writer, but Blanchard was deeply unhappy about what happened to his witty and elegant scripts once Harris got his hands on them. Harris had hit on the idea of hiring music-hall stars for Drury Lane pantomimes. He wasn't the first manager to do this, but he was the first to bring people like Marie Lloyd, Little Tich and Vesta Tilley to Drury Lane.[11] Music hall was very popular and produced its own stars who had major celebrity status, but it wasn't respectable, so middle-class families couldn't go. They could, however, go to the Drury Lane pantomime to see the people they kept hearing about, while working-class patrons were also glad to see their favourites in more extended roles.

However, the music-hall artistes altered the tone. They brought with them their popular songs, often of a vulgar and suggestive nature, and they wanted to introduce their own comic routines. Blanchard found that his scripts were being hacked about to suit these new requirements and he was deeply unhappy. 'My smooth and pointed lines are turned into ragged prose and arrant nonsense. Consider the payment made to me as an equivalent for the harm done to my literary reputation' he wrote in his diary of *Robinson Crusoe* (1881). 'For the... grossly interpolated book I am in no way responsible,' he complained of *Sinbad the Sailor* (1882), 'though exquisitely got up, it is a very dreary music-hall entertainment... the music-hall element crushing out the rest and the good old fairy tales never to be again illustrated as they should be'.[12] Blanchard was far from being a lone voice. After watching *Little Bo Peep* (1892) in which 'it wasn't the sheep that strayed but Bo Peep herself',[13] the critic of *The Athenaeum* pleaded: 'Oh, Sir Augustus!... Leave our children their fairy tales... your little shepherdesses of the music hall, with their vulgar fancies and style, have nothing to do with pantomime nor with childhood.'[14] From the advent of pantomime in the eighteenth century, cultural commentators had been warning of its corrosive effects upon the culture of the nation. Now they were calling for a return to the good old days of the harlequinade and faery fantasies in opposition to the coarsening of what had become the main theatrical entertainment for children.

Harris was dismissive of this harking back to the good old days. 'The dear old ladies and gentlemen who now insist that this class of performance should be played today, because it met with the approval of their generation, forget that the School Board was not invented when they were young. Whereas in the olden times a pantomime ran a few weeks, it now runs as many months.'[15] At the beginning of Chatterton's management, pantomimes had still been afterpieces, starting at around 9:30 p.m. By the end, Chatterton had made the pantomime the main part of the evening's entertainment, following a curtain-raiser. Harris soon did away with the curtain-raiser, starting at 7:00 p.m. or 7:30 p.m.✤

✤ Harris similarly dispensed with the tradition of mainpiece and afterpiece for his melodramas. Initially he had a curtain-raiser, beginning at 7:15 p.m. or 7:30 p.m., with the melodrama starting at 8:00 p.m., but he soon dropped the curtain-raiser altogether.

Furthermore, the occasional 'morning performances' of Smith and Chatterton – two or three times a week for a few weeks after Boxing Day – were replaced with a more taxing regime of two performances a day throughout January and most of February, followed by evening performances with Saturday and occasional mid-week matinées until March. Harris knew that Blanchard didn't approve of what he was doing, and found his scripts less and less useful. Nevertheless, Blanchard was still a 'name' and it was worth having him on the bills, even if other people were getting co-authorship credits. Harris called Blanchard 'The Old Man of the Sea' because of the way he hung on until the bitter end, which came with *Babes in the Wood* in 1891. There was a certain symbolism in Blanchard's departure after this – he died in the following year – because *Babes in the Wood* introduced Dan Leno, the biggest music-hall star of them all to make the crossover to pantomime. He would become the mainstay of Drury Lane pantomimes for the rest of his life.

The funniest man on earth

Dan Leno was born into a music-hall family and began performing at the age of three as 'the Infant Wonder, Contortionist and Posturer'. He made his first appearance in pantomime at four as a 'juvenile clown' and became part of the family act, specialising in singing and dancing. He excelled in Irish jigs and clog dancing, becoming Champion Clog Dancer of the World at the Whit Week championships in Leeds in 1880. His clog dancing became the main feature of his music-hall act, but he also developed his talent for comic songs, sometimes in female characters. His cross-dressing was not of the outrageous burlesque style, but depended on closely observed depictions of often downtrodden working-class women who would have been familiar to many in his audience. In 1885, Leno's cousin Johnny Danvers, another music-hall artiste, came to London to appear in the pantomime at the Surrey Theatre. One morning, Leno mentioned that he had never seen the

'National Theatre', Drury Lane, so they went to have a look at the outside. Leno crossed the road and knelt down on the steps. Returning to his cousin, he said: 'Johnny, I shall act there some day!'[16]

In 1886, Dan and Johnny were appearing together in *Jack and the Beanstalk* at the Surrey Theatre, in which Dan played the downtrodden Dame Durden, a plain lady of a certain age who was given to doing unexpected little dances. Dan's music-hall career was leading him to develop studies of working-class women in songs like 'Young Men Taken in and Done For' and 'My Old Man'. Augustus Harris saw him performing at the Empire, Leicester Square, and thought Dan would make an ideal Dame for his next pantomime.

Leno made his Drury Lane début as the Naughty Baroness in *Babes in the Wood* (1888/89) and was back the next year as Jack's mother in *Jack and the Beanstalk*. For the 1890/91 pantomime, *Beauty and the Beast*, he played Beauty's father, Mr Lombarde Streete, but the following year he was back in drag as the Queen of Hearts in *Humpty Dumpty*. It had a strong cast of music-hall performers, including Marie Lloyd and Little Tich, but the significance of the show for Dan was his first pairing with Herbert Campbell as the King of Hearts. Campbell was huge – over six foot tall and weighing twenty stone – while Leno was small. They both came from the same music-hall background and seemed to relate to each other intuitively. They made a perfect double act and would go down in comedy legend as one of the greatest double acts of all, on a par with Laurel and Hardy and Morecambe and Wise. Their popularity was such that they soon dominated the Drury Lane pantomimes. Just as Grimaldi had altered the balance of pantomime at the beginning of the nineteenth century, making Clown more important than Harlequin, so Leno altered it at the end. He was not the first man to play Dame in drag but he was the most important. He made the Dame the leading figure in pantomime, which she remains.

As Drury Lane pantomimes turned into what must have seemed like irresistible forces, Harris could afford to be complacent about his critics who accused him of vulgarising and commercialising it. He believed that universal education was changing everything. He argued that modern audiences demanded standards unknown to previous generations of managers, and that the creation of a successful stage spectacle involved skills and research in the areas of costume, scenery, machinery, music and dance that deserved as much respect as the writing of the words. In the old days, 'the same throne did for Cleopatra, Julius Caesar or Henry V', but now everything had to be accurate. Harris admitted that only a minority of his vast audience would appreciate the attention to detail, and asked rhetorically: 'Why not follow the old Boucicaultian managerial axiom, "never try to educate your audience"? Because the minority is fast becoming a majority, thanks to the march of education.'[17] Harris was progressive in his views and welcomed the increasing equality that education was bringing. One of the songs in *Cinderella* (1895), his last pantomime, contained the lines:

> *Progressive legislation and the School Board and the Press,*
> *Now are lev'lling up the masses with remarkable success...*
> *It's a very thin partition now that class from class divides.*

Harris's pantomimes looked to the future, not some Arcadian past of faery lore. His last Cinderella went to the ball in a car powered by electricity.

Druriodramas

The autumn melodramas were on the same trajectory as the pantomimes: each one was bigger and better than the last. *Youth*, in 1881, featured a recreation of the Defence of Hawke's Point which was so convincing that Lord Wolseley, Commander-in-Chief of the Armed Forces, wrote to Harris to say that the military scenes were staged with 'a vividness and reality quite startling'.[18] The show was so successful that, although it had to be taken off for the pantomime, it was put back on afterwards for another 69 performances. *Pluck* (1882) featured a train crash, a house on fire and snow falling in Piccadilly Circus, while for *The Prodigal Daughter* (1892) Harris came up with a real show-stopper: the Grand National run onstage. The horses were racing on a treadmill, suspended in harnesses from the flies. The harnesses were mounted on tracks so that one horse could be moved in relation to another. Harris arranged for an actual winner of the Grand National, called Voluptuary, to win the stage version, and it was such a success that Harris tried the same thing two years later. For *The Derby Winner* (1894) it was a different race but the same sensation. On the first night there was an unfortunate oversight and the hero's horse didn't actually win the race. Nothing daunted, Harris went before the curtain to tell the audience that the section of the race-track they were looking at did not contain the winning post, which was half-a-mile further on, and that Clipstone (the hero's horse) had won by a neck.

In 1888, the tercentenary of the defeat of the Spanish Armada persuaded Harris to depart from his usual run of stories from modern life to depict the great naval victory onstage. Following a tableau vivant of Sir Francis Drake playing bowls on Plymouth Hoe, Spanish galleons were seen at anchor in the twilight, only to be suddenly illuminated by the flames of Drake's fireships. Through the smoke appeared the English vessels which came alongside the galleons and boarded them, to much cheering from the audience. This was far from being the end of the story. The fiancée of the hero had been abducted to Spain by a dastardly villain who handed her over to the Inquisition when she refused to marry him. The hero, having defeated the Armada, hotfoots it to Cadiz where he arrives to find his beloved tied to the stake with the torches about to be applied to the faggots. Needless to say, the Spanish Inquisition proves to be no match for a few true-hearted Englishmen who save the lady and return to London. When Queen Elizabeth hears of his bravery, she invites the young couple to join her triumphal procession to St Paul's Cathedral for a service of thanksgiving. The authentic representation of the front of Old St Paul's, as well as the hundreds of completely authentic Elizabethan costumes of the extras, provided a splendid climax to the patriotic drama.

The end of repertory

Harris had found the formula that would turn Drury Lane into a serious money-making venture for the first time since the days of David Garrick. From the beginning of his management to the end, Harris's theatrical year followed a fixed pattern: autumn melodrama (July/August to December), followed by Christmas pantomime (Boxing Day to March) followed by visiting companies to fill the gap until the next melodrama. These visiting companies supplied the high culture. In 1881, the Saxe-Meiningen company from Germany demonstrated their influential staging of *Julius Caesar*[19] and, in the following year, Herr Hans Richter and the Hamburg Theatre presented a season of German opera that included the first performances in Britain of Wagner's *Die Meistersinger von Nürnberg* and *Tristan und Isolde*.[20] For several years the Carl Rosa Opera Company, dedicated to opera in English, did summer seasons. The *Comédie-Française* did a season in 1893, as did Eleanora Duse in 1895. These visiting companies did not always make money, but they didn't lose a lot either,[21] and the important thing was that they didn't tie up the resources of the theatre, which were dedicated to producing the thousands of costumes and acres of scenery required for the melodramas and pantomimes. If Harris could have run his melodramas throughout the year he would have done so, but such long runs were still rare at the time and Drury Lane had a lot of seats to fill.

Harris's management did, however, see the end of the repertory system and its replacement by the system of long, continuous runs that we know today. Some of the visiting companies, like the Carl Rosa Opera Company, still performed in repertory, changing the bill every night or every few nights, but as far as in-house productions were concerned, repertory had come to an end. In fact, it had more or less finished under Chatterton, who had found it less and less profitable to put on shows for a few nights. We can see this by comparing two of Chatterton's seasons, early and late.

Chatterton's 1867/68 season opened on 23 September with an adaptation of Goethe's *Faust* followed by the 50-year-old melodrama *The Miller and His Men*. *Faust* closed after two weeks. *The Miller and His Men* was kept on as the afterpiece to *King John* for a week, then to

Macbeth for two weeks, then to *The Lady of Lyons* for a week, closing on 1 November. The following night, Chatterton opened his big show of the season, *The Doge of Venice*. It was an expensive flop, closing after less than three weeks. The theatre was then dark until the opening of the pantomime, *Jack the Giant Killer*, on Boxing Day. This ran until 29 February, following a variety of mainpieces including *Richard III* and *The School for Scandal*. Chatterton filled up the rest of the season with 'good old English comedies',[22] closing early on 20 March.

Chatterton's 1877/78 season looked different. It opened on 22 September with a triple bill: *Barbazon* (at 7:00 p.m.) followed by *England* (at 8:00 p.m.) followed by *The Conscription* (at 10:45 p.m.). On 29 September, *Sarah's Young Man* replaced *Barbazon*. On 20 October, a revival of *Amy Robsart* replaced *England*, and the three plays ran until 8 December. The theatre was then dark until the opening of the pantomime, *The White Cat*, which ran until 2 March, when the season once again closed early. The pantomime was now the main entertainment of the evening, starting at 7:45 p.m. after a curtain-raiser called *After the Wedding*, which began at 7:00 p.m. In the course of the season, Chatterton had presented only a handful of productions compared with the dozens of mainpieces and afterpieces that would have comprised a normal season for Colley Cibber or David Garrick.

Chatterton had clearly found it no longer economical to put on plays for a few nights, and closed the theatre rather than do this. Harris copied him and established the system which still prevails at Drury Lane and at all commercial theatres in London of running a show until the public stop coming, then closing it permanently. The only exceptions occurred when there was sufficient pent-up demand to bring the melodrama back after the pantomime.

Passing the baton

Harris's workload at Drury Lane was tremendous as he not only produced the shows but co-wrote many of them and acted in some. As if this weren't enough, Harris took over the management of Covent Garden in 1888 and displayed the same energetic approach to managing the affairs of the Royal Italian Opera House that he had applied across the road. He presented the London début of Nellie Melba, popularised the operas of Wagner and arranged for visits by Mascagni and Puccini. Harris adopted a policy of staging operas in their native language, as a result of which 'Italian' was dropped from the name and the theatre became the Royal Opera House, which it remains.

Harris was also a London County Councillor and Sheriff of the City of London: he received his knighthood for arranging the entertainments for a successful visit to London by the German Emperor. He controlled the Empire, Leicester Square and the Olympia exhibition halls, as well as owning *The Sunday Times* which he bought partly in order to respond to the unceasing attacks on his vulgar and populist influence on Drury Lane. In June 1896 he died from a combination of cancer, diabetes and overwork at the age of forty-four.

In the last years of his life, Harris had secured an immensely valuable benefit for Drury Lane in the form of a new lease from the Duke of Bedford. The lease issued by the sixth Duke to the Drury Lane Company of Proprietors in 1812 was set to expire at Christmas 1894, so the question arose of negotiating a new lease – and to whom it should be issued. The proprietors were, of course, anxious for a renewal, and pointed out that, without a new lease, all the capital invested by them in the building would be lost. As most of this capital investment had been made eighty years before by people who were long dead, this wasn't a very strong argument. Augustus Harris, who wanted the lease for himself, was making a much more generous offer, and the policy of the Bedford estate was to renew leases to the tenant in occupation. However, the newly-formed London County Council (LCC) was attempting to take the Covent Garden market into public ownership and had introduced a bill in parliament to give themselves powers of compulsory purchase. They therefore requested the Duke not to issue any lease for Drury Lane for longer than seven years as they intended to demolish it to extend the market.

Rent charged for the lease by the
Drury Lane Company of Proprietors

YEAR	LESSEE	RENT PER ANNUM
1819	Robert Elliston	£10,200
1826	Stephen Price	£10,600
1830	Captain Polehill/Alexander Lee	£9,000
1833	Captain Polehill	£8,000
1835	Alfred Bunn	£6,500
1836	Alfred Bunn	£6,000
1839	William Hammond	£5,000
1852	Edward Smith	£3,500
1853	Edward Smith	£4,000
1862	Edmund Falconer	£4,500
1866	Frederick Chatterton	£6,000
1878	Frederick Chatterton	£6,000
1879	Augustus Harris	£6,000
1894	The lease issued by the Duke of Bedford to the Drury Lane Company of Proprietors in 1812 expires. A new lease is issued to Augustus Harris, the tenant in occupation, and the Company of Proprietors is dissolved.	

In August 1893, therefore, Herbrand Russell, the eleventh Duke of Bedford, offered Harris a seven-year lease at £6,300 per annum. (The proprietors had been offering £2,000.) The lease, executed in May 1894, contained a number of restrictive covenants: Drury Lane was not to be used for circuses, music hall or variety acts, promenade concerts or dancing – nothing at all, in fact, apart from plays and operas. There was to be no sub-letting, except for short seasons of opera or drama, without the Duke's express permission. Successive Dukes of Bedford had clearly been deeply unimpressed by some of the shows put on by lessees throughout the nineteenth century. The Committee of Proprietors now had no reason to exist and dissolved itself in November 1897, issuing a final dividend of £4 9s. to the shareholders. They still had one asset, however: the Killigrew patent. In spite of the fact that both patents had been devalued by the 1843 Theatre Regulation Act, which deprived

Drury Lane and Covent Garden of their monopoly powers to present plays, the patents conferred one last privilege: they absolved the holders from the necessity, under which every other place of entertainment in London laboured, to obtain an annual licence from the Lord Chamberlain. Harris therefore purchased the Killigrew patent from the proprietors. Augustus Harris became the first person since Sheridan to be at once patentee, head-leaseholder and manager of Drury Lane, but within two years he was dead. His mantle descended to Arthur Collins, his stage manager, but the structure of the organisation changed.

Collins had joined the Drury Lane company as a scene painter in 1881 and was working in the paint frame under Henry Emden when the great William Beverley was still sometimes to be found there. He wanted to act, and persuaded Harris to give him a part in the provincial tour of the 1886 melodrama about the turf, *A Run of Luck*. According to legend, Harris turned up at the theatre where the tour was playing late at night, after the show had closed, and found Collins repainting the set on his own initiative. Harris was so impressed by this dedication above and beyond the call of duty that he made Collins stage manager at Drury Lane.

Collins admired his boss and saw himself as the natural heir. He persuaded Harris's executors to allow him to take over the interest in the remaining term of the seven-year lease and applied to the Duke of Bedford for a new lease. The Duke's agent told him that the Duke was agreeable in principle, but that Collins needed to show some evidence of substantial financial backing. In May 1896, Collins applied to the Board of Trade for registration of a company called Theatre Royal, Drury Lane Limited, and a few days later received agreement from the Duke of Bedford for a forty-year lease at a rent rising to £6,550 per annum. (The attempt by the LCC to demolish the theatre and extend the market had now failed.) As a condition of this lease, Collins had to create a passageway along the south side of the theatre with a high wall to separate it from the blocks of flats that had been built on the north side of Russell Street. As this made the site slightly smaller, Collins received as compensation the lease to more land on the Drury Lane frontage for a rebuilt paint-shop and property room.

In May 1897, Collins transferred the building and contents, his forty-year lease and the Killigrew patent to the new company, which received its certificate of incorporation on 28 May 1897. Collins became one of six directors of the company, of which the share capital of 125,000 £1 shares was fully subscribed by the end of August. From now on, no one would be able to inscribe himself, like Chatterton, as 'sole lessee and manager' of Drury Lane, as it belonged to a company controlled by a board of directors.

The directors completed the building work agreed by Collins with the Duke of Bedford and also took a lease on the three houses on Drury Lane which stood between the paint-shop and the corner of the alleyway, which kept its old name of Vinegar Yard. For the first time since 1663, the theatre management now controlled the entire island site from Drury Lane to what was now Catherine Street. In 1903, after more structural alterations, the theatre's board was issued with a new lease extending to 1977 at a rent of £6,450 per annum, but long before this expired, the Russell family would have severed their connection with Drury Lane by selling the whole Covent Garden estate.

It is pleasing to relate that, in the midst of all these changes, permission was given to the committee of the Sir Augustus Harris Memorial Fund to erect a drinking fountain against the front wall of the theatre. The Duke of Bedford was persuaded to donate £50 to the fund by his steward, who pointed out that: 'By his enterprise and pluck [Harris] resuscitated Drury Lane Theatre when it had fallen on evil times and there is no doubt whatever that he has added materially to the market value of the theatre'.[23] The drinking fountain is still there, but more importantly, so is the theatre. Its survival, which had been by no means a foregone conclusion, was owing, in large measure, to the man who was proud to be known as Druriolanus. Augustus Harris had defied the jinx of Drury Lane and made his last exit looking so sleek and prosperous that he was often compared to the Prince of Wales. As the playwright George Sims put it, he was 'the Napoleon of Theatreland without having the worry of Waterloo or the ennui of Elba'.[24] It was a remarkable turnaround.

27

Only a Great Nation Could Have Done Such a Thing

Arthur Collins opened his management on 16 September 1897 with that year's autumn melodrama, *The White Heather*. He could scarcely have got off to a better start, as it proved a spectacular success with one of the most famous scenes in any Druriodrama. The hero realises that the proof of the villain's wrongdoing is to be found in a shipwreck on the seabed. He puts on a diving suit and jumps over the side of his ship, unaware that the villain has seen him and intends to prevent the evidence from being brought to light. Both men descend to the seabed, then fight to the death, with the hero cutting the air supply to the baddie, who drowns. To achieve the effect, the first ship was hoisted up into the flies as the shipwreck rose up from beneath the stage while the men were 'diving'. A green gauze descended, and real fish could be seen swimming in glass tanks placed between bits of scenery. It was so impressive that people would pay to come in and stand at the back of the circle just to see the fight again.

It was the creation of the scenic artist Bruce Smith, who was known as 'Sensation' Smith[1] because he created the sensations for most of the Drury Lane melodramas during the Collins management. Smith was not a complete newcomer to Drury Lane: he had painted some scenes for the pantomimes under Harris, but Harris appears not to have been a great admirer, and it wasn't until Collins took over that Smith was given his own corner in the Drury Lane paintshop. The spectacular effects he created there are legendary. In *The Great Ruby* (1898) the villain falls to his death from a balloon over Hampstead Heath; in *Hearts Are Trumps* an avalanche in the Alps does the job; in *The Great Millionaire* (1901) the baddie's car plunges over a cliff. Plays involving horse races were still popular, and the most famous one of all was *The Whip* (1909) in which the eponymous equine hero wins the Two Thousand Guineas at Newmarket. The villain plans to derail his victory (literally) by uncoupling the horse-box from the train taking the horse to Newmarket so that it will be smashed to pieces by the express train following it down the track. The dastardly plot is concocted in the Chamber of Horrors of Madame Tussaud's Waxworks, where it is overheard by the horse's trainer, posing as the waxwork of the murderer Charles Pearce. In one continuous sequence, the audience saw the horse loaded into the horse-box; the train leave the station; the villain uncouple the horse-box which remains on the track as the train moves ahead; and the trainer climb down an embankment and release the horse, just as the express train emerges from a tunnel and smashes the horse-box to bits, coming off the rails in the process. It was so exciting that members of the audience were screaming advice to the trainer as he struggled to free the horse, with the noise of the approaching train coming through the tunnel. When the villainess Mrs D'Aquila was told that people had died in the crash, she replied: 'They were only third-class passengers – something always happens to people like that,' which got a terrific response from the gallery. Needless to say, The Whip goes on to win the Two Thousand Guineas, although not on the first night. In a repeat of the mix-up on the first night of *The Derby Winner* (1894), the horse was put into the wrong harness and came in a very poor fifth. Arthur Collins had to appear before the curtain to assure the audience that The Whip would be sure to win the race at all subsequent performances. The play was so popular that it was put on again after that year's pantomime, then transferred to the Adelphi and went out on tour.

Two years later, Bruce Smith decided to top even this stunning achievement with another horse-racing drama, *The Hope*, in which the

Derby would be run by horses facing towards the audience. The set represented a bend on the racetrack, with a diorama on both sides winding through the scenes on either side of the track during the race. Arthur Collins knew he had a hit on his hands when the cleaning ladies fled screaming from the stalls at the dress rehearsal, thinking they were going to be trampled to death. Unfortunately, the first-night jinx struck again. The mechanics all worked and the race was run, with the right horse winning this time, but there was no audience reaction. The stage manager had forgotten to raise the curtain, so the audience heard the race but didn't see it. It had to be run again, but Bruce Smith insisted on slowing the pace of the treadmills, as the horses were now exhausted and 'the nags had no understudies'.[2]

The most famous equestrian spectacle of all was probably the chariot race in *Ben Hur*, staged in 1902 and revived in 1912. This involved five teams of four horses each pulling chariots against a panoramic moving backcloth representing the arena, with both painted and live spectators cheering them on. The most applauded scene, however, was not the chariot race but the sinking of a Roman galley on the high seas and the survival of the hero on a raft, tossed about on the waves by an army of carefully drilled 'strong men' using a variety of gymnastic movements to make the canvas sea heave.

Here we are again

The pantomimes were by no means lagging behind the melodramas in magnificence. Drury Lane pantomimes had become famous for being the biggest and most expensive in the world, until they symbolised the might of the British Empire itself. A critic in *The Star* wrote in 1900:

> The Drury Lane pantomime, that national institution, is a symbol of our Empire. It is the biggest thing of its kind in the world, it is prodigal of money, of invention, of splendour, of men and women; but it is without the sense of beauty or the restraining

influence of taste. It is impossible to sit in the theatre for five hours without being filled with weary admiration. Only a great nation could have done such a thing; only an undisciplined one would have done it.[3]

This is the sort of grudging, half-admiring tone that intellectuals use nowadays to describe Las Vegas. You might not like it, but criticism is pointless because it is so big it makes its own rules. There is no doubt that the values of the Empire would never lack a champion at Drury Lane. The atmosphere was so patriotic that both the National Anthem and 'Rule Britannia' were played at every performance of the pantomime, and a 'plant' would be hired to hiss during the National Anthem just to whip the audience up into a patriotic frenzy.[4]

The 1899 pantomime *Jack and the Beanstalk* provides a good example of Drury Lane imperialism. The Boer War had broken out two months before and the British were doing badly, so it was decided to give the giant the features of Kruger, the Boer leader, and to call him Blunderboer (instead of the more usual Blunderbore). After the giant had fallen down the beanstalk, instead of showing only his legs or hand, Bruce Smith constructed a complete fifty-foot corpse, sprawled across the stage. While Jack sat on his knee singing a patriotic song called 'Pretoria', hundreds of children dressed in differently coloured military uniforms and representing various army regiments began to march out of his pocket. The 'cavalry' regiments rode on Shetland ponies. This was in reference to Kruger's claim that he could put the British army into his pocket. When the miniature soldiers raised their helmets on their rifles and sang 'Rule Britannia', the audience loved it. The finale was called 'The End of the Century' and 'represented, in allegorical fashion, all the wonders, discoveries and inventions of this, the best of all centuries'.[5] No *fin de siècle* exhaustion here, then. *Jack and the Beanstalk* ran until April, which was exceptional even for a Drury Lane pantomime.

Jack and the Beanstalk featured Dan Leno as Mrs Kelly, Jack's mother, and the very large Herbert Campbell as 'Little Bobbie'. They were at the height of their powers and popularity, and Leno was regarded as the greatest clown since Grimaldi. His salary reflected his drawing power, having risen from £28 to £240 a week. In November 1898 it was announced that Leno had been signed to appear in the Drury Lane pantomimes until 1935, by which time he would have been seventy-five. In fact, he wouldn't see forty-five.

Many of Leno's admirers felt that his best-ever Dame was Mother Goose in the 1902 pantomime of the same name. The part was really three parts: the poor and homely Mother Goose is magically transformed into a rich but vulgar social-climber, and then into a beautiful but penniless girl desperate to find a husband. After a visit to 'The Magic Pool', she returns to her old self, and decides that this is what suits her best. As Leno's biographer, Barry Anthony, puts it: 'with her tattered shawl, crumpled apron and battered boots, Mother Goose was the final summation of Dan's working-class female characters'.[6]

Mother Goose was the expected great success, but by the end of the run Leno was exhibiting disturbing behaviour which, whatever its cause, was certainly exacerbated by his heavy drinking. Amongst other eccentricities, he conceived the idea of founding his own company in which he would play the leading roles of Shakespeare, starting with Richard III. He turned up at Her Majesty's Theatre, built and run by Sir Herbert Beerbohm Tree, and asked for Tree's help. Tree kept him talking while the call-boy was sent to fetch Leno's manager, who turned up with two heavies to take him away. Tree's reaction was characteristically paradoxical. He told Constance Collier, his leading lady: 'If this is madness, what is the point of being sane? If he ever plays Richard III it will be the greatest performance of the part we have ever seen.'[7]

Leno was confined in a private asylum for two months, then went to Dorset to recuperate. It was so uncertain whether or not he would be able to do the pantomime that another comic, Harry Randall, was signed to appear. In the event, Leno was pronounced well enough in December, and the script of *Humpty Dumpty* had to be hurriedly rewritten to accommodate him. Leno's health had been a national news story, with the King himself sending to the asylum for reports, and when Leno made his first entrance on Boxing Day the house rose to give him a five-minute ovation. He managed to cope with the strains of the run, doing two four-hour shows a day for six weeks then another six weeks of evenings plus occasional matinees, but his behaviour was erratic, involving furious backstage outbursts against his good friend Herbert Campbell. At the end of each performance the two of them would come down to the footlights to sing:

> *In the panto of Old Drury Lane*
> *We have both come together again,*
> *And we hope to appear*
> *For many a year*
> *In the panto of Old Drury Lane.*

This silly little ditty has a dreadful poignancy now, because *Humpty Dumpty*, which had begun their partnership in 1891, would also end it. Before the start of the next pantomime season they would both be dead. In July 1904, Herbert Campbell bumped his leg and broke the skin. Blood poisoning set in, leading to a fatal seizure. Three months later, Leno died of what was described on his death certificate as 'general paralysis of the insane', a medical euphemism for syphilis.[8]

Leno was sorely missed, but nothing could stop the juggernaut of the Drury Lane pantomime. Harry Randall was taken on as comic for *The White Cat* in 1904, but it was a thankless role and the pantomime was judged to be below par, mainly because audiences wanted Leno. Nevertheless, the pantomimes kept coming, with an apparently endless supply of transformations, harlequinades, fairy bowers, giants, dames and principal boys. Even the outbreak of the World War I had very little impact on the Drury Lane routine, apart from the fact that the 1914 *Sleeping Beauty Beautified* was put together with stock scenery because of shortages.

Pageants

The tercentenary of the death of Shakespeare occurred in 1916 and it was decided that, in spite of the War, or perhaps because of it, the opportunity to celebrate the Bard should not be allowed to pass. Drury Lane was chosen for a royal gala performance of *Julius Caesar*, with an all-star cast, followed by a Shakespeare Pageant. A huge black and gold staircase was built, descending from the flies into the orchestra pit, down which came groups of actors representing, in dumb-show to music, scenes from nine Shakespeare plays. The president of the actors' committee organising the whole thing was Sir Herbert Beerbohm Tree, but he was in America so the actual organisation was done by the actor-manager Sir George Alexander, famous for his association with the St James Theatre. Alexander's secretary was Hesketh Pearson, an actor who later became a writer, and, according to Pearson, Alexander found it the toughest assignment of his life.[9] Everyone who was anyone in the profession wanted to be in the performance, and no one wanted to carry the spears. The all-star *Julius Caesar* kept a lot of them happy, but the pageant was a masterstroke. Alexander appointed a different luminary to direct each of the sequences, so Lady Tree was in charge of *The Merry Wives of Windsor*, Dion Boucicault of *As You Like It*, and matinée idol Owen Nares of *Romeo and Juliet*. Alexander took *Much Ado About Nothing* and appeared as Benedick.

The part of Julius Caesar was taken by Frank Benson, who also appeared as Coriolanus in the pageant. Benson was a much-loved and somewhat eccentric character who, without any training at all, had spent his life barnstorming the country with productions of Shakespeare's plays. Operating without subsidy, he put all of his own money into the venture and touched everyone he knew for loans that were never repaid. The shows were distinctly ropey and Benson was a terrible actor, whose ranting style tore the verse to shreds. Nevertheless, a generation of Shakespearean actors graduated from his company, and he was the director of the annual Shakespeare Festival in Stratford-upon-Avon from 1891 to 1919. He put on every one of Shakespeare's plays except for *Titus Andronicus* and *Troilus and Cressida*. He seldom appeared in London, partly because he genuinely believed that it was important to take Shakespeare to all of the people and partly because his productions were nowhere near a West End standard, but he was greatly admired in the profession for his dedication.

On the morning of the gala performance, Benson was sitting in the lounge of a hotel in Victoria reading mail that had been pursuing him around the country for weeks. One of the letters came from the Palace and asked if he would accept a knighthood. As he was to perform before King George V a few hours later, he thought this was too good a chance to miss and sent a messenger to the Palace to say yes. The messenger was told that His Majesty was at lunch and could not be disturbed, so when Benson turned up at Drury Lane he asked Arthur Collins if he could sort something out. As soon as the King and Queen were seated in the royal box, Collins explained the situation to Sir Charles Cust, the aide-de-camp, and asked if Benson could be knighted in the theatre. Sir Charles explained that the King was not in uniform and had no sword, but Collins sent a messenger to B.J. Simmons, the theatrical costumiers in Covent Garden, for a real sword. Sir Charles spoke to the King who, in spite of being a stickler for protocol, agreed to this highly irregular procedure, so Benson was summoned to the royal retiring room after dying onstage as Julius Caesar. Kneeling before George V in his bloodstained toga, he became the first person to be knighted in a theatre. George Alexander went in front of the curtain to announce the news to the audience, and when Benson descended the staircase as Coriolanus shortly afterwards he received a standing ovation.[10]

There was another pageant two years later to celebrate the end of World War I. The 1918 pantomime, *Babes in the Wood*, included 'The Pageant of Peace', in which an all-white tableau of Peace surrounded by angels and classical columns framed the groups representing the allies: 'There are wild shouts for the Stars and Stripes, there is a deep roar for the Tricolor of France, but when the Union Jack and the other colours of the British Empire are at last seen the whole house bursts into a prolonged and deafening cheer of triumph.'[11]

However, the Pageant of Peace was not the first pageant to be staged at Drury Lane in 1918. On 19 September the theatre had presented a 'Pageant of Drury Lane' to commemorate the 21 years of management of the theatre by Arthur Collins. It began with Apollo and the muses in the clouds and progressed to a scene in Whitehall, in which Thomas

Killigrew, Charles II and Samuel Pepys decided that it would be a good idea to build a theatre in Drury Lane. This was followed by excerpts from *The Humorous Lieutenant* by Beaumont and Fletcher, which opened the first theatre, and *Macbeth*, which opened the third. Dr Johnson, Boswell, Garrick, Sir Joshua Reynolds and Peg Woffington were discovered chatting in the Green Room on the first night of *Irene*, then Robert Baddeley appeared with the idea for his Baddeley Cake on Twelfth Night. The pageant ended with extracts from *The Bohemian Girl* and *The Best of Luck*, the 1916 autumn melodrama. Arthur Collins appeared on the stage at the end for a round of applause.

Collins had now been managing Drury Lane for longer than any of his predecessors apart from Garrick (29 years) and Sheridan (33 years). He had taken over the policy of his predecessor, Sir Augustus Harris, and carried it out, without the slightest change in artistic direction, throughout his management. The result was that Drury Lane had the air of Sleeping Beauty's castle over which Aurora had waved her wand to stop the passage of time. Any show from the 1910s could have been put on in the 1880s, and vice versa, without anyone noticing the difference, apart from the appearance of things like motor cars and airships. This is a most unusual situation in showbusiness, in which successful entrepreneurs normally have to be slightly ahead of public taste, anticipating the next big thing. However, the policy had been successful. No one had gone bankrupt and, although there had been a few flops, the losses were easily recovered as the annual cycle of melodrama and pantomime followed each other with the inevitability of the liturgical seasons of the year.

By the end of the Great War, however, there was a feeling that this Victorian idyll had had its day, and that it was time to open a few windows onto the modern world. The spirit of modernity appeared, like the genie through one of the many traps in the stage, in the form of Alfred Butt.

The breeze of change

Butt had begun his career in the accounts department of Harrods, but at the age of nineteen he was hired by Charles Morton, who had got himself into financial problems by building the Palace Theatre in Cambridge Circus as a home for popular opera. The young Butt made such a success of sorting out the finances that he became manager in 1904, at the age of twenty-six. Opera was ditched in favour of music hall and Butt made the Palace into a successful and upmarket home of variety. He took over a circuit of music halls and formed the Variety Theatres Controlling Company which was able seriously to challenge the dominance of Oswald Stoll's Moss Empires. He took over the management of the Globe, Queen's, Gaiety, Adelphi and other London theatres and built the Victoria Palace.

By the end of the First World War, Butt had acquired a backer in the person of Solly Joel, the South African diamond millionaire, and was able to turn his attention to the most famous theatre of them all. In November 1918, Butt offered to buy the original £1 shares in Drury Lane, which were at that time valued at 12s., for 17s. 6d. He upped the offer to £1, then to £1 10s. On 25 February 1919, the board announced that Alfred Butt had been elected to the board and appointed as chairman and joint managing director with Arthur Collins. Their joint managing-directorship would extend to 30 June 1924, and during that time they would receive a joint salary of £4,000 per annum, divided into £3,000 for Collins and £1,000 for Butt. There was also a profit-sharing arrangement.[12] A group of shareholders representing the interests of Oswald Stoll, a rival bidder, called an EGM on 1 April to remove the entire board apart from Arthur Collins, but this motion was defeated and Collins refused to support any move against the board's decision.[13]

Another great change had occurred in 1918 affecting the site. Herbrand Russell, the eleventh Duke of Bedford, had decided, like many other aristocrats, that it was necessary to concentrate resources on the maintenance of the ancestral estate – in his case Woburn Abbey – in order to combat the threat of death duties. The Covent Garden estate was sold to Sir Joseph Beecham, whose fortune came from the famous pills and who wanted to acquire an opera house for his son, Thomas. Sir Joseph died in 1916, before the transaction was completed, and in 1918 the whole estate was conveyed to The Covent Garden Estate Company, controlled by the Beecham family.[14] The estate included Drury Lane as well as the opera house, which meant that, for the first time since Thomas Killigrew had opened with *The Humorous Lieutenant* in May 1663, the owners of the theatre were not paying rent to a member of the Russell family. Thomas Beecham had become a director of Drury Lane in the same boardroom shake-up that brought in Alfred Butt, and would direct seasons of opera there, but he was more interested in the opera house. Consequently, Drury Lane was put up for auction in January 1920 but had failed to reach its reserve of £160,000 when bidding stopped at £134,500.[15] It was withdrawn and, two months later, Drury Lane was sold privately to the Ellerman Property Trust Limited.

There was no dramatic change of direction under the new arrangements, and the 1919 autumn melodrama, *The Great Day*, included the expected sensation scene designed by Bruce Smith. This time it was an underground night refuge in Paris that gets flooded by the Seine.✢ *Cinderella* was back for the pantomime season, then in June 1920 there was a rather different melodrama. Alfred Butt was keen to give Robert Hitchens's best-selling novel *The Garden of Allah* the Drury Lane treatment. The plot concerns a Trappist monk who struggles with his vows and escapes from his monastery in Algeria into the desert. He is the only monk to know the recipe for the liqueur which the monks support themselves by selling. He meets and marries a European heiress, who is unaware of his monastic background, but when they are caught in a sandstorm and rescued by the French Foreign Legion, one of the Legionnaires recognises the liqueur that the

---

✢ George Claremont, a 73-year-old actor, died in a fall from the stage level onto the cellar floor whilst taking his place for a scene. The coroner reached a verdict of accidental death, observing that 'there were always exciting incidents in Drury Lane dramas, and actors knew they were exposed to considerable risks and would have to protect themselves'. ('Drury Lane Actor's Death', *The Times*, 24 December 1919.)

grateful husband serves him. Everything comes out, and the monk/ husband abandons his pregnant wife to return to the monastery.

This rather daring tale was closer to the spirit of the times than some of the other Druriodramas, without being too shocking. However, the big attraction was the sandstorm, for which a caravan of real camels was imported from Algeria.✤ On the first night, it was so realistic that patrons in the front stalls were left with their black evening suits and tiaras covered with a fine white dust. This attracted considerable publicity and led to a debate about what the 'sand' was made of. Suggestions included cork dust, pea flour and tobacco ash. The truth was not known until Dennis Castle wrote the biography of his grandfather, Bruce 'Sensation' Smith, in which he revealed that the 'sand' was in fact oatmeal. Smith had carefully set up the effect so that nothing would get into the auditorium, but the first night was a hot night in June and somebody had left the scene dock doors open to cool the stage. This created the necessary draft for audience participation. Nobody complained, but a gauze was used at subsequent performances.[16]

The Garden of Allah was so successful that Collins and Butt didn't want to take it off for the pantomime, but on the other hand they didn't feel they could allow Christmas to come and go without a Drury Lane pantomime. They compromised by mounting *Cinderella* for the second year running as the Drury Lane pantomime, but with performances taking place at Covent Garden. Inevitably, so many parents turned up in Catherine Street wondering what the displays of camels and North Africa had to do with the glass slipper that guides had to be employed to take them across to Bow Street.

The Garden of Allah finally closed on 2 April 1921 after a continuous run of nearly ten months, the longest in the history of the theatre. The theatre then closed down for a complete reconstruction of the auditorium and stage that would take a year.

✤ On 20 August the theatre management was summoned to appear at Bow Street Police Court on a charge of animal cruelty. An RSPCA inspector had found the camels to be mangy and emaciated to the point that their humps had disappeared. Their keeper blamed this on the distress caused by their long sea-voyage from Algeria. (*The Times*, 20 August 1920.)

A new auditorium

The architects for this major building work were J. Emblin Walker, F. Edward Jones and Robert Cromie. Benjamin Dean Wyatt's auditorium of 1812 had been extensively remodelled by Samuel Beazley in 1822, and tinkered with a few more times since then, but the new work was not remodelling but complete reconstruction that entailed tearing out everything to the outer walls of the auditorium shell. The auditorium that emerged, which is the one we know now, represents what we think of as a 'normal' theatre interior, but was different in significant ways from Wyatt's original, largely owing to changes in building techniques.

When Wyatt built his theatre, iron had been in use for over half a century and formed the core of the columns that held up the tiers of seats. However, supporting the weight of a large number of people over a void was still a tricky business, so each tier was shallow – only four rows of seats deep. The pit ended where the tiers began to rise, each one lined up above the other: there was no overhang. As the nineteenth century progressed, boxes in theatres became less popular and were replaced with rows of seating. The boxes which lined the pit in Wyatt's Drury Lane eventually disappeared, with the pit seating extending underneath the first tier, thus creating an overhang. Towards the end of the nineteenth century, steel began to be used in construction as it has a much greater load-bearing capacity than iron. In 1901 the Drury Lane auditorium was rebuilt using steel girders and concrete floors which enabled the fronts of each tier to be brought forward, allowing for two more rows of seats and creating a deeper overhang. The 1921 auditorium made much more extensive use of steel, cantilevering the beams supporting each tier into the outside walls of the building so that each of the three tiers – grand circle, upper circle and balcony – now had eleven rows of seats and no supporting columns. All views were now unobstructed, as each tier 'floats' above the one below. The four levels of the present auditorium replace what had been six, in the same volume of space, which says a lot about the amount of space allowed for each spectator under the old system. Wyatt's top gallery, which had been so far from the stage that it actually started behind the ceiling over the auditorium, had been done away with at the request of the London County Council by the end of Augustus Harris's management, but that still left five levels of quite cramped seating. Although people complain about legroom in all of the old West End theatres, there is more than there used to be in most parts of the house, and of course we all expect to have a seat now, rather than be squashed onto a bench. These changes reduced the capacity from approximately 3,000 to 2,600. Alterations to the auditorium since 1922 have reduced this still further to around 2,200, depending on technical requirements in the auditorium.

The work cost £150,000, plus the loss of revenue for a whole year, and the new auditorium opened on 20 April 1922 with *Decameron Nights*, a £40,000 musical spectacle set in Venice and Damascus and very loosely based on Boccaccio's *Decameron*. A moment of high drama involved the heroine being sentenced to be stripped and whipped for adultery (which she didn't commit, of course) in the public square. When her executioner started to tear at her clothing, her sleeve came away to reveal her bare arm, but then her modesty was preserved by a total eclipse of the sun. The joke backstage was that if the first night jinx had struck again, the blackout might have been late and provided the audience with a greater sensation than planned.

Decameron Nights was succeeded in March 1923 by *Angelo – the Life of a Great Composer*, loosely based on the life of Hoffman. This closed after 29 performances, to be succeeded by *Ned Kean of Old Drury*. This also flopped and closed after 61 performances. Arthur Collins, who was scheduled to retire in 1924, was worried that he might go out on a low note, so all the stops were pulled out for that year's autumn melodrama, *Good Luck*, which featured a shipwreck, Parkhurst Prison in flames and the Ascot Gold Cup. This was the last in the line of Druriodramas, and considering how antiquated the formula had become, it was surprisingly successful. It ran until 10 May 1924, so Arthur Collins was able to retire in triumph.

He had worked at Drury Lane for 43 years, being manager or joint manager for 27 of them. That was a long stint at the Lane, which makes it surprising that we know so little about him. There is no biography and no entry in *The Oxford Dictionary of National Biography*. He was a good businessman and he was responsible for improving the backstage facilities. Apart from that, there is little to say. He never really emerged from the shadow of Druriolanus, whose policies he had been happy to carry forward. He seems to have been pompous and humourless, and, according to Bruce Smith, ungenerous in acknowledging the work of colleagues. He wasn't involved in any of those spectacular feuds that enliven so much theatre history, but nor was he the subject of affectionate or amusing anecdotes in other people's memoirs. At the dinner to celebrate his 21 years in management, he had told a story about how he needed to put up £1,000 to secure the lease after Harris's death and managed to borrow it from a man he met in a restaurant.[17] The tale was so similar to Augustus Harris's legendary account of how he got the lease in 1879 that it seems unlikely that Collins's fellow diners could have been taken in by it. Arthur Collins seems, paradoxically, to have been not only one of the most successful but also one of the dullest people in the history of Drury Lane.

28

Last Chance as
the National Theatre

Alfred Butt knew that Drury Lane had to change to reflect the massive changes that had taken place in society since Augustus Harris had established his routine of autumn melodrama and Boxing Day pantomime. The Drury Lane audience had traditionally been drawn from all sections of society, with the gentry in the boxes, the middle classes in the pit and the working classes in the gallery. It made for some rowdy houses, but it also made Drury Lane an inclusive theatre, where members of different classes could come together to watch the same play. As landlord, the Duke of Bedford had his private box, with its own entrance on Russell Street and an attendant to look after his family and guests, while the porters from Covent Garden market, of which he was also the landlord, would have been in the first or second gallery.[1] This tradition of mixing the classes persisted longer at Drury Lane than at other London theatres, partly because it had so many seats to sell that it could only be filled by coming up with a formula that had wide appeal. The melodramas, in particular, reflected that.

By the 1920s, the cinema had largely taken away the working class audience from the theatre. This was especially true for melodrama, as film producers could make a much better job of the avalanches, car crashes, sinking ships and trains hurtling down the track than any stage show. The aristocracy were no longer an important part of the theatre audience, which left the middle classes and visitors to London, either from the provinces or from abroad as international tourism became more important.

Butt knew that Drury Lane needed to change its old-fashioned image and he decided to replace Arthur Collins, after his retirement, with an up-and-coming young man of the theatre, Basil Dean. Dean, who was thirty-six at the time, had made a name for himself as an actor, playwright and director, first of all with Annie Horniman's company in Manchester, then as the founder director of the Liverpool Repertory Theatre, now the Liverpool Playhouse. He had set up a production company called ReandeaN (*sic*) and taken the lease on the St Martin's Theatre where he staged plays by Galsworthy, Somerset Maugham, J.M. Barrie and Clemence Dane. In 1924, when Butt approached him about Drury Lane, he had three productions running successfully in the West End. He was already well known to Butt, as the two of them were in partnership to run the Queen's Theatre in Shaftesbury Avenue.

Dean has left an account of his Drury Lane episode, which turned into a complete debâcle, in his autobiography, *Seven Ages*. As always with autobiographical accounts, it is necessary to do a bit of reading between the lines to fill in the bits the author doesn't want to share, but it is a good account of what would turn out to be the last, doomed attempt to run Drury Lane as the National Theatre.

Dean was initially sceptical about taking on a theatre that was regarded by younger people in the profession as a dinosaur that had somehow survived the Ice Age. Everything exciting in theatre was happening at smaller, newer venues. However, Dean was aware of the Lane's great historical legacy and was tempted by the chance of making it, once again, the home of great drama 'by presenting some of our leading actors in Shakespeare and the English classics'.[2] He outlined his terms to Butt: complete artistic control and the hiring and firing of all technical staff. Butt's response was that this would depend on the profitability of his first productions. Dean was engaged as joint managing director on 30 January 1924, subject to approval by the board. At the time, Collins's last melodrama *Good Luck* was running, and Butt led him to believe that it would run until the autumn, giving Dean time to prepare a programme. Dean heard nothing for several weeks, then the business for *Good Luck* began to tail off. An emergency board meeting was called to confirm his appointment, which was announced to the press before any artistic policy had been agreed.

Good Luck closed in May, and another production was needed in a hurry. Dean was already making arrangements to stage Arnold Bennett's new play *London Life* at the Queen's, so this was switched to Drury Lane. It was given a big production, with a scene on the terrace of the House of Commons and a grand reception in Grosvenor Square, but the play flopped. 'No horse-races, no burning houses, or falling roofs, no sea voyages,' lamented *The Daily Telegraph*.[3] After two weeks, the actors were persuaded to take half-pay and after five weeks it closed.

Drury Lane was now dark, with nothing ready for production. Dean was dreaming of a great classical repertoire, with a historically accurate production of *The School for Scandal, A Midsummer Night's Dream* with the Mendelssohn score, and a new spectacular production about the French Revolution written by Hilaire Belloc and Louis Parker, the leading pageant master of the day. 'All this time,' he claimed, 'I remained blissfully unaware of the chairman's adamantine opposition to the production of any but obvious box-office attractions.'[4] With Drury Lane dark for several weeks, Butt put in a screen to show Douglas Fairbanks in *The Thief of Bagdad*, which seemed like an admission of defeat. At this critical moment, Dean went to America to direct *Peter Pan* on Broadway, leaving Drury Lane with no show.

By this stage, Butt must have been regretting his choice and seems to have begun scheming to get rid of Dean. Whist in America, Dean was planning his Christmas production of *A Midsummer Night's Dream* (instead of the eternal Drury Lane pantomime) and issued a contract to Michael Fokine to stage the ballet sequences. Butt sent an angry telegram saying that Dean had no right to issue such a contract and that the board was extremely unlikely to agree to the Christmas production of the *Dream*. Meanwhile, Butt wanted Dean to report on a new show that had just opened in New York called *Rose Marie*.

Dean's view was that *Rose Marie* was good but not right for Drury Lane. Butt ignored his advice and began negotiating to get *Rose Marie* into Drury Lane for Christmas.

A dream of what might have been

By the time Dean returned to London in the autumn, business for *The Thief of Bagdad* was tailing off and it was clear that *Rose Marie* wouldn't be ready by Christmas. Butt therefore agreed that the Christmas production of *A Midsummer Night's Dream* could go ahead, but on unusual terms: Dean had to write his letter of resignation which Butt would keep in his safe. If the production were a success, he would tear the letter up. If not, the resignation would be accepted. However, there was no agreed measure of success, which was unfortunate as, by the time the *Dream* opened, *Rose Marie* was already booked into the Lane for March.

When *A Midsummer Night's Dream* opened on Boxing Day 1924, it was a historic occasion. It was the first in-house Shakespearean production for 46 years, the last one being F.B. Chatterton's disastrous *Winter's Tale* that racked up losses at the start of his doomed final season in 1878. Dean had a reputation for being modern and progressive, but he knew how to do spectacle as well and was a pioneer of stage lighting techniques. The production looked magnificent and had a strong cast: Edith Evans and Athene Seyler as Helena and Hermia, and Gwen Frangçon-Davies as Titania. There was the Mendelssohn music, the Fokine ballets and a splendid final effect as the walls and columns of the palace became transparent to reveal a tableau of the fairies, hoisted aloft on the stage's largest hydraulic lift.

The reviews were good and the box-office takings excellent, but Dean wasn't surprised to read on newspaper hoardings in February that he had resigned from Drury Lane. It was no secret that Dean and Butt had fallen out and Dean was pressed on his plan to turn Drury Lane into the National Theatre. Would that require a government subsidy? He prevaricated, saying: 'Not necessarily. That might lead to interference in the theatre's internal affairs.' As he admitted later, this was disingenuous, because it had become obvious to everyone interested in the idea of a national theatre, the campaign for which was gaining ground, that it would be impossible without some form of subsidy. The time, however, was not right. *The Yorkshire Post* summed it up: 'Sir Alfred Butt wants to earn dividends for his shareholders, Dean wants it to become a national theatre with a policy. Winston Churchill [then Chancellor of the Exchequer] will tell him promptly that the country has no money to spare for intellectual luxuries at present.'[5] Looking back, nearly half-a-century later, Dean was philosophical about it:

> When I was appointed, the old theatre was at the parting of the ways. I have no doubt at all that if I had had the wisdom and experience to carry Sir Alfred Butt with me, and if the idea of subsidy had been ripe for acceptance, I might have succeeded in my attempt to wean Drury Lane away from a purely commercial outlook.[6]

There were too many 'ifs'. Political acceptance of the idea of subsidy for the theatre was decades in the future, and in any case, it wasn't very likely that Alfred Butt, who had saved the Palace Theatre by replacing opera with music hall, would agree to take Drury Lane in the opposite direction. Its history was littered with too many horrible examples of what happened to people who tried, like Alfred Bunn, to be 'extra legitimate'.

29

The Coming of the Musicals

On 20 March 1925, *Rose Marie* opened at Drury Lane and proved that Alfred Butt's instinct for what the public wanted was a good deal stronger than Basil Dean's. It broke all records and ran for two years, easily outstripping the ten months of *The Garden of Allah* and the eleven months of *Decameron Nights*. The hit of the show was 'The Indian Love-Call' and it was said that George V, who saw the show three times, could be heard singing 'When I'm calling you-oo-oo-oo-oo-oo-oo' as he walked around Buckingham Palace. *Rose Marie* would establish the reputation of Drury Lane as the house for big musicals that survives to the present day. With the exception of a brief attempt by Ivor Novello to bring Shakespeare back to the Lane in 1938, the idea of Drury Lane as a temple of the national drama was now finished.

Rose Marie was followed by Sigmund Romberg's *The Desert Song*, a ludicrous tale about the son of the governor of a French Moroccan province who becomes the Red Shadow by night. Romberg conducted the orchestra on the opening night and it ran for over a year. The next musical, opening on 3 May 1928, was the first London production of *Show Boat* with music by Jerome Kern and lyrics by Oscar Hammerstein II. Based on Edna Ferber's best-selling novel about the lives of the cast and crew of a Mississippi paddle-steamer called the Cotton Blossom, it was the first piece of musical theatre to integrate plot and songs into an artistic whole. Instead of sub-Viennese operetta with fairy-tale plots and characters, *Show Boat* dealt with serious issues, particularly racism. The quality of the score was far in advance of other musicals and included classics such as 'Can't Help Lovin' Dat Man' and 'Ol' Man River', performed by Paul Robeson.

Show Boat ran for a year to be replaced by *The New Moon*, starring Evelyn Laye. It was another Sigmund Romberg show, but in spite of the inclusion of 'Softly, as in a morning sunrise' and 'Lover, come back to me', plus a sea fight with a blazing pirate ship, it didn't do good business. Butt was quoted as saying that it was taking £4,000 a week – the second best box office in London – but showing profits of only a couple of hundred.[1] It was taken off for a revival of *Rose Marie*, followed by a musical version of *The Three Musketeers*, followed in short order by a Vivian Ellis musical called *The Song of the Drum*. These two shows had a combined loss of £20,000 and on 15 April 1931 Butt called a board meeting at which he dramatically resigned, saying that the advent of talking pictures meant that stage musicals could no longer compete with the cinema.[2]

He was replaced by George Grossmith, a successful actor/manager/lyricist who had been involved with many hits at the Gaiety Theatre and had built the Winter Garden Theatre in Drury Lane on what is now the site of the New London Theatre. Grossmith was undeterred by Butt's gloomy prophecy and produced the Franz Lehár musical *Land of Smiles* with the famous Austrian tenor Richard Tauber. Tauber, already an acclaimed opera singer and said to have one of the most perfect voices of the time, was receiving a reported £1,500 a week for the show, which was unheard of. His arrival in London was a story in itself, and it is said that this was the first time that publicity had focused on a performer rather than the show. This backfired on the management because Tauber's operatic training had not prepared him for the rigours of eight shows a week in a commercial musical. He missed so many performances that the audience had more chance of seeing his understudy than Tauber, and this led to a falling off at the box office. His personal success was undoubted, and one night he was forced to sing 'You Are My Heart's Delight' six times before the show could continue, but *Land of Smiles* ran for only two months.

It was followed by a show that has acquired legendary status, partly because the scale on which it was produced has made any full-scale revival of it impossible: Noël Coward's *Cavalcade*. Coward was already a major figure in the theatre. He had written *Hay Fever, Fallen Angels* and *Private Lives*, as well as songs and sketches for musical revues that seemed to sum up the zeitgeist of the roaring twenties: 'Poor Little Rich Girl', 'Dance Little Lady' and 'Room With a View'. His play *The Vortex* (1924) had shocked London with its depiction of a woman who takes a much younger lover while her son takes a great deal of heroin. Coward played the son, Nicky Lancaster, and took care to cultivate an air of decadence that was just enough to get publicity without getting him prosecuted, telling the *Evening Standard*: 'I am never out of opium dens, cocaine dens, and other evil places... My mind is a mass of corruption'.[3] This was all a tongue-in-cheek pose: Coward was solidly lower-middle class in his background and beliefs, and as patriotic as his characters in *This Happy Breed*. The famous photograph of Coward reclining on a bed in a silk dressing gown, smoking a cigarette in a long holder, was actually taken in one of the rooms of his mother's guest-house in Pimlico.

Cavalcade was the result of a collaboration between Coward and the impresario C.B. Cochran to do something really big. Before either of them knew what it was going to be, Cochran tried to book the Coliseum, but the long run of *The White Horse Inn* made that impossible, so he took Drury Lane. Coward is supposed to have had the idea for *Cavalcade* when he came across a photograph of troops embarking for the Boer War in *The Illustrated London News*. He conceived the plan for a drama that would follow the fortunes of one family, the Marryotts, and their servants from 1900 to New Year's Eve 1929. It was an upstairs/downstairs story that reflected the state of the nation, moving from the Relief of Mafeking and the death of Queen Victoria to the sinking of the Titanic and World War I. Coward interwove the popular songs of each period into the script and wrote new ones of his own. The enormous cast of 400 filled massive sets depicting troopships, Petticoat Lane and Trafalgar Square. The closing words of the play were: 'Let's drink to the hope that one day this country of ours, which we love so much, will find dignity and greatness and peace again.' This led into Coward's composition 'Twentieth Century Blues' which was in turn replaced by the whole cast singing the National Anthem underneath a Union Jack. Coward said in his first night speech: 'I hope that this play has made us feel that despite our national troubles it is still a pretty exciting thing to be English.' The audience were on their feet cheering every night for eleven months, and the show's original investment of £30,000 brought a return of £300,000.

Coward's rival for the title of king of the London stage was Ivor Novello. Both men were multi-talented as actors, composers and authors. Novello had become famous at the age of 21 when he wrote 'Keep the Home Fires Burning', which became the song of World War I. He would live to write 'We'll Gather Lilacs', which acquired the same status in World War II. In between, he had been a star of silent films, talkies and the stage. He had composed popular songs for revues and had written over a dozen plays, starring in many of them himself. At two points in his career he had three plays running concurrently in the West End. He was amazingly good-looking and had a profile in the days when profiles were more important than they are now. Coward used to say that there were only two perfect things in the world, his mind and Ivor Novello's profile.

In 1934, H.M. (Harry) Tennent had been appointed as General Manager of Drury Lane and was in desperate need of some product. The last few shows had flopped and there were no big American musicals of the sort Drury Lane had been relying on ready to come over. Tennent took Novello to lunch at the Ivy and explained his predicament, asking if Ivor had anything for him. Ivor replied that he had almost finished work on a musical play, so of course Tennent was all ears. Ivor outlined a preposterous story about a handsome young inventor (of the television) who visits Ruritania (actually called Krasnia in the show) where he falls in love with a beautiful gypsy prima donna who happens to be the beloved of King Stefan of Krasnia. She returns the passion of the young inventor and they leave on a liner which sinks. They survive and are married in a glamorous gypsy wedding. But then the gypsy Militza learns that her beloved country is in danger and decides that she must do her duty and return to marry King Stefan. (Presumably the gypsy wedding was invalid.) The heartbroken young inventor returns to England alone, where he watches her marriage on his new-fangled television set.

Harry Tennent must have been desperate because he immediately said this was just what they wanted for Drury Lane, and asked if Ivor could give him the script to read to the board meeting the following afternoon. Ivor said yes, but he hadn't actually written the show, so he went back to his flat above what was then the Strand Theatre (now renamed the Novello) and stayed up all night putting together a draft script. He sent it round just as the board meeting was about to begin, and heard a few hours later that it had been given the green light for production in May 1935. Ivor went into seclusion to write the show at his house, Redroofs in Maidenhead, seeing no one but his lyricist, Christopher Hassall. The Drury Lane board gave him everything he needed: Mary Ellis, the beautiful American operatic soprano, to star; a cast of 150 actors, singers and dancers; Oliver Messel to design; and Leontine Sagan, the first woman to direct a show at Drury Lane.

The first night was a very emotional moment for Novello because, as he said later: 'no thrill that I have ever known and no adventure that I have ever undertaken has given me the tremendous thrill which Drury Lane has provided. For I, like every other member of my profession, have the greatest veneration and respect for this great theatre, which is more national than any specially founded "National Theatre" could ever be... Drury Lane has always obsessed me. I have always loved it, and even as a small child of nine my ambition was to play there, and, if possible, to write a play for its historic boards.'[4] The romance of Old Drury chimed with his own view of theatre. One of the characters in his 1933 play *Proscenium* had said: 'I believe in the theatre: I believe in beauty in the theatre; I believe that in the theatre lies one of the roads back to sanity. I want to give people the chance to dream again.' His show, which was called *Glamorous Night,* would certainly do that. And it was his show: he had conceived it, written the music and the book, and he was starring in it, displaying the beautiful profile for all it was worth.

Glamorous Night was a huge success that changed Novello's status in the theatre. He had written hit songs before, but this was his first piece of musical theatre, and it seemed to suggest that the British could now compete in a form that had been an American monopoly. In his speech to the AGM of shareholders in 1927, Alfred Butt had broached the objection that Drury Lane, the national theatre, should not be putting on American musicals: 'the answer was that they only did so because, unfortunately, no British authors or composers brought forward books or music which, in the board's judgement, were likely to succeed... after all, the company was not a philanthropic institution'.[5] With its record-breaking box office, *Glamorous Night* had no need of philanthropy. When George V and Queen Mary came to see it, they summoned Novello to the royal box and told him that they enjoyed the show, but that it was too sad. 'You made the Queen cry,' said the King. 'We wondered if you couldn't change the ending and write a happy one, so that you both meet again and go away happily together.'[6] Wisely, Novello left the ending as it was.

Glamorous Night was the hottest ticket in town, so Novello was astonished to discover that the board planned to close it in order to make way for a Christmas pantomime. He thought this was madness when they were still turning away hundreds of people a night, and he offered a guarantee of £8,000 against any losses they might sustain by keeping it on. The board demanded £10,000 which Novello refused, so *Glamorous Night* closed after six months, when it was still at the height of its success. Novello had already written his next show, *Careless Rapture*, which, astonishingly, the board turned down.

The show which followed the pantomime into Drury Lane was another musical called *Rise and Shine* which closed after five weeks. Harry Tennent contacted Novello to say that the board was having second thoughts about *Careless Rapture* and would like to stage it. Novello agreed on condition that he would co-produce, to ensure that there was no question of it being taken off for a pantomime again.

It opened on 11 September 1936 and enjoyed the same success as *Glamorous Night*, with a fun fair on Hampstead Heath, an earthquake in China and much more lush, romantic music. It also had a happy ending, to avoid making Queen Mary cry.

Careless Rapture ran for a year, to make way for Novello's third musical, *Crest of the Wave*. Novello played the impoverished Duke of Cheviot who goes to Hollywood and becomes a movie star to retrieve the family fortunes. He marries a Cockney film extra but she is injured in a train crash. She greets the tenants at the Christmas Ball from her wheelchair. The train crash was in the best Drury Lane tradition and the scene in the ruins of a gothic cathedral in which the ghosts of the men who have prayed there sing the patriotic song 'Rose of England' was very moving. However, *Crest of the Wave* was not such a success as the two previous shows and closed after six months. Novello sent the show out on tour while he embarked on a risky and surprising project: to star as Henry V at Drury Lane.

Shakespeare in the Last Chance Saloon

As a matinée idol and musical comedy star, Novello was setting himself up for a fall with the critics. The 5,000 good-luck telegrams he had received on the first night of *Crest of the Wave* testified to the size of his following and the affection in which he was held by the profession, but the keepers of Shakespeare's flame would be a harder bunch to please. He pulled out all the stops, engaging Lewis Casson to direct a spectacular production with lavish sets and a large company. It was scheduled for ten weeks, after which Novello intended to put on ten weeks of *As You Like It* and ten weeks of *Much Ado About Nothing*. Shakespeare was by this stage in the last chance saloon at Drury Lane: if Ivor, with his enormous fan base, couldn't make the Bard pay at the Lane, no one could.

Henry V opened on 16 September 1938 to excellent reviews and good business for the first two weeks, but the timing couldn't have been worse. Everyone was worried about war with Nazi Germany, which seemed to be imminent, and Chamberlain made his 'Peace In Our Time' speech in the third week of the run. People desperately wanted peace, even as Drury Lane, like other public buildings, was being sand-bagged in preparation for bombing raids. It wasn't the best time to be putting on a play about a warlike king who calls upon his people to stiffen their sinews and summon up the blood. In its third week, *Henry V* was playing to empty rows and had to come off. It cost Novello and his producer Tom Arnold a great deal of money and represented both the beginning and end of Novello as a classical actor. He must have been disappointed, but he didn't complain of public taste, having once said of himself: 'I am not a highbrow. I am an entertainer. Empty seats and good opinions mean nothing to me.'

Ivor Novello's *Henry V* was the very last in-house production of Shakespeare in the theatre that had, more than any other, been responsible for his rise in status from so-so writer of a few dependable plays to Greatest Englishman and Greatest Author Who Has Ever Lived. The shades of David Garrick and Sarah Siddons must have shed a ghostly tear as they watched *Henry V* being dismantled, to say nothing of the managers who had struggled, from Betterton to Chatterton, to make Drury Lane a shrine of Bardolatry.

Novello, meanwhile, set about writing another hit show in which the public would want to see him in larger numbers. *The Dancing Years*, which opened at Drury Lane on 23 March 1939, is, in the opinion of many, his best musical. It is not set in Ruritania but in the real world of Austria, in which Jews are threatened by the rise of Nazism. Novello played Rudi Kleiber, a talented composer discovered by the prima donna of the Viennese Opera. They fall in love and she bears him a son, but he is already promised to someone else. The prima donna marries an aristocrat and many years later is able to use her connections to save Rudi from execution on a charge of helping Jews to escape from Austria. This was pretty strong stuff for Drury Lane and Novello was under pressure to remove the last scene, which he refused to do, although there was no overt reference to Hitler in the script. *The Dancing Years* represented Novello's view that music, art and beauty can heal a world torn apart by conflict, which was not an insignificant thing to be saying in 1939 (or now). The score included many of his most beautiful melodies such as 'My Dearest Dear', 'Waltz of My Heart', 'I Can Give You the Starlight' and 'When It's Spring in Vienna'.

It was a triumphant success, but once again, the timing was wrong. With war now imminent, theatre audiences were falling off, and the last performance of *The Dancing Years* took place on 31 August 1939 when there were so few people in the auditorium that Novello asked the patrons in the circles and gallery to come down to the stalls to fill it up.

The stage manager at Drury Lane was a man called Abingdon who had been hired by Basil Dean during his very brief stint as manager in 1924. Abingdon knew that Dean was looking for a base for the Entertainments National Service Association (ENSA) that he had set up to provide entertainment for the members of the armed forces in the event of war, so he rang Dean and suggested that ENSA should take over Drury Lane. Within a few days, Drury Lane had been requisitioned, so there would be no more shows there until the end of the war.

Novello was unwilling to give up on *The Dancing Years*, so in the following year he and producer Tom Arnold took it out on a regional tour. Originally planned for a few months, the tour lasted for a year-and-a-half, then came back into London at the Adelphi Theatre, where it played for two more years.

Novello's next show, *Arc de Triomphe*, opened on 9 November 1943 at the Phoenix Theatre, as Drury Lane was unavailable, to be followed by *Perchance to Dream*, which opened on 21 April 1945 at the London Hippodrome. This contained the song 'We'll Gather Lilacs'. Novello played three parts in a sequence of stories set in an English country house called Huntersmoon as it passes through generations of the same family, the first in the Regency period, then early Victorian, then present day (i.e. the 1930s). In the first two stories, the lovers are torn apart by an eternal triangle, but in the final section, the lovers come together, watched over by the ghosts of Huntersmoon.

Novello's final show, *King's Rhapsody*, opened on 15 September 1949 at the Palace Theatre. Drury Lane was still not available, but for a different reason. Shortly after the theatre had re-opened for public performances after its occupation by ENSA, *Oklahoma!* received its British première. It launched a run of Rodgers and Hammerstein musicals that would last for nine years and cause the critic Milton Schulman to ask if someone could inspect the deeds of Drury Lane to find out if it had actually been annexed by the USA. Over at the Palace, Novello's audience found themselves once again in Ruritania, where Novello, now fifty-six, was still playing the romantic lead. As Crown Prince Nikki of Murania, he is persuaded by his mother to make a marriage of convenience with Princess Christine of Norseland, but he ignores his wife, preferring the company of his mistress, Marta. Meeting Christine by chance in the palace, he takes her for a maid and seduces her. This results in the birth of another Crown Prince, so Nikki decides he must do his duty and reign over Murania where he tries to introduce some liberal reforms. He is forced to abdicate by a reactionary prime minister but turns up incognito at the cathedral to watch the coronation of his son.

King's Rhapsody was Novello's greatest commercial success. He was so pleased with the record-breaking box office that he would write the nightly gross on his dressing room mirror in lipstick. (It was said that producer Tom Arnold asked him not to do this in case other people in the show started asking for more money.) However, his health began to deteriorate during the run and he took time off to spend Christmas 1950 at his house in Montego Bay, Jamaica. In February 1951 he returned to the show, against medical advice, and after the performance on 5 March he returned to his flat over the Strand Theatre where he had a heart attack and died during the night. The year before, he had told a magazine interviewer how he wanted to die: 'I should like to make an enchanting curtain speech at the end of a wildly successful first night and – to the sound of cheers and applause – drop gracefully dead. If possible, before the curtain falls!'[7] His wish was nearly granted.

His role in *King's Rhapsody* was taken over by Jack Buchanan and the show ran for another seven months, closing on 6 October 1951. Since then, with the exception of an unsuccessful production of *The Dancing Years* at the Savile Theatre in the 1960s, there has been no major revival of any Ivor Novello show in London, where he had dominated the stage for thirty years. If his name is remembered at all now, it is probably in connection with the music awards ceremony named after him. The dramatic fall from grace is not hard to understand, given the changing direction of musical theatre. His admirers had believed that he could hold back the American invasion: 'Mr Novello, author, composer, and actor, can with his tranquillity stand up to all the bounding Oklahomans and Brigadooners in the world,' as Ivor Brown put it in his *Observer* review of *King's Rhapsody*, but there was a lot of wishful thinking in this.[8] The problem with Novello's shows was not just the Ruritanian settings and saccharine sentimentality, it was the structure. He was still working in a tradition in which songs had to be catchy and charming without necessarily being related to the plot. Any of his songs could come from any of his shows, and his last leading lady, Vanessa Lee, told a story that demonstrated this. She was touring with Novello in *Perchance to Dream* while he was working on *King's Rhapsody*. One night, as she was about to go on and sing 'A Woman's Heart', he told her to sing 'Someday My Heart Will Awake' from *King's Rhapsody* instead. The next actor to appear was also told to switch her song. Novello then went down to the footlights to tell the audience that they had just heard two numbers from his next show.[9] They were delighted, but the fact that two numbers could be transposed like this without anyone noticing that something was wrong says a lot about Novello's style. It would be hard to transpose a number from *Oklahoma!* to *The King and I*, or from *South Pacific* to *The Sound of Music*. The future of musical theatre would belong to writers who could use the songs to develop character and advance the plot.

Nevertheless, it seems appropriate that Clemence Dane's bust of Novello, which used to stand in his Aldwych flat, is now in the rotunda at Drury Lane. Novello provided the Lane with a string of big money-making hits when it needed them, and paved the way for others who would show that musical theatre is a form not necessarily exclusive to America.

30

Basil Dean Returns to the Lane

When Basil Dean left Drury Lane at the beginning of 1925, after his bruising experience with Alfred Butt, the stage carpenter tried to console him with an old theatrical superstition: 'Never mind, guv'nor, you'll be back... every producer works in a theatre three times.'[1] Fourteen years later, Dean was back, as director of the Entertainments National Service Association (ENSA) which took over Drury Lane for the duration of World War II.

Dean had served in World War I, when his involvement with the stage had led to a request from his commanding officer to organise entertainment for the troops of his division. His shows were so successful that he was asked to operate on a wider scale and soon controlled 15 theatres and ten touring companies for the armed forces. At the time, the government was being criticised over the way in which the commercial contractors who were running troop canteens were making excessive profits in return for poor service. As a result, a new organisation was set up called the Army Canteen Committee, which became the Navy and Army Canteen Board (NACB) and then, in recognition of all three branches of the armed forces, the Navy, Army and Air Force Institutes (NAAFI). Profits from the sale of food and drink would be used to fund welfare projects for the forces, including support for widows and orphans. As Dean had been staging shows in the canteens, entertainment for the forces came under the remit of the new canteen organisation. He was thus in at the start of what would become a very large organisation with a rather unusual status within the armed forces. The canteen organisation was neither a government department nor a charity but a trading co-operative that distributed its profits between the services in proportion to the extent to which each of the services contributed towards those profits.

As the 1930s drew to a close, Dean realised that, with another war looming, it was important for the entertainment industry to be better organised than it had been for World War I. He undertook to organise and co-ordinate the industry's contribution towards the war effort and approached NAAFI about starting a new organisation under its auspices. This was agreed, and the new body was originally to be called the Actors' National Service Association (ANSA), soon changed to the Entertainments National Service Association (ENSA). As ENSA grew into what was probably the largest provider of entertainment ever seen at that time, there was inevitable friction when the parent body found it was being overwhelmed by the cuckoo in its nest. Nevertheless, in spite of all the problems and Dean's frantic attempts to free ENSA from NAAFI as the war progressed, he acknowledged that ENSA might not have happened at all had he not been able to draw on his involvement with this canteen organisation of World War I.

Dean was not the only person to be thinking about entertaining the troops in the event of hostilities, and there was considerable resentment at the way in which he had taken it upon himself to speak for the whole profession. He recognised that he had to secure the co-operation of numerous parties such as the theatre managers and producers, agents and trades unions, but he was unfortunately not the best person to build such an alliance. He had an abrasive manner and a reputation for falling out with people. There was a particularly stormy meeting on 8 September 1939 at which almost all present complained bitterly about Dean's high-handed approach, and it looked as if the meeting would break up in disarray. At a critical point, Dean was called out of the room to take a phone call telling him that it had been agreed that ENSA should requisition the Theatre Royal, Drury Lane as its headquarters. When he returned to the meeting to share this news, things became quieter. There was no doubt that the Theatre Royal conferred a certain status on ENSA that set it apart from other organisations and individuals working in the field, but the friction was by no means over.

ENSA completely colonised the theatre, taking over its offices and creating more in all the space available until they were being built on the stage. It spread across the street to the Fortune Theatre and took over more office space in the surrounding area. The theatre's workshops were as busy as they had ever been in the days when they were manufacturing melodramas and pantomimes, only now it was portable stages and lighting rigs in addition to costumes and scenery for travelling revues, plays and concert parties. ENSA began broadcasting to the forces, setting up a studio in the stalls bar and then, when the scale of its broadcasting outgrew that, another one in the Fortune Theatre. Variety shows, films and plays were joined by concerts of classical music involving some of the greatest musical talent of the time. 'Never before,' as Dean observed, 'had such eminent artistes found themselves working side by side with patter comedians, crooners and dancers.'[2] For the most part, they took it well.

ENSA started by entertaining the troops stationed in the UK, waiting for action; then, as soon as hostilities began, ENSA followed the Allied advance. Wherever British forces were fighting, ENSA was somehow there, in Europe, Africa, the Middle East – 'from Iceland to Madagascar' as Dean put it.[3] Conditions were difficult and often dangerous, but seemed to bring out the best in those involved. Cancelling shows or curtailing tours had to be avoided at all cost, as the disappointment to troops who had been away from home in remote parts of the world for long periods would have been intense. Chorus girls slapped on glamorous masks of Max Factor in the melting heat of North Africa while musicians whose sheet music had been blown overboard had to do the best they could from memory. One story must serve for many. The concert pianist Solomon Cutner, always known simply as Solomon, worked tirelessly for ENSA throughout the war. He was never perturbed by inadequate facilities, and once told a piano tuner who was struggling to get sand out of the high notes of a piano in Iran while the troops were becoming impatient: 'Don't worry, I won't play them.' On another occasion, he arrived in Bangkok to give two performances but neglected to try out the piano first. As he started to play, lit by a brilliant spotlight overhead, insects began to crawl out from between the keys, up his sleeves and under his collar. He endured it for half an hour, trying to squash them on the keyboard, then fled the stage tearing off his collar and saying he couldn't stand it. Someone suggested switching off the light, which seemed to be attracting the bugs, and he played the rest of the concert in complete darkness. Unsurprisingly, Solomon was not eager to go through this again the next day, but the ENSA officer in charge had the piano soaked with DDT and promised there would be no more insects. This was true, but the effect of the spotlight this time was to draw out the fumes of DDT until Solomon's playing became extremely erratic and he ended the concert exhibiting all the signs of intoxication.[4]

These tours of every theatre of war were all being organised from the Theatre Royal, Drury Lane, where the logistics of the organisation would have crushed anyone less resilient than Basil Dean. By the end of the war, ENSA had given 2,656,565 shows to an estimated audience of 300,000,000 people.[5] This included not just the forces overseas and in the UK, but workers in munitions factories and other essential branches of the war effort. Dean was often accused of being dictatorial in his manner and, from everything we know about him, the charge was almost certainly true. Nevertheless, a tendency to give orders is not necessarily inappropriate in a wartime environment. It is difficult to see how else it would have been possible to keep so many thousands of shows (literally) on the road.

In 1956, Dean published his own account of the ENSA years under the title *Theatre at War*. It is useful to have a detailed account of everything that happened from the man who was at the centre of it, but Dean's book is hard work for the modern reader. This is partly because he tells you more than you really want to know, going into great detail about the feuds that dogged the organisation throughout the war: feuds between ENSA and NAAFI over resources; between ENSA and government departments over discipline and command; between ENSA and commercial managers and agents, unwilling to release their performers; between ENSA and the BBC, uneasy about giving an independent body access to the airwaves; between ENSA and the newly-formed Council for the Encouragement of Music and the Arts (CEMA) that wanted to muscle in on its territory. In Dean's account of these seemingly endless and bitter struggles, he presents himself as the innocent observer (the default setting of autobiography), but there may have been more to it than that.

We have another, much shorter, account of ENSA in W. Macqueen-Pope's 1955 book *Pillars of Drury Lane*. Macqueen-Pope had worked as business manager for Alfred Butt at several of his theatres, then as manager of Alexandra Palace and a number of West End theatres. He became press representative of Drury Lane in 1935 and would retain the position for 21 years, so he was there when ENSA moved in. He agreed to be the public relations officer for ENSA and his expertise in handling the press was of great benefit to the organisation, which was given a rough ride by Fleet Street from the start. There were so many false and damaging stories about ENSA that Macqueen-Pope took the extremely unusual step of issuing a writ for libel against a paper that had run an article calling into question his 'veracity and integrity'. The editor published a partial retraction of the article, and after that things got slightly better for ENSA in the press.[6]

Macqueen-Pope wrote a series of history books about theatres, including the first modern history of Drury Lane. His qualifications as a historian are open to challenge (*see* Appendix 1) but his passion for theatre in general, and Drury Lane in particular, is not. His lush, romantic style makes it hard to enjoy these books now, especially when he is writing about people still alive, when praise spills over into gross flattery. The sole exception to this was Basil Dean. Macqueen-Pope had no hesitation in laying the blame for ENSA's problems at the feet of its supremo: 'He is not an easy man to know or work with... he was all for frontal attack when strategy would have proved more successful... He never received the support of the great ones of the world of the theatre. It is to be feared that a great deal of personal feeling and jealousy went into that.'[7] It says a great deal for Dean's personal qualities that when he published his own account of ENSA, a year after Macqueen-Pope's book, he paid generous tribute to his former PRO and even acknowledged the fault of needlessly upsetting people. The playwright Clemence Dane had asked him, after the war, if he would do it all again and what, if anything, he would do differently. He answered 'yes' to the first part of the question and said that, were he to have the chance again: 'I should pray for greater insights into the situations I was called upon to face, so that I might proceed with less exigence and so avoid hurting people's feelings and raising unnecessary opposition.'[8]

Dean realised, early on in the war, that the relationship with NAAFI, that had been useful to get ENSA launched, was now a drag on its operations. The NAAFI management became increasingly concerned about the scale of ENSA's activities and the extent to which it was draining funds that were needed for other work, like support for the wounded. NAAFI made restrictions, some of them petty like which name was to be on the posters, but others more serious. NAAFI's policy was to allocate its profits in proportion to the amounts contributed by each of the services, so the RAF, as the newest and smallest service, received the least. Dean argued that this was unacceptable to ENSA as RAF pilots in bomber command were under intense strain and deserved some relaxation. Furthermore, men stationed in remote areas should be given priority over those stationed near large towns with their own entertainment.[9] He lobbied to have ENSA constituted as a government department reporting to a minister, and an inquiry was set up to look into this proposal. Dean was hopeful about the outcome, but in the end he was defeated by politics. When the inquiry's report was published in March 1941, it stated that ENSA should continue to operate under the supervision of NAAFI and a new body called the National Service Entertainments Board, with Basil Dean as Director of National Service Entertainment. The new Board was 'to be recognised as the sole source of supply of professional entertainments for any section of the community for whom entertainments (other than concerts promoted by the Council for the Encouragement of Music and the Arts) are provided out of public or semi-public funds'.[10]

Dropping the PR man

Dean regarded this as a victory of sorts that freed him to a certain extent from interference by NAAFI and saw off the challenge from others who were trying to get involved with entertaining the troops, although the exception made in the case of CEMA would prove to be significant. He organised a lunch at the Savoy to celebrate what he regarded as 'a turning-point in the muddled history of the relations between the state and the professional worlds of music and drama'.[11] Macqueen-Pope took a different view. During the course of the lunch, some dramatic news had arrived: the *Bismarck* had been sunk, and this coloured Macqueen-Pope's reaction to the report. 'The German battleship *Bismarck* was sunk – and so was ENSA… Old Drury was, for the time being, a government department. It did not think much of that position, nor did its old inhabitants. In their opinion, a Theatre Royal was better than a government department.' Macqueen-Pope resigned, saying that he didn't want to be a civil servant, as he had never been a servant and was rarely civil. At least, that was his story.[12]

Dean gives more detail about Macqueen-Pope's departure, which he claims was in response to disagreements about the broadcasting work. ENSA had a Broadcasting Council, of which Macqueen-Pope was director of programmes, under the chairmanship of Revd Sir Herbert Dunnico. Dunnico was a Welsh Baptist minister who had been a Labour MP. He had been involved with ENSA from its early days and had been a lot of help with his political connections, even though he had lost his seat in the House of Commons in 1931. ENSA broadcasts always began with the announcement: 'ENSA calling all theatres of war'[13] and comprised music, sketches, interviews and messages from the troops to their families. Macqueen-Pope had his own programme called 'London Carries On' which he wrote himself and which always began with the words: 'From the world's most famous playhouse, Theatre Royal, Drury Lane, we who work there send you half an hour of London'.[14] This was broadcast from the studio in the stalls bar of the theatre, while the bigger programmes came from the Fortune Theatre across the road. Macqueen-Pope complained constantly to Dean about interference in his work, especially from Dunnico. Macqueen-Pope was suffering from ill-health at the time, so Dean put his querulousness down to physical causes and refused to back him up against Dunnico – a decision Dean would come to regret. Macqueen-Pope wasn't the only person to point out that Dunnico behaved as if he weren't accountable to anyone. He was bad-tempered and abusive until in 1945, after the war had ended, Dean decided to make a stand. He passed Dunnico, carrying his ENSA uniform, in the corridor of Drury Lane and discovered that he was preparing for a trip to Brussels to organise a Sports Brains Trust which would open a NAAFI Club. This was beyond his remit and Dean forbade him to go. Dunnico resigned and issued a statement calling for a public inquiry before a High Court judge into the affairs of ENSA which, he claimed, was run by Dean wielding 'sole executive authority over an expenditure of £4,000,000 per annum' and behaving as an 'absolute dictator overriding the decisions of his executives'.

Dunnico was able to persuade Ernest Millington, MP for Chelmsford, to initiate an adjournment debate on 29 November 1945 calling for an inquiry into ENSA. Millington gave a lurid and inaccurate account of ENSA's affairs, heavily implying that Dean had been guilty of incompetence and corruption. Dean had been hoping that Herbert Morrison would reply on behalf of the government, but that task was given to John Strachey, Under-Secretary of State for Air, who had no particular knowledge of ENSA and no great interest in defending Dean's reputation. Strachey simply said that the case for a public inquiry had not been made. Matters were thus left with serious charges hanging in the air, unresolved. Dean wrote to *The Times* stating that, if Millington would care to repeat his charges outside the privileged arena of the House of Commons, Dean would bring an action for libel and it could be resolved in court. This didn't happen and, as a result, Dean's seven years of tireless service on behalf of the war effort were tarnished. Dictatorial and tactless he may have been, and some of the other charges about ENSA shows being a bit rough around the edges may have been true,✤ but for Dean to be accused of corruption was grossly defamatory and should have been dealt with at the time.

State funding for the arts

Dean had been hoping to keep ENSA in existence after the war, as he saw it as the means of persuading the government to allocate public money to the arts, but he was defeated in this aim. NAAFI didn't want to continue with ENSA and, more importantly, it was announced that the Council for the Encouragement of Music and the Arts (CEMA) was to be renamed the Arts Council of Great Britain with Maynard Keynes as its first chairman. Keynes had set up CEMA as a rival to ENSA during the war and was able to use his immense prestige and influence to out-manoeuvre Dean. ENSA was formally closed down at a meeting held at Drury Lane on 18 July 1946.

The principle of subsidy for the arts had been accepted, but Dean was to play no part in the scheme. He was now 58 and had been out of the professional theatre for seven years. Theatre, like all of the performing arts, had experienced a boom during the war years and new, younger talents had emerged. Dean was unable to pick up his career where he had left it off and, although he would live for another thirty years, he never regained his position of eminence and did comparatively little. He received a CBE for services to the war effort, but as Macqueen-Pope observed, 'they could not have given him much less'.[15]

✤ It was sometimes said that ENSA stood for 'Every Night Something Awful', but Macqueen-Pope claimed that the negative view of ENSA derived from its association with NAAFI, which was deeply unpopular with the troops. (Macqueen-Pope [1955] 217.)

Ten years after the closure of ENSA, with Dunnico by then in his grave, Dean wrote his book explaining what had happened. He welcomed the formation of the Arts Council as 'the most forward step in the advancement of British culture that a British government has yet taken', and he claimed that ENSA was due at least some of the credit for it.[16] He believed that ENSA had shown how the performing arts could be used to raise morale and strengthen a sense of national identity. There may have been something in that, and there is no doubt that the gratitude felt towards the artistes, from John Gielgud to George Formby, who had thrown themselves into the war effort, often at great financial loss, played a part in changing official attitudes towards subsidy. However, the more relevant factor in the decision to allocate public money to the arts was the mindset that emerged in the aftermath of the war that favoured government involvement in important areas of life. There was a feeling that Britain had led the Allies to victory against the Nazi tyranny by getting everyone to pull together, pool resources and accept a larger role for the government in the organisation of national life. What had worked in the war was thought to be good for the peace, and the formation of the Arts Council has to be seen as part of the same process that gave us the National Health Service and the welfare state.

Dean concluded his book with a 'Testament in Postscript', written in the character of an old man of the theatre passing on the baton to the younger generation. He argued that, now that state aid for the arts had been accepted in principle, this must be extended to the theatre. (Keynes had kept Arts Council funding closely focused on his own particular interests, especially opera and ballet at the Royal Opera House, of which he was also the chairman.) 'The cornerstone of state aid for the drama should be a National Theatre,' Dean wrote, and where better than at Drury Lane? He called upon the government to do for Drury Lane what it had already done for the Royal Opera House: set up a trust to acquire the freehold of the theatre. Alternatively, if that were regarded as going too far, the Old Vic and Stratford-upon-Avon companies could be presented there from time to time under the auspices of the trust. 'One immediate effect of the scheme... would be to break the stranglehold of American musical comedy over what is still regarded as the national shrine of our theatrical tradition.'[17]

Dean tells of a meeting he had with a member of the Royal Academy committee set up by Sir Edwin Lutyens to report on the future development of London. Dean was asked what he would recommend for the Covent Garden area and he suggested what we would now call a cultural hub, based on the Royal Opera House and Drury Lane. He wanted to clear away the market, introduce smart restaurants and academies for drama, opera and ballet, with a central booking hall. He envisaged a new approach to Drury Lane from Waterloo Bridge: a sweeping avenue adorned with fountains and statuary leading to the National Theatre. Dean was delighted to hear later that Lutyens had incorporated his ideas in the grand plan.[18]

Many of Dean's proposals have been carried out: the market has gone and Covent Garden is a smart area, with much improved public access to the Royal Opera House through the new facilities in the Floral Hall. But there are no statues or fountains in front of Drury Lane because in 1976, 20 years after the publication of Basil Dean's book, the National Theatre opened on the other side of the Thames.❖

❖ Lord Goodman, Chairman of the Arts Council at the time the decision was taken to build the National Theatre on its present site, admitted later that he would have been happy with either Drury Lane or the Haymarket. However, Denys Lasdun's designs for the new building were already in existence and 'we would have been cowardly not to build it'. (Elsom and Tomalin, 179.)

31

More Musicals

Drury Lane took a direct hit during the Blitz. Just before midnight on 15 October 1940, a 500 lb bomb hit the roof and ploughed through the gallery, upper circle and dress circle, exploding at the back of the pit. The blast tore out the front of the circle and caused the iron safety curtain to buckle. The nosecap became detached from the main part of the bomb and went through the floor into the stalls bar below, where members of the theatre's ARP team were sleeping. No one was hurt, as the explosion only affected the floor above. Incendiary bombs followed, burning out the pit and stalls, but the ARP team kept the fire under control and no lives were lost or injuries sustained. When Basil Dean arrived at the theatre the next day, he insisted that work should continue as usual, since the offices were unaffected, so not a day was lost. The nosecap of the bomb is still on display in the stalls bar.

During the war, Associated Theatre Properties had acquired a majority shareholding in Theatre Royal, Drury Lane Ltd. The chairman and managing director of ATP, Prince Littler, was therefore in charge of opening Drury Lane to the public again after the war. He would remain in charge until his death in 1973.

There was a great deal of work to do in order to make Drury Lane fit for the public again after the war, repairing the bomb damage and clearing away all of the temporary offices set up for ENSA's occupation. Considering that ENSA had only moved out in July, and wartime restrictions made it difficult to obtain building supplies, Prince Littler did a remarkably quick refit and was able to re-open on 19 December 1946 with a Noel Coward show called *Pacific 1860*. It was a flop, and the first indicator of the fact that Coward's leading position in the pre-war London theatre would not survive the changes of the post-war world. However, the show that followed it would change the direction of musical theatre.

A bright golden haze

***Oklahoma!* was the first collaboration** between the composer Richard Rodgers and the lyricist Oscar Hammerstein II. It followed the example of *Show Boat* as a 'book musical', which is to say a piece of musical theatre that tells a story with believable characters and convincing situations, in which the music, singing and choreography all carry the narrative forward. It had been produced on Broadway in 1943 by the Theatre Guild, an organisation set up to produce non-commercial works by American and foreign playwrights. *Oklahoma!*, based on the 1931 play *Green Grow the Lilacs* that had also been produced by the Guild, was a sensational success that flagged the emergence of a brilliant new writing partnership that would transform musical theatre. In 1944, Rodgers and Hammerstein received a special Pulitzer Prize for their contribution to 'Letters'.

Prince Littler negotiated to bring the original Broadway production to Drury Lane, but it was regarded as such a big risk that, for the first time in the theatre's history, it was decided to start the show out of London, at the Opera House in Manchester. In many ways, *Oklahoma!* just didn't look like a Drury Lane show. The cast were unknown, as was the music which, for copyright reasons, had never been released in the UK.✤ It was a small show: no shipwrecks, avalanches or horse races. Instead of opening with a big chorus number, the curtain went up on an old lady sitting in a rocking chair and a man's voice offstage singing 'There's a bright golden haze on the meadow'. Its success at Drury Lane was regarded as far from assured.

There were considerable problems with getting the cast and production across the Atlantic. First of all, the ship that was to carry cast, production team and costumes burnt out completely before it set sail. The costumes and some of the company were transferred to the Queen Elizabeth, which ran aground on a sandbank. When they arrived, the costumes were impounded by customs. Some of the cast were booked onto flights, but eight others had to travel on a freighter. The weather was bad and they were stuck in fog. Rehearsals in Manchester were dogged with issues surrounding the 'unregistered alien' status of the company, the need for ration books and the fact that they were not members of British Equity. The first night was postponed, although it was sold out, as the eight missing cast members were still at sea, no one knew where. Another opening night was announced and the management was determined to stick to it, but the situation was so bad that Macqueen-Pope exercised his considerable influence with the press corps to persuade journalists to give up their first night tickets and review the second night, which was unprecedented. Eventually the missing freighter was located off Dungeness. A tug-boat was hired to get the actors off the ship and into cars which drove at top speed to Manchester, where they arrived three-quarters of an hour before curtain-up.[1]

The first night in Manchester was a success, and the first night at Drury Lane, on 30 April 1947, was an even greater one. J.C. Trewin described *Oklahoma!* in *The Observer* as 'the sunrise score that dawns so freshly after the stuffy night of the mammoth musical'.[2] It replaced crown princes and Viennese prima donnas with the sort of characters

---

✤ In 1943, Gertrude Lawrence, a tireless representative of ENSA's interests in the USA, had recorded some of the numbers from *Oklahoma!* for her radio programme *Broadway Calling: The New York ENSA Half-hour*. When the British copyright-holders found out, they forbade its transmission.

whom the audience might know, and the public responded. The initial investment of £42,740 showed a return of £1,583,000. There were 1,375 performances over three years, making it the longest running show in the theatre's history at that time, and it was followed by three more shows from the Rodgers and Hammerstein partnership: *Carousel* (1950-51); *South Pacific* (1951-53); and *The King and I* (1953-56).[3] By the time Rodgers and Hammerstein ended their nine-year occupancy of Drury Lane, its status as the home of big musicals appeared to be set in stone. However, Shakespeare would make a last stand there, holding the curtain as London awaited the arrival of *My Fair Lady*.

My Fair Lady had opened on Broadway in January 1956 to an unprecedented reaction. Critics were hailing it as the greatest musical in years and punters had to wait months for tickets. With music by Frederick Loewe and lyrics by Alan Jay Lerner, it was the musical version of George Bernard Shaw's *Pygmalion*, with Julie Andrews as Eliza Doolittle, Rex Harrison as Henry Higgins and Stanley Holloway as Alfred Doolittle. Cecil Beaton's costumes were almost stars in their own right, with the famous black-and-white Ascot, and the score yielded so many hits that it seemed as if every number were not only perfect for its moment in the plot but could be extracted to become a standard of popular music.

While arrangements were being made for a London production, a couple of very unsuccessful musicals were put into Drury Lane, followed by short visits of companies from other countries. Then, on 5 December 1957, Peter Brook's Stratford-upon-Avon production of *The Tempest*, with John Gielgud as Prospero, opened at the Lane for a seven-week run. Everyone knew that this was just filling time, and Peter Brook complained that his actors were being used as guinea pigs to try out the new lighting rig for *My Fair Lady* (which was probably true),[4] but it was a significant moment. There had been no Shakespeare production at Drury Lane since Ivor Novello's ill-fated *Henry V* in 1938, and if, as seems likely, this one was destined to be the very last, there was a certain appropriateness in the choice of play. *The Tempest* has often been taken to be Shakespeare's farewell to the stage. When Prospero breaks his staff and renounces his magic powers, we can sense Shakespeare giving up on the theatre to retire to the life of a prosperous burgher in the town of his birth. This interpretation has been challenged, but whether or not Shakespeare really was saying goodbye to the theatre with *The Tempest*, he was certainly saying goodbye to Drury Lane, the temple where he had been worshipped for so many generations.

My Fair Lady opened at Drury Lane on 30 April 1958 and its reception was, if anything, even warmer than the one it had received on Broadway. It was hailed by critics as near perfection, and many aficionados of musical theatre still regard it as the perfect musical. *My Fair Lady*, with its original three stars, became the first show in London for which people had to book six months ahead. It clocked up 2,281 performances over five-and-a-half years, breaking the record of *Oklahoma!*

It had been hoped to follow *My Fair Lady* with Lerner and Loewe's next Broadway success, *Camelot*, the story of King Arthur, Guinevere and Lancelot based on T.H. White's *The Once and Future King*. However, *Camelot* was postponed for a year, so *My Fair Lady* was followed by the Richard Rodgers and Lorenz Hart musical *The Boys from Syracuse*, based on Shakespeare's *Comedy of Errors*. The show was already 25 years old and had never been seen in London. When it opened, the reason became obvious. It received some of the worst reviews in living memory and was described by *The Times* as 'less a revival than an exhumation'.[5] It closed after a short run, to be followed by short seasons of music and dance companies, including a month-long residency by the company from the Royal Opera House, which had the builders in.

Camelot finally opened on 19 August 1964 to poor reviews, which were no doubt partly due to the impossibility of living up to the reputation of *My Fair Lady*. It was the first show of which it was said that you came out humming the scenery, as the sets by John Truscott looked splendid. *Camelot* ran for just over a year, to be followed by more musicals, including *Hello Dolly!*, *Mame* and *The Great Waltz*. The latter, known as *The Great Schmaltz*, opened in July 1970 and featured the supposed rivalry between Viennese Waltz Kings Johann

Strauss, father and son. It was still running two years later when Brian Dobbs published his history of Drury Lane, and he drew a gloomy conclusion from its success. He felt that musicals were overwhelming the theatre, and that the vast amounts of money required to stage them, coupled with the vast profits that could be derived from them, meant that the money-men were in control at the expense of the creative team. The temptation would always be to use the tried-and-tested formula rather than take any risks, with the result that 'we may see the musical become a moribund museum piece as out-of-touch with its time and audience as the melodrama'.[6]

It is easy to understand how anyone might take this view after sitting through *The Great Waltz*, a show not so much preserved in aspic as pickled in formaldehyde. Fortunately, Brian Dobbs's prediction of musical doom failed to materialise, as musical theatre explored new territory in the following decades that would take it a long way from the 'icing sugar and double cream'[7] sweetness of *The Great Waltz*.

British musical theatre had laboured for a long time in the shadow of *Oliver!*, turning classics of literature – often by Dickens or Shakespeare – into musicals, with very mixed results. In the 1970s there was a revolutionary new approach, spear-headed by Andrew Lloyd-Webber, Tim Rice and Cameron Mackintosh. Lloyd-Webber and Rice went to more unusual sources for their material: the Old Testament (*Joseph and The Amazing Technicolor Dreamcoat*); the New Testament (*Jesus Christ Superstar*); and Latin-American politics (*Evita*). Lloyd-Webber then took T.S. Eliot's poems from *Old Possum's Book of Practical Cats* as the basis for *Cats*, which he co-produced with Cameron Mackintosh at the New London Theatre. He followed this in 1986 with *The Phantom of the Opera* at Her Majesty's, also co-produced with Mackintosh, who, the year before, had produced *Les Misérables*, based on Victor Hugo's nineteenth century novel. *Les Misérables* was written by the French team of Alain Boublil and Claude-Michel Schönberg, whose next show, *Miss Saigon*, was produced by Mackintosh at Drury Lane. It opened on 20 September 1989 and ran until 30 October 1999, clocking up 4,263 performances and becoming the longest-running show in the history of Drury Lane.

With the exception of *Miss Saigon*, none of the shows mentioned in the previous paragraph were staged at Drury Lane, but their influence was felt throughout musical theatre, including Drury Lane. Michael Bennett's *A Chorus Line*, which was a long way from the take-a-literary-classic-and-add-twelve-numbers formula, ran from 1976 to 1979. Stephen Sondheim's *Sweeney Todd* is a dark masterpiece that is so far removed from *The Great Waltz* that it seems improper to describe them both as musicals, which is probably why we now speak of musical theatre. It ran for only 20 weeks at Drury Lane in 1980, but it won the Olivier Award for Best New Musical and is regarded as a classic. More recent offerings have included *The Producers* (the stage musical version of the Mel Brooks film), *Lord of the Rings, Shrek* and the stage musical version of Roald Dahl's *Charlie and the Chocolate Factory*. The theatre-going public shows no indication of losing its taste for musicals, sweet or sour.

Changing hands

As well as being chairman and managing director of Associated Theatre Properties, which controlled Theatre Royal, Drury Lane Ltd, Prince Littler occupied the same position in the Stoll Theatres Corporation. He merged the two companies, and in 1965 Stoll Theatres was taken over by Lord (Lew) Grade's company Associated Television (ATV). This made Lew Grade an important figure in theatre as well as commercial television, and he became chairman of Drury Lane on the death of Prince Littler in 1973. In 1982 the Australian businessman Robert Holmes á Court acquired the company, now known as Stoll Moss Theatres, and became chairman until his death in 1990, when his widow, Janet Holmes á Court, took over. In 2000, Andrew Lloyd-Webber's Really Useful Group acquired the Stoll Moss Theatre Group, making Lord Lloyd-Webber the current owner of Drury Lane.[8] His well known passion for art and architecture makes him the ideal curator of a Grade 1 listed building with the finest art collection of any London theatre.

Conclusion

The National Theatre
in Drury Lane?

Purpose-built public theatres appeared in London in the last part of the sixteenth century. Like the inn-yards in which the actors had been accustomed to performing, they were open-air structures in which scenery had to be of the simplest nature, with little more than a few props to indicate the difference between a bedroom and a forest. At the beginning of a new reign and a new century, there would be a dramatic development in staging techniques, but it took place not in the public theatres but at the court.

James I and his Queen, Anne of Denmark, were fond of lavish shows and instigated a series of extravaganzas known as the court masques. Charles I inherited the taste from his parents, and masques were performed, often on Twelfth Night or some other feast day in January or February, from 1605 to 1640. These productions were short musical performances with allegorical storylines designed to ram home the image of the King as wise, just, merciful and so on, ruling over his people by the divine right conferred on him by God. Their constant theme was the triumph of good over evil, of order over chaos and of beauty over ugliness. They bore little relation to the political realities of the time, and the last of them, *Salmacida Spolia*, represented Charles I as Philogenes ('Lover of his People') doomed to rule in

482

evil times. It was performed in 1640, on the verge of the series of events that led to the outbreak of the English Civil War. A few years later, Charles would be led onto the scaffold through the Banqueting House in Whitehall that had been built to accommodate these masques.

What gave these performances their tremendous symbolic value was the fact that the King, Queen, members of the royal family and leading members of the nobility were appearing in them. They were not, of course, open to the public. Each masque would be given only once or twice, before an invited audience of courtiers and diplomats. In spite of this, the budgets were huge and the spectacle was breath-taking. The costumes and scenery were designed by Inigo Jones, who had travelled in Italy where he had studied the classical architecture of the ancient world. He had also been able to witness the spectacles that were being staged at the courts of Renaissance Europe. Jones brought back with him an approach to both theatre and architecture that was revolutionary, introducing the classical style into a country where it was almost unknown.

In 1604, the Queen decided that she wanted to put on a show for Twelfth Night on 6 January 1605. She asked Ben Jonson, one of the most successful playwrights in London, to write the script, and she called on Inigo Jones to design the scenery and costumes. Jones was 31, completely unknown and lacking in any relevant experience, but it seems he had visited the court of the Queen's brother, who was King of Denmark and who may have recommended this brilliant young man to his sister. The show that Jones designed must have been a revelation to his first audience on Twelfth Night, as it was unlike anything that had been seen in Britain before. One of the ideas that Jones had brought back with him from Italy was a proscenium arch with a curtain which fell to reveal a billowing sea with tritons, mermaids and sea-monsters. The moon sat on a silver throne in the clouds. The really revolutionary thing was that the scenery was painted in perspective, using wings and a backcloth, with a vanishing point designed to work perfectly for the King, sitting in his throne in the middle of the hall watching it.

The masque was a success, and Jones and Jonson found themselves required to come up with a masque or two every year, each one needing to be more astonishing than the last. Using everything he had learned of stagecraft in Italy, Jones set the wings and the backdrop (or shutter) in grooves so that they could slide off, each set revealing another one behind. Stormy landscapes could change into peaceful valleys; the Prison of the Night drew back to reveal the Queen and her ladies as the Daughters of the Morn; a rock parted to reveal a throne lit by countless lights on which sat the Prince of Wales as Oberon, the Fairy Prince. Then there was the wonderful machinery that Jones had invented himself, far in advance of anything he could have seen in Italy, that allowed gods and goddesses to descend in chariots and thrones until, in *Salmacida Spolia*, whole pantheons of deities could appear in the skies to lend their moral support to Charles I, on the verge of a civil war.

For 26 years, Ben Jonson wrote the scripts for these masques. Initially, he was enthusiastic about the form, which he used to promote the ideals of neo-Platonism, imaging a perfect world that existed somewhere and that could be referenced as a means of improving the world we live in.[1] However, Jonson became uneasy about the way in which the scenery was drowning out his words, because he believed that the words were the most important part. The scenery and costumes would ravish the senses of the spectators, coming to them through their eyes, but this was all transitory. It lasted only a moment. The words, impressing themselves upon the spectators' understanding, made a more lasting impression. He drew an analogy between body and soul: the spectacle was the body of the masque but the poetry was its soul.[2]

Jonson was a great playwright and a very learned man – perhaps a bit too learned. The published scripts of his masques are so dense with notes explaining all the classical allusions that they are difficult to read. Even at the time, most of the erudition must have gone over the heads of the audience, who were, nevertheless, stunned by the spectacle. Jonson's feeling that he was being upstaged by the designer boiled over in 1631 when he published the scripts of two masques on which they had just collaborated, *Love's Triumph Through Callipolis* and *Chloridia*. Normally, the published versions were not credited to anyone, but these two both stated on their title pages: 'The Inventors: Ben Jonson Inigo Jones'. The problem was the order: Jones felt he should have come first. It is difficult for people who don't work in theatre to appreciate the intensity with which people treat arrangements over billing, the negotiations for which are often conducted with more passion than those relating to salary. No one else knows what you are being paid, but everyone can see where your name is on the poster. It seems that Jones complained to the King or Queen, or both, and it is certain that Jonson never worked on a court masque again, thus losing a significant part of his income.

The resentment that Jonson had long been nurturing against Inigo Jones boiled over into fury. He caricatured Jones as 'Vitruvius Hoop' in his play *A Tale of a Tub* and wrote a poetic diatribe which was so venomous that he was warned by a friend not to publish it, as it would draw repercussions from the court. It contains the lines:

> *O shows! Shows! Mighty shows!*
> *The eloquence of masques! What need of prose*
> *Or verse, or sense, t'express immortal you?...*
> *O to make boards to speak! There is a task!*
> *Painting and carpentry are the soul of masque.*[3]

Ben Jonson was a proud, arrogant and sometimes violent man (he was convicted of murder and only escaped hanging by pleading the 'benefit of the clergy' because he could read Latin). He had a high regard for his own talents and a low regard for most other people's. The surprising thing is not that he fell out with Inigo Jones, but that the partnership lasted so long. However, Jonson's personal failings should not blind us to the real issue here. Jonson was a professional man of the theatre – the public theatre, not the aristocratic amateur dramatics over which Jones was presiding. He believed passionately in the power of the spoken word on the stage and he didn't want to see it overwhelmed by costumes and machinery. In 1626 he wrote a prologue to his play *The Staple of News* in which an actor delivers a message to the audience from the playwright:

For your own sakes, not his, he bad me say,
Would you were come to hear, not see, a play.
…he'd have you wise,
Much rather by your ears than by your eyes.

The distinction Ben Jonson drew between what comes in through our ears and through our eyes would frame the debate about the role and purpose of theatre for the next three centuries. So would slagging off the carpenters.

Painting and carpentry

During Ben Jonson's lifetime, there was not much danger that the script was going to be submerged by scenery in the public theatres because, even in the indoor theatres that opened at the beginning of the seventeenth century, the staging was very simple. When the theatres re-opened after the Restoration in 1660, the situation changed. Sir William Davenant, in charge of the Duke's Company, was able to profit by the knowledge he had acquired from working with Inigo Jones on court masques before the Civil War. When he opened his theatre in Lincoln's Inn Fields in 1661, he installed the moveable, perspective scenery that had been familiar to pre-Civil War courtiers, but never seen on a public stage (if we except his brief attempts to stage operas without being shut down by the army during the Commonwealth). The impact of this novelty was so great that Samuel Pepys noted the falling-off in business at the rival King's Company as a result.[4] No doubt in response to this, Thomas Killigrew moved out of his converted tennis court in Vere Street and into the first Theatre Royal, Drury Lane, where he had the space to compete with Davenant's new scenery. The stage was then set (literally) for a rivalry between the two theatre companies in which, to the alarm of those who loved plays, the audience would be tempted by music, dancing, opera, pantomime and spectacle – anything but the words. As Colley Cibber wrote of

486

opera: 'The sensual supply of sight and sound, coming in to the assistance of the weaker party, it was no wonder they should grow too hard for sense and simple nature, when it is consider'd how many more people there are, that can see and hear, than think and judge... the crowd... fluctuated, from one house to another, as their eyes were more, or less, regaled than their ears.'[5] According to Cibber's ranking of bodily organs, the ears were good when they were listening to plays, bad when they were soaking up the lush sounds of opera. Plays made you think, but operas didn't.

Exactly a century after the publication of *An Apology for the Life of Colley Cibber*, Alfred Bunn was using the same cultural taxonomy of organs in his own apologia, *The Stage, Both Before and Behind the Curtain*. He drew up a list of authors whose work could be brought 'under the head of LEGITIMATE DRAMA... most of whose writings are of a high mental order, and most of them appealing to the ear rather than the eye'.[6] Bunn wrote his book to defend himself against the charge of cultural vandalism, or 'having neglected the legitimate drama, and infected its dominions with gewgaw and pageantry, wherein SENSE had been compelled to give way to SHOW'.[7]

The banner under which the champions of 'the legitimate drama' rallied was inscribed with the words 'sense' and 'nature'. Good plays embody both: they represent 'nature' by showing us how men and women really think and behave; and they increase our store of common sense by teaching us how the world works. Pantomimes, operas, performing animals and other forms of 'illegitimate' entertainment are unnatural and nonsensical. We learn nothing useful from the warbling of the Italian *castrati* or the transformations conjured up by Harlequin's wand. Sense and nature were perceived to be threatened by the cupidity of managers who would put on whatever rubbish the public wanted to see. 'It is said a most excellent comedy of Sir Richard Steele's [*The Conscious Lovers*] is to be prohibited acting,' wrote Dr Thomas Rundle to a friend in 1720, 'lest it should draw away good company and spoil their relish for operas, by seducing them with wit, sense and humour.'[8] This was a joke, but you can see where he was going with it.

Sir Richard Steele himself had plenty to say on this subject, starting with the prologue to his first play, *The Funeral*, performed at Drury Lane in December 1701:

> *Nature's deserted and dramatick art,*
> *To dazzle now the eye, has left the heart;*
> *Gay lights and dresses, long extended scenes,*
> *Daemons and angels moving in machines,*
> *All that can now, or please, or fright the fair,*
> *May be performed without a writer's care,*
> *And is the skill of carpenter, not player.*

Concern about what the carpenters were getting up to became a *leitmotif* of this discussion, not to mention the dressmakers, machinists and other backstage trades that were thought to be invading the rightful territory of the author. A puff for Henry Fielding's season at the Little Theatre in the Haymarket in 1737 had informed the public that: 'a certain author... has taken it into his head... to explode the reigning taste for dumb shew and machinery, and has declared open war against Harlequin, Punch, Pierrot, and all modern poets, *viz.* joiners, dancing-masters, and scene painters'.[9] Popular as his plays were, Fielding could scarcely have hoped really to 'explode' this reigning taste, and in 1772 a review of Garrick's Christmas pantomime *The Witches or a Trip to Naples* described it as 'one of those mummeries in which the carpenters, painters and taylors belonging to the theatre are the principal projectors; who torture dull brains to furnish out most contemptible pieces of entertainment'.[10]

More than a century later, George Bernard Shaw, the doughty champion of authors' rights, was making the same point about the 1897 pantomime *Babes in the Wood*, produced by Arthur Collins and starring Dan Leno:

> The spectacular scenes exhibit Mr Collins as a manager to whom a thousand pounds is as five shillings. The dramatic scenes exhibit him as one to whom a crown-piece is as a million. If Mr Dan Leno

had asked for a hundred-guinea tunic to wear during a single walk across the stage, no doubt he would have got it, with a fifty-guinea hat and sword-belt to boot. If he had asked for ten guineas' worth of a competent dramatic humorist to provide him with at least one line that might not have been pirated from the nearest Cheap Jack, he would I suspect, have been asked whether he wished to make Drury Lane bankrupt for the sake of dramatic authors.[11]

Shaw's rebuke to the management over the quality of the script provides us with one of those strange moments when the generations link hands across centuries at Drury Lane. This is because, 165 years earlier, Aaron Hill had made exactly the same point about the pantomime scripts to Barton Booth. On Christmas Day 1732, Hill wrote to his old school-friend Booth, trying to cheer him up in his last illness with a bit of theatre talk. Booth had been forced into retirement by ill health in 1728, but he still possessed half of his original one-third share in Drury Lane, so Hill encouraged him to use his influence to make the pantomimes more intelligent. There was no reason, according to Hill, for the superiority of the Lincoln's Inn Fields company in pantomime: Drury Lane had more talent in every area, but the scripts were poor:

...there ought to be a *purpose* and a *point*. It is impossible, that any man should laugh, with less pleasure, only because he has *reason*, as well as *humour*, for laughing; and were the tricks of *Harlequin* connected into a *thread*, and the consequences of some story and design, they might, undoubtedly, be more lively, more various, more extravagant, and suprizing; and, yet, give *pleasure* without *shame*; both which we now receive, together.[12]

We don't have Booth's answer to this letter, but we can form a reasonably good idea of how he might have defended himself from an anecdote related by Theophilus Cibber, Colley Cibber's son, in his book *Lives and Characters of Actors*. Cibber recalls a time when he and Booth were in a coffee-house together after a show and Booth was approached by some fans. They thanked him for the pleasure he had given them that night with his performance of Varanes in Nathaniel Lee's tragedy *Theodosius*, but gently took him to task for bringing down the tone of the evening by following the tragedy with the 'senseless' pantomime of *Perseus and Andromeda*:

> Mr Booth frankly answered that he thought a thin audience was a much greater indignity to the stage than any they mentioned and a full one most likely to keep up the spirits of the actor, and consequently heighten the representation. He begged them to consider there were many more spectators than men of taste and judgement; and if, by the artifice of a pantomime, they could induce a greater number to partake... of a good play than could be drawn without it, he could not see any great harm in it... For his part, he confessed he considered profit as well as fame;... He desired them to recollect what sums were expended on operas, how much it was the fashion to subscribe to them, how high were their prices, and what a train of nobility and gentry were drawn to them, to the no small prejudice of the playhouse, as appeared by the melancholy testimony of their receipts, till by those auxiliary pantomimes they not only found their pit and galleries were fuller, but their boxes made a nobler appearance; and as Mr Hill had justly observed, he could not think it was the business of the directors to be wise to empty boxes.[13]

Theophilus Cibber was recalling this event after a gap of 30 years, and some of the details are wrong. (*Theodosius* was often followed by a pantomime, but *Perseus and Andromeda* didn't appear until November 1728, by which time Booth had retired from the stage.) However, the wisdom of the old stager rings true. The division of shows into legitimate/illegitimate or artistic/commercial or serious/frivolous is more appealing to literary critics than to actors, who just want a good house to play to. As a member of the triumvirate, sharing in both the profits and the losses of Drury Lane, it was clearly in Booth's interest to keep the benches full and, if pantomime did the trick, so be it.

Furthermore, the way in which he cites Aaron Hill's opinion in support of his own view is significant, because Hill was one of the most important theorists of drama of the eighteenth century.

Harlequin, darkness and corruption

Aaron Hill had by no means lost interest in theatre after being ejected from Drury Lane by rebellious actors at the end of his seven months as manager in June 1710. As a poet, playwright and journalist, he waged a passionate campaign to reform the stage by finding ways to put on good plays, properly staged, with acting of a much higher standard than was customary. In 1721 he tried to rent the Little Theatre in the Haymarket to try out his theories, but that fell through. Ten years later, he wrote a poem called 'Advice to the Poets', published with a dedicatory epistle 'To the few great spirits of Great Britain' in which he called for public subsidy of the stage. He advised the government to follow the example of ancient Athens, where playwrights were honoured and supported because their tragedies played such an important part in the moral formation of the people. 'Their youth grew up in a spirit of greatness and liberty, an aversion against tyranny, a propensity to arms and eloquence… and an impatient emulation of what they daily heard and saw'. If only the British government would support the theatre, it would soon become apparent that 'there is no part of learning… so capable as this branch of poetry to serve the wise and the national views of a great and able politician… how immortal would be the name of that minister to whose influence we should owe such an establishment of a stage in London, redeemed from the narrow limitations of the present'.[14] This is one of the first calls (if not the first) for public subsidy of theatre. It would be more than three centuries before any minister of the British government would seek the sort of immortality Hill was promising, but he wasn't deterred from trying to reform the stage, even under 'the narrow limitations of the present'.

In 1733, with the break-up of the triumvirate who had been ruling Drury Lane for twenty years, Hill tried to 'rent' the shares of the patent owned by Barton Booth and Robert Wilks's widow, but both wanted to sell. He was offered a half-share of the patent for £8,000 but couldn't raise that sort of money. When John Highmore gained control of Drury Lane and fell out with his rebellious actors, Hill, no doubt remembering his own drubbing at the hands of the actors in 1710, supported Highmore and warned that, as soon as you let actors interfere in the management of a theatre, you can expect 'something scandalously silly or impertinently partial'.[15] Hill offered to help Highmore out of his difficulties by taking over the running of Drury Lane from the opening of the season in autumn 1733 until Christmas.[16] He offered to guarantee Highmore against loss in return for a quarter of the profits, but Highmore refused.

Balked of the opportunity to manage, Hill continued to harangue. He started a journal called *The Prompter* that appeared twice a week from November 1734 to July 1736, promoting his ideas for reforming the stage. He blasted the taste of town for the nonsensical follies of pantomime and opera, especially the Italian *castrati*, whose presence on the stage he described as 'only fit for nations of corrupt and dissolute morals'.[17] *The Prompter* for 29 November 1734 described a 'wanted' poster which was supposed to have said: 'Hunted or strayed out of the theatres of this great city, and supposed to be lurking in some private and remote part of the country, a lean, ragged, un-curried creature called Common Sense.' It was reported that Common Sense had found shelter with 'Verax', who turned out to be Henry Fielding. Hill welcomed Fielding's plays because they attracted support 'by the single power of satire, wit and common sense'.[18] Eventually, Hill decided that no one was listening to him and he gave up. In one of the later issues of *The Prompter*, he described the stage as 'a dead body without hope of resurrection… Farewell all prospects of reviving SENSE! Hail Harlequin! and Wantonness! and Darkness! and Corruption!'[19]

Fielding was no doubt pleased to have the support of Aaron Hill, who was highly respected in the world of letters even if he couldn't get into theatre management. Fielding shared Hill's fear that the theatre was going to the dogs because of the abysmal level of public taste, and he wrote several satires using the play-within-a-play format to ridicule popular entertainments, especially pantomime. On 29 April 1736, when he was running the Little Theatre in the Haymarket, Fielding put on his burlesque *Tumble-Down Dick or Phaeton in the Suds* which ridiculed a pantomime called *The Fall of Phaeton* that had opened at Drury Lane in February. *The Fall of Phaeton* was what we would now call a posh panto, with music by Thomas Arne and scenery by Francis Hayman. It was described as 'a new dramatic masque' rather than a pantomime or 'entertainment' (the more usual term) and enjoyed great success, being visited by the entire royal family. Fielding decided to ridicule its pretensions by rewriting the story in a less elevated style. In Greek mythology, Phaeton is the son of Phoebus Apollo, the sun god, and the nymph Clymene. Phaeton seeks a favour from Apollo and is allowed to drive the chariot of the sun for a day. He is unable to control the horses and, to prevent the earth from being burnt up, Apollo is forced to kill his son with a thunderbolt. In Fielding's version, Phoebus is a nightwatchman. He lets Phaeton carry his lantern for one night to prove that he really is the boy's father, rather than a sergeant of the Foot-Guards, as the local lads are saying. Phaeton falls asleep and tumbles out of his wheelbarrow with his lantern.

The hero of *Tumble-Down Dick* is Fustian, a playwright who is struggling to find a theatre manager willing to stage a serious play, because of the taste for pantomime. Fustian is shocked when Machine, the author of the forthcoming pantomime, insists on cutting *Othello* to make more time for his entertainment:

MACHINE: Mr Prompter, I must insist that you cut out a great deal of *Othello*, if my pantomime is performed with it, or the audience will be pall'd before the entertainment begins.

PROMPTER: We'll cut out the fifth act, sir, if you please.

MACHINE: Sir, that's not enough. I'll have the first cut out too.

FUSTIAN: Death and the devil! Can I bear this? Shall Shakespeare be mangled to introduce this trumpery?

PROMPTER: Sir, this gentleman brings more money to the house,
             than all the poets put together.[20]

Fielding was creating the most absurd and extreme situation he could think of to give his satire bite. On 29 April 1836, a hundred years to the day after the first performance of *Tumble-Down Dick*, the fantastic insult to Shakespeare that Fielding had dreamt up actually happened at Drury Lane. Alfred Bunn cut two acts of *Richard III* to make time for two musical extravaganzas, resulting in the famous fisticuffs with William Charles Macready. As Fielding might have said, you couldn't make it up.

Royal status

Ever since it had opened its doors in 1663, Drury Lane enjoyed a status unlike that of any other theatre. With regard to its patent, it enjoyed the same privileges as the rival company, but the rival company was called the Duke's Company while Drury Lane was the King's Company. What happened at Drury Lane was important in a way that is difficult to appreciate now that theatre plays such a small part in the culture, relative to other forces, and this was the reason for the intense political interference in its early years. Charles II persuaded Betterton to develop an English school of opera that would enable him to compete with Louis XIV. When Christopher Rich brought his ruthless capitalist approach to bear on Betterton's traditional methods, the Lord Chamberlain violated the terms of Rich's patent to allow Betterton and his company of rebel actors to set up a new company in opposition. A Tory MP, William Collier, was able to take the control of Drury Lane away from Rich when the Tories were in government, and Collier was in turn thrown out to make way for the Whig MP Richard Steele when George of Hanover ascended the throne and the Whigs won the general election. When the Duke of Newcastle became Lord Chamberlain, he silenced Drury Lane and banned first Colley

Cibber then Richard Steele from playing any part in its management until they acknowledged the power of his office to control the theatre.

Because what was happening at Drury Lane was significant, the court and government wanted to feel that the theatre was in a safe pair of hands. Plays that threatened to undermine government policy would be banned. Dryden's play *The Duke of Guise* was forbidden by Charles II because it was thought to reflect on the Duke of Monmouth (who would lead a rebellion against Charles's brother James II a few years later); Colley Cibber's adaptation of *Richard III* would have its whole first act cut out in case the lamentations of Henry VI caused the audience to reflect on James II, living in exile in France. This censorship was understandable in a period of great political instability and upheaval which saw the replacement of James II by his daughter and son-in-law in 1688; the replacement of the Stuart dynasty by the House of Hanover in 1714; and the invasion of the country by the son of James II in 1715.

With the increasing prosperity and stability of Britain in the eighteenth century, the political imperative to control Drury Lane diminished, but it was replaced by a cultural imperative. Sir Richard Steele's appointment as governor, then patentee, of Drury Lane was a reward for his staunch support for the House of Hanover, but it was more than that. Steele was regarded as a credible reformer of the stage, who would save it from the rising tide of filth and atheism so luridly depicted by Jeremy Collier in his *Short View of the Immorality and Profaneness of the English Stage*. Steele didn't do that much to clean up Drury Lane, and the bawdy old comedies were still being performed, although in 1722 he did produce *The Conscious Lovers*, a smash-hit play that featured a hero who exhibited all the Christian virtues in place of the debauched rakes of the Restoration stage.

The much greater cultural concern was the threat to straight plays from pantomime, which emerged at Drury Lane in 1717 with *The Loves of Mars and Venus*. Pantomime established itself so quickly as the dominant popular form in theatre that there was a genuine fear that serious plays might not survive at all, and the fact that John Rich established the rival house as supreme in pantomime just made the situation worse for the Drury Lane management. In 1724 the triumvirate were proposing to Steele that they should sell the patent, as the competition from 'nonsense of different kinds' at the other theatres was too tough.[21] That didn't happen, and managers succeeded in balancing the demand for pantomime and spectacle with the drama, none more successfully than Garrick, who made Drury Lane a temple to Shakespeare while staying afloat financially with crowd-pleasers like the pantomime *Harlequin's Invasion* (which glorified Shakespeare).

Sheridan rebuilt Drury Lane on a scale that made it problematic for serious plays and more suited to spectacle and melodrama. By the early part of the nineteenth century, there was a feeling that the time had come to abolish the monopoly privileges of the two patent houses, as neither were felt to be fulfilling their remit of safeguarding 'the national drama'. Attempts at reform were defeated by vested interests in 1810 and 1833, but in 1843 the Theatre Regulation Act abolished the exclusive right of Drury Lane and Covent Garden to present plays in London. As *The Times* put it: 'In the drama, as in all things else, the world has arrived a period when the order of the day is Free Trade.'[22]

Under the new dispensation, any theatre in London could put on any sort of show, from burlesque to Ben Jonson. The strange thing is, this in no way diminished the view that Drury Lane had a special place in the culture of the nation, and what went on there was still an issue. The most powerful testimony we have to this is the little pamphlet produced by F.B. Chatterton called *Poets and Profits*, in which he sought to defend himself against charges of philistinism. Chatterton became lessee of Drury Lane in 1866, long after the abolition of the monopoly, but he regarded himself as being in charge of 'a national institution' and 'the leading theatre of the kingdom'.[23] He acknowledged that he was under an obligation 'to keep up the glorious traditions of its past history [and] to pay a due tribute of reverence to its high intellectual and artistic associations' by 'balancing legitimacy and high art that will not pay with the sensational drama and realism that will'.[24] But why did Chatterton feel this need to put on 'legitimate' productions that lost money, when he bore the entire financial risk? His sense of cultural obligation led him to mount loss-making productions of *Antony and Cleopatra* and *The Winter's Tale* that pushed him towards bankruptcy. Following his ruin and the loss of Drury Lane, Chatterton lived for seven years, dependent on the charity of his fellow professionals and fearing that his contribution towards 'the history of the English drama' was already forgotten.[25]

Chatterton's successor as lessee, Augustus Harris, had no time for this sort of cultural baggage. In 1885, by which time he had been in charge of Drury Lane for six years, he wrote an article called 'The National Theatre' for *The Fortnightly Review* in which he tackled head-on these claims about the status of Drury Lane and the obligations of the manager to support them:

> The fact that Drury Lane has been known from time immemorial as the National Theatre seems to have given a section of the public a prescriptive right to interfere in its management, and even to dictate to its proprietors and lessees the bill of fare which they should provide for its gratification. This benevolent intervention has usually taken the form of a more or less imperious demand for the exclusive performance at all risks of what its patrons are pleased to designate the legitimate drama, and a vigorous attempt to declare the intrusion of all other classes of entertainment little less than the wanton desecration of a time-honoured shrine.[26]

The note of irritation that Harris felt towards dramatic theorists who expect other people to risk their money for the sake of 'the legitimate drama' is audible. Harris maintained that his successful policy of pantomime and melodrama had been devised before he even got hold of the lease, and that any deviation towards 'high art' had lost money. George Rignold's *Henry V* and Marie Litton's *As You Like It* both resulted in deficits; the Saxe-Meiningen company drew the admiration of theatre professionals but was only 'a magnificent succès d'estime' as far as the box office was concerned; while Harris referred to the Wagner season as 'the disasters of the German opera'.[27] Harris was unapologetic about taking 'the taste of those I endeavour to please' as his guiding star, and he was very clear in his own mind about what would and wouldn't work at Drury Lane. Small-scale 'cup-and-saucer' plays were no good: Drury Lane demanded 'strong situations and striking spectacle… a performance which must be… dramatic, full of life, novelty and movement; treating, as a rule, of the age in which we live'. 'Literati and antiquarians' might pine for Shakespeare at Drury Lane, 'but the practical and prudent theatrical manager will ever learn a lesson from the eventful history of Drury Lane and carefully frame his programme in accordance with the tastes of the majority of his paying patrons and the old law of supply and demand'. Of course, if the 'literati and antiquarians' were prepared to put their hands in their pockets and offer a subsidy, Harris would take a different view – 'or perhaps they might be influential enough to secure the realisation of their hobby at the expense of the State'.[28]

The campaign for a National Theatre

Harris mentions the possibility of a state subsidy for the theatre as something remote and almost incredible, which it was in the nineteenth century. One or two people, most notably Matthew Arnold, had begun to speak of the need for a national theatre that would function in a different way to commercial enterprises, where profit was the driving force, but philanthropy was supposed to plug the gap between income and expenditure. In 1903, the actor/playwright/director Harley Granville Barker and William Archer, the critic and translator of Ibsen, produced *A National Theatre: Scheme and Estimates*. This proposal, described as the 'blueprint and bible for the National Theatre movement',[29] laid out in great detail the arrangements that would be necessary for a national theatre, in terms of building, management structure, hiring of actors, choice of director and plays. 'It may be asked why… we do not suggest going direct to the government… for the money required. The reason is simply that we believe it would be a waste of time… We must look to private liberality to present a central theatre in London.'[30] Fundraising got under way and a site was purchased in Bloomsbury. The outbreak of World War I put a stop to this, and after the war the Bloomsbury site was sold and another one purchased in Kensington, opposite the Victoria and Albert Museum. Once again, war brought operations to a standstill, and after World War II the Kensington site was exchanged with the London County Council for a site on the South Bank. The LCC had plans to redevelop the South Bank and it was hoped that the presence of a National Theatre would play an important part in reclaiming what had become a notorious and insalubrious area on the doorstep of central London. The establishment of the Arts Council of Great Britain in 1946 introduced public funding of the arts, and although the site was moved twice, the National Theatre opened next to Waterloo Bridge in 1976.

There is a certain irony in the fact that, after having 'been known from time immemorial as the National Theatre',[31] as Augustus Harris put it, Drury Lane was never seriously in the running to be the actual National Theatre when the movement got into its stride. This was because Barker and Archer claimed that their vision could never be realised in any existing London theatre, so a new building was required. In 1930, Barker published a revised version of the *Scheme* in which he insisted that there must be two auditoria, suitable for both domestic and epic drama, so that members of the large permanent company that he envisaged would not be idle when a small-cast play was being performed. Clearly neither Drury Lane nor any other London theatre could fit this brief and, in any case, the size of the Drury Lane auditorium had been regarded as problematic for straight plays since the days of Sheridan.

Nevertheless, Drury Lane still had its champions amongst those who were dubious about the idea of a specially established National Theatre. James Agate, the influential drama critic of *The Sunday Times*, was so overwhelmed by Ivor Novello's *Glamorous Night* that he asked 'why one should bother about the National Theatre when one has this'. Novello himself believed Drury Lane, with its rich historical associations, to be 'more national than any specially founded "National

Theatre" could ever be'.[32] As late as 1956, Basil Dean still believed that Drury Lane would make the ideal National Theatre, and that the whole National Theatre movement had been bedevilled by 'cranks and enthusiasts', most notably George Bernard Shaw, who 'never understood the theatre in the professional sense'.[33] As an experienced actor, playwright, director and producer, Dean believed that Drury Lane was just as well qualified to be the state-subsided theatre as Covent Garden was to be the state-subsidised opera house, and it galled him that opera had achieved this status first. The old rivalry between Bow Street and Drury Lane that had animated Garrick and Sheridan was still alive.

Of course, it was not to be. With the establishment of an actual National Theatre in 1962, appearing in the Old Vic before moving into Denys Lasdun's new building in 1976, the whole question of the appropriateness or otherwise of what Drury Lane was putting on fell into abeyance. It is now the National Theatre's status which adds significance to the choice of plays like *England People Very Nice* or *Can We Talk About This?* Drury Lane can put on whatever it likes, which for the foreseeable future will be musicals.

Does it matter? Are the shades of John Dryden, Colley Cibber, David Garrick, William Charles Macready and F.B. Chatterton shaking their heads in sadness at the disappearance of their beloved Shakespeare from the Lane? Perhaps, but they were all professional men of the theatre who understood the need to get bums on seats. Drury Lane has never received any public or private subsidy, and this is just as much a part of its history as the brilliant comedies of Sheridan and the glorious tragedies of Shakespeare. A comparison with the fortunes of Covent Garden tells us a lot.

The profit motive

From its opening in 1732, Covent Garden was the deadly rival of Drury Lane. The proprietors of each theatre would go to any lengths to undermine those of the other, poaching actors and using 'spoilers'. Although they were the only two theatres that could legally put on plays in London, it sometimes seemed as if there were one too many, and both struggled to attract support. Both were occasionally faced with the prospect of closure and demolition, and by 1843, when the Theatre Regulation Act was passed, Covent Garden had ceased to function as a theatre.[34] Four years later, it became an opera house, which it has remained ever since, and this changed the financial dynamics. Opera has always, since its first introduction into London at the end of the seventeenth century, enjoyed the support of wealthy and aristocratic patrons. With the exception of a few very brief periods, opera has always struggled to pay its way at the box office, so another form of support was found for it: the subscription, under which wealthy opera lovers would guarantee an income to the management for a set period of time in return for seats. This was a private rather than a public subsidy, but it created a very different managerial environment in which the box office was no longer paramount.

From 1888 until his death in 1896, Augustus Harris was manager of Covent Garden as well as Drury Lane, but whereas he had to cover his costs at Drury Lane from ticket sales, at Covent Garden he had the backing of a group of wealthy aristocrats. In 1914, Sir Joseph Beecham used the fortune derived from the famous pills to buy the entire Covent Garden Estate from the Duke of Bedford, so that his son Thomas could have an opera house to conduct in. Even the Beecham fortune was insufficient to sustain the losses indefinitely, and in 1932 it was announced that Sir Thomas Beecham would conduct the very last season at Covent Garden before it was demolished for redevelopment. Once again, a group of wealthy supporters formed a new company to take over the management, so Covent Garden was saved at the eleventh hour. During World War II, it was used as a Mecca dance hall, and after the war it became the first recipient of public funds from the newly established Arts Council. It has always remained the Council's biggest 'client'.

There is no parallel in the history of Drury Lane. There have been no bailouts by wealthy admirers and no grants from the government.

When Drury Lane has faced its crises, the answer has always been found in the emergence of someone who could put on shows that the public wanted to see, from Colley Cibber and David Garrick to Augustus Harris and Ivor Novello. The message of Samuel Johnson's great prologue to David Garrick's management seems to be buried in the building's foundations:

> Ah! let not Censure term our Fate our Choice,
> The Stage but echoes back the publick Voice.
> The Drama's Laws the Drama's Patrons give,
> For we that live to please, must please to live.

Drury Lane has been echoing back the public voice for three-and-a-half centuries. It has seen the triumphs of Garrick, Siddons and Kean as well as those of Carlo the Newfoundland dog and Isaac Van Amburgh's lions. They are all part of its history, threads in a theatrical tapestry that has no equal in the annals of the stage. There is no reason to doubt that Drury Lane will survive for as long as men and women who love theatre continue to be inspired by its remarkable story.

APPENDICES

APPENDIX ONE

Exorcising the Ghost

In spite of its legacy, Drury Lane has attracted little attention from historians. When the Survey of London volume on Drury Lane and Covent Garden was published in 1970, it was noted that: 'in spite of its long career and its association with almost every name famous in the history of the English stage, Drury Lane Theatre still lacks an adequate account of its history'.[1]

In fact, a history of Drury Lane had been published in 1945 by W. Macqueen-Pope, the theatre's publicist for 21 years. Macqueen-Pope, known as Popie, claimed descent from the actress Jane Pope, who had been a member of Garrick's company, and he was the author of numerous books on the theatre. None of these books are taken seriously by theatre historians, owing to what Raymond Mander and Joe Mitchenson described as his tendency towards 'Edwardian nostalgia and a romantic aura in which research and truth have little place'.[2] As a publicist, Macqueen-Pope didn't allow facts to stand in the way of a good story, which is why so many of the tales he tells about Drury Lane belong in the realm of fantasy. Unfortunately, some of them have entered the twilight zone of legends repeated so often they are taken to have some basis in reality. Here are a few.

George II receives news of the defeat of Bonnie Prince Charlie whilst in the Royal Box at Drury Lane

The romance of Macqueen-Pope:

> It was a night in 1746. Rebellion and bloodshed were wracking the land, but the King showed spirit by going to the play. He was in the Royal Box when a dispatch rider, a mask of dust and blood, demanded audience with His Majesty... The rider, sinking to his knees, handed to His Majesty the dispatches from the Duke of Cumberland, announcing the complete defeat and rout of the Young Pretender at Culloden Moor. The King, overjoyed and excited, rushed back into the box... The house gazed at him in amazement, even the players stopped and stared at the foreign gentleman who ruled over them, and now stood frantically waving papers in his hand. George wanted to tell them; but in his frenzy of excitement his little English played him false. All he could do was to yell: 'Hey, hey, hey'.[3]

Fact:

The Battle of Culloden was fought on 16 April 1746. News of the victory reached London several days later. George II was not at Drury Lane when he received it.

Why does Drury Lane have two royal boxes, approached by separate staircases named 'The King's Side' and 'The Prince's Side'?

The romance of Macqueen-Pope:

> Old King George [III] disliked his son heartily. One night, shortly after the new building was opened, the King and the Prince, in separate parties, both visited Drury Lane. The rotunda, then as now the crush room of the theatre, was crowded with nobility and gentry. The Royal father and the Royal son met face to face. Before he could be prevented... old King George got hold of his son, set about him, and soundly smacked his face and boxed his ears. The management decided that such a thing must never happen again. So over the left-hand door went up the words 'King's Side', and over the right 'Prince's Side'. The rotunda was made no man's land for the Royal parties, who were tactfully persuaded to keep in future to the territory allotted to them. And there today you may read those signs, one of Drury Lane's unique curiosities.⁴

Fact:

The incident described by Macqueen-Pope never happened. In 1810, George III suffered his final onset of what was regarded as insanity but was probably porphyria. He never appeared in public again and consequently never visited the present Drury Lane, which opened in 1812. The tradition of having two royal boxes, one for the monarch and one for the Prince of Wales, went back to George II. Because he was hard of hearing, George II asked for the royal box to be moved from the centre of the dress tier of boxes (which had the best view of the stage) to a position adjoining the proscenium arch. At the same time, a 'balancing' box was created on the opposite side of the auditorium for the Prince of Wales. This was partly because all of the first three Georges were on bad terms with their eldest sons and didn't necessarily want to sit with them at the theatre. Furthermore, by the early eighteenth century the Prince of Wales was an important patron of both politics and the arts in his own right.

Who is The Man In Grey?

The romance of Macqueen-Pope:

> It is natural that the grand theatre, so rich in history, so full of years, so colourful of story, should have its own supernatural inhabitant... He is a man of medium height, dressed in a long grey riding cloak of the early eighteenth century, wearing a powdered wig of the period and a three-

cornered hat... Who is this uneasy spirit and why does he walk?... About a century ago, when some work was proceeding in the theatre, workmen employed on the Russell Street side of the upper circle... came to a portion of what seemed to them the main wall, which rang hollow. They called the attention of the foreman in charge to this, and he decided to break through and see what was wrong. It was far more wrong than he had imagined. For when the workmen had hewed their way through the wall, they found themselves suddenly bursting into a small room, which had been bricked up. In that room was a skeleton, and in that skeleton's ribs was a dagger... An inquest was held, an open verdict returned; and the skeleton, which was that of a male, was interred in the little graveyard on the corner of Russell Street and Drury Lane.[5]

Fact:

No skeleton has even been found at Drury Lane; consequently there was no inquest and no burial. Even if a corpse had been bricked up in the theatre in the early part of the eighteenth century, that building was demolished in 1791 and its successor burnt to the ground in 1809. It is inconceivable that anything would have survived at upper circle level. Like the previous stories, this one originates with Macqueen-Pope, so the ghost had waited a long time to put in an appearance. The strongest evidence – that the ghost was seen by the whole cast of *The Dancing Years* in 1939 – is hardly convincing, as Macqueen-Pope was the theatre's publicist at the time. Hiring an actor to dress up in a cloak and three-cornered hat and stand at the back of the upper circle would have been an easy matter.

***

For W. Macqueen-Pope, theatre was about glamour and romance. His breathless prose style reflected the way he spoke about theatre to people who knew that the profession was not really lit by rose-tinted gelatines. One day, Bruce Smith, creator of the spectacular effects Popie admired so much in the Drury Lane melodramas, cut short his gushing by saying: 'Popie, you sound like a pantomime dame auditioning for good fairy.'[6] As a result, Smith was never mentioned in any of Popie's books. Basil Dean was kinder about his ENSA publicist: 'It is enough for this master of collated incident to make some innocent and romantic (in a theatre sense) adornment to a story he is telling and to repeat it two or three times for it to become unalterably fixed in his mind as verifiable fact.'[7]

Having said all of which, Macqueen-Pope had a deep sense of the historical and cultural significance of Drury Lane, which is why his words form the epigraph to this book.

APPENDIX TWO

The Four Theatres Royal

The first Theatre Royal, Drury Lane opened in 1663 on a site behind the back-yards of properties fronting onto Bridges Street (now Catherine Street), Russell Street, Drury Lane and Vinegar Yard. The land (like the whole Covent Garden estate) belonged to the Earls (later the Dukes) of Bedford, but some plots surrounding the site had been sold off under an arrangement known as fee-farm.

Following the fire of 1672, the second Theatre Royal opened in 1674. When David Garrick took over the management of this building in 1747, he regarded the auditorium, which seated about 1,000, as too small. Garrick was unable to expand the main structure, so he acquired the leases on surrounding properties into which he moved features of the theatre such as foyers, staircases, refreshment rooms and offices. This enabled the expansion of the auditorium, which grew in capacity to about 2,300. In the summer of 1775, Garrick commissioned Robert Adam to rebuild the auditorium and to put a grand frontage onto the entrance from Bridges Street.

When Sheridan took over the theatre from Garrick, he persuaded the Duke of Bedford to buy back the surrounding land that his family had once controlled and to issue a lease for a much larger site. The third Theatre Royal, which opened in 1794, was therefore significantly bigger than its predecessors. It burned down in 1809.

The fourth Theatre Royal, which opened in 1812, had its front wall on Bridges Street and a scene room at the back on Drury Lane, which took the theatre building from one end of the block to the other for the first time. In 1897 the theatre gave up some land on the Vinegar Yard side and, in return, the Duke of Bedford granted a lease on further land fronting onto Drury Lane. The theatre had also acquired the leases of houses at 67-70 Drury Lane. Although they were not incorporated into the theatre, the Drury Lane management now controlled the entire island site bounded by Drury Lane, Russell Street, Catherine Street and Vinegar Yard (which still exists as a narrow passage onto which the fire exits disgorge theatregoers at the end of the show).

The Four Theatres Royal

Site plan 1661–1748

Based on leases and fee-farm grants in the Greater London Record Office. Hatched areas represent land sold by the Earls of Bedford before 1661. Unhatched areas represent land owned by the Earls and Dukes of Bedford.

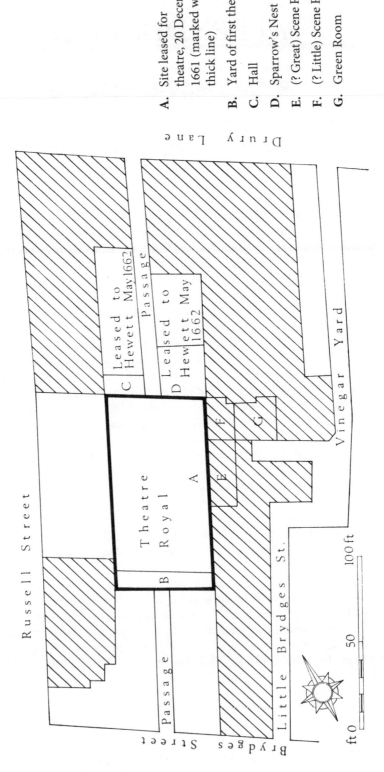

A. Site leased for theatre, 20 December 1661 (marked with thick line)

B. Yard of first theatre

C. Hall

D. Sparrow's Nest

E. (? Great) Scene Room

F. (? Little) Scene Room

G. Green Room

From *Survey of London* XXXV, Athlone Press/GLC/English Heritage, 1970.

The First Theatre Royal: Killigrew's Drury Lane

Opened 7 May 1663

First performance
The Humorous Lieutenant by Beaumont and Fletcher

Architect
Richard Ryder?
Christopher Wren?

Cost £2,505 0s. 6d.

Seating capacity
Unknown

Closed
25 January 1672

Reason for closure Burnt down

Last performance
The Miser by Thomas Shadwell, an adaptation of *L'Avare* by Molière.*

*We do not have the date of this performance, but the preface to the published edition of the play claims that it was the last play to be performed in Drury Lane before the fire. This could mean the last *new* play.

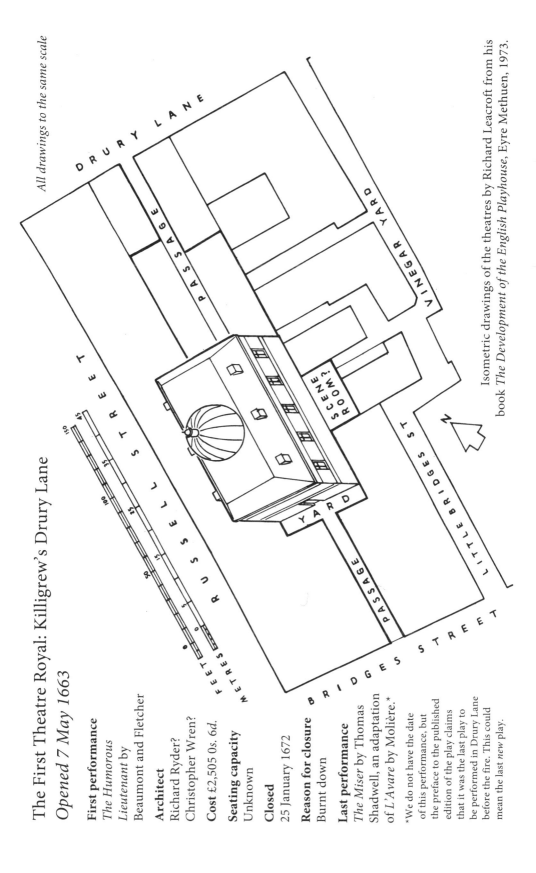

All drawings to the same scale

Isometric drawings of the theatres by Richard Leacroft from his book *The Development of the English Playhouse*, Eyre Methuen, 1973.

All drawings to the same scale

The Second Theatre Royal: Garrick's Drury Lane
Opened 26 March 1674

Robert Adam's rebuilding – Opened 23 September 1775

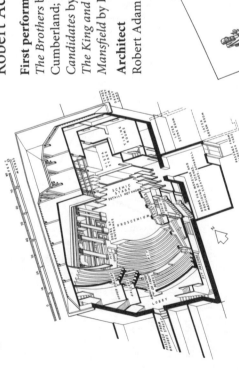

First performance
The Brothers by Richard
Cumberland; *The Theatrical
Candidates* by Garrick;
*The King and the Miller of
Mansfield* by Robert Dodsley

Architect
Robert Adam

Cost £4,000 guineas (£4,200)

Seating capacity
Less than 2,362

Closed Saturday
4 June 1791

Reason for closure
Demolished

Last performance
The Country Girl by David Garrick/
William Wycherley; *No Song No Supper*
by Prince Hoare and Stephen Storace

First performance
Beggar's Bush by
Fletcher (Massinger?
Beaumont?)

Architect
Christopher Wren?

Cost £3,908

Seating capacity
1,001 before 1747;
1,268 after 1747;
2,362 (max) after 1762

Closed
Saturday 27 May 1775

Reason for closure
Reconstruction of
auditorium

Last performance
Matilda by Thomas
Francklin and *Bon
Ton* by David Garrick

All drawings to the same scale

The Third Theatre Royal: Sheridan's Drury Lane
Opened 21 April 1794

First performance
Macbeth by William Shakespeare;
The Virgin Unmask'd by Henry Fielding

Architect
Henry Holland

Cost £78,730 10s. 6d.

Seating capacity
3,611

Closed
Friday 24 February 1809

Reason for closure
Burnt down

Last performance
The Circassian Bride, music by
Henry Bishop, libretto by C.
Ward, on 23 February 1809,
the night before the fire. *

*The fire occurred on a Friday night. There were no
performances on Wednesdays or Fridays during Lent.

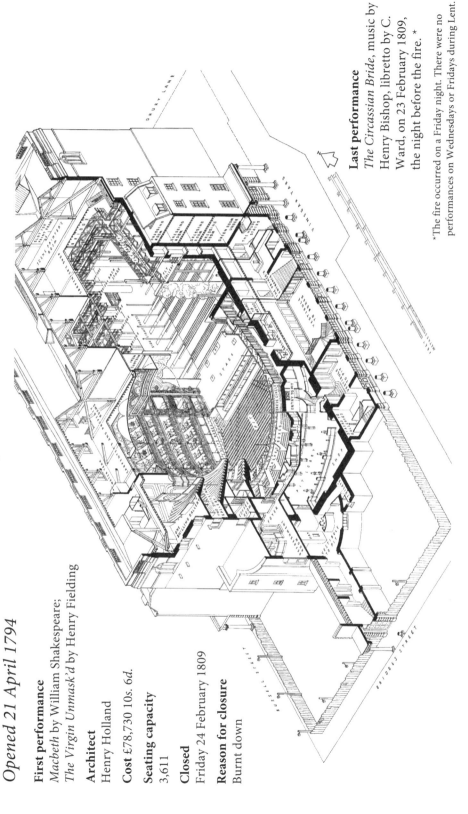

All drawings to the same scale

The Fourth Theatre Royal: Our Drury Lane
Opened 10 October 1812

First performance
Hamlet by William Shakespeare;
The Devil to Pay by Charles Coffey

Architect
Benjamin Dean Wyatt

Cost £151,672

Seating capacity
3,214; 3,060 after remodelling
by Beazley in 1822

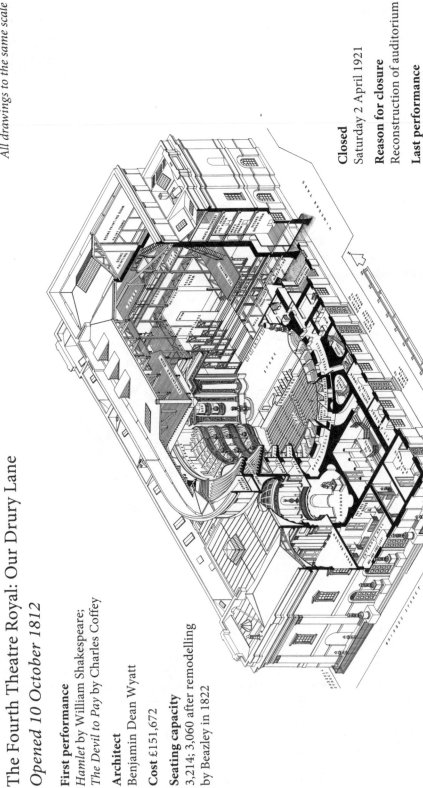

Closed
Saturday 2 April 1921

Reason for closure
Reconstruction of auditorium

Last performance
The Garden of Allah, by
Robert Hitchens and Mary
Anderson

All drawings to the same scale

Remodelling of auditorium
Opened 20 April 1922

First performance
Decameron Nights by
Robert McLaughlin

Architect
J. Emblin Walker, F.
Edward Jones, Robert
Cromie

Cost £150,000

Seating capacity
2,600. Reduced on several remodellings to 2,283 (1971)
and currently 2,200

Bibliography

G.A. Aitken (ed.) *Richard Steele: Plays* (The Mermaid Series), London: T. Fisher Unwin, 1926

Barry Anthony, *The King's Jester: The life of Dano Leno, Victorian comic genius*, London: I.B. Tauris, 2010

William Archer, *William Charles Macready*, London: Kegan Paul, Trench, Trübner and Co, 1890

Emmett L. Avery, 'The Shakespeare Ladies Club', *Shakespeare Quarterly*, 7 (1956) 153-58

H. Barton Baker, *The London Stage: Its history and traditions from 1576 to 1888*, London, W.H. Allen, 2 vols, 1889

Martin C. Battestin, 'Fielding, Henry (1707–1754)', *Oxford Dictionary of National Biography*, Oxford University Press, 2004

Mark Batty, 'Booth, Barton (1681–1733)', *Oxford Dictionary of National Biography*, Oxford University Press, 2004

Kate Bennett, 'Wycherley, William (bap. 1641, d. 1716)', *Oxford Dictionary of National Biography*, Oxford University Press, 2004

George Biddlecombe, 'Bunn, Alfred (1796–1860)', *Oxford Dictionary of National Biography*, Oxford University Press, 2004

Michael R. Booth, *Theatre in the Victorian Age*, Cambridge: Cambridge University Press, 1991

Gyles Brandreth, *The Funniest Man on Earth: The Story of Dan Leno*, London: Hamish Hamilton, 1977

Charles Brayne, 'Fleetwood, Charles (d. 1747)', *Oxford Dictionary of National Biography*, Oxford University Press, 2004

Andrew Brown, 'Lytton, Edward George Earle Lytton Bulwer, first Baron Lytton (1803–1873)', *Oxford Dictionary of National Biography*, Oxford University Press, 2004

Clive Brown, 'Balfe, Michael William (1808–1870)', *Oxford Dictionary of National Biography*, Oxford University Press, 2004; online edn, Oct 2007

Reed Browning, 'Holles, Thomas Pelham-, duke of Newcastle-upon-Tyne and first duke of Newcastle-under-Lyme (1693–1768)', *Oxford Dictionary of National Biography*, Oxford University Press, 2004; online edn, May 2011

Alfred Bunn, *The Stage: Both Before and Behind the Curtain, From 'Observations Taken on the Spot'*, 2 vols, Lea and Blanchard: Philadelphia, 1840

William J. Burling, 'Doggett, Thomas (c.1670–1721)', *Oxford Dictionary of National Biography*, Oxford University Press, 2004

Dennis Castle, *'Sensation' Smith of Drury Lane*, London: Charles Skilton, 1984

W.D. Christie (ed.) *The Poetical Works of John Dryden*, London: Macmillan and Co., 1881

Colley Cibber, *An Apology for the Life of Colley Cibber: with an historical view of the stage during his own time, written by himself* (ed. B.R.S. Fone) Ann Arbor: University of Michigan Press, [1740] 1968

John Coleman, *Players and Playwrights I Have Known: A review of the English stage from 1840 to 1880*, London: Chatto & Windus, 2 vols, 1888

Andrew Crowhurst, 'Butt, Sir Alfred, first baronet (1878–1962)', *Oxford Dictionary of National Biography*, Oxford University Press, 2004

Jim Davis (ed.), *Victorian Pantomime: A Collection of Critical Essays*, Basingstoke: Palgrave Macmillan, 2010

Basil Dean, *Seven Ages: an autobiography 1888-1927*, London: Hutchinson, 1970

Basil Dean, *The Theatre at War*, London: George Harrap, 1956

Christian Deelman, *The Great Shakespeare Jubilee*, London: Michael Joseph, 1964

Phyllis T. Dircks, 'Rich, John (1692–1761)', *Oxford Dictionary of National Biography*, Oxford University Press, 2004; online edn, May 2011

Brian Dobbs, *Drury Lane: Three centuries of the Theatre Royal 1663-1971*, London: Cassell, 1972

Alan S. Downer, *The Eminent Tragedian: William Charles Macready*, Cambridge, MA: Harvard University Press, 1966

John Downes, *Roscius Anglicanus*, (eds. Judith Milhous and Robert D. Hume) London: The Society for Theatre Research, 1987

John Dryden, *John Dryden: Of Dramatic Poesy and Other Critical Essays* (ed. George Watson) London: J.M. Dent and Sons Ltd, 2 vols, 1962

Mary Edmond, 'Davenant, Sir William (1606–1668)', *Oxford Dictionary of National Biography*, Oxford University Press, 2004; online edn, Oct 2009

John Elsom and Nicholas Tomalin, *The History of the National Theatre*, London: Jonathan Cape, 1978

Richard Fawkes, *Dion Boucicault: A Biography*, London: Quartet Books, 1979

C.Y. Ferdinand and D.F. McKenzie, 'William Congreve', *Oxford Dictionary of National Biography*, Oxford: Oxford University Press, 2004; online edn, Jan 2008

John Field, *The King's Nurseries: The Story of Westminster School*, London: James and James, 1987

Ophelia Field, *The Kit-Cat Club: Friends who imagined a nation*, London: Harper Press, 2008

D. R. Fisher, 'Whitbread, Samuel (1764–1815)', *Oxford Dictionary of National Biography*, Oxford University Press, 2004; online edn, Jan 2008

Percy Fitzgerald, *A New History of the English Stage: From the Restoration to the liberty of the theatres, in connection with the patent houses*, London: Tinsley Brothers, 2 vols, 1882

Richard Foulkes, 'Macready, William Charles (1793–1873)', *Oxford Dictionary of National Biography*, Oxford University Press, 2004; online edn, Jan 2008

Mark Fox, *Theatre Royal Drury Lane*, London: Really Useful Group, 2000

Roger Fulford, *Samuel Whitbread: A study in opposition*, London: Macmillan, 1967

John Genest, *Some Account of the English Stage From the Restoration in 1660 to 1830*, 10 vols, London: Thomas Rodd, 1832

Christine Gerrard, *Aaron Hill: the Muses' Projector 1685-1750*, Oxford: Oxford University Press, 2003

Elizabeth Gibson, 'Swiny, Owen (1676–1754)', *Oxford Dictionary of National Biography*, Oxford University Press, 2004; online edn, Jan 2008

Jane Girdham, *English Opera in Late Eighteenth-Century London: Stephen Storace at Drury Lane*, Oxford: Clarendon Press, 1997

David J. Golby, 'Arne, Thomas Augustine (1710–1778)', *Oxford Dictionary of National Biography*, Oxford University Press, 2004; online edn, May 2009

Robert Gore-Browne, *Gay Was the Pit: The life and times of Anne Oldfield, actress (1683-1730)* London: Max Reinhardt, 1957

Joseph Grimaldi, *The Memoirs of Joseph Grimaldi, edited by 'Boz'*, London: 1838

Paul Hammond, 'Dryden, John (1631–1700)', *Oxford Dictionary of National Biography*, Oxford University Press, 2004; online edn, Oct 2009

Augustus Harris, 'The National Theatre', *The Fortnightly Review*, **18**, July-December 1885, 630-636

Augustus Harris, 'Spectacle', *The Magazine of Art*, **12**, 1889, 109-113

John Harris, Stephen Orgel, Roy Strong, *The King's Arcadia: Inigo Jones and the Stuart Court*, London: Arts Council of Great Britain, 1973

William Hazlitt, *The Selected Writings of William Hazlitt*, iii, 'A View of the English Stage', Duncan Wu (ed.), London: Pickering and Chatto, 1998

Philip Hoare, 'Coward, Sir Noël Peirce (1899–1973)', *Oxford Dictionary of National Biography*, Oxford University Press, 2004; online edn, Jan 2011

Leslie Hotson, *The Commonwealth and Restoration Stage*, Cambridge, MA: Harvard University Press, 1928

Robert D. Hume, 'The Nature of the Dorset Garden Theatre', *Theatre Notebook*, **36**, 1982, 99-109

Robert D. Hume, *Henry Fielding and the London Theatre 1728–1737*, Oxford: The Clarendon Press, 1988

Robert D. Hume and Harold Love (eds.) *Plays, Poems and Miscellaneous Writings associated with George Villiers, Second Duke of Buckingham*, Oxford: Oxford University Press, 2007

Norman Jeffares, 'Sheridan, Richard Brinsley (1751–1816)', *Oxford Dictionary of National Biography*, Oxford University Press, 2004; online edn, Jan 2008

Norman Jeffares, 'Sheridan, Thomas (1775–1817)', *Oxford Dictionary of National Biography*, Oxford University Press, 2004; online edn, Jan 2008

Samuel Johnson, *Lives of the English Poets*, [1779-1781] London: Oxford University Press, 2 vols, originally published 1906. Edition used 1967-1968

Ben Jonson, *Ben Jonson*, edited by C.H. Herford, Percy and Evelyn Simpson, Oxford: Clarendon Press, vol. vii & vol. viii, 1941 & 1947

Linda Kelly, *The Kemble Era: John Philip Kemble, Sarah Siddons and the London Stage*, London: The Bodley Head, 1980

Linda Kelly, *Richard Brinsley Sheridan: A Life*, London: Faber & Faber, [1997] 2008

Michael Kelly, *Reminiscences*, (ed. Roger Fiske) London: Oxford University Press, [1826] 1975

Charles Lamb Kenney, *Poets and Profits at Drury Lane Theatre: A theatrical narrative*, London: Aubert's Steam Printing Works, 1875

Shirley Strum Kenny, 'Farquhar, George (1676/7–1707)', *Oxford Dictionary of National Biography*, Oxford University Press, 2004

Richard Leacroft, *The Development of the English Playhouse*, London: Eyre Methuen, 1973

Michael Leapman, *Inigo: The troubled life of Inigo Jones, architect of the English Renaissance*, London: Review, 2003

Martin J. Levy, 'Robinson, Mary [Perdita] (1756/1758?–1800)', *Oxford Dictionary of National Biography*, Oxford University Press, 2004; online edn, Jan 2008

John Levitt, 'King, Thomas (1730–1805)', *Oxford Dictionary of National Biography*, Oxford University Press, 2004; online edn, Jan 2007

Thomas Lockwood (ed.) *Henry Fielding: Plays, Volume Three 1734-1742*, Oxford: Clarendon Press, 2011

John Loftis, *Steele at Drury Lane*, Berkeley and Los Angeles: University of California Press, 1952

Harold Love, 'Sackville, Charles, sixth earl of Dorset and first earl of Middlesex (1643–1706)', *Oxford Dictionary of National Biography*, Oxford University Press, 2004; online edn, Jan 2008

Jack Lynch, *Becoming Shakespeare: How a dead poet became the world's foremost literary genius*, London: Constable, 2007

Fiona MacCarthy, *Byron: Life and Legend*, London: John Murray, 2002

Ian McIntyre, *Garrick*, London: Allen Lane, Penguin, 1999

Dougald MacMillan, *Drury Lane Calendar 1747-1776*, Oxford: The Clarendon Press, 1938

W.J. Macqueen-Pope, *Pillars of Drury Lane*, London: Hutchinson, 1955

W.J. Macqueen-Pope, *Theatre Royal Drury Lane*, London: W.H. Allen, 1945

William Charles Macready, *The Journal of William Charles Macready, 1832-1851*, abridged and edited by J. C. Trewin, London: Longmans, 1967

David Mayer III, *Harlequin in His Element*, Cambridge, MA: Harvard University Press, 1969

Judith Milhous, 'Christopher Rich', *Oxford Dictionary of National Biography*, Oxford: Oxford University Press, 2004; online edn, Jan 2008

Judith Milhous, 'Betterton, Thomas (bap. 1635, d. 1710)', *Oxford Dictionary of National Biography*, Oxford University Press, 2004; online edn, Sept 2010

Judith Milhous and Robert D. Hume (eds.) *A Register of English Theatrical Documents 1660-1737*, Carbondale and Edwardsville, Southern Illinois: University Press, 2 vols, 1991

Judith Milhous and Robert D. Hume (eds.) *Vice-Chamberlain Coke's Theatrical Papers 1706-1715*, Carbondale and Edwardsville Southern Illinois: University Press, 1982

Jane Moody, 'Grimaldi, Joseph (1778–1837)', *Oxford Dictionary of National Biography*, Oxford University Press, 2004, online edn, Jan 2008

Christopher Murray, *Robert William Elliston, Manager*, London: Society for Theatre Research, 1975

Christopher Murray, 'Elliston, Robert William (1774–1831)', *Oxford Dictionary of National Biography*, Oxford University Press, 2004

Allardyce Nicoll, *A History of Restoration Drama: 1660-1700*, Ann Arbor: University of Michigan Press, 1952

Watson Nicholson, *The Struggle for a Free Stage in London*, Boston and New York: Houghton, Mifflin and Company, 1906

Peter Noble, *Ivor Novello: Man of the Theatre*, London: Falcon Press, 1951

John O'Brien, *Harlequin Britain: Pantomime and Entertainment, 1690-1760*, Johns Hopkins University Press, 2004

Edward Pearce, *The Great Man: Scoundrel, Genius and Britain's First Prime Minister*, London: Jonathan Cape, 2007

Hesketh Pearson, *The Last Actor-Managers*, London: White Lion Publishers, [1950] 1974

Harry William Pedicord, *By Their Majesties' Command: The House of Hanover at the London Theatres, 1714-1800*, London: The Society for Theatre Research, 1991

Harry William Pedicord, *The Theatrical Public in the Time of Garrick*, Carbondale and Edwardsville: Southern Illinois University Press, 1954

Harry William Pedicord and Frederick Louis Bergmann (eds.) *The Plays of David Garrick*, Carbondale and Edwardsville: Southern Illinois University Press, vol. 2, 1980

Gill Perry with Joseph Roach and Shearer West, *The First Actresses: Nell Gwyn to Sarah Siddons*, London: National Portrait Gallery, 2011

J.R. Planché, *The Extravaganzas of J. R. Planché*, London: Samuel French, vol. 2, 1879

J.R. Planché, *The Jewess: A Grand Operatic Drama*, London: Porter and Wright, 1835

J.R. Planché, *The Recollections and Reflections of J.R. Planché*, 2 vols, Cambridge: Cambridge University Press, [1872] 2011

Giles Playfair, *Kean: The life and paradox of a great actor*, London: Columbus Books, [1939] 1988

Giles Playfair, *The Prodigy: A Study of the Strange Life of Master Betty*, London: Secker and Warburg, 1967

Jonathan Pritchard, 'Dennis, John (1658–1734)', *Oxford Dictionary of National Biography*, Oxford University Press, 2004

Leslie du S. Read, 'Weaver, John (1673–1760)', *Oxford Dictionary of National Biography*, Oxford University Press, 2004

Frederick Reynolds, *The Life and Times of Frederick Reynolds, written by himself*, London: Henry Colburn, 2 vols, 1826

Marcus Risdell (ed.) *The Face and Figure of Shakespeare: How Britain's 18th century sculptors invented a national hero*, catalogue of an exhibition at Orleans House Gallery, Twickenham, 18 April – 7 June 2009, Orleans House Gallery, 2009

David Roberts, *Thomas Betterton: The Greatest Actor of the Restoration Stage*, Cambridge: Cambridge University Press, 2010

James Roose-Evans, 'Dean, Basil Herbert (1888–1978)', *Oxford Dictionary of National Biography*, Oxford University Press, 2004; online edn, Jan 2011

Richard Rose, *The World of Ivor Novello: Perchance to Dream*, London: Leslie Frewin, 1974

George Rowell (ed.) *Victorian Dramatic Criticism*, London: Methuen, 1971

Eric Salmon, 'Cibber, Colley (1671–1757)', *Oxford Dictionary of National Biography*, Oxford University Press, 2004, online edn, May 2012

Eric Salmon, 'Cibber, Theophilus (1703–1758)', *Oxford Dictionary of National Biography*, Oxford University Press, 2004; online edn, May 2005

Eric Salmon, 'Collier, Jeremy (1650–1726)', *Oxford Dictionary of National Biography*, Oxford University Press, 2004

Virginia P. Scott, 'The Infancy of English Pantomime: 1716-1723', *Educational Theatre Journal*, **24**, no. 2, 125-134, May 1972

Robert Shaughnessy, 'Macklin, Charles (1699?–1797)', *Oxford Dictionary of National Biography*, Oxford University Press, 2004

George R. Sims, *My Life: Sixty years' recollections of bohemian London*, London: Eveleigh Nash Co., 1917

Edward Stirling, *Old Drury Lane: Fifty years' recollections of author, actor and manager*, 2 vols., London: Chatto & Windus, 1881

Andrew McConnell Stott, *The Pantomime Life of Joseph Grimaldi: Laughter, Madness and the Story of Britain's Greatest Comedian*, Edinburgh: Canongate, 2009

Maureen Sullivan (ed.) *Colley Cibber: Three sentimental comedies*, New Haven: Yale University Press, 1973

Survey of London XXXV: The Theatre Royal Drury Lane and the Royal Opera House Covent Garden, General Editor F.H.W. Sheppard, London: The Athlone Press, 1970

C. M. P. Taylor, 'Hammond, William John (1797x9–1848)', *Oxford Dictionary of National Biography*, Oxford University Press, 2004; online edn, Jan 2008

Daniel Crane Taylor, *William Congreve*, New York: Russell and Russell, 1963

Peter Thomson, 'Farren, Elizabeth [married name Elizabeth Smith Stanley, countess of Derby] (1759x62–1829)', *Oxford Dictionary of National Biography*, Oxford University Press, 2004

Peter Thomson, 'Kean, Edmund (1787–1833)', *Oxford Dictionary of National Biography*, Oxford University Press, 2004; online edn, Jan 2008

Simon Thurley, 'Theatre Royal: Drury Lane: The Crucible of Modern Theatre' in *Lost Buildings of Britain*, London: Viking, 2004

Claire Tomalin, *Mrs Jordan's Profession: The story of a great actress and a future King*, London: Penguin Books, [1994] 1995

J.C. Trewin, *Benson and the Bensonians*, London: Barrie and Rockliff, 1960

John M. Turner, 'Smith, Edward Tyrrel (1804–1877)', *Oxford Dictionary of National Biography*, Oxford University Press, 2004

Jenny Uglow, *A Gambling Man: Charles II and the Restoration*, London: Faber and Faber, 2009

J. P. Vander Motten, 'Killigrew, Thomas (1612–1683)', *Oxford Dictionary of National Biography*, Oxford University Press, 2004; online edn, Jan 2008

William Van Lennep (ed.) *The London Stage 1660-1800: A calendar of plays, entertainments & afterpieces together with casts, box-receipts and contemporary comment compiled from the playbills, newspapers and theatrical diaries of the period*, edited in five parts by Emmett L. Avery, Arthur H. Scouten, George Winchester Stone, Jr and Charles Beecher Hogan, 11 vols, Carbondale, Illinois: Southern Illinois University Press, 1960-68

Eugene Waith (ed.) *Restoration Drama*, New York: Bantam , 1968

W.C. Ward (ed.) *William Wycherley* (The Mermaid Series) London: Ernest Benn, 1948

Gerald Weales, *The Complete Plays of William Wycherley*, New York: Anchor Books, 1966

Staring B. Wells (ed.) *A Comparison Between the Two Stages,* Princeton: Princeton University Press, [1702] 1942

John Harold Wilson, *All the King's Ladies: Actresses of the Restoration*, Chicago: University of Chicago Press, 1958

M. Glen Wilson, 'Kean, Charles John (1811–1868)', *Oxford Dictionary of National Biography*, Oxford University Press, 2004; online edn, Jan 2008

Sandy Wilson, *Ivor*, London: Michael Joseph, 1975

James Anderson Winn, *John Dryden and His World*, New Haven & London: Yale University Press, 1987

James Winston, *Drury Lane Journal: Selections from James Winston's Diaries 1819-1827*, Alfred L. Nelson and Gilbert B. Cross (eds.), London: Society for Theatre Research, 1974

Calhoun Winton, 'Steele, Sir Richard (bap. 1672, d. 1729)', *Oxford Dictionary of National Biography*, Oxford University Press, 2004; online edn, Oct 2005

James Wright, *Historia Histrionica: An historical account of the English stage shewing the ancient use, improvement, and perfection of dramatick representations in this nation. In a dialogue of plays and players*, first printed in 1699 by G. Groom for William Hawes. Later republished as 'A Dialogue on Plays and Players' in *A Select Collection of Old Plays*, London: Robert Dodsley, 1744, xi, and subsequent editions of that work; also reprinted in Robert Lowe's 1889 edition of Cibber's *Apology*

S. M. Wynne, 'Gwyn, Eleanor (1651?–1687)', *Oxford Dictionary of National Biography*, Oxford University Press, 2004; online edn, Sept 2010

Notes

INTRODUCTION

1 Quoted in *The London Stage*, Part I, lxxviii.
2 BM E1115.15 quoted in Hotson, 5.
3 Inigo Jones supported Charles I in the Civil War and was taken prisoner by the Roundheads when they stormed Basing House in 1645. He was described in the news-sheets as 'the King's Surveyor, and contriver of scenes for the Queen's Dancing Barne'. (Harris *et al.* 209.) On 16 July 1645 the House of Commons ordered the pulling down of 'the boarded masque-house at Whitehall'. (Hotson, 13.)
4 Prologue written by Sir William Davenant for the performance of *The Silent Woman* by Ben Jonson before the King in the Cockpit at Whitehall Palace, 19 November 1660, quoted in Hotson, 208.
5 Samuel Pepys, Diary, 24 May 1660.
6 Samuel Pepys, Diary, 13 February 1668.
7 The full texts of the Davenant and Killigrew patents are reproduced in Fitzgerald, i, 73-80.
8 John Evelyn, Diary, 18 October 1666.
9 Samuel Pepys, Diary, 15 August 1661.
10 Samuel Pepys, Diary, 24 August 1661.
11 The full text of the warrant, which passed the privy signet on 21 August 1660, is given in Fitzgerald, i, 23-24.
12 Samuel Pepys, Diary, 4 July 1661.

1: CURTAIN UP

1 Samuel Pepys, Diary, 8 May 1663.
2 Balthasar de Monconys, *Journal des Voyages de Monsieur de Monconys*, Lyons, 1666, Part 2, 25-6.
3 The visitor was Prince Cosmo III of Tuscany. Conte Lorenzo Magalotti, *The Travels of Cosmo the Third*, London, 1821, 190-1.
4 Samuel Pepys, Diary, 1 May 1668.

2: WHICH SHOW GOES ON?

1 Calculation by A.R.Botica, 'Audience, Playhouse and Play in English Restoration Theatre, 1660-1700', unpublished DPhil Thesis, Oxford University, 1985, 35; quoted in Roberts, 73.
2 'Thomas Otway' in Samuel Johnson, *Lives of the English Poets,* i, 166.
3 Quoted in Winn, 145. In fact, *Henry V* would appear at Lincoln's Inn Fields, not the new Theatre Royal.
4 Memoirs of Dr Robert Creighton, preserved in the Muniments of Trinity College, Cambridge, quoted in Winn, 68.
5 Dryden, *Of Dramatic Poesy*, i, 85.
6 Dryden, 'To My Dear Friend Mr Congreve, on his Comedy Called *The Double Dealer*', 1693, in Christie, 315.
7 Dryden, *Of Dramatic Poesy*, i, 44.
8 Dryden, *Of Dramatic Poesy*, i, 67.
9 Dryden, *Of Dramatic Poesy*, i, 76.
10 Quoted in Uglow, 9.
11 'Defence of the Epilogue' [to *The Conquest of Granada*, 1672], in Dryden, *Of Dramatic Poesy*, i, 169.
12 Johnson, 'John Dryden', *Lives of the Poets*, i, 248.
13 John Dryden, *The Conquest of Grenada*, Part 1, Act I, Scene 1.
14 Printed in *A Royal Arbour of Loyal Poesie* by Thomas Jordan, 1664.
15 Samuel Pepys, Diary, 2 March 1667.

16 'Nell Gwyn and Covent Garden
   Goddesses' by Joseph Roach in
   Perry, Roach and West, 71.

3: THE ANNUS MIRABILIS OF 1671

1 Mrs Mary Evelyn to Mr Bohun, circa
  January 1671, *The Diary and
  Correspondence of John Evelyn*, ed.
  William Bray, iv, 25.
2 Johnson, 'Dryden', *Lives of the Poets*,
  i, 247.
3 John Evelyn, Diary, 10 February
  1671, referred to 'very glorious
  scenes and perspectives'.
4 William Wycherley, *Love in a Wood*,
  Act II, Scene 1.
5 William Wycherley, *Love in a Wood*,
  Act V, Scene 6.
6 William Wycherley, *Love in a Wood*,
  Act I, Scene 2.
7 John Dryden, *Marriage à la Mode*,
  Act IV, Scene 3
8 John Dryden, *Marriage à la Mode*,
  Act II, Scene 1.
9 Fitzgerald, i, 22.
10 George Villiers, Duke of Buckingham,
   The Rehearsal, Act I, Scene 2.
11 The account of the character's
   costume and mannerisms emerged
   in 1730, while the story about
   Dryden sitting in the box, between
   the Duke of Buckingham and the
   Earl of Dorset, doesn't appear in
   print until Thomas Davies's
   Dramatic Miscellanies, 1784.
12 John Dryden, *Absalom and
   Achitophel*, lines 545-550.

4: A DOWNWARD SPIRAL

1 The site today is covered by the
  Victoria Embankment and no longer
  has a river frontage.
2 John Dryden, Prologue and Epilogue
  to the University of Oxford, 1673. In
  Christie, 422.
3 Downes, 74 (page 35 of Downes's
  original pamphlet).

4 John Wilson (*All The King's Ladies*,
  32-33) found evidence of such
  proceedings against 22 actors in the
  King's Company, some of them many
  times over, but only nine against
  members of the Duke's Company.
5 John Dryden, 'Prologue to the
  University of Oxford' (1681), in
  Christie, 450.
6 11 May 1681: £3 14*s*. 6d; 30 May
  1681: £3 2*s*.; 18 June 1681: £3.13*s*.
  Hotson, 267.

5: THE UNITED COMPANY

1 Cibber, 59-60.
2 Wells, 11.
3 Cibber, 139.
4 'Upon a run of good audiences, he
  was more frightened to be thought a
  gainer, which might make him
  accountable to others, than he was
  dejected with bad houses, which at
  worst, he knew, would make others
  accountable to him.' Cibber, 185.
5 Downes, 89. The page number in
  Downes's pamphlet was 43.
6 Cibber, 145.
7 Roberts, 159.
8 Nicoll, 1952, 378.
9 The full text of 'The Petition of the
  Players' is printed in Judith Milhous,
  *Thomas Betterton and the Management
  of Lincoln's Inn Fields, 1695-1708*,
  Carbondale: Southern Illinois
  University Press, 1979, Appendix A.
10 *Memoirs Relating to Mr Congreve
   Written by Mr Thomas Southern*,
   quoted in *The London Stage* Part 1, 419.
11 Dryden to Walsh, quoted in Taylor
   (1963) 45.
12 When it had last been used as a
   theatre, it had been the Duke of
   York's. With the Duke, who became
   James II, now living in exile as a
   guest of Louis XIV, no one wanted
   to remember that connection.
13 Cibber, 115.

14 Cibber, 46.

15 Cibber, 102.

16 Cibber doesn't record this story in his *Apology*. It first appears in print in *Dramatic Miscellanies* by Thomas Davies, published in 1784.

6: SENTIMENTAL COMEDY AND THE LAST OF THE RAKES

1 Wells, 16.

2 Pepys, Diary, 27 December 1662.

3 Cibber, 126.

4 Samuel Johnson, 'Congreve', *Lives of the English Poets*, ii, 27.

5 John Dryden, 'A Defence of *An Essay of Dramatic Poesy*, being an answer to the preface of *The Great Favourite or the Duke of Lerma'*, prefixed to *The Indian Emperor* (1668). Reprinted in Dryden, *Of Dramatic Poesy*, i, 113.

6 John Vanbrugh, *A Short Vindication of* The Relapse *and* The Provok'd Wife *from Immorality and Profaneness*, London, 1698, 46 & 4.

7 Letter from John Dryden to Mrs Steward dated 4 March 1699. *The Letters of John Dryden*, ed. C.E. Ward, Durham, North Carolina, 1942, 113.

8 Cibber, 151.

9 Wells, 52.

10 Letter from John Dryden to Mrs Steward dated 12 March 1699. *The Letters of John Dryden*, ed. C.E. Ward, Durham, North Carolina, 1942, 133-34.

11 John Dryden, from the dedication of *Amphitryon* (1690) for which Purcell had written the music. Quoted in Winn, 444.

12 Wells, 7.

7: A TUMULTUOUS DECADE

1 Horace Walpole, *Anecdotes of Painting in England*, 1761-1771, quoted in Field, 271.

2 Field, 137.

3 BL Landsdowne MS 1,024, quoted in Field, 138.

4 Quoted in Taylor (1963) 185.

5 Downes, 99. (Page 48 in Downes's original pamphlet.)

6 Letter from Congreve to Joseph Keally, 15 December 1705.

7 Cibber, 180.

8 The composite was called *Marriage à la Mode or The Comical Lovers*.

9 The full text of the conveyance, dated 6 October 1707, is reprinted in Fitzgerald, i, 252-57.

10 The immediate complaint was from Mrs Oldfield regarding her benefit performance of *The Beaux' Stratagem* on 3 March 1709. Receipts came to £134 3s., from which £40 were deducted for house charges plus an additional charge of £31 7s. 8d. This represented a third of the balance.

11 Cibber relates the story in the third person, but he is obviously 'the actor' described.

12 Cibber, 222. The line in Shakespeare's *Henry VIII* is: 'Read o'er this,/ and after, this, and then to breakfast with/What appetite you have.' (Act III, Scene 2, 202-03.)

13 By Edmund Curll in his 1731 biography of Anne Oldfield.

14 *Tatler,* vol. 2, No 99, 26 November 1709.

15 Cibber, 206 &213

8: A TRIUMVIRATE (PLUS ONE)

1 Cibber, 234.

2 Gerrard, 35.

3 Cibber, 236.

4 Milhous & Hume (1982) 184-85.

5 Milhous & Hume (1982) 148, 178.

6 Cibber, 241.

7 Cibber, 245.

8 Cibber, 248.

9 Cibber, 249.

10 *The Spectator*, no. 10, 12 March 1711.

11 Joseph Addison, *Cato*, Act II, Scene 1.

12 Cibber, 251.

13 *The Spectator,* no. 65, 15 May 1711.

14 The full text of the patent is reproduced in Fitzgerald, i, 401-404.

15 *Town Talk* no. 6, 20 January 1716. Steele reproduces his patent in the same issue.

9: A CHRISTIAN HERO AT DRURY LANE

1 R. Ralph, *The Life and Works of John Weaver,* 1985, ix, quoted in Read, ODNB.

2 John Weaver, *Anatomical and Mechanical Lectures Upon Dancing,* London (1721) 4, quoted in O'Brien, 87.

3 Quoted in *The London Stage*, Part 2, 439. *The Loves of Mars and Venus* opened on 2 March 1717.

4 Quoted in Scott, 131. *The Shipwreck* opened on 2 April 1717.

5 Cibber, 227.

6 Cibber, 50.

7 Cibber, 279.

8 Cibber, 256. 'He that will have a May-pole shall have a May-pole' was a proverbial saying.

9 'He had an easier access, and a more regarded audience at court, than our low station of life could pretend to.' Cibber, 290-91.

10 *Town Talk*, no. 6, 20 January 1716.

11 'Silent' because of the mime element in pantomime. Quoted in Loftis, 75. The anecdote is related in an unidentified newspaper, dated 1763, in the British Museum.

12 *Town Talk*, no. 2, 23 December 1715.

13 Fitzgerald, i, 24.

14 Cibber, 152-53. Cibber tells the story with his usual panache, although we have to make allowances for the way in which actors can always construct narratives in such as way as to give themselves all the best lines.

15 An account of this critical conversation is given in an anonymous pamphlet called *The State of the Case Restated*, published on 29 March 1720, but Cibber's designation of Drury Lane as 'a separate ministry' had become well known by the time John Dennis quoted it in his bitter attack on the Drury Lane management, contained in the preface to his play *The Invader of His Country* on 20 November 1719. The *Invader of His Country* was Dennis's 'improved' version of Shakespeare's *Coriolanus* that had flopped at Drury Lane. Dennis blamed the triumvirate for its failure. See Loftis, 131-32.

16 Letter from Sir John Vanbrugh to Jacob Tonson, dated 18 February 1720, quoted in Loftis, 151.

17 See Loftis, 153.

18 *The Tatler* of 8 June 1710 seems to refer to the plot of *The Conscious Lovers.*

19 *The First Ode of the Second Book of Horace Paraphras'd: And Address'd to Sir Richard Steele* by Jonathan Swift, published January 1714.

20 John Dennis, *A Defence of Sir Fopling Flutter*, quoted in Loftis, 194.

21 *The Tatler*, 8 June 1710.

22 Richard Steele, *The Concious Lovers*, Act II, Scene 1.

23 Richard Steele, *The Concious Lovers*, Act V, Scene 3.

24 Richard Steele, *The Concious Lovers*, Act II, Scene 2.

25 *Sir Fopling Flutter* was the title by which Etherege's *The Man of Mode* was generally known at the time. By defending the wicked Dorimant, based on the Earl of Rochester, Dennis was diving in at the deep end.

26 Richard Steele, *The Concious Lovers*, Act IV, Scene 2.

27 *The Spectator*, no. 10, 12 March 1711.

28 Milhous and Hume (1991) ii, 863.

29 Milhous and Hume (1991) ii, 822.

10: THE GREAT PLAYWRIGHT WE NEVER HAD

1 Henry Fielding, *Pasquin*, in Lockwood, 259-60.

2 Things got worse on the Monday night when the footmen began chopping down the door to the passage admitting them to 'what they call their gallery', threatening to burn the house down. Colonel Deveil, who happened to be in the audience, read them the Riot Act, whereupon they dispersed. (*Weekly Journal,* 26 February 1737, quoted in *The London Stage*, Part 3, 640.) An anonymous letter was sent to Fleetwood, still threatening to burn the place down if footmen were not admitted to their gallery, and a reward was offered for identification of the author. A guard was mounted at the theatre and a magistrate stationed on the premises to read the Riot Act if required. (*Daily Advertiser*, 14 March 1737, quoted in *The London Stage*, Part 3, 647.) In April, two footmen were convicted of riot and sentenced to six months of hard labour. (*London Magazine*, 23 April 1737, quoted in Milhous & Hume [1991] ii, 902-03.)

3 Henry Fielding, *Pasquin*, in Lockwood, 263 & 272.

4 *Daily Gazetteer*, 7 May 1737, quoted in Hume (1988) 237.

5 The Lord Chamberlain's powers of stage censorship would not be revoked until 1968.

6 Fielding was certainly of this opinion, describing *The Golden Rump* as an 'obscure piece which was never exhibited upon the stage, and pretended to be suppress'd; so that it may have been written on purpose, for aught we know with such a particular design.' The official story was that the script had been sent to Henry Giffard, proprietor of the illegal theatre in Goodman's Fields, who took it to Walpole in a state of great distress, saying that his financial problems might make it necessary for him to stage this filth. Walpole gave him £1,000 to compensate him. Writing in 1740, Fielding alleged that Giffard might have been promised a special licence to continue performances at Goodman's Fields as a reward for helping Walpole, and it is suspicious that Giffard's theatre was allowed to re-open later that year. The play itself was never performed or published, and probably never existed except as a few sheets of filthy speeches that Walpole could read out in the House of Commons. *The Golden Rump* was defamatory of the royal family and gave Walpole a better excuse to muzzle the stage than a play like *The Political Register* that attacked Walpole but not the royals. See Pearce, 351-54 and *The London Stage*, Part 3, l.

7 Quoted in Milhous & Hume (1991) ii, 904.

8 In his introduction to the published text, Gay gave an account of the suppression of the play on the orders of the Lord Chamberlain, denying that the play had any political slant and insisting that his only intention had been: 'to lash in general the reigning and fashionable vices, and to recommend and set virtue in as amiable a light as I could.'

9 The Licensing Act received royal assent on 21 June and took effect on 24 June. The only significant opposition to it had been a magnificent speech by Lord Chesterfield against censorship during the debate in the House of Lords.

10 Arthur Murphy, 'An Essay on the Life and Genius of Henry Fielding Esq.' in his edition of Fielding's *Works,* London, 1762, i, 26, quoted in Hume (1988) 259.

11 George Bernard Shaw, *Plays*, i, xviii, quoted in Lockwood, x-xi.

12 Cibber, 156.

13 Erostratus set fire to the Temple of Artemis at Ephesus, one of the wonders of the ancient world, simply in order to achieve immortal fame. The Ephesians responded by making it an offence, punishable by death, ever to name him.

14 Cibber, 157.

15 Salmon, 'Colley Cibber', ODNB (2004).

16 Cibber, 224.

17 Cibber, 185.

11: THE COMING OF GARRICK

1 Henry Fielding, *The Historical Register for the Year 1736*, Act III, Scene 1.

2 W.W.Appleton, *Charles Macklin: An Actor's Life*, 1961, 33, quoted in Shaughnessy, ODNB, 2004.

3 Percival Stockdale, *The Memoirs of the Life, and Writings of Percival Stockdale*, London, 1809, ii, 153-54, quoted in McIntyre, 41.

4 Quoted McIntyre, 40.

5 McIntyre, 51.

6 The same logic is behind the difference in ticket prices today for a musical compared with a straight play.

7 These figures are taken from McIntyre's biography of Garrick and Charles Brayne's entry on Fleetwood in the *Oxford Dictionary of National Biography. Survey of London XXXV* gives the purchase price as £6,750 against an outstanding mortgage of £5,000 and an annuity of £600 (15). Owing to the fraud and dishonesty that were Fleetwood's normal way of doing business, it is difficult to establish exact figures for anything.

8 Walpole, *Correspondence*, London and Newhaven, 48 vols, 1937-83, xix, 42, quoted in McIntyre, 128.

12: THE FOURTH ESTATE

1 The full title of the play is *Mahomet and Irene*, but everyone from Boswell onwards has referred to it as *Irene*.

2 All figures are taken from *The Theatrical Public in the Time of Garrick* by Harry William Pedicord (1954).

3 A newspaper reported that 'from the several alterations... the house will contain £90 more' (McIntyre, 320).

4 Arthur Murphy, *The Life of David Garrick Esq.*, ii, 201, 1801, quoted in Kelly (2008) 71.

5 Quoted by Theophilus Cibber in *Lives and Characters of Actors*, 2 vols, 1753. The passage is reproduced in Fitzgerald, i, 430.

6 In 1938 Dougald MacMillan published his *Drury Lane Calendar 1747-1776*, in which he listed every performance of every production with their cast lists. In 1954 Harry Pedicord, in *The Theatrical Public in the Time of Garrick*, analysed and refined MacMillan's data to create a ranking of all productions over the period. I am indebted to the work of both men. I have silently corrected some small errors in Pedicord's calculations that do not affect his conclusions. He shows a total of 376 shows, but has omitted Etherege's *The Man of Mode* which received nine performances over three seasons, so I have given a total of 377.

7 Dryden, 'Essay of Dramatic Poesy' in *Of Dramatic Poesy*, i, 85.

8 'Upon the New Performances Exhibited at the Two Theatres This Winter', *The Gentleman's Magazine*, January 1767, quoted in Pedicord (1954) 133.

9 He doesn't say who commanded it, but tells us that the request was delivered 'in a manner that could not be resisted', implying a royal command (Cibber, 308).

10 Horace Walpole, *Correspondence*, xix, 27, quoted in McIntyre, 100.

11 Garrick put the words into the mouth of Sir Macaroni Virtu in his theatrical satire *A Peep Behind the Curtain* (1767), but they represent his own sentiments. Quoted in McIntyre, 398.

12 Letter to Reverend Charles Jenner, quoted in McIntyre, 444.

13 Boswell records the remark, made at dinner with Sir Joshua Reynolds. Quoted in McIntyrre, 93.

14 Oliver Goldsmith, 'An Essay on the theatre: or, a comparison between sentimental and laughing comedy', in *The Westminster Magazine*, January 1773.

15 Quoted in McIntyre, 493.

16 Calculations from Avery, 156.

17 *The Daily Advertiser*, 26 May 1737, quoted in Avery, 155.

18 Prologue to *Marina,* George Lillo's adaptation of *Pericles*, staged at Covent Garden 1 August 1738, quoted in Avery, 157.

19 F.W. Bateson wrote in *English Comic Drama* (1929, 134-5), that it is hard today to 'recapture the extraordinary animosity Rich inspired among the people of culture of his own day'.

20 From the prologue written by Garrick to open the 1750/51 season at Drury Lane.

21 The word was coined by George Bernard Shaw in his preface to *Plays for Puritans* in 1901, but the concept was a familiar one by the end of the eighteenth century.

22 Quoted in Deelman, 61.

23 *St James's Chronicle*, 6 – 9 May 1769, quoted in Deelman, 74.

24 Quoted in Deelman, 284-85.

25 Calculation by George Stone, quoted in Deelman, 286.

13: THE LAST YEARS OF GARRICK'S DRURY LANE

1 Walter Sichel, *Sheridan*, Constable, 1909, i, 525, quoted in Kelly (2008) 70-71.

2 Letter to Hannah More, quoted in McIntyre, 562.

3 Quoted in McIntyre, 563.

4 Quoted in McIntyre, 564.

5 From Boswell's *Life of Johnson*, quoted in McIntyre, 594.

6 Quoted in Kelly (2008) 88.

7 Quoted in MacMillan, 199.

8 Michael Kelly (1975) 340.

9 Reynolds, ii, 306-07.

10 Michael Kelly (1975) 339.

11 Reynolds, i, 110.

12 *The Letters of Richard Brinsley Sheridan*, ed. Cecil Price, 1966, iii, 293-307, quoted in Tomalin, 50.

13 *David Garrick* by Carola Oman, 1958, 360, quoted in Kelly (2008) 85.

14 Michael Kelly (1975) 345.

15 Michael Kelly (1975) 338.

16 Reynolds, ii, 226-27.

17 *Creevey* by John Gore (ed.), 1949, 36, quoted in Kelly (2008) 99.

18 'We then, indeed, knew all the luxury of grief,' wrote her biographer James Boaden, 'but the nerves of many a gentle being gave way before the intensity of such appeals; and fainting fits long and frequently alarmed the decorum of the house.' James Boaden, *The Memoirs of Mrs Siddons*, 1827, 161.

19 Kelly (1980) 22.

20 *Sheridaniana*, 283, quoted in Kelly (2008) 118.

21 *Memoirs of the Life of John Philip Kemble* by James Boaden, i, 403, quoted in Kelly (2008) 155.

14: OLD MADAM DRURY'S SUCCESSOR

1   Michael Kelly (1975) 180.
2   *The London Stage*, Part 5, ii, 1360-01.
3   All scenery had to be newly constructed for the new theatre to fill Holland's enormous stage. It was one of the extra costs that hadn't been foreseen.
4   *European Magazine*, March 1794, 236, quoted in *The London Stage*, Part 5, iii, 1625.
5   Sheridan's Letters, i, 218, cited in *Survey of London XXXV*, 19.
6   *The Morning Herald*, 1 December 1797, cited in *The London Stage*, Part 5, iii, 1568-69.
7   *Survey of London XXXV*, 56.
8   Sheridan's letters, i, 218, cited in *Survey of London XXXV*, 19.
9   *Survey of London XXXV*, 19.
10 *The Times*, 22 April 1794.
11 Percy Fitzgerald, *The Kembles*, 1871, i, 309, quoted in Kelly (1980) 99.
12 Richard Brinsley Peake, *Memoirs of the Colman Family*, 1841, ii, 20, quoted in *The London Stage*, Part 5, iii, 1473.
13 Richard Cumberland, *Memoirs*, 1807, ii, 384, quoted in Kelly (1980) 99.
14 *The Torrington Diaries, Containing the Tours through England and Wales of the Hon. John Byng (Later Fifth Viscount Torrington) Between the Years 1781 and 1794*, iv, 18, quoted in Girdham, 40.

15: SPECTACLE AND MELODRAMA

1   Michael Kelly (1975) 188. Kelly's account of the *Lodoiska* incident occurs on page 209 of his memoirs.
2   *The London Stage*, Part 5, iii, 1727, quoting the playbill.
3   W. Macqueen-Pope (1955) 113.
4   Michael Kelly (1975) 218.
5   Fanny Kemble, *Record of a Girlhood*, 1878, i, 283, quoted in Kelly (1980) 111.

6   Kelly (1980) 101.
7   There is a good account of the Ireland forgeries in Lynch, 209-28.
8   *Morning Herald*, 16 December 1797, quoted in *The London Stage*, Part 5, iii, 2030.
9   Although the Pizarro experience was extreme, Sheridan had left things late even when writing *The School for Scandal*. The last pages of the original manuscript show signs of having been written in a hurry, and Sheridan wrote at the bottom: 'Finished at last. Thank God. R.B. Sheridan.' Underneath the prompter has written: 'Amen! W. Hopkins.' Kelly (2008) 77.
10 Michael Kelly records that 'the exhaustion of the audience was so complete' that, when the afterpiece started, there were 17 people left in the dress circle and 22 in the pit. *Reminiscences*, 255.
11 Michael Kelly (1975) 210.
12 Quoted in Kelly (1980) 140.
13 MS letters in the Harvard Theatre collection, 27 November 1800 and one undated, plus James Boaden, *Memoirs of the Life of John Philip Kemble*, 1825, ii, 47; all quoted in Kelly (1980) 140-41.
14 Leslie Marchand (ed.), *Lord Byron: Letters and Journals*, John Murray, 1979, ix, 57, quoted in Kelly (2008) 205.
15 Michael Kelly (1975) 201-02.
16 Reynolds, ii, 364. Reynolds, who was well in with the Covent Garden management, was in a position to know the true amount.
17 'Young Roscius', *The Times*, 3 December 1804.
18 Quoted in Playfair (1967) 73.
19 James Boaden, *The Life of Mrs Jordan*, 1831, ii, 181, quoted in Stott, 138.
20 Quoted in Playfair (1967) 80.
21 Quoted in Playfair (1967) 72.

16: THE RAVAGES OF FIRE

1 The theatre historian and biographer James Boaden claimed that the tanks had been full when they were inspected two days before the fire, but there were no hoses attached to them. The real problem, in his view, was that the theatre was empty when it caught alight and there was no watchman to activate the fire precautions. (James Boaden, *The Life of Mrs Jordan*, 1831, ii, 225, quoted in Leacroft, 156.)

2 Michael Kelly gives this vivid account in his *Reminiscences*, 309-10.

3 Michael Kelly tells the story in his *Reminiscences*, 295.

4 Downes, 55.

5 By Peter Pindar, quoted in Tomalin, 123.

6 See Tomalin, 186 & 166. Claire Tomalin notes that the loan of £2,400 led to a charming understatement by the Duke to his banker, Mr Coutts, that 'Mrs Jordan has never been to me the least cause of expense'.

7 Anonymous, *The Life of Mrs Jordan*, 1886, 35, quoted in Tomalin, 163. The 1886 *Life* had originally been published in a slightly longer, illustrated form in 1832, supposedly by 'a confidential friend of the departed'.

8 *The Memoirs of Joseph Grimaldi, Edited by 'Boz'*, London, 1838, quoted in Stott, 147. Grimaldi's *Memoirs* were adapted by Charles Dickens from a first-person narrative left by Grimaldi at his death in 1837 and turned into a third-person narrative.

9 Richard Findlater, *Joe Grimaldi: His Life and Theatre*, Cambridge University Press, 1977, 120, quoted in Stott, 180.

10 The doctor was John Abertheny. Stott, 200 & 269.

11 Stott, 254.

12 Stott, 291.

17: FROM THE ASHES

1 Fulford, 277. The letter is reproduced in Thomas Moore's *Memoirs of the Life of Sheridan* (1826), but Moore changed the wording to make it match what happened afterwards.

2 Fulford, 278-79.

3 *Sheridan Letters*, iii, 131, quoted in *Survey of London XXXV*, 21.

4 Nicholson, 23.

5 Fulford, 284.

6 See 'Drury Lane Addresses by Byron and Others', edited by Peter Cochran at http://petercochran.files.wordpress .com/2009/03/c

7 Benjamin Dean Wyatt, *Observations on the Design for the Theatre Royal, Drury Lane*, London, 1813, 10, quoted in *Survey of London XXXV*, 60. See also Leacroft, 173.

8 Benjamin Dean Wyatt, *Observations on the Design for the Theatre Royal, Drury Lane*, London, 1813, quoted in Leacroft, 172.

9 Benjamin Dean Wyatt, *Observations on the Design for the Theatre Royal, Drury Lane*, London, 1813, 3, quoted in *Survey of London XXXV*, 60.

10 Reynolds, ii, 393.

11 Benjamin Dean Wyatt, *Observations on the Design for the Theatre Royal, Drury Lane*, London, 1813, 42-43, quoted in *Survey of London XXXV*, 60-61.

18: A THEATRE RUN BY A COMMITTEE

1 From a short memoir, probably written by Whitbread's son-in-law, quoted in Fulford, 278.

2 Michael Kelly tells the story in his *Reminiscences*, 208. He also claims to have chosen the four-year-old Edmund to play Cupid in his revival of the opera *Cymon* in 1791.

'I consider my having been the means of introducing this great genius to the stage, one of my most pleasurable recollections' (188). Kean's biographer Giles Playfair was sceptical about this story, and in fact another child was listed as Cupid in the playbill.

3 Playfair (1988) 82.

4 Playfair (1988) 83.

5 William Hazlitt, *The Morning Chronicle*, 27 January 1814, reprinted in Rowell, 50-51.

6 Playfair (1988) 98 & 106.

7 Fulford, 290.

8 Playfair (1988) 150-51.

9 Fulford, 306.

10 Fulford, 302.

11 *The Letters of Richard Brinsley Sheridan*, ed. Cecil Price, Oxford: OUP, 1966, iii, 188, quoted in Kelly (2008) 299.

12 Fisher, ODNB, 2004.

13 MacCarthy, 250.

14 MacCarthy, 256.

15 Garrick had revived it for the 1748/49 season, but it only made four performances.

16 *The Examiner*, 14 January 1816, Hazlitt, 104-06.

17 *The Examiner*, 5 May 1816, Hazlitt, 134-35.

18 *The Examiner*, 8 December 1816, Hazlitt, 178-80.

19 The story comes from Thomas Moore's *Memoirs of the Life of the right honourable Richard Brinsley Sheridan*, 1825, quoted in Kelly (2008) 303.

20 H. G. Bennett MP, quoted in Kelly (2008) 307.

21 Michael Kelly (1975) 303.

22 The story was taken from Byron's journal for 1812-13 by Thomas Moore for his *Memoirs of the Life of the right honourable Richard Brinsley Sheridan*, 1825, quoted in Kelly (1997) 301-02.

19: THE GREAT LESSEE

1 *Theatrical Inquisitor XIV*, 1819, 428, quoted in Murray (1975) 83.

2 'Drury-Lane Theatre', *The Times*, 5 October 1819.

3 'Drury-Lane Theatre', *The Times*, 5 October 1819.

4 From Elliston's published version of the play, quoted in Murray (1975) 90. Murray points out that Elliston did stage the play with its original tragic ending three years later on 10 February 1823. However, apart from Act V, most of the text was from the Nahum Tate version and did not include the Fool. (*The Times*, 11 February 1823.)

5 George Raymond, *Memoirs of Robert William Elliston*, 1845, ii, 475n. quoted in *Survey of London XXXV*, 65.

6 From Byron's letters to John Murray, quoted in MacCarthy, 396.

7 Murray (1975) 96.

8 The story is told by William Oxberry in 'Memoir of Robert Elliston', contained in *Oxberry's Dramatic Biography*, 5 vols, 1825/26, iii, 88, quoted in Murray (1975) 4. Oxberry wasn't a fan.

9 George Raymond, *op.cit.*, ii, 315, quoted in *Survey of London XXXV*, 64.

10 Letter from Elliston to James Winston, his manager at the Olympic Theatre, 26 September 1815, Elliston papers, quoted in Murray (1975) 52.

11 Quoted in Murray (1975) 104.

12 Quoted in Murray (1975) 107. The author of *Faustus* was George Soane, son of the theatre's famous supervisory architect. Soane junior was a German scholar, and the first part of his translation of Goethe's work had been approved by the author himself. The version that

reached the stage of Drury Lane bore almost no relation to it.

13 The warning was given by his friend Warner Phipps, who told him: 'Your respectability is expiring – your energies declining – your estate wasting – and your very hopes are themselves becoming hopeless.' Murray (1975) 109.

14 13 March 1824, Winston, *Drury Lane Journal*, 83.

15 14 July 1824, Winston, *Drury Lane Journal*, 93.

16 4 December 1824, Winston, *Drury Lane Journal*, 101.

17 10 May 1824, Winston, *Drury Lane Journal*, 86.

18 16 July 1825, Winston, *Drury Lane Journal*, 113.

19 Murray (1975) 116.

20 24 May 1826, Winston, *Drury Lane Journal*, 123.

21 Murray (1975) 137.

22 Charles Lamb, 'Ellistoniana', *The Englishman's Magazine*, August 1831, reproduced in Rowell, 45-48.

20: THE MONOPOLY UNDER ATTACK

1 James Winston, *Drury Lane Journal*, 17 January 1820, 4.

2 James Winston, *Drury Lane Journal*, 16 August 1820, 16.

3 James Winston, *Drury Lane Journal*, 16 July 1825, 112.

4 James Winston, *Drury Lane Journal*, 6 February 1827, 142.

5 *The Times*, 18 January 1825, quoted in Playfair (1988) 239.

6 Playfair (1988) 294.

7 James Winston, *Drury Lane Journal*, 2 July 1827, 151.

8 James Winston, *Drury Lane Journal*, 12 November 1826; 31 January 1827; 136, 141.

9 James Winston, *Drury Lane Journal*, 30 June 1827; 2 July 1827, 150, 151.

10 Fitzgerald, ii, 427 and *Survey of London XXXV*, 24.

11 Planché (1872) i, 178 & 238.

12 James Winston, *Drury Lane Journal*, 25 July 1824, 97.

13 James Winston, *Drury Lane Journal*, 20 April 1824, 85.

14 According to J. R. Planché, Bunn had been presenting himself as the lessee, rather than manager, of Drury Lane ever since the Lee/Polehill partnership had broken up in 1831. Polehill was content to remain 'behind the curtain' as the financial backer, leaving Bunn to front the operation (Planché [1872] i, 238).

15 Bunn only assumed financial responsibility for Drury Lane when he took over Polehill's lease in December 1834, but as far as the public and the profession were concerned, he was in charge of both Drury Lane and Covent Garden from the opening of the 1833 season in October.

16 Bunn, i, 86.

17 Bunn, i, 105.

18 J.R. Planché maintained that Bunn failed to give the two theatres distinct profiles, and 'actually put up tragedy against tragedy, dividing, instead of combining, his forces'. (Planché [1872] i, 240.) Planché, however, was unsympathetic to Bunn's style of management which he described as 'sheer gambling' (Planché [1872] ii, 200).

19 George Raymond, the biographer of Robert Elliston, quoted in Fitzgerald, ii, 429.

20 George Raymond, the biographer of Robert Elliston, quoted in Planché (1872) i, 239.

21 Planché (1872) i, 239.

22 Bunn, i, 59.

23 'Two sets of actors, tolerated in the same place, have constantly ended in the corruption of the theatre.' Cibber, 278.

24 Jane Moody, *Illegitimate Theatre in London, 1770-1840*, Cambridge University Press, 2000, 24, quoted in Stott, 40.

25 *Timour the Tartar* by Matthew 'Monk' Lewis was first performed at Covent Garden in April 1811 and featured many stunts involving horses. 'The white horse which carried the heroine (Mrs H. Johnston) plays admirably', reported *The European Magazine*, in a review which, as Lewis's biographer Louis F. Peck points out, any horse would be proud to read.

26 R.W. Elliston, *Copy of a Memorial Presented to the Lord Chamberlain by the Committee of Management of Theatre-Royal, Drury Lane and by the Proprietors of Theatre-Royal, Covent Garden, against the Olympic and Sans Souci Theatres, with Copies of Two Letters in Reply to the Contents of Such Memoirs, Addressed to the Lord Chamberlain by Robert William Elliston, Comedian,* London, 1818, quoted in Nicholson, 300-01.

27 Quoted in Nicholson, 326-27.

28 Bunn, i, 135

29 Bunn, i, 87.

21: BUNN FIGHT

1 Macready, *Journal*, 1 December 1834, 36.

2 Macready, *Journal*, 10 January 1835 & 18 July 1835, 38 & 42.

3 Macready, *Journal*, 25 April & 27 April 1833, 9.

4 Macready, *Journal*, 19 September 1833, 1 November 1833, 3 April 1834, 31 October 1835; 16, 17, 24, 48.

5 Bunn, i, 100.

6 Bunn, i, 101.

7 Bunn, i, 150.

8 Bunn, i, 155-56.

9 Bunn, i, 187. Bunn reproduces the contract with Macready on 186-87.

10 Quoted in Downer, 143.

11 Quoted in Downer, 144.

12 Macready, *Journal*, 28 April 1836, 61.

13 Macready, *Journal*, 11 May 1836, 68.

14 Bunn, i, 209.

15 Bunn, i, 230.

16 Bunn, i, 172.

17 Bunn, ii, 53.

18 Bunn, ii, 54.

19 Bunn, ii, 147.

20 Bunn, ii, 40.

21 Bunn, ii, 42.

22 Bunn, ii, 168.

23 Nicholson, 399.

24 Nicholson, 402-03.

25 Bunn, ii, 82.

26 Bunn, ii, 47.

22: THE FIRST THEATRE OF THE EMPIRE

1 Bunn, i, 50 & ii, 159.

2 Macready would later claim that he had actually paid the proprietors £5,500 in rent for the first Covent Garden season and £7,000 in rent for the second. (Report of Macready's farewell speech at the end of his Drury Lane management, *The Illustrated London News*, 17 June 1843, 422.)

3 The two manifestoes are printed in Bunn, ii, 74-78.

4 *The Examiner*, 4 February 1838. Edmund Kean had acted *King Lear* with the original tragic ending but without the Fool on 10 February 1823. See note 4, chapter 19, 532.

5 Downer, 176.

6 Macready, *Journal*, 31 May 1838, 121.

7 Macready, *Journal*, 3 August 1838, 123.

8 Diary entry for 30 July 1838. Bunn, ii, 134.

9 Macready, *Journal*, 22 October 1838, 125.

10 This phrase has entered the language, but the actual passage, from Isaiah 11:6, states: 'The wolf also shall dwell

with the lamb, and the leopard shall lie down with the kid; and the calf and the young lion and the fatling between them; and a little child shall lead them.'

11 Bunn, ii, 164.
12 Bunn, ii, 249.
13 Bunn, ii, 223.
14 Planché (1879) 13.
15 Bunn, ii, 224.
16 Bunn, ii, 229.
17 Bunn, ii, 159.

23: THE END OF THE MONOPOLY

1 Bunn, ii, 229. *The Road to Ruin* by Thomas Holcroft had first been performed at Covent Garden in 1792.
2 Bunn, i, 234.
3 Bunn, ii, 239-42.
4 Macready, *Journal*, 137.
5 Macready, *Journal*, 30 June 1839, 140. Emphasis in original.
6 Macready, *Journal*, 23 March 1841, 171.
7 Report of Macready's farewell speech at the end of his Drury Lane management, *The Illustrated London News*, 17 June 1843, 422.
8 Macready, *Journal*, 26 August 1842, 185.
9 Macready, *Journal*, 4 October 1841, 175.
10 Macready, *Journal*, 23 May 1842, 183.
11 Downer, 222. The actor was James Anderson, who would later take over the lease of Drury Lane.
12 Quoted in Downer, 238.
13 Archer, 139.
14 James Anderson, actor, who was also Macready's stage manager, quoted in Archer, 131. Anderson added: 'He had his own way, but he lost his money.'
15 Archer, 140.
16 Report of Macready's farewell speech at the end of his Drury Lane management, *The Illustrated London News*, 17 June 1843, 422.

17 *The Times*, 10 June 1848.
18 *The Spectator*, 10 June 1843, quoted in Nicholson, 418-19.
19 Planché (1879) 289.

24: MORE LESSEES

1 Macready, *Journal*, 1 December 1842, 189.
2 Macready, *Journal*, 22 February 1843, 194.
3 Macready, *Journal*, 29 April 1840, 196.
4 Macready, *Journal*, 3 August 1843, 199.
5 Quoted in Fawkes, 66.
6 Macready, *Journal*, 104.
7 Macready, *Journal*, 292.
8 James Anderson, *An Actor's Life*, London, 1902, 192-93, quoted in Downer, 317.
9 Macready, *Journal*, 26 February 1851, 293. Macready recorded the whole text of his speech in the diary entry for the day.
10 Baker, i, 113
11 J.R. Planché, (1872) ii, 200.
12 Bedford Office London, Annual Report, 1852, 5, quoted in *Survey of London XXXV*, 26.
13 Bedford Office London, Annual Report, 1853, 3, quoted in *Survey of London XXXV*, 26
14 Baker, 115.
15 *George Barnwell* was originally the sub-title of George Lillo's 1731 play *The London Merchant* which had been performed annually on the holiday of the London apprentices, usually around Easter, until 1819.
16 Stirling, i, 267. Stirling was an actor, stage manager and general factotum at Drury Lane during the 1850s and 1860s, and claims to have been present at the dinner party at which this exchange took place.
17 Letter to the Editor of *The Times*, dated 29 September 1862, published 2 October 1862.
18 Booth, 13.

19 Turner, ODNB.

25: POETS AND PROFITS

1 Baker, i, 116.
2 Kenney, 11.
3 John Coleman, *Players and Playwrights I Have Known*, London: Chatto and Windus, 1888, ii, 345, quoted in Jeffrey Richards, 'E.L. Blanchard and "The Golden Age of Pantomime"' in Davis (ed.) 2010, 30.
4 Kenney, iii.
5 Kenney, v.
6 Kenney, 13.
7 See Jeffrey Richards, *op. cit.*, 26.
8 Kenney, 16.
9 Kenney, 19.
10 Kenney, 22.
11 Fawkes, 176-77. According to an article in *The New York Times* that appeared after Chatterton's death (5 January 1890): 'He is remembered now for a saying of his which... has been bandied about wherever the English language is spoken', which is ironic as Fawkes takes the view that the letter was actually written by Boucicault, although signed by Chatterton.
12 Stirling, i, 291.
13 Kenney, 39.
14 Kenney, 40.
15 Kenney, 44.
16 John Ruskin, *Fors Clavigera*, Letter 39, March 1874.
17 See Jeffrey Richards, *op.cit.*, 27.
18 Kenney, iii.
19 Dobbs, 151.
20 Quoted in Townsend Walsh, *The Career of Dion Boucicault*, New York, 1915, 95-6, and Fawkes, 148.
21 Kenney, 50-51.
22 Coleman, ii. 345.
23 *The Daily News*, 15 February 1879, quoted in Jeffrey Richards, *op.cit.*, 31.
24 *The Times*, 3 April 1879.

25 Coleman, ii, 358, 345, 376. Quoted in Jeffrey Richards, *op.cit.*, 30.

26: DRURIOLANUS

1 Sims, 287.
2 Quoted in Macqueen-Pope (1955) 189.
3 Quoted in Dobbs, 158.
4 Stirling, i, 322.
5 Stirling, i, 322-23.
6 The description comes from H.G. Hibbert, *A Playgoer's Memories*, London: Grant Richards, 1920, 78, quoted in Jeffrey Richards, 'E.L. Blanchard and "The golden age of pantomime"', in Davis, 31.
7 'Victorian Pantomime' article on the Victoria and Albert Museum website, http://www.vam.ac.uk/content/articles/v/victorian-pantomime/
8 *The Times*, 27 December 1893.
9 *The Times*, 27 December 1884.
10 Augustus Harris, 'Spectacle', *The Magazine of Art*, xii, 1889, 112.
11 Although Augustus Harris was widely blamed by traditionalists for starting the custom of importing music-hall artistes into pantomime, that honour probably belongs to his father, Augustus senior, who had been stage manager at Covent Garden. He had introduced the music-hall star G.H. Macdermott into *Bluebeard* there in 1871. The practice was rapidly adopted by theatres in both the East and West End. (Jeffrey Richards, 'E.L. Blanchard and "The golden age of pantomime"', in Davis, 33.)
12 Clement Scott and Cecil Howard (eds.) *The Life and Reminscences of E.L. Blanchard*, London: Hutchinson, 1891, 2 vols, ii, 528 & 541-42, quoted in Jeffrey Richards, 'E.L. Blanchard and "The golden age of pantomime"', in Davis, 35.
13 Jim Davis, '"Only an undisciplined [nation] would have done it": Drury

Lane pantomime in the late nineteenth century', in Davis, 101.

14 *The Athenaeum*, 31 December 1892.

15 Augustus Harris, 'Spectacle', *The Magazine of Art*, vol. 12, 1889, 112.

16 Anthony, 63.

17 Augustus Harris, 'Spectacle', *The Magazine of Art*, vol. 12, 1889, 109-12.

18 Macqueen-Pope (1955) 192.

19 In his 1889 history of *The London Stage*, H. Barton Baker described the visit of the Saxe-Meiningen company as 'the most notable event of Mr Harris's management... their perfection of detail gave a lesson to London managers by which the latter have largely profited, and the effects of which, especially in the handling of supers [extras], have been very conspicuous in recent productions.' (Baker, 118). Baker was not a fan of Harris's style of management and asked rhetorically: 'if audiences flock to see shipwrecks, processions and earthquakes, who can blame him for considering the perfection of the histrionic department a matter of minor importance?'

20 'The German Opera Season', *The Times*, 26 April 1882. The first performance of *Die Meistersinger von Nürnberg* was on 30 May and the first performance of *Tristan und Isolde* was on 20 June. The German Opera Season also involved staging the whole of the ring cycle at Her Majesty's. Wagner's entire oeuvre could be seen in London over the course of the season, 'a feat, by the way, which we believe is unprecedented, even in Germany', according to the *Times's* critic (22 June 1882).

21 The exception was the 1887 season of opera starring Jean de Reske, the current singing sensation, which lost

£10,000. Harris seems to have regarded it as his contribution to Queen Victoria's golden jubilee.

22 Kenney, 18.

23 Quoted in *Survey of London XXXV*, 28.

24 Sims, 288.

27: ONLY A GREAT NATION COULD HAVE DONE SUCH A THING

1 He acquired the name after Bernard Shaw wrote in a review of a show Smith had designed that he had walked out as soon as 'that silly sensation scene came on'. (Castle, 101.)

2 Castle, 182.

3 *The Star*, 27 December 1900, quoted in Jim Davis, 'Only an Undisciplined [Nation] Would Have Done It: Drury Lane pantomime in the late nineteenth century', in Davis (ed.) 105.

4 Jimmy Glover, *Jimmy Glover His Book*, London: Methuen and Co, 1911, 174, quoted in Davis, *op. cit.*, 116. Jimmy Glover was the musical director at Drury Lane for many years.

5 *The Sketch*, 27 December 1899, quoted in Davis, *op. cit.*, 103.

6 Anthony, 191.

7 Anthony, 192.

8 Anthony, 193.

9 Pearson, 32.

10 Trewin, 215-17.

11 'Babes in the Wood: Drury Lane Pantomime', *The Times*, 27 December 1918.

12 'Future of Drury Lane: Sir Alfred Butt as Chairman', *The Times*, 26 February 1919.

13 'The Future of Drury Lane: Another Shareholders' Meeting', *The Times*, 21 March 1919; 'The Drury Lane Dispute; Present Directors to Remain', *The Times*, 2 April 1919; 'Company Meetings: Theatre Royal, Drury Lane', *The Times*, 2 April 1919.

14 *Survey of London XXXV*, 84.
15 'Covent Garden Auction', *The Times*, 22 January 1920.
16 Castle, 213-14.
17 'Mr Arthur Collins's Story of £1,000', *The Times*, 7 October 1918.

28: LAST CHANCE FOR THE NATIONAL THEATRE
1 *Survey of London XXXV*, 38n. 'When the eleventh Duke sold the Covent Garden estate in 1918 he retained his box at Drury Lane subject to paying a rent of £400 per annum to the purchaser. He eventually gave up the right to the box in 1940.'
2 Dean (1970), 227.
3 Dean (1970) 229.
4 Dean (1970) 230.
5 Dean (1970) 244.
6 Dean (1970) 244.

29: THE COMING OF THE MUSICALS
1 Quoted in Dobbs, 182.
2 Quoted in Dobbs, 182.
3 Hoare, ODNB.
4 Noble, 204-06.
5 'Drury Lane Theatre', *The Times*, 30 September 1927.
6 Rose, 148.
7 *Women's Pictorial*, 8 April 1950, quoted in Noble, 292.
8 Quoted in Noble, 259-60.
9 Wilson (1975) 249.

30: BASIL DEAN RETURNS TO THE LANE
1 Dean (1970) 245.
2 Dean (1956) 225.
3 Dean (1956) 387.
4 Dean (1956) 495-96.
5 Dean (1956) 541.
6 Dean (1956) 203.
7 Macqueen-Pope (1955) 227-28.
8 Dean (1956) 534.
9 Dean (1956) 61.
10 Dean (1956) 167.

11 Dean (1956) 170.
12 Macqueen-Pope (1955) 226.
13 Dean (1956) 277.
14 Macqueen-Pope (1955) 225.
15 Macqueen-Pope (1955) 230.
16 Dean (1956) 530.
17 Dean (1956) 538.
18 Dean (1956) 539

31: MORE MUSICALS
1 Macqueen-Pope (1955) 234-37.
2 Fox, 28.
3 Dobbs, 203.
4 Dobbs, 202.
5 Dobbs, 203.
6 Dobbs, 213.
7 Dobbs, 211.
8 Fox, 28, 30, 33 & 35.

CONCLUSION: THE NATIONAL THEATRE IN DRURY LANE?
1 Jonson was credited with being the first person to describe the shows as 'masques', because so many of the performers were wearing masks.
2 Jonson makes this analogy in the introduction to the printed text of *Hymenaei*, performed to celebrate the marriage of the Earl of Essex to the daughter of the Earl of Suffolk in January 1606. (Jonson, vii, 209.)
3 'Expostulation with Inigo Jones', Jonson, viii, 403-04. Spelling modernised. The poem was circulating in manuscript form when Jonson was warned by his friend, the diplomat James Howell, that he was being criticised at court for writing 'with a porcupine's quill dipped in too much gall'. Jonson destroyed all the manuscript copies he could get back, but one survived and was published after his death. (Leapman, 252-53.)
4 Samuel Pepys, Diary, 4 July 1661.
5 Cibber, 57 & 171.
6 Bunn, ii, 224.
7 Bunn, ii, 223.

8 Dr Thomas Rundle, letter, 24 March 1720, quoted in Loftis, 190-91.

9 *The Daily Advertiser*, 7 January 1737, quoted in Hume (1988) 221.

10 *Theatrical Review*, 26 December 1772, quoted in McIntyre, 463.

11 George Bernard Shaw, 'Peace and Goodwill to All Managers', 1 January 1898, *The Saturday Review*, review of *Babes in the Wood* by Arthur Sturgess and Arthur Collins, 27 December 1897.

12 Aaron Hill, letter to Barton Booth, 25 December 1732, in *The Works of the Late Aaron Hill Esq*, 1754, i, 181-84, quoted in Gerrard, 156.

13 Theophilus Cibber, *Lives and Characters of Actors*, 2 vols (1753) quoted in Fitzgerald, i, 430.

14 Aaron Hill, *Advice to the Poets. A poem. To which is prefix'd an epistle dedicatory to the few great spirits of Great Britain*. London, 1731, xii-xiii.

15 Letter from Hill to Benjamin Victor, 22 March 1733, quoted in Gerrard, 149.

16 Letter from Hill to John Highmore, 5 July 1733, Hill, *Works*, i, 129-34, quoted in Gerrard, 150.

17 *The Prompter*, no. 7, 4 December 1734, quoted in Gerrard, 157.

18 *The Prompter*, no. 147, 2 April 1736, quoted in Gerrard, 162.

19 *The Prompter*, 129, 2 February 1736, quoted in Gerrard, 171.

20 Henry Fielding, *Tumble-Down Dick or Phaeton in the Suds*, in Lockwood, 336.

21 Loftis, 227.

22 *The Times*, 10 June 1848.

23 Kenney, v.

24 Kenney, 50-51.

25 Coleman, ii, chapter 6.

26 Harris (1885) 630.

27 Harris (1885) 634-35.

28 Harris (1885) 634-35.

29 Elsom and Tomalin, 28.

30 William Archer and Harley Granville Barker, *A National Theatre*, London, 1907, xix, quoted in Elsom and Tomalin, 30.

31 Harris (1885) 630.

32 Noble, 204.

33 Dean (1956) 537. Dean used the fact that the Queen had actually laid the foundation stone on a site that everyone knew was not going to be used, next to County Hall, as proof of the incompetence of the National Theatre movement.

34 *Survey of London XXXV*, 80.

APPENDIX 1:
EXORCISING THE GHOST

1 *Survey of London XXXV*, 9.

2 Raymond Mander and Joe Mitchenson, *Musical Comedy*, London: Peter Davies (1969) quoted in Dobbs, xii.

3 Macqueen-Pope (1945) 152.

4 Macqueen-Pope (1945) 238.

5 Macqueen-Pope (1945) 89-91.

6 Castle, 244.

7 Dean (1956) 107.

Index

The growth of the Theatre Royal:

Russell Street

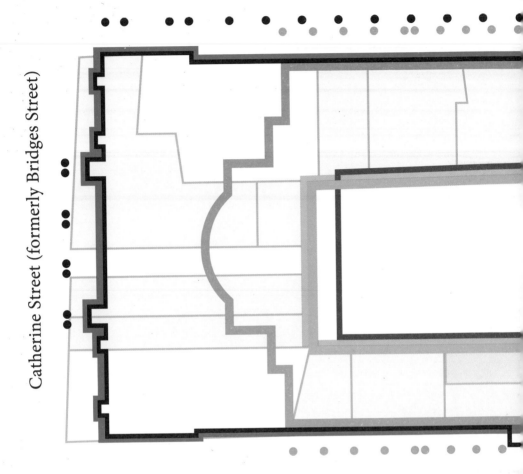

Catherine Street (formerly Bridges Street)

Vinegar Yard (formerly Little Bridges Street and Vinegar Yard)

The First Theatre Royal (opened 1663)

The Second Theatre Royal (opened 1674)

Boundaries of plots used for the scenic workshops and green room of the second Theatre Royal

The Second Theatre Royal in 1776 after expansion by Garrick and rebuilding by Robert Adam

Boundaries of plots surrounding the second Theatre Royal acquired by Garrick and used to provide new entrances and facilities outside the walls of the main structure.